A THEORY OF JUSTICE

A THEORY OF JUSTICE

JOHN RAWLS

THE BELKNAP PRESS OF
HARVARD UNIVERSITY PRESS
CAMBRIDGE, MASSACHUSETTS

For Mard

after initial allocation, how is
distribution regulated ?

PREFACE

In presenting a theory of justice I have tried to bring together into one coherent view the ideas expressed in the papers I have written over the past dozen years or so. All of the central topics of these essays are taken up again, usually in considerably more detail. The further questions required to round out the theory are also discussed. The exposition falls into three parts. The first part covers with much greater elaboration the same ground as "Justice as Fairness" (1958) and "Distributive Justice: Some Addenda" (1968), while the three chapters of the second part correspond respectively, but with many additions, to the topics of "Constitutional Liberty" (1963), "Distributive Justice" (1967), and "Civil Disobedience" (1966). The second chapter of the last part covers the subjects of "The Sense of Justice" (1963). Except in a few places, the other chapters of this part do not parallel the published essays. Although the main ideas are much the same, I have tried to eliminate inconsistencies and to fill out and strengthen the argument at many points.

Perhaps I can best explain my aim in this book as follows. During much of modern moral philosophy the predominant systematic theory has been some form of utilitarianism. One reason for this is that it has been espoused by a long line of brilliant writers who have built up a body of thought truly impressive in its scope and refinement. We sometimes forget that the great utilitarians, Hume and Adam Smith, Bentham and Mill, were social theorists and economists of the first rank; and the moral doctrine they worked out was framed to meet the needs of their wider interests and to fit into a comprehensive scheme. Those who criticized them often did so on a much narrower front. They pointed out the obscurities of the principle of utility and noted the apparent incongruities between many of its implications and our moral sentiments. But they failed, I believe, to construct a workable and systematic moral conception to oppose it. The outcome is that we often seem forced to choose between utilitarianism and intuitionism. Most likely we finally settle upon a variant of the utility principle circumscribed and restricted in certain ad hoc ways by intuitionistic constraints. Such a view is not irrational; and there is no assurance that we can do better. But this is no reason not to try.

What I have attempted to do is to generalize and carry to a higher order of abstraction the traditional theory of the social contract as represented by Locke, Rousseau, and Kant. In this way I hope that the theory can be developed so that it is no longer open to the more obvious objections often thought fatal to it. Moreover, this theory seems to offer an alternative systematic account of justice that is superior, or so I argue, to the dominant utilitarianism of the tradition. The theory that results is highly Kantian in nature. Indeed, I must disclaim any originality for the views I put forward. The leading ideas are classical and well known. My intention has been to organize them into a general framework by using certain simplifying devices so that their full force can be appreciated. My ambitions for the book will be completely realized if it enables one to see more clearly the chief structural features of the alternative conception of justice that is implicit in the contract tradition and points the way to its further elaboration. Of the traditional views, it is this conception, I believe, which best approximates our considered judgments of justice and constitutes the most appropriate moral basis for a democratic society.

This is a long book, not only in pages. Therefore, to make things easier for the reader, a few remarks by way of guidance. The fundamental intuitive ideas of the theory of justice are presented in §§ 1–4 of Chapter I. From here it is possible to go directly to the discussion of the two principles of justice for institutions in §§ 11–17 of Chapter II, and then to the account of the original position in Chapter III, the whole chapter. A glance at § 8 on the priority problem may prove necessary if this notion is unfamiliar. Next, parts of Chapter IV, §§ 33–35 on equal liberty and §§ 39–40 on the meaning of the priority of liberty and the Kantian interpretation, give the best picture of the doctrine. So far this is about a third of the whole and comprises most of the essentials of the theory.

There is a danger, however, that without consideration of the argument of the last part, the theory of justice will be misunderstood. In particular, the following sections should be emphasized: § § 66–67 of Chapter VII on moral worth and self-respect and related notions; § 77 of Chapter VIII on the basis of equality; and §§ 78–79 on autonomy and social union, § 82 on the priority of liberty, and §§ 85–86 on the unity of the self and congruence, all in Chapter IX. Adding these sections to the others still comes to considerably less than half the text.

The section headings, the remarks that preface each chapter, and the index will guide the reader to the contents of the book. It seems superfluous to comment on this except to say that I have avoided extensive methodological discussions. There is a brief consideration of the nature of moral theory in § 9, and of justification in § 4 and § 87. A short digression on the meaning of "good" is found in § 62. Occasionally there are methodological comments and asides, but for the most part I try to work out a substantive theory of justice. Comparisons and contrasts with other theories, and criticisms thereof now and then, especially of utilitarianism, are viewed as means to this end.

By not including most of Chapters IV–VIII in the more basic parts of the book, I do not mean to suggest that these chapters are peripheral, or merely applications. Rather, I believe that an important test of a theory of justice is how well it introduces order and system into our considered judgments over a wide range of questions. Therefore the topics of these chapters need to be taken up, and the conclusions reached modify in turn the view proposed. But in this regard the reader is more free to follow his preferences and to look at the problems which most concern him.

In writing this book I have acquired many debts in addition to those indicated in the text. Some of these I should like to acknowledge here. Three different versions of the manuscript have passed among students and colleagues, and I have benefited beyond estimation from the innumerable suggestions and criticisms that I have received. I am grateful to Allan Gibbard for his criticism of the first version (1964–1965). To meet his objections to the veil of ignorance as then presented, it seemed necessary to include a theory of the good. The notion of primary goods based on the conception discussed in Chapter VII is the result. I also owe him thanks, along with Norman Daniels, for pointing out difficulties with my account of utilitarianism as a basis for individual duties and obligations. Their objections led me to eliminate much of this topic and to simplify the treatment of this part of the theory. David Diamond objected forcefully to my discussion of equality, particularly to its failure to consider the relevance of status. I eventually included an account of self-respect as a primary good to try to deal with this and other questions, including those of society as a social union of social unions and the priority of liberty. I had profitable discussions with David Richards on the problems of political duty and obligation. Although supererogation is not a central topic of the book, I have been helped in my comments on it by Barry Curtis and John Troyer; even so they may still object to what I say. Thanks should also go to Michael Gardner and Jane English for several corrections which I managed to make in the final text.

I have been fortunate in receiving valuable criticisms from persons who have discussed the essays in print.[1] I am indebted to Brian Barry, Michael Lessnoff, and R. P. Wolff for their discussions of the formulation of and the argument for the two principles of justice.[2] Where I have not accepted their conclusions I have had to

1. In the order mentioned in the first paragraph, the references for the six essays are as follows: "Justice as Fairness," *The Philosophical Review*, vol. 57 (1958); "Distributive Justice: Some Addenda," *Natural Law Forum*, vol. 13 (1968); "Constitutional Liberty and the Concept of Justice," *Nomos VI: Justice*, ed. C. J. Friedrich and John Chapman (New York, Atherton Press, 1963); "Distributive Justice," *Philosophy, Politics, and Society*, Third Series, ed. Peter Laslett and W. G. Runciman (Oxford, Basil Blackwell, 1967); "The Justification of Civil Disobedience," *Civil Disobedience*, ed. H. A. Bedau (New York, Pegasus, 1969); "The Sense of Justice," *The Philosophical Review*, vol. 62 (1963).

2. See Brian Barry, "On Social Justice," *The Oxford Review* (Trinity Term, 1967), pp. 29–52; Michael Lessnoff, "John Rawls' Theory of Justice," *Political Studies*, vol. 19 (1971), pp. 65–80; and R. P. Wolff, "A Refutation of Rawls' Theorem on Justice," *Journal of Philosophy*, vol. 63 (1966), pp. 179–190. While "Distributive Justice" (1967) was completed and sent to the publisher before Wolff's article appeared, I regret that from oversight I failed to add a reference to it in proof.

amplify the argument to meet their objections. I hope the theory as now presented is no longer open to the difficulties they raised, nor to those urged by John Chapman.[3] The relation between the two principles of justice and what I call the general conception of justice is similar to that proposed by S. I. Benn.[4] I am grateful to him, and to Lawrence Stern and Scott Boorman, for suggestions in this direction. The substance of Norman Care's criticisms of the conception of moral theory found in the essays seems sound to me, and I have tried to develop the theory of justice so that it avoids his objections.[5] In doing this, I have learned from Burton Dreben, who made W. V. Quine's view clear to me and persuaded me that the notions of meaning and analyticity play no essential role in moral theory as I conceive of it. Their relevance for other philosophical questions need not be disputed here one way or the other; but I have tried to make the theory of justice independent of them. Thus I have followed with some modifications the point of view of my "Outline for Ethics."[6] I should also like to thank A. K. Sen for his searching discussion and criticisms of the theory of justice.[7] These have enabled me to improve the presentation at various places. His book will prove indispensable to philosophers who wish to study the more formal theory of social choice as economists think of it. At the same time, the philosophical problems receive careful treatment.

Many persons have volunteered written comments on the several versions of the manuscript. Gilbert Harman's on the earliest one

3. See John Chapman, "Justice and Fairness," in *Nomos VI: Justice*.

4. See S. I. Benn, "Egalitarianism and the Equal Consideration of Interests," *Nomos IX: Equality*, ed. J. R. Pennock and John Chapman (New York, Atherton Press, 1967), pp. 72–78.

5. See Norman Care, "Contractualism and Moral Criticism," *The Review of Metaphysics*, vol. 23 (1969), pp. 85–101. I should also like to acknowledge here the criticisms of my work by R. L. Cunningham, "Justice: Efficiency or Fairness," *The Personalist*, vol. 52 (1971); Dorothy Emmett, "Justice," *Proceedings of the Aristotelian Society*, supp. vol. (1969); Charles Frankel, "Justice and Rationality," in *Philosophy, Science, and Method*, ed. Sidney Morgenbesser, Patrick Suppes, and Morton White (New York, St. Martin's Press, 1969); and Ch. Perelman, *Justice* (New York, Random House, 1967), esp. pp. 39–51.

6. *The Philosophical Review*, vol. 50 (1951).

7. See *Collective Choice and Social Welfare* (San Francisco, Holden-Day, 1970), esp. pp. 136–141, 156–160.

were fundamental and forced me to abandon a number of views and to make basic changes at many points. I received others while at the Philosophical Institute at Boulder (summer 1966), from Leonard Krimerman, Richard Lee, and Huntington Terrell; and from Terrell again later. I have tried to accommodate to these, and to the very extensive and instructive comments of Charles Fried, Robert Nozick, and J. N. Shklar, each of whom has been of great help throughout. In developing the account of the good, I have gained much from J. M. Cooper, T. M. Scanlon, and A. T. Tymoczko, and from discussions over many years with Thomas Nagel, to whom I am also indebted for clarification about the relation between the theory of justice and utilitarianism. I must also thank R. B. Brandt and Joshua Rabinowitz for their many useful ideas for improvements in the second manuscript (1967–1968), and B. J. Diggs, J. C. Harsanyi, and W. G. Runciman for illuminating correspondence.

During the writing of the third version (1969–1970), Brandt, Tracy Kendler, E. S. Phelps, and Amélie Rorty were a constant source of advice, and their criticisms were of great assistance. On this manuscript I received many valuable comments and suggestions for changes from Herbert Morris, and from Lessnoff and Nozick; these have saved me from a number of lapses and have made the book much better. I am particularly grateful to Nozick for his unfailing help and encouragement during the last stages. Regrettably I have not been able to deal with all criticisms received, and I am well aware of the faults that remain; but the measure of my debt is not the shortfall from what might be but the distance traveled from the beginnings.

The Center for Advanced Study at Stanford provided the ideal place for me to complete my work. I should like to express my deep appreciation for its support in 1969–1970, and for that of the Guggenheim and Kendall foundations in 1964–1965. I am grateful to Anna Tower and to Margaret Griffin for helping me with the final manuscript.

Without the good will of all these good people I never could have finished this book.

John Rawls

Cambridge, Massachusetts
August 1971

CONTENTS

Part One. Theory

Contents

Part Two. Institutions

Part Three. Ends

PART ONE. THEORY

CHAPTER I. JUSTICE AS FAIRNESS

In this introductory chapter I sketch some of the main ideas of the theory of justice I wish to develop. The exposition is informal and intended to prepare the way for the more detailed arguments that follow. Unavoidably there is some overlap between this and later discussions. I begin by describing the role of justice in social cooperation and with a brief account of the primary subject of justice, the basic structure of society. I then present the main idea of justice as fairness, a theory of justice that generalizes and carries to a higher level of abstraction the traditional conception of the social contract. The compact of society is replaced by an initial situation that incorporates certain procedural constraints on arguments designed to lead to an original agreement on principles of justice. I also take up, for purposes of clarification and contrast, the classical utilitarian and intuitionist conceptions of justice and consider some of the differences between these views and justice as fairness. My guiding aim is to work out a theory of justice that is a viable alternative to these doctrines which have long dominated our philosophical tradition.

1. THE ROLE OF JUSTICE

Justice is the first virtue of social institutions, as truth is of systems of thought. A theory however elegant and economical must be rejected or revised if it is untrue; likewise laws and institutions no matter how efficient and well-arranged must be reformed or abolished if they are unjust. Each person possesses an inviolability founded on justice that even the welfare of society as a whole cannot override. For this reason justice denies that the loss of freedom for some is made right

3

by a greater good shared by others. It does not allow that the sacrifices imposed on a few are outweighed by the larger sum of advantages enjoyed by many. Therefore in a just society the liberties of equal citizenship are taken as settled; the rights secured by justice are not subject to political bargaining or to the calculus of social interests. The only thing that permits us to acquiesce in an erroneous theory is the lack of a better one; analogously, an injustice is tolerable only when it is necessary to avoid an even greater injustice. Being first virtues of human activities, truth and justice are uncompromising.

These propositions seem to express our intuitive conviction of the primacy of justice. No doubt they are expressed too strongly. In any event I wish to inquire whether these contentions or others similar to them are sound, and if so how they can be accounted for. To this end it is necessary to work out a theory of justice in the light of which these assertions can be interpreted and assessed. I shall begin by considering the role of the principles of justice. Let us assume, to fix ideas, that a society is a more or less self-sufficient association of persons who in their relations to one another recognize certain rules of conduct as binding and who for the most part act in accordance with them. Suppose further that these rules specify a system of cooperation designed to advance the good of those taking part in it. Then, although a society is a cooperative venture for mutual advantage, it is typically marked by a conflict as well as by an identity of interests. There is an identity of interests since social cooperation makes possible a better life for all than any would have if each were to live solely by his own efforts. There is a conflict of interests since persons are not indifferent as to how the greater benefits produced by their collaboration are distributed, for in order to pursue their ends they each prefer a larger to a lesser share. A set of principles is required for choosing among the various social arrangements which determine this division of advantages and for underwriting an agreement on the proper distributive shares. These principles are the principles of social justice: they provide a way of assigning rights and duties in the basic institutions of society and they define the appropriate distribution of the benefits and burdens of social cooperation.

Now let us say that a society is well-ordered when it is not only designed to advance the good of its members but when it is also effectively regulated by a public conception of justice. That is, it is a society in which (1) everyone accepts and knows that the others accept the same principles of justice, and (2) the basic social institutions generally satisfy and are generally known to satisfy these principles. In this case while men may put forth excessive demands on one another, they nevertheless acknowledge a common point of view from which their claims may be adjudicated. If men's inclination to self-interest makes their vigilance against one another necessary, their public sense of justice makes their secure association together possible. Among individuals with disparate aims and purposes a shared conception of justice establishes the bonds of civic friendship; the general desire for justice limits the pursuit of other ends. One may think of a public conception of justice as constituting the fundamental charter of a well-ordered human association.

Existing societies are of course seldom well-ordered in this sense, for what is just and unjust is usually in dispute. Men disagree about which principles should define the basic terms of their association. Yet we may still say, despite this disagreement, that they each have a conception of justice. That is, they understand the need for, and they are prepared to affirm, a characteristic set of principles for assigning basic rights and duties and for determining what they take to be the proper distribution of the benefits and burdens of social cooperation. Thus it seems natural to think of the concept of justice as distinct from the various conceptions of justice and as being specified by the role which these different sets of principles, these different conceptions, have in common.[1] Those who hold different conceptions of justice can, then, still agree that institutions are just when no arbitrary distinctions are made between persons in the assigning of basic rights and duties and when the rules determine a proper balance between competing claims to the advantages of social life. Men can agree to this description of just institutions since the notions of an arbitrary distinction and of a proper balance, which are included in the concept of justice, are left open for each to interpret according to the principles of justice that he accepts. These principles single out which similarities and differences among per-

1. Here I follow H. L. A. Hart, *The Concept of Law* (Oxford, The Clarendon Press, 1961), pp. 155–159.

sons are relevant in determining rights and duties and they specify which division of advantages is appropriate. Clearly this distinction between the concept and the various conceptions of justice settles no important questions. It simply helps to identify the role of the principles of social justice.

Some measure of agreement in conceptions of justice is, however, not the only prerequisite for a viable human community. There are other fundamental social problems, in particular those of coordination, efficiency, and stability. Thus the plans of individuals need to be fitted together so that their activities are compatible with one another and they can all be carried through without anyone's legitimate expectations being severely disappointed. Moreover, the execution of these plans should lead to the achievement of social ends in ways that are efficient and consistent with justice. And finally, the scheme of social cooperation must be stable: it must be more or less regularly complied with and its basic rules willingly acted upon; and when infractions occur, stabilizing forces should exist that prevent further violations and tend to restore the arrangement. Now it is evident that these three problems are connected with that of justice. In the absence of a certain measure of agreement on what is just and unjust, it is clearly more difficult for individuals to coordinate their plans efficiently in order to insure that mutually beneficial arrangements are maintained. Distrust and resentment corrode the ties of civility, and suspicion and hostility tempt men to act in ways they would otherwise avoid. So while the distinctive role of conceptions of justice is to specify basic rights and duties and to determine the appropriate distributive shares, the way in which a conception does this is bound to affect the problems of efficiency, coordination, and stability. We cannot, in general, assess a conception of justice by its distributive role alone, however useful this role may be in identifying the concept of justice. We must take into account its wider connections; for even though justice has a certain priority, being the most important virtue of institutions, it is still true that, other things equal, one conception of justice is preferable to another when its broader consequences are more desirable.

2. THE SUBJECT OF JUSTICE

Many different kinds of things are said to be just and unjust: not only laws, institutions, and social systems, but also particular actions of many kinds, including decisions, judgments, and imputations. We also call the attitudes and dispositions of persons, and persons themselves, just and unjust. Our topic, however, is that of social justice. For us the primary subject of justice is the basic structure of society, or more exactly, the way in which the major social institutions distribute fundamental rights and duties and determine the division of advantages from social cooperation. By major institutions I understand the political constitution and the principal economic and social arrangements. Thus the legal protection of freedom of thought and liberty of conscience, competitive markets, private property in the means of production, and the monogamous family are examples of major social institutions. Taken together as one scheme, the major institutions define men's rights and duties and influence their life-prospects, what they can expect to be and how well they can hope to do. The basic structure is the primary subject of justice because its effects are so profound and present from the start. The intuitive notion here is that this structure contains various social positions and that men born into different positions have different expectations of life determined, in part, by the political system as well as by economic and social circumstances. In this way the institutions of society favor certain starting places over others. These are especially deep inequalities. Not only are they pervasive, but they affect men's initial chances in life; yet they cannot possibly be justified by an appeal to the notions of merit or desert. It is these inequalities, presumably inevitable in the basic structure of any society, to which the principles of social justice must in the first instance apply. These principles, then, regulate the choice of a political constitution and the main elements of the economic and social system. The justice of a social scheme depends essentially on how fundamental rights and duties are assigned and on the economic opportunities and social conditions in the various sectors of society.

The scope of our inquiry is limited in two ways. First of all, I am concerned with a special case of the problem of justice. I shall not consider the justice of institutions and social practices generally, nor except in passing the justice of the law of nations and of relations between states (§ 58). Therefore, if one supposes that the concept of justice applies whenever there is an allotment of something rationally regarded as advantageous or disadvantageous, then we are interested in only one instance of its application. There is no reason to suppose ahead of time that the principles satisfactory for the basic structure hold for all cases. These principles may not work for the rules and practices of private associations or for those of less comprehensive social groups. They may be irrelevant for the various informal conventions and customs of everyday life; they may not elucidate the justice, or perhaps better, the fairness of voluntary cooperative arrangements or procedures for making contractual agreements. The conditions for the law of nations may require different principles arrived at in a somewhat different way. I shall be satisfied if it is possible to formulate a reasonable conception of justice for the basic structure of society conceived for the time being as a closed system isolated from other societies. The significance of this special case is obvious and needs no explanation. It is natural to conjecture that once we have a sound theory for this case, the remaining problems of justice will prove more tractable in the light of it. With suitable modifications such a theory should provide the key for some of these other questions.

The other limitation on our discussion is that for the most part I examine the principles of justice that would regulate a well-ordered society. Everyone is presumed to act justly and to do his part in upholding just institutions. Though justice may be, as Hume remarked, the cautious, jealous virtue, we can still ask what a perfectly just society would be like.[2] Thus I consider primarily what I call strict compliance as opposed to partial compliance theory (§§ 25, 39). The latter studies the principles that govern how we are to deal with injustice. It comprises such topics as the theory of punishment, the doctrine of just war, and the justification of the various ways of opposing unjust regimes, ranging from civil disobedience and militant resistance to revolution and rebellion. Also included here are questions of compensatory justice and of weighing one form of institutional injustice against another. Obviously the problems of partial

2. *An Enquiry Concerning the Principles of Morals,* sec. III, pt. I, par. 3, ed. L. A. Selby-Bigge, 2nd edition (Oxford, 1902), p. 184.

compliance theory are the pressing and urgent matters. These are the things that we are faced with in everyday life. The reason for beginning with ideal theory is that it provides, I believe, the only basis for the systematic grasp of these more pressing problems. The discussion of civil disobedience, for example, depends upon it (§§ 55–59). At least, I shall assume that a deeper understanding can be gained in no other way, and that the nature and aims of a perfectly just society is the fundamental part of the theory of justice.

Now admittedly the concept of the basic structure is somewhat vague. It is not always clear which institutions or features thereof should be included. But it would be premature to worry about this matter here. I shall proceed by discussing principles which do apply to what is certainly a part of the basic structure as intuitively understood; I shall then try to extend the application of these principles so that they cover what would appear to be the main elements of this structure. Perhaps these principles will turn out to be perfectly general, although this is unlikely. It is sufficient that they apply to the most important cases of social justice. The point to keep in mind is that a conception of justice for the basic structure is worth having for its own sake. It should not be dismissed because its principles are not everywhere satisfactory.

A conception of social justice, then, is to be regarded as providing in the first instance a standard whereby the distributive aspects of the basic structure of society are to be assessed. This standard, however, is not to be confused with the principles defining the other virtues, for the basic structure, and social arrangements generally, may be efficient or inefficient, liberal or illiberal, and many other things, as well as just or unjust. A complete conception defining principles for all the virtues of the basic structure, together with their respective weights when they conflict, is more than a conception of justice; it is a social ideal. The principles of justice are but a part, although perhaps the most important part, of such a conception. A social ideal in turn is connected with a conception of society, a vision of the way in which the aims and purposes of social cooperation are to be understood. The various conceptions of justice are the outgrowth of different notions of society against the background of opposing views of the natural necessities and opportunities of human life. Fully to understand a conception of justice we must make explicit the conception of social cooperation from which it derives. But in doing this we should not lose sight of the special role of the principles of justice or of the primary subject to which they apply.

In these preliminary remarks I have distinguished the concept of justice as meaning a proper balance between competing claims from a conception of justice as a set of related principles for identifying the relevant considerations which determine this balance. I have also characterized justice as but one part of a social ideal, although the theory I shall propose no doubt extends its everyday sense. This theory is not offered as a description of ordinary meanings but as an account of certain distributive principles for the basic structure of society. I assume that any reasonably complete ethical theory must include principles for this fundamental problem and that these principles, whatever they are, constitute its doctrine of justice. The concept of justice I take to be defined, then, by the role of its principles in assigning rights and duties and in defining the appropriate division of social advantages. A conception of justice is an interpretation of this role.

Now this approach may not seem to tally with tradition. I believe, though, that it does. The more specific sense that Aristotle gives to justice, and from which the most familiar formulations derive, is that of refraining from *pleonexia*, that is, from gaining some advantage for oneself by seizing what belongs to another, his property, his reward, his office, and the like, or by denying a person that which is due to him, the fulfillment of a promise, the repayment of a debt, the showing of proper respect, and so on.[3] It is evident that this definition is framed to apply to actions, and persons are thought to be just insofar as they have, as one of the permanent elements of their character, a steady and effective desire to act justly. Aristotle's definition clearly presupposes, however, an account of what properly belongs to a person and of what is due to him. Now such entitlements are, I believe, very often derived from social institutions and the legitimate expectations to which they give rise. There is no reason to

3. *Nicomachean Ethics*, 1129b–1130b5. I have followed the interpretation of Gregory Vlastos, "Justice and Happiness in *The Republic*," in *Plato: A Collection of Critical Essays*, edited by Vlastos (Garden City, N.Y., Doubleday and Company, 1971), vol. 2, pp. 70f. For a discussion of Aristotle on justice, see W. F. R. Hardie, *Aristotle's Ethical Theory* (Oxford, The Clarendon Press, 1968), ch. X.

think that Aristotle would disagree with this, and certainly he has a conception of social justice to account for these claims. The definition I adopt is designed to apply directly to the most important case, the justice of the basic structure. There is no conflict with the traditional notion.

3. THE MAIN IDEA OF THE THEORY OF JUSTICE

My aim is to present a conception of justice which generalizes and carries to a higher level of abstraction the familiar theory of the social contract as found, say, in Locke, Rousseau, and Kant.[4] In order to do this we are not to think of the original contract as one to enter a particular society or to set up a particular form of government. Rather, the guiding idea is that the principles of justice for the basic structure of society are the object of the original agreement. They are the principles that free and rational persons concerned to further their own interests would accept in an initial position of equality as defining the fundamental terms of their association. These principles are to regulate all further agreements; they specify the kinds of social cooperation that can be entered into and the forms of government that can be established. This way of regarding the principles of justice I shall call justice as fairness.

Thus we are to imagine that those who engage in social cooperation choose together, in one joint act, the principles which are to assign basic rights and duties and to determine the division of social benefits. Men are to decide in advance how they are to regulate their claims against one another and what is to be the foundation charter of their society. Just as each person must decide by rational reflection what constitutes his good, that is, the system of ends which

4. As the text suggests, I shall regard Locke's *Second Treatise of Government*, Rousseau's *The Social Contract*, and Kant's ethical works beginning with *The Foundations of the Metaphysics of Morals* as definitive of the contract tradition. For all of its greatness, Hobbes's *Leviathan* raises special problems. A general historical survey is provided by J. W. Gough, *The Social Contract*, 2nd ed. (Oxford, The Clarendon Press, 1957), and Otto Gierke, *Natural Law and the Theory of Society*, trans. with an introduction by Ernest Barker (Cambridge, The University Press, 1934). A presentation of the contract view as primarily an ethical theory is to be found in G. R. Grice, *The Grounds of Moral Judgment* (Cambridge, The University Press, 1967). See also §19, note 30.

it is rational for him to pursue, so a group of persons must decide once and for all what is to count among them as just and unjust. The choice which rational men would make in this hypothetical situation of equal liberty, assuming for the present that this choice problem has a solution, determines the principles of justice.

In justice as fairness the original position of equality corresponds to the state of nature in the traditional theory of the social contract. This original position is not, of course, thought of as an actual historical state of affairs, much less as a primitive condition of culture. It is understood as a purely hypothetical situation characterized so as to lead to a certain conception of justice.[5] Among the essential features of this situation is that no one knows his place in society, his class position or social status, nor does any one know his fortune in the distribution of natural assets and abilities, his intelligence, strength, and the like. I shall even assume that the parties do not know their conceptions of the good or their special psychological propensities. The principles of justice are chosen behind a veil of ignorance. This ensures that no one is advantaged or disadvantaged in the choice of principles by the outcome of natural chance or the contingency of social circumstances. Since all are similarly situated and no one is able to design principles to favor his particular condition, the principles of justice are the result of a fair agreement or bargain. For given the circumstances of the original position, the symmetry of everyone's relations to each other, this initial situation is fair between individuals as moral persons, that is, as rational beings with their own ends and capable, I shall assume, of a sense of justice. The original position is, one might say, the appropriate initial status quo, and thus the fundamental agreements reached in it are fair. This explains the propriety of the name "justice as fairness": it conveys the idea that the principles of justice are agreed to in an initial situation that is fair. The name does not mean that the con-

5. Kant is clear that the original agreement is hypothetical. See *The Metaphysics of Morals,* pt. I (*Rechtslehre*), especially §§ 47, 52; and pt. II of the essay "Concerning the Common Saying: This May Be True in Theory but It Does Not Apply in Practice," in *Kant's Political Writings,* ed. Hans Reiss and trans. by H. B. Nisbet (Cambridge, The University Press, 1970), pp. 73–87. See Georges Vlachos, *La Pensée politique de Kant* (Paris, Presses Universitaires de France, 1962), pp. 326–335; and J. G. Murphy, *Kant: The Philosophy of Right* (London, Macmillan, 1970), pp. 109–112, 133–136, for a further discussion.

cepts of justice and fairness are the same, any more than the phrase "poetry as metaphor" means that the concepts of poetry and metaphor are the same.

Justice as fairness begins, as I have said, with one of the most general of all choices which persons might make together, namely, with the choice of the first principles of a conception of justice which is to regulate all subsequent criticism and reform of institutions. Then, having chosen a conception of justice, we can suppose that they are to choose a constitution and a legislature to enact laws, and so on, all in accordance with the principles of justice initially agreed upon. Our social situation is just if it is such that by this sequence of hypothetical agreements we would have contracted into the general system of rules which defines it. Moreover, assuming that the original position does determine a set of principles (that is, that a particular conception of justice would be chosen), it will then be true that whenever social institutions satisfy these principles those engaged in them can say to one another that they are cooperating on terms to which they would agree if they were free and equal persons whose relations with respect to one another were fair. They could all view their arrangements as meeting the stipulations which they would acknowledge in an initial situation that embodies widely accepted and reasonable constraints on the choice of principles. The general recognition of this fact would provide the basis for a public acceptance of the corresponding principles of justice. No society can, of course, be a scheme of cooperation which men enter voluntarily in a literal sense; each person finds himself placed at birth in some particular position in some particular society, and the nature of this position materially affects his life prospects. Yet a society satisfying the principles of justice as fairness comes as close as a society can to being a voluntary scheme, for it meets the principles which free and equal persons would assent to under circumstances that are fair. In this sense its members are autonomous and the obligations they recognize self-imposed.

One feature of justice as fairness is to think of the parties in the initial situation as rational and mutually disinterested. This does not mean that the parties are egoists, that is, individuals with only certain kinds of interests, say in wealth, prestige, and domination. But they are conceived as not taking an interest in one another's interests.

They are to presume that even their spiritual aims may be opposed, in the way that the aims of those of different religions may be opposed. Moreover, the concept of rationality must be interpreted as far as possible in the narrow sense, standard in economic theory, of taking the most effective means to given ends. I shall modify this concept to some extent, as explained later (§ 25), but one must try to avoid introducing into it any controversial ethical elements. The initial situation must be characterized by stipulations that are widely accepted.

In working out the conception of justice as fairness one main task clearly is to determine which principles of justice would be chosen in the original position. To do this we must describe this situation in some detail and formulate with care the problem of choice which it presents. These matters I shall take up in the immediately succeeding chapters. It may be observed, however, that once the principles of justice are thought of as arising from an original agreement in a situation of equality, it is an open question whether the principle of utility would be acknowledged. Offhand it hardly seems likely that persons who view themselves as equals, entitled to press their claims upon one another, would agree to a principle which may require lesser life prospects for some simply for the sake of a greater sum of advantages enjoyed by others. Since each desires to protect his interests, his capacity to advance his conception of the good, no one has a reason to acquiesce in an enduring loss for himself in order to bring about a greater net balance of satisfaction. In the absence of strong and lasting benevolent impulses, a rational man would not accept a basic structure merely because it maximized the algebraic sum of advantages irrespective of its permanent effects on his own basic rights and interests. Thus it seems that the principle of utility is incompatible with the conception of social cooperation among equals for mutual advantage. It appears to be inconsistent with the idea of reciprocity implicit in the notion of a well-ordered society. Or, at any rate, so I shall argue.

I shall maintain instead that the persons in the initial situation would choose two rather different principles: the first requires equality in the assignment of basic rights and duties, while the second holds that social and economic inequalities, for example inequalities of wealth and authority, are just only if they result in compensating

14

benefits for everyone, and in particular for the least advantaged members of society. These principles rule out justifying institutions on the grounds that the hardships of some are offset by a greater good in the aggregate. It may be expedient but it is not just that some should have less in order that others may prosper. But there is no injustice in the greater benefits earned by a few provided that the situation of persons not so fortunate is thereby improved. The intuitive idea is that since everyone's well-being depends upon a scheme of cooperation without which no one could have a satisfactory life, the division of advantages should be such as to draw forth the willing cooperation of everyone taking part in it, including those less well situated. Yet this can be expected only if reasonable terms are proposed. The two principles mentioned seem to be a fair agreement on the basis of which those better endowed, or more fortunate in their social position, neither of which we can be said to deserve, could expect the willing cooperation of others when some workable scheme is a necessary condition of the welfare of all.[6] Once we decide to look for a conception of justice that nullifies the accidents of natural endowment and the contingencies of social circumstance as counters in quest for political and economic advantage, we are led to these principles. They express the result of leaving aside those aspects of the social world that seem arbitrary from a moral point of view.

The problem of the choice of principles, however, is extremely difficult. I do not expect the answer I shall suggest to be convincing to everyone. It is, therefore, worth noting from the outset that justice as fairness, like other contract views, consists of two parts: (1) an interpretation of the initial situation and of the problem of choice posed there, and (2) a set of principles which, it is argued, would be agreed to. One may accept the first part of the theory (or some variant thereof), but not the other, and conversely. The concept of the initial contractual situation may seem reasonable although the particular principles proposed are rejected. To be sure, I want to maintain that the most appropriate conception of this situation does lead to principles of justice contrary to utilitarianism and perfectionism, and therefore that the contract doctrine provides an alternative to these views. Still, one may dispute this contention even though

6. For the formulation of this intuitive idea I am indebted to Allan Gibbard.

one grants that the contractarian method is a useful way of studying ethical theories and of setting forth their underlying assumptions.

Justice as fairness is an example of what I have called a contract theory. Now there may be an objection to the term "contract" and related expressions, but I think it will serve reasonably well. Many words have misleading connotations which at first are likely to confuse. The terms "utility" and "utilitarianism" are surely no exception. They too have unfortunate suggestions which hostile critics have been willing to exploit; yet they are clear enough for those prepared to study utilitarian doctrine. The same should be true of the term "contract" applied to moral theories. As I have mentioned, to understand it one has to keep in mind that it implies a certain level of abstraction. In particular, the content of the relevant agreement is not to enter a given society or to adopt a given form of government, but to accept certain moral principles. Moreover, the undertakings referred to are purely hypothetical: a contract view holds that certain principles would be accepted in a well-defined initial situation.

The merit of the contract terminology is that it conveys the idea that principles of justice may be conceived as principles that would be chosen by rational persons, and that in this way conceptions of justice may be explained and justified. The theory of justice is a part, perhaps the most significant part, of the theory of rational choice. Furthermore, principles of justice deal with conflicting claims upon the advantages won by social cooperation; they apply to the relations among several persons or groups. The word "contract" suggests this plurality as well as the condition that the appropriate division of advantages must be in accordance with principles acceptable to all parties. The condition of publicity for principles of justice is also connoted by the contract phraseology. Thus, if these principles are the outcome of an agreement, citizens have a knowledge of the principles that others follow. It is characteristic of contract theories to stress the public nature of political principles. Finally there is the long tradition of the contract doctrine. Expressing the tie with this line of thought helps to define ideas and accords with natural piety. There are then several advantages in the use of the term "contract." With due precautions taken, it should not be misleading.

A final remark. Justice as fairness is not a complete contract theory. For it is clear that the contractarian idea can be extended to the choice of more or less an entire ethical system, that is, to a system including principles for all the virtues and not only for justice. Now for the most part I shall consider only principles of justice and others closely related to them; I make no attempt to discuss the virtues in a systematic way. Obviously if justice as fairness succeeds reasonably well, a next step would be to study the more general view suggested by the name "rightness as fairness." But even this wider theory fails to embrace all moral relationships, since it would seem to include only our relations with other persons and to leave out of account how we are to conduct ourselves toward animals and the rest of nature. I do not contend that the contract notion offers a way to approach these questions which are certainly of the first importance; and I shall have to put them aside. We must recognize the limited scope of justice as fairness and of the general type of view that it exemplifies. How far its conclusions must be revised once these other matters are understood cannot be decided in advance.

4. THE ORIGINAL POSITION AND JUSTIFICATION

I have said that the original position is the appropriate initial status quo which insures that the fundamental agreements reached in it are fair. This fact yields the name "justice as fairness." It is clear, then, that I want to say that one conception of justice is more reasonable than another, or justifiable with respect to it, if rational persons in the initial situation would choose its principles over those of the other for the role of justice. Conceptions of justice are to be ranked by their acceptability to persons so circumstanced. Understood in this way the question of justification is settled by working out a problem of deliberation: we have to ascertain which principles it would be rational to adopt given the contractual situation. This connects the theory of justice with the theory of rational choice.

If this view of the problem of justification is to succeed, we must, of course, describe in some detail the nature of this choice problem. A problem of rational decision has a definite answer only if we know the beliefs and interests of the parties, their relations with respect to one another, the alternatives between which they are to choose, the procedure whereby they make up their minds, and so on. As the circumstances are presented in different ways, correspondingly different principles are accepted. The concept of the original position, as I shall refer to it, is that of the most philosophically favored interpretation of this initial choice situation for the purposes of a theory of justice.

But how are we to decide what is the most favored interpretation? I assume, for one thing, that there is a broad measure of agreement that principles of justice should be chosen under certain conditions. To justify a particular description of the initial situation one shows that it incorporates these commonly shared presumptions. One argues from widely accepted but weak premises to more specific conclusions. Each of the presumptions should by itself be natural and plausible; some of them may seem innocuous or even trivial. The aim of the contract approach is to establish that taken together they impose significant bounds on acceptable principles of justice. The ideal outcome would be that these conditions determine a unique set of principles; but I shall be satisfied if they suffice to rank the main traditional conceptions of social justice.

One should not be misled, then, by the somewhat unusual conditions which characterize the original position. The idea here is simply to make vivid to ourselves the restrictions that it seems reasonable to impose on arguments for principles of justice, and therefore on these principles themselves. Thus it seems reasonable and generally acceptable that no one should be advantaged or disadvantaged by natural fortune or social circumstances in the choice of principles. It also seems widely agreed that it should be impossible to tailor principles to the circumstances of one's own case. We should insure further that particular inclinations and aspirations, and persons' conceptions of their good do not affect the principles adopted. The aim is to rule out those principles that it would be rational to propose for acceptance, however little the chance of success, only if one knew certain things that are irrelevant from the standpoint of justice. For example, if a man knew that he was wealthy, he might find it rational to advance the principle that various taxes for welfare measures be counted unjust; if he knew that he was poor, he would most likely propose the contrary principle. To represent the desired restrictions one imagines a situation in which everyone is deprived of this sort of information. One excludes the knowledge of those contingencies which sets men at odds and allows them to be guided by their prejudices. In this manner the veil of ignorance is arrived at in a natural way. This concept should cause no difficulty if we keep in mind the constraints on arguments that it is meant to express. At any time we can enter the original position, so to speak, simply by following a certain procedure, namely, by arguing for principles of justice in accordance with these restrictions.

It seems reasonable to suppose that the parties in the original position are equal. That is, all have the same rights in the procedure for choosing principles; each can make proposals, submit reasons for their acceptance, and so on. Obviously the purpose of these conditions is to represent equality between human beings as moral persons, as creatures having a conception of their good and capable of a sense of justice. The basis of equality is taken to be similarity in these two respects. Systems of ends are not ranked in value; and each man is presumed to have the requisite ability to understand and to act upon whatever principles are adopted. Together with the veil of ignorance, these conditions define the principles of justice as those which rational persons concerned to advance their interests would consent to as equals when none are known to be advantaged or disadvantaged by social and natural contingencies.

There is, however, another side to justifying a particular description of the original position. This is to see if the principles which would be chosen match our considered convictions of justice or extend them in an acceptable way. We can note whether applying these principles would lead us to make the same judgments about the basic structure of society which we now make intuitively and in which we have the greatest confidence; or whether, in cases where our present judgments are in doubt and given with hesitation, these principles offer a resolution which we can affirm on reflection. There are questions which we feel sure must be answered in a certain way. For example, we are confident that religious intolerance and racial discrimination are unjust. We think that we have examined these things with care and have reached what we believe is an impartial judgment not likely to be distorted by an excessive attention to our own interests. These convictions are provisional fixed points which we presume any conception of justice must fit. But we have much less assurance as to what is the correct distribution of wealth and authority. Here we may be looking for a way to remove our doubts. We can check an interpretation of the initial situation, then, by the capacity of its principles to accommodate our firmest convictions and to provide guidance where guidance is needed.

In searching for the most favored description of this situation we work from both ends. We begin by describing it so that it represents generally shared and preferably weak conditions. We then see if these conditions are strong enough to yield a significant set of principles. If not, we look for further premises equally reasonable. But if so, and these principles match our considered convictions of justice, then so far well and good. But presumably there will be discrepancies. In this case we have a choice. We can either modify the account of the initial situation or we can revise our existing judgments, for even the judgments we take provisionally as fixed points are liable to revision. By going back and forth, sometimes altering the conditions of the contractual circumstances, at others withdrawing our judgments and conforming them to principle, I assume that eventually we shall find a description of the initial situation that both expresses reasonable conditions and yields principles which match our considered judgments duly pruned and adjusted. This state of affairs I refer to as reflective equilibrium.[7] It is an equilibrium because at last our principles and judgments coincide; and it is reflective since we know to what principles our judgments conform and the premises of their derivation. At the moment everything is in order. But this equilibrium is not necessarily stable. It is liable to be upset by further examination of the conditions which should be imposed on the contractual situation and by particular

7. The process of mutual adjustment of principles and considered judgments is not peculiar to moral philosophy. See Nelson Goodman, *Fact, Fiction, and Forecast* (Cambridge, Mass., Harvard University Press, 1955), pp. 65–68, for parallel remarks concerning the justification of the principles of deductive and inductive inference.

cases which may lead us to revise our judgments. Yet for the time being we have done what we can to render coherent and to justify our convictions of social justice. We have reached a conception of the original position.

I shall not, of course, actually work through this process. Still, we may think of the interpretation of the original position that I shall present as the result of such a hypothetical course of reflection. It represents the attempt to accommodate within one scheme both reasonable philosophical conditions on principles as well as our considered judgments of justice. In arriving at the favored interpretation of the initial situation there is no point at which an appeal is made to self-evidence in the traditional sense either of general conceptions or particular convictions. I do not claim for the principles of justice proposed that they are necessary truths or derivable from such truths. A conception of justice cannot be deduced from self-evident premises or conditions on principles; instead, its justification is a matter of the mutual support of many considerations, of everything fitting together into one coherent view.

A final comment. We shall want to say that certain principles of justice are justified because they would be agreed to in an initial situation of equality. I have emphasized that this original position is purely hypothetical. It is natural to ask why, if this agreement is never actually entered into, we should take any interest in these principles, moral or otherwise. The answer is that the conditions embodied in the description of the original position are ones that we do in fact accept. Or if we do not, then perhaps we can be persuaded to do so by philosophical reflection. Each aspect of the contractual situation can be given supporting grounds. Thus what we shall do is to collect together into one conception a number of conditions on principles that we are ready upon due consideration to recognize as reasonable. These constraints express what we are prepared to regard as limits on fair terms of social cooperation. One way to look at the idea of the original position, therefore, is to see it as an expository device which sums up the meaning of these conditions and helps us to extract their consequences. On the other hand, this conception is also an intuitive notion that suggests its own elaboration, so that led on by it we are drawn to define more clearly the standpoint

thought experiment

from which we can best interpret moral relationships. We need a conception that enables us to envision our objective from afar: the intuitive notion of the original position is to do this for us.[8]

5. CLASSICAL UTILITARIANISM

There are many forms of utilitarianism, and the development of the theory has continued in recent years. I shall not survey these forms here, nor take account of the numerous refinements found in contemporary discussions. My aim is to work out a theory of justice that represents an alternative to utilitarian thought generally and so to all of these different versions of it. I believe that the contrast between the contract view and utilitarianism remains essentially the same in all these cases. Therefore I shall compare justice as fairness with familiar variants of intuitionism, perfectionism, and utilitarianism in order to bring out the underlying differences in the simplest way. With this end in mind, the kind of utilitarianism I shall describe here is the strict classical doctrine which receives perhaps its clearest and most accessible formulation in Sidgwick. The main idea is that society is rightly ordered, and therefore just, when its major institutions are arranged so as to achieve the greatest net balance of satisfaction summed over all the individuals belonging to it.[9]

8. Henri Poincaré remarks: "Il nous faut une faculté qui nous fasse voir le but de loin, et, cette faculté, c'est l'intuition." *La Valeur de la science* (Paris, Flammarion, 1909), p. 27.

9. I shall take Henry Sidgwick's *The Methods of Ethics,* 7th ed. (London, 1907), as summarizing the development of utilitarian moral theory. Book III of his *Principles of Political Economy* (London, 1883) applies this doctrine to questions of economic and social justice, and is a precursor of A. C. Pigou, *The Economics of Welfare* (London, Macmillan, 1920). Sidgwick's *Outlines of the History of Ethics,* 5th ed. (London, 1902), contains a brief history of the utilitarian tradition. We may follow him in assuming, somewhat arbitrarily, that it begins with Shaftesbury's *An Inquiry Concerning Virtue and Merit* (1711) and Hutcheson's *An Inquiry Concerning Moral Good and Evil* (1725). Hutcheson seems to have been the first to state clearly the principle of utility. He says in *Inquiry,* sec. III, §8, that "that action is best, which procures the greatest happiness for the greatest numbers; and that, worst, which, in like manner, occasions misery." Other major eighteenth century works are Hume's *A Treatise of Human Nature* (1739), and *An Enquiry Concerning the Principles of Morals* (1751); Adam Smith's *A Theory of the Moral*

We may note first that there is, indeed, a way of thinking of society which makes it easy to suppose that the most rational conception of justice is utilitarian. For consider: each man in realizing his own interests is certainly free to balance his own losses against his own gains. We may impose a sacrifice on ourselves now for the sake of a greater advantage later. A person quite properly acts, at least when others are not affected, to achieve his own greatest good, to advance his rational ends as far as possible. Now why should not a society act on precisely the same principle applied to the group and therefore regard that which is rational for one man as right for an association of men? Just as the well-being of a person is constructed from the series of satisfactions that are experienced at different moments in the course of his life, so in very much the same way the well-being of society is to be constructed from the fulfillment of the systems of desires of the many individuals who belong to it. Since the principle for an individual is to advance as far as possible his own welfare, his own system of desires, the principle for society is to advance as far as possible the welfare of the group, to realize to the

Sentiments (1759); and Bentham's The Principles of Morals and Legislation (1789). To these we must add the writings of J. S. Mill represented by Utilitarianism (1863) and F. Y. Edgeworth's Mathematical Psychics (London, 1888).

The discussion of utilitarianism has taken a different turn in recent years by focusing on what we may call the coordination problem and related questions of publicity. This development stems from the essays of R. F. Harrod, "Utilitarianism Revised," Mind, vol. 45 (1936); J. D. Mabbott, "Punishment," Mind, vol. 48 (1939); Jonathan Harrison, "Utilitarianism, Universalisation, and Our Duty to Be Just," Proceedings of the Aristotelian Society, vol. 53 (1952–53); and J. O. Urmson, "The Interpretation of the Philosophy of J. S. Mill," Philosophical Quarterly, vol. 3 (1953). See also J. J. C. Smart, "Extreme and Restricted Utilitarianism," Philosophical Quarterly, vol. 6 (1956), and his An Outline of a System of Utilitarian Ethics (Cambridge, The University Press, 1961). For an account of these matters, see David Lyons, Forms and Limits of Utilitarianism (Oxford, The Clarendon Press, 1965); and Allan Gibbard, "Utilitarianisms and Coordination" (dissertation, Harvard University, 1971). The problems raised by these works, as important as they are, I shall leave aside as not bearing directly on the more elementary question of distribution which I wish to discuss.

Finally, we should note here the essays of J. C. Harsanyi, in particular, "Cardinal Utility in Welfare Economics and in the Theory of Risk-Taking," Journal of Political Economy, 1953, and "Cardinal Welfare, Individualistic Ethics, and Interpersonal Comparisons of Utility," Journal of Political Economy, 1955; and R. B. Brandt, "Some Merits of One Form of Rule-Utilitarianism," University of Colorado Studies (Boulder, Colorado, 1967). See below §§27–28.

greatest extent the comprehensive system of desire arrived at from the desires of its members. Just as an individual balances present and future gains against present and future losses, so a society may balance satisfactions and dissatisfactions between different individuals. And so by these reflections one reaches the principle of utility in a natural way: a society is properly arranged when its institutions maximize the net balance of satisfaction. The principle of choice for an association of men is interpreted as an extension of the principle of choice for one man. Social justice is the principle of rational prudence applied to an aggregative conception of the welfare of the group (§ 30).[10]

This idea is made all the more attractive by a further consideration. The two main concepts of ethics are those of the right and the good; the concept of a morally worthy person is, I believe, derived from them. The structure of an ethical theory is, then, largely determined by how it defines and connects these two basic notions. Now it seems that the simplest way of relating them is taken by teleological theories: the good is defined independently from the right, and then the right is defined as that which maximizes the good.[11] More precisely, those institutions and acts are right which of the available alternatives produce the most good, or at least as much good as any of the other institutions and acts open as real possibilities (a rider needed when the maximal class is not a singleton). Teleological theories have a deep intuitive appeal since they seem to embody the idea of rationality. It is natural to think that

10. On this point see also D. P. Gauthier, *Practical Reasoning* (Oxford, Clarendon Press, 1963), pp. 126f. The text elaborates the suggestion found in "Constitutional Liberty and the Concept of Justice," *Nomos VI: Justice*, ed. C. J. Friedrich and J. W. Chapman (New York, Atherton Press, 1963), pp. 124f, which in turn is related to the idea of justice as a higher-order administrative decision. See "Justice as Fairness," *Philosophical Review*, 1958, pp. 185–187. For references to utilitarians who explicitly affirm this extension, see §30, note 37. That the principle of social integration is distinct from the principle of personal integration is stated by R. B. Perry, *General Theory of Value* (New York, Longmans, Green, and Company, 1926), pp. 674–677. He attributes the error of overlooking this fact to Emile Durkheim and others with similar views. Perry's conception of social integration is that brought about by a shared and dominant benevolent purpose. See below, §24.

11. Here I adopt W. K. Frankena's definition of teleological theories in *Ethics* (Englewood Cliffs, N.J., Prentice Hall, Inc., 1963), p. 13.

rationality is maximizing something and that in morals it must be maximizing the good. Indeed, it is tempting to suppose that it is self-evident that things should be arranged so as to lead to the most good.

It is essential to keep in mind that in a teleological theory the good is defined independently from the right. This means two things. First, the theory accounts for our considered judgments as to which things are good (our judgments of value) as a separate class of judgments intuitively distinguishable by common sense, and then proposes the hypothesis that the right is maximizing the good as already specified. Second, the theory enables one to judge the goodness of things without referring to what is right. For example, if pleasure is said to be the sole good, then presumably pleasures can be recognized and ranked in value by criteria that do not presuppose any standards of right, or what we would normally think of as such. Whereas if the distribution of goods is also counted as a good, perhaps a higher order one, and the theory directs us to produce the most good (including the good of distribution among others), we no longer have a teleological view in the classical sense. The problem of distribution falls under the concept of right as one intuitively understands it, and so the theory lacks an independent definition of the good. The clarity and simplicity of classical teleological theories derives largely from the fact that they factor our moral judgments into two classes, the one being characterized separately while the other is then connected with it by a maximizing principle.

Teleological doctrines differ, pretty clearly, according to how the conception of the good is specified. If it is taken as the realization of human excellence in the various forms of culture, we have what may be called perfectionism. This notion is found in Aristotle and Nietzsche, among others. If the good is defined as pleasure, we have hedonism; if as happiness, eudaimonism, and so on. I shall understand the principle of utility in its classical form as defining the good as the satisfaction of desire, or perhaps better, as the satisfaction of rational desire. This accords with the view in all essentials and provides, I believe, a fair interpretation of it. The appropriate terms of social cooperation are settled by whatever in the circumstances will achieve the greatest sum of satisfaction of the rational desires of individuals. It is impossible to deny the initial plausibility and attractiveness of this conception.

The striking feature of the utilitarian view of justice is that it does not matter, except indirectly, how this sum of satisfactions is distributed among individuals any more than it matters, except indirectly, how one man distributes his satisfactions over time. The correct distribution in either case is that which yields the maximum fulfillment. Society must allocate its means of satisfaction whatever these are, rights and duties, opportunities and privileges, and various forms of wealth, so as to achieve this maximum if it can. But in itself no distribution of satisfaction is better than another except that the more equal distribution is to be preferred to break ties.[12] It is true that certain common sense precepts of justice, particularly those which concern the protection of liberties and rights, or which express the claims of desert, seem to contradict this contention. But from a utilitarian standpoint the explanation of these precepts and of their seemingly stringent character is that they are those precepts which experience shows should be strictly respected and departed from only under exceptional circumstances if the sum of advantages is to be maximized.[13] Yet, as with all other precepts, those of justice are derivative from the one end of attaining the greatest balance of satisfaction. Thus there is no reason in principle why the greater gains of some should not compensate for the lesser losses of others; or more importantly, why the violation of the liberty of a few might not be made right by the greater good shared by many. It simply happens that under most conditions, at least in a reasonably advanced stage of civilization, the greatest sum of advantages is not attained in this way. No doubt the strictness of common sense precepts of justice has a certain usefulness in limiting men's propensities to injustice and to socially injurious actions, but the utilitarian believes that to affirm this strictness as a first principle of morals is a mistake. For just as it is rational for one man to maximize the fulfillment of his system of desires, it is right for a society to maximize the net balance of satisfaction taken over all of its members.

The most natural way, then, of arriving at utilitarianism (although not, of course, the only way of doing so) is to adopt for society as a

12. On this point see Sidgwick, *The Methods of Ethics*, pp. 416f.
13. See J. S. Mill, *Utilitarianism*, ch. V, last two pars.

whole the principle of rational choice for one man. Once this is recognized, the place of the impartial spectator and the emphasis on sympathy in the history of utilitarian thought is readily understood. For it is by the conception of the impartial spectator and the use of sympathetic identification in guiding our imagination that the principle for one man is applied to society. It is this spectator who is conceived as carrying out the required organization of the desires of all persons into one coherent system of desire; it is by this construction that many persons are fused into one. Endowed with ideal powers of sympathy and imagination, the impartial spectator is the perfectly rational individual who identifies with and experiences the desires of others as if these desires were his own. In this way he ascertains the intensity of these desires and assigns them their appropriate weight in the one system of desire the satisfaction of which the ideal legislator then tries to maximize by adjusting the rules of the social system. On this conception of society separate individuals are thought of as so many different lines along which rights and duties are to be assigned and scarce means of satisfaction allocated in accordance with rules so as to give the greatest fulfillment of wants. The nature of the decision made by the ideal legislator is not, therefore, materially different from that of an entrepreneur deciding how to maximize his profit by producing this or that commodity, or that of a consumer deciding how to maximize his satisfaction by the purchase of this or that collection of goods. In each case there is a single person whose system of desires determines the best allocation of limited means. The correct decision is essentially a question of efficient administration. This view of social cooperation is the consequence of extending to society the principle of choice for one man, and then, to make this extension work, conflating all persons into one through the imaginative acts of the impartial sympathetic spectator. Utilitarianism does not take seriously the distinction between persons.

6. SOME RELATED CONTRASTS

It has seemed to many philosophers, and it appears to be supported by the convictions of common sense, that we distinguish as a matter of principle between the claims of liberty and right on the one hand and the desirability of increasing aggregate social welfare on the other; and that we give a certain priority, if not absolute weight, to the former. Each member of society is thought to have an inviolability founded on justice or, as some say, on natural right, which even the welfare of every one else cannot override. Justice denies that the loss of freedom for some is made right by a greater good shared by others. The reasoning which balances the gains and losses of different persons as if they were one person is excluded. Therefore in a just society the basic liberties are taken for granted and the rights secured by justice are not subject to political bargaining or to the calculus of social interests.

Justice as fairness attempts to account for these common sense convictions concerning the priority of justice by showing that they are the consequence of principles which would be chosen in the original position. These judgments reflect the rational preferences and the initial equality of the contracting parties. Although the utilitarian recognizes that, strictly speaking, his doctrine conflicts with these sentiments of justice, he maintains that common sense precepts of justice and notions of natural right have but a subordinate validity as secondary rules; they arise from the fact that under the conditions of civilized society there is great social utility in following them for the most part and in permitting violations only under exceptional circumstances. Even the excessive zeal with which we are apt to affirm these precepts and to appeal to these rights is itself granted a certain usefulness, since it counterbalances a natural human tendency to violate them in ways not sanctioned by utility. Once we understand this, the apparent disparity between the utilitarian principle and the strength of these persuasions of justice is no longer a philosophical difficulty. Thus while the contract doctrine accepts our convictions about the priority of justice as on the whole sound, utilitarianism seeks to account for them as a socially useful illusion.

A second contrast is that whereas the utilitarian extends to society the principle of choice for one man, justice as fairness, being a contract view, assumes that the principles of social choice, and so the principles of justice, are themselves the object of an original agreement. There is no reason to suppose that the principles which should regulate an association of men is simply an extension of the principle of choice for one man. On the contrary: if we assume that the correct regulative principle for anything depends on the nature of that thing, and that the plurality of distinct persons with separate systems of ends is an essential feature of human societies, we should not expect the principles of social choice to be utilitarian. To be sure, it has not been shown by anything said so far that the parties in the original position would not choose the principle of utility to define the terms of social cooperation. This is a difficult question which I shall examine later on. It is perfectly possible, from all that one knows at this point, that some form of the principle of utility would be adopted, and therefore that contract theory leads eventually to a deeper and more roundabout justification of utilitarianism. In fact a derivation of this kind is sometimes suggested by Bentham and Edgeworth, although it is not developed by them in any systematic way and to my knowledge it is not found in Sidgwick.[14] For the present I shall simply assume that the persons in the original position would reject the utility principle and that they would adopt instead, for the kinds of reasons previously sketched, the two principles of justice already mentioned. In any case, from the standpoint of contract theory one cannot arrive at a principle of social choice merely by extending the principle of rational prudence to the system of desires constructed by the impartial spectator. To do this is not to take seriously the plurality and distinctness of individuals, nor to recognize as the basis of justice that to which men would consent. Here we may note a curious anomaly. It is customary to think of utilitarianism as individualistic, and certainly there are good reasons for this. The utilitarians were strong defenders of liberty and freedom of thought, and they held that the good of society is constituted by the advantages enjoyed by individuals. Yet utilitarianism is not individualistic, at least when arrived at by the more natural course of reflection, in that, by conflating all systems of desires, it applies to society the principle of choice for **one** man. And thus we see that the second contrast is

14. For Bentham see *The Principles of International Law*, Essay I, in *The Works of Jeremy Bentham*, ed. John Bowring (Edinburgh, 1838–1843), vol. II, p. 537; for Edgeworth see *Mathematical Psychics*, pp. 52–56, and also the first pages of "The Pure Theory of Taxation," *Economic Journal*, vol. 7 (1897), where the same argument is presented more briefly. See below, §28.

related to the first, since it is this conflation, and the principle based upon it, which subjects the rights secured by justice to the calculus of social interests.

The last contrast that I shall mention now is that utilitarianism is a teleological theory whereas justice as fairness is not. By definition, then, the latter is a deontological theory, one that either does not specify the good independently from the right, or does not interpret the right as maximizing the good. (It should be noted that deontological theories are defined as non-teleological ones, not as views that characterize the rightness of institutions and acts independently from their consequences. All ethical doctrines worth our attention take consequences into account in judging rightness. One which did not would simply be irrational, crazy.) Justice as fairness is a deontological theory in the second way. For if it is assumed that the persons in the original position would choose a principle of equal liberty and restrict economic and social inequalities to those in everyone's interests, there is no reason to think that just institutions will maximize the good. (Here I suppose with utilitarianism that the good is defined as the satisfaction of rational desire.) Of course, it is not impossible that the most good is produced but it would be a coincidence. The question of attaining the greatest net balance of satisfaction never arises in justice as fairness; this maximum principle is not used at all.

There is a further point in this connection. In utilitarianism the satisfaction of any desire has some value in itself which must be taken into account in deciding what is right. In calculating the greatest balance of satisfaction it does not matter, except indirectly, what the desires are for.[15] We are to arrange institutions so as to obtain the greatest sum of satisfactions; we ask no questions about their source or quality but only how their satisfaction would affect the total of well-being. Social welfare depends directly and solely upon the levels of satisfaction or dissatisfaction of individuals. Thus if men take a certain pleasure in discriminating against one another, in subjecting others to a lesser liberty as a means of enhancing their self-respect, then the satisfaction of these desires must be weighed in our

15. Bentham, *The Principles of Morals and Legislation*, ch. I, sec. IV.

deliberations according to their intensity, or whatever, along with other desires. If society decides to deny them fulfillment, or to suppress them, it is because they tend to be socially destructive and a greater welfare can be achieved in other ways.

In justice as fairness, on the other hand, persons accept in advance a principle of equal liberty and they do this without a knowledge of their more particular ends. They implicitly agree, therefore, to conform their conceptions of their good to what the principles of justice require, or at least not to press claims which directly violate them. An individual who finds that he enjoys seeing others in positions of lesser liberty understands that he has no claim whatever to this enjoyment. The pleasure he takes in other's deprivations is wrong in itself: it is a satisfaction which requires the violation of a principle to which he would agree in the original position. The principles of right, and so of justice, put limits on which satisfactions have value; they impose restrictions on what are reasonable conceptions of one's good. In drawing up plans and in deciding on aspirations men are to take these constraints into account. Hence in justice as fairness one does not take men's propensities and inclinations as given, whatever they are, and then seek the best way to fulfill them. Rather, their desires and aspirations are restricted from the outset by the principles of justice which specify the boundaries that men's systems of ends must respect. We can express this by saying that in justice as fairness the concept of right is prior to that of the good. A just social system defines the scope within which individuals must develop their aims, and it provides a framework of rights and opportunities and the means of satisfaction within and by the use of which these ends may be equitably pursued. The priority of justice is accounted for, in part, by holding that the interests requiring the violation of justice have no value. Having no merit in the first place, they cannot override its claims.[16]

This priority of the right over the good in justice as fairness turns

16. The priority of right is a central feature of Kant's ethics. See, for example, *The Critique of Practical Reason*, ch. II, bk. I of *pt. I*, esp. pp. 62–65 of vol. 5 of *Kants Gesammelte Schriften, Preussische Akademie der Wissenschaften* (Berlin, 1913). A clear statement is to be found in "Theory and Practice" (to abbreviate the title), *Political Writings*, pp. 67f.

out to be a central feature of the conception. It imposes certain criteria on the design of the basic structure as a whole; these arrangements must not tend to generate propensities and attitudes contrary to the two principles of justice (that is, to certain principles which are given from the first a definite content) and they must insure that just institutions are stable. Thus certain initial bounds are placed upon what is good and what forms of character are morally worthy, and so upon what kinds of persons men should be. Now any theory of justice will set up some limits of this kind, namely, those that are required if its first principles are to be satisfied given the circumstances. Utilitarianism excludes those desires and propensities which if encouraged or permitted would, in view of the situation, lead to a lesser net balance of satisfaction. But this restriction is largely formal, and in the absence of fairly detailed knowledge of the circumstances it does not give much indication of what these desires and propensities are. This is not, by itself, an objection to utilitarianism. It is simply a feature of utilitarian doctrine that it relies very heavily upon the natural facts and contingencies of human life in determining what forms of moral character are to be encouraged in a just society. The moral ideal of justice as fairness is more deeply embedded in the first principles of the ethical theory. This is characteristic of natural rights views (the contractarian tradition) in comparison with the theory of utility.

In setting forth these contrasts between justice as fairness and utilitarianism, I have had in mind only the classical doctrine. This is the view of Bentham and Sidgwick and of the utilitarian economists Edgeworth and Pigou. The kind of utilitarianism espoused by Hume would not serve my purpose; indeed, it is not strictly speaking utilitarian. In his well-known arguments against Locke's contract theory, for example, Hume maintains that the principles of fidelity and allegiance both have the same foundation in utility, and therefore that nothing is gained from basing political obligation on an original contract. Locke's doctrine represents, for Hume, an unnecessary shuffle: one might as well appeal directly to utility.[17] But all Hume seems to mean by utility is the general interests and necessities of society. The

17. "Of the Original Contract," *Essays: Moral, Political, and Literary,* ed. T. H. Green and T. H. Grose, vol. 1 (London, 1875), pp. 454f.

32

principles of fidelity and allegiance derive from utility in the sense that the maintenance of the social order is impossible unless these principles are generally respected. But then Hume assumes that each man stands to gain, as judged by his long-term advantage, when law and government conform to the precepts founded on utility. No mention is made of the gains of some outweighing the disadvantages of others. For Hume, then, utility seems to be identical with some form of the common good; institutions satisfy its demands when they are to everyone's interests, at least in the long run. Now if this interpretation of Hume is correct, there is offhand no conflict with the priority of justice and no incompatibility with Locke's contract doctrine. For the role of equal rights in Locke is precisely to ensure that the only permissible departures from the state of nature are those which respect these rights and serve the common interest. It is clear that all the transformations from the state of nature which Locke approves of satisfy this condition and are such that rational men concerned to advance their ends could consent to them in a state of equality. Hume nowhere disputes the propriety of these constraints. His critique of Locke's contract doctrine never denies, or even seems to recognize, its fundamental contention.

The merit of the classical view as formulated by Bentham, Edgeworth, and Sidgwick is that it clearly recognizes what is at stake, namely, the relative priority of the principles of justice and of the rights derived from these principles. The question is whether the imposition of disadvantages on a few can be outweighed by a greater sum of advantages enjoyed by others; or whether the weight of justice requires an equal liberty for all and permits only those economic and social inequalities which are to each person's interests. Implicit in the contrasts between classical utilitarianism and justice as fairness is a difference in the underlying conceptions of society. In the one we think of a well-ordered society as a scheme of cooperation for reciprocal advantage regulated by principles which persons would choose in an initial situation that is fair, in the other as the efficient administration of social resources to maximize the satisfaction of the system of desire constructed by the impartial spectator from the many individual systems of desires accepted as given. The comparison with classical utilitarianism in its more natural derivation brings out this contrast.

7. INTUITIONISM

I shall think of intuitionism in a more general way than is customary: namely, as the doctrine that there is an irreducible family of first principles which have to be weighed against one another by asking ourselves which balance, in our considered judgment, is the most just. Once we reach a certain level of generality, the intuitionist maintains that there exist no higher-order constructive criteria for determining the proper emphasis for the competing principles of justice. While the complexity of the moral facts requires a number of distinct principles, there is no single standard that accounts for them or assigns them their weights. Intuitionist theories, then, have two features: first, they consist of a plurality of first principles which may conflict to give contrary directives in particular types of cases; and second, they include no explicit method, no priority rules, for weighing these principles against one another: we are simply to strike a balance by intuition, by what seems to us most nearly right. Or if there are priority rules, these are thought to be more or less trivial and of no substantial assistance in reaching a judgment.[18]

Various other contentions are commonly associated with intuitionism, for example, that the concepts of the right and the good are

18. Intuitionist theories of this type are found in Brian Barry, *Political Argument* (London, Routledge and Kegan Paul, 1965), see esp. pp. 4–8, 286f; R. B. Brandt, *Ethical Theory* (Englewood Cliffs, N.J., Prentice-Hall, Inc. 1959), pp. 404, 426, 429f, where the principle of utility is combined with a principle of equality; and Nicholas Rescher, *Distributive Justice* (New York, Bobbs-Merrill, 1966), pp. 35–41, 115–121, where analogous restrictions are introduced by the concept of the effective average. Robert Nozick discusses some of the problems in developing this kind of intuitionism in "Moral Complications and Moral Structures," *Natural Law Forum*, vol. 13 (1968).

Intuitionism in the traditional sense includes certain epistemological theses, for example, those concerning the self-evidence and necessity of moral principles. Here representative works are G. E. Moore, *Principia Ethica* (Cambridge, The University Press, 1903), esp. chs. I and VI; H. A. Prichard's essays and lectures in *Moral Obligation* (Oxford, The Clarendon Press, 1949), especially the first essay, "Does Moral Philosophy Rest on a Mistake?" (1912); W. D. Ross, *The Right and the Good* (Oxford, The Clarendon Press, 1930), especially chs. I and II, and *The Foundations of Ethics* (Oxford, The Clarendon Press, 1939). See also the eighteenth century treatise by Richard Price, *A Review of the Principal Questions of Morals*, 3rd ed., 1787, ed. D. D. Raphael (Oxford, The Clarendon Press, 1948). For a recent discussion of this classical form of intuitionism, see H. J. McCloskey, *Meta-Ethics and Normative Ethics* (The Hague, Martinus Nijhoff, 1969).

unanalyzable, that moral principles when suitably formulated express self-evident propositions about legitimate moral claims, and so on. But I shall leave these matters aside. These characteristic epistemological doctrines are not a necessary part of intuitionism as I understand it. Perhaps it would be better if we were to speak of intuitionism in this broad sense as pluralism. Still, a conception of justice can be pluralistic without requiring us to weigh its principles by intuition. It may contain the requisite priority rules. To emphasize the direct appeal to our considered judgment in the balancing of principles, it seems appropriate to think of intuitionism in this more general fashion. How far such a view is committed to certain epistemological theories is a separate question.

Now so understood, there are many kinds of intuitionism. Not only are our everyday notions of this type but so perhaps are most philosophical doctrines. One way of distinguishing between intuitionist views is by the level of generality of their principles. Common sense intuitionism takes the form of groups of rather specific precepts, each group applying to a particular problem of justice. There is a group of precepts which applies to the question of fair wages, another to that of taxation, still another to punishment, and so on. In arriving at the notion of a fair wage, say, we are to balance somehow various competing criteria, for example, the claims of skill, training, effort, responsibility, and the hazards of the job, as well as to make some allowance for need. No one presumably would decide by any one of these precepts alone, and some compromise between them must be struck. The determination of wages by existing institutions also represents, in effect, a particular weighting of these claims. This weighting, however, is normally influenced by the demands of different social interests and so by relative positions of power and influence. It may not, therefore, conform to any one's conception of a fair wage. This is particularly likely to be true since persons with different interests are likely to stress the criteria which advance their ends. Those with more ability and education are prone to emphasize the claims of skill and training, whereas those lacking these advantages urge the claim of need. But not only are our everyday ideas of justice influenced by our own situation, they are also strongly colored by custom and current expectations. And by what criteria are we to judge the justice of custom itself and the legitimacy of these expectations? To reach some measure of understanding and agreement which goes beyond a mere de facto resolution of competing interests and a reliance on existing conventions and established expectations, it is necessary to move to a more general scheme for determining the balance of precepts, or at least for confining it within narrower limits.

Thus we can consider the problems of justice by reference to certain ends of social policy. Yet this approach also is likely to rely on intuition, since it normally takes the form of balancing various economic and social objectives. For example, suppose that allocative efficiency, full employment, a larger national income, and its more equal distribution are accepted as social ends. Then, given the desired weighting of these aims, and the existing institutional setup, the precepts of fair wages, just taxation, and so on will receive their due emphasis. In order to achieve greater efficiency and equity, one may follow a policy which has the effect of stressing skill and effort in the payment of wages, leaving the precept of need to be handled in some other fashion, perhaps by welfare transfers. An intuitionism of social ends provides a basis for deciding whether the determination of fair wages makes sense in view of the taxes to be imposed. How we weigh the precepts in one group is adjusted to how we weigh them in another. In this way we have managed to introduce a certain coherence into our judgments of justice; we have moved beyond the narrow de facto compromise of interests to a wider view. Of course we are still left with an appeal to intuition in the balancing of the higher-order ends of policy themselves. Different weightings for these are not by any means trivial variations but often correspond to profoundly opposed political convictions.

The principles of philosophical conceptions are of the most general kind. Not only are they intended to account for the ends of social policy, but the emphasis assigned to these principles should correspondingly determine the balance of these ends. For purposes of illustration, let us discuss a rather simple yet familiar conception based on the aggregative-distributive dichotomy. It has two principles: the basic structure of society is to be designed first to produce the most good in the sense of the greatest net balance of satisfaction, and second to distribute satisfactions equally. Both principles have, of course, *ceteris paribus* clauses. The first principle, the principle of

utility, acts in this case as a standard of efficiency, urging us to produce as large a total as we can, other things equal; whereas the
second principle serves as a standard of justice constraining the pursuit of aggregate well-being and evening out of the distribution of
advantages.

This conception is intuitionist because no priority rule is provided
for determining how these two principles are to be balanced against
each other. Widely different weights are consistent with accepting
these principles. No doubt it is natural to make certain assumptions
about how most people would in fact balance them. For one thing, at
different combinations of total satisfaction and degrees of equality,
we presumably would give these principles different weights. For
example, if there is a large total satisfaction but it is unequally distributed, we would probably think it more urgent to increase equality
than if the large aggregate well-being were already rather evenly
shared. This can be put more formally by using the economist's device of indifference curves.[19] Assume that we can measure the extent
to which particular arrangements of the basic structure satisfy these
principles; and represent total satisfaction on the positive X-axis and
equality on the positive Y-axis. (The latter may be supposed to have
an upper bound at perfect equality.) The extent to which an arrangement of the basic structure fulfills these principles can now be
represented by a point in the plane.

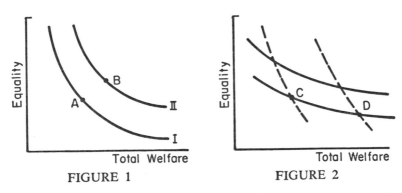

FIGURE 1   FIGURE 2

19. For the use of this device to illustrate intuitionist conceptions, see Barry,
Political Argument, pp. 3–8. Most any book on demand theory or welfare economics will contain an exposition. W. J. Baumol, *Economic Theory and Operations
Analysis*, 2nd ed. (Englewood Cliffs N.J., Prentice-Hall, Inc., 1965), ch. IX is
an accessible account.

Now clearly a point which is northeast of another is a better arrangement: it is superior on both counts. For example, the point B is better than the point A in figure 1. Indifference curves are formed by connecting points judged equally just. Thus curve I in figure 1 consists of the points rated equally with point A which lies on that curve; curve II consists of the points ranked along with point B, and so on. We may assume that these curves slope downward to the right; and also that they do not intersect, otherwise the judgments they represent would be inconsistent. The slope of the curve at any point expresses the relative weights of equality and total satisfaction at the combination the point represents; the changing slope along an indifference curve shows how the relative urgency of the principles shifts as they are more or less satisfied. Thus, moving along either of the indifference curves in figure 1, we see that as equality decreases a larger and larger increase in the sum of satisfactions is required to compensate for a further decrease in equality.

Moreover, very different weightings are consistent with these principles. Let figure 2 represent the judgments of two different persons. The solid lines depict the judgments of the one who gives a relatively strong weight to equality, while the dashed lines depict the judgments of the other who gives a relatively strong weight to total welfare. Thus while the first person ranks arrangement D equal with C, the second judges D superior. This conception of justice imposes no limitations on what are the correct weightings; and therefore it allows different persons to arrive at a different balance of principles. Nevertheless such an intuitionist conception, if it were to fit our considered judgments on reflection, would be by no means without importance. At least it would single out the criteria which are significant, the apparent axes, so to speak, of our considered judgments of social justice. The intuitionist hopes that once these axes, or principles, are identified, men will in fact balance them more or less similarly, at least when they are impartial and not moved by an excessive attention to their own interests. Or if this is not so, then at least they can agree to some scheme whereby their assignment of weights can be compromised.

It is essential to observe that the intuitionist does not deny that we can describe how we balance competing principles, or how any one man does so, supposing that we weigh them differently. The intuitionist grants the possibility that these weights can be depicted by indifference curves. Knowing the description of these weights, the judgments which will be made can be foreseen. In this sense these judgments have a consistent and definite structure. Of course, it may be claimed that in the assignment of weights we are guided, without being aware of it, by certain further standards or by how best to realize a certain end. Perhaps the weights we assign are those which would result if we were to apply these standards or to pursue this end. Admittedly any given balancing of principles is subject to interpretation in this way. But the intuitionist claims that, in fact, there is no such interpretation. He contends that there exists no expressible ethical conception which underlies these weights. A geometrical figure or a mathematical function may describe them, but there are no constructive moral criteria that establish their reasonableness. Intuitionism holds that in our judgments of social justice we must eventually reach a plurality of first principles in regard to which we can only say that it seems to us more correct to balance them this way rather than that.

Now there is nothing intrinsically irrational about this intuitionist doctrine. Indeed, it may be true. We cannot take for granted that there must be a complete derivation of our judgments of social justice from recognizably ethical principles. The intuitionist believes to the contrary that the complexity of the moral facts defies our efforts to give a full account of our judgments and necessitates a plurality of competing principles. He contends that attempts to go beyond these principles either reduce to triviality, as when it is said that social justice is to give every man his due, or else lead to falsehood and oversimplification, as when one settles everything by the principle of utility. The only way therefore to dispute intuitionism is to set forth the recognizably ethical criteria that account for the weights which, in our considered judgments, we think appropriate to give to the plurality of principles. A refutation of intuitionism consists in presenting the sort of constructive criteria that are said not to exist. To be sure, the notion of a recognizably ethical principle is vague, although it is easy to give many examples drawn from tradition and common sense. But it is pointless to discuss this matter in the abstract. The intuitionist and his critic will have to settle this question once the latter has put forward his more systematic account.

39

It may be asked whether intuitionistic theories are teleological or deontological. They may be of either kind, and any ethical view is bound to rely on intuition to some degree at many points. For example, one could maintain, as Moore did, that personal affection and human understanding, the creation and the contemplation of beauty, and the gaining and appreciation of knowledge are the chief good things, along with pleasure.[20] And one might also maintain (as Moore did not) that these are the sole intrinsic goods. Since these values are specified independently from the right, we have a teleological theory of a perfectionist type if the right is defined as maximizing the good. Yet in estimating what yields the most good, the theory may hold that these values have to be balanced against each other by intuition: it may say that there are no substantive criteria for guidance here. Often, however, intuitionist theories are deontological. In the definitive presentation of Ross, the distribution of good things according to moral worth (distributive justice) is included among the goods to be advanced; and while the principle to produce the most good ranks as a first principle, it is but one such principle which must be balanced by intuition against the claims of the other prima facie principles.[21] The distinctive feature, then, of intuitionistic views is not their being teleological or deontological, but the especially prominent place that they give to the appeal to our intuitive capacities unguided by constructive and recognizably ethical criteria. Intuitionism denies that there exists any useful and explicit solution to the priority problem. I now turn to a brief discussion of this topic.

8. THE PRIORITY PROBLEM

We have seen that intuitionism raises the question of the extent to which it is possible to give a systematic account of our considered judgments of the just and the unjust. In particular, it holds that no constructive answer can be given to the problem of assigning weights to competing principles of justice. Here at least we must rely on our intuitive capacities. Classical utilitarianism tries, of course, to avoid

20. See *Principia Ethica*, ch. VI. The intuitionist nature of Moore's doctrine is assured by his principle of organic unity, pp. 27-31.
21. See W. D. Ross, *The Right and the Good*, pp. 21-27.

the appeal to intuition altogether. It is a single-principle conception with one ultimate standard; the adjustment of weights is, in theory anyway, settled by reference to the principle of utility. Mill thought that there must be but one such standard, otherwise there would be no umpire between competing criteria, and Sidgwick argues at length that the utilitarian principle is the only one which can assume this role. They maintain that our moral judments are implicitly utilitarian in the sense that when confronted with a clash of precepts, or with notions which are vague and imprecise, we have no alternative except to adopt utilitarianism. Mill and Sidgwick believe that at some point we must have a single principle to straighten out and to systematize our judgments.[22] Undeniably one of the great attractions of the classical doctrine is the way it faces the priority problem and tries to avoid relying on intuition.

As I have already remarked, there is nothing necessarily irrational in the appeal to intuition to settle questions of priority. We must recognize the possibility that there is no way to get beyond a plurality of principles. No doubt any conception of justice will have to rely on intuition to some degree. Nevertheless, we should do what we can to reduce the direct appeal to our considered judgments. For if men balance final principles differently, as presumably they often do, then their conceptions of justice are different. The assignment of weights is an essential and not a minor part of a conception of justice. If we cannot explain how these weights are to be determined by reasonable ethical criteria, the means of rational discussion have come to an end. An intuitionist conception of justice is, one might say, but half a conception. We should do what we can to formulate explicit principles for the priority problem, even though the dependence on intuition cannot be eliminated entirely.

In justice as fairness the role of intuition is limited in several ways. Since the whole question is rather difficult, I shall only make a few comments here the full sense of which will not be clear until later on. The first point is connected with the fact that the principles of justice are those which would be chosen in the original position. They are

22. For Mill, see *A System of Logic*, bk. VI, ch. XII, sec. 7; and *Utilitarianism*, ch. V, pars. 26–31, where this argument is made in connection with common sense precepts of justice. For Sidgwick, see *The Methods of Ethics*, for example, bk. IV, chs. II and III, which summarize much of the argument of bk. III.

the outcome of a certain choice situation. Now being rational, the persons in the original position recognize that they should consider the priority of these principles. For if they wish to establish agreed standards for adjudicating their claims on one another, they will need principles for assigning weights. They cannot assume that their intuitive judgments of priority will in general be the same; given their different positions in society they surely will not. Thus I suppose that in the original position the parties try to reach some agreement as to how the principles of justice are to be balanced. Now part of the value of the notion of choosing principles is that the reasons which underlie their adoption in the first place may also support giving them certain weights. Since in justice as fairness the principles of justice are not thought of as self-evident, but have their justification in the fact that they would be chosen, we may find in the grounds for their acceptance some guidance or limitation as to how they are to be balanced. Given the situation of the original position, it may be clear that certain priority rules are preferable to others for much the same reasons that principles are initially assented to. By emphasizing the role of justice and the special features of the initial choice situation, the priority problem may prove more tractable.

A second possibility is that we may be able to find principles which can be put in what I shall call a serial or lexical order.[23] (The correct

23. The term "lexicographical" derives from the fact that the most familiar example of such an ordering is that of words in a dictionary. To see this, substitute numerals for letters, putting "1" for "a" "2" for "b" and so on, and then rank the resulting strings of numerals from left to right, moving to the right only when necessary to break ties. In general, a lexical ordering cannot be represented by a continuous real-valued utility function; such a ranking violates the assumption of continuity. See I. F. Pearce, *A Contribution to Demand Analysis* (Oxford, The Clarendon Press, 1946), pp. 22–27; and A. K. Sen, *Collective Choice and Social Welfare* (San Francisco, Holden-Day, 1970), pp. 34f. For further references, see H. S. Houthakker, "The Present State of Consumption Theory," *Econometrica*, vol. 29 (1961), pp. 710f.

In the history of moral philosophy the conception of a lexical order occasionally appears though it is not explicitly discussed. A clear example may be found in Hutcheson, *A System of Moral Philosophy* (1755). He proposes that in comparing pleasures of the same kind, we use their intensity and duration; in comparing pleasures of different kinds, we must consider their duration and dignity jointly. Pleasures of higher kinds may have a worth greater than those of lower kinds however great the latter's intensity and duration. See L. A. Selby-Bigge, term is "lexicographical," but it is too cumbersome.) This is an order which requires us to satisfy the first principle in the ordering before we can move on to the second, the second before we consider the third, and so on. A principle does not come into play until those previous to it are either fully met or do not apply. A serial ordering avoids, then, having to balance principles at all; those earlier in the ordering have an absolute weight, so to speak, with respect to later ones, and hold without exception. We can regard such a ranking as analogous to a sequence of constrained maximum principles. For we can suppose that any principle in the order is to be maximized subject to the condition that the preceding principles are fully satisfied. As an important special case I shall, in fact, propose an ordering of this kind by ranking the principle of equal liberty prior to the principle regulating economic and social inequalities. This means, in effect, that the basic structure of society is to arrange the inequalities of wealth and authority in ways consistent with the equal liberties required by the preceding principle. Certainly the concept of a lexical, or serial, order does not offhand seem very promising. Indeed, it appears to offend our sense of moderation and good judgment. Moreover, it presupposes that the principles in the order be of a rather special kind. For example, unless the earlier principles have but a limited application and establish definite requirements which can be fulfilled, later principles will never come into play. Thus the principle of equal liberty can assume a prior position since it may, let us suppose, be satisfied. Whereas if the principle of utility were first,

British Moralists, vol. I (Oxford, 1897), pp. 421–423. J. S. Mill's well-known view in Utilitarianism, ch. II, pars. 6–8, is similar to Hutcheson's. It also is natural to rank moral worth as lexically prior to non-moral values. See for example Ross, The Right and the Good, pp. 149–154. And of course the primacy of justice noted in §1, as well as the priority of right as found in Kant, are further cases of such an ordering.

The theory of utility in economics began with an implicit recognition of the hierarchical structure of wants and the priority of moral considerations. This is clear in W. S. Jevons, The Theory of Political Economy, (London, 1871), pp. 27–32. Jevons states a conception analogous to Hutcheson's and confines the economist's use of the utility calculus to the lowest rank of feelings. For a discussion of the hierarchy of wants and its relation to utility theory, see Nicholas Georgescu-Roegen, "Choice, Expectations, and Measurability," Quarterly Journal of Economics, vol. 68 (1954), esp. pp. 510–520.

it would render otiose all subsequent criteria. I shall try to show that at least in certain social circumstances a serial ordering of the principles of justice offers an approximate solution to the priority problem.

Finally, the dependence on intuition can be reduced by posing more limited questions and by substituting prudential for moral judgment. Thus someone faced with the principles of an intuitionist conception may reply that without some guidelines for deliberation he does not know what to say. He might maintain, for example, that he could not balance total utility against equality in the distribution of satisfaction. Not only are the notions involved here too abstract and comprehensive for him to have any confidence in his judgment, but there are enormous complications in interpreting what they mean. The aggregative-distributive dichotomy is no doubt an attractive idea, but in this instance it seems unmanageable. It does not factor the problem of social justice into small enough parts. In justice as fairness the appeal to intuition is focused in two ways. First we single out a certain position in the social system from which the system is to be judged, and then we ask whether, from the standpoint of a representative man in this position, it would be rational to prefer this arrangement of the basic structure rather than that. Given certain assumptions, economic and social inequalities are to be judged in terms of the long-run expectations of the least advantaged social group. Of course, the specification of this group is not very exact, and certainly our prudential judgments likewise give considerable scope to intuition, since we may not be able to formulate the principle which determines them. Nevertheless, we have asked a much more limited question and have substituted for an ethical judgment a judgment of rational prudence. Often it is quite clear how we should decide. The reliance on intuition is of a different nature and much less than in the aggregative-distributive dichotomy of the intuitionist conception.

In addressing the priority problem the task is that of reducing and not of eliminating entirely the reliance on intuitive judgments. There is no reason to suppose that we can avoid all appeals to intuition, of whatever kind, or that we should try to. The practical aim is to reach a reasonably reliable agreement in judgment in order to provide a common conception of justice. If men's intuitive priority judgments are similar, it does not matter, practically speaking, that they cannot formulate the principles which account for these convictions, or even whether such principles exist. Contrary judgments, however, raise a difficulty, since the basis for adjudicating claims is to that extent obscure. Thus our object should be to formulate a conception of justice which, however much it may call upon intuition, ethical or prudential, tends to make our considered judgments of justice converge. If such a conception does exist, then, from the standpoint of the original position, there would be strong reasons for accepting it, since it is rational to introduce further coherence into our common convictions of justice. Indeed, once we look at things from the standpoint of the initial situation, the priority problem is not that of how to cope with the complexity of already given moral facts which cannot be altered. Instead, it is the problem of formulating reasonable and generally acceptable proposals for bringing about the desired agreement in judgments. On a contract doctrine the moral facts are determined by the principles which would be chosen in the original position. These principles specify which considerations are relevant from the standpoint of social justice. Since it is up to the persons in the original position to choose these principles, it is for them to decide how simple or complex they want the moral facts to be. The original agreement settles how far they are prepared to compromise and to simplify in order to establish the priority rules necessary for a common conception of justice.

I have reviewed two obvious and simple ways of dealing constructively with the priority problem: namely, either by a single overall principle, or by a plurality of principles in lexical order. Other ways no doubt exist, but I shall not consider what they might be. The traditional moral theories are for the most part single-principled or intuitionistic, so that the working out of a serial ordering is novelty enough for a first step. While it seems clear that, in general, a lexical order cannot be strictly correct, it may be an illuminating approximation under certain special though significant conditions (§ 82). In this way it may indicate the larger structure of conceptions of justice and suggest the directions along which a closer fit can be found.

45

9. SOME REMARKS ABOUT MORAL THEORY

It seems desirable at this point, in order to prevent misunderstanding, to discuss briefly the nature of moral theory. I shall do this by explaining in more detail the concept of a considered judgment in reflective equilibrium and the reasons for introducing it.[24]

Let us assume that each person beyond a certain age and possessed of the requisite intellectual capacity develops a sense of justice under normal social circumstances. We acquire a skill in judging things to be just and unjust, and in supporting these judgments by reasons. Moreover, we ordinarily have some desire to act in accord with these pronouncements and expect a similar desire on the part of others. Clearly this moral capacity is extraordinarily complex. To see this it suffices to note the potentially infinite number and variety of judgments that we are prepared to make. The fact that we often do not know what to say, and sometimes find our minds unsettled, does not detract from the complexity of the capacity we have.

Now one may think of moral philosophy at first (and I stress the provisional nature of this view) as the attempt to describe our moral capacity; or, in the present case, one may regard a theory of justice as describing our sense of justice. This enterprise is very difficult. For by such a description is not meant simply a list of the judgments on institutions and actions that we are prepared to render, accompanied with supporting reasons when these are offered. Rather, what is required is a formulation of a set of principles which, when conjoined to our beliefs and knowledge of the circumstances, would lead us to make these judgments with their supporting reasons were we to apply these principles conscientiously and intelligently. A conception of justice characterizes our moral sensibility when the everyday judgments we do make are in accordance with its principles. These principles can serve as part of the premises of an argument which arrives at the matching judgments. We do not understand our sense of justice until we know in some systematic way covering a wide range of cases what these principles are. Only a deceptive familiarity with our everyday judgments and our natural readiness to make them

24. In this section I follow the general point of view of "Outline of a Procedure for Ethics," *Philosophical Review*, vol. 60 (1951). The comparison with linguistics is of course new.

could conceal the fact that characterizing our moral capacities is an intricate task. The principles which describe them must be presumed to have a complex structure, and the concepts involved will require serious study.

A useful comparison here is with the problem of describing the sense of grammaticalness that we have for the sentences of our native language.[25] In this case the aim is to characterize the ability to recognize well-formed sentences by formulating clearly expressed principles which make the same discriminations as the native speaker. This is a difficult undertaking which, although still unfinished, is known to require theoretical constructions that far outrun the ad hoc precepts of our explicit grammatical knowledge. A similar situation presumably holds in moral philosophy. There is no reason to assume that our sense of justice can be adequately characterized by familiar common sense precepts, or derived from the more obvious learning principles. A correct account of moral capacities will certainly involve principles and theoretical constructions which go much beyond the norms and standards cited in everyday life; it may eventually require fairly sophisticated mathematics as well. This is to be expected, since on the contract view the theory of justice is part of the theory of rational choice. Thus the idea of the original position and of an agreement on principles there does not seem too complicated or unnecessary. Indeed, these notions are rather simple and can serve only as a beginning.

So far, though, I have not said anything about considered judgments. Now, as already suggested, they enter as those judgments in which our moral capacities are most likely to be displayed without distortion. Thus in deciding which of our judgments to take into account we may reasonably select some and exclude others. For example, we can discard those judgments made with hesitation, or in which we have little confidence. Similarly, those given when we are upset or frightened, or when we stand to gain one way or the other can be left aside. All these judgments are likely to be erroneous or to be influenced by an excessive attention to our own interests. Considered judgments are simply those rendered under conditions favorable to the exercise of the sense of justice, and therefore in circum-

25. See Noam Chomsky, *Aspects of the Theory of Syntax* (Cambridge, Mass., The M.I.T. Press, 1965), pp. 3–9.

stances where the more common excuses and explanations for making a mistake do not obtain. The person making the judgment is presumed, then, to have the ability, the opportunity, and the desire to reach a correct decision (or at least, not the desire not to). Moreover, the criteria that identify these judgments are not arbitrary. They are, in fact, similar to those that single out considered judgments of any kind. And once we regard the sense of justice as a mental capacity, as involving the exercise of thought, the relevant judgments are those given under conditions favorable for deliberation and judgment in general.

I now turn to the notion of reflective equilibrium. The need for this idea arises as follows. According to the provisional aim of moral philosophy, one might say that justice as fairness is the hypothesis that the principles which would be chosen in the original position are identical with those that match our considered judgments and so these principles describe our sense of justice. But this interpretation is clearly oversimplified. In describing our sense of justice an allowance must be made for the likelihood that considered judgments are no doubt subject to certain irregularities and distortions despite the fact that they are rendered under favorable circumstances. When a person is presented with an intuitively appealing account of his sense of justice (one, say, which embodies various reasonable and natural presumptions), he may well revise his judgments to conform to its principles even though the theory does not fit his existing judgments exactly. He is especially likely to do this if he can find an explanation for the deviations which undermines his confidence in his original judgments and if the conception presented yields a judgment which he finds he can now accept. From the standpoint of moral philosophy, the best account of a person's sense of justice is not the one which fits his judgments prior to his examining any conception of justice, but rather the one which matches his judgments in reflective equilibrium. As we have seen, this state is one reached after a person has weighed various proposed conceptions and he has either revised his judgments to accord with one of them or held fast to his initial convictions (and the corresponding conception).

The notion of reflective equilibrium introduces some complications that call for comment. For one thing, it is a notion characteristic of the study of principles which govern actions shaped by self-examination. Moral philosophy is Socratic: we may want to change our present considered judgments once their regulative principles are brought to light. And we may want to do this even though these principles are a perfect fit. A knowledge of these principles may suggest further reflections that lead us to revise our judgments. This feature is not peculiar though to moral philosophy, or to the study of other philosophical principles such as those of induction and scientific method. For example, while we may not expect a substantial revision of our sense of correct grammar in view of a linguistic theory the principles of which seem especially natural to us, such a change is not inconceivable, and no doubt our sense of grammaticalness may be affected to some degree anyway by this knowledge. But there is a contrast, say, with physics. To take an extreme case, if we have an accurate account of the motions of the heavenly bodies that we do not find appealing, we cannot alter these motions to conform to a more attractive theory. It is simply good fortune that the principles of celestial mechanics have their intellectual beauty.

There are, however, several interpretations of reflective equilibrium. For the notion varies depending upon whether one is to be presented with only those descriptions which more or less match one's existing judgments except for minor discrepancies, or whether one is to be presented with all possible descriptions to which one might plausibly conform one's judgments together with all relevant philosophical arguments for them. In the first case we would be describing a person's sense of justice more or less as it is although allowing for the smoothing out of certain irregularities; in the second case a person's sense of justice may or may not undergo a radical shift. Clearly it is the second kind of reflective equilibrium that one is concerned with in moral philosophy. To be sure, it is doubtful whether one can ever reach this state. For even if the idea of all possible descriptions and of all philosophically relevant arguments is well-defined (which is questionable), we cannot examine each of them. The most we can do is to study the conceptions of justice known to us through the tradition of moral philosophy and any further ones that occur to us, and then to consider these. This is pretty much what I shall do, since in presenting justice as fairness I shall compare its principles and arguments with a few other familiar views. In light of these remarks, justice as fairness can be understood

49

as saying that the two principles previously mentioned would be chosen in the original position in preference to other traditional conceptions of justice, for example, those of utility and perfection; and that these principles give a better match with our considered judgments on reflection than these recognized alternatives. Thus justice as fairness moves us closer to the philosophical ideal; it does not, of course, achieve it.

This explanation of reflective equilibrium suggests straightway a number of further questions. For example, does a reflective equilibrium (in the sense of the philosophical ideal) exist? If so, is it unique? Even if it is unique, can it be reached? Perhaps the judgments from which we begin, or the course of reflection itself (or both), affect the resting point, if any, that we eventually achieve. It would be useless, however, to speculate about these matters here. They are far beyond our reach. I shall not even ask whether the principles that characterize one person's considered judgments are the same as those that characterize another's. I shall take for granted that these principles are either approximately the same for persons whose judgments are in reflective equilibrium, or if not, that their judgments divide along a few main lines represented by the family of traditional doctrines that I shall discuss. (Indeed, one person may find himself torn between opposing conceptions at the same time.) If men's conceptions of justice finally turn out to differ, the ways in which they do so is a matter of first importance. Of course we cannot know how these conceptions vary, or even whether they do, until we have a better account of their structure. And this we now lack, even in the case of one man, or homogeneous group of men. Here too there is likely to be a similarity with linguistics: if we can describe one person's sense of grammar we shall surely know many things about the general structure of language. Similarly, if we should be able to characterize one (educated) person's sense of justice, we would have a good beginning toward a theory of justice. We may suppose that everyone has in himself the whole form of a moral conception. So for the purposes of this book, the views of the reader and the author are the only ones that count. The opinions of others are used only to clear our own heads.

I wish to stress that a theory of justice is precisely that, namely, a theory. It is a theory of the moral sentiments (to recall an eighteenth century title) setting out the principles governing our moral powers, or, more specifically, our sense of justice. There is a definite if limited class of facts against which conjectured principles can be checked, namely, our considered judgments in reflective equilibrium. A theory of justice is subject to the same rules of method as other theories. Definitions and analyses of meaning do not have a special place: definition is but one device used in setting up the general structure of theory. Once the whole framework is worked out, definitions have no distinct status and stand or fall with the theory itself. In any case, it is obviously impossible to develop a substantive theory of justice founded solely on truths of logic and definition. The analysis of moral concepts and the a priori, however traditionally understood, is too slender a basis. Moral philosophy must be free to use contingent assumptions and general facts as it pleases. There is no other way to give an account of our considered judgments in reflective equilibrium. This is the conception of the subject adopted by most classical British writers through Sidgwick. I see no reason to depart from it.[26]

Moreover, if we can find an accurate account of our moral conceptions, then questions of meaning and justification may prove much easier to answer. Indeed some of them may no longer be real questions at all. Note, for example, the extraordinary deepening of our understanding of the meaning and justification of statements in logic and mathematics made possible by developments since Frege and Cantor. A knowledge of the fundamental structures of logic and set theory and their relation to mathematics has transformed the

26. I believe that this view goes back in its essentials to Aristotle's procedure in the *Nicomachean Ethics*. See W. F. R. Hardie, *Aristotle's Ethical Theory*, ch. III, esp. pp. 37–45. And Sidgwick thought of the history of moral philosophy as a series of attempts to state "in full breadth and clearness those primary intuitions of Reason, by the scientific application of which the common moral thought of mankind may be at once systematized and corrected." *The Methods of Ethics*, pp. 373f. He takes for granted that philosophical reflection will lead to revisions in our considered judgments, and although there are elements of epistemological intuitionism in his doctrine, these are not given much weight when unsupported by systematic considerations. For an account of Sidgwick's methodology, see J. B. Schneewind, "First Principles and Common Sense Morality in Sidgwick's Ethics," *Archiv für Geschichte der Philosophie*, Bd. 45 (1963).

philosophy of these subjects in a way that conceptual analysis and linguistic investigations never could. One has only to observe the effect of the division of theories into those which are decidable and complete, undecidable yet complete, and neither complete nor decidable. The problem of meaning and truth in logic and mathematics is profoundly altered by the discovery of logical systems illustrating these concepts. Once the substantive content of moral conceptions is better understood, a similar transformation may occur. It is possible that convincing answers to questions of the meaning and justification of moral judgments can be found in no other way.

I wish, then, to stress the central place of the study of our substantive moral conceptions. But the corollary to recognizing their complexity is accepting the fact that our present theories are primitive and have grave defects. We need to be tolerant of simplifications if they reveal and approximate the general outlines of our judgments. Objections by way of counterexamples are to be made with care, since these may tell us only what we know already, namely that our theory is wrong somewhere. The important thing is to find out how often and how far it is wrong. All theories are presumably mistaken in places. The real question at any given time is which of the views already proposed is the best approximation overall. To ascertain this some grasp of the structure of rival theories is surely necessary. It is for this reason that I have tried to classify and to discuss conceptions of justice by reference to their basic intuitive ideas, since these disclose the main differences between them.

In presenting justice as fairness I shall contrast it with utilitarianism. I do this for various reasons, partly as an expository device, partly because the several variants of the utilitarian view have long dominated our philosophical tradition and continue to do so. And this dominance has been maintained despite the persistent misgivings that utilitarianism so easily arouses. The explanation for this peculiar state of affairs lies, I believe, in the fact that no constructive alternative theory has been advanced which has the comparable virtues of clarity and system and which at the same time allays these doubts. Intuitionism is not constructive, perfectionism is unacceptable. My conjecture is that the contract doctrine properly worked out can fill this gap. I think justice as fairness an endeavor in this direction.

Of course the contract theory as I shall present it is subject to the strictures that we have just noted. It is no exception to the primitiveness that marks existing moral theories. It is disheartening, for example, how little can now be said about priority rules; and while a lexical ordering may serve fairly well for some important cases, I assume that it will not be completely satisfactory. Nevertheless, we are free to use simplifying devices, and this I have often done. We should view a theory of justice as a guiding framework designed to focus our moral sensibilities and to put before our intuitive capacities more limited and manageable questions for judgment. The principles of justice identify certain considerations as morally relevant and the priority rules indicate the appropriate precedence when these conflict, while the conception of the original position defines the underlying idea which is to inform our deliberations. If the scheme as a whole seems on reflection to clarify and to order our thoughts, and if it tends to reduce disagreements and to bring divergent convictions more in line, then it has done all that one may reasonably ask. Understood as parts of a framework that does indeed seem to help, the numerous simplifications may be regarded as provisionally justified.

CHAPTER II. THE PRINCIPLES OF JUSTICE

The theory of justice may be divided into two main parts: (1) an interpretation of the initial situation and a formulation of the various principles available for choice there, and (2) an argument establishing which of these principles would in fact be adopted. In this chapter two principles of justice for institutions and several principles for individuals are discussed and their meaning explained. Thus I am concerned for the present with only one aspect of the first part of the theory. Not until the next chapter do I take up the interpretation of the initial situation and begin the argument to show that the principles considered here would indeed be acknowledged. A variety of topics are discussed: institutions as subjects of justice and the concept of formal justice; three kinds of procedural justice; the place of the theory of the good; and the sense in which the principles of justice are egalitarian, among others. In each case the aim is to explain the meaning and application of the principles.

10. INSTITUTIONS AND FORMAL JUSTICE

The primary subject of the principles of social justice is the basic structure of society, the arrangement of major social institutions into one scheme of cooperation. We have seen that these principles are to govern the assignment of rights and duties in these institutions and they are to determine the appropriate distribution of the benefits and burdens of social life. The principles of justice for institutions must not be confused with the principles which apply to individuals and their actions in particular circumstances. These two kinds of principles apply to different subjects and must be discussed separately.

Now by an institution I shall understand a public system of rules which defines offices and positions with their rights and duties, powers and immunities, and the like. These rules specify certain forms of action as permissible, others as forbidden; and they provide for certain penalties and defenses, and so on, when violations occur. As examples of institutions, or more generally social practices, we may think of games and rituals, trials and parliaments, markets and systems of property. An institution may be thought of in two ways: first as an abstract object, that is, as a possible form of conduct expressed by a system of rules; and second, as the realization in the thought and conduct of certain persons at a certain time and place of the actions specified by these rules. There is an ambiguity, then, as to which is just or unjust, the institution as realized or the institution as an abstract object. It seems best to say that it is the institution as realized and effectively and impartially administered which is just or unjust. The institution as an abstract object is just or unjust in the sense that any realization of it would be just or unjust.

An institution exists at a certain time and place when the actions specified by it are regularly carried out in accordance with a public understanding that the system of rules defining the institution is to be followed. Thus parliamentary institutions are defined by a certain system of rules (or family of such systems to allow for variations). These rules enumerate certain forms of action ranging from holding a session of parliament to taking a vote on a bill to raising a point of order. Various kinds of general norms are organized into a coherent scheme. A parliamentary institution exists at a certain time and place when certain people perform the appropriate actions, engage in these activities in the required way, with a reciprocal recognition of one another's understanding that their conduct accords with the rules they are to comply with.[1]

In saying that an institution, and therefore the basic structure of society, is a public system of rules, I mean then that everyone en-

1. See H. L. A. Hart, *The Concept of Law* (Oxford, The Clarendon Press, 1961), pp. 59f, 106f, 109–114, for a discussion of when rules and legal systems may be said to exist.

gaged in it knows what he would know if these rules and his participation in the activity they define were the result of an agreement. A person taking part in an institution knows what the rules demand of him and of the others. He also knows that the others know this and that they know that he knows this, and so on. To be sure, this condition is not always fulfilled in the case of actual institutions, but it is a reasonable simplifying assumption. The principles of justice are to apply to social arrangements understood to be public in this sense. Where the rules of a certain subpart of an institution are known only to those belonging to it, we may assume that there is an understanding that those in this part can make rules for themselves as long as these rules are designed to achieve ends generally accepted and others are not adversely affected. The publicity of the rules of an institution insures that those engaged in it know what limitations on conduct to expect of one another and what kinds of actions are permissible. There is a common basis for determining mutual expectations. Moreover, in a well-ordered society, one effectively regulated by a shared conception of justice, there is also a public understanding as to what is just and unjust. Later I assume that the principles of justice are chosen subject to the knowledge that they are to be public (§ 23). This condition is a natural one in a contractarian theory.

It is necessary to note the distinction between the constitutive rules of an institution, which establish its various rights and duties, and so on, and strategies and maxims for how best to take advantage of the institution for particular purposes.[2] Rational strategies and maxims are based upon an analysis of which permissible actions individuals and groups will decide upon in view of their interests, beliefs, and conjectures about one another's plans. These strategies and maxims are not themselves part of the institution. Rather they belong to the theory of it, for example, to the theory of parliamentary politics. Normally the theory of an institution, just as that of a game, takes the constitutive rules as given and analyzes the way in which power is distributed and explains how those engaged in it are likely

2. On constitutive rules and institutions, see J. R. Searle, *Speech Acts* (Cambridge, The University Press, 1969), pp. 33–42. See also G. E. M. Anscombe, "On Brute Facts," *Analysis*, vol. 18 (1958); and B. J. Diggs, "Rules and Utilitarianism," *American Philosophical Quarterly*, vol. 1 (1964), where various interpretations of rules are discussed.

to avail themselves of its opportunities. In designing and reforming social arrangements one must, of course, examine the schemes and tactics it allows and the forms of behavior which it tends to encourage. Ideally the rules should be set up so that men are led by their predominant interests to act in ways which further socially desirable ends. The conduct of individuals guided by their rational plans should be coordinated as far as possible to achieve results which although not intended or perhaps even foreseen by them are nevertheless the best ones from the standpoint of social justice. Bentham thinks of this coordination as the artificial identification of interests, Adam Smith as the work of the invisible hand.[3] It is the aim of the ideal legislator in enacting laws and of the moralist in urging their reform. Still, the strategies and tactics followed by individuals, while essential to the assessment of institutions, are not part of the public systems of rules which define them.

We may also distinguish between a single rule (or group of rules), an institution (or a major part thereof), and the basic structure of the social system as a whole. The reason for doing this is that one or several rules of an arrangement may be unjust without the institution itself being so. Similarly, an institution may be unjust although the social system as a whole is not. There is the possibility not only that single rules and institutions are not by themselves sufficiently important but that within the structure of an institution or social system one apparent injustice compensates for another. The whole is less unjust than it would be if it contained but one of the unjust parts. Further, it is conceivable that a social system may be unjust even though none of its institutions are unjust taken separately: the injustice is a consequence of how they are combined together into a single system. One institution may encourage and appear to justify expectations which are denied or ignored by another. These distinctions are obvious enough. They simply reflect the fact that in appraising institutions we may view them in a wider or a narrower context.

There are, it should be remarked, institutions in regard to which

3. The phrase "the artificial identification of interests" is from Elie Halévy's account of Bentham in *La Formation du radicalisme philosophique*, vol. 1 (Paris, Felix Alcan, 1901), pp. 20–24. On the invisible hand, see *The Wealth of Nations*, ed. Edwin Cannan (New York, The Modern Library, 1937), p. 423.

the concept of justice does not ordinarily apply. A ritual, say, is not usually regarded as either just or unjust, although cases can no doubt be imagined in which this would not be true, for example, the ritual sacrifice of the first-born or of prisoners of war. A general theory of justice would consider when rituals and other practices not commonly thought of as just or unjust are indeed subject to this form of criticism. Presumably they must involve in some way the allocation among persons of certain rights and values. I shall not, however, pursue this larger inquiry. Our concern is solely with the basic structure of society and its major institutions and therefore with the standard cases of social justice.

Now let us suppose a certain basic structure to exist. Its rules satisfy a certain conception of justice. We may not ourselves accept its principles; we may even find them odious and unjust. But they are principles of justice in the sense that for this system they assume the role of justice: they provide an assignment of fundamental rights and duties and they determine the division of advantages from social cooperation. Let us also imagine that this conception of justice is by and large accepted in the society and that institutions are impartially and consistently administered by judges and other officials. That is, similar cases are treated similarly, the relevant similarities and differences being those identified by the existing norms. The correct rule as defined by institutions is regularly adhered to and properly interpreted by the authorities. This impartial and consistent administration of laws and institutions, whatever their substantive principles, we may call formal justice. If we think of justice as always expressing a kind of equality, then formal justice requires that in their administration laws and institutions should apply equally (that is, in the same way) to those belonging to the classes defined by them. As Sidgwick emphasized, this sort of equality is implied in the very notion of a law or institution, once it is thought of as a scheme of general rules.[4] Formal justice is adherence to principle, or as some have said, obedience to system.[5]

4. *The Methods of Ethics*, 7th ed. (London, Macmillan, 1907), p. 267.
5. See Ch. Perelman, *The Idea of Justice and the Problem of Argument*, trans. J. Petrie (London, Routledge and Kegan Paul, 1963), p. 41 All of the first two chapters, a translation of *De la Justice* (Brussels, 1943), is relevant here, but especially pp. 36–45.

It is obvious, Sidgwick adds, that law and institutions may be equally executed and yet be unjust. Treating similar cases similarly is not a sufficient guarantee of substantive justice. This depends upon the principles in accordance with which the basic structure is framed. There is no contradiction in supposing that a slave or caste society, or one sanctioning the most arbitrary forms of discrimination, is evenly and consistently administered, although this may be unlikely. Nevertheless, formal justice, or justice as regularity, excludes significant kinds of injustices. For if it is supposed that institutions are reasonably just, then it is of great importance that the authorities should be impartial and not influenced by personal, monetary, or other irrelevant considerations in their handling of particular cases. Formal justice in the case of legal institutions is simply an aspect of the rule of law which supports and secures legitimate expectations. One kind of injustice is the failure of judges and others in authority to adhere to the appropriate rules or interpretations thereof in deciding claims. A person is unjust to the extent that from character and inclination he is disposed to such actions. Moreover, even where laws and institutions are unjust, it is often better that they should be consistently applied. In this way those subject to them at least know what is demanded and they can try to protect themselves accordingly; whereas there is even greater injustice if those already disadvantaged are also arbitrarily treated in particular cases when the rules would give them some security. On the other hand, it might be still better in particular cases to alleviate the plight of those unfairly treated by departures from the existing norms. How far we are justified in doing this, especially at the expense of expectations founded in good faith on current institutions, is one of the tangled questions of political justice. In general, all that can be said is that the strength of the claims of formal justice, of obedience to system, clearly depend upon the substantive justice of institutions and the possibilities of their reform.

Some have held that in fact substantive and formal justice tend to go together and therefore that at least grossly unjust institutions are never, or at any rate rarely, impartially and consistently administered.[6] Those who uphold and gain from unjust arrangements,

6. See Lon Fuller, *The Morality of Law* (New Haven, Yale University Press, 1964), ch. IV.

59

and who deny with contempt the rights and liberties of others, are not likely, it is said, to let scruples concerning the rule of law interfere with their interests in particular cases. The inevitable vagueness of laws in general and the wide scope allowed for their interpretation encourages an arbitrariness in reaching decisions which only an allegiance to justice can allay. Thus it is maintained that where we find formal justice, the rule of law and the honoring of legitimate expectations, we are likely to find substantive justice as well. The desire to follow rules impartially and consistently, to treat similar cases similarly, and to accept the consequences of the application of public norms is intimately connected with the desire, or at least the willingness, to recognize the rights and liberties of others and to share fairly in the benefits and burdens of social cooperation. The one desire tends to be associated with the other. This contention is certainly plausible but I shall not examine it here. For it cannot be properly assessed until we know what are the most reasonable principles of substantive justice and under what conditions men come to affirm and to live by them. Once we understand the content of these principles and their basis in reason and human attitudes, we may be in a position to decide whether substantive and formal justice are tied together.

11. TWO PRINCIPLES OF JUSTICE

I shall now state in a provisional form the two principles of justice that I believe would be chosen in the original position. In this section I wish to make only the most general comments, and therefore the first formulation of these principles is tentative. As we go on I shall run through several formulations and approximate step by step the final statement to be given much later. I believe that doing this allows the exposition to proceed in a natural way.

The first statement of the two principles reads as follows.

First: each person is to have an equal right to the most extensive basic liberty compatible with a similar liberty for others.

Second: social and economic inequalities are to be arranged so that they are both (a) reasonably expected to be to everyone's advantage, and (b) attached to positions and offices open to all.

60

There are two ambiguous phrases in the second principle, namely "everyone's advantage" and "open to all." Determining their sense more exactly will lead to a second formulation of the principle in § 13. The final version of the two principles is given in § 46; § 39 considers the rendering of the first principle.

By way of general comment, these principles primarily apply, as I have said, to the basic structure of society. They are to govern the assignment of rights and duties and to regulate the distribution of social and economic advantages. As their formulation suggests, these principles presuppose that the social structure can be divided into two more or less distinct parts, the first principle applying to the one, the second to the other. They distinguish between those aspects of the social system that define and secure the equal liberties of citizenship and those that specify and establish social and economic inequalities. The basic liberties of citizens are, roughly speaking, political liberty (the right to vote and to be eligible for public office) together with freedom of speech and assembly; liberty of conscience and freedom of thought; freedom of the person along with the right to hold (personal) property; and freedom from arbitrary arrest and seizure as defined by the concept of the rule of law. These liberties are all required to be equal by the first principle, since citizens of a just society are to have the same basic rights.

The second principle applies, in the first approximation, to the distribution of income and wealth and to the design of organizations that make use of differences in authority and responsibility, or chains of command. While the distribution of wealth and income need not be equal, it must be to everyone's advantage, and at the same time, positions of authority and offices of command must be accessible to all. One applies the second principle by holding positions open, and then, subject to this constraint, arranges social and economic inequalities so that everyone benefits.

These principles are to be arranged in a serial order with the first principle prior to the second. This ordering means that a departure from the institutions of equal liberty required by the first principle cannot be justified by, or compensated for, by greater social and economic advantages. The distribution of wealth and income, and the hierarchies of authority, must be consistent with both the liberties of equal citizenship and equality of opportunity.

It is clear that these principles are rather specific in their content, and their acceptance rests on certain assumptions that I must eventually try to explain and justify. A theory of justice depends upon a theory of society in ways that will become evident as we proceed. For the present, it should be observed that the two principles (and this holds for all formulations) are a special case of a more general conception of justice that can be expressed as follows.

All social values—liberty and opportunity, income and wealth, and the bases of self-respect—are to be distributed equally unless an unequal distribution of any, or all, of these values is to everyone's advantage.

Injustice, then, is simply inequalities that are not to the benefit of all. Of course, this conception is extremely vague and requires interpretation.

As a first step, suppose that the basic structure of society distributes certain primary goods, that is, things that every rational man is presumed to want. These goods normally have a use whatever a person's rational plan of life. For simplicity, assume that the chief primary goods at the disposition of society are rights and liberties, powers and opportunities, income and wealth. (Later on in Part Three the primary good of self-respect has a central place.) These are the social primary goods. Other primary goods such as health and vigor, intelligence and imagination, are natural goods; although their possession is influenced by the basic structure, they are not so directly under its control. Imagine, then, a hypothetical initial arrangement in which all the social primary goods are equally distributed: everyone has similar rights and duties, and income and wealth are evenly shared. This state of affairs provides a benchmark for judging improvements. If certain inequalities of wealth and organizational powers would make everyone better off than in this hypothetical starting situation, then they accord with the general conception.

Now it is possible, at least theoretically, that by giving up some of their fundamental liberties men are sufficiently compensated by the resulting social and economic gains. The general conception of justice imposes no restrictions on what sort of inequalities are permissible; it only requires that everyone's position be improved. We need not suppose anything so drastic as consenting to a condition of slavery. Imagine instead that men forego certain political rights when the economic returns are significant and their capacity to influence the course of policy by the exercise of these rights would be marginal in any case. It is this kind of exchange which the two principles as stated rule out; being arranged in serial order they do not permit exchanges between basic liberties and economic and social gains. The serial ordering of principles expresses an underlying preference among primary social goods. When this preference is rational so likewise is the choice of these principles in this order.

In developing justice as fairness I shall, for the most part, leave aside the general conception of justice and examine instead the special case of the two principles in serial order. The advantage of this procedure is that from the first the matter of priorities is recognized and an effort made to find principles to deal with it. One is led to attend throughout to the conditions under which the acknowledgment of the absolute weight of liberty with respect to social and economic advantages, as defined by the lexical order of the two principles, would be reasonable. Offhand, this ranking appears extreme and too special a case to be of much interest; but there is more justification for it than would appear at first sight. Or at any rate, so I shall maintain (§82). Furthermore, the distinction between fundamental rights and liberties and economic and social benefits marks a difference among primary social goods that one should try to exploit. It suggests an important division in the social system. Of course, the distinctions drawn and the ordering proposed are bound to be at best only approximations. There are surely circumstances in which they fail. But it is essential to depict clearly the main lines of a reasonable conception of justice; and under many conditions anyway, the two principles in serial order may serve well enough. When necessary we can fall back on the more general conception.

The fact that the two principles apply to institutions has certain consequences. Several points illustrate this. First of all, the rights and liberties referred to by these principles are those which are defined by the public rules of the basic structure. Whether men are free is determined by the rights and duties established by the major institutions of society. Liberty is a certain pattern of social forms. The first principle simply requires that certain sorts of rules, those defining basic liberties, apply to everyone equally and that they allow the most extensive liberty compatible with a like liberty for all. The only reason for circumscribing the rights defining liberty and making men's freedom less extensive than it might otherwise be is that these equal rights as institutionally defined would interfere with one another.

Another thing to bear in mind is that when principles mention persons, or require that everyone gain from an inequality, the reference is to representative persons holding the various social positions, or offices, or whatever, established by the basic structure. Thus in applying the second principle I assume that it is possible to assign an expectation of well-being to representative individuals holding these positions. This expectation indicates their life prospects as viewed from their social station. In general, the expectations of representative persons depend upon the distribution of rights and duties throughout the basic structure. When this changes, expectations change. I assume, then, that expectations are connected: by raising the prospects of the representative man in one position we presumably increase or decrease the prospects of representative men in other positions. Since it applies to institutional forms, the second principle (or rather the first part of it) refers to the expectations of representative individuals. As I shall discuss below, neither principle applies to distributions of particular goods to particular individuals who may be identified by their proper names. The situation where someone is considering how to allocate certain commodities to needy persons who are known to him is not within the scope of the principles. They are meant to regulate basic institutional arrangements. We must not assume that there is much similarity from the standpoint of justice between an administrative allotment of goods to specific persons and the appropriate design of society. Our common sense intuitions for the former may be a poor guide to the latter.

Now the second principle insists that each person benefit from permissible inequalities in the basic structure. This means that it must be reasonable for each relevant representative man defined by this structure, when he views it as a going concern, to prefer his prospects with the inequality to his prospects without it. One is not allowed to justify differences in income or organizational powers on the ground that the disadvantages of those in one position are outweighed by the greater advantages of those in another. Much less can infringements of liberty be counterbalanced in this way. Applied to the basic structure, the principle of utility would have us maximize the sum of expectations of representative men (weighted by the number of persons they represent, on the classical view); and this would permit us to compensate for the losses of some by the gains of others. Instead, the two principles require that everyone benefit from economic and social inequalities. It is obvious, however, that there are indefinitely many ways in which all may be advantaged when the initial arrangement of equality is taken as a benchmark. How then are we to choose among these possibilities? The principles must be specified so that they yield a determinate conclusion. I now turn to this problem.

12. INTERPRETATIONS OF THE SECOND PRINCIPLE

I have already mentioned that since the phrases "everyone's advantage" and "equally open to all" are ambiguous, both parts of the second principle have two natural senses. Because these senses are independent of one another, the principle has four possible meanings. Assuming that the first principle of equal liberty has the same sense throughout, we then have four interpretations of the two principles. These are indicated in the table below.

	"Everyone's advantage"	
"Equally open"	Principle of efficiency	Difference principle
Equality as careers open to talents	System of Natural Liberty	Natural Aristocracy
Equality as equality of fair opportunity	Liberal Equality	Democratic Equality

I shall sketch in turn these three interpretations: the system of natural liberty, liberal equality, and democratic equality. In some respects this sequence is the more intuitive one, but the sequence via

65

the interpretation of natural aristocracy is not without interest and I shall comment on it briefly. In working out justice as fairness, we must decide which interpretation is to be preferred. I shall adopt that of democratic equality, explaining in this chapter what this notion means. The argument for its acceptance in the original position does not begin until the next chapter.

The first interpretation (in either sequence) I shall refer to as the system of natural liberty. In this rendering the first part of the second principle is understood as the principle of efficiency adjusted so as to apply to institutions or, in this case, to the basic structure of society; and the second part is understood as an open social system in which, to use the traditional phrase, careers are open to talents. I assume in all interpretations that the first principle of equal liberty is satisfied and that the economy is roughly a free market system, although the means of production may or may not be privately owned. The system of natural liberty asserts, then, that a basic structure satisfying the principle of efficiency and in which positions are open to those able and willing to strive for them will lead to a just distribution. Assigning rights and duties in this way is thought to give a scheme which allocates wealth and income, authority and responsibility, in a fair way whatever this allocation turns out to be. The doctrine includes an important element of pure procedural justice which is carried over to the other interpretations.

At this point it is necessary to make a brief digression to explain the principle of efficiency. This principle is simply that of Pareto optimality (as economists refer to it) formulated so as to apply to the basic structure.[7] I shall always use the term "efficiency" instead because this is literally correct and the term "optimality" suggests

7. There are expositions of this principle in most any work on price theory or social choice. A perspicuous account is found in T. C. Koopmans, *Three Essays on the State of Economic Science* (New York, McGraw-Hill, 1957), pp. 41–66. See also A. K. Sen, *Collective Choice and Social Welfare* (San Francisco, Holden-Day Inc., 1970), pp. 21f. These works contain everything (and more) that is required for our purposes in this book; and the latter takes up the relevant philosophical questions. The principle of efficiency was introduced by Vilfredo Pareto in his *Manuel d'économie politique* (Paris, 1909), ch. VI, §53, and the appendix, §89. A translation of the relevant passages can be found in A. N. Page, *Utility Theory: A Book of Readings* (New York, John Wiley, 1968), pp. 38f. The related concept of indifference curves goes back to F. Y. Edgeworth, *Mathematical Psychics* (London, 1888), pp. 20–29; also in Page, pp. 160–167.

that the concept is much broader than it is in fact.[8] To be sure, this principle was not originally intended to apply to institutions but to particular configurations of the economic system, for example, to distributions of goods among consumers or to modes of production. The principle holds that a configuration is efficient whenever it is impossible to change it so as to make some persons (at least one) better off without at the same time making other persons (at least one) worse off. Thus a distribution of a stock of commodities among certain individuals is efficient if there exists no redistribution of these goods that improves the circumstances of at least one of these individuals without another being disadvantaged. The organization of production is efficient if there is no way to alter inputs so as to produce more of some commodity without producing less of another. For if we could produce more of one good without having to give up some of another, the larger stock of goods could be used to better the circumstances of some persons without making that of others any worse. These applications of the principle show that it is, indeed, a principle of efficiency. A distribution of goods or a scheme of production is inefficient when there are ways of doing still better for some individuals without doing any worse for others. I shall assume that the parties in the original position accept this principle to judge the efficiency of economic and social arrangements. (See the accompanying discussion of the principle of efficiency.)

THE PRINCIPLE OF EFFICIENCY

Assume that there is a fixed stock of commodities to be distributed between two persons, x_1 and x_2. Let the line AB represent the points such that given x_1's gain at the corresponding level, there is no way to distribute the commodities so as to make x_2 better off than the point indicated by the curve. Consider the point D = (a,b). Then holding x_1 at the level a, the best that can be done for x_2 is the level b. In figure 3 the point O, the origin, represents the position before any commodities are distributed. The points on the line AB are the efficient points. Each point on AB can be seen to satisfy Pareto's criterion: there is no redistribution that makes either person better off without making the other worse

---

8. On this point see Koopmans, *Three Essays on the State of Economic Science*, p. 49. Koopmans remarks that a term like "allocative efficiency" would have been a more accurate name.

67

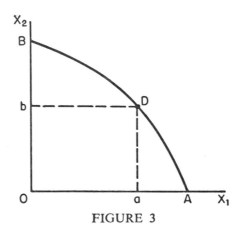

FIGURE 3

off. This is conveyed by the fact that the line AB slopes downward to the right. Since there is but a fixed stock of items, it is supposed that as one person gains the other loses. (Of course, this assumption is dropped in the case of the basic structure which is a system of co-operation producing a sum of positive advantages.) Normally the region OAB is taken to be a convex set. This means that given any pair of points in the set, the points on the straight line joining these two points are also in the set. Circles, ellipses, squares, triangles, and so on are convex sets.

It is clear that there are many efficient points, in fact, all the points on the line AB. The principle of efficiency does not by itself select one particular distribution of commodities as the efficient one. To select among the efficient distributions some other principle, a principle of justice, say, is necessary.

Of two points, if one is northeast of the other, this point is superior by the principle of efficiency. Points to the northwest or southeast cannot be compared. The ordering defined by the principle of efficiency is but a partial one. Thus in figure 4 while C is superior to E, and D is superior to F, none of the points on the line AB are either superior or inferior to one another. The class of efficient points cannot be ranked. Even the extreme points A and B at which one of the parties has everything are efficient, just as other points on AB.

Observe that we cannot say that any point on the line AB is superior to *all* points in the interior of OAB. Each point on AB is superior only

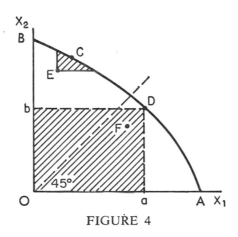

FIGURE 4

to those points in the interior southwest of it. Thus the point D is superior to all points inside the rectangle indicated by the dotted lines joining D to the points a and b. The point D is not superior to the point E. These points cannot be ordered. The point C, however, is superior to E and so are all the points on the line AB belonging to the small shaded triangular region that has the point E as a corner.

On the other hand, if one takes the 45° line as indicating the locus of equal distribution (this assumes an interpersonal cardinal interpretation of the axes, something not supposed in the preceding remarks), and if one counts this as an additional basis of decision, then all things considered, the point D may be preferable to both C and E. It is much closer to this line. One may even decide that an interior point such as F is to be preferred to C which is an efficient point. Actually, in justice as fairness the principles of justice are prior to considerations of efficiency and therefore, roughly speaking, the interior points that represent just distributions will generally be preferred to efficient points which represent unjust distributions. Of course, figure 4 depicts a very simple situation and cannot be applied to the basic structure.

There are, however, many configurations which are efficient. For example, the distributions in which one person receives the entire stock of commodities is efficient, since there is no rearrangement that will make some better off and none worse off. The person who holds the whole stock must lose out. But of course not every distribution is efficient, as might be suggested by the efficiency of such disparities. As long as a distribution leaves some persons willing to swap goods with others, it cannot be efficient; for the willingness to trade shows that there is a rearrangement which improves the situation of some without hurting that of anyone else. Indeed, an efficient distribution is one in which it is not possible to find further profitable exchanges. In that sense, the allocation of goods in which one man has everything is efficient because the others have nothing to give him in return. The principle of efficiency allows then that there are many efficient configurations. Each efficient arrangement is better than some other arrangements, but none of the efficient arrangements is better than another.

Now the principle of efficiency can be applied to the basic structure by reference to the expectations of representative men.[9] Thus we can say that an arrangement of rights and duties in the basic structure is efficient if and only if it is impossible to change the rules, to redefine the scheme of rights and duties, so as to raise the expectations of any representative man (at least one) without at the same time lowering the expectations of some (at least one) other representative man. Of course, these alterations must be consistent with the other principles. That is, in changing the basic structure we are not permitted to violate the principle of equal liberty or the requirement of open positions. What can be altered is the distribution of income and wealth and the way in which organizational powers, and various other forms of authority, regulate cooperative activities. Consistent with the constraints of liberty and accessibility, the allocation of these primary goods may be adjusted to modify the expectations of representative individuals. An arrangement of the basic structure is efficient when there is no way to change this distribution so as to raise the prospects of some without lowering the prospects of others.

There are, I shall assume, many efficient arrangements of the basic

9. For the application of the Pareto criterion to systems of public rules, see J. M. Buchanan, "The Relevance of Pareto Optimality," *Journal of Conflict Resolution,* vol. 6 (1962), as well as his book with Gordon Tullock, *The Calculus of Consent* (Ann Arbor, The University of Michigan Press, 1962). In applying this and other principles to institutions I follow one of the points of "Two Concepts of Rules," *Philosophical Review,* vol. 64 (1955). Doing this has the advantage, among other things, of constraining the employment of principles by publicity effects. See §23, note 8.

structure. Each of these specifies a particular division of advantages from social cooperation. The problem is to choose between them, to find a conception of justice that singles out one of these efficient distributions as also just. If we succeed in this, we shall have gone beyond mere efficiency yet in a way compatible with it. Now it is natural to try out the idea that as long as the social system is efficient there is no reason to be concerned with distribution. All efficient arrangements are in this case declared equally just. Of course, this suggestion would be outlandish for the allocation of particular goods to known individuals. No one would suppose that it is a matter of indifference from the standpoint of justice whether any one of a number of men happens to have everything. But the suggestion seems equally unreasonable for the basic structure. Thus it may be that under certain conditions serfdom cannot be significantly reformed without lowering the expectations of some representative man, say that of landowners, in which case serfdom is efficient. Yet it may also happen under the same conditions that a system of free labor cannot be changed without lowering the expectations of some representative man, say that of free laborers, so this arrangement is likewise efficient. More generally, whenever a society is relevantly divided into a number of classes, it is possible, let us suppose, to maximize with respect to each one of its representative men at a time. These maxima give at least this many efficient positions, for none of them can be departed from to raise the expectations of any one representative man without lowering those of another, namely, the representative man with respect to whom the maximum is defined. Thus each of these extremes is efficient but they surely cannot be all just, and equally so. These remarks simply parallel for social systems the situation in distributing particular goods to given individuals where the distributions in which a single person has everything is efficient.

Now these reflections show only what we knew all along, that is, that the principle of efficiency cannot serve alone as a conception of justice.[10] Therefore it must be supplemented in some way. Now in

10. This fact is generally recognized in welfare economics, as when it is said that efficiency is to be balanced against equity. See for example Tibor Scitovsky, *Welfare and Competition* (London, George Allen and Unwin, 1952), pp. 60–69 and I. M. D. Little, *A Critique of Welfare Economics,* 2nd ed. (Oxford, The

the system of natural liberty the principle of efficiency is constrained by certain background institutions; when these constraints are satisfied, any resulting efficient distribution is accepted as just. The system of natural liberty selects an efficient distribution roughly as follows. Let us suppose that we know from economic theory that under the standard assumptions defining a competitive market economy, income and wealth will be distributed in an efficient way, and that the particular efficient distribution which results in any period of time is determined by the initial distribution of assets, that is, by the initial distribution of income and wealth, and of natural talents and abilities. With each initial distribution, a definite efficient outcome is arrived at. Thus it turns out that if we are to accept the outcome as just, and not merely as efficient, we must accept the basis upon which over time the initial distribution of assets is determined.

In the system of natural liberty the initial distribution is regulated by the arrangements implicit in the conception of careers open to talents (as earlier defined). These arrangements presuppose a background of equal liberty (as specified by the first principle) and a free market economy. They require a formal equality of opportunity in that all have at least the same legal rights of access to all advantaged social positions. But since there is no effort to preserve an equality, or similarity, of social conditions, except insofar as this is necessary to preserve the requisite background institutions, the initial distribution of assets for any period of time is strongly influenced by natural and social contingencies. The existing distribution of income and wealth, say, is the cumulative effect of prior distributions of natural assets—that is, natural talents and abilities—as these have been developed or left unrealized, and their use favored or disfavored over time by social circumstances and such chance contingencies as accident and good fortune. Intuitively, the most obvious injustice of the system of natural liberty is that it permits distributive shares to be improperly influenced by these factors so arbitrary from a moral point of view.

Clarendon Press, 1957), ch. VI, esp. pp. 112–116. See Sen's remarks on the limitations of the principle of efficiency, *Collective Choice and Social Welfare*, pp. 22, 24–26, 83–86.

The liberal interpretation, as I shall refer to it, tries to correct for this by adding to the requirement of careers open to talents the further condition of the principle of fair equality of opportunity. The thought here is that positions are to be not only open in a formal sense, but that all should have a fair chance to attain them. Offhand it is not clear what is meant, but we might say that those with similar abilities and skills should have similar life chances. More specifically, assuming that there is a distribution of natural assets, those who are at the same level of talent and ability, and have the same willingness to use them, should have the same prospects of success regardless of their initial place in the social system, that is, irrespective of the income class into which they are born. In all sectors of society there should be roughly equal prospects of culture and achievement for everyone similarly motivated and endowed. The expectations of those with the same abilities and aspirations should not be affected by their social class.[11]

The liberal interpretation of the two principles seeks, then, to mitigate the influence of social contingencies and natural fortune on distributive shares. To accomplish this end it is necessary to impose further basic structural conditions on the social system. Free market arrangements must be set within a framework of political and legal institutions which regulates the overall trends of economic events and preserves the social conditions necessary for fair equality of opportunity. The elements of this framework are familiar enough, though it may be worthwhile to recall the importance of preventing excessive accumulations of property and wealth and of maintaining equal opportunities of education for all. Chances to acquire cultural knowledge and skills should not depend upon one's class position, and so the school system, whether public or private, should be designed to even out class barriers.

While the liberal conception seems clearly preferable to the system of natural liberty, intuitively it still appears defective. For one thing, even if it works to perfection in eliminating the influence of social contingencies, it still permits the distribution of wealth and income

11. This definition follows Sidgwick's suggestion in *The Methods of Ethics,* p. 285n. See also R. H. Tawney, *Equality* (London, George Allen and Unwin, 1931), ch. II, sec. ii; and B. A. O. Williams, "The Idea of Equality," in *Philosophy, Politics, and Society,* ed. Peter Laslett and W. G. Runciman (Oxford, Basil Blackwell, 1962), pp. 125f.

to be determined by the natural distribution of abilities and talents. Within the limits allowed by the background arrangements, distributive shares are decided by the outcome of the natural lottery; and this outcome is arbitrary from a moral perspective. There is no more reason to permit the distribution of income and wealth to be settled by the distribution of natural assets than by historical and social fortune. Furthermore, the principle of fair opportunity can be only imperfectly carried out, at least as long as the institution of the family exists. The extent to which natural capacities develop and reach fruition is affected by all kinds of social conditions and class attitudes. Even the willingness to make an effort, to try, and so to be deserving in the ordinary sense is itself dependent upon happy family and social circumstances. It is impossible in practice to secure equal chances of achievement and culture for those similarly endowed, and therefore we may want to adopt a principle which recognizes this fact and also mitigates the arbitrary effects of the natural lottery itself. That the liberal conception fails to do this encourages one to look for another interpretation of the two principles of justice.

Before turning to the conception of democratic equality, we should note that of natural aristocracy. On this view no attempt is made to regulate social contingencies beyond what is required by formal equality of opportunity, but the advantages of persons with greater natural endowments are to be limited to those that further the good of the poorer sectors of society. The aristocratic ideal is applied to a system that is open, at least from a legal point of view, and the better situation of those favored by it is regarded as just only when less would be had by those below, if less were given to those above.[12] In this way the idea of *noblesse oblige* is carried over to the conception of natural aristocracy.

Now both the liberal conception and that of natural aristocracy are unstable. For once we are troubled by the influence of either

12. This formulation of the aristocratic ideal is derived from Santayana's account of aristocracy in ch. IV of *Reason and Society* (New York, Charles Scribner, 1905), pp. 109f. He says, for example, "an aristocratic regimen can only be justified by radiating benefit and by proving that were less given to those above, less would be attained by those beneath them." I am indebted to Robert Rodes for pointing out to me that natural aristocracy is a possible interpretation of the two principles of justice and that an ideal feudal system might also try to fulfill the difference principle.

social contingencies or natural chance on the determination of distributive shares, we are bound, on reflection, to be bothered by the influence of the other. From a moral standpoint the two seem equally arbitrary. So however we move away from the system of natural liberty, we cannot be satisfied short of the democratic conception. This conception I have yet to explain. And, moreover, none of the preceding remarks are an argument for this conception, since in a contract theory all arguments, strictly speaking, are to be made in terms of what it would be rational to choose in the original position. But I am concerned here to prepare the way for the favored interpretation of the two principles so that these criteria, especially the second one, will not strike the reader as too eccentric or bizarre. I have tried to show that once we try to find a rendering of them which treats everyone equally as a moral person, and which does not weight men's share in the benefits and burdens of social cooperation according to their social fortune or their luck in the natural lottery, it is clear that the democratic interpretation is the best choice among the four alternatives. With these comments as a preface, I now turn to this conception.

13. DEMOCRATIC EQUALITY AND THE DIFFERENCE PRINCIPLE

The democratic interpretation, as the table suggests, is arrived at by combining the principle of fair equality of opportunity with the difference principle. This principle removes the indeterminateness of the principle of efficiency by singling out a particular position from which the social and economic inequalities of the basic structure are to be judged. Assuming the framework of institutions required by equal liberty and fair equality of opportunity, the higher expectations of those better situated are just if and only if they work as part of a scheme which improves the expectations of the least advantaged members of society. The intuitive idea is that the social order is not to establish and secure the more attractive prospects of those better off unless doing so is to the advantage of those less fortunate. (See the discussion of the difference principle that follows.)

75

THE DIFFERENCE PRINCIPLE

Assume that indifference curves now represent distributions that are judged equally just. Then the difference principle is a strongly egalitarian conception in the sense that unless there is a distribution that makes both persons better off (limiting ourselves to the two-person case for simplicity), an equal distribution is to be preferred. The indifference curves take the form depicted in figure 5. These curves are actually made up of vertical and straight lines that intersect at right angles at the 45° line (again supposing an interpersonal and cardinal interpretation of the axes). No matter how much either person's situation is improved, there is no gain from the standpoint of the difference principle unless the other gains also.

Suppose that x_1 is the most favored representative man in the basic structure. As his expectations are increased so are the prospects of x_2, the least advantaged man. In figure 6 let the curve OP represent the

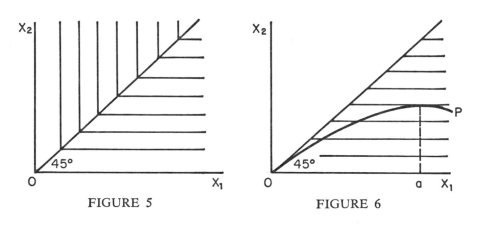

FIGURE 5   FIGURE 6

contribution to x_2's expectations made by the greater expectations of x_1. The point O, the origin, represents the hypothetical state in which all social primary goods are distributed equally. Now the OP curve is always below the 45° line, since x_1 is always better off. Thus the only relevant parts of the indifference curves are those below this line, and for this reason the upper left-hand part of figure 6 is not drawn in. Clearly the difference principle is perfectly satisfied only when the OP curve is just tangent to the highest indifference curve that it touches. In figure 6 this is at the point a.

Note that the contribution curve, the curve OP, supposes that the

76

social cooperation defined by the basic structure is mutually advantageous. It is no longer a matter of shuffling about a fixed stock of goods. Also, nothing is lost if an accurate interpersonal comparison of benefits is impossible. It suffices that the least favored person can be identified and his rational preference determined.

A view less egalitarian than the difference principle, and perhaps more plausible at first sight, is one in which the indifference lines for just distributions (or for all things considered) are smooth curves convex to the origin, as in figure 7. The indifference curves for social welfare functions are often depicted in this fashion. This shape of the curves expresses the fact that as either person gains relative to the other, further benefits to him become less valuable from a social point of view.

A classical utilitarian, on the other hand, is indifferent as to how a constant sum of benefits is distributed. He appeals to equality only to break ties. If there are but two persons, then assuming an interpersonal cardinal interpretation of the axes, the utilitarian's indifference lines for distributions are straight lines perpendicular to the 45° line. Since, however, x_1 and x_2 are representative men, the gains to them have to be weighted by the number of persons they each represent. Since presumably x_2 represents rather more persons than x_1, the indifference lines become more horizontal, as seen in figure 8. The ratio of the num-

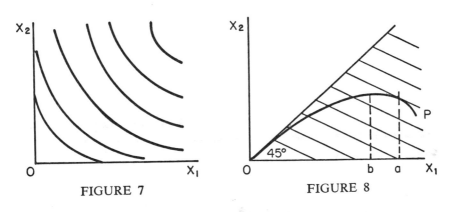

FIGURE 7   FIGURE 8

ber of advantaged to the number of disadvantaged defines the slope of these straight lines. Drawing the same contribution curve OP as before, we see that the best distribution from a utilitarian point of view is reached at the point which is beyond the point b where the OP curve reaches its maximum. Since the difference principle selects the point b and b is always to the left of a, utilitarianism allows, other things equal, larger inequalities.

To illustrate the difference principle, consider the distribution of income among social classes. Let us suppose that the various income groups correlate with representative individuals by reference to whose expectations we can judge the distribution. Now those starting out as members of the entrepreneurial class in property-owning democracy, say, have a better prospect than those who begin in the class of unskilled laborers. It seems likely that this will be true even when the social injustices which now exist are removed. What, then, can possibly justify this kind of initial inequality in life prospects? According to the difference principle, it is justifiable only if the difference in expectation is to the advantage of the representative man who is worse off, in this case the representative unskilled worker. The inequality in expectation is permissible only if lowering it would make the working class even more worse off. Supposedly, given the rider in the second principle concerning open positions, and the principle of liberty generally, the greater expectations allowed to entrepreneurs encourages them to do things which raise the long-term prospects of laboring class. Their better prospects act as incentives so that the economic process is more efficient, innovation proceeds at a faster pace, and so on. Eventually the resulting material benefits spread throughout the system and to the least advantaged. I shall not consider how far these things are true. The point is that something of this kind must be argued if these inequalities are to be just by the difference principle.

I shall now make a few remarks about this principle. First of all, in applying it, one should distinguish between two cases. The first case is that in which the expectations of the least advantaged are indeed maximized (subject, of course, to the mentioned constraints). No changes in the expectations of those better off can improve the situation of those worst off. The best arrangement obtains, what I shall call a perfectly just scheme. The second case is that in which the expectations of all those better off at least contribute to the welfare of the more unfortunate. That is, if their expectations were decreased, the prospects of the least advantaged would likewise fall. Yet the maximum is not yet achieved. Even higher expectations for the more advantaged would raise the expectations of those in the lowest position. Such a scheme is, I shall say, just throughout, but not the best just arrangement. A scheme is unjust when the higher expectations, one or more of them, are excessive. If these expectations were decreased, the situation of the least favored would be improved. How unjust an arrangement is depends on how excessive the higher expectations are and to what extent they depend upon the violation of the other principles of justice, for example, fair equality of opportunity; but I shall not attempt to measure in any exact way the degrees of injustice. The point to note here is that while the difference principle is, strictly speaking, a maximizing principle, there is a significant distinction between the cases that fall short of the best arrangement. A society should try to avoid the region where the marginal contributions of those better off are negative, since, other things equal, this seems a greater fault than falling short of the best scheme when these contributions are positive. The even larger difference between rich and poor makes the latter even worse off, and this violates the principle of mutual advantage as well as democratic equality (§ 17).

A further point is this. We saw that the system of natural liberty and the liberal conception attempt to go beyond the principle of efficiency by moderating its scope of operation, by constraining it by certain background institutions and leaving the rest to pure procedural justice. The democratic conception holds that while pure procedural justice may be invoked to some extent at least, the way previous interpretations do this still leaves too much to social and natural contingency. But it should be noted that the difference principle is compatible with the principle of efficiency. For when the former is fully satisfied, it is indeed impossible to make any one representative man better off without making another worse off, namely, the least advantaged representative man whose expectations we are to maximize. Thus justice is defined so that it is consistent with efficiency, at least when the two principles are perfectly fulfilled. Of course, if the basic structure is unjust, these principles will authorize changes that may lower the expectations of some of those better off; and therefore the democratic conception is not consistent with the principle of efficiency if this principle is taken to mean that only changes which improve everyone's prospects are allowed. Justice is prior to efficiency and requires some changes that are not efficient in this sense. Consistency obtains only in the sense that a perfectly just scheme is also efficient.

Next, we may consider a certain complication regarding the meaning of the difference principle. It has been taken for granted that if the principle is satisfied, everyone is benefited. One obvious sense in which this is so is that each man's position is improved with respect to the initial arrangement of equality. But it is clear that nothing depends upon being able to identify this initial arrangement; indeed, how well off men are in this situation plays no essential role in applying the difference principle. We simply maximize the expectations of the least favored position subject to the required constraints. As long as doing this is an improvement for everyone, as we assume it is, the estimated gains from the situation of hypothetical equality are irrelevant, if not largely impossible to ascertain anyway. There may be, however, a further sense in which everyone is advantaged when the difference principle is satisfied, at least if we make certain natural assumptions. Let us suppose that inequalities in expectations are chain-connected: that is, if an advantage has the effect of raising the expectations of the lowest position, it raises the expectations of all positions in between. For example, if the greater expectations for entrepreneurs benefit the unskilled worker, they also benefit the semiskilled. Notice that chain connection says nothing about the case where the least advantaged do not gain, so that it does not mean that all effects move together. Assume further that expectations are close-knit: that is, it is impossible to raise or lower the expectation of any representative man without raising or lowering the expectation of every other representative man, especially that of the least advantaged. There is no loose-jointedness, so to speak, in the way expectations hang together. Now with these assumptions there is a sense in which everyone benefits when the difference principle is satisfied. For the representative man who is better off in any two-way comparison gains by the advantages offered him, and the man who is worse off gains from the contributions which these inequalities make. Of course, these conditions may not hold. But in this case those who are better off should not have a veto over the benefits available for the least favored. We are still to maximize the expectations of those most disadvantaged. (See the accompanying discussion of chain connection.)

CHAIN CONNECTION

For simplicity assume that there are three representative men. Let x_1 be the most favored and x_3 the least favored with x_2 in between. Let the expectations of x_1 be marked off along the horizontal axis, the expectations of x_2 and x_3 along the vertical axis. The curves showing the contribution of the most favored to the other groups begin at the origin as the hypothetical position of equality. Moreover, there is a maximum gain permitted to the most favored on the assumption that, even if the difference principle would allow it, there would be unjust effects on the political system and the like excluded by the priority of liberty.

The difference principle selects the point where the curve for x_3 reaches its maximum, for example, the point a in figure 9.

Chain connection means that at any point where the x_3 curve is rising to the right, the x_2 curve is also rising, as in the intervals left of the points a and b in figures 9 and 10. Chain connection says nothing about the case where the x_3 curve is falling to the right, as in the interval to the right of the point a in figure 9. The x_2 curve may be either rising or falling (as indicated by the dashed line x'_2). Chain connection does not hold to the right of b in figure 10.

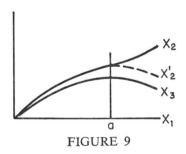 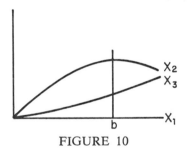

FIGURE 9   FIGURE 10

Intervals in which both the x_2 and the x_3 curves are rising define the intervals of position contributions. Any more to the right increases the average expectation (average utility if utility is measured by expectations) and also satisfies the principle of efficiency as a criterion of change, that is, points to the right improve everyone's situation.

In figure 9 the average expectations may be rising beyond the point a, although the expectations of the least favored are falling. (This depends on the weights of the several groups.) The difference principle excludes this and selects the point a.

Close-knitness means that there are no flat stretches on the curves for

x_2 and x_3. At each point both curves are either rising or falling. All the curves illustrated are close-knit.

I shall not examine how likely it is that chain connection and close-knitness hold. The difference principle is not contingent on these relations being satisfied. However, one may note that when the contributions of the more favored positions spread generally throughout society and are not confined to particular sectors, it seems plausible that if the least advantaged benefit so do others in between. Moreover, a wide diffusion of benefits is favored by two features of institutions both exemplified by the basic structure: first, they are set up to advance certain fundamental interests which everyone has in common, and second, offices and positions are open. Thus it seems probable that if the privileges and powers of legislators and judges, say, improve the situation of the less favored, they improve that of citizens generally. Chain connection may often be true, provided the other principles of justice are fulfilled. If this is so, then we may observe that within the region of positive contributions (the region where the advantages of all those in favored positions raise the prospects of the least fortunate), any movement toward the perfectly just arrangement both increases average well-being and improves everyone's expectation. Given these special assumptions, the difference principle has the same practical consequences as the principles of average utility and efficiency. Of course, if chain connection rarely holds and these cases are unimportant, this coincidence between principles is only a curiosity. But we often suppose that within just social arrangements something like a general diffusion of gains does take place, at least in the longer run. Should this be true, these remarks indicate how the difference principle can account for these more familiar notions as special cases. It remains to be shown, though, that this principle is the more fundamental one from a moral point of view.

There is a further complication. Close-knitness is assumed in order to simplify the statement of the difference principle. It is clearly conceivable, however likely or important in practice, that the least advantaged are not affected one way or the other by some changes in expectations of the best off although these changes benefit others. In this sort of case close-knitness fails, and to cover the situation we can express a more general principle as follows: in a basic structure with n relevant representatives, first maximize the welfare of the worst off representative man; second, for equal welfare of the worst-off representative, maximize the welfare of the second worst-off representative man, and so on until the last case which is, for equal welfare of all the preceding n—1 representatives, maximize the welfare of the best-off representative man. We may think of this as the lexical difference principle.[13] However, I shall always use the difference principle in the simpler form. And therefore, as the outcome of the last several sections, the second principle is to read as follows.

Social and economic inequalities are to be arranged so that they are both (a) to the greatest benefit of the least advantaged and (b) attached to offices and positions open to all under conditions of fair equality of opportunity.

Finally, it should be observed that the difference principle, or the idea expressed by it, can easily be accommodated to the general conception of justice. In fact, the general conception is simply the difference principle applied to all primary goods including liberty and opportunity and so no longer constrained by other parts of the special conception. This is evident from the earlier brief discussion of the principles of justice. These principles in serial order are, as I shall indicate from time to time, the form that the general conception finally assumes as social conditions improve. This question ties up with that of the priority of liberty which I shall discuss later on (§§ 39, 82). For the moment it suffices to remark that in one form or another the difference principle is basic throughout.

14. FAIR EQUALITY OF OPPORTUNITY AND PURE PROCEDURAL JUSTICE

I should now like to comment upon the second part of the second principle, henceforth to be understood as the liberal principle of fair equality of opportunity. It must not then be confused with the notion of careers open to talents; nor must one forget that since it is tied in with the difference principle its consequences are quite distinct from the liberal interpretation of the two principles taken to-

13. On this point, see Sen, *Collective Choice and Social Welfare*, p. 138n.

gether. In particular, I shall try to show further on (§ 17) that this principle is not subject to the objection that it leads to a meritocratic society. Here I wish to consider a few other points, especially its relation to the idea of pure procedural justice.

First, though, I should note that the reasons for requiring open positions are not solely, or even primarily, those of efficiency. I have not maintained that offices must be open if in fact everyone is to benefit from an arrangement. For it may be possible to improve everyone's situation by assigning certain powers and benefits to positions despite the fact that certain groups are excluded from them. Although access is restricted, perhaps these offices can still attract superior talent and encourage better performance. But the principle of open positions forbids this. It expresses the conviction that if some places were not open on a basis fair to all, those kept out would be right in feeling unjustly treated even though they benefited from the greater efforts of those who were allowed to hold them. They would be justified in their complaint not only because they were excluded from certain external rewards of office such as wealth and privilege, but because they were debarred from experiencing the realization of self which comes from a skillful and devoted exercise of social duties. They would be deprived of one of the main forms of human good.

Now I have said that the basic structure is the primary subject of justice. This means, as we have seen, that the first distributive problem is the assignment of fundamental rights and duties and the regulation of social and economic inequalities and of the legitimate expectations founded on these. Of course, any ethical theory recognizes the importance of the basic structure as a subject of justice, but not all theories regard its importance in the same way. In justice as fairness society is interpreted as a cooperative venture for mutual advantage. The basic structure is a public system of rules defining a scheme of activities that leads men to act together so as to produce a greater sum of benefits and assigns to each certain recognized claims to a share in the proceeds. What a person does depends upon what the public rules say he will be entitled to, and what a person is entitled to depends on what he does. The distribution which results is arrived at by honoring the claims determined by what persons undertake to do in the light of these legitimate expectations.

These considerations suggest the idea of treating the question of distributive shares as a matter of pure procedural justice.[14] The intuitive idea is to design the social system so that the outcome is just whatever it happens to be, at least so long as it is within a certain range. The notion of pure procedural justice is best understood by a comparison with perfect and imperfect procedural justice. To illustrate the former, consider the simplest case of fair division. A number of men are to divide a cake: assuming that the fair division is an equal one, which procedure, if any, will give this outcome? Technicalities aside, the obvious solution is to have one man divide the cake and get the last piece, the others being allowed their pick before him. He will divide the cake equally, since in this way he assures for himself the largest share possible. This example illustrates the two characteristic features of perfect procedural justice. First, there is an independent criterion for what is a fair division, a criterion defined separately from and prior to the procedure which is to be followed. And second, it is possible to devise a procedure that is sure to give the desired outcome. Of course, certain assumptions are made here, such as that the man selected can divide the cake equally, wants as large a piece as he can get, and so on. But we can ignore these details. The essential thing is that there is an independent standard for deciding which outcome is just and a procedure guaranteed to lead to it. Pretty clearly, perfect procedural justice is rare, if not impossible, in cases of much practical interest.

Imperfect procedural justice is exemplified by a criminal trial. The desired outcome is that the defendant should be declared guilty if and only if he has committed the offense with which he is charged. The trial procedure is framed to search for and to establish the truth in this regard. But it seems impossible to design the legal rules so that they always lead to the correct result. The theory of trials examines which procedures and rules of evidence, and the like, are best calculated to advance this purpose consistent with the other ends of the law. Different arrangements for hearing cases may reasonably be expected in different circumstances to yield the right results, not

14. For a general discussion of procedural justice, see Brian Barry, *Political Argument* (London, Routledge and Kegan Paul, 1965), ch. VI. On the problem of fair division, see R. D. Luce and Howard Raiffa, *Games and Decisions* (New York, John Wiley and Sons, Inc., 1957), pp. 363–368; and Hugo Steinhaus, "The Problem of Fair Division," *Econometrica,* vol. 16 (1948).

always but at least most of the time. A trial, then, is an instance of imperfect procedural justice. Even though the law is carefully followed, and the proceedings fairly and properly conducted, it may reach the wrong outcome. An innocent man may be found guilty, a guilty man may be set free. In such cases we speak of a miscarriage of justice: the injustice springs from no human fault but from a fortuitous combination of circumstances which defeats the purpose of the legal rules. The characteristic mark of imperfect procedural justice is that while there is an independent criterion for the correct outcome, there is no feasible procedure which is sure to lead to it.

By contrast, pure procedural justice obtains when there is no independent criterion for the right result: instead there is a correct or fair procedure such that the outcome is likewise correct or fair, whatever it is, provided that the procedure has been properly followed. This situation is illustrated by gambling. If a number of persons engage in a series of fair bets, the distribution of cash after the last bet is fair, or at least not unfair, whatever this distribution is. I assume here that fair bets are those having a zero expectation of gain, that the bets are made voluntarily, that no one cheats, and so on. The betting procedure is fair and freely entered into under conditions that are fair. Thus the background circumstances define a fair procedure. Now any distribution of cash summing to the initial stock held by all individuals could result from a series of fair bets. In this sense all of these particular distributions are equally fair. A distinctive feature of pure procedural justice is that the procedure for determining the just result must actually be carried out; for in these cases there is no independent criterion by reference to which a definite outcome can be known to be just. Clearly we cannot say that a particular state of affairs is just because it could have been reached by following a fair procedure. This would permit far too much and would lead to absurdly unjust consequences. It would allow one to say that almost any distribution of goods is just, or fair, since it could have come about as a result of fair gambles. What makes the final outcome of betting fair, or not unfair, is that it is the one which has arisen after a series of fair gambles. A fair procedure translates its fairness to the outcome only when it is actually carried out.

In order, therefore, to apply the notion of pure procedural justice to distributive shares it is necessary to set up and to administer impartially a just system of institutions. Only against the background of a just basic structure, including a just political constitution and a just arrangement of economic and social institutions, can one say that the requisite just procedure exists. In Part Two I shall describe in some detail a basic structure that has the necessary features. Its various institutions are explained and connected with the two principles of justice. The intuitive idea is familiar. Suppose that law and government act effectively to keep markets competitive, resources fully employed, property and wealth (especially if private ownership of the means of production is allowed) widely distributed by the appropriate forms of taxation, or whatever, and to guarantee a reasonable social minimum. Assume also that there is fair equality of opportunity underwritten by education for all; and that the other equal liberties are secured. Then it would appear that the resulting distribution of income and the pattern of expectations will tend to satisfy the difference principle. In this complex of institutions, which we think of as establishing social justice in the modern state, the advantages of the better situated improve the condition of the least favored. Or when they do not, they can be adjusted to do so, for example, by setting the social minimum at the appropriate level. As these institutions presently exist they are riddled with grave injustices. But there presumably are ways of running them compatible with their basic design and intention so that the difference principle is satisfied consistent with the demands of liberty and fair equality of opportunity. It is this fact which underlies our assurance that these arrangements can be made just.

It is evident that the role of the principle of fair opportunity is to insure that the system of cooperation is one of pure procedural justice. Unless it is satisfied, distributive justice could not be left to take care of itself, even within a restricted range. Now the great practical advantage of pure procedural justice is that it is no longer necessary in meeting the demands of justice to keep track of the endless variety of circumstances and the changing relative positions of particular persons. One avoids the problem of defining principles to cope with the enormous complexities which would arise if such details were relevant. It is a mistake to focus attention on the varying relative positions of individuals and to require that every change, considered as a single transaction viewed in isolation, be in itself just. It is the arrangement of the basic structure which is to be judged, and judged from a general point of view. Unless we are prepared to criticize it from the standpoint of a relevant representative man in some particular position, we have no complaint against it. Thus the acceptance of the two principles constitutes an understanding to discard as irrelevant as a matter of social justice much of the information and many of the complications of everyday life.

In pure procedural justice, then, distributions of advantages are not appraised in the first instance by confronting a stock of benefits available with given desires and needs of known individuals. The allotment of the items produced takes place in accordance with the public system of rules, and this system determines what is produced, how much is produced, and by what means. It also determines legitimate claims the honoring of which yields the resulting distribution. Thus in this kind of procedural justice the correctness of the distribution is founded on the justice of the scheme of cooperation from which it arises and on answering the claims of individuals engaged in it. A distribution cannot be judged in isolation from the system of which it is the outcome or from what individuals have done in good faith in the light of established expectations. If it is asked in the abstract whether one distribution of a given stock of things to definite individuals with known desires and preferences is better than another, then there is simply no answer to this question. The conception of the two principles does not interpret the primary problem of distributive justice as one of allocative justice.

By contrast the allocative conception of justice seems naturally to apply when a given collection of goods is to be divided among definite individuals with known desires and needs. The goods to be allotted are not produced by these individuals, nor do these individuals stand in any existing cooperative relations. Since there are no prior claims on the things to be distributed, it is natural to share them out according to desires and needs, or even to maximize the net balance of satisfaction. Justice becomes a kind of efficiency, unless equality is preferred. Suitably generalized, the allocative conception leads to the classical utilitarian view. For as we have seen, this doctrine assimilates justice to the benevolence of the impartial spectator and the latter in turn to the most efficient design of institutions to promote the greatest balance of satisfaction. As I observed earlier, on this conception society is thought of as so many separate individuals each defining a separate line along which rights and duties are to be assigned and scarce means of satisfaction allocated in accordance with rules so as to give the most complete fulfillment of desire. I shall put aside consideration of the other aspects of this notion until later. The point to note here is that utilitarianism does not interpret the basic structure as a scheme of pure procedural justice. For the utilitarian has, in principle anyway, an independent standard for judging all distributions, namely, whether they produce the greatest net balance of satisfaction. In his theory, institutions are more or less imperfect arrangements for bringing about this end. Thus given existing desires and preferences, and the natural continuations into the future which they allow, the statesman's aim is to set up those social schemes that will best approximate an already specified goal. Since these arrangements are subject to the unavoidable constraints and hindrances of everyday life, the basic structure is a case of imperfect procedural justice.

For the time being I shall suppose that the two parts of the second principle are lexically ordered. Thus we have one lexical ordering within another. But when necessary, this ordering can be modified in the light of the general conception of justice. The advantage of the special conception is that it has a definite shape and suggests certain questions for investigation, for example, under what conditions if any would the lexical ordering be chosen? Our inquiry is given a particular direction and is no longer confined to generalities. Of course, this conception of distributive shares is obviously a great simplification. It is designed to characterize in a clear way a basic structure that makes use of the idea of pure procedural justice. But all the same we should attempt to find simple concepts that can be assembled to give a reasonable conception of justice. The notions of the basic structure, of the veil of ignorance, of a lexical order, of the least favored position, as well as of pure procedural justice are all examples of this. By themselves none of these could be expected to work, but properly put together they may serve well enough. It is too much to suppose that there exists for all or even most moral problems a reasonable solution. Perhaps only a few can be satisfactorily answered. In any case social wisdom consists in framing institutions so that intractable difficulties do not often arise and in accepting the need for clear and simple principles.

15. PRIMARY SOCIAL GOODS AS THE BASIS OF EXPECTATIONS

So much, then, for a brief statement and explanation of the two principles of justice and of the procedural conception which they express. In later chapters I shall present further details by describing an arrangement of institutions that realizes this conception. At the moment, however, there are several preliminary matters that must be faced. I begin with a discussion of expectations and how they are to be estimated.

The significance of this question can be brought out by a comparison with utilitarianism. When applied to the basic structure the principle of utility requires us to maximize the algebraic sum of expectations taken over all relevant positions. (The classical principle weights these expectations by the number of persons in these positions, the average principle by the fraction of persons.) Leaving aside for the next section the question as to what defines a relevant position, it is clear that utilitarianism assumes some fairly accurate measure of these expectations. Not only is it necessary to have a cardinal measure for each representative individual but these measures must make sense in interpersonal comparisons. Some method of correlating the scales of different persons is presupposed if we are to say that the gains of some are to outweigh the losses of others. It is unreasonable to demand great precision, yet these estimates cannot be left to our unguided intuition. For judgments of a greater balance of interests leave too much room for conflicting claims. Moreover, these judgments may be based on ethical and other notions, not to mention bias and self-interest, which puts their validity in question. Simply because we do in fact make what we call interpersonal comparisons of well-being does not mean that we understand the basis of these comparisons or that we should accept them as sound. To settle these matters we need to give an account of these judgments, to set out the criteria that underlie them (§ 49). For questions of social justice we should try to find some objective grounds for these comparisons, ones that men can recognize and agree to. At the present time, there appears to be no satisfactory answer to these difficulties from a utilitarian point of view. Therefore it seems that, for the time being at least, the principle of utility makes such heavy demands on our ability to estimate the balance of advantages that it defines at best an ambiguous court of appeal for questions of justice.

I do not assume, though, that a satisfactory solution to these problems is impossible. While these difficulties are real, and the difference principle is framed to circumvent them, I do not wish to stress its relative merits on this score. For one thing, skepticism about interpersonal comparisons is often based on questionable views: for example, that the intensity of pleasure or of the enjoyment which indicates well-being is the intensity of pure sensation; and that while the intensity of such sensations can be experienced and known by the subject, it is impossible for others to know it or to infer it with reasonable certainty. Both these contentions seem wrong. Indeed, the second is simply part of a skepticism about the existence of other minds, unless it is shown why judgments of well-being present special problems which cannot be overcome.[15] I believe that the real difficulties with utilitarianism lie elsewhere. The main point is that even if interpersonal comparisons of satisfaction can be made, these comparisons must reflect values which it makes sense to pursue. It is irrational to advance one end rather than another simply because it can be more accurately estimated. The controversy about interpersonal comparisons tends to obscure the real question, namely, whether the total (or average) happiness is to be maximized in the first place.

The difference principle meets some of the difficulties in making interpersonal comparisons. This it does in two ways. First of all, as long as we can identify the least advantaged representative man, only ordinal judgments of well-being are required from then on. We know from what position the social system is to be judged. It does not matter how much worse off this representative individual is than the others. If positions can be ranked as better or worse, the lowest can be found. The further difficulties of cardinal measurement do not arise since no other interpersonal comparisons are necessary. And,

15. See H. L. A. Hart, "Bentham," *Proceedings of the British Academy,* vol. 48 (London, 1962), pp. 340f, and Little, *Critique of Welfare Economics,* pp. 54f.

of course, in maximizing with respect to the least favored representative man, we need not go beyond ordinal judgments. If we can decide whether a change in the basic structure makes him better or worse off, we can determine his best situation. We do not have to know how much he prefers one situation to another. The difference principle, then, asks less of our judgments of welfare. We never have to calculate a sum of advantages involving a cardinal measure. While qualitative interpersonal comparisons are made in finding the bottom position, for the rest the ordinal judgments of one representative man suffice.

The difference principle also avoids difficulties by introducing a simplification for the basis of interpersonal comparisons. These comparisons are made in terms of expectations of primary social goods. In fact, I define these expectations simply as the index of these goods which a representative individual can look forward to. One man's expectations are greater than another's if this index for some one in his position is greater. Now primary goods, as I have already remarked, are things which it is supposed a rational man wants whatever else he wants. Regardless of what an individual's rational plans are in detail, it is assumed that there are various things which he would prefer more of rather than less. With more of these goods men can generally be assured of greater success in carrying out their intentions and in advancing their ends, whatever these ends may be. The primary social goods, to give them in broad categories, are rights and liberties, opportunities and powers, income and wealth. (A very important primary good is a sense of one's own worth; but for simplicity I leave this aside until much later, §67.) It seems evident that in general these things fit the description of primary goods. They are social goods in view of their connection with the basic structure; liberties and powers are defined by the rules of major institutions and the distribution of income and wealth is regulated by them.

The theory of the good adopted to account for primary goods will be presented more fully in Chapter VII. It is a familiar one going back to Aristotle, and something like it is accepted by philosophers so different in other respects as Kant and Sidgwick. It is not in dispute between the contract doctrine and utilitarianism. The main idea is that a person's good is determined by what is for him the most rational long-term plan of life given reasonably favorable circumstances. A man is happy when he is more or less successfully in the way of carrying out this plan. To put it briefly, the good is the satisfaction of rational desire. We are to suppose, then, that each individual has a rational plan of life drawn up subject to the conditions that confront him. This plan is designed to permit the harmonious satisfaction of his interests. It schedules activities so that various desires can be fulfilled without interference. It is arrived at by rejecting other plans that are either less likely to succeed or do not provide for such an inclusive attainment of aims. Given the alternatives available, a rational plan is one which cannot be improved upon; there is no other plan which, taking everything into account, would be preferable.

Now the assumption is that though men's rational plans do have different final ends, they nevertheless all require for their execution certain primary goods, natural and social. Plans differ since individual abilities, circumstances, and wants differ; rational plans are adjusted to these contingencies. But whatever one's system of ends, primary goods are necessary means. Greater intelligence, wealth and opportunity, for example, allow a person to achieve ends he could not rationally contemplate otherwise. The expectations of representative men are, then, to be defined by the index of primary social goods available to them. While the persons in the original position do not know their conception of the good, they do know, I assume, that they prefer more rather than less primary goods. And this information is sufficient for them to know how to advance their interests in the initial situation.

Let us consider several difficulties. One problem clearly is the construction of the index itself. How are the different primary social goods to be weighed? Assuming that the two principles of justice are serially ordered, this problem is greatly simplified. The fundamental liberties are always equal, and there is fair equality of opportunity; one does not need to balance these liberties and rights against other values. The primary social goods that vary in their distribution are the powers and prerogatives of authority, and income and wealth. But the difficulties are not so great as they might seem at first because of the nature of the difference principle. The only index problem that concerns us is that for the least advantaged group. The primary goods

an awful lot of assumptions

enjoyed by other representative individuals are adjusted to raise this index, subject of course to the usual constraints. It is unnecessary to define weights for the more favored positions in any detail, as long as we are sure that they are more favored. But often this is easy since they frequently have more of every primary good, greater powers and wealth tending to go together. If we know how the distribution of goods to the more favored affects the expectations of the most disfavored, this is sufficient. The index problem largely reduces, then, to that of weighting primary goods for the least advantaged, for those with the least authority and the lowest income, since these also tend to be associated. We try to do this by taking up the standpoint of the representative individual from this group and asking which combination of primary social goods it would be rational for him to prefer. In doing this we admittedly rely upon our intuitive capacities. This cannot be avoided entirely, however. The aim is to replace moral judgments by those of rational prudence and to make the appeal to intuition more limited in scope, more sharply focused.

Another difficulty is this. It may be objected that expectations should not be defined as an index of primary goods anyway but rather as the satisfactions to be expected when plans are executed using these goods. After all, it is in the fulfillment of these plans that men gain happiness, and therefore the estimate of expectations should not be founded on the available means. Justice as fairness, however, takes a different view. For it does not look behind the use which persons make of the rights and opportunities available to them in order to measure, much less to maximize, the satisfactions they achieve. Nor does it try to evaluate the relative merits of different conceptions of the good. Instead, it is assumed that the members of society are rational persons able to adjust their conceptions of the good to their situation. There is no necessity to compare the worth of the conceptions of different persons once it is supposed they are compatible with the principles of justice. Everyone is assured an equal liberty to pursue whatever plan of life he pleases as long as it does not violate what justice demands. Men share in primary goods on the principle that some can have more if they are acquired in ways which improve the situation of those who have less. Once the whole arrangement is set up and going no questions are asked about the totals of satisfaction or perfection. Things work themselves out according to the principles that would be chosen in the original position. On this conception of social justice, then, expectations are defined as the index of primary goods that a representative man can reasonably look forward to. A person's prospects are improved when he can anticipate a preferred collection of these goods.

It is worth noting that this interpretation of expectations represents, in effect, an agreement to compare men's situations solely by reference to things which it is assumed they all prefer more of. This seems the most feasible way to establish a publicly recognized objective measure, that is, a common measure that reasonable persons can accept. Whereas there cannot be a similar agreement on how to estimate happiness as defined, say, by men's success in executing their rational plans, much less on the intrinsic value of these plans. Now founding expectations on primary goods is another simplifying device. I should like to comment in passing that this and other simplifications are accompanied by some sort of philosophical explanation, though this is not strictly necessary. Theoretical assumptions must, of course, do more than simplify; they must identify essential elements that explain the facts we want to understand. Similarly, the parts of a theory of justice must represent basic moral features of the social structure, and if it appears that some of these are being left aside, it is desirable to assure ourselves that such is not the case. I shall try to follow this rule. But even so, the soundness of the theory of justice is shown as much in its consequences as in the prima facie acceptability of its premises. Indeed, these cannot be usefully separated and therefore the discussion of institutional questions, particularly in Part Two, which may seem at first unphilosophical, is in fact unavoidable.

16. RELEVANT SOCIAL POSITIONS

In applying the two principles of justice to the basic structure of society one takes the position of certain representative individuals and considers how the social system looks to them. The difference principle, for example, requires that the higher expectations of the more advantaged contribute to the prospects of the least advantaged. Or as I sometimes say more loosely, social and economic inequalities must be in the interest of the representative men in all relevant social positions. The perspective of those in these situations defines a suitably general point of view. But certainly not all social positions are relevant. For not only are there farmers, say, but dairy farmers, wheat farmers, farmers working on large tracts of land, and so on for other occupations and groups indefinitely. We cannot have a coherent and manageable theory if we must take such a multiplicity of positions into account. The assessment of so many competing claims is impossible. Therefore we need to identify certain positions as more basic than the others and as providing an appropriate standpoint for judging the social system. Thus the choice of these positions becomes part of the theory of justice. On what principle, though, are they to be identified?

To answer this question we must keep in mind the fundamental problem of justice and the manner in which the two principles cope with it. The primary subject of justice, as I have emphasized, is the basic structure of society. The reason for this is that its effects are so profound and pervasive, and present from birth. This structure favors some starting places over others in the division of the benefits of social cooperation. It is these inequalities which the two principles are to regulate. Once these principles are satisfied, other inequalities are allowed to arise from men's voluntary actions in accordance with the principle of free association. Thus the relevant social positions are, so to speak, the starting places properly generalized and aggregated. By choosing these positions to specify the general point of view one follows the idea that the two principles attempt to mitigate the arbitrariness of natural contingency and social fortune.

I suppose, then, that for the most part each person holds two relevant positions: that of equal citizenship and that defined by his place in the distribution of income and wealth. The relevant representative men, therefore, are the representative citizen and those who stand for the various levels of well-being. Since I assume that in general other positions are entered into voluntarily, we need not consider the point of view of men in these positions in judging the basic structure. Indeed, we are to adjust the whole scheme to suit the preferences of those in the so-called starting places. In judging the social system we are to disregard our more specific interests and associations and look at our situation from the standpoint of these representative men.

Now as far as possible the basic structure should be appraised from the position of equal citizenship. This position is defined by the rights and liberties required by the principle of equal liberty and the principle of fair equality of opportunity. When the two principles are satisfied, all are equal citizens, and so everyone holds this position. In this sense, equal citizenship defines a general point of view. The problems of adjudicating among the fundamental liberties are settled by reference to it. These matters I shall discuss in Chapter IV. But it should be noted here that many questions of social policy can also be considered from this position. For there are matters which concern the interests of everyone and in regard to which distributive effects are immaterial or irrelevant. In these cases the principle of the common interest can be applied. According to this principle institutions are ranked by how effectively they guarantee the conditions necessary for all equally to further their aims, or by how efficiently they advance shared ends that will similarly benefit everyone. Thus reasonable regulations to maintain public order and security, or efficient measures for public health and safety, promote the common interest in this sense. So do collective efforts for national defense in a just war. It may be suggested that maintaining public health and safety or achieving victory in a just war have distributive effects: the rich benefit more than the poor since they have more to lose. But if social and economic inequalities are just, these effects may be left aside and the principle of the common interest applied. The standpoint of equal citizenship is the appropriate one.

The definition of representative men for judging social and economic inequalities is less satisfactory. For one thing, taking these individuals as specified by the levels of income and wealth, I assume that these primary social goods are sufficiently correlated with those of power and authority to avoid an index problem. That is, I suppose that those with greater political authority, say, or those higher in institutional forms, are in general better off in other respects. On the whole, this assumption seems safe enough for our purposes. There is also a question about how many such representative men

97

to single out, but this is not crucial because the difference principle selects one representative for a special role. The serious difficulty is how to define the least fortunate group.

Here it seems impossible to avoid a certain arbitrariness. One possibility is to choose a particular social position, say that of the unskilled worker, and then to count as the least advantaged all those with the average income and wealth of this group, or less. The expectation of the lowest representative man is defined as the average taken over this whole class. Another alternative is a definition solely in terms of relative income and wealth with no reference to social position. Thus all persons with less than half of the median income and wealth may be taken as the least advantaged segment. This definition depends only upon the lower half of the distribution and has the merit of focusing attention on the social distance between those who have least and the average citizen.[16] Surely this gap is an essential feature of the situation of the less favored members of society. I suppose that either of these definitions, or some combination of them, will serve well enough.

In any case we are to aggregate to some degree over the expectations of the worst off, and the figure selected on which to base these computations is to a certain extent ad hoc. Yet we are entitled at some point to plead practical considerations in formulating the difference principle. Sooner or later the capacity of philosophical or other arguments to make finer discriminations is bound to run out. I assume therefore that the persons in the original position understand the difference principle to be defined in one of these ways. They interpret it from the first as a limited aggregative principle and assess it as such in comparison with other standards. It is not as if they agreed to think of the least advantaged as literally the worst off individual and then in order to make this criterion work adopted in practice some form of averaging. Rather, it is the practicable criterion itself that is to be evaluated from the perspective of the original position.[17] It may turn out that a more exact definition of the least favored proves unnecessary.

16. For this definition, see M. J. Bowman's discussion of the so-called Fuchs criterion in "Poverty in an Affluent Society," an essay in *Contemporary Economic Issues,* ed. N. W. Chamberlain (Homewood, Ill., R. D. Irwin, 1969), pp. 53–56.
17. I am indebted to Scott Boorman for clarification on this point.

As far as possible, then, justice as fairness appraises the social system from the position of equal citizenship and the various levels of income and wealth. Sometimes, however, other positions may need to be taken into account. If, for example, there are unequal basic rights founded on fixed natural characteristics, these inequalities will single out relevant positions. Since these characteristics cannot be changed, the positions they define count as starting places in the basic structure. Distinctions based on sex are of this type, and so are those depending upon race and culture. Thus if, say, men are favored in the assignment of basic rights, this inequality is justified by the difference principle (in the general interpretation) only if it is to the advantage of women and acceptable from their standpoint. And the analogous condition applies to the justification of caste systems, or racial and ethnic inequalities (§39). Such inequalities multiply relevant positions and complicate the application of the two principles. On the other hand, these inequalities are seldom, if ever, to the advantage of the less favored, and therefore in a just society the smaller number of relevant positions should ordinarily suffice.

Now it is essential that the judgments made from the perspective of the relevant positions override the claims that we are prone to make in more particular situations. Not everyone always benefits by what the two principles require if we think of ourselves in terms of our more specific positions. And unless the viewpoint of the relevant positions has priority, one still has a chaos of competing claims. Thus the two principles express, in effect, an understanding to order our interests by giving certain of them a special weight. For example, persons engaged in a particular industry often find that free trade is contrary to their interests. Perhaps the industry cannot remain prosperous without tariffs or other restrictions. But if free trade is desirable from the point of view of equal citizens or of the least advantaged, it is justified even though more specific interests suffer. For we are to agree in advance to the principles of justice and their consistent application from the standpoint of certain positions. There is no way to guarantee the protection of everyone's interests over each period of time once the situation of representative men is defined more narrowly. Having acknowledged certain principles and a certain way of applying them, we are bound to *no sense + contra-dict yourself! you make*

accept the consequences. This does not mean, of course, that the rigors of free trade should be allowed to go unchecked. But the arrangements for softening them are to be considered from an appropriately general perspective.

The relevant social positions specify, then, the general point of view from which the two principles of justice are to be applied to the basic structure. In this way everyone's interests are taken into account, for each person is an equal citizen and all have a place in the distribution of income and wealth or in the range of fixed natural characteristics upon which distinctions are based. Some selection of relevant positions is necessary for a coherent theory of social justice and the ones chosen should accord with its first principles. By selecting the so-called starting places one follows out the idea of mitigating the effects of natural accident and social circumstance. No one is to benefit from these contingencies except in ways that redound to the well-being of others.

17. THE TENDENCY TO EQUALITY

I wish to conclude this discussion of the two principles by explaining the sense in which they express an egalitarian conception of justice. Also I should like to forestall the objection to the principle of fair opportunity that it leads to a callous meritocratic society. In order to prepare the way for doing this, I note several aspects of the conception of justice that I have set out.

First we may observe that the difference principle gives some weight to the considerations singled out by the principle of redress. This is the principle that undeserved inequalities call for redress; and since inequalities of birth and natural endowment are undeserved, these inequalities are to be somehow compensated for.[18] Thus the principle holds that in order to treat all persons equally, to provide genuine equality of opportunity, society must give more attention to those with fewer native assets and to those born into the less favorable social positions. The idea is to redress the bias

18. See Herbert Spiegelberg, "A Defense of Human Equality," *Philosophical Review*, vol. 53 (1944), pp. 101, 113–123; and D. D. Raphael, "Justice and Liberty," *Proceedings of the Aristotelian Society*, vol. 51 (1950–1951), pp. 187f.

of contingencies in the direction of equality. In pursuit of this principle greater resources might be spent on the education of the less rather than the more intelligent, at least over a certain time of life, say the earlier years of school.

Now the principle of redress has not to my knowledge been proposed as the sole criterion of justice, as the single aim of the social order. It is plausible as most such principles are only as a prima facie principle, one that is to be weighed in the balance with others. For example, we are to weigh it against the principle to improve the average standard of life, or to advance the common good.[19] But whatever other principles we hold, the claims of redress are to be taken into account. It is thought to represent one of the elements in our conception of justice. Now the difference principle is not of course the principle of redress. It does not require society to try to even out handicaps as if all were expected to compete on a fair basis in the same race. But the difference principle would allocate resources in education, say, so as to improve the long-term expectation of the least favored. If this end is attained by giving more attention to the better endowed, it is permissible; otherwise not. And in making this decision, the value of education should not be assessed solely in terms of economic efficiency and social welfare. Equally if not more important is the role of education in enabling a person to enjoy the culture of his society and to take part in its affairs, and in this way to provide for each individual a secure sense of his own worth.

Thus although the difference principle is not the same as that of redress, it does achieve some of the intent of the latter principle. It transforms the aims of the basic structure so that the total scheme of institutions no longer emphasizes social efficiency and technocratic values. We see then that the difference principle represents, in effect, an agreement to regard the distribution of natural talents as a common asset and to share in the benefits of this distribution whatever it turns out to be. Those who have been favored by nature, whoever they are, may gain from their good fortune only on terms that improve the situation of those who have lost out. The naturally advantaged are not to gain merely because they are more gifted, but only to

19. See, for example, Spiegelberg, pp. 120f.

cover the costs of training and education and for using their endowments in ways that help the less fortunate as well. No one deserves
his greater natural capacity nor merits a more favorable starting place
in society. But it does not follow that one should eliminate these distinctions. There is another way to deal with them. The basic structure can be arranged so that these contingencies work for the good
of the least fortunate. Thus we are led to the difference principle if
we wish to set up the social system so that no one gains or loses
from his arbitrary place in the distribution of natural assets or his
initial position in society without giving or receiving compensating
advantages in return.

In view of these remarks we may reject the contention that the
ordering of institutions is always defective because the distribution
of natural talents and the contingencies of social circumstance are
unjust, and this injustice must inevitably carry over to human arrangements. Occasionally this reflection is offered as an excuse for
ignoring injustice, as if the refusal to acquiesce in injustice is on a
par with being unable to accept death. The natural distribution is
neither just nor unjust; nor is it unjust that persons are born into
society at some particular position. These are simply natural facts.
What is just and unjust is the way that institutions deal with these
facts. Aristocratic and caste societies are unjust because they make
these contingencies the ascriptive basis for belonging to more or
less enclosed and privileged social classes. The basic structure of
these societies incorporates the arbitrariness found in nature. But
there is no necessity for men to resign themselves to these contingencies. The social system is not an unchangeable order beyond
human control but a pattern of human action. In justice as fairness
men agree to share one another's fate. In designing institutions they
undertake to avail themselves of the accidents of nature and social
circumstance only when doing so is for the common benefit. The
two principles are a fair way of meeting the arbitrariness of fortune;
and while no doubt imperfect in other ways, the institutions which
satisfy these principles are just.

A further point is that the difference principle expresses a conception of reciprocity. It is a principle of mutual benefit. We have
seen that, at least when chain connection holds, each representative
man can accept the basic structure as designed to advance his in-

terests. The social order can be justified to everyone, and in particular to those who are least favored; and in this sense it is egalitarian. But it seems necessary to consider in an intuitive way how the condition of mutual benefit is satisfied. Consider any two representative men A and B, and let B be the one who is less favored. Actually, since we are most interested in the comparison with the least favored man, let us assume that B is this individual. Now B can accept A's being better off since A's advantages have been gained in ways that improve B's prospects. If A were not allowed his better position, B would be even worse off than he is. The difficulty is to show that A has no grounds for complaint. Perhaps he is required to have less than he might since his having more would result in some loss to B. Now what can be said to the more favored man? To begin with, it is clear that the well-being of each depends on a scheme of social cooperation without which no one could have a satisfactory life. Secondly, we can ask for the willing cooperation of everyone only if the terms of the scheme are reasonable. The difference principle, then, seems to be a fair basis on which those better endowed, or more fortunate in their social circumstances, could expect others to collaborate with them when some workable arrangement is a necessary condition of the good of all.

There is a natural inclination to object that those better situated deserve their greater advantages whether or not they are to the benefit of others. At this point it is necessary to be clear about the notion of desert. It is perfectly true that given a just system of cooperation as a scheme of public rules and the expectations set up by it, those who, with the prospect of improving their condition, have done what the system announces that it will reward are entitled to their advantages. In this sense the more fortunate have a claim to their better situation; their claims are legitimate expectations established by social institutions, and the community is obligated to meet them. But this sense of desert presupposes the existence of the cooperative scheme; it is irrelevant to the question whether in the first place the scheme is to be designed in accordance with the difference principle or some other criterion.

Perhaps some will think that the person with greater natural endowments deserves those assets and the superior character that made their development possible. Because he is more worthy in

103

this sense, he deserves the greater advantages that he could achieve with them. This view, however, is surely incorrect. It seems to be one of the fixed points of our considered judgments that no one deserves his place in the distribution of native endowments, any more than one deserves one's initial starting place in society. The assertion that a man deserves the superior character that enables him to make the effort to cultivate his abilities is equally problematic; for his character depends in large part upon fortunate family and social circumstances for which he can claim no credit. The notion of desert seems not to apply to these cases. Thus the more advantaged representative man cannot say that he deserves and therefore has a right to a scheme of cooperation in which he is permitted to acquire benefits in ways that do not contribute to the welfare of others. There is no basis for his making this claim. From the standpoint of common sense, then, the difference principle appears to be acceptable both to the more advantaged and to the less advantaged individual. Of course, none of this is strictly speaking an argument for the principle, since in a contract theory arguments are made from the point of view of the original position. But these intuitive considerations help to clarify the nature of the principle and the sense in which it is egalitarian.

I noted earlier (§ 13) that a society should try to avoid the region where the marginal contributions of those better off to the well-being of the less favored are negative. It should operate only on the upward rising part of the contribution curve (including of course the maximum). One reason for this, we can now see, is that on this segment of the curve the criterion of mutual benefit is always fulfilled. Moreover, there is a natural sense in which the harmony of social interests is achieved; representative men do not gain at one another's expense since only reciprocal advantages are allowed. To be sure, the shape and slope of the contribution curve is determined in part at least by the natural lottery in native assets, and as such it is neither just nor unjust. But suppose we think of the forty-five degree line as representing the ideal of a perfect harmony of interests; it is the contribution curve (a straight line in this case) along which everyone gains equally. Then it seems that the consistent realization of the two principles of justice tends to raise the curve closer to the ideal of a perfect harmony of in-

Excludes problems again

terests. Once a society goes beyond the maximum it operates along the downward sloping part of the curve and a harmony of interests no longer exists. As the more favored gain the less advantaged lose, and vice versa. The situation is analogous to being on an efficiency frontier. This is far from desirable when the justice of the basic structure is involved. Thus it is to realize the ideal of the harmony of interests on terms that nature has given us, and to meet the criterion of mutual benefit, that we should stay in the region of positive contributions.

A further merit of the difference principle is that it provides an interpretation of the principle of fraternity. In comparison with liberty and equality, the idea of fraternity has had a lesser place in democratic theory. It is thought to be less specifically a political concept, not in itself defining any of the democratic rights but conveying instead certain attitudes of mind and forms of conduct without which we would lose sight of the values expressed by these rights.[20] Or closely related to this, fraternity is held to represent a certain equality of social esteem manifest in various public conventions and in the absence of manners of deference and servility.[21] No doubt fraternity does imply these things, as well as a sense of civic friendship and social solidarity, but so understood it expresses no definite requirement. We have yet to find a principle of justice that matches the underlying idea. The difference principle, however, does seem to correspond to a natural meaning of fraternity: namely, to the idea of not wanting to have greater advantages unless this is to the benefit of others who are less well off. The family, in its ideal conception and often in practice, is one place where the principle of maximizing the sum of advantages is rejected. Members of a family commonly do not wish to gain unless they can do so in ways that further the interests of the rest. Now wanting to act on the difference principle has precisely this consequence. Those better circumstanced are willing to have their greater advantages only under a scheme in which this works out for the benefit of the less fortunate.

20. See J. R. Pennock, *Liberal Democracy: Its Merits and Prospects* (New York, Rinehart, 1950), pp. 94f.
21. See R. B. Perry, *Puritanism and Democracy* (New York, The Vanguard Press, 1944), ch. XIX, sec. 8.

The ideal of fraternity is sometimes thought to involve ties of sentiment and feeling which it is unrealistic to expect between members of the wider society. And this is surely a further reason for its relative neglect in democratic theory. Many have felt that it has no proper place in political affairs. But if it is interpreted as incorporating the requirements of the difference principle, it is not an impracticable conception. It does seem that the institutions and policies which we most confidently think to be just satisfy its demands, at least in the sense that the inequalities permitted by them contribute to the well-being of the less favored. Or at any rate, so I shall try to make plausible in Chapter V. On this interpretation, then, the principle of fraternity is a perfectly feasible standard. Once we accept it we can associate the traditional ideas of liberty, equality, and fraternity with the democratic interpretation of the two principles of justice as follows: liberty corresponds to the first principle, equality to the idea of equality in the first principle together with equality of fair opportunity, and fraternity to the difference principle. In this way we have found a place for the conception of fraternity in the democratic interpretation of the two principles, and we see that it imposes a definite requirement on the basic structure of society. The other aspects of fraternity should not be forgotten, but the difference principle expresses its fundamental meaning from the standpoint of social justice.

Now it seems evident in the light of these observations that the democratic interpretation of the two principles will not lead to a meritocratic society.[22] This form of social order follows the principle of careers open to talents and uses equality of opportunity as a way of releasing men's energies in the pursuit of economic prosperity and political dominion. There exists a marked disparity between the upper and lower classes in both means of life and the rights and privileges of organizational authority. The culture of the poorer strata is impoverished while that of the governing and technocratic elite is securely based on the service of the national ends of power and wealth. Equality of opportunity means an equal chance to leave the less fortunate behind in the personal quest for

22. The problem of a meritocratic society is the subject of Michael Young's fantasy, *The Rise of Meritocracy* (London, Thames and Hudson, 1958).

influence and social position.[23] Thus a meritocratic society is a danger for the other interpretations of the principles of justice but not for the democratic conception. For, as we have just seen, the difference principle transforms the aims of society in fundamental respects. This consequence is even more obvious once we note that we must when necessary take into account the essential primary good of self-respect and the fact that a well-ordered society is a social union of social unions (§79). It follows that the confident sense of their own worth should be sought for the least favored and this limits the forms of hierarchy and the degrees of inequality that justice permits. Thus, for example, resources for education are not to be allotted solely or necessarily mainly according to their return as estimated in productive trained abilities, but also according to their worth in enriching the personal and social life of citizens, including here the less favored. As a society progresses the latter consideration becomes increasingly more important.

These remarks must suffice to sketch the conception of social justice expressed by the two principles for institutions. Before taking up the principles for individuals I should mention one further question. I have assumed so far that the distribution of natural assets is a fact of nature and that no attempt is made to change it, or even to take it into account. But to some extent this distribution is bound to be affected by the social system. A caste system, for example, tends to divide society into separate biological populations, while an open society encourages the widest genetic diversity.[24] In addition, it is possible to adopt eugenic policies, more or less explicit. I shall not consider questions of eugenics, confining myself throughout to the traditional concerns of social justice. We should note, though, that it is not in general to the advantage of the less fortunate to propose policies which reduce the talents of others. Instead, by accepting the difference principle, they view the greater abilities as a social asset to be used for the common advantage. But

23. For elaborations of this point to which I am indebted, see John Schaar, "Equality of Opportunity and Beyond," *Nomos IX: Equality*, ed. by J. R. Pennock and J. W. Chapman (New York, Atherton Press, 1967); and B. A. O. Williams, "The Idea of Equality," pp. 125–129.

24. See Theodosius Dobzhansky, *Mankind Evolving* (New Haven, Yale University Press, 1962), pp. 242–252, for a discussion of this question.

it is also in the interest of each to have greater natural assets. This enables him to pursue a preferred plan of life. In the original position, then, the parties want to insure for their descendants the best genetic endowment (assuming their own to be fixed). The pursuit of reasonable policies in this regard is something that earlier generations owe to later ones, this being a question that arises between generations. Thus over time a society is to take steps at least to preserve the general level of natural abilities and to prevent the diffusion of serious defects. These measures are to be guided by principles that the parties would be willing to consent to for the sake of their successors. I mention this speculative and difficult matter to indicate once again the manner in which the difference principle is likely to transform problems of social justice. We might conjecture that in the long run, if there is an upper bound on ability, we would eventually reach a society with the greatest equal liberty the members of which enjoy the greatest equal talent. But I shall not pursue this thought further.

18. PRINCIPLES FOR INDIVIDUALS: THE PRINCIPLE OF FAIRNESS

In the discussion so far I have considered the principles which apply to institutions or, more exactly, to the basic structure of society. It is clear, however, that principles of another kind must also be chosen, since a complete theory of right includes principles for individuals as well. In fact, as the accompanying diagram indicates, one needs in addition principles for the law of nations and of course priority rules for assigning weights when principles conflict. I shall not take up the principles for the law of nations, except in passing (§58); nor shall I attempt any systematic discussion of the principles for individuals. But certain principles of this type are an essential part of any theory of justice. In this and the next section the meaning of several of these principles is explained, although the examination of the reasons for choosing them is postponed until later (§§51–52).

The accompanying diagram is purely schematic. It is not suggested that the principles associated with the concepts lower down

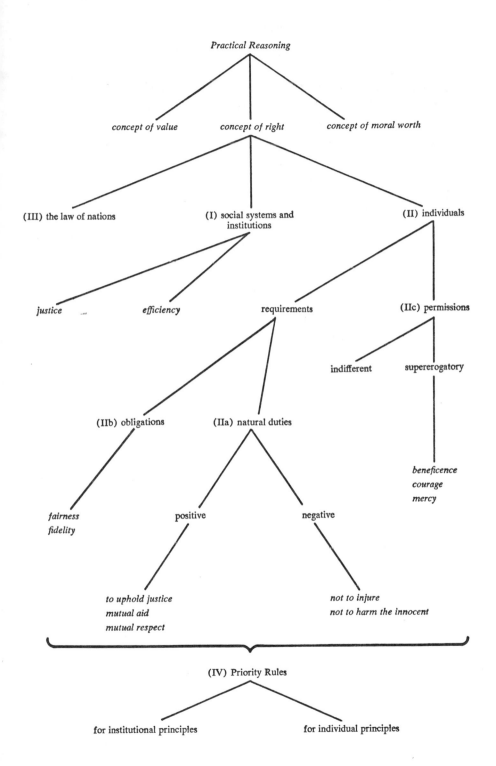

in the tree are deduced from the higher ones. The diagram simply indicates the kinds of principles that must be chosen before a full conception of right is on hand. The Roman numerals express the order in which the various sorts of principles are to be acknowledged in the original position. Thus the principles for the basic structure of society are to be agreed to first, principles for individuals next, followed by those for the law of nations. Last of all the priority rules are adopted, although we may tentatively choose these earlier contingent on subsequent revision.

Now the order in which principles are chosen raises a number of questions which I shall skip over. The important thing is that the various principles are to be adopted in a definite sequence and the reasons for this ordering are connected with the more difficult parts of the theory of justice. To illustrate: while it would be possible to choose many of the natural duties before those for the basic structure without changing the principles in any substantial way, the sequence in either case reflects the fact that obligations presuppose principles for social forms. And some natural duties also presuppose such principles, for example, the duty to support just institutions. For this reason it seems simpler to adopt all principles for individuals after those for the basic structure. That principles for institutions are chosen first shows the social nature of the virtue of justice, its intimate connection with social practices so often noted by idealists. When Bradley says that the individual is a bare abstraction, he can be interpreted to say, without too much distortion, that a person's obligations and duties presuppose a moral conception of institutions and therefore that the content of just institutions must be defined before the requirements for individuals can be set out.[25] And this is to say that, in most cases, the principles for obligations and duties should be settled upon after those for the basic structure.

Therefore, to establish a complete conception of right, the parties in the original position are to choose in a definite order not only a conception of justice but also principles to go with each major concept falling under the concept of right. These concepts are I assume relatively few in number and have a determinate relation

25. See F. H. Bradley, *Ethical Studies*, 2nd ed. (Oxford, The Clarendon Press, 1927), pp. 163–189.

to each other. Thus, in addition to principles for institutions there must be an agreement on principles for such notions as fairness and fidelity, mutual respect and beneficence as these apply to individuals, as well as on principles for the conduct of states. The intuitive idea is this: the concept of something's being right is the same as, or better, may be replaced by, the concept of its being in accordance with the principles that in the original position would be acknowledged to apply to things of its kind. I do not interpret this concept of right as providing an analysis of the meaning of the term "right" as normally used in moral contexts. It is not meant as an analysis of the concept of right in the traditional sense. Rather, the broader notion of rightness as fairness is to be understood as a replacement for existing conceptions. There is no necessity to say that sameness of meaning holds between the word "right" (and its relatives) in its ordinary use and the more elaborate locutions needed to express this ideal contractarian concept of right. For our purposes here I accept the view that a sound analysis is best understood as providing a satisfactory substitute, one that meets certain desiderata while avoiding certain obscurities and confusions. In other words, explication is elimination: we start with a concept the expression for which is somehow troublesome; but it serves certain ends that cannot be given up. An explication achieves these ends in other ways that are relatively free of difficulty.[26] Thus if the theory of justice as fairness, or more generally of rightness as fairness, fits our considered judgments in reflective equilibrium, and if it enables us to say all that on due examination we want to say, then it provides a way of eliminating customary phrases in favor of other expressions. So understood one may think of justice as fairness and rightness as fairness as providing a definition or explication of the concepts of justice and right.

I now turn to one of the principles that applies to individuals, the principle of fairness. I shall try to use this principle to account for all requirements that are obligations as distinct from natural duties. This principle holds that a person is required to do his part as defined by the rules of an institution when two conditions are met: first, the institution is just (or fair), that is, it satisfies the two

26. See W. V. Quine, *Word and Object* (Cambridge, Mass., M.I.T. Press, 1960), pp. 257–262, whom I follow here.

principles of justice; and second, one has voluntarily accepted the benefits of the arrangement or taken advantage of the opportunities it offers to further one's interests. The main idea is that when a number of persons engage in a mutually advantageous cooperative venture according to rules, and thus restrict their liberty in ways necessary to yield advantages for all, those who have submitted to these restrictions have a right to a similar acquiescence on the part of those who have benefited from their submission.[27] We are not to gain from the cooperative labors of others without doing our fair share. The two principles of justice define what is a fair share in the case of institutions belonging to the basic structure. So if these arrangements are just, each person receives a fair share when all (himself included) do their part.

Now by definition the requirements specified by the principle of fairness are the obligations. All obligations arise in this way. It is important, however, to note that the principle of fairness has two parts, the first which states that the institutions or practices in question must be just, the second which characterizes the requisite voluntary acts. The first part formulates the conditions necessary if these voluntary acts are to give rise to obligations. By the principle of fairness it is not possible to be bound to unjust institutions, or at least to institutions which exceed the limits of tolerable injustice (so far undefined). In particular, it is not possible to have an obligation to autocratic and arbitrary forms of government. The necessary background does not exist for obligations to arise from consensual or other acts, however expressed. Obligatory ties presuppose just institutions, or ones reasonably just in view of the circumstances. It is, therefore, a mistake to argue against justice as fairness and contract theories generally that they have the consequence that citizens are under an obligation to unjust regimes which coerce their consent or win their tacit acquiescence in more refined ways. Locke especially has been the object of this mistaken criticism which overlooks the necessity for certain background conditions.[28]

27. I am indebted here to H. L. A. Hart, "Are There Any Natural Rights?" *Philosophical Review*, vol. 64 (1955), pp. 185f.

28. Locke holds that conquest gives no right, nor does violence and injury however much "colored with the name, pretences, or forms of law." *Second*

There are several characteristic features of obligations which distinguish them from other moral requirements. For one thing, they arise as a result of our voluntary acts; these acts may be the giving of express or tacit undertakings, such as promises and agreements, but they need not be, as in the case of accepting benefits. Further, the content of obligations is always defined by an institution or practice the rules of which specify what it is that one is required to do. And finally, obligations are normally owed to definite individuals, namely, those who are cooperating together to maintain the arrangement in question.[29] As an example illustrating these features, consider the political act of running for and (if successful) holding public office in a constitutional regime. This act gives rise to the obligation to fulfill the duties of office, and these duties determine the content of the obligation. Here I think of duties not as moral duties but as tasks and responsibilities assigned to certain institutional positions. It is nevertheless the case that one may have a moral reason (one based on a moral principle) for discharging these duties, as when one is bound to do so by the principle of fairness. Also, one who assumes public office is obligated to his fellow citizens whose trust and confidence he has sought and with whom he is cooperating in running a democratic society. Similarly, we assume obligations when we marry as well as when we accept positions of judicial, administrative, or other authority. We acquire obligations by promising and by tacit understandings, and even when we join a game, namely, the obligation to play by the rules and to be a good sport.

All of these obligations are, I believe, covered by the principle of fairness. There are two important cases though that are somewhat problematical, namely, political obligation as it applies to

Treatise of Government, pars. 176, 20. See Hanna Pitkin's discussion of Locke in "Obligation and Consent I," *American Political Science Review,* vol. 59 (1965), esp. pp. 994–997, the essentials of which I accept.

29. In distinguishing between obligations and natural duties I have drawn upon H. L. A. Hart, "Legal and Moral Obligation," in *Essays in Moral Philosophy,* ed. by A. I. Melden (Seattle, University of Washington Press, 1958), pp. 100–105; C. H. Whiteley, "On Duties," *Proceedings of the Aristotelian Society,* vol. 53 (1952–53); and R. B. Brandt, "The Concepts of Obligation and Duty," *Mind,* vol. 73 (1964).

the average citizen, rather than, say, to those who hold office, and the obligation to keep promises. In the first case it is not clear what is the requisite binding action or who has performed it. There is, I believe, no political obligation, strictly speaking, for citizens generally. In the second case an explanation is needed as to how fiduciary obligations arise from taking advantage of a just practice. We need to look into the nature of the relevant practice in this instance. These matters I shall discuss at another place (§§51–52).

19. PRINCIPLES FOR INDIVIDUALS: THE NATURAL DUTIES

Whereas all obligations are accounted for by the principle of fairness, there are many natural duties, positive and negative. I shall make no attempt to bring them under one principle. Admittedly this lack of unity runs the risk of putting too much strain on priority rules, but I shall have to leave this difficulty aside. The following are examples of natural duties: the duty of helping another when he is in need or jeopardy, provided that one can do so without excessive risk or loss to oneself; the duty not to harm or injure another; and the duty not to cause unnecessary suffering. The first of these duties, the duty of mutual aid, is a positive duty in that it is a duty to do something good for another; whereas the last two duties are negative in that they require us not to do something that is bad. The distinction between positive and negative duties is intuitively clear in many cases, but often gives way. I shall not put any stress upon it. The distinction is important only in connection with the priority problem, since it seems plausible to hold that, when the distinction is clear, negative duties have more weight than positive ones. But I shall not pursue this question here.

Now in contrast with obligations, it is characteristic of natural duties that they apply to us without regard to our voluntary acts. Moreover, they have no necessary connection with institutions or social practices; their content is not, in general, defined by the rules of these arrangements. Thus we have a natural duty not to be cruel, and a duty to help another, whether or not we have com-

114

mitted ourselves to these actions. It is no defense or excuse to say that we have made no promise not to be cruel or vindictive, or to come to another's aid. Indeed, a promise not to kill, for example, is normally ludicrously redundant, and the suggestion that it establishes a moral requirement where none already existed is mistaken. Such a promise is in order, if it ever is so, only when for special reasons one has the right to kill, perhaps in a situation arising in a just war. A further feature of natural duties is that they hold between persons irrespective of their institutional relationships; they obtain between all as equal moral persons. In this sense the natural duties are owed not only to definite individuals, say to those cooperating together in a particular social arrangement, but to persons generally. This feature in particular suggests the propriety of the adjective "natural." One aim of the law of nations is to assure the recognition of these duties in the conduct of states. This is especially important in constraining the means used in war, assuming that, in certain circumstances anyway, wars of self-defense are justified (§ 58).

From the standpoint of justice as fairness, a fundamental natural duty is the duty of justice. This duty requires us to support and to comply with just institutions that exist and apply to us. It also constrains us to further just arrangements not yet established, at least when this can be done without too much cost to ourselves. Thus if the basic structure of society is just, or as just as it is reasonable to expect in the circumstances, everyone has a natural duty to do his part in the existing scheme. Each is bound to these institutions independent of his voluntary acts, performative or otherwise. Thus even though the principles of natural duty are derived from a contractarian point of view, they do not presuppose an act of consent, express or tacit, or indeed any voluntary act, in order to apply. The principles that hold for individuals, just as the principles for institutions, are those that would be acknowledged in the original position. These principles are understood as the outcome of a hypothetical agreement. If their formulation shows that no binding action, consensual or otherwise, is a presupposition of their application, then they apply unconditionally. The reason why obligations depend upon voluntary acts is given by the second part of the principle of fairness which states this condition. It has nothing to do with the contractual nature of justice as fairness.[30] In fact, once the full set of principles, a complete conception of right, is on hand, we can simply forget about the conception of original position and apply these principles as we would any others.

There is nothing inconsistent, or even surprising, in the fact that justice as fairness allows unconditional principles. It suffices to show that the parties in the original position would agree to principles defining the natural duties which as formulated hold unconditionally. We should note that, since the principle of fairness may establish a bond to existing just arrangements, the obligations covered by it can support a tie already present that derives from the natural duty of justice. Thus a person may have both a natural duty and an obligation to comply with an institution and to do his part. The thing to observe here is that there are several ways in which one may be bound to political institutions. For the most part the natural duty of justice is the more fundamental, since it binds citizens generally and requires no voluntary acts in order to apply. The principle of fairness, on the other hand, binds only those who assume public office, say, or those who, being better situated, have advanced their aims within the system. There is, then, another sense of *noblesse oblige:* namely, that those who are more privileged are likely to acquire obligations tying them even more strongly to a just scheme.

I shall say very little about the other kind of principles for individuals. For while permissions are not an unimportant class of actions, I must limit the discussion to the theory of social justice. It may be observed, though, that once all the principles defining requirements are chosen, no further acknowledgments are necessary to define permissions. This is so because permissions are those acts

30. For clarification on these points I am indebted to Robert Amdur. Views seeking to derive political ties solely from consensual acts are found in Michael Walzer, *Obligations: Essays on Disobedience, War, and Citizenship* (Cambridge, Mass., Harvard University Press, 1970), esp. pp. ix–xvi, 7–10, 18–21, and ch. 5; and Joseph Tussman, *Obligation and the Body Politic* (New York, Oxford University Press, 1960). On the latter, see Hanna Pitkin, "Obligation and Consent I," pp. 997f. For further discussions of the problems of consent theory in addition to Pitkin, see Alan Gewirth, "Political Justice." in *Social Justice,* ed. R. B. Brandt (Englewood Cliffs, N.J., Prentice-Hall, Inc., 1962), pp. 128–141; and J. P. Plamenatz, *Consent, Freedom, and Political Obligation,* 2nd ed. (London, Oxford University Press, 1968).

which we are at liberty both to do and not to do. They are acts which violate no obligation or natural duty. In studying permissions one wishes to single out those that are significant from a moral point of view and to explain their relation to duties and obligations. Many such actions are morally indifferent or trivial. But among permissions is the interesting class of supererogatory actions. These are acts of benevolence and mercy, of heroism and self-sacrifice. It is good to do these actions but it is not one's duty or obligation. Supererogatory acts are not required, though normally they would be were it not for the loss or risk involved for the agent himself. A person who does a supererogatory act does not invoke the exemption which the natural duties allow. For while we have a natural duty to bring about a great good, say, if we can do so relatively easily, we are released from this duty when the cost to ourselves is considerable. Supererogatory acts raise questions of first importance for ethical theory. For example, it seems offhand that the classical utilitarian view cannot account for them. It would appear that we are bound to perform actions which bring about a greater good for others whatever the cost to ourselves provided that the sum of advantages altogether exceeds that of other acts open to us. There is nothing corresponding to the exemptions included in the formulation of the natural duties. Thus some of the actions which justice as fairness counts as supererogatory may be required by the utility principle. I shall not, however, pursue this matter further. Supererogatory acts are mentioned here for the sake of completeness. We must now turn to the interpretation of the initial situation.

CHAPTER III. THE ORIGINAL POSITION

In this chapter I discuss the favored philosophical interpretation of the initial situation. I refer to this interpretation as the original position. I begin by sketching the nature of the argument for conceptions of justice and explaining how the alternatives are presented so that the parties are to choose from a definite list of traditional conceptions. Then I describe the conditions which characterize the initial situation under several headings: the circumstances of justice, the formal constraints of the concept of right, the veil of ignorance, and the rationality of the contracting parties. In each case I try to indicate why the features adopted for the favored interpretation are reasonable from a philosophical point of view. Next the natural lines of reasoning leading to the two principles of justice and to the principle of average utility are examined prior to a consideration of the relative advantages of these conceptions of justice. I argue that the two principles would be acknowledged and set out some of the main grounds to support this contention. In order to clarify the differences between the various conceptions of justice, the chapter concludes with another look at the classical principle of utility.

20. THE NATURE OF THE ARGUMENT
FOR CONCEPTIONS OF JUSTICE

The intuitive idea of justice as fairness is to think of the first principles of justice as themselves the object of an original agreement in a suitably defined initial situation. These principles are those which rational persons concerned to advance their interests would accept in this position of equality to settle the basic terms of their

118

association. It must be shown, then, that the two principles of justice are the solution for the problem of choice presented by the original position. In order to do this, one must establish that, given the circumstances of the parties, and their knowledge, beliefs, and interests, an agreement on these principles is the best way for each person to secure his ends in view of the alternatives available.

Now obviously no one can obtain everything he wants; the mere existence of other persons prevents this. The absolutely best for any man is that everyone else should join with him in furthering his conception of the good whatever it turns out to be. Or failing this, that all others are required to act justly but that he is authorized to exempt himself as he pleases. Since other persons will never agree to such terms of association these forms of egoism would be rejected. The two principles of justice, however, seem to be a reasonable proposal. In fact, I should like to show that these principles are everyone's best reply, so to speak, to the corresponding demands of the others. In this sense, the choice of this conception of justice is the unique solution to the problem set by the original position.

By arguing in this way one follows a procedure familiar in social theory. That is, a simplified situation is described in which rational individuals with certain ends and related to each other in certain ways are to choose among various courses of action in view of their knowledge of the circumstances. What these individuals will do is then derived by strictly deductive reasoning from these assumptions about their beliefs and interests, their situation and the options open to them. Their conduct is, in the phrase of Pareto, the resultant of tastes and obstacles.[1] In the theory of price, for example, the equilibrium of competitive markets is thought of as arising when many individuals each advancing his own interests give way to each other what they can best part with in return for what they most desire. Equilibrium is the result of agreements freely struck between willing traders. For each person it is the best situation that he can reach by free exchange consistent with the right and freedom of others to further their interests in the same way. It is for this reason that this state of affairs is an equilibrium, one that will persist in the absence of further changes in the circumstances. No

---

1. *Manuel d'économie politique* (Paris, 1909), ch. III, §23. Pareto says: "L'equilibre résulte précisément de cette opposition des goûts et des obstacles."

119

one has any incentive to alter it. If a departure from this situation sets in motion tendencies which restore it, the equilibrium is stable.

Of course, the fact that a situation is one of equilibrium, even a stable one, does not entail that it is right or just. It only means that given men's estimate of their position, they act effectively to preserve it. Clearly a balance of hatred and hostility may be a stable equilibrium; each may think that any feasible change will be worse. The best that each can do for himself may be a condition of lesser injustice rather than of greater good. The moral assessment of equilibrium situations depends upon the background circumstances which determine them. It is at this point that the conception of the original position embodies features peculiar to moral theory. For while the theory of price, say, tries to account for the movements of the market by assumptions about the actual tendencies at work, the philosophically favored interpretation of the initial situation incorporates conditions which it is thought reasonable to impose on the choice of principles. By contrast with social theory, the aim is to characterize this situation so that the principles that would be chosen, whatever they turn out to be, are acceptable from a moral point of view. The original position is defined in such a way that it is a status quo in which any agreements reached are fair. It is a state of affairs in which the parties are equally represented as moral persons and the outcome is not conditioned by arbitrary contingencies or the relative balance of social forces. Thus justice as fairness is able to use the idea of pure procedural justice from the beginning.

It is clear, then, that the original position is a purely hypothetical situation. Nothing resembling it need ever take place, although we can by deliberately following the constraints it expresses simulate the reflections of the parties. The conception of the original position is not intended to explain human conduct except insofar as it tries to account for our moral judgments and helps to explain our having a sense of justice. Justice as fairness is a theory of our moral sentiments as manifested by our considered judgments in reflective equilibrium. These sentiments presumably affect our thought and action to some degree. So while the conception of the original position is part of the theory of conduct, it does not follow at all that there are actual situations that resemble it. What is necessary is that the principles that would be accepted play the requisite part in our moral reasoning and conduct.

One should note also that the acceptance of these principles is not conjectured as a psychological law or probability. Ideally anyway, I should like to show that their acknowledgment is the only choice consistent with the full description of the original position. The argument aims eventually to be strictly deductive. To be sure, the persons in the original position have a certain psychology, since various assumptions are made about their beliefs and interests. These assumptions appear along with other premises in the description of this initial situation. But clearly arguments from such premises can be fully deductive, as theories in politics and economics attest. We should strive for a kind of moral geometry with all the rigor which this name connotes. Unhappily the reasoning I shall give will fall far short of this, since it is highly intuitive throughout. Yet it is essential to have in mind the ideal one would like to achieve.

A final remark. There are, as I have said, many possible interpretations of the initial situation. This conception varies depending upon how the contracting parties are conceived, upon what their beliefs and interests are said to be, upon which alternatives are available to them, and so on. In this sense, there are many different contract theories. Justice as fairness is but one of these. But the question of justification is settled, as far as it can be, by showing that there is one interpretation of the initial situation which best expresses the conditions that are widely thought reasonable to impose on the choice of principles yet which, at the same time, leads to a conception that characterizes our considered judgments in reflective equilibrium. This most favored, or standard, interpretation I shall refer to as the original position. We may conjecture that for each traditional conception of justice there exists an interpretation of the initial situation in which its principles are the preferred solution. Thus, for example, there are interpretations that lead to the classical as well as the average principle of utility. These variations of the initial situation will be mentioned as we go along. The procedure of contract theories provides, then, a general analytic method for the comparative study of conceptions of justice. One tries to set out the different conditions embodied in the contractual situation in which their principles would be chosen. In this way one formulates the various underlying assumptions on which these conceptions seem to depend. But if one interpretation is philosophically most favored, and if its principles characterize our considered judgments, we have a procedure for justification as well. We cannot know at first whether such an interpretation exists, but at least we know what to look for.

21. THE PRESENTATION OF ALTERNATIVES

Let us now turn from these remarks on method to the description of the original position. I shall begin with the question of the alternatives open to the persons in this situation. Ideally of course one would like to say that they are to choose among all possible conceptions of justice. One obvious difficulty is how these conceptions are to be characterized so that those in the original position can be presented with them. Yet granting that these conceptions could be defined, there is no assurance that the parties could make out the best option; the principles that would be most preferred might be overlooked. Indeed, there may exist no best alternative: conceivably for each conception of justice there is another that is better. Even if there is a best alternative, it seems difficult to describe the parties' intellectual powers so that this optimum, or even the more plausible conceptions, are sure to occur to them. Some solutions to the choice problem may be clear enough on careful reflection; it is another matter to describe the parties so that their deliberations generate these alternatives. Thus although the two principles of justice may be superior to those conceptions known to us, perhaps some hitherto unformulated set of principles is still better.

In order to handle this problem I shall resort to the following device. I shall simply take as given a short list of traditional conceptions of justice, for example those discussed in the first chapter, together with a few other possibilities suggested by the two principles of justice. I then assume that the parties are presented with this list and required to agree unanimously that one conception is the best among those enumerated. We may suppose that this decision is arrived at by making a series of comparisons in pairs. Thus the two principles would be shown to be preferable once all agree that they are to be chosen over each of the other alternatives. In this chapter I shall consider for the most part the choice between the two principles of justice and two forms of the principle of utility (the classical and the average principle). Later on, the comparisons with perfectionism and mixed theories are discussed. In this manner I try to show that the two principles would be chosen from the list.

Now admittedly this is an unsatisfactory way to proceed. It would be better if we could define necessary and sufficient conditions for a uniquely best conception of justice and then exhibit a conception that fulfilled these conditions. Eventually one may be able to do this. For the time being, however, I do not see how to avoid rough and ready methods. Moreover, using such procedures may point to a general solution of our problem. Thus it may turn out that, as we run through these comparisons, the reasoning of the parties singles out certain features of the basic structure as desirable, and that these features have natural maximum and minimum properties. Suppose, for example, that it is rational for the persons in the original position to prefer a society with the greatest equal liberty. And suppose further that while they prefer social and economic advantages to work for the common good they insist that they mitigate the ways in which men are advantaged or disadvantaged by natural and social contingencies. If these two features are the only relevant ones, and if the principle of equal liberty is the natural maximum of the first feature, and the difference principle (constrained by fair equality of opportunity) the natural maximum of the second, then, leaving aside the problem of priority, the two principles are the optimum solution. The fact that one cannot constructively characterize or enumerate all possible conceptions of justice, or describe the parties so that they are bound to think of them, is no obstacle to this conclusion.

It would not be profitable to pursue these speculations any further. For the present, no attempt is made to deal with the general problem of the best solution. I limit the argument throughout to the weaker contention that the two principles would be chosen from the conceptions of justice on the following list.

A. The Two Principles of Justice (in serial order)
   1. The principle of greatest equal liberty
   2. (a) The principle of (fair) equality of opportunity
      (b) The difference principle
B. Mixed Conceptions. Substitute one for A2 above
   1. The principle of average utility; or
   2. The principle of average utility, subject to a constraint, either:
      (a) That a certain social minimum be maintained, or
      (b) That the overall distribution not be too wide; or
   3. The principle of average utility subject to either constraint in B2 plus that of equality of fair opportunity
C. Classical Teleological Conceptions
   1. The classical principle of utility
   2. The average principle of utility
   3. The principle of perfection
D. Intuitionistic Conceptions
   1. To balance total utility against the principle of equal distribution
   2. To balance average utility against the principle of redress
   3. To balance a list of prima facie principles (as appropriate)
E. Egoistic Conceptions (See §23 where it is explained why strictly speaking the egoistic conceptions are not alternatives.)
   1. First-person dictatorship: Everyone is to serve my interests
   2. Free-rider: Everyone is to act justly except for myself, if I choose not to
   3. General: Everyone is permitted to advance his interests as he pleases

The merits of these traditional theories surely suffice to justify the effort to rank them. And in any case, the study of this ranking is a useful way of feeling one's way into the larger question. Now each of these conceptions presumably has its assets and liabilities; there are reasons for and against any alternative one selects. The fact that a conception is open to criticism is not necessarily decisive against it, nor are certain desirable features always conclusive in its favor. The decision of the persons in the original position hinges, as we shall see, on a balance of various considerations. In this sense, there is an appeal to intuition at the basis of the theory of justice. Yet when everything is tallied up, it may be perfectly clear where the balance of reason lies. The relevant reasons may have been so factored and analyzed by the description of the original position that one conception of justice is distinctly preferable to the others. The argument for it is not strictly speaking a proof, not yet anyway; but, in Mill's phrase, it may present considerations capable of determining the intellect.[2]

The list of conceptions is largely self-explanatory. A few brief comments, however, may be useful. Each conception is expressed in a reasonably simple way, and each holds unconditionally, that is, whatever the circumstances or state of society. None of the principles is contingent upon certain social or other conditions. Now one reason for this is to keep things simple. It would be easy to formulate a family of conceptions each designed to apply only if special circumstances obtain, these various conditions being exhaustive and mutually exclusive. For example one conception might hold at one stage of culture, a different conception at another. Such a family could be counted as itself a conception of justice; it would consist of a set of ordered pairs, each pair being a conception of justice matched with the circumstances in which it applies. But if conceptions of this kind were added to the list, our problem would become very complicated if not unmanageable. Moreover, there is a reason for excluding alternatives of this kind, for it is natural to ask what underlying principle determines the ordered pairs. Here I assume that some recognizably ethical conception specifies the appropriate principles given each of the conditions. It is really this unconditional principle that defines the conception expressed by the set of ordered pairs. Thus to allow such families on the list is to include alternatives that conceal their proper basis. So for this reason as well I shall exclude them. It also turns out to be desirable to characterize the original position so that the parties are to choose principles that hold unconditionally whatever the circumstances. This fact is connected with the Kantian interpretation of justice as fairness. But I leave this matter aside until later (§40).

Finally, an obvious point. An argument for the two principles, or

2. *Utilitarianism*, ch. I, par. 5.

indeed for any conception, is always relative to some list of alternatives. If we change the list, the argument will, in general, have to be different. A similar sort of remark applies to all features of the original position. There are indefinitely many variations of the initial situation and therefore no doubt indefinitely many theorems of moral geometry. Only a few of these are of any philosophical interest, since most variations are irrelevant from a moral point of view. We must try to steer clear of side issues while at the same time not losing sight of the special assumptions of the argument.

22. THE CIRCUMSTANCES OF JUSTICE

The circumstances of justice may be described as the normal conditions under which human cooperation is both possible and necessary.[3] Thus, as I noted at the outset, although a society is a cooperative venture for mutual advantage, it is typically marked by a conflict as well as an identity of interests. There is an identity of interests since social cooperation makes possible a better life for all than any would have if each were to try to live solely by his own efforts. There is a conflict of interests since men are not indifferent as to how the greater benefits produced by their collaboration are distributed, for in order to pursue their ends they each prefer a larger to a lesser share. Thus principles are needed for choosing among the various social arrangements which determine this division of advantages and for underwriting an agreement on the proper distributive shares. These requirements define the role of justice. The background conditions that give rise to these necessities are the circumstances of justice.

These conditions may be divided into two kinds. First, there are the objective circumstances which make human cooperation both possible and necessary. Thus, many individuals coexist together at the same time on a definite geographical territory. These individ-

3. My account largely follows that of Hume in *A Treatise of Human Nature*, bk. III, pt. II, sec. ii, and *An Enquiry Concerning the Principles of Morals*, sec. III, pt. I. But see also H. L. A. Hart, *The Concept of Law* (Oxford, The Clarendon Press, 1961), pp. 189–195, and J. R. Lucas, *The Principles of Politics* (Oxford, The Clarendon Press, 1966), pp. 1–10.

uals are roughly similar in physical and mental powers; or at any rate, their capacities are comparable in that no one among them can dominate the rest. They are vulnerable to attack, and all are subject to having their plans blocked by the united force of others. Finally, there is the condition of moderate scarcity understood to cover a wide range of situations. Natural and other resources are not so abundant that schemes of cooperation become superfluous, nor are conditions so harsh that fruitful ventures must inevitably break down. While mutually advantageous arrangements are feasible, the benefits they yield fall short of the demands men put forward.

The subjective circumstances are the relevant aspects of the subjects of cooperation, that is, of the persons working together. Thus while the parties have roughly similar needs and interests, or needs and interests in various ways complementary, so that mutually advantageous cooperation among them is possible, they nevertheless have their own plans of life. These plans, or conceptions of the good, lead them to have different ends and purposes, and to make conflicting claims on the natural and social resources available. Moreover, although the interests advanced by these plans are not assumed to be interests in the self, they are the interests of a self that regards its conception of the good as worthy of recognition and that advances claims in its behalf as deserving satisfaction. I shall emphasize this aspect of the circumstances of justice by assuming that the parties take no interest in one another's interests. I also suppose that men suffer from various shortcomings of knowledge, thought, and judgment. Their knowledge is necessarily incomplete, their powers of reasoning, memory, and attention are always limited, and their judgment is likely to be distorted by anxiety, bias, and a preoccupation with their own affairs. Some of these defects spring from moral faults, from selfishness and negligence; but to a large degree, they are simply part of men's natural situation. As a consequence individuals not only have different plans of life but there exists a diversity of philosophical and religious belief, and of political and social doctrines.

Now this constellation of conditions I shall refer to as the circumstances of justice. Hume's account of them is especially perspicuous and the preceding summary adds nothing essential to his much fuller discussion. For simplicity I often stress the condition of moderate scarcity (among the objective circumstances), and that of mutual disinterest, or individuals taking no interest in one another's interests (among the subjective circumstances). Thus, one can say, in brief, that the circumstances of justice obtain whenever mutually disinterested persons put forward conflicting claims to the division of social advantages under conditions of moderate scarcity. Unless these circumstances existed there would be no occasion for the virtue of justice, just as in the absence of threats of injury to life and limb there would be no occasion for physical courage.

Several clarifications should be noted. First of all, I shall, of course, assume that the persons in the original position know that these circumstances of justice obtain. This much they take for granted about the conditions of their society. A further assumption is that the parties try to advance their conception of the good as best they can, and that in attempting to do this they are not bound by prior moral ties to each other.

The question arises, however, whether the persons in the original position have obligations and duties to third parties, for example, to their immediate descendants. To say that they do would be one way of handling questions of justice between generations. However, the aim of justice as fairness is to derive all duties and obligations from other conditions; so this way out should be avoided. Instead, I shall make a motivational assumption. The parties are thought of as representing continuing lines of claims, as being, so to speak, deputies for a kind of everlasting moral agent or institution. They need not take into account its entire life span in perpetuity, but their goodwill stretches over at least two generations. Thus representatives from periods adjacent in time have overlapping interests. For example, we may think of the parties as heads of families, and therefore as having a desire to further the welfare of their nearest descendants. As representatives of families their interests are opposed as the circumstances of justice imply. It is not necessary to think of the parties as heads of families, although I shall generally follow this interpretation. What is essential is that each person in the original position should care about the well-being of some of those in the next generation, it being presumed that their concern

128

is for different individuals in each case. Moreover for anyone in the next generation, there is someone who cares about him in the present generation. Thus the interests of all are looked after and, given the veil of ignorance, the whole strand is tied together.

It should be noted that I make no restrictive assumptions about the parties' conceptions of the good except that they are rational long-term plans. While these plans determine the aims and interests of a self, the aims and interests are not presumed to be egoistic or selfish. Whether this is the case depends upon the kinds of ends which a person pursues. If wealth, position, and influence, and the accolades of social prestige, are a person's final purposes, then surely his conception of the good is egoistic. His dominant interests are in himself, not merely, as they must always be, interests of a self.[4] There is no inconsistency, then, in supposing that once the veil of ignorance is removed, the parties find that they have ties of sentiment and affection, and want to advance the interests of others and to see their ends attained. But the postulate of mutual disinterest in the original position is made to insure that the principles of justice do not depend upon strong assumptions. Recall that the original position is meant to incorporate widely shared and yet weak conditions. A conception of justice should not presuppose, then, extensive ties of natural sentiment. At the basis of the theory, one tries to assume as little as possible.

Finally, when it is supposed that the parties are severally disinterested, and are not willing to have their interests sacrificed to the others, the intention is to express men's conduct and motives in cases where questions of justice arise. The spiritual ideals of saints and heroes can be as irreconcilably opposed as any other interests. Conflicts in pursuit of these ideals are the most tragic of all. Thus justice is the virtue of practices where there are competing interests and where persons feel entitled to press their rights on each other. In an association of saints agreeing on a common ideal, if such a community could exist, disputes about justice would not occur. Each would work selflessly for one end as determined by their common religion, and reference to this end (assuming it to be clearly defined) would settle every question of right. But a human

4. On this point see W. T. Stace, *The Concept of Morals* (London, Macmillan, 1937), pp. 221–223.

129

society is characterized by the circumstances of justice. The account of these conditions involves no particular theory of human motivation. Rather, its aim is to include in the description of the original position the relations of individuals to one another which set the stage for questions of justice.

23. THE FORMAL CONSTRAINTS OF THE CONCEPT OF RIGHT

The situation of the persons in the original position reflects certain constraints. The alternatives open to them and their knowledge of their circumstances are limited in various ways. These restrictions I refer to as the constraints of the concept of right since they hold for the choice of all ethical principles and not only for those of justice. If the parties were to acknowledge principles for the other virtues as well, these constraints would also apply.

I shall consider first the constraints on the alternatives. There are certain formal conditions that it seems reasonable to impose on the conceptions of justice that are to be allowed on the list presented to the parties. I do not claim that these conditions follow from the concept of right, much less from the meaning of morality. I avoid an appeal to the analysis of concepts at crucial points of this kind. There are many constraints that can reasonably be associated with the concept of right, and different selections can be made from these and counted as definitive within a particular theory. The merit of any definition depends upon the soundness of the theory that results; by itself, a definition cannot settle any fundamental question.[5]

5. Various interpretations of the concept of morality are discussed by W. K. Frankena, "Recent Conceptions of Morality," in *Morality and the Language of Conduct,* ed. H. N. Castañeda and George Nakhnikian (Detroit, Wayne State University Press, 1965), and "The Concept of Morality," *Journal of Philosophy,* vol. 63 (1966). The first of these essays contains numerous references. The account in the text is perhaps closest to that of Kurt Baier in *The Moral Point of View* (Ithaca, N.Y., Cornell University Press, 1958), ch. VIII. I follow Baier in emphasizing the conditions of publicity (he does not use this term, but it is implied by his stipulation of universal teachability, pp. 195f), ordering, finality, and material content (although on the contract view the last condition follows as a

The propriety of these formal conditions is derived from the task of principles of right in adjusting the claims that persons make on their institutions and one another. If the principles of justice are to play their role, that of assigning basic rights and duties and determining the division of advantages, these requirements are natural enough. Each of them is suitably weak and I assume that they are satisfied by the traditional conceptions of justice. These conditions do, however, exclude the various forms of egoism, as I note below, which shows that they are not without moral force. This makes it all the more necessary that the conditions not be justified by definition or the analysis of concepts, but only by the reasonableness of the theory of which they are a part. I arrange them under five familiar headings.

First of all, principles should be general. That is, it must be possible to formulate them without the use of what would be intuitively recognized as proper names, or rigged definite descriptions. Thus the predicates used in their statement should express general properties and relations. Unfortunately deep philosophical difficulties seem to bar the way to a satisfactory account of these matters.[6] I shall not try to deal with them here. In presenting a theory of justice one is entitled to avoid the problem of defining general properties and relations and to be guided by what seems reasonable. Further, since the parties have no specific information about themselves or their situation, they cannot identify themselves anyway. Even if a person could get others to agree, he does not know how to tailor principles to his advantage. The parties are effectively forced to stick to general principles, understanding the notion here in an intuitive fashion.

The naturalness of this condition lies in part in the fact that first principles must be capable of serving as a public charter of a well-ordered society in perpetuity. Being unconditional, they always hold (under the circumstances of justice), and the knowledge of them must be open to individuals in any generation. Thus, to un-

---

consequence, see §25 and note 16 below). For other discussions, see W. D. Falk, "Morality, Self, and Others," also in *Morality and the Language of Conduct,* and P. F. Strawson, "Social Morality and Individual Ideal," *Philosophy,* vol. 36 (1961).

6. See, for example, W. V. Quine, *Ontological Relativity and Other Essays* (New York, Columbia University Press, 1969), ch. 5 entitled "Natural Kinds."

derstand these principles should not require a knowledge of contingent particulars, and surely not a reference to individuals or associations. Traditionally the most obvious test of this condition is the idea that what is right is that which accords with God's will. But in fact this doctrine is normally supported by an argument from general principles. For example, Locke held that the fundamental principle of morals is the following: if one person is created by another (in the theological sense), then that person has a duty to comply with the precepts set to him by his creator.[7] This principle is perfectly general and given the nature of the world on Locke's view, it singles out God as the legitimate moral authority. The generality condition is not violated, although it may appear so at first sight.

Next, principles are to be universal in application. They must hold for everyone in virtue of their being moral persons. Thus I assume that each can understand these principles and use them in his deliberations. This imposes an upper bound of sorts on how complex they can be, and on the kinds and number of distinctions they draw. Moreover, a principle is ruled out if it would be self-contradictory, or self-defeating, for everyone to act upon it. Similarly, should a principle be reasonable to follow only when others conform to a different one, it is also inadmissible. Principles are to be chosen in view of the consequences of everyone's complying with them.

As defined, generality and universality are distinct conditions. For example, egoism in the form of first-person dictatorship (Everyone is to serve my—or Pericles'—interests) satisfies universality but not generality. While all could act in accordance with this principle, and the results might in some cases not be at all bad, depending on the interests of the dictator, the personal pronoun (or the name) violates the first condition. Again, general principles may not be universal. They may be framed to hold for a restricted class of individuals, for instance those singled out by special biological or social characteristics, such as hair color or class situation, or whatever. To be sure, in the course of their lives individuals acquire obligations and assume duties that are peculiar to them. Neverthe-

7. See *Essays on the Laws of Nature*, ed. W. von Leyden (Oxford, the Clarendon Press, 1954), the fourth essay, especially pp. 151–157.

less these various duties and obligations are the consequence of first principles that hold for all as moral persons; the derivation of these requirements has a common basis.

A third condition is that of publicity, which arises naturally from a contractarian standpoint. The parties assume that they are choosing principles for a public conception of justice.[8] They suppose that everyone will know about these principles all that he would know if their acceptance were the result of an agreement. Thus the general awareness of their universal acceptance should have desirable effects and support the stability of social cooperation. The difference between this condition and that of universality is that the latter leads one to assess principles on the basis of their being intelligently and regularly followed by everyone. But it is possible that all should understand and follow a principle and yet this fact not be widely known or explicitly recognized. The point of the publicity condition is to have the parties evaluate conceptions of justice as publicly acknowledged and fully effective moral constitutions of social life. The publicity condition is clearly implicit in Kant's doctrine of the categorical imperative insofar as it requires us to act in accordance with principles that one would be willing as a rational being to enact as law for a kingdom of ends. He thought of this kingdom as an ethical commonwealth, as it were, which has such moral principles for its public charter.

A further condition is that a conception of right must impose an

8. Publicity is clearly implied in Kant's notion of the moral law, but the only place I know of where he discusses it expressly is in *Perpetual Peace*, appendix II; see *Political Writings*, ed. Hans Reiss and trans. H. B. Nisbet (Cambridge, The University Press, 1970), pp. 125–130. There are of course brief statements elsewhere. For example, in *The Metaphysics of Morals*, pt. I (*Rechtslehre*), §43, he says: "Public Right is the sum total of those laws which require to be made universally public in order to produce a state of right." In "Theory and Practice" he remarks in a footnote: "No right in a state can be tacitly and treacherously included by a secret reservation, and least of all a right which the people claim to be a part of the constitution, for all laws within it must be thought of as arising out of a public will. Thus if a constitution allowed rebellion, it would have to declare this right publicly and make clear how it might be implemented." *Political Writings*, pp. 136, 84n, respectively. I believe Kant intends this condition to apply to a society's conception of justice. See also note 4, §51, below; and Baier, cited in note 5 above. There is a discussion of common knowledge and its relation to agreement in D. K. Lewis, *Convention* (Cambridge, Mass., Harvard University Press, 1969), esp. pp. 52–60, 83–88.

ordering on conflicting claims. This requirement springs directly from the role of its principles in adjusting competing demands. There is a difficulty, however, in deciding what counts as an ordering. It is clearly desirable that a conception of justice be complete, that is, able to order all the claims that can arise (or that are likely to in practice). And the ordering should in general be transitive: if, say, a first arrangement of the basic structure is ranked more just than a second, and the second more just than a third, then the first should be more just than the third. These formal conditions are natural enough, though not always easy to satisfy.[9] But is trial by combat a form of adjudication? After all, physical conflict and resort to arms result in an ordering; certain claims do win out over others. The main objection to this ordering is not that it may be intransitive. Rather, it is to avoid the appeal to force and cunning that the principles of right and justice are accepted. Thus I assume that to each according to his threat advantage is not a conception of justice. It fails to establish an ordering in the required sense, an ordering based on certain relevant aspects of persons and their situation which are independent from their social position, or their capacity to intimidate and coerce.[10]

9. For a discussion of orderings and preference relations, see A. K. Sen, *Collective Choice and Social Welfare* (San Francisco, Holden-Day Inc., 1970), chs. 1 and 1*; and K. J. Arrow, *Social Choice and Individual Values,* 2nd ed. (New York, John Wiley, 1963), ch. II.

10. To illustrate this point, consider R. B. Braithwaite's study, *Theory of Games as a Tool for the Moral Philosopher* (Cambridge, The University Press, 1955). On the analysis he presents, it turns out that the fair division of playing time between Matthew and Luke depends on their preferences, and these in turn are connected with the instruments they wish to play. Since Matthew has a threat advantage over Luke, arising from the fact that Matthew, the trumpeter, prefers both of them playing at once to neither of them playing, whereas Luke, the pianist, prefers silence to cacophony, Matthew is allotted twenty-six evenings of play to Luke's seventeen. If the situation were reversed, the threat advantage would be with Luke. See pp. 36f. But we have only to suppose that Matthew is a jazz enthusiast who plays the drums, and Luke a violinist who plays sonatas, in which case it will be fair on this analysis for Matthew to play whenever and as often as he likes, assuming as it is plausible to assume that he does not care whether Luke plays or not. Clearly something has gone wrong. What is lacking is a suitable definition of a status quo that is acceptable from a moral point of view. We cannot take various contingencies as known and individual preferences as given and expect to elucidate the concept of justice (or fairness) by theories

134

The fifth and last condition is that of finality. The parties are to assess the system of principles as the final court of appeal in practical reasoning. There are no higher standards to which arguments in support of claims can be addressed; reasoning successfully from these principles is conclusive. If we think in terms of the fully general theory which has principles for all the virtues, then such a theory specifies the totality of relevant considerations and their appropriate weights, and its requirements are decisive. They override the demands of law and custom, and of social rules generally. We are to arrange and respect social institutions as the principles of right and justice direct. Conclusions from these principles also override considerations of prudence and self-interest. This does not mean that these principles insist upon self-sacrifice; for in drawing up the conception of right the parties take their interests into account as best they can. The claims of personal prudence are already given an appropriate weight within the full system of principles. The complete scheme is final in that when the course of practical reasoning it defines has reached its conclusion, the question is settled. The claims of existing social arrangements and of self-interest have been duly allowed for. We cannot at the end count them a second time because we do not like the result.

Taken together, then, these conditions on conceptions of right come to this: a conception of right is a set of principles, general in form and universal in application, that is to be publicly recognized as a final court of appeal for ordering the conflicting claims of moral persons. Principles of justice are identified by their special role and the subject to which they apply. Now by themselves the five conditions exclude none of the traditional conceptions of justice. It should be noted, however, that they do rule out the listed variants of egoism. The generality condition eliminates both

---

of bargaining. The conception of the original position is designed to meet the problem of the appropriate status quo. A similar objection to Braithwaite's analysis is found in J. R. Lucas, "Moralists and Gamesmen," *Philosophy,* vol. 34 (1959), pp. 9f. For another discussion, consult Sen, *Collective Choice and Social Welfare,* pp. 118–123, who argues that the solution of J. F. Nash in "The Bargaining Problem," *Econometrica,* vol. 18 (1950), is similarly defective from an ethical point of view.

first-person dictatorship and the free-rider forms, since in each case a proper name, or pronoun, or a rigged definite description is needed, either to single out the dictator or to characterize the free-rider. Generality does not, however, exclude general egoism, for each person is allowed to do whatever, in his judgment, is most likely to further his own aims. The principle here can clearly be expressed in a perfectly general way. It is the ordering condition which renders general egoism inadmissible, for if everyone is authorized to advance his aims as he pleases, or if everyone ought to advance his own interests, competing claims are not ranked at all and the outcome is determined by force and cunning.

The several kinds of egoism, then, do not appear on the list presented to the parties. They are eliminated by the formal constraints. Of course, this is not a surprising conclusion, since it is obvious that by choosing one of the other conceptions the persons in the original position can do much better for themselves. Once they ask which principles all should agree to, no form of egoism is a serious candidate for consideration in any case. This only confirms what we knew already, namely, that although egoism is logically consistent and in this sense not irrational, it is incompatible with what we intuitively regard as the moral point of view. The significance of egoism philosophically is not as an alternative conception of right but as a challenge to any such conception. In justice as fairness this is reflected in the fact that we can interpret general egoism as the no-agreement point. It is what the parties would be stuck with if they were unable to reach an understanding.

24. THE VEIL OF IGNORANCE

The idea of the original position is to set up a fair procedure so that any principles agreed to will be just. The aim is to use the notion of pure procedural justice as a basis of theory. Somehow we must nullify the effects of specific contingencies which put men at odds and tempt them to exploit social and natural circumstances to their own advantage. Now in order to do this I assume that the parties are situated behind a veil of ignorance. They do not know how the various alternatives will affect their own particular case

136

and they are obliged to evaluate principles solely on the basis of general considerations.[11]

It is assumed, then, that the parties do not know certain kinds of particular facts. First of all, no one knows his place in society, his class position or social status; nor does he know his fortune in the distribution of natural assets and abilities, his intelligence and strength, and the like. Nor, again, does anyone know his conception of the good, the particulars of his rational plan of life, or even the special features of his psychology such as his aversion to risk or liability to optimism or pessimism. More than this, I assume that the parties do not know the particular circumstances of their own society. That is, they do not know its economic or political situation, or the level of civilization and culture it has been able to achieve. The persons in the original position have no information as to which generation they belong. These broader restrictions on knowledge are appropriate in part because questions of social justice arise between generations as well as within them, for example, the question of the appropriate rate of capital saving and of the conservation of natural resources and the environment of nature. There is also, theoretically anyway, the question of a reasonable genetic policy. In these cases too, in order to carry through the idea of the original position, the parties must not know the contingencies that set them in opposition. They must choose principles the consequences of which they are prepared to live with whatever generation they turn out to belong to.

As far as possible, then, the only particular facts which the parties know is that their society is subject to the circumstances of justice and whatever this implies. It is taken for granted, however, that they know the general facts about human society. They understand political affairs and the principles of economic theory; they know the basis of social organization and the laws of human psychology. Indeed, the parties are presumed to know whatever general facts affect the choice of the principles of justice. There are

11. The veil of ignorance is so natural a condition that something like it must have occurred to many. The closest explicit statement of it known to me is found in J. C. Harsanyi, "Cardinal Utility in Welfare Economics and in the Theory of Risk-Taking," *Journal of Political Economy,* vol. 61 (1953). Harsanyi uses it to develop a utilitarian theory, as I discuss below in §§27–28.

no limitations on general information, that is, on general laws and theories, since conceptions of justice must be adjusted to the characteristics of the systems of social cooperation which they are to regulate, and there is no reason to rule out these facts. It is, for example, a consideration against a conception of justice that, in view of the laws of moral psychology, men would not acquire a desire to act upon it even when the institutions of their society satisfied it. For in this case there would be difficulty in securing the stability of social cooperation. It is an important feature of a conception of justice that it should generate its own support. That is, its principles should be such that when they are embodied in the basic structure of society men tend to acquire the corresponding sense of justice. Given the principles of moral learning, men develop a desire to act in accordance with its principles. In this case a conception of justice is stable. This kind of general information is admissible in the original position.

The notion of the veil of ignorance raises several difficulties. Some may object that the exclusion of nearly all particular information makes it difficult to grasp what is meant by the original position. Thus it may be helpful to observe that one or more persons can at any time enter this position, or perhaps, better, simulate the deliberations of this hypothetical situation, simply by reasoning in accordance with the appropriate restrictions. In arguing for a conception of justice we must be sure that it is among the permitted alternatives and satisfies the stipulated formal constraints. No considerations can be advanced in its favor unless they would be rational ones for us to urge were we to lack the kind of knowledge that is excluded. The evaluation of principles must proceed in terms of the general consequences of their public recognition and universal application, it being assumed that they will be complied with by everyone. To say that a certain conception of justice would be chosen in the original position is equivalent to saying that rational deliberation satisfying certain conditions and restrictions would reach a certain conclusion. If necessary, the argument to this result could be set out more formally. I shall, however, speak throughout in terms of the notion of the original position. It is more economical and suggestive, and brings out certain essential features that otherwise one might easily overlook.

These remarks show that the original position is not to be thought of as a general assembly which includes at one moment everyone who will live at some time; or, much less, as an assembly of everyone who could live at some time. It is not a gathering of all actual or possible persons. To conceive of the original position in either of these ways is to stretch fantasy too far; the conception would cease to be a natural guide to intuition. In any case, it is important that the original position be interpreted so that one can at any time adopt its perspective. It must make no difference when one takes up this viewpoint, or who does so: the restrictions must be such that the same principles are always chosen. The veil of ignorance is a key condition in meeting this requirement. It insures not only that the information available is relevant, but that it is at all times the same.

It may be protested that the condition of the veil of ignorance is irrational. Surely, some may object, principles should be chosen in the light of all the knowledge available. There are various replies to this contention. Here I shall sketch those which emphasize the simplifications that need to be made if one is to have any theory at all. (Those based on the Kantian interpretation of the original position are given later, § 40.) To begin with, it is clear that since the differences among the parties are unknown to them, and everyone is equally rational and similarly situated, each is convinced by the same arguments. Therefore, we can view the choice in the original position from the standpoint of one person selected at random. If anyone after due reflection prefers a conception of justice to another, then they all do, and a unanimous agreement can be reached. We can, to make the circumstances more vivid, imagine that the parties are required to communicate with each other through a referee as intermediary, and that he is to announce which alternatives have been suggested and the reasons offered in their support. He forbids the attempt to form coalitions, and he informs the parties when they have come to an understanding. But such a referee is actually superfluous, assuming that the deliberations of the parties must be similar.

Thus there follows the very important consequence that the parties have no basis for bargaining in the usual sense. No one knows his situation in society nor his natural assets, and therefore no one is in a position to tailor principles to his advantage. We might imagine that one of the contractees threatens to hold out unless the others agree to principles favorable to him. But how does he know which principles are especially in his interests? The same holds for the formation of coalitions: if a group were to decide to band together to the disadvantage of the others, they would not know how to favor themselves in the choice of principles. Even if they could get everyone to agree to their proposal, they would have no assurance that it was to their advantage, since they cannot identify themselves either by name or description. The one case where this conclusion fails is that of saving. Since the persons in the original position know that they are contemporaries (taking the present time of entry interpretation), they can favor their generation by refusing to make any sacrifices at all for their successors; they simply acknowledge the principle that no one has a duty to save for posterity. Previous generations have saved or they have not; there is nothing the parties can now do to affect that. So in this instance the veil of ignorance fails to secure the desired result. Therefore I resolve the question of justice between generations in a different way by altering the motivation assumption. But with this adjustment no one is able to formulate principles especially designed to advance his own cause. Whatever his temporal position, each is forced to choose for everyone.[12]

The restrictions on particular information in the original position are, then, of fundamental importance. Without them we would not be able to work out any definite theory of justice at all. We would have to be content with a vague formula stating that justice is what would be agreed to without being able to say much, if anything, about the substance of the agreement itself. The formal constraints of the concept of right, those applying to principles directly, are not sufficient for our purpose. The veil of ignorance makes possible a unanimous choice of a particular conception of justice. Without these limitations on knowledge the bargaining problem of the original position would be hopelessly complicated. Even if theoretically a solution were to exist, we would not, at present anyway, be able to determine it.

The notion of the veil of ignorance is implicit, I think, in Kant's

12. Rousseau, *The Social Contract*, bk. II, ch. IV, par. 5.

ethics (§40). Nevertheless the problem of defining the knowledge of the parties and of characterizing the alternatives open to them has often been passed over, even by contract theories. Sometimes the situation definitive of moral deliberation is presented in such an indeterminate way that one cannot ascertain how it will turn out. Thus Perry's doctrine is essentially contractarian: he holds that social and personal integration must proceed by entirely different principles, the latter by rational prudence, the former by the concurrence of persons of good will. He would appear to reject utilitarianism on much the same grounds suggested earlier: namely, that it improperly extends the principle of choice for one person to choices facing society. The right course of action is characterized as that which best advances social aims as these would be formulated by reflective agreement given that the parties have full knowledge of the circumstances and are moved by a benevolent concern for one another's interests. No effort is made, however, to specify in any precise way the possible outcomes of this sort of agreement. Indeed, without a far more elaborate account, no conclusions can be drawn.[13] I do not wish here to criticize others; rather, I want to explain the necessity for what may seem at times like so many irrelevant details.

Now the reasons for the veil of ignorance go beyond mere simplicity. We want to define the original position so that we get the desired solution. If a knowledge of particulars is allowed, then the outcome is biased by arbitrary contingencies. As already observed, to each according to his threat advantage is not a principle of justice. If the original position is to yield agreements that are just, the parties must be fairly situated and treated equally as moral persons. The arbitrariness of the world must be corrected for by adjusting the circumstances of the initial contractual situation. Moreover, if in choosing principles we required unanimity even when there is full information, only a few rather obvious cases could be decided. A conception of justice based on unanimity in these circumstances would indeed be weak and trivial. But once knowledge is excluded, the requirement of unanimity is not out of place and the fact that

---

13. See R. B. Perry, *The General Theory of Value* (New York, Longmans, Green and Company, 1926), pp. 674–682.

it can be satisfied is of great importance. It enables us to say of the preferred conception of justice that it represents a genuine reconciliation of interests.

A final comment. For the most part I shall suppose that the parties possess all general information. No general facts are closed to them. I do this mainly to avoid complications. Nevertheless a conception of justice is to be the public basis of the terms of social cooperation. Since common understanding necessitates certain bounds on the complexity of principles, there may likewise be limits on the use of theoretical knowledge in the original position. Now clearly it would be very difficult to classify and to grade for complexity the various sorts of general facts. I shall make no attempt to do this. We do however recognize an intricate theoretical construction when we meet one. Thus it seems reasonable to say that other things equal one conception of justice is to be preferred to another when it is founded upon markedly simpler general facts, and its choice does not depend upon elaborate calculations in the light of a vast array of theoretically defined possibilities. It is desirable that the grounds for a public conception of justice should be evident to everyone when circumstances permit. This consideration favors, I believe, the two principles of justice over the criterion of utility.

25. THE RATIONALITY OF THE PARTIES

I have assumed throughout that the persons in the original position are rational. In choosing between principles each tries as best he can to advance his interests. But I have also assumed that the parties do not know their conception of the good. This means that while they know that they have some rational plan of life, they do not know the details of this plan, the particular ends and interests which it is calculated to promote. How, then, can they decide which conceptions of justice are most to their advantage? Or must we suppose that they are reduced to mere guessing? To meet this difficulty, I postulate that they accept the account of the good touched upon in the preceding chapter: they assume that they would prefer more primary social goods rather than less. Of course, it may turn out, once the veil of ignorance is removed, that some of them for religious or other reasons may not, in fact, want more of these goods.

142

But from the standpoint of the original position, it is rational for the parties to suppose that they do want a larger share, since in any case they are not compelled to accept more if they do not wish to, nor does a person suffer from a greater liberty. Thus even though the parties are deprived of information about their particular ends, they have enough knowledge to rank the alternatives. They know that in general they must try to protect their liberties, widen their opportunities, and enlarge their means for promoting their aims whatever these are. Guided by the theory of the good and the general facts of moral psychology, their deliberations are no longer guesswork. They can make a rational decision in the ordinary sense.

The concept of rationality invoked here, with the exception of one essential feature, is the standard one familiar in social theory.[14] Thus in the usual way, a rational person is thought to have a coherent set of preferences between the options open to him. He ranks these options according to how well they further his purposes; he follows the plan which will satisfy more of his desires rather than less, and which has the greater chance of being successfully executed. The special assumption I make is that a rational individual does not suffer from envy. He is not ready to accept a loss for himself if only others have less as well. He is not downcast by the knowledge or perception that others have a larger index of primary social goods. Or at least this is true as long as the differences between himself and others do not exceed certain limits, and he does not believe that the existing inequalities are founded on injustice or are the result of letting chance work itself out for no compensating social purpose (§ 80).

14. For this notion of rationality, see the references to Sen and Arrow above, §23, note 9. The discussion in I. M. D. Little, *The Critique of Welfare Economics,* 2nd ed. (Oxford, Clarendon Press, 1957), ch. II, is also relevant here. For rational choice under uncertainty, see below §26, note 18. II. A. Simon discusses the limitations of the classical conceptions of rationality and the need for a more realistic theory in "A Behavioral Model of Rational Choice," *Quarterly Journal of Economics,* vol. 69 (1955). See also his essay in *Surveys of Economic Theory,* vol. 3 (London, Macmillan, 1967). For philosophical discussions see Donald Davidson, "Actions, Reasons, and Causes," *Journal of Philosophy,* vol. 60 (1963); C. G. Hempel, *Aspects of Scientific Explanation* (New York, The Free Press, 1965), pp. 463–486; Jonathan Bennett, *Rationality* (London, Routledge and Kegan Paul, 1964), and J. D. Mabbott, "Reason and Desire," *Philosophy,* vol. 28 (1953).

The assumption that the parties are not moved by envy raises certain questions. Perhaps we should also assume that they are not liable to various other feelings such as shame and humiliation (§ 67). Now a satisfactory account of justice will eventually have to deal with these matters too, but for the present I shall leave these complications aside. Another objection to our procedure is that it is too unrealistic. Certainly men are afflicted with these feelings. How can a conception of justice ignore this fact? I shall meet this problem by dividing the argument for the principles of justice into two parts. In the first part, the principles are derived on the supposition that envy does not exist; while in the second, we consider whether the conception arrived at is feasible in view of the circumstances of human life.

One reason for this procedure is that envy tends to make everyone worse off. In this sense it is collectively disadvantageous. Presuming its absence amounts to supposing that in the choice of principles men should think of themselves as having their own plan of life which is sufficient for itself. They have a secure sense of their own worth so that they have no desire to abandon any of their aims provided others have less means to further theirs. I shall work out a conception of justice on this stipulation to see what happens. Later I shall try to show that when the principles adopted are put into practice, they lead to social arrangements in which envy and other destructive feelings are not likely to be strong. The conception of justice eliminates the conditions that give rise to disruptive attitudes. It is, therefore, inherently stable (§§ 80–81).

The assumption of mutually disinterested rationality, then, comes to this: the persons in the original position try to acknowledge principles which advance their system of ends as far as possible. They do this by attempting to win for themselves the highest index of primary social goods, since this enables them to promote their conception of the good most effectively whatever it turns out to be. The parties do not seek to confer benefits or to impose injuries on one another; they are not moved by affection or rancor. Nor do they try to gain relative to each other; they are not envious or vain. Put in terms of a game, we might say: they strive for as high an absolute score as possible. They do not wish a high or a low score for their opponents, nor do they seek to maximize or minimize the difference between their successes and those of others. The idea of a game does not really apply, since the parties are not concerned to win but to get as many points as possible judged by their own system of ends.

There is one further assumption to guarantee strict compliance. The parties are presumed to be capable of a sense of justice and this fact is public knowledge among them. This condition is to insure the integrity of the agreement made in the original position. It does not mean that in their deliberations the parties apply some particular conception of justice, for this would defeat the point of the motivation assumption. Rather, it means that the parties can rely on each other to understand and to act in accordance with whatever principles are finally agreed to. Once principles are acknowledged the parties can depend on one another to conform to them. In reaching an agreement, then, they know that their undertaking is not in vain: their capacity for a sense of justice insures that the principles chosen will be respected. It is essential to observe, however, that this assumption still permits the consideration of men's capacity to act on the various conceptions of justice. The general facts of human psychology and the principles of moral learning are relevant matters for the parties to examine. If a conception of justice is unlikely to generate its own support, or lacks stability, this fact must not be overlooked. For then a different conception of justice might be preferred. The assumption only says that the parties have a capacity for justice in a purely formal sense: taking everything relevant into account, including the general facts of moral psychology, the parties will adhere to the principles eventually chosen. They are rational in that they will not enter into agreements they know they cannot keep, or can do so only with great difficulty. Along with other considerations, they count the strains of commitment (§ 29). Thus in assessing conceptions of justice the persons in the original position are to assume that the one they adopt will be strictly complied with. The consequences of their agreement are to be worked out on this basis.

With the preceding remarks about rationality and motivation of the parties the description of the original position is for the most part complete. We can summarize this description with the following list of elements of the initial situation and their variations. (The asterisks mark the interpretations that constitute the original position.)

1. The Nature of the Parties (§ 22)
   *a. continuing persons (family heads, or genetic lines)
   b. single individuals
   c. associations (states, churches, or other corporate bodies)

2. Subject of Justice (§ 2)
   *a. basic structure of society
   b. rules of corporate associations
   c. law of nations

3. Presentation of Alternatives (§ 21)
   *a. shorter (or longer) list
   b. general characterization of the possibilities

4. Time of Entry (§ 24)
   *a. any time (during age of reason) for living persons
   b. all actual persons (those alive at some time) simultaneously
   c. all possible persons simultaneously

5. Circumstances of Justice (§ 22)
   *a. Hume's conditions of moderate scarcity
   b. the above plus further extremes

6. Formal Conditions on Principles (§ 23)
   *a. generality, universality, publicity, ordering, and finality
   b. the above less publicity, say

7. Knowledge and Beliefs (§ 24)
   *a. veil of ignorance
   b. full information
   c. partial knowledge

8. Motivation of the Parties (§ 25)
   *a. mutual disinterestedness (limited altruism)
   b. elements of social solidarity and good will
   c. perfect altruism

9. Rationality (§§ 25, 28)
   *a. taking effective means to ends with unified expectations and objective interpretation of probability
   b. as above but without unified expectations and using the principle of insufficient reason

10. Agreement Condition (§ 24)
    *a. unanimity in perpetuity
    b. majority acceptance, or whatever, for limited period
11. Compliance Condition (§ 25)
    *a. strict compliance
    b. partial compliance in various degrees
12. No Agreement Point (§ 23)
    *a. general egoism
    b. the state of nature

We can turn now to the choice of principles. But first I shall mention a few misunderstandings to be avoided. First of all, we must keep in mind that the parties in the original position are theoretically defined individuals. The grounds for their consent are set out by the description of the contractual situation and their preference for primary goods. Thus to say that the principles of justice would be adopted is to say how these persons would decide being moved in ways our account describes. Of course, when we try to simulate the original position in everyday life, that is, when we try to conduct ourselves in moral argument as its constraints require, we will presumably find that our deliberations and judgments are influenced by our special inclinations and attitudes. Surely it will prove difficult to correct for our various propensities and aversions in striving to adhere to the conditions of this idealized situation. But none of this affects the contention that in the original position rational persons so characterized would make a certain decision. This proposition belongs to the theory of justice. It is another question how well human beings can assume this role in regulating their practical reasoning.

Since the persons in the original position are assumed to take no interest in one another's interests (although they may have a concern for third parties), it may be thought that justice as fairness is itself an egoistic theory. It is not, of course, one of the three forms of egoism mentioned earlier, but some may think, as Scho-penhauer thought of Kant's doctrine, that it is egoistic neverthe-less.[15] Now this is a misconception. For the fact that in the original

15. See *On the Basis of Ethics* (1840), trans. E. F. J. Payne (New York, The Liberal Arts Press, Inc., 1965), pp. 89–92.

147

position the parties are characterized as not interested in one another's concerns does not entail that persons in ordinary life who hold the principles that would be agreed to are similarly disinterested in one another. Clearly the two principles of justice and the principles of obligation and natural duty require us to consider the rights and claims of others. And the sense of justice is a normally effective desire to comply with these restrictions. The motivation of the persons in the original position must not be confused with the motivation of persons in everyday life who accept the principles that would be chosen and who have the corresponding sense of justice. In practical affairs an individual does have a knowledge of his situation and he can, if he wishes, exploit contingencies to his advantage. Should his sense of justice move him to act on the principles of right that would be adopted in the original position, his desires and aims are surely not egoistic. He voluntarily takes on the limitations expressed by this interpretation of the moral point of view.

This conclusion is supported by a further reflection. Once we consider the idea of a contract theory it is tempting to think that it will not yield the principles we want unless the parties are to some degree at least moved by benevolence, or an interest in one another's interests. Perry, as I mentioned before, thinks of the right standards and decisions as those promoting the ends reached by reflective agreement under circumstances making for impartiality and good will. Now the combination of mutual disinterest and the veil of ignorance achieves the same purpose as benevolence. For this combination of conditions forces each person in the original position to take the good of others into account. In justice as fairness, then, the effects of good will are brought about by several conditions working jointly. The feeling that this conception of justice is egoistic is an illusion fostered by looking at but one of the elements of the original position. Furthermore, this pair of assumptions has enormous advantages over that of benevolence plus knowledge. As I have noted, the latter is so complex that no definite theory at all can be worked out. Not only are the complications caused by so much information insurmountable, but the motivational assumption requires clarification. For example, what is the relative strength of benevolent desires? In brief, the combination of mutual disinterestedness plus the veil of ignorance has the merits of simplicity and clarity while at the same time insuring the effects of what are at first sight morally more attractive assumptions. And if it is asked why one should not postulate benevolence with the veil of ignorance, the answer is that there is no need for so strong a condition. Moreover, it would defeat the purpose of grounding the theory of justice on weak stipulations, as well as being incongruous with the circumstances of justice.

Finally, if the parties are conceived as themselves making proposals, they have no incentive to suggest pointless or arbitrary principles. For example, none would urge that special privileges be given to those exactly six feet tall or born on a sunny day. Nor would anyone put forward the principle that basic rights should depend on the color of one's skin or the texture of one's hair. No one can tell whether such principles would be to his advantage. Furthermore, each such principle is a limitation of one's liberty of action, and such restrictions are not to be accepted without a reason. Certainly we might imagine peculiar circumstances in which these characteristics are relevant. Those born on a sunny day might be blessed with a happy temperament, and for some positions of authority this might be a qualifying attribute. But such distinctions would never be proposed in first principles, for these must have some rational connection with the advancement of human interests broadly defined. The rationality of the parties and their situation in the original position guarantees that ethical principles and conceptions of justice have this general content.[16] Inevitably, then, racial and sexual discrimination presupposes that some hold a favored place in the social system which they are willing to exploit to their advantage. From the standpoint of persons similarly situated in an initial situation which is fair, the principles of explicit racist doctrines are not only unjust. They are irrational. For this reason we could say that they are not moral conceptions at all, but simply means of suppression. They have no place on a reason-

16. For a different way of reaching this conclusion, see Philippa Foot, "Moral Arguments," *Mind*, vol. 67 (1958), and "Moral Beliefs," *Proceedings of the Aristotelian Society*, vol. 59 (1958–1959); and R. W. Beardsmore, *Moral Reasoning* (New York, Schocken Books, 1969), especially ch. IV. The problem of content is discussed briefly in G. F. Warnock, *Contemporary Moral Philosophy* (London, Macmillan, 1967), pp. 55–61.

able list of traditional conceptions of justice.[17] Of course, this contention is not at all a matter of definition. It is rather a consequence of the conditions characterizing the original position, especially the conditions of the rationality of the parties and the veil of ignorance. That conceptions of right have a certain content and exclude arbitrary and pointless principles is, therefore, an inference from the theory.

26. THE REASONING LEADING TO THE TWO PRINCIPLES OF JUSTICE

In this and the next two sections I take up the choice between the two principles of justice and the principle of average utility. Determining the rational preference between these two options is perhaps the central problem in developing the conception of justice as fairness as a viable alternative to the utilitarian tradition. I shall begin in this section by presenting some intuitive remarks favoring the two principles. I shall also discuss briefly the qualitative structure of the argument that needs to be made if the case for these principles is to be conclusive.

It will be recalled that the general conception of justice as fairness requires that all primary social goods be distributed equally unless an unequal distribution would be to everyone's advantage. No restrictions are placed on exchanges of these goods and therefore a lesser liberty can be compensated for by greater social and economic benefits. Now looking at the situation from the standpoint of one person selected arbitrarily, there is no way for him to win special advantages for himself. Nor, on the other hand, are there grounds for his acquiescing in special disadvantages. Since it is not reasonable for him to expect more than an equal share in the division of social goods, and since it is not rational for him to agree to less, the sensible thing for him to do is to acknowledge as the first principle of justice one requiring an equal distribution.

17. For a similar view, see B. A. O. Williams, "The Idea of Equality," *Philosophy, Politics, and Society*, Second Series, ed. Peter Laslett and W. G. Runciman (Oxford, Basil Blackwell, 1962), p. 113.

Indeed, this principle is so obvious that we would expect it to occur to anyone immediately.

Thus, the parties start with a principle establishing equal liberty for all, including equality of opportunity, as well as an equal distribution of income and wealth. But there is no reason why this acknowledgment should be final. If there are inequalities in the basic structure that work to make everyone better off in comparison with the benchmark of initial equality, why not permit them? The immediate gain which a greater equality might allow can be regarded as intelligently invested in view of its future return. If, for example, these inequalities set up various incentives which succeed in eliciting more productive efforts, a person in the original position may look upon them as necessary to cover the costs of training and to encourage effective performance. One might think that ideally individuals should want to serve one another. But since the parties are assumed not to take an interest in one another's interests, their acceptance of these inequalities is only the acceptance of the relations in which men stand in the circumstances of justice. They have no grounds for complaining of one another's motives. A person in the original position would, therefore, concede the justice of these inequalities. Indeed, it would be shortsighted of him not to do so. He would hesitate to agree to these regularities only if he would be dejected by the bare knowledge or perception that others were better situated; and I have assumed that the parties decide as if they are not moved by envy. In order to make the principle regulating inequalities determinate, one looks at the system from the standpoint of the least advantaged representative man. Inequalities are permissible when they maximize, or at least all contribute to, the long-term expectations of the least fortunate group in society.

Now this general conception imposes no constraints on what sorts of inequalities are allowed, whereas the special conception, by putting the two principles in serial order (with the necessary adjustments in meaning), forbids exchanges between basic liberties and economic and social benefits. I shall not try to justify this ordering here. From time to time in later chapters this problem will be considered (§§ 39, 82). But roughly, the idea underlying this ordering is that if the parties assume that their basic liberties

151

can be effectively exercised, they will not exchange a lesser liberty for an improvement in economic well-being. It is only when social conditions do not allow the effective establishment of these rights that one can concede their limitation; and these restrictions can be granted only to the extent that they are necessary to prepare the way for a free society. The denial of equal liberty can be defended only if it is necessary to raise the level of civilization so that in due course these freedoms can be enjoyed. Thus in adopting a serial order we are in effect making a special assumption in the original position, namely, that the parties know that the conditions of their society, whatever they are, admit the effective realization of the equal liberties. The serial ordering of the two principles of justice eventually comes to be reasonable if the general conception is consistently followed. This lexical ranking is the long-run tendency of the general view. For the most part I shall assume that the requisite circumstances for the serial order obtain.

It seems clear from these remarks that the two principles are at least a plausible conception of justice. The question, though, is how one is to argue for them more systematically. Now there are several things to do. One can work out their consequences for institutions and note their implications for fundamental social policy. In this way they are tested by a comparison with our considered judgments of justice. Part II is devoted to this. But one can also try to find arguments in their favor that are decisive from the standpoint of the original position. In order to see how this might be done, it is useful as a heuristic device to think of the two principles as the maximin solution to the problem of social justice. There is an analogy between the two principles and the maximin rule for choice under uncertainty.[18] This is evident from the fact that the two principles are those a person would choose for the design of a society in which his enemy is to assign him his place. The maximin rule tells us to rank alternatives by their worst pos-

18. An accessible discussion of this and other rules of choice under uncertainty can be found in W. J. Baumol, *Economic Theory and Operations Analysis,* 2nd ed. (Englewood Cliffs, N.J., Prentice-Hall Inc., 1965), ch. 24. Baumol gives a geometric interpretation of these rules, including the diagram used in §13 to illustrate the difference principle. See pp. 558–562. See also R. D. Luce and Howard Raiffa, *Games and Decisions* (New York, John Wiley and Sons, Inc., 1957), ch. XIII, for a fuller account.

sible outcomes: we are to adopt the alternative the worst outcome of which is superior to the worst outcomes of the others. The persons in the original position do not, of course, assume that their initial place in society is decided by a malevolent opponent. As I note below, they should not reason from false premises. The veil of ignorance does not violate this idea, since an absence of information is not misinformation. But that the two principles of justice would be chosen if the parties were forced to protect themselves against such a contingency explains the sense in which this conception is the maximin solution. And this analogy suggests that if the original position has been described so that it is rational for the parties to adopt the conservative attitude expressed by this rule, a conclusive argument can indeed be constructed for these principles. Clearly the maximin rule is not, in general, a suitable guide for choices under uncertainty. But it is attractive in situations marked by certain special features. My aim, then, is to show that a good case can be made for the two principles based on the fact that the original position manifests these features to the fullest possible degree, carrying them to the limit, so to speak.

Consider the gain-and-loss table below. It represents the gains and losses for a situation which is not a game of strategy. There is no one playing against the person making the decision; instead he is faced with several possible circumstances which may or may not obtain. Which circumstances happen to exist does not depend upon what the person choosing decides or whether he announces his moves in advance. The numbers in the table are monetary values (in hundreds of dollars) in comparison with some initial situation. The gain (g) depends upon the individual's decision (d) and the circumstances (c). Thus $g = f(d, c)$. Assuming that there are three possible decisions and three possible circumstances, we might have this gain-and-loss table.

Decisions	Circumstances		
	c_1	c_2	c_3
d_1	-7	8	12
d_2	-8	7	14
d_3	5	6	8

153

The maximin rule requires that we make the third decision. For in this case the worst that can happen is that one gains five hundred dollars, which is better than the worst for the other actions. If we adopt one of these we may lose either eight or seven hundred dollars. Thus, the choice of d_3 maximizes $f(d,c)$ for that value of c, which for a given d, minimizes f. The term "maximin" means the *maximum minimorum;* and the rule directs our attention to the worst that can happen under any proposed course of action, and to decide in the light of that.

Now there appear to be three chief features of situations that give plausibility to this unusual rule.[19] First, since the rule takes no account of the likelihoods of the possible circumstances, there must be some reason for sharply discounting estimates of these probabilities. Offhand, the most natural rule of choice would seem to be to compute the expectation of monetary gain for each decision and then to adopt the course of action with the highest prospect. (This expectation is defined as follows: let us suppose that g_{ij} represent the numbers in the gain-and-loss table, where i is the row index and j is the column index; and let p_j, $j = 1, 2, 3$, be the likelihoods of the circumstances, with $\Sigma p_j = 1$. Then the expectation for the ith decision is equal to $\Sigma p_j g_{ij}$.) Thus it must be, for example, that the situation is one in which a knowledge of likelihoods is impossible, or at best extremely insecure. In this case it is unreasonable not to be skeptical of probabilistic calculations unless there is no other way out, particularly if the decision is a fundamental one that needs to be justified to others.

The second feature that suggests the maximin rule is the following: the person choosing has a conception of the good such that he cares very little, if anything, for what he might gain above the minimum stipend that he can, in fact, be sure of by following the maximin rule. It is not worthwhile for him to take a chance for the sake of a further advantage, especially when it may turn out that he loses much that is important to him. This last provision brings in the third feature, namely, that the rejected alternatives have outcomes that one can hardly accept. The situation involves grave risks. Of course these features work most effectively in combina-

19. Here I borrow from William Fellner, *Probability and Profit* (Homewood, Ill., R. D. Irwin, Inc., 1965), pp. 140–142, where these features are noted.

tion. The paradigm situation for following the maximin rule is when all three features are realized to the highest degree. This rule does not, then, generally apply, nor of course is it self-evident. Rather, it is a maxim, a rule of thumb, that comes into its own in special circumstances. Its application depends upon the qualitative structure of the possible gains and losses in relation to one's conception of the good, all this against a background in which it is reasonable to discount conjectural estimates of likelihoods.

It should be noted, as the comments on the gain-and-loss table say, that the entries in the table represent monetary values and not utilities. This difference is significant since for one thing computing expectations on the basis of such objective values is not the same thing as computing expected utility and may lead to different results. The essential point though is that in justice as fairness the parties do not know their conception of the good and cannot estimate their utility in the ordinary sense. In any case, we want to go behind de facto preferences generated by given conditions. Therefore expectations are based upon an index of primary goods and the parties make their choice accordingly. The entries in the example are in terms of money and not utility to indicate this aspect of the contract doctrine.

Now, as I have suggested, the original position has been defined so that it is a situation in which the maximin rule applies. In order to see this, let us review briefly the nature of this situation with these three special features in mind. To begin with, the veil of ignorance excludes all but the vaguest knowledge of likelihoods. The parties have no basis for determining the probable nature of their society, or their place in it. Thus they have strong reasons for being wary of probability calculations if any other course is open to them. They must also take into account the fact that their choice of principles should seem reasonable to others, in particular their descendants, whose rights will be deeply affected by it. There are further grounds for discounting that I shall mention as we go along. For the present it suffices to note that these considerations are strengthened by the fact that the parties know very little about the gain-and-loss table. Not only are they unable to conjecture the likelihoods of the various possible circumstances, they cannot say much about what the possible circumstances are, much less enumerate them and foresee the outcome of each alternative available. Those deciding are much more in the dark than the illustration by a numerical table suggests. It is for this reason that I have spoken of an analogy with the maximin rule.

Several kinds of arguments for the two principles of justice illustrate the second feature. Thus, if we can maintain that these principles provide a workable theory of social justice, and that they are compatible with reasonable demands of efficiency, then this conception guarantees a satisfactory minimum. There may be, on reflection, little reason for trying to do better. Thus much of the argument, especially in Part Two, is to show, by their application to the main questions of social justice, that the two principles are a satisfactory conception. These details have a philosophical purpose. Moreover, this line of thought is practically decisive if we can establish the priority of liberty, the lexical ordering of the two principles. For this priority implies that the persons in the original position have no desire to try for greater gains at the expense of the equal liberties. The minimum assured by the two principles in lexical order is not one that the parties wish to jeopardize for the sake of greater economic and social advantages. In parts of Chapters IV and IX the case for this ordering is discussed.

Finally, the third feature holds if we can assume that other conceptions of justice may lead to institutions that the parties would find intolerable. For example, it has sometimes been held that under some conditions the utility principle (in either form) justifies, if not slavery or serfdom, at any rate serious infractions of liberty for the sake of greater social benefits. We need not consider here the truth of this claim, or the likelihood that the requisite conditions obtain. For the moment, this contention is only to illustrate the way in which conceptions of justice may allow for outcomes which the parties may not be able to accept. And having the ready alternative of the two principles of justice which secure a satisfactory minimum, it seems unwise, if not irrational, for them to take a chance that these outcomes are not realized.

So much, then, for a brief sketch of the features of situations in which the maximin rule comes into its own and of the way in which the arguments for the two principles of justice can be subsumed under them. Thus if the list of traditional views (§ 21) represents the possible decisions, these principles would be selected by the rule. The original position clearly exhibits these special features to a very high degree in view of the fundamental character of the choice of a conception of justice. These remarks about the maximin rule are intended only to clarify the structure of the choice problem in the original position. They depict its qualitative anatomy. The arguments for the two principles will be presented more fully as we proceed. I want to conclude this section by taking up an objection which is likely to be made against the difference principle and which leads into an important question. The objection is that since we are to maximize (subject to the usual constraints) the long-term prospects of the least advantaged, it seems that the justice of large increases or decreases in the expectations of the more advantaged may depend upon small changes in the prospects of those worst off. To illustrate: the most extreme disparities in wealth and income are allowed provided that the expectations of the least fortunate are raised in the slightest degree. But at the same time similar inequalities favoring the more advantaged are forbidden when those in the worst position lose by the least amount. Yet it seems extraordinary that the justice of increasing the expectations of the better placed by a billion dollars, say, should turn on whether the prospects of the least favored increase or decrease by a penny. This objection is analogous to the following difficulty with the maximin rule. Consider the sequence of gain-and-loss tables:

$$
\begin{array}{cc}
0 & n \\
1/n & 1
\end{array}
$$

for all natural numbers n. Even if for some smallish number it is reasonable to select the second row, surely there is another point later in the sequence when it is irrational not to choose the first row contrary to the rule.

Part of the answer is that the difference principle is not intended to apply to such abstract possibilities. As I have said, the problem of social justice is not that of allocating *ad libitum* various amounts of something, whether it be money, or property, or whatever, among given individuals. Nor is there some substance of which *what ?!*

expectations are made that can be shuffled from one representative man to another in all possible combinations. The possibilities which the objection envisages cannot arise in real cases; the feasible set is so restricted that they are excluded.[20] The reason for this is that the two principles are tied together as one conception of justice which applies to the basic structure of society as a whole. The operation of the principles of equal liberty and open positions prevents these contingencies from occurring. For as we raise the expectations of the more advantaged the situation of the worst off is continuously improved. Each such increase is in the latter's interest, up to a certain point anyway. For the greater expectations of the more favored presumably cover the costs of training and encourage better performance thereby contributing to the general advantage. While nothing guarantees that inequalities will not be significant, there is a persistent tendency for them to be leveled down by the increasing availability of educated talent and ever widening opportunities. The conditions established by the other principles insure that the disparities likely to result will be much less than the differences that men have often tolerated in the past.

We should also observe that the difference principle not only assumes the operation of other principles, but it presupposes as well a certain theory of social institutions. In particular, as I shall discuss in some detail in Chapter V, it relies on the idea that in a competitive economy (with or without private ownership) with an open class system excessive inequalities will not be the rule. Given the distribution of natural assets and the laws of motivation, great disparities will not long persist. Now the point to stress here is that there is no objection to resting the choice of first principles upon the general facts of economics and psychology. As we have seen, the parties in the original position are assumed to know the general facts about human society. Since this knowledge enters into the premises of their deliberations, their choice of principles is relative to these facts. What is essential, of course, is that these premises be true and sufficiently general. It is often objected, for example, that utilitarianism may allow for slavery and serfdom, and for other infractions of liberty. Whether these institutions are justified is

20. I am indebted to S. A. Marglin for this point.

made to depend upon whether actuarial calculations show that they yield a higher balance of happiness. To this the utilitarian replies that the nature of society is such that these calculations are normally against such denials of liberty. Utilitarians seek to account for the claims of liberty and equality by making certain standard assumptions, as I shall refer to them. Thus they suppose that persons have similar utility functions which satisfy the condition of diminishing marginal utility. It follows from these stipulations that, given a fixed amount of income say, the distribution should be equal, once we leave aside effects on future production. For so long as some have more than others, total utility can be increased by transfers to those who have less. The assignment of rights and liberties can be regarded in much the same way. There is nothing wrong with this procedure provided the assumptions are sound.

Contract theory agrees, then, with utilitarianism in holding that the fundamental principles of justice quite properly depend upon the natural facts about men in society. This dependence is made explicit by the description of the original position: the decision of the parties is taken in the light of general knowledge. Moreover, the various elements of the original position presuppose many things about the circumstances of human life. Some philosophers have thought that ethical first principles should be independent of all contingent assumptions, that they should take for granted no truths except those of logic and others that follow from these by an analysis of concepts. Moral conceptions should hold for all possible worlds. Now this view makes moral philosophy the study of the ethics of creation: an examination of the reflections an omnipotent deity might entertain in determining which is the best of all possible worlds. Even the general facts of nature are to be chosen. Certainly we have a natural religious interest in the ethics of creation. But it would appear to outrun human comprehension. From the point of view of contract theory it amounts to supposing that the persons in the original position know nothing at all about themselves or their world. How, then, can they possibly make a decision? A problem of choice is well defined only if the alternatives are suitably restricted by natural laws and other constraints, and those deciding already have certain inclinations to choose among them. Without a definite structure of this kind the question posed

159

contradiction

is indeterminate. For this reason we need have no hesitation in making the choice of the principles of justice presuppose a certain theory of social institutions. Indeed, one cannot avoid assumptions about general facts any more than one can do without a conception of the good on the basis of which the parties rank alternatives. If these assumptions are true and suitably general, everything is in order, for without these elements the whole scheme would be pointless and empty.

It is evident from these remarks that both general facts as well as moral conditions are needed even in the argument for the first principles of justice. (Of course, it has always been obvious that secondary moral rules and particular ethical judgments depend upon factual premises as well as normative principles.) In a contract theory, these moral conditions take the form of a description of the initial contractual situation. It is also clear that there is a division of labor between general facts and moral conditions in arriving at conceptions of justice, and this division can be different from one theory to another. As I have noted before, principles differ in the extent to which they incorporate the desired moral ideal. It is characteristic of utilitarianism that it leaves so much to arguments from general facts. The utilitarian tends to meet objections by holding that the laws of society and of human nature rule out the cases offensive to our considered judgments. Justice as fairness, by contrast, embeds the ideals of justice, as ordinarily understood, more directly into its first principles. This conception relies less on general facts in reaching a match with our judgments of justice. It insures this fit over a wider range of possible cases.

There are two reasons that justify this embedding of ideals into first principles. First of all, and most obviously, the utilitarian's standard assumptions that lead to the wanted consequences may be only probably true, or even doubtfully so. Moreover, their full meaning and application may be highly conjectural. And the same may hold for all the requisite general suppositions that support the principle of utility. From the standpoint of the original position it may be unreasonable to rely upon these hypotheses and therefore far more sensible to embody the ideal more expressly in the principles chosen. Thus it seems that the parties would prefer to secure their liberties straightway rather than have them depend upon what may be uncertain and speculative actuarial calculations. These remarks are further confirmed by the desirability of avoiding complicated theoretical arguments in arriving at a public conception of justice (§ 24). In comparison with the reasoning for the two principles, the grounds for the utility criterion trespass upon this constraint. But secondly, there is a real advantage in persons' announcing to one another once and for all that even though theoretical computations of utility always happen to favor the equal liberties (assuming that this is indeed the case here), they do not wish that things had been different. Since in justice as fairness moral conceptions are public, the choice of the two principles is, in effect, such an announcement. And the benefits of this collective profession favor these principles even though the standard utilitarian assumptions should be true. These matters I shall consider in more detail in connection with publicity and stability (§ 29). The relevant point here is that while, in general, an ethical theory can certainly invoke natural facts, there may nevertheless be good reasons for embedding convictions of justice more directly into first principles than a theoretically complete grasp of the contingencies of the world may actually require.

27. THE REASONING LEADING TO THE PRINCIPLE OF AVERAGE UTILITY

I now wish to examine the reasoning that favors the principle of average utility. The classical principle is discussed later (§ 30). One of the merits of contract theory is that it reveals these principles to be markedly distinct conceptions, however much their practical consequences may coincide. Their underlying analytic assumptions are far apart in the sense that they are associated with contrasting interpretations of the initial situation. Or so I shall try to show.

Applied to the basic structure, the classical principle requires that institutions be arranged to maximize the absolute weighted sum of the expectations of the relevant representative men. This sum is arrived at by weighting each expectation by the number of persons in the corresponding position and then adding. Thus, other

161

things equal, when the number of persons in society doubles, total utility is twice as great. (Of course, on the utilitarian view expectations are to measure total satisfactions enjoyed and foreseen. They are not, as in justice as fairness, merely indexes of primary goods.) By contrast, the principle of average utility directs society to maximize not the total but the average utility (per capita). This seems to be a more modern view: it was held by Mill and Wicksell, and recently others have given it a new foundation.[21] To apply this conception to the basic structure, institutions are set up so as to maximize the percentage weighted sum of the expectations of representative individuals. To compute this sum we multiply expectations by the fraction of society at the corresponding position. Thus it is no longer true that, other things equal, when a community doubles its population the utility is twice as great. To the contrary, as long as the percentages in the various positions are unchanged, the utility remains the same.

Which of these principles of utility would be preferred in the original position? To answer this question, one should note that both variations come to the same thing if population size is constant. But when population is subject to change, there is a difference. The classical principle requires that so far as institutions affect the size of families, the age of marriage, and the like, they should be arranged so that the maximum of total utility is achieved. This entails that so long as the average utility per person falls slowly enough when the number of individuals increases, the population should be encouraged to grow indefinitely no matter how

21. For Mill and Wicksell, see Gunnar Myrdal, *The Political Element in the Development of Economic Theory*, trans. Paul Streeten (London, Routledge and Kegan Paul, Ltd., 1953), pp. 38f. J. J. C. Smart in *An Outline of a System of Utilitarian Ethics* (Cambridge, The University Press, 1961), p. 18, leaves the matter unsettled, but affirms the classical principle in the case where it is necessary to break ties. As unambiguous proponents of the average doctrine, see J. C. Harsanyi, "Cardinal Utility in Welfare Economics and the Theory of Risk Taking," *Journal of Political Economy*, vol. 61 (1953), and "Cardinal Welfare, Individualistic Ethics, and Interpersonal Comparisons of Utility," *Journal of Political Economy*, vol. 63 (1955); and R. B. Brandt, "Some Merits of One Form of Rule Utilitarianism," in *University of Colorado Studies* (Boulder, Colo., 1967), pp. 39–65. But note the qualification regarding Brandt's view in §29 below, note 31. For a discussion of Harsanyi, see P. K. Pattanaik, "Risk, Impersonality, and the Social Welfare Function," *Journal of Political Economy*, vol. 76 (1968), and Sen, *Collective Choice and Social Welfare*, pp. 141–146.

low the average has fallen. In this case the sum of utilities added by the greater number of persons is sufficiently great to make up for the decline in the share per capita. As a matter of justice and not of preference, a very low average of well-being may be required. (See the following figure.)

INDEFINITE INCREASE OF POPULATION

Formally the condition for increasing population size indefinitely is that the curve $y = F(x)$, where y is average per capita and x is population size, should be flatter than the rectangular hyperbola

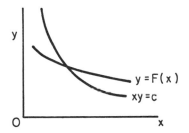

$xy = c$. For xy equals the total utility, and the area of the rectangle representing this total increases as x increases whenever the curve $y = F(x)$ is flatter than $xy = c$.

Now this consequence of the classical principle seems to show that it would be rejected by the parties in favor of the average principle. The two principles would be equivalent only if it is supposed that average well-being always falls sufficiently fast (beyond a certain point anyway) so that there is no serious conflict between them. But this assumption seems questionable. From the standpoint of the persons in the original position, it would appear more rational to agree to some sort of floor to hold up average welfare. Since the parties aim to advance their own interests, they have no desire in any event to maximize the sum total of satisfaction. I assume, therefore, that the more plausible utilitarian alternative to the two principles of justice is the average and not the classical principle.

I now wish to consider how the parties might arrive at the average principle. The reasoning I shall sketch is perfectly general and if it were sound it would sidestep entirely the problem of how to present the alternatives. The average principle would be recognized as the only reasonable candidate. Imagine a situation in which a single rational individual can choose which of several societies to enter.[22] To fix ideas, assume first that the members of these societies all have the same preferences. And assume also that these preferences satisfy conditions that enable one to define a cardinal utility. Further, each society has the same resources and the same distribution of natural talents. Nevertheless, individuals with different talents have different incomes; and each society has a redistribution policy which if pushed beyond a certain point weakens incentives and thereby lowers production. Supposing that different policies are followed in these societies, how will a single individual decide which society to join? If he knows his own abilities and interests precisely, and if he has detailed information about these societies, he may be able to foresee the well-being that he will almost certainly enjoy in each one. He can then decide on this basis. There is no need for him to make any probabilistic calculations.

But this case is rather special. Let us alter it step by step so that it increasingly resembles that of someone in the original position. Thus, suppose first that the hypothetical joiner is unsure about the role his talents will enable him to fill in these various societies. If he assumes that his preferences are the same as everyone else, he may decide by trying to maximize his expected well-being. He computes his prospect for a given society by taking as the alternative utilities those of the representative members of that society and as the likelihoods for each position his estimates of his chances of attaining it. His expectation is defined, then, by a weighted sum of utilities of representative individuals, that is, by the expression $\Sigma p_i u_i$, where p_i is the likelihood of his achieving the ith position,

22. Here I follow the first stages of W. S. Vickrey's presentation in "Utility, Strategy, and Social Decision Rules," *Quarterly Journal of Economics*, vol. 74 (1960), pp. 523f.

and u_i the utility of the corresponding representative man. He then chooses the society offering the highest prospect.

Several further modifications bring the situation closer to that of the original position. Assume that the hypothetical joiner knows nothing about either his abilities or the place he is likely to hold in each society. It is still assumed, though, that his preferences are the same as the people in these societies. Now suppose that he continues to reason along probabilistic lines by holding that he has an equal chance of being any individual (that is, that his chance of falling under any representative man is the fraction of society that this man represents). In this case his prospects are still identical with the average utility for each society. These modifications have at last brought his expected gains for each society in line with its average welfare.

So far we have assumed that all individuals have similar preferences whether or not they belong to the same society. Their conceptions of the good are roughly the same. Once this highly restrictive assumption is dropped, we take the final step and arrive at a variation of the initial situation. Nothing is known, let us say, about the particular preferences of the members of these societies or of the person deciding. These facts as well as a knowledge of the structure of these societies are ruled out. The veil of ignorance is now complete. But one can still imagine that the hypothetical newcomer reasons much as before. He assumes that there is an equal likelihood of his turning out to be anyone, fully endowed with that person's preferences, abilities, and social position. Once again his prospect is highest for that society with the greatest average utility. We can see this in the following way. Let n be the number of persons in a society. Let their levels of well-being be $u_1, u_2, \ldots, u_n$. Then the total utility is Σu_i and the average is $\Sigma u_i/n$. Assuming that one has an equal chance of being any person, one's prospect is: $1/n\ u_1 + 1/n\ u_2 + \ldots + 1/n\ u_n$ or $\Sigma u_i/n$. The value of the prospect is identical with the average utility.

Thus if we waive the problem of interpersonal comparisons of utility, and if the parties are viewed as rational individuals who have no aversion to risk and who follow the principle of insufficient reason in computing likelihoods (the principle that underlies the preceding probabilistic calculations), then the idea of the initial situation leads naturally to the average principle. By choosing it the parties maximize their expected well-being as seen from this point of view. Some form of contract theory provides, then, a way of arguing for the average over the classical view. In fact, how else is the average principle to be accounted for? After all, it is not a teleological doctrine, strictly speaking, as the classical view is, and therefore it lacks some of the intuitive appeal of the idea of maximizing the good. Presumably one who held the average principle would want to invoke the contract theory at least to this extent.

Moreover, there is no loss of generality in taking up the standpoint of a hypothetical newcomer. To be sure, the persons in the original position know that they already hold a place in some particular society. But from the perspective of the initial situation there is no essential difference between reasoning how things have happened and reasoning how they will happen. The veil of ignorance removes any basis for the distinction. Thus either way, the same arguments for the average principle can be made.[23] In accepting it the parties would agree to arrange their society as best they could to accord with the principle they would use as hypothetical newcomers to choose between societies in circumstances analogous to the original position. The average principle appeals to those in the initial situation once they are conceived as single rational individuals prepared to gamble on the most abstract probabilistic reasoning in all cases. To argue for the two principles of justice I must show that the conditions defining the original position exclude this conception of the parties. Indeed, we face here one of the main problems of justice as fairness: namely, to define the original position in such a way that, while a meaningful agreement can be reached (the veil of ignorance along with other conditions removing the bases for bargaining and bias), the constraints imposed to achieve this result still lead to principles characteristic of the contractarian tradition.

23. I am indebted here to G. H. Harman.

28. SOME DIFFICULTIES WITH THE AVERAGE PRINCIPLE

Before taking up the arguments for the two principles of justice I wish to mention several difficulties with the average principle of utility. First, though, we should note an objection which turns out to be only apparent. As we have seen, this principle may be viewed as the ethics of a single rational individual prepared to take whatever chances necessary to maximize his prospects from the standpoint of the initial situation. (If there is no objective basis for probabilities, they are computed by the principle of insufficient reason.) Now it is tempting to argue against this principle that it presupposes a real and equal acceptance of risk by all members of society. At some time, one wants to say, everyone must actually have agreed to take the same chances. Since clearly there was no such occasion, the principle is unsound. Consider an extreme case: a slaveholder when confronted by his slaves attempts to justify his position to them by claiming that, first of all, given the circumstances of their society, the institution of slavery is in fact necessary to produce the greatest average happiness; and secondly, that in the initial contractual situation he would choose the average principle even at the risk of its subsequently happening that he is justifiably held a slave. Now offhand we are inclined to reject the slaveholder's argument as beside the point, if not outrageous. One may think that it makes no difference what he would choose. Unless individuals have actually agreed to a conception of justice subject to real risks, no one is bound by its requirements.

On the contract view, however, the general form of the slaveholder's argument is correct. It would be a mistake for the slaves to retort that his contentions are irrelevant since there has been no actual occasion of choice, no equal sharing of risk as to how things would turn out. The contract doctrine is purely hypothetical: if a conception of justice would be agreed to in the original position, its principles are the right ones to apply. It is no objection that such an understanding has never been nor ever will be entered into. We cannot have it both ways: we cannot interpret the theory of justice hypothetically when the appropriate occasions of consent cannot be found to explain individuals' duties and obligations, and then insist upon real situations of risk-bearing to throw out principles of justice that we do not want.[24] Thus in justice as fairness the way to refute the slaveholder's argument is to show that the principle he invokes would be rejected in the original position. We have no alternative but to exploit the various aspects of this initial situation (on the favored interpretation) to establish that the balance of reasons favors the two principles of justice. In the next section I shall start on this task.

The first difficulty with the average principle I have already mentioned in discussing the maximin rule as a heuristic device for arranging the arguments favoring the two principles. It concerns the way that a rational individual is to estimate probabilities. This question arises because there seem to be no objective grounds in the initial situation for assuming that one has an equal chance of turning out to be anybody. That is, this assumption is not founded upon known features of one's society. In the early stages of the argument leading to the average principle, the hypothetical newcomer does have some knowledge of his abilities and of the design of the societies among which he is choosing. The estimates of his chances are based upon this information. But at the last stage there is complete ignorance of particular facts (with the exception of those implied by the circumstances of justice). The construction of the individual's prospect depends at this stage solely upon the principle of insufficient reason. This principle is used to assign probabilities to outcomes in the absence of any information. When we have no evidence at all, the possible cases are taken to be equally probable. Thus Laplace reasoned that when we are drawing from two urns each containing a different ratio of black to red balls, but we have no information as to which urn we are faced with, then we should assume initially that the chance of drawing from each of these urns is the same. The idea is that the state of ignorance on the basis of which these prior probabilities are assigned presents the same sort of problem as the situation where one has a lot of evidence showing that a particular coin is unbiased.

24. I have myself been in error on this matter. See "Constitutional Liberty and the Concept of Justice," *Nomos VI: Justice,* ed. C. J. Friedrich and J. W. Chapman (New York, Atherton Press, 1963), pp. 109–114. I am grateful to G. H. Harman for clarification on this point.

What is distinctive about the use of the principle is that it enables one to incorporate different kinds of information within one strictly probabilistic framework and to draw inferences about probabilities even in the absence of knowledge. Prior probabilities however arrived at are part of one theory along with estimates of chances based on random sampling. The limiting case of no information does not pose a theoretical problem.[25] As evidence accumulates the prior probabilities are revised anyway and the principle of insufficient reason at least insures that no possibilities are excluded from the outset.

Now I shall assume that the parties discount likelihoods arrived at solely on the basis of this principle. This supposition is plausible in view of the fundamental importance of the original agreement and the desire to have one's decision appear responsible to one's descendants who will be affected by it. We are more reluctant to take great risks for them than for ourselves; and we are willing to do so only when there is no way to avoid these uncertainties, or when the probable gains, as estimated by objective information, are so large that it would appear to them irresponsible to have refused the chance offered even though accepting it should actually turn out badly. Since the parties have the alternative of the two principles of justice, they can in large part sidestep the uncertainties of the original position. They can guarantee the protection of their liberties and a reasonably satisfactory standard of life as the conditions of their society permit. In fact, as I argue in the next section, it is questionable whether the choice of the average principle really offers a better prospect anyway, waiving the fact that it is based on the principle of insufficient reason. It seems, then, that the effect of the veil of ignorance is to favor the two principles. This conception of justice is better suited to the situation of complete ignorance.

There are, to be sure, assumptions about society that, if they were sound, would allow the parties to arrive at objective estimates

25. See William Fellner, *Probability and Profit,* pp. 27f. The principle of insufficient reason in its classical form is known to lead to difficulties. See J. M. Keynes, *A Treatise on Probability* (London, Macmillan, 1921), ch. IV. Part of Rudolf Carnap's aim in his *Logical Foundations of Probability,* 2nd ed. (Chicago: University of Chicago Press, 1962), is to construct a system of inductive logic by finding other theoretical means to do what the classical principle was intended to do. See pp. 344f.

of equal probability. To see this one can convert an argument of Edgeworth for the classical principle into one for average utility.[26] In fact, his reasoning can be adjusted to support nearly any general standard of policy. Edgeworth's idea is to formulate certain reasonable assumptions under which it would be rational for self-interested parties to agree to the standard of utility as a political principle to assess social policies. The necessity for such a principle arises because the political process is not a competitive one and these decisions cannot be left to the market. Some other method must be found to reconcile divergent interests. Edgeworth believes that the principle of utility would be agreed to by self-interested parties as the desired criterion. His thought seems to be that over the long run of many occasions, the policy of maximizing utility on each occasion is most likely to give the greatest utility for any person individually. Consistent application of this standard to taxation and property legislation, and so on, is calculated to give the best results from any one man's point of view. Therefore by adopting this principle self-interested parties have reasonable assurance that they will not lose out in the end and, in fact, will best improve their prospects.

The flaw in Edgeworth's idea is that the necessary assumptions are extremely unrealistic, especially in the case of the basic structure.[27] To state these assumptions is to see how implausible they are. We must suppose that the effects of the decisions which make up the political process are not only more or less independent, but roughly of the same order in their social results, which cannot be very great in any event, otherwise these effects could not be independent. Moreover, it must be assumed either that men move from one social position to another in random fashion and live long enough for gains and losses to average out, or else that there is some mechanism which insures that legislation guided by the principle of utility distributes its favors evenly over time. But clearly society is not a stochastic process of this type; and some questions

26. See F. Y. Edgeworth, *Mathematical Psychics* (London, 1888), pp. 52–56, and the first pages of "The Pure Theory of Taxation," *Economic Journal*, vol. 7 (1897). See also R. B. Brandt, *Ethical Theory* (Englewood Cliffs, N.J., Prentice Hall, Inc., 1959), pp. 376f.
27. Here I apply to Edgeworth an argument used by I. M. D. Little in his *Critique of Welfare Economics*, 2nd ed. (Oxford, The Clarendon Press, 1957), against a proposal of J. R. Hicks. See pp. 93f, 113f.

of social policy are much more vital than others, often causing large and enduring shifts in the institutional distribution of advantages.

Consider, for example, the case where a society is contemplating a historic change in its trade policies with foreign countries. The question is whether it shall remove long-standing tariffs on the import of agricultural products in order to obtain cheaper foodstuffs for workers in new industries. The fact that the change is justified on utilitarian grounds does not mean that it will not permanently affect the relative positions of those belonging to the landed and the industrial classes. Edgeworth's reasoning holds only when each of the many decisions has a relatively small and temporary influence on distributive shares and there is some institutional device insuring randomness. Under realistic assumptions, then, his argument can establish at best only that the principle of utility has a subordinate place as a legislative standard for lesser questions of policy. But this clearly implies that the principle fails for the main problems of social justice. The pervasive and continuing influence of our initial place in society and of our native endowments, and of the fact that the social order is one system, is what characterizes the problem of justice in the first place. We must not be enticed by mathematically attractive assumptions into pretending that the contingencies of men's social positions and the asymmetries of their situations somehow even out in the end. Rather, we must choose our conception of justice fully recognizing that this is not and cannot be the case.

It seems, then, that if the principle of average utility is to be accepted, the parties must reason from the principle of insufficient reason. They must follow what some have called the Laplacean rule for choice under uncertainty. The possibilities are identified in some natural way and each assigned the same likelihood. No general facts about society are offered to support these assignments; the parties carry on with probabilistic calculations as if information had not run out. Now I cannot discuss here the concept of probability, but a few points should be noted.[28] First of all, it may be

28. William Fellner, *Probability and Profit*, pp. 210–233, contains a useful bibliography with brief commentaries. Particularly important for the recent development of the so-called Bayesian point of view is L. J. Savage, *The Foundations*

surprising that the meaning of probability should arise as a problem in moral philosophy, especially in the theory of justice. It is, however, the inevitable consequence of the contract doctrine which conceives of moral philosophy as part of the theory of rational choice. Considerations of probability are bound to enter in given the way in which the initial situation is defined. The veil of ignorance leads directly to the problem of choice under uncertainty. Of course, it is possible to regard the parties as perfect altruists and to assume that they reason as if they are certain to be in the position of each person. This interpretation of the initial situation removes the element of risk and uncertainty (§ 30).

In justice as fairness, however, there is no way to avoid this question entirely. The essential thing is not to allow the principles chosen to depend on special attitudes toward risk. For this reason the veil of ignorance also rules out the knowledge of these inclinations: the parties do not know whether or not they have a characteristic aversion to taking chances. As far as possible the choice of a conception of justice should depend on a rational assessment of accepting risks unaffected by peculiar individual preferences for taking chances one way or the other. Of course, a social system may take advantage of these varying propensities by having institutions that permit them full play for common ends. But ideally anyway, the basic design of the system should not depend on one of these attitudes (§ 81). Therefore, it is not an argument for the two principles of justice that they express a peculiarly conservative point of view about taking chances in the original position. What must be shown is that choosing as if one had such an aversion is rational given the unique features of that situation irrespective of any special attitudes toward risk.

Secondly, I have simply assumed that judgments of probability, if they are to be grounds of rational decision, must have an objective basis, that is, a basis in knowledge of particular facts (or in reasonable beliefs). This evidence need not take the form of reports of relative frequencies but it should provide grounds for estimating the relative strength of the various tendencies that affect the out-

---

of Statistics (New York, John Wiley and Sons, Inc., 1954). For a guide to the philosophical literature, see H. E. Kyburg, *Probability and Inductive Logic* (Riverside, N.J., Macmillan, 1970).

come. The necessity for objective reasons is all the more urgent in view of the fundamental significance of the choice in the original position and the fact that the parties want their decision to appear well founded to others. I shall assume, therefore, to fill out the description of the original position, that the parties discount estimates of likelihoods not supported by a knowledge of particular facts and that derive largely if not solely from the principle of insufficient reason. The requirement of objective grounds does not seem to be in dispute between neo-Bayesian theorists and those adhering to more classical ideas. The controversy in this case is how far intuitive and imprecise estimates of likelihoods based on common sense and the like should be incorporated into the formal apparatus of the theory of probability rather than used in an ad hoc way to adjust the conclusions reached by methods that leave this information out of account.[29] Here neo-Bayesians have a strong case. Surely it is better when possible to use our intuitive knowledge and common sense hunches in a systematic and not in an irregular and unexplained manner. But none of this affects the contention that judgments of probability must have some objective basis in the known facts about society if they are to be rational grounds of decision in the special situation of the original position.

The last difficulty I shall mention here raises a deep problem. Although I cannot deal with it properly, it should not be passed over. The trouble arises from the peculiarity of the expectation in the final step of the reasoning for the average principle. When expectations are computed in the normal case, the utilities of the alternatives (the u_i in the expression $\Sigma p_i u_i$) are derived from a single system of preferences, namely those of the individual making the choice. The utilities represent the worth of the alternatives for this person as estimated by his scheme of values. In the present case, however, each utility is based on the preferences of a different person. There are as many distinct persons as there are utilities. Of course, it is clear that this reasoning presupposes interpersonal comparisons. But leaving aside for the moment the problem of defining these, the point to notice here is that the individual is thought to choose as if he has no aims at all which he counts as his own.

29. See Fellner, *Probability and Profit*, pp. 48–67, and Luce and Raiffa, *Games and Decisions*, pp. 318–334.

doesn't his idea assume this also

He takes a chance on being any one of a number of persons complete with each individual's system of ends, abilities, and social position. We may wonder then whether this expectation is a meaningful one. Since there is no one scheme of preferences by which its estimates have been arrived at, it appears to lack the necessary unity.

To clarify this problem, let us distinguish between evaluating objective situations and evaluating aspects of the person: abilities, traits of character, and system of aims. Now from our point of view it is often easy enough to appraise another individual's situation as specified say by his social position, wealth, and the like, or by his prospects in terms of primary goods. We put ourselves in his shoes, complete with our character and preferences (not his), and take account of how our plans would be affected. We can go much further. We can assess the worth to us of being in another's place with at least some of his traits and aims. Knowing our plan of life, we can decide whether it would be rational for us to have those traits and aims, and therefore advisable for us to develop and encourage them if we can. These matters I shall discuss in Chapter VII. It suffices to observe here that what we cannot do is to evaluate another person's total circumstances, his objective situation plus his character and system of ends, without any reference to the details of our conception of our good. If we are to judge these things from our standpoint at all, we must know what our plan of life is. The worth to us of the circumstances of others is not, as the constructed expectation assumes, its value to them.

Furthermore, as we have seen, the clearest basis for interpersonal comparisons is in terms of primary goods, things that every rational person is presumed to want whatever else he wants. The more we ascend to the higher aims and aspects of the person and try to assess their worth to us, the more tenuous the procedure becomes. The reason for this is that these evaluations contemplate more fundamental changes in our way of life, more far-reaching revisions in our plans. Indeed, it seems pointless to try to define a measure between persons which includes the full range of final ends. The problem is similar to comparing different styles of art. There are simply many things in which human beings become engaged and find fully worthwhile depending upon their inclinations. Of course, the utilitarian could concede this objection, accept the account of primary goods, and then define his principle in terms of the relevant indexes of these. This involves a major change in the theory which I shall not follow up. I shall confine the discussion to the standard view.

Thus the expectation finally arrived at in the reasoning for the average principle seems spurious for two reasons: it is not, as expectations should be, founded on one system of aims; and since the veil of ignorance excludes the knowledge of the parties' conception of their good, the worth to a person of the circumstances of others simply cannot be assessed. The argument ends up with a purely formal expression for an expectation that is without meaning. This difficulty about expectations is analogous to that concerning the knowledge of probabilities. In both instances the reasoning carries on with these notions after the basis for their legitimate use has been ruled out by the conditions of the original position.

29. SOME MAIN GROUNDS FOR THE TWO PRINCIPLES OF JUSTICE

In this section my aim is to use the conditions of publicity and finality to give some of the main arguments for the two principles of justice. I shall rely upon the fact that for an agreement to be valid, the parties must be able to honor it under all relevant and foreseeable circumstances. There must be a rational assurance that one can carry through. The arguments I shall adduce fit under the heuristic schema suggested by the reasons for following the maximin rule. That is, they help to show that the two principles are an adequate minimum conception of justice in a situation of great uncertainty. Any further advantages that might be won by the principle of utility, or whatever, are highly problematical, whereas the hardship if things turn out badly are intolerable. It is at this point that the concept of a contract has a definite role: it suggests the condition of publicity and sets limits upon what can be agreed to. Thus justice as fairness uses the concept of contract to a greater extent than the discussion so far might suggest.

The first confirming ground for the two principles can be explained in terms of what I earlier referred to as the strains of commitment. I said (§ 25) that the parties have a capacity for justice in the sense that they can be assured that their undertaking is not in vain. Assuming that they have taken everything into account, including the general facts of moral psychology, they can rely on one another to adhere to the principles adopted. Thus they consider the strains of commitment. They cannot enter into agreements that may have consequences they cannot accept. They will avoid those that they can adhere to only with great difficulty. Since the original agreement is final and made in perpetuity, there is no second chance. In view of the serious nature of the possible consequences, the question of the burden of commitment is especially acute. A person is choosing once and for all the standards which are to govern his life prospects. Moreover, when we enter an agreement we must be able to honor it even should the worst possibilities prove to be the case. Otherwise we have not acted in good faith. Thus the parties must weigh with care whether they will be able to stick by their commitment in all circumstances. Of course, in answering this question they have only a general knowledge of human psychology to go on. But this information is enough to tell which conception of justice involves the greater stress.

In this respect the two principles of justice have a definite advantage. Not only do the parties protect their basic rights but they insure themselves against the worst eventualities. They run no chance of having to acquiesce in a loss of freedom over the course of their life for the sake of a greater good enjoyed by others, an undertaking that in actual circumstances they might not be able to keep. Indeed, we might wonder whether such an agreement can be made in good faith at all. Compacts of this sort exceed the capacity of human nature. How can the parties possibly know, or be sufficiently sure, that they can keep such an agreement? Certainly they cannot base their confidence on a general knowledge of moral psychology. To be sure, any principle chosen in the original position may require a large sacrifice for some. The beneficiaries of clearly unjust institutions (those founded on principles which have no claim to acceptance) may find it hard to reconcile themselves to the changes that will have to be made. But in this case they will know that they could not have maintained their position anyway.

Yet should a person gamble with his liberties and substantive interests hoping that the application of the principle of utility might secure him a greater well-being, he may have difficulty abiding by his undertaking. He is bound to remind himself that he had the two principles of justice as an alternative. If the only possible candidates all involved similar risks, the problem of the strains of commitment would have to be waived. This is not the case, and judged in this light the two principles seem distinctly superior.

A second consideration invokes the condition of publicity as well as that of the constraints on agreements. I shall present the argument in terms of the question of psychological stability. Earlier I stated that a strong point in favor of a conception of justice is that it generates its own support. When the basic structure of society is publicly known to satisfy its principles for an extended period of time, those subject to these arrangements tend to develop a desire to act in accordance with these principles and to do their part in institutions which exemplify them. A conception of justice is stable when the public recognition of its realization by the social system tends to bring about the corresponding sense of justice. Now whether this happens depends, of course, on the laws of moral psychology and the availability of human motives. I shall discuss these matters later on (§§ 75–76). At the moment we may observe that the principle of utility seems to require a greater identification with the interests of others than the two principles of justice. Thus the latter will be a more stable conception to the extent that this identification is difficult to achieve. When the two principles are satisfied, each person's liberties are secured and there is a sense defined by the difference principle in which everyone is benefited by social cooperation. Therefore we can explain the acceptance of the social system and the principles it satisfies by the psychological law that persons tend to love, cherish, and support whatever affirms their own good. Since everyone's good is affirmed, all acquire inclinations to uphold the scheme.

When the principle of utility is satisfied, however, there is no such assurance that everyone benefits. Allegiance to the social system may demand that some should forgo advantages for the sake of the greater good of the whole. Thus the scheme will not be stable unless those who must make sacrifices strongly identify with interests broader than their own. But this is not easy to bring about. The sacrifices in question are not those asked in times of social emergency when all or some must pitch in for the common good. The principles of justice apply to the basic structure of the social system and to the determination of life prospects. What the principle of utility asks is precisely a sacrifice of these prospects. We are to accept the greater advantages of others as a sufficient reason for lower expectations over the whole course of our life. This is surely an extreme demand. In fact, when society is conceived as a system of cooperation designed to advance the good of its members, it seems quite incredible that some citizens should be expected, on the basis of political principles, to accept lower prospects of life for the sake of others. It is evident then why utilitarians should stress the role of sympathy in moral learning and the central place of benevolence among the moral virtues. Their conception of justice is threatened with instability unless sympathy and benevolence can be widely and intensely cultivated. Looking at the question from the standpoint of the original position, the parties recognize that it would be highly unwise if not irrational to choose principles which may have consequences so extreme that they could not accept them in practice. They would reject the principle of utility and adopt the more realistic idea of designing the social order on a principle of reciprocal advantage. We need not suppose, of course, that persons never make substantial sacrifices for one another, since moved by affection and ties of sentiment they often do. But such actions are not demanded as a matter of justice by the basic structure of society.

Furthermore, the public recognition of the two principles gives greater support to men's self-respect and this in turn increases the effectiveness of social cooperation. Both effects are reasons for choosing these principles. It is clearly rational for men to secure their self-respect. A sense of their own worth is necessary if they are to pursue their conception of the good with zest and to delight in its fulfillment. Self-respect is not so much a part of any rational plan of life as the sense that one's plan is worth carrying out. Now our self-respect normally depends upon the respect of others. Unless we feel that our endeavors are honored by them, it is difficult if not impossible for us to maintain the conviction that our ends are worth advancing (§ 67). Hence for this reason the parties would accept the natural duty of mutual respect which asks them to treat one another civilly and to be willing to explain the grounds of their actions, especially when the claims of others are overruled (§ 51). Moreover, one may assume that those who respect themselves are more likely to respect each other and conversely. Self-contempt leads to contempt of others and threatens their good as much as envy does. Self-respect is reciprocally self-supporting.

Thus a desirable feature of a conception of justice is that it should publicly express men's respect for one another. In this way they insure a sense of their own value. Now the two principles achieve this end. For when society follows these principles, everyone's good is included in a scheme of mutual benefit and this public affirmation in institutions of each man's endeavors supports men's self-esteem. The establishment of equal liberty and the operation of the difference principle are bound to have this effect. The two principles are equivalent, as I have remarked, to an undertaking to regard the distribution of natural abilities as a collective asset so that the more fortunate are to benefit only in ways that help those who have lost out. I do not say that the parties are moved by the ethical propriety of this idea. But there are reasons for them to accept this principle. For by arranging inequalities for reciprocal advantage and by abstaining from the exploitation of the contingencies of nature and social circumstance within a framework of equal liberty, persons express their respect for one another in the very constitution of their society. In this way they insure their self-esteem as it is rational for them to do.

Another way of putting this is to say that the principles of justice manifest in the basic structure of society men's desire to treat one another not as means only but as ends in themselves. I cannot examine Kant's view here.[30] Instead I shall freely interpret it in the light of the contract doctrine. The notion of treating men as ends in themselves and never as only a means obviously needs an explanation. There is even a question whether it is possible to realize. How can we always treat everyone as an end and never as a means only?

30. See *The Foundations of the Metaphysics of Morals,* pp. 427–430 of vol. IV of *Kants Gesammelten Schriften,* Preussische Akademie der Wissenschaften (Berlin, 1913), where the second formulation of the categorical imperative is introduced.

Certainly we cannot say that it comes to treating everyone by the same general principles, since this interpretation makes the concept equivalent to formal justice. On the contract interpretation treating men as ends in themselves implies at the very least treating them in accordance with the principles to which they would consent in an original position of equality. For in this situation men have equal representation as moral persons who regard themselves as ends and the principles they accept will be rationally designed to protect the claims of their person. The contract view as such defines a sense in which men are to be treated as ends and not as means only.

But the question arises whether there are substantive principles which convey this idea. If the parties wish to express this notion visibly in the basic structure of their society in order to secure each man's rational interest in his self-respect, which principles should they choose? Now it seems that the two principles of justice achieve this aim: for all have an equal liberty and the difference principle explicates the distinction between treating men as a means only and treating them also as ends in themselves. To regard persons as ends in themselves in the basic design of society is to agree to forgo those gains which do not contribute to their representative expectations. By contrast, to regard persons as means is to be prepared to impose upon them lower prospects of life for the sake of the higher expectations of others. Thus we see that the difference principle, which at first appears rather extreme, has a reasonable interpretation. If we further suppose that social cooperation among those who respect each other and themselves as manifest in their institutions is likely to be more effective and harmonious, the general level of expectations, assuming we could estimate it, may be higher when the two principles of justice are satisfied than one might otherwise have thought. The advantage of the principle of utility in this respect is no longer so clear.

The principle of utility presumably requires some to forgo greater life prospects for the sake of others. To be sure, it is not necessary that those having to make such sacrifices rationalize this demand by having a lesser appreciation of their own worth. It does not follow from the utilitarian doctrine that it is because their aims are trivial or unimportant that some individuals' expectations are less. Yet this may often be the case, and there is a sense, as we have just noted, in which utilitarianism does not regard persons as ends in themselves. And in any event, the parties must consider the general facts of moral psychology. Surely it is natural to experience a loss of self-esteem, a weakening of our sense of the value of accomplishing our aims, when we must accept a lesser prospect of life for the sake of others. This is particularly likely to be so when social cooperation is arranged for the good of individuals. That is, those with greater advantages do not claim that they are necessary to preserve certain religious or cultural values which everyone has a duty to maintain. We are not here considering a doctrine of traditional order nor the principle of perfectionism, but rather the principle of utility. In this instance, then, men's self-esteem hinges on how they regard one another. If the parties accept the utility criterion, they will lack the support to their self-respect provided by the public commitment of others to arrange inequalities to everyone's advantage and to guarantee an equal liberty for all. In a public utilitarian society men will find it more difficult to be confident of their own worth.

The utilitarian may answer that in maximizing the average utility these matters are already taken into account. If, for example, the equal liberties are necessary for men's self-respect and the average utility is higher when they are affirmed, then of course they should be established. So far so good. But the point is that we must not lose sight of the publicity condition. This requires that in maximizing the average utility we do so subject to the constraint that the utilitarian principle is publicly accepted and followed as the fundamental charter of society. What we cannot do is to raise the average utility by encouraging men to adopt and apply non-utilitarian principles of justice. If, for whatever reasons, the public recognition of utilitarianism entails some loss of self-esteem, there is no way around this drawback. It is an unavoidable cost of the utilitarian scheme given our stipulations. Thus suppose that the average utility is actually greater should the two principles of justice be publicly affirmed and realized as the basis of the social structure. For the reasons mentioned, this may conceivably be the case. These principles would then represent the most attractive prospect, and on both lines of reasoning just examined, the two principles would be accepted. The utilitarian cannot reply that one is now really maximizing the average utility. In fact, the parties would have chosen the two principles of justice.

We should note, then, that utilitarianism, as I have defined it, is the view that the principle of utility is the correct principle for society's public conception of justice. And to show this one must argue that this criterion would be chosen in the original position. If we like, we can define a different variation of the initial situation in which the motivation assumption is that the parties want to adopt those principles that maximize average utility. The preceding remarks indicate that the two principles of justice may still be chosen. But if so, it is a mistake to call these principles—and the theory in which they appear—utilitarian. The motivation assumption by itself does not determine the character of the whole theory. In fact, the case for the principles of justice is strengthened if they would be chosen under different motivation assumptions. This indicates that the theory of justice is firmly grounded and not sensitive to slight changes in this condition. What we want to know is which conception of justice characterizes our considered judgments in reflective equilibrium and best serves as the public moral basis of society. Unless one maintains that this conception is given by the principle of utility, one is not a utilitarian.[31]

The advocate of utility can maintain, however, that this principle also gives a sense to the Kantian idea, namely, the sense provided by Bentham's formula "everybody to count for one, nobody for more than one." This means, as Mill remarks, that one person's happiness assumed to be equal in degree to another person's is to be counted exactly the same.[32] The weights in the additive function that represents the utility principle are identical for all individuals, and it is natural to take them as one. The principle of utility, one might say, treats persons both as ends and as means. It treats them as ends by assigning the same (positive) weight to the welfare of

31. Thus while Brandt holds that a society's moral code is to be publicly recognized, and that the best code from a philosophical standpoint is the one that maximizes average utility, he does not maintain that the principle of utility must belong to the code itself. In fact, he denies that within the public morality the final court of appeal need be to utility. Thus by the definition in the text, his view is not utilitarian. See "Some Merits of One Form of Rule Utilitarianism," *University of Colorado Studies* (Boulder, Colo., 1967), pp. 58f.

32. *Utilitarianism*, ch. V, par. 36.

each; it treats them as means by allowing higher life prospects for some to counterbalance lower life prospects for others who are already less favorably situated. The two principles of justice give a stronger and more characteristic interpretation to Kant's idea. They rule out even the tendency to regard men as means to one another's welfare. In the design of the social system we must treat persons solely as ends and not in any way as means. The preceding arguments draw upon this more stringent interpretation.

I shall conclude this section by observing that the conditions of generality of principle, universality of application, and limited information as to natural and social status are not enough by themselves to characterize the original position of justice as fairness. The reasoning for the average principle of utility shows this. These conditions are necessary but not sufficient. The original position requires the parties to make a collective agreement, and therefore the restrictions on valid undertakings as well as the publicity and finality conditions are an essential part of the argument for the two principles. I have discussed the role of these constraints in connection with the strains of commitment and the problem of stability. Once these considerations are established the doubts about the reasoning for the average principle become more serious.

The tentative conclusion, then, is that the balance of reasons clearly favors the two principles of justice over the principle of average utility, and assuming transitivity, over the classical doctrine as well. Insofar as the conception of the original position is used in the justification of principles in everyday life, the claim that one would agree to the two principles of justice is perfectly credible. There is no reason offhand to think that it is not sincere. In order for this profession to be convincing, it is not necessary that one should have actually given and honored this undertaking. Thus it is able to serve as a conception of justice in the public acceptance of which persons can recognize one another's good faith.

30. CLASSICAL UTILITARIANISM, IMPARTIALITY, AND BENEVOLENCE

I now want to compare classical utilitarianism with the two principles of justice. As we have seen, the parties in the original position would reject the classical principle in favor of that of maximizing average utility. Since they are concerned to advance their own interests, they have no desire to maximize the total (or the net balance) of satisfactions. For similar reasons they would prefer the two principles of justice. From a contractarian point of view, then, the classical principle ranks below both of these alternatives. It must, therefore, have an entirely different derivation, for it is historically the most important form of utilitarianism. The great utilitarians who espoused it were certainly under no misapprehension that it would be chosen in what I have called the original position. Some of them, particularly Sidgwick, clearly recognized the average principle as an alternative and rejected it.[33] We saw in the first chapter that the classical view is closely related to the concept of the impartial sympathetic spectator. I now want to look at this concept in order to clarify the intuitive basis of the traditional doctrine.

Consider the following definition reminiscent of Hume and Adam Smith. Something is right, a social system say, when an ideally rational and impartial spectator would approve of it from a general point of view should he possess all the relevant knowledge of the circumstances. A rightly ordered society is one meeting the approval of such an ideal observer.[34] Now there may be several problems with this definition, for example, whether the notions of approval and relevant knowledge can be specified without circularity. But I shall leave these questions aside. The essential point here is that there is no conflict so far between this definition and justice as fairness. For suppose we define the concept of right by saying that something is right if and only if it satisfies the principles which would be chosen in the original position to apply to things of its kind. It may well be the case that an ideally rational and impartial

33. *Methods of Ethics*, pp. 415f.

34. See Roderick Firth, "Ethical Absolutism and the Ideal Observer," *Philosophy and Phenomenological Research*, vol. 12 (1952); and F. C. Sharp, *Good and Ill Will* (Chicago, University of Chicago Press, 1950), pp. 156–162. For Hume's account, see *Treatise of Human Nature*, ed. L. A. Selby-Bigge (Oxford, 1888), bk. III, pt. III, sec. I, especially pp. 574–584; and for Adam Smith, *The Theory of Moral Sentiments*, in L. A. Selby-Bigge, *British Moralists*, vol. I (Oxford, 1897), pp. 257–277. A general discussion is found in C. D. Broad, "Some Reflections on Moral-Sense Theories in Ethics," *Proceedings of the Aristotelian Society*, vol. 45 (1944–45). See also W. K. Kneale, "Objectivity in Morals," *Philosophy*, vol. 25 (1950)

spectator would approve of a social system if and only if it satisfies the principles of justice which would be adopted in the contract scheme. The definitions may both be true of the same things. This possibility is not ruled out by the ideal observer definition. Since this definition makes no specific psychological assumptions about the impartial spectator, it yields no principles to account for his approvals under ideal conditions. One who accepts this definition is free to accept justice as fairness for this purpose: one simply allows that an ideal observer would approve of social systems to the extent that they satisfy the two principles of justice. There is an essential difference, then, between these two definitions of right. The impartial spectator definition makes no assumptions from which the principles of right and justice may be derived.[35] It is designed instead to single out certain central features characteristic of moral discussion, the fact that we try to appeal to our considered judgments after conscientious reflection, and the like. The contractarian definition is more ambitious: it attempts to provide a deductive basis for the principles that account for these judgments. The conditions of the initial situation and the motivation of the parties are intended to set out the necessary premises to achieve this end.

Now while it is possible to supplement the impartial spectator definition with the contract point of view, there are other ways of giving it a deductive basis. Thus suppose that the ideal observer is thought of as a perfectly sympathetic being. Then there is a natural derivation of the classical principle of utility along the following lines. An institution is right, let us say, if an ideally sympathetic and impartial spectator would approve of it more strongly than any other institution feasible in the circumstances. For simplicity we may assume, as Hume sometimes does, that approval is a special kind of pleasure which arises more or less intensely in contemplating the workings of institutions and their consequences for the happiness of those engaged in them. This special pleasure is the result of sympathy. In Hume's account it is quite literally a reproduction in

35. Thus Firth holds, for example, that an ideal observer has various general interests though not particular ones; and that these interests are indeed necessary if such an observer is to have any significant moral reactions. But nothing specific is said about the content of these interests that enables one to work out how the approvals and disapprovals of an ideal observer would be determined. See "Ethical Absolutism and the Ideal Observer," pp. 336–341.

our experience of the satisfactions and pleasures which we recognize to be felt by others.[36] Thus an impartial spectator experiences this pleasure in contemplating the social system in proportion to the net sum of pleasure felt by those affected by it. The strength of his approval corresponds to, or measures, the amount of satisfaction in the society surveyed. Therefore his expressions of approval will be given according to the classical principle of utility. To be sure, as Hume observes, sympathy is not a strong feeling. Not only is self-interest likely to inhibit the frame of mind in which we experience it, but self-interest tends to override its dictates in determining our actions. Yet when men do regard their institutions from a general point of view, Hume thought that sympathy is the main psychological propensity at work, and it will at least guide our considered moral judgments. However weak sympathy may be, it nevertheless constitutes a common ground for bringing our moral opinions into agreement. Men's natural capacity for sympathy suitably generalized provides the perspective from which they can reach an understanding on a common conception of justice.

Thus we arrive at the following view. A rational and impartial sympathetic spectator is a person who takes up a general perspective: he assumes a position where his own interests are not at stake and he possesses all the requisite information and powers of reasoning. So situated he is equally responsive and sympathetic to the desires and satisfactions of everyone affected by the social system. His own interests do not thwart his natural sympathy for the aspirations of others and he has perfect knowledge of these endeavors and what they mean for those who have them. Responding to the interests of each person in the same way, an impartial spectator gives free reign to his capacity for sympathetic identification by viewing each person's situation as it affects that person. Thus he imagines himself in the place of each person in turn, and when he has done this for everyone, the strength of his approval is determined by the balance of satisfactions to which he has sympathetically responded. When he has made the rounds of all the affected parties, so to speak, his

36. See *A Treatise of Human Nature*, bk. II, pt. I, sec. XI, and bk. III, pt. I, sec. I, the first parts of each, and sec. VI. In the edition of L. A. Selby-Bigge, this is pp. 316–320, 575–580, and 618f.

approval expresses the total result. Sympathetically imagined pains cancel out sympathetically imagined pleasures, and the final intensity of approval corresponds to the net sum of positive feeling.

It is instructive to note a contrast between the features of the sympathetic spectator and the conditions defining the original position. The elements of the sympathetic spectator definition, impartiality, possession of relevant knowledge, and powers of imaginative identification, are to assure the complete and accurate response of natural sympathy. Impartiality prevents distortions of bias and self-interest; knowledge and the capacity for identification guarantee that the aspirations of others will be accurately appreciated. We can understand the point of the definition once we see that its parts are designed to give free scope to the operation of fellow feeling. In the original position, by contrast, the parties are mutually disinterested rather than sympathetic; but lacking knowledge of their natural assets or social situation, they are forced to view their arrangements in a general way. In the one case perfect knowledge and sympathetic identification result in a correct estimate of the net sum of satisfaction; in the other, mutual disinterestedness subject to a veil of ignorance leads to the two principles of justice.

Now, as I mentioned in the first chapter, there is a sense in which classical utilitarianism fails to take seriously the distinction between persons. The principle of rational choice for one man is taken as the principle of social choice as well. How does this view come about? It is the consequence, as we can now see, of wanting to give a deductive basis to an ideal observer definition of right, and of presuming that men's natural capacity for sympathy provides the only perspective from which their moral judgments can be brought into agreement. With this background, it is tempting to adopt the approvals of the impartial sympathetic spectator as the standard of justice. The one person of the classical doctrine is, then, identical with the impartial sympathetic spectator. This spectator is the one self who includes all desires and satisfactions within one experience as he imaginatively identifies in turn with the members of society. It is he who compares their aspirations and approves of institutions according to the extent to which they satisfy the one system of desire that he constructs as he views everyone's desires as if they were

187

his own. The classical view results, then, in impersonality, in the conflation of all desires into one system of desire.[37]

From the standpoint of justice as fairness there is no reason why the persons in the original position would agree to the approvals of an impartial sympathetic spectator as the standard of justice. This agreement has all the drawbacks of the classical principle of utility to which it is equivalent. If, however, the parties are conceived as perfect altruists, that is, as persons whose desires conform to the

37. The most explicit and developed statement of this view I know of is that found in C. I. Lewis, *The Analysis of Knowledge and Valuation* (La Salle, Ill., Open Court Publishing Co., 1946). The whole of sec. 13 of ch. 18 is relevant here. Lewis says: "Value to more than one person is to be assessed as if their several experiences of value were included in that of a single person." Page 550. J. J. C. Smart, in reply to the idea that fairness is a constraint on maximizing happiness, puts the point neatly when he asks: "if it is rational for me to choose the pain of a visit to the dentist in order to prevent the pain of toothache, why is it not rational of me to choose a pain for Jones, similar to that of my visit to the dentist, if that is the only way in which I can prevent a pain, equal to that of my toothache, for Robinson?" *An Outline of a System of Utilitarian Ethics*, p. 26. Another brief statement is in R. M. Hare, *Freedom and Reason* (Oxford, The Clarendon Press, 1963), p. 123.

Among the classical writers the conflation of all desires into one system is not to my knowledge clearly asserted. But it seems implicit in Edgeworth's comparison between "mécanique celeste" and "mécanique sociale" and in his idea that someday the latter may take its place with the former, both being founded upon one maximum principle, "the supreme pinnacle of moral as of physical science." He says: "As the movements of each particle, constrained or loose, in a material cosmos are continually subordinated to one maximum sum-total of accumulated energy, so the movements of each soul, whether selfishly isolated or linked sympathetically, may continually be realising the maximum energy of pleasure, the Divine love of the universe." *Mathematical Psychics*, p. 12. Sidgwick is always more restrained and there are only hints of the doctrine in *The Methods of Ethics*. Thus at one point he may be read to say that the notion of universal good is constructed from the goods of different individuals in the same way as the good (on the whole) of a single individual is constructed from the different goods that succeed one another in the temporal series of his conscious states (p. 382). This interpretation is confirmed by his saying later: "If, then, when any one hypothetically concentrates his attention on himself, Good is naturally and almost inevitably conceived to be pleasure, we may reasonably conclude that the Good of any number of similar beings, whatever their mutual relations may be, cannot be essentially different in quality." Page 405. Sidgwick also believed that the axiom of rational prudence is no less problematical than that of rational benevolence. We can equally well ask why we should concern ourselves about our own future feelings as about the feelings of other persons. Pages 418f. Presumably he thought the answer identical in each case: it is necessary to achieve the greatest sum of satisfaction. These remarks seem to suggest the conflation view.

approvals of such a spectator, then the classical principle would, of course, be adopted. The greater net balance of happiness with which to sympathize, the more a perfect altruist achieves his desire. Thus we arrive at the unexpected conclusion that while the average principle of utility is the ethic of a single rational individual (with no aversion to risk) who tries to maximize his own prospects, the classical doctrine is the ethic of perfect altruists. A surprising contrast indeed! By looking at these principles from the standpoint of the original position, we see that a different complex of ideas underlies them. Not only are they based upon contrary motivational assumptions, but the notion of taking chances has a part in one view yet none in the other. In the classical conception one chooses as if one will for certain live through the experiences of each individual, seriatim as Lewis says, and then sum up the result.[38] The idea of taking a chance on which person one will turn out to be does not arise. Thus even if the concept of the original position served no other purpose, it would be a useful analytic device. Although the various principles of utility may often have similar practical consequences, we can see that these conceptions derive from markedly distinct assumptions.

There is, however, a peculiar feature of perfect altruism that deserves mention. A perfect altruist can fulfill his desire only if someone else has independent, or first-order, desires. To illustrate this fact, suppose that in deciding what to do all vote to do what everyone else wants to do. Obviously nothing gets settled; in fact, there is nothing to decide. For a problem of justice to arise at least two persons must want to do something other than whatever everyone else wants to do. It is impossible, then, to assume that the parties are simply perfect altruists. They must have some separate interests which may conflict. Justice as fairness makes this assumption, in the form of mutual disinterest, the main motivational condition of the original position. While this may prove to be an oversimplification, one can develop a reasonably comprehensive conception of justice on this basis.

Some philosophers have accepted the utilitarian principle because they believed that the idea of an impartial sympathetic spectator is the correct interpretation of impartiality. Indeed, Hume thought

38. See *The Analysis of Knowledge and Valuation*, p. 547.

that it offered the only perspective from which moral judgments could be made coherent and brought into line. Now moral judgments are, or should be, impartial; but there is another way to achieve this, another point of view by reference to which our judgments of justice may be organized. Justice as fairness provides what we want. An impartial judgment, we can say, is one rendered in accordance with the principles which would be chosen in the original position. An impartial person is one whose situation and character enable him to judge in accordance with these principles without bias or prejudice. Instead of defining impartiality from the standpoint of a sympathetic observer who responds to the conflicting interests of others as if they were his own, we define impartiality from the standpoint of the litigants themselves. It is they who must choose their conception of justice once and for all in an original position of equality. They must decide by which principles their claims against one another are to be settled, and he who is to judge between men serves as their agent. The fault of the utilitarian doctrine is that it mistakes impersonality for impartiality.

The preceding remarks naturally lead one to ask what sort of theory of justice would result if one adopted the sympathetic spectator idea but did not characterize this spectator as conflating all desires into one system. Hume's conception provides one modus operandi for benevolence, but is it the only possibility? Now love clearly has among its main elements the desire to advance the other person's good as this person's rational self-love would require. Very often how one is to realize this desire is clear enough. The difficulty is that the love of several persons is thrown into confusion once the claims of these persons conflict. If we reject the classical doctrine, what does the love of mankind enjoin? It is quite pointless to say that one is to judge the situation as benevolence dictates. This assumes that we are wrongly swayed by self-concern. Our problem lies elsewhere. Benevolence is at sea as long as its many loves are in opposition in the persons of its many objects.

We might try out here the idea that a benevolent person is to be guided by the principles someone would choose if he knew that he is to split, so to speak, into the many members of society.[39] That is, he

39. This idea is found in Thomas Nagel, *The Possibility of Altruism* (Oxford, The Clarendon Press, 1970), pp. 140f.

is to imagine that he is to divide into a plurality of persons whose life and experiences will be distinct in the usual way. Experiences and memories are to remain each person's own; and there is to be no conflation of desires and memories into those of one person. Since a single individual is literally to become many persons, there is no question of guessing which one; once again the problem of taking chances does not arise. Now knowing this (or believing it), which conception of justice would a person choose for a society comprised of these individuals? As this person would, let us suppose, love this plurality of persons as he loves himself, perhaps the principles he would choose characterize the aims of benevolence.

Leaving aside the difficulties in the idea of splitting that may arise from problems about personal identity, two things seem evident. First of all, it is still unclear what a person would decide, since the situation does not offhand provide an answer. But secondly, the two principles of justice now seem a relatively more plausible choice than the classical principle of utility. The latter is no longer the natural preference, and this suggests that the conflation of persons into one is indeed at the root of the classical view. The reason why the situation remains obscure is that love and benevolence are second-order notions: they seek to further the good of beloved individuals that is already given. If the claims of these goods clash, benevolence is at a loss as to how to proceed, as long anyway as it treats these individuals as separate persons. These higher-order sentiments do not include principles of right to adjudicate these conflicts. Therefore a love of mankind that wishes to preserve the distinction of persons, to recognize the separateness of life and experience, will use the two principles of justice to determine its aims when the many goods it cherishes are in opposition. This is simply to say that this love is guided by what individuals themselves would consent to in a fair initial situation which gives them equal representation as moral persons. We now see why nothing would have been gained by attributing benevolence to the parties in the original position.

We must, however, distinguish between the love of mankind and the sense of justice. The difference is not that they are guided by different principles, since both include a desire to give justice. Rather, the former is manifest by the greater intensity and pervasiveness of this desire, and in a readiness to fulfill all the natural duties in addition to that of justice, and even to go beyond their requirements. The love of mankind is more comprehensive than the sense of justice and prompts to acts of supererogation, whereas the latter does not. Thus we see that the assumption of the mutual disinterestedness of the parties does not prevent a reasonable interpretation of benevolence and of the love of mankind within the framework of justice as fairness. The fact that we start out assuming that the parties are mutually disinterested and have conflicting first-order desires still allows us to construct a comprehensive account. For once the principles of right and justice are on hand, they may be used to define the moral virtues just as in any other theory. The virtues are sentiments, that is, related families of dispositions and propensities regulated by a higher-order desire, in this case a desire to act from the corresponding moral principles. Although justice as fairness begins by taking the persons in the original position as individuals, or more accurately as continuing strands, this is no obstacle to explicating the higher-order moral sentiments that serve to bind a community of persons together. In Part Three I shall return to these matters.

These remarks conclude the theoretical part of our discussion. I shall make no attempt to summarize this long chapter. Having set out the initial arguments in favor of the two principles of justice over the two forms of utility, it is time to see how these principles apply to institutions and how well they seem to match our considered judgments. Only in this way can we become clearer about their meaning and find out whether they are an improvement over other conceptions.

PART TWO. INSTITUTIONS

CHAPTER IV. EQUAL LIBERTY

In the three chapters of Part Two my aim is to illustrate the content of the principles of justice. I shall do this by describing a basic structure that satisfies these principles and by examining the duties and obligations to which they give rise. The main institutions of this structure are those of a constitutional democracy. I do not argue that these arrangements are the only ones that are just. Rather my intention is to show that the principles of justice, which so far have been discussed in abstraction from institutional forms, define a workable political conception, and are a reasonable approximation to and extension of our considered judgments. In this chapter I begin by setting out a four-stage sequence that clarifies how the principles for institutions are to be applied. Two parts of the basic structure are briefly described and the concept of liberty defined. After this, three problems of equal liberty are discussed: equal liberty of conscience, political justice and equal political rights, and equal liberty of the person and its relation to the rule of law. I then take up the meaning of the priority of liberty, and conclude with a brief account of the Kantian interpretation of the original position.

31. THE FOUR-STAGE SEQUENCE

It is evident that some sort of framework is needed to simplify the application of the two principles of justice. For consider three kinds of judgments that a citizen has to make. First of all, he must judge the justice of legislation and social policies. But he also knows that his opinions will not always coincide with those of others, since men's judgments and beliefs are likely to differ especially when their interests are engaged. Therefore secondly, a citizen must decide which constitutional arrangements are just for reconciling conflicting opinions of justice. We may think of the political process as a machine which makes social decisions when the views of representatives and their constituents are fed into it. A citizen will regard some ways of designing this machine as more just than others. So a complete conception of justice is not only able to assess laws and policies but it can also rank procedures for selecting which political opinion is to be enacted into law. There is still a third problem. The citizen accepts a certain constitution as just, and he thinks that certain traditional procedures are appropriate, for example, the procedure of majority rule duly circumscribed. Yet since the political process is at best one of imperfect procedural justice, he must ascertain when the enactments of the majority are to be complied with and when they can be rejected as no longer binding. In short, he must be able to determine the grounds and limits of political duty and obligation. Thus a theory of justice has to deal with at least three types of questions, and this indicates that it may be useful to think of the principles as applied in a several-stage sequence.

At this point, then, I introduce an elaboration of the original position. So far I have supposed that once the principles of justice are chosen the parties return to their place in society and henceforth judge their claims on the social system by these principles. But if several intermediate stages are imagined to take place in a definite sequence, this sequence may give us a schema for sorting out the complications that must be faced. Each stage is to represent an appropriate point of view from which certain kinds of questions are considered.[1] Thus I suppose that after the parties have adopted the principles of justice in the original position, they move to a constitutional convention. Here they are to decide upon the justice of political forms and choose a constitution: they are delegates, so to speak, to such a convention. Subject to the constraints of the principles of justice already chosen, they are to design a system for the constitutional

1. The idea of a four-stage sequence is suggested by the United States Constitution and its history. For some remarks as to how this sequence might be interpreted theoretically and related to procedural justice, see K. J. Arrow, *Social Choice and Individual Values*, 2nd ed. (New York, John Wiley and Sons, 1963), pp. 89–91.

powers of government and the basic rights of citizens. It is at this stage that they weigh the justice of procedures for coping with diverse political views. Since the appropriate conception of justice has been agreed upon, the veil of ignorance is partially lifted. The persons in the convention have, of course, no information about particular individuals: they do not know their own social position, their place in the distribution of natural attributes, or their conception of the good. But in addition to an understanding of the principles of social theory, they now know the relevant general facts about their society, that is, its natural circumstances and resources, its level of economic advance and political culture, and so on. They are no longer limited to the information implicit in the circumstances of justice. Given their theoretical knowledge and the appropriate general facts about their society, they are to choose the most effective just constitution, the constitution that satisfies the principles of justice and is best calculated to lead to just and effective legislation.[2]

At this point we need to distinguish two problems. Ideally a just constitution would be a just procedure arranged to insure a just outcome. The procedure would be the political process governed by the constitution, the outcome the body of enacted legislation, while the principles of justice would define an independent criterion for both procedure and outcome. In pursuit of this ideal of perfect procedural justice (§ 14), the first problem is to design a just procedure. To do this the liberties of equal citizenship must be incorporated into and protected by the constitution. These liberties include those of liberty of conscience and freedom of thought, liberty of the person, and equal political rights. The political system, which I assume to be some form

2. It is important to distinguish the four-stage sequence and its conception of a constitutional convention from the kind of view of constitutional choice found in social theory and exemplified by J. M. Buchanan and Gordon Tullock, *The Calculus of Consent* (Ann Arbor, University of Michigan Press, 1963). The idea of the four-stage sequence is part of a moral theory, and does not belong to an account of the working of actual constitutions, except insofar as political agents are influenced by the conception of justice in question. In the contract doctrine, the principles of justice have already been agreed to, and our problem is to formulate a schema that will assist us in applying them. The aim is to characterize a just constitution and not to ascertain which sort of constitution would be adopted, or acquiesced in, under more or less realistic (though simplified) assumptions about political life, much less on individualistic assumptions of the kind characteristic of economic theory.

197

of constitutional democracy, would not be a just procedure if it did not embody these liberties.

Clearly any feasible political procedure may yield an unjust outcome. In fact, there is no scheme of procedural political rules which guarantees that unjust legislation will not be enacted. In the case of a constitutional regime, or indeed of any political form, the ideal of perfect procedural justice cannot be realized. The best attainable scheme is one of imperfect procedural justice. Nevertheless some schemes have a greater tendency than others to result in unjust laws. The second problem, then, is to select from among the procedural arrangements that are both just and feasible those which are most likely to lead to a just and effective legal order. Once again this is Bentham's problem of the artificial identification of interests, only here the rules (just procedure) are to be framed to give legislation (just outcome) likely to accord with the principles of justice rather than the principle of utility. To solve this problem intelligently requires a knowledge of the beliefs and interests that men in the system are liable to have and of the political tactics that they will find it rational to use given their circumstances. The delegates are assumed, then, to know these things. Provided they have no information about particular individuals including themselves, the idea of the original position is not affected.

In framing a just constitution I assume that the two principles of justice already chosen define an independent standard of the desired outcome. If there is no such standard, the problem of constitutional design is not well posed, for this decision is made by running through the feasible just constitutions (given, say, by enumeration on the basis of social theory) looking for the one that in the existing circumstances will most probably result in effective and just social arrangements. Now at this point we come to the legislative stage, to take the next step in the sequence. The justice of laws and policies is to be assessed from this perspective. Proposed bills are judged from the position of a representative legislator who, as always, does not know the particulars about himself. Statutes must satisfy not only the principles of justice but whatever limits are laid down in the constitution. By moving back and forth between the stages of the constitutional convention and the legislature, the best constitution is found.

Now the question whether legislation is just or unjust, especially in connection with economic and social policies, is commonly subject to reasonable differences of opinion. In these cases judgment frequently depends upon speculative political and economic doctrines and upon social theory generally. Often the best that we can say of a law or policy is that it is at least not clearly unjust. The application of the difference principle in a precise way normally requires more information than we can expect to have and, in any case, more than the application of the first principle. It is often perfectly plain and evident when the equal liberties are violated. These violations are not only unjust but can be clearly seen to be unjust: the injustice is manifest in the public structure of institutions. But this state of affairs is comparatively rare with social and economic policies regulated by the difference principle.

I imagine then a division of labor between stages in which each deals with different questions of social justice. This division roughly corresponds to the two parts of the basic structure. The first principle of equal liberty is the primary standard for the constitutional convention. Its main requirements are that the fundamental liberties of the person and liberty of conscience and freedom of thought be protected and that the political process as a whole be a just procedure. Thus the constitution establishes a secure common status of equal citizenship and realizes political justice. The second principle comes into play at the stage of the legislature. It dictates that social and economic policies be aimed at maximizing the long-term expectations of the least advantaged under conditions of fair equality of opportunity, subject to the equal liberties being maintained. At this point the full range of general economic and social facts is brought to bear. The second part of the basic structure contains the distinctions and hierarchies of political, economic, and social forms which are necessary for efficient and mutually beneficial social cooperation. Thus the priority of the first principle of justice to the second is reflected in the priority of the constitutional convention to the legislative stage.

The last stage is that of the application of rules to particular cases by judges and administrators, and the following of rules by citizens generally. At this stage everyone has complete access to all the facts. No limits on knowledge remain since the full system of rules has now been adopted and applies to persons in virtue of their characteristics and circumstances. However, it is not from this standpoint that we are

199

to decide the grounds and limits of political duty and obligation. This third type of problem belongs to partial compliance theory, and its principles are discussed from the point of view of the original position after those of ideal theory have been chosen (§ 39). Once these are on hand, we can view our particular situation from the perspective of the last stage, as for example in the cases of civil disobedience and conscientious refusal (§§ 57–59).

The availability of knowledge in the four-stage sequence is roughly as follows. Let us distinguish between three kinds of facts: the first principles of social theory (and other theories when relevant) and their consequences; general facts about society, such as its size and level of economic advance, its institutional structure and natural environment, and so on; and finally, particular facts about individuals such as their social position, natural attributes, and peculiar interests. In the original position the only particular facts known to the parties are those that can be inferred from the circumstances of justice. While they know the first principles of social theory, the course of history is closed to them; they have no information about how often society has taken this or that form, or which kinds of societies presently exist. In the next stages, however, the general facts about their society are made available to them but not the particularities of their own condition. Limitations on knowledge can be relaxed since the principles of justice are already chosen. The flow of information is determined at each stage by what is required in order to apply these principles intelligently to the kind of question of justice at hand, while at the same time any knowledge that is likely to give rise to bias and distortion and to set men against one another is ruled out. The notion of the rational and impartial application of principles defines the kind of knowledge that is admissible. At the last stage, clearly, there are no reasons for the veil of ignorance in any form, and all restrictions are lifted.

It is essential to keep in mind that the four-stage sequence is a device for applying the principles of justice. This scheme is part of the theory of justice as fairness and not an account of how constitutional conventions and legislatures actually proceed. It sets out a series of points of view from which the different problems of justice are to be settled, each point of view inheriting the constraints adopted at the preceding stages. Thus a just constitution is one that rational delegates subject to the restrictions of the second stage would adopt for their society. And similarly just laws and policies are those that would be enacted at the legislative stage. Of course, this test is often indeterminate: it is not always clear which of several constitutions, or economic and social arrangements, would be chosen. But when this is so, justice is to that extent likewise indeterminate. Institutions within the permitted range are equally just, meaning that they could be chosen; they are compatible with all the constraints of the theory. Thus on many questions of social and economic policy we must fall back upon a notion of quasi-pure procedural justice: laws and policies are just provided that they lie within the allowed range, and the legislature, in ways authorized by a just constitution, has in fact enacted them. This indeterminacy in the theory of justice is not in itself a defect. It is what we should expect. Justice as fairness will prove a worthwhile theory if it defines the range of justice more in accordance with our considered judgments than do existing theories, and if it singles out with greater sharpness the graver wrongs a society should avoid.

32. THE CONCEPT OF LIBERTY

In discussing the application of the first principle of justice I shall try to bypass the dispute about the meaning of liberty that has so often troubled this topic. The controversy between the proponents of negative and positive liberty as to how freedom should be defined is one I shall leave aside. I believe that for the most part this debate is not concerned with definitions at all, but rather with the relative values of the several liberties when they come into conflict. Thus one might want to maintain, as Constant did, that the so-called liberty of the moderns is of greater value than the liberty of the ancients. While both sorts of freedom are deeply rooted in human aspirations, freedom of thought and liberty of conscience, freedom of the person and the civil liberties, ought not to be sacrificed to political liberty, to the freedom to participate equally in political affairs.[3] This question

3. See Constant's essay *Ancient and Modern Liberty* (1819). His ideas on this are discussed by Guido de Ruggiero, *The History of European Liberalism*, trans. R. G. Collingwood (Oxford, The Clarendon Press, 1927), pp. 159–164,

is clearly one of substantive political philosophy, and a theory of right and justice is required to answer it. Questions of definition can have at best but an ancillary role.

Therefore I shall simply assume that liberty can always be explained by a reference to three items: the agents who are free, the restrictions or limitations which they are free from, and what it is that they are free to do or not to do. Complete explanations of liberty provide the relevant information about these three things.[4] Very often certain matters are clear from the context and a full explanation is unnecessary. The general description of liberty, then, has the following form: this or that person (or persons) is free (or not free) from this or that constraint (or set of constraints) to do (or not to do) so and so. Associations as well as natural persons may be free or not free, and constraints may range from duties and prohibitions defined by law to the coercive influences arising from public opinion and social pressure. For the most part I shall discuss liberty in connection with constitutional and legal restrictions. In these cases liberty is a certain structure of institutions, a certain system of public rules defining rights and duties. Set in this background, liberty always has the above three-part form. Moreover, just as there are various kinds of agents who may be free—persons, associations, and states—so there are many kinds of conditions that constrain them and innumerable sorts of things that they are or are not free to do. In this sense there are many different liberties which on occasion it may be useful to distinguish. Yet these distinctions can be made without introducing different senses of liberty.

Thus persons are at liberty to do something when they are free from certain constraints either to do it or not to do it and when their doing it or not doing it is protected from interference by other persons. If, for example, we consider liberty of conscience as defined by law, then individuals have this liberty when they are free to pursue

---

167–169. For a general discussion, see Isaiah Berlin, *Four Essays on Liberty* (London, Oxford University Press, 1969), esp. the third essay and pp. xxxvii–lxiii of the introduction; and G. G. MacCallum, "Negative and Positive Freedom," *Philosophical Review,* vol. 76 (1967).

4. Here I follow MacCallum, "Negative and Positive Freedom." See further Felix Oppenheim, *Dimensions of Freedom* (New York, St. Martin's Press, 1961), esp. pp. 109–118, 132–134, where a notion of social freedom is also triadically defined.

their moral, philosophical, or religious interests without legal restrictions requiring them to engage or not to engage in any particular form of religious or other practice, and when other men have a legal duty not to interfere. A rather intricate complex of rights and duties characterizes any particular liberty. Not only must it be permissible for individuals to do or not to do something, but government and other persons must have a legal duty not to obstruct. I shall not delineate these rights and duties in any detail, but shall suppose that we understand their nature well enough for our purposes.

Several brief comments. First of all, it is important to recognize that the basic liberties must be assessed as a whole, as one system. That is, the worth of one liberty normally depends upon the specification of the other liberties, and this must be taken into account in framing a constitution and in legislation generally. While it is by and large true that a greater liberty is preferable, this holds primarily for the system of liberty as a whole, and not for each particular liberty. Clearly when the liberties are left unrestricted they collide with one another. To illustrate by an obvious example, certain rules of order are necessary for intelligent and profitable discussion. Without the acceptance of reasonable procedures of inquiry and debate, freedom of speech loses its value. It is essential in this case to distinguish between rules of order and rules restricting the content of speech.[5] While rules of order limit our freedom, since we cannot speak whenever we please, they are required to gain the benefits of this liberty. Thus the delegates to a constitutional convention, or the members of the legislature, must decide how the various liberties are to be specified so as to yield the best total system of equal liberty. They have to balance one liberty against another. The best arrangement of the several liberties depends upon the totality of limitations to which they are subject, upon how they hang together in the whole scheme by which they are defined.

While the equal liberties may, therefore, be restricted, these limits are subject to certain criteria expressed by the meaning of equal liberty and the serial order of the two principles of justice. Offhand there are two ways of contravening the first principle. Liberty is unequal as when one class of persons has a greater liberty than another,

5. See Alexander Meiklejohn, *Free Speech and Its Relation to Self-Government* (New York, Harper and Brothers, 1948), ch. I, sec. 6.

or liberty is less extensive than it should be. Now all the liberties of equal citizenship must be the same for each member of society. Nevertheless some of the equal liberties may be more extensive than others, assuming that their extensions can be compared. More realistically, if it is supposed that at best each liberty can be measured on its own scale, then the various liberties can be broadened or narrowed according to how they affect one another. When lexical order holds, a basic liberty covered by the first principle can be limited only for the sake of liberty itself, that is, only to insure that the same liberty or a different basic liberty is properly protected and to adjust the one system of liberties in the best way. The adjustment of the complete scheme of liberty depends solely upon the definition and extent of the particular liberties. Of course, this scheme is always to be assessed from the standpoint of the representative equal citizen. From the perspective of the constitutional convention or the legislative stage (as appropriate) we are to ask which system it would be rational for him to prefer.

A final point. The inability to take advantage of one's rights and opportunities as a result of poverty and ignorance, and a lack of means generally, is sometimes counted among the constraints definitive of liberty. I shall not, however, say this, but rather I shall think of these things as affecting the worth of liberty, the value to individuals of the rights that the first principle defines. With this understanding, and assuming that the total system of liberty is drawn up in the manner just explained, we may note that the two-part basic structure allows a reconciliation of liberty and equality. Thus liberty and the worth of liberty are distinguished as follows: liberty is represented by the complete system of the liberties of equal citizenship, while the worth of liberty to persons and groups is proportional to their capacity to advance their ends within the framework the system defines. Freedom as equal liberty is the same for all; the question of compensating for a lesser than equal liberty does not arise. But the worth of liberty is not the same for everyone. Some have greater authority and wealth, and therefore greater means to achieve their aims. The lesser worth of liberty is, however, compensated for, since the capacity of the less fortunate members of society to achieve their aims would be even less were they not to accept the existing inequalities whenever the difference principle is satisfied. But compensating for the lesser worth of freedom is not to be confused with making good an unequal liberty. Taking the two principles together, the basic structure is to be arranged to maximize the worth to the least advantaged of the complete scheme of equal liberty shared by all. This defines the end of social justice.

These remarks about the concept of liberty are unhappily abstract. At this stage it would serve no purpose to classify systematically the various liberties. Instead I shall assume that we have a clear enough idea of the distinctions between them, and that in the course of taking up various cases these matters will gradually fall into place. In the next sections I discuss the first principle of justice in connection with liberty of conscience and freedom of thought, political liberty, and liberty of the person as protected by the rule of law. These applications provide an occasion to clarify the meaning of equal liberty and to present further grounds for the first principle. Moreover, each case illustrates the use of the criteria for limiting and adjusting the various freedoms and thereby exemplifies the meaning of the priority of liberty.

33. EQUAL LIBERTY OF CONSCIENCE

In the preceding chapter I remarked that one of the attractive features of the principles of justice is that they guarantee a secure protection for the equal liberties. In the next several sections I wish to examine the argument for the first principle in more detail by considering the grounds for freedom of conscience.[6] So far, while it has been sup-

6. The notion of equal right is, of course, well known in one form or another and appears in numerous analyses of justice even where the writers differ widely on other matters. Thus if the principle of an equal right to freedom is commonly associated with Kant—see *The Metaphysical Elements of Justice,* trans. John Ladd (New York, The Library of Liberal Arts, 1965), pp. 43–45—it may be claimed that it can also be found in J. S. Mill's *On Liberty* and elsewhere in his writings, and in those of many other liberal thinkers. H. L. A. Hart has argued for something like it in "Are There Any Natural Rights?" *Philosophical Review,* vol. 64 (1955); and similarly Richard Wollheim in the symposium "Equality," *Proceedings of the Aristotelian Society,* vol. 56 (1955–1956). The principle of equal liberty as I shall use it may acquire, though, special features in view of the theory of which it is a part. In particular, it enjoins a certain structure of institutions to be departed from only as the priority rules allow (§39). It is far

posed that the parties represent continuing lines of claims and care for their immediate descendants, this feature has not been stressed. Nor have I emphasized that the parties must assume that they may have moral, religious, or philosophical interests which they cannot put in jeopardy unless there is no alternative. One might say that they regard themselves as having moral or religious obligations which they must keep themselves free to honor. Of course, from the standpoint of justice as fairness, these obligations are self-imposed; they are not bonds laid down by this conception of justice. The point is rather that the persons in the original position are not to view themselves as single isolated individuals. To the contrary, they assume that they have interests which they must protect as best they can and that they have ties with certain members of the next generation who will also make similar claims. Once the parties consider these matters, the case for the principles of justice is very much strengthened, as I shall now try to show.

The question of equal liberty of conscience is settled. It is one of the fixed points of our considered judgments of justice. But precisely because of this fact it illustrates the nature of the argument for the principle of equal liberty. The reasoning in this case can be generalized to apply to other freedoms, although not always with the same force. Turning then to liberty of conscience, it seems evident that the parties must choose principles that secure the integrity of their religious and moral freedom. They do not know, of course, what their religious or moral convictions are, or what is the particular content of their moral or religious obligations as they interpret them. Indeed, they do not know that they think of themselves as having such obligations. The possibility that they do suffices for the argument, although I shall make the stronger assumption. Further, the parties do not know how their religious or moral view fares in their society, whether, for example, it is in the majority or the minority. All they know is that they have obligations which they interpret in this way. The question they are to decide is which principle they should adopt to regulate the liberties of citizens in regard to their fundamental religious, moral, and philosophical interests.

---

removed from a principle of equal consideration, since the intuitive idea is to generalize the principle of religious toleration to a social form, thereby arriving at equal liberty in public institutions.

Now it seems that equal liberty of conscience is the only principle that the persons in the original position can acknowledge. They cannot take chances with their liberty by permitting the dominant religious or moral doctrine to persecute or to suppress others if it wishes. Even granting (what may be questioned) that it is more probable than not that one will turn out to belong to the majority (if a majority exists), to gamble in this way would show that one did not take one's religious or moral convictions seriously, or highly value the liberty to examine one's beliefs. Nor on the other hand, could the parties consent to the principle of utility. In this case their freedom would be subject to the calculus of social interests and they would be authorizing its restriction if this would lead to a greater net balance of satisfaction. Of course, as we have seen, a utilitarian may try to argue from the general facts of social life that when properly carried out the computation of advantages never justifies such limitations, at least under reasonably favorable conditions of culture. But even if the parties were persuaded of this, they might as well guarantee their freedom straightway by adopting the principle of equal liberty. There is nothing gained by not doing so, and to the extent that the outcome of the actuarial calculation is unclear a great deal may be lost. Indeed, if we give a realistic interpretation to the general knowledge available to the parties (see the end of § 26), they are forced to reject the utilitarian principle. These considerations have all the more force in view of the complexity and vagueness of these calculations (if we can so describe them) as they are bound to be made in practice.

Moreover, the initial agreement on the principle of equal liberty is final. An individual recognizing religious and moral obligations regards them as binding absolutely in the sense that he cannot qualify his fulfillment of them for the sake of greater means for promoting his other interests. Greater economic and social benefits are not a sufficient reason for accepting less than an equal liberty. It seems possible to consent to an unequal liberty only if there is a threat of coercion which it is unwise to resist from the standpoint of liberty itself. For example, the situation may be one in which a person's religion or his moral view will be tolerated provided that he does not protest, whereas claiming an equal liberty will bring greater repression that cannot be effectively opposed. But from the perspective of the original position there is no way of ascertaining the relative strength of various doctrines and so these considerations do not arise. The veil of ignorance leads to an agreement on the principle of equal liberty; and the strength of religious and moral obligations as men interpret them seems to require that the two principles be put in serial order, at least when applied to freedom of conscience.

It may be said against the principle of equal liberty that religious sects, say, cannot acknowledge any principle at all for limiting their claims on one another. The duty to religious and divine law being absolute, no understanding among persons of different faiths is permissible from a religious point of view. Certainly men have often acted as if they held this doctrine. It is unnecessary, however, to argue against it. It suffices that if any principle can be agreed to, it must be that of equal liberty. A person may indeed think that others ought to recognize the same beliefs and first principles that he does, and that by not doing so they are grievously in error and miss the way to their salvation. But an understanding of religious obligation and of philosophical and moral first principles shows that we cannot expect others to acquiesce in an inferior liberty. Much less can we ask them to recognize us as the proper interpreter of their religious duties or moral obligations.

We should now observe that these reasons for the first principle receive further support once the parties' concern for the next generation is taken into account. Since they have a desire to obtain similar liberties for their descendants, and these liberties are also secured by the principle of equal liberty, there is no conflict of interests between generations. Moreover, the next generation could object to the choice of this principle only if the prospects offered by some other conception, say that of utility or perfection, were so attractive that the persons in the original position must not have properly considered their descendants when they rejected it. We can express this by noting that were a father, for example, to assert that he would accept the principle of equal liberty, a son could not object that were he (the father) to do so he would be neglecting his (the son's) interests. The advantages of the other principles are not this great and appear in fact uncertain and conjectural. The father could reply that when the choice of principles affects the liberty of others, the decision must, if possible, seem reasonable and responsible to them once they come of age. Those who care for others must choose for them in the light of what they will want whatever else they want once they reach maturity. Therefore following the account of primary goods, the parties presume that their descendants will want their liberty protected.

At this point we touch upon the principle of paternalism that is to guide decisions taken on behalf of others (§ 39). We must choose for others as we have reason to believe they would choose for themselves if they were at the age of reason and deciding rationally. Trustees, guardians, and benefactors are to act in this way, but since they usually know the situation and interests of their wards and beneficiaries, they can often make accurate estimates as to what is or will be wanted. The persons in the original position, however, are prevented from knowing any more about their descendants than they do about themeslves, and so in this case too they must rely upon the theory of primary goods. Thus the father can say that he would be irresponsible if he were not to guarantee the rights of his descendants by adopting the principle of equal liberty. From the perspective of the original position, he must assume that this is what they will come to recognize as for their good.

I have tried to show, by taking liberty of conscience as an example, how justice as fairness provides strong arguments for equal liberty. The same kind of reasoning applies, I believe, in other cases, though it is not always so convincing. I do not deny, however, that persuasive arguments for liberty are forthcoming on other views. As understood by Mill, the principle of utility often supports freedom. Mill defines the concept of value by reference to the interests of man as a progressive being. By this idea he means the interests men would have and the activities they would rather pursue under conditions encouraging freedom of choice. He adopts, in effect, a choice criterion of value: one activity is better than another if it is preferred by those who are capable of both and who have experienced each of them under circumstances of liberty.[7]

Using this principle Mill adduces essentially three grounds for

7. Mill's definition of utility as grounded on the permanent interests of man as a progressive being is in *On Liberty*, ch. I, par. 11. Originally I read the passage as "the permanent interests of a man," following a number of editions. I am grateful to David Spitz for telling me that Mill almost certainly wrote "man" and not "a man," and therefore the later variant, stemming from an early low-priced edition, is very probably a typesetter's error. I have revised the text accordingly. For the choice criterion of value, see *Utilitarianism*, ch. II, pars. 2–10. I heard this interpretation stated by G. A. Paul (1953) and am indebted to his remarks.

free institutions. For one thing, they are required to develop men's capacities and powers, to arouse strong and vigorous natures. Unless their abilities are intensely cultivated and their natures enlivened, men will not be able to engage in and to experience the valuable activities of which **they** are capable. Secondly, the institutions of liberty and the opportunity for experience which they allow are necessary, at least to some degree, if men's preferences among different activities are to be rational and informed. Human beings have no other way of knowing what things they can do and which of them are most rewarding. Thus if the pursuit of value, estimated in terms of the progressive interests of mankind, is to be rational, that is, guided by a knowledge of human capacities and well-formed preferences, certain freedoms are indispensable. Otherwise society's attempt to follow the principle of utility proceeds blindly. The suppression of liberty is always likely to be irrational. Even if the general capacities of mankind were known (as they are not), each person has still to find himself, and for this freedom is a prerequisite. Finally, Mill believes that human beings prefer to live under institutions of liberty. Historical experience shows that men desire to be free whenever they have not resigned themselves to apathy and despair; whereas those who are free never want to abdicate their liberty. Although men may complain of the burdens of freedom and culture, they have an overriding desire to determine how they shall live and to settle their own affairs. Thus by Mill's choice criterion, free institutions have value in themselves as basic aspects of rationally preferred forms of life.[8]

These are certainly forceful arguments and under some circumstances anyway they might justify many if not most of the equal liberties. They clearly guarantee that in favorable conditions a considerable degree of liberty is a precondition of the rational pursuit of value. But even Mill's contentions, as cogent as they are, will not, it seems, justify an equal liberty for all. We still need analogues of the standard utilitarian assumptions. One must suppose a certain similarity among individuals, say their equal capacity for the activities and interests of men as progressive beings, and in addition a principle of the diminishing marginal value of basic rights when assigned to in-

8. These three grounds are found in *On Liberty*, ch. III. They are not to be confused with the reasons Mill gives elsewhere, in ch. II for example, which urge the beneficial effects of free institutions.

dividuals. In the absence of these presumptions the advancement of human ends may be compatible with some persons' being oppressed, or at least granted but a restricted liberty. Whenever a society sets out to maximize the sum of intrinsic value or the net balance of the satisfaction of interests, it is liable to find that the denial of liberty for some is justified in the name of this single end. The liberties of equal citizenship are insecure when founded upon teleological principles. The argument for them relies upon precarious calculations as well as controversial and uncertain premises.

Moreover, nothing is gained by saying that persons are of equal intrinsic value unless this is simply a way of using the standard assumptions as if they were part of the principle of utility. That is, one applies this principle as if these assumptions were true. Doing this certainly has the merit of recognizing that we have more confidence in the principle of equal liberty than in the truth of the premises from which a perfectionist or utilitarian view would derive it. The grounds for this confidence, according to the contract view, is that the equal liberties have a different basis altogether. They are not a way of maximizing the sum of intrinsic value or of achieving the greatest net balance of satisfaction. The notion of maximizing a sum of value by adjusting the rights of individuals does not arise. Rather these rights are assigned to fulfill the principles of cooperation that citizens would acknowledge when each is fairly represented as a moral person. The conception defined by these principles is not that of maximizing anything, except in the vacuous sense of best meeting the requirements of justice, all things considered.

34. TOLERATION AND THE COMMON INTEREST

Justice as fairness provides, as we have now seen, strong arguments for an equal liberty of conscience. I shall assume that these arguments can be generalized in suitable ways to support the principle of equal liberty. Therefore the parties have good grounds for adopting this principle. It is obvious that these considerations are also important in making the case for the priority of liberty. From the perspective of the constitutional convention these arguments lead to the choice of a regime guaranteeing moral liberty and freedom of thought and belief, and of religious practice, although these may be regulated as always by the state's interest in public order and security. The state can favor no particular religion and no penalties or disabilities may be attached to any religious affiliation or lack thereof. The notion of a confessional state is rejected. Instead, particular associations may be freely organized as their members wish, and they may have their own internal life and discipline subject to the restriction that their members have a real choice of whether to continue their affiliation. The law protects the right of sanctuary in the sense that apostasy is not recognized, much less penalized, as a legal offense, any more than is having no religion at all. In these ways the state upholds moral and religious liberty.

Liberty of conscience is limited, everyone agrees, by the common interest in public order and security. This limitation itself is readily derivable from the contract point of view. First of all, acceptance of this limitation does not imply that public interests are in any sense superior to moral and religious interests; nor does it require that government view religious matters as things indifferent or claim the right to suppress philosophical beliefs whenever they conflict with affairs of state. The government has no authority to render associations either legitimate or illegitimate any more than it has this authority in regard to art and science. These matters are simply not within its competence as defined by a just constitution. Rather, given the principles of justice, the state must be understood as the association consisting of equal citizens. It does not concern itself with philosophical and religious doctrine but regulates individuals' pursuit of their moral and spiritual interests in accordance with principles to which they themselves would agree in an initial situation of equality. By exercising its powers in this way the government acts as the citizens' agent and satisfies the demands of their public conception of justice. Therefore the notion of the omnicompetent laicist state is also denied, since from the principles of justice it follows that government has neither the right nor the duty to do what it or a majority (or whatever) wants to do in questions of morals and religion. Its duty is limited to underwriting the conditions of equal moral and religious liberty.

Granting all this, it now seems evident that, in limiting liberty by reference to the common interest in public order and security, the government acts on a principle that would be chosen in the original position. For in this position each recognizes that the disruption of these conditions is a danger for the liberty of all. This follows once the maintenance of public order is understood as a necessary condition for everyone's achieving his ends whatever they are (provided they lie within certain limits) and for his fulfilling his interpretation of his moral and religious obligations. To restrain liberty of conscience at the boundary, however inexact, of the state's interest in public order is a limit derived from the principle of the common interest, that is, the interest of the representative equal citizen. The government's right to maintain public order and security is an enabling right, a right which the government must have if it is to carry out its duty of impartially supporting the conditions necessary for everyone's pursuit of his interests and living up to his obligations as he understands them.

Furthermore, liberty of conscience is to be limited only when there is a reasonable expectation that not doing so will damage the public order which the government should maintain. This expectation must be based on evidence and ways of reasoning acceptable to all. It must be supported by ordinary observation and modes of thought (including the methods of rational scientific inquiry where these are not controversial) which are generally recognized as correct. Now this reliance on what can be established and known by everyone is itself founded on the principles of justice. It implies no particular metaphysical doctrine or theory of knowledge. For this criterion appeals to what everyone can accept. It represents an agreement to limit liberty only by reference to a common knowledge and understanding of the world. Adopting this standard does not infringe upon anyone's equal freedom. On the other hand, a departure from generally recognized ways of reasoning would involve a privileged place for the views of some over others, and a principle which permitted this could not be agreed to in the original position. Furthermore, in holding that the consequences for the security of public order should not be merely possible or in certain cases even probable, but reasonably certain or imminent, there is again no implication of a particular philosophical theory. Rather this requirement expresses the high place which must be accorded to liberty of conscience and freedom of thought.

We may note at this point an analogy with the method of making interpersonal comparisons of well-being. These are founded on the index of primary goods that one may reasonably expect (§ 15), primary goods being those which everyone is presumed to want. This basis of comparison is one to which the parties can agree for the purposes of social justice. It does not require subtle estimates of men's capacity for happiness, much less of the relative worth of their plans of life. We need not question the meaningfulness of these notions; but they are inappropriate for designing just institutions. Similarly, the parties consent to publicly recognized criteria to determine what counts as evidence that their equal liberty is pursued in ways injurious to the common interest in public order and to the liberty of others. These principles of evidence are adopted for the aims of justice; they are not intended to apply to all questions of meaning and truth. How far they are valid in philosophy and science is a separate matter.

The characteristic feature of these arguments for liberty of conscience is that they are based solely on a conception of justice. Toleration is not derived from practical necessities or reasons of state. Moral and religious freedom follows from the principle of equal liberty; and assuming the priority of this principle, the only ground for denying the equal liberties is to avoid an even greater injustice, an even greater loss of liberty. Moreover, the argument does not rely on any special metaphysical or philosophical doctrine. It does not presuppose that all truths can be established by ways of thought recognized by common sense; nor does it hold that everything is, in some definable sense, a logical construction out of what can be observed or evidenced by rational scientific inquiry. The appeal is indeed to common sense, to generally shared ways of reasoning and plain facts accessible to all, but it is framed in such a way as to avoid these larger presumptions. Nor, on the other hand, does the case for liberty imply skepticism in philosophy or indifference to religion. Perhaps arguments for liberty of conscience can be given that have one or more of these doctrines as a premise. There is no reason to be surprised at this, since different arguments can have the same conclusion. But we need not pursue this question. The case for liberty is at least as strong as its strongest argument; the weak and fallacious ones are best forgotten. Those who would deny liberty of conscience cannot justify their action by condemning philosophical skepticism and indifference to religion, nor by appealing to social interests and affairs of state. The limitation of liberty is justified only when it is necessary for liberty itself, to prevent an invasion of freedom that would be still worse.

The parties in the constitutional convention, then, must choose a constitution that guarantees an equal liberty of conscience regulated solely by forms of argument generally accepted, and limited only when such argument establishes a reasonably certain interference with the essentials of public order. Liberty is governed by the necessary conditions for liberty itself. Now by this elementary principle alone many grounds of intolerance accepted in past ages are mistaken. Thus, for example, Aquinas justified the death penalty for heretics on the ground that it is a far graver matter to corrupt the faith, which is the life of the soul, than to counterfeit money which sustains life. So if it is just to put to death forgers and other criminals, heretics may a fortiori be similarly dealt with.[9] But the premises on which Aquinas relies cannot be established by modes of reasoning commonly recognized. It is a matter of dogma that faith is the life of the soul and that the suppression of heresy, that is, departures from ecclesiastical authority, is necessary for the safety of souls.

Again, the reasons given for limited toleration often run afoul of this principle. Thus Rousseau thought that people would find it impossible to live in peace with those whom they regarded as damned, since to love them would be to hate God who punishes them. He believed that those who regard others as damned must either torment or convert them, and therefore sects preaching this conviction cannot be trusted to preserve civil peace. Rousseau would not, then, tolerate those religions which say that outside the church there is no salvation.[10] But the consequences of such dogmatic belief which Rousseau conjectures are not borne out by experience. A priori psychological argument, however plausible, is not sufficient to abandon the principle of toleration, since justice holds that the disturbance to public order and to liberty itself must be securely established by common experience. There is, however,

9. *Summa Theologica*, II–II, q. 11, art. 3.
10. *The Social Contract*, bk. IV, ch. VIII.

an important difference between Rousseau and Locke, who advocated a limited toleration, and Aquinas and the Protestant Reformers who did not.[11] Locke and Rousseau limited liberty on the basis of what they supposed were clear and evident consequences for the public order. If Catholics and atheists were not to be tolerated it was because it seemed evident that such persons could not be relied upon to observe the bonds of civil society. Presumably a greater historical experience and a knowledge of the wider possibilities of political life would have convinced them that they were mistaken, or at least that their contentions were true only under special circumstances. But with Aquinas and the Protestant Reformers the grounds of intolerance are themselves a matter of faith, and this difference is more fundamental than the limits actually drawn to toleration. For when the denial of liberty is justified by an appeal to public order as evidenced by common sense, it is always possible to urge that the limits have been drawn incorrectly, that experience does not in fact justify the restriction. Where the suppression of liberty is based upon theological principles or matters of faith, no argument is possible. The one view recognizes the priority of principles which would be chosen in the original position whereas the other does not.

35. TOLERATION OF THE INTOLERANT

Let us now consider whether justice requires the toleration of the intolerant, and if so under what conditions. There are a variety of situations in which this question arises. Some political parties in democratic states hold doctrines that commit them to suppress the constitutional liberties whenever they have the power. Again, there are those who reject intellectual freedom but who nevertheless hold positions in the university. It may appear that toleration in these cases is inconsistent with the principles of justice, or at any rate not

11. For the views of the Protestant Reformers, see J. E. E. D. (Lord) Acton, "The Protestant Theory of Persecution" in *The History of Freedom and Other Essays* (London, Macmillan, 1907). For Locke, see *A Letter Concerning Toleration,* included along with *The Second Treatise of Government,* ed. J. W. Gough (Oxford, Basil Blackwell, 1946), pp. 156–158.

required by them. I shall discuss the matter in connection with religious toleration. With appropriate alterations the argument can be extended to these other instances.

Several questions should be distinguished. First, there is the question whether an intolerant sect has any title to complain if it is not tolerated; second, under what conditions tolerant sects have a right not to tolerate those which are intolerant; and last, when they have the right not to tolerate them, for what ends it should be exercised. Beginning with the first question, it seems that an intolerant sect has no title to complain when it is denied an equal liberty. At least this follows if it is assumed that one has no title to object to the conduct of others that is in accordance with principles one would use in similar circumstances to justify one's actions toward them. A person's right to complain is limited to violations of principles he acknowledges himself. A complaint is a protest addressed to another in good faith. It claims a violation of a principle that both parties accept. Now, to be sure, an intolerant man will say that he acts in good faith and that he does not ask anything for himself that he denies to others. His view, let us suppose, is that he is acting on the principle that God is to be obeyed and the truth accepted by all. This principle is perfectly general and by acting on it he is not making an exception in his own case. As he sees the matter, he is following the correct principle which others reject.

The reply to this defense is that, from the standpoint of the original position, no particular interpretation of religious truth can be acknowledged as binding upon citizens generally; nor can it be agreed that there should be one authority with the right to settle questions of theological doctrine. Each person must insist upon an equal right to decide what his religious obligations are. He cannot give up this right to another person or institutional authority. In fact, a man exercises his liberty in deciding to accept another as an authority even when he regards this authority as infallible, since in doing this he in no way abandons his equal liberty of conscience as a matter of constitutional law. For this liberty as secured by justice is imprescriptible: a person is always free to change his faith and this right does not depend upon his having exercised his powers of choice regularly or intelligently. We may observe that men's having an equal liberty of conscience is consistent with the idea that all men ought to obey God and accept the truth. The problem of liberty is that of choosing a principle by which the claims men make on one another in the name of their religion are to be regulated. Granting that God's will should be followed and the truth recognized does not as yet define a principle of adjudication. From the fact that God's intention is to be complied with, it does not follow that any person or institution has authority to interfere with another's interpretation of his religious obligations. This religious principle justifies no one in demanding in law or politics a greater liberty for himself. The only principles which authorize claims on institutions are those that would be chosen in the original position.

Let us suppose, then, that an intolerant sect has no title to complain of intolerance. We still cannot say that tolerant sects have the right to suppress them. For one thing, others may have a right to complain. They may have this right not as a right to complain on behalf of the intolerant, but simply as a right to object whenever a principle of justice is violated. For justice is infringed whenever equal liberty is denied without sufficient reason. The question, then, is whether being intolerant of another is grounds enough for limiting someone's liberty. To simplify things, assume that the tolerant sects have the right not to tolerate the intolerant in at least one circumstance, namely, when they sincerely and with reason believe that intolerance is necessary for their own security. This right follows readily enough since, as the original position is defined, each would agree to the right of self-preservation. Justice does not require that men must stand idly by while others destroy the basis of their existence. Since it can never be to men's advantage, from a general point of view, to forgo the right of self-protection, the only question, then, is whether the tolerant have a right to curb the intolerant when they are of no immediate danger to the equal liberties of others.

Suppose that, in some way or other, an intolerant sect comes to exist within a well-ordered society accepting the two principles of justice. How are the citizens of this society to act in regard to it? Now certainly they should not suppress it simply because the members of the intolerant sect could not complain were they to do so. Rather, since a just constitution exists, all citizens have a natural duty of justice to uphold it. We are not released from this duty whenever others are disposed to act unjustly. A more stringent condition is required: there must be some considerable risks to our own legitimate interests. Thus just citizens should strive to preserve the constitution with all its equal liberties as long as liberty itself and their own freedom are not in danger. They can properly force the intolerant to respect the liberty of others, since a person can be required to respect the rights established by principles that he would acknowledge in the original position. But when the constitution itself is secure, there is no reason to deny freedom to the intolerant.

The question of tolerating the intolerant is directly related to that of the stability of a well-ordered society regulated by the two principles. We can see this as follows. It is from the position of equal citizenship that persons join the various religious associations, and it is from this position that they should conduct their discussions with one another. Citizens in a free society should not think one another incapable of a sense of justice unless this is necessary for the sake of equal liberty itself. If an intolerant sect appears in a well-ordered society, the others should keep in mind the inherent stability of their institutions. The liberties of the intolerant may persuade them to a belief in freedom. This persuasion works on the psychological principle that those whose liberties are protected by and who benefit from a just constitution will, other things equal, acquire an allegiance to it over a period of time (§ 72). So even if an intolerant sect should arise, provided that it is not so strong initially that it can impose its will straightway, or does not grow so rapidly that the psychological principle has no time to take hold, it will tend to lose its intolerance and accept liberty of conscience. This is the consequence of the stability of just institutions, for stability means that when tendencies to injustice arise other forces will be called into play that work to preserve the justice of the whole arrangement. Of course, the intolerant sect may be so strong initially or growing so fast that the forces making for stability cannot convert it to liberty. This situation presents a practical dilemma which philosophy alone cannot resolve. Whether the liberty of the intolerant should be limited to preserve freedom under a just constitution depends on the circumstances. The theory of justice only characterizes the just constitution, the end of political action by reference to which practical decisions are to be made. In pursuing this end the natural strength of free institutions must not be forgotten, nor should it be

219

supposed that tendencies to depart from them go unchecked and always win out. Knowing the inherent stability of a just constitution, members of a well-ordered society have the confidence to limit the freedom of the intolerant only in the special cases when it is necessary for preserving equal liberty itself.

The conclusion, then, is that while an intolerant sect does not itself have title to complain of intolerance, its freedom should be restricted only when the tolerant sincerely and with reason believe that their own security and that of the institutions of liberty are in danger. The tolerant should curb the intolerant only in this case. The leading principle is to establish a just constitution with the liberties of equal citizenship. The just should be guided by the principles of justice and not by the fact that the unjust cannot complain. Finally, it should be noted that even when the freedom of the intolerant is limited to safeguard a just constitution, this is not done in the name of maximizing liberty. The liberties of some are not suppressed simply to make possible a greater liberty for others. Justice forbids this sort of reasoning in connection with liberty as much as it does in regard to the sum of advantages. It is only the liberty of the intolerant which is to be limited, and this is done for the sake of equal liberty under a just constitution the principles of which the intolerant themselves would acknowledge in the original position.

The argument in this and the preceding sections suggests that the adoption of the principle of equal liberty can be viewed as a limiting case. Even though their differences are profound and no one knows how to reconcile them by reason, men can, from the standpoint of the original position, still agree on this principle if they can agree on any principle at all. This idea which arose historically with religious toleration can be extended to other instances. Thus we can suppose that the persons in the original position know that they have moral convictions although, as the veil of ignorance requires, they do not know what these convictions are. They understand that the principles they acknowledge are to override these beliefs when there is a conflict; but otherwise they need not revise their opinions nor give them up when these principles do not uphold them. In this way the principles of justice can adjudicate between opposing moralities just as they regulate the claims of rival religions.

Within the framework that justice establishes, moral conceptions with different principles, or conceptions representing a different balancing of the same principles, may be adopted by various parts of society. What is essential is that when persons with different convictions make conflicting demands on the basic structure as a matter of political principle, they are to judge these claims by the principles of justice. The principles that would be chosen in the original position are the kernel of political morality. They not only specify the terms of cooperation between persons but they define a pact of reconciliation between diverse religions and moral beliefs, and the forms of culture to which they belong. If this conception of justice now seems largely negative, we shall see that it has a happier side.

36. POLITICAL JUSTICE AND THE CONSTITUTION

I now wish to consider political justice, that is, the justice of the constitution, and to sketch the meaning of equal liberty for this part of the basic structure. Political justice has two aspects arising from the fact that a just constitution is a case of imperfect procedural justice. First, the constitution is to be a just procedure satisfying the requirements of equal liberty; and second, it is to be framed so that of all the feasible just arrangements, it is the one more likely than any other to result in a just and effective system of legislation. The justice of the constitution is to be assessed under both headings in the light of what circumstances permit, these assessments being made from the standpoint of the constitutional convention.

The principle of equal liberty, when applied to the political procedure defined by the constitution, I shall refer to as the principle of (equal) participation. It requires that all citizens are to have an equal right to take part in, and to determine the outcome of, the constitutional process that establishes the laws with which they are to comply. Justice as fairness begins with the idea that where common principles are necessary and to everyone's advantage, they are to be worked out from the viewpoint of a suitably defined initial situation of equality in which each person is fairly represented. The principle of participation transfers this notion from the original position to the constitution as the highest-order system of social rules for making rules. If the state is to exercise a final and coercive authority over a certain territory, and if it is in this way to affect permanently men's prospects in life, then the constitutional process should preserve the equal representation of the original position to the degree that this is practicable.

For the time being I assume that a constitutional democracy can be arranged so as to satisfy the principle of participation. But we need to know more exactly what this principle requires under favorable circumstances, when taken to the limit so to speak. These requirements are, of course, familiar, comprising what Constant called the liberty of the ancients in contrast to the liberty of the moderns. Nevertheless, it is worthwhile to see how these liberties fall under the principle of participation. The adjustments that need to be made to existing conditions, and the reasoning that regulates these compromises, I discuss in the following section.

We may begin by recalling certain elements of a constitutional regime. First of all, the authority to determine basic social policies resides in a representative body selected for limited terms by and ultimately accountable to the electorate. This representative body has more than a purely advisory capacity. It is a legislature with lawmaking powers and not simply a forum of delegates from various sectors of society to which the executive explains its actions and discerns the movements of public sentiment. Nor are political parties mere interest groups petitioning the government on their own behalf; instead, to gain enough support to win office, they must advance some conception of the public good. The constitution may, of course, circumscribe the legislature in numerous respects; and constitutional norms define its actions as a parliamentary body. But in due course a firm majority of the electorate is able to achieve its aims, by constitutional amendment if necessary.

All sane adults, with certain generally recognized exceptions, have the right to take part in political affairs, and the precept one elector one vote is honored as far as possible. Elections are fair and free, and regularly held. Sporadic and unpredictable tests of public sentiment by plebiscite or other means, or at such times as may suit the convenience of those in office, do not suffice for a representative regime. There are firm constitutional protections for certain liberties, particularly freedom of speech and assembly, and liberty to form political associations. The principle of loyal opposition is recognized, the clash of political beliefs, and of the interests and attitudes that are likely to influence them, are accepted as a normal condition of human life. A lack of unanimity is part of the circumstances of justice, since disagreement is bound to exist even among honest men who desire to follow much the same political principles. Without the conception of loyal opposition, and an attachment to constitutional rules which express and protect it, the politics of democracy cannot be properly conducted or long endure.

Three points concerning the equal liberty defined by the principle of participation call for discussion: its meaning, its extent, and the measures that enhance its worth. Starting with the question of meaning, the precept of one elector one vote implies, when strictly adhered to, that each vote has approximately the same weight in determining the outcome of elections. And this in turn requires, assuming single member territorial constituencies, that members of the legislature (with one vote each) represent the same number of electors. I shall also suppose that the precept necessitates that legislative districts be drawn up under the guidance of certain general standards specified in advance by the constitution and applied as far as possible by an impartial procedure. These safeguards are needed to prevent gerrymandering, since the weight of the vote can be as much affected by feats of gerrymander as by districts of disproportionate size. The requisite standards and procedures are to be adopted from the standpoint of the constitutional convention in which no one has the knowledge that is likely to prejudice the design of constituencies. Political parties cannot adjust boundaries to their advantage in the light of voting statistics; districts are defined by means of criteria already agreed to in the absence of this sort of information. Of course, it may be necessary to introduce certain random elements, since the criteria for designing constituencies are no doubt to some extent arbitrary. There may be no other fair way to deal with these contingencies.[12]

The principle of participation also holds that all citizens are to have an equal access, at least in the formal sense, to public office.

12. For a discussion of this problem, see W. S. Vickrey, "On the Prevention of Gerrymandering," *Political Science Quarterly,* vol. 76 (1961).

Each is eligible to join political parties, to run for elective positions, and to hold places of authority. To be sure, there may be qualifications of age, residency, and so on. But these are to be reasonably related to the tasks of office; presumably these restrictions are in the common interest and do not discriminate unfairly among persons or groups in the sense that they fall evenly on everyone in the normal course of life.

The second point concerning equal political liberty is its extent. How broadly are these liberties to be defined? Offhand it is not clear what extent means here. Each of the political liberties can be more or less widely defined. Somewhat arbitrarily, but nevertheless in accordance with tradition, I shall assume that the main variation in the extent of equal political liberty lies in the degree to which the constitution is majoritarian. The definition of the other liberties I take to be more or less fixed. Thus the most extensive political liberty is established by a constitution that uses the procedure of so-called bare majority rule (the procedure in which a minority can neither override nor check a majority) for all significant political decisions unimpeded by any constitutional constraints. Whenever the constitution limits the scope and authority of majorities, either by requiring a greater plurality for certain types of measures, or by a bill of rights restricting the powers of the legislature, and the like, equal political liberty is less extensive. The traditional devices of constitutionalism—bicameral legislature, separation of powers mixed with checks and balances, a bill of rights with judicial review —limit the scope of the principle of participation. I assume, however, that these arrangements are consistent with equal political liberty provided that similar restrictions apply to everyone and that the constraints introduced are likely over time to fall evenly upon all sectors of society. And this seems probable if the fair value of political liberty is maintained. The main problem, then, is how extensive equal participation should be. This question I leave aside for the next section.

Turning now to the worth of political liberty, the constitution must take steps to enhance the value of the equal rights of participation for all members of society. It must underwrite a fair opportunity to take part in and to influence the political process. The distinction here is analogous to that made before (§ 12): ideally, those similarly endowed and motivated should have roughly the same chance of attaining positions of political authority irrespective of their economic and social class. But how is this fair value of these liberties to be secured?

We may take for granted that a democratic regime presupposes freedom of speech and assembly, and liberty of thought and conscience. These institutions are not only required by the first principle of justice but, as Mill argued, they are necessary if political affairs are to be conducted in a rational fashion. While rationality is not guaranteed by these arrangements, in their absence the more reasonable course seems sure to be rejected in favor of policies sought by special interests. If the public forum is to be free and open to all, and in continuous session, everyone should be able to make use of it. All citizens should have the means to be informed about political issues. They should be in a position to assess how proposals affect their well-being and which policies advance their conception of the public good. Moreover, they should have a fair chance to add alternative proposals to the agenda for political discussion.[13] The liberties protected by the principle of participation lose much of their value whenever those who have greater private means are permitted to use their advantages to control the course of public debate. For eventually these inequalities will enable those better situated to exercise a larger influence over the development of legislation. In due time they are likely to acquire a preponderant weight in settling social questions, at least in regard to those matters upon which they normally agree, which is to say in regard to those things that support their favored circumstances.

Compensating steps must, then, be taken to preserve the fair value for all of the equal political liberties. A variety of devices can be used. For example, in a society allowing private ownership of the means of production, property and wealth must be kept widely distributed and government monies provided on a regular basis to encourage free public discussion. In addition, political parties are

13. See R. A. Dahl, *A Preface to Democratic Theory* (Chicago, University of Chicago Press, 1956), pp. 67–75, for a discussion of the conditions necessary to achieve political equality.

to be made independent from private economic interests by allotting them sufficient tax revenues to play their part in the constitutional scheme. (Their subventions might, for example, be based by some rule on the number of votes received in the last several elections, and the like.) What is necessary is that political parties be autonomous with respect to private demands, that is, demands not expressed in the public forum and argued for openly by reference to a conception of the public good. If society does not bear the costs of organization, and party funds need to be solicited from the more advantaged social and economic interests, the pleadings of these groups are bound to receive excessive attention. And this is all the more likely when the less favored members of society, having been effectively prevented by their lack of means from exercising their fair degree of influence, withdraw into apathy and resentment.

Historically one of the main defects of constitutional government has been the failure to insure the fair value of political liberty. The necessary corrective steps have not been taken, indeed, they never seem to have been seriously entertained. Disparities in the distribution of property and wealth that far exceed what is compatible with political equality have generally been tolerated by the legal system. Public resources have not been devoted to maintaining the institutions required for the fair value of political liberty. Essentially the fault lies in the fact that the democratic political process is at best regulated rivalry; it does not even in theory have the desirable properties that price theory ascribes to truly competitive markets. Moreover, the effects of injustices in the political system are much more grave and long lasting than market imperfections. Political power rapidly accumulates and becomes unequal; and making use of the coercive apparatus of the state and its law, those who gain the advantage can often assure themselves of a favored position. Thus inequities in the economic and social system may soon undermine whatever political equality might have existed under fortunate historical conditions. Universal suffrage is an insufficient counterpoise; for when parties and elections are financed not by public funds but by private contributions, the political forum is so constrained by the wishes of the dominant interests that the basic measures needed to establish just constitutional rule are seldom properly presented. These questions, however, belong to political sociology.[14] I mention them here as a way of emphasizing that our discussion is part of the theory of justice and must not be mistaken for a theory of the political system. We are in the way of describing an ideal arrangement, comparison with which defines a standard for judging actual institutions, and indicates what must be maintained to justify departures from it.

By way of summing up the account of the principle of participation, we can say that a just constitution sets up a form of fair rivalry for political office and authority. By presenting conceptions of the public good and policies designed to promote social ends, rival parties seek the citizens' approval in accordance with just procedural rules against a background of freedom of thought and assembly in which the fair value of political liberty is assured. The principle of participation compels those in authority to be responsive to the felt interests of the electorate. Representatives are not, to be sure, mere agents of their constituents, since they have a certain discretion and they are expected to exercise their judgment in enacting legislation. In a well-ordered society they must, nevertheless, represent their constituents in the substantive sense: they must seek first to pass just and effective legislation, since this is a citizen's first interest in government, and secondly, they must further their constituents' other interests insofar as these are consistent with justice.[15] The principles of justice are among the main criteria to be used in judging a representative's record and the reasons he gives in defense of it. Since the constitution is the foundation of the social structure, the highest-order system of rules that regulates and controls other institutions, everyone has the same access to the political procedure that it sets up. When the principle of participation is satisfied, all have the common status of equal citizen.

Finally, to avoid misunderstanding, it should be kept in mind that the principle of participation applies to institutions. It does not define an ideal of citizenship; nor does it lay down a duty requiring all to take an active part in political affairs. The duties and obligations

14. My remarks draw upon F. H. Knight, *The Ethics of Competition and Other Essays* (New York, Harper and Brothers, 1935), pp. 293–305.

15. See H. F. Pitkin, *The Concept of Representation* (Berkeley, University of California Press, 1967), pp. 221–225, for a discussion of representation to which I am indebted.

of individuals are a separate question that I shall discuss later (see Chapter VI). What is essential is that the constitution should establish equal rights to engage in public affairs and that measures be taken to maintain the fair value of these liberties. In a well-governed state only a small fraction of persons may devote much of their time to politics. There are many other forms of human good. But this fraction, whatever its size, will most likely be drawn more or less equally from all sectors of society. The many communities of interests and centers of political life will have their active members who look after their concerns.

37. LIMITATIONS ON THE PRINCIPLE OF PARTICIPATION

It is evident from the preceding account of the principle of participation that there are three ways to limit its application. The constitution may define a more or a less extensive freedom of participation; it may allow inequalities in political liberties; and greater or smaller social resources may be devoted to insuring the worth of these freedoms to the representative citizen. I shall discuss these kinds of limitations in order, all with a view to clarifying the meaning of the priority of liberty.

The extent of the principle of participation is defined as the degree to which the procedure of (bare) majority rule is restricted by the mechanisms of constitutionalism. These devices serve to limit the scope of majority rule, the kinds of matters on which majorities have final authority, and the speed with which the aims of the majority are put into effect. A bill of rights may remove certain liberties from majority regulation altogether, and the separation of powers with judicial review may slow down the pace of legislative change. The question, then, is how these mechanisms might be justified consistent with the two principles of justice. We are not to ask whether these devices are in fact justified, but what kind of an argument for them is required.

To begin with, however, we should observe that the limits on the extent of the principle of participation are assumed to fall equally upon everyone. For this reason these restrictions are easier to justify than unequal political liberties. If all could have a greater liberty, at least each loses equally, other things the same; and if this lesser liberty is unnecessary and not imposed by some human agency, the scheme of liberty is to this degree irrational rather than unjust. Unequal liberty, as when the precept one man one vote is violated, is another matter and immediately raises a question of justice.

Supposing for the time being that the constraints on majority rule bear equally on all citizens, the justification for the devices of constitutionalism is that they presumably protect the other freedoms. The best arrangement is found by noting the consequences for the complete system of liberty. The intuitive idea here is straightforward. We have said that the political process is a case of imperfect procedural justice. A constitution that restricts majority rule by the various traditional devices is thought to lead to a more just body of legislation. Since the majority principle must as a practical necessity be relied upon to some degree, the problem is to find which constraints work best in given circumstances to further the ends of liberty. Of course, these matters lie outside the theory of justice. We need not consider which if any of the constitutional mechanisms is effective in achieving its aim, or how far its successful working presupposes certain underlying social conditions. The relevant point is that to justify these restrictions one must maintain that from the perspective of the representative citizen in the constitutional convention the less extensive freedom of participation is sufficiently outweighed by the greater security and extent of the other liberties. Unlimited majority rule is often thought to be hostile to these liberties. Constitutional arrangements compel a majority to delay putting its will into effect and force it to make a more considered and deliberate decision. In this and other ways procedural constraints are said to mitigate the defects of the majority principle. The justification appeals to a greater equal liberty. At no point is there a reference to compensating economic and social benefits.

One of the tenets of classical liberalism is that the political liberties are of less intrinsic importance than liberty of conscience and freedom of the person. Should one be forced to choose between the political liberties and all the others, the governance of a good sovereign who recognized the latter and who upheld the rule of law would be far preferable. On this view, the chief merit of the principle of participation is to insure that the government respects the rights and welfare of the governed.[16] Fortunately however, we do not often have to assess the relative total importance of the different liberties. Usually the way to proceed is to apply the principle of equal advantage in adjusting the complete system of freedom. We are not called upon either to abandon the principle of participation entirely or to allow it unlimited sway. Instead, we should narrow or widen its extent up to the point where the danger to liberty from the marginal loss in control over those holding political power just balances the security of liberty gained by the greater use of constitutional devices. The decision is not an all or nothing affair. It is a question of weighing against one another small variations in the extent and definition of the different liberties. The priority of liberty does not exclude marginal exchanges within the system of freedom. Moreover, it allows although it does not require that some liberties, say those covered by the principle of participation, are less essential in that their main role is to protect the remaining freedoms. Different opinions about the value of the liberties will, of course, affect how different persons think the full scheme of freedom should be arranged. Those who place a higher worth on the principle of participation will be prepared to take greater risks with the freedoms of the person, say, in order to give political liberty a larger place. Ideally these conflicts will not occur and it should be possible, under favorable conditions anyway, to find a constitutional procedure that allows a sufficient scope for the value of participation without jeopardizing the other liberties.

It is sometimes objected to majority rule that, however circumscribed, it fails to take account of the intensity of desire, since the larger part may override the strong feelings of a minority. This criticism rests upon the mistaken view that the intensity of desire is a relevant consideration in enacting legislation (see § 54). To the contrary, whenever questions of justice are raised, we are not to go by the strength of feeling but must aim instead for the greater justice of the legal order. The fundamental criterion for judging any procedure is the justice of its likely results. A similar reply may be given to the propriety of majority rule when the vote is rather evenly

16. See Isaiah Berlin, *Four Essays on Liberty*, pp. 130, 165.

divided. Everything depends on the probable justice of the outcome. If the various sectors of society have reasonable confidence in one another and share a common conception of justice, the rule by bare majorities may succeed fairly well. To the extent that this underlying agreement is lacking, the majority principle becomes more difficult to justify because it is less probable that just policies will be followed. There may, however, be no procedures that can be relied upon once distrust and enmity pervade society. I do not wish to pursue these matters further. I mention these familiar points about majority rule only to emphasize that the test of constitutional arrangements is always the overall balance of justice. Where issues of justice are involved, the intensity of desires should not be taken into account. Of course, as things are, legislators must reckon with strong public feelings. Men's sense of outrage however irrational will set boundaries upon what is politically attainable; and popular views will affect the strategies of enforcement within these limits. But questions of strategy are not to be confused with those of justice. If a bill of rights guaranteeing liberty of conscience and freedom of thought and assembly would be effective, then it should be adopted. Whatever the depth of feeling against them, these rights should if possible be made to stand. The force of opposing attitudes has no bearing on the question of right but only on the feasibility of arrangements of liberty.

The justification of unequal political liberty proceeds in much the same way. One takes up the point of view of the representative citizen in the constitutional convention and assesses the total system of freedom as it looks to him. But in this case there is an important difference. We must now reason from the perspective of those who have the lesser political liberty. An inequality in the basic structure must always be justified to those in the disadvantaged position. This holds whatever the primary social good and especially for liberty. Therefore the priority rule requires us to show that the inequality of right would be accepted by the less favored in return for the greater protection of their other liberties that results from this restriction.

Perhaps the most obvious political inequality is the violation of the precept one person one vote. Yet until recent times most writers rejected equal universal suffrage. Indeed, persons were not regarded as the proper subjects of representation at all. Often it was interests that were to be represented, with Whig and Tory differing as to whether the interest of the rising middle class should be given a place alongside the landed and ecclesiastical interests. For others it is regions that are to be represented, or forms of culture, as when one speaks of the representation of the agricultural and urban elements of society. At the first sight, these kinds of representation appear unjust. How far they depart from the precept one person one vote is a measure of their abstract injustice, and indicates the strength of the countervailing reasons that must be forthcoming.[17]

Now it frequently turns out that those who oppose equal political liberty put forward justifications of the required form. They are at least prepared to argue that political inequality is to the benefit of those with the lesser liberty. Consider as an illustration Mill's view that persons with greater intelligence and education should have extra votes in order that their opinions may have a greater influence.[18] Mill believed that in this case plural voting accords with the natural order of human life, for whenever persons conduct a common enterprise in which they have a joint interest, they recognize that while all should have a voice, the say of everyone need not be equal. The judgment of the wiser and more knowledgeable should have a superior weight. Such an arrangement is in the interest of each and conforms to men's sentiment of justice. National affairs are precisely such a joint concern. Although all should indeed have the vote, those with a greater capacity for the management of the public interest should have a larger say. Their influence should be great enough to protect them from the class legislation of the uneducated, but not so large as to allow them to enact class legislation in their own behalf. Ideally, those with superior wisdom and judgment should act as a constant force on the side of justice and the common good, a force that, although always weak by itself, can often tip the scale in the right direction if the larger forces cancel out. Mill was persuaded that everyone would gain from this arrangement, including those whose votes count for less. Of course, as it

17. See J. R. Pole, *Political Representation in England and the Origin of the American Republic* (London, Macmillan, 1966), pp. 535–537.

18. *Representative Government,* ed. R. B. McCallum, together with *On Liberty* (Oxford, Basil Blackwell, 1946). pp. 216–222. (This is much of the latter half of ch. VIII.)

stands, this argument does not go beyond the general conception of justice as fairness. Mill does not state explicitly that the gain to the uneducated is to be estimated in the first instance by the larger security of their other liberties, although his reasoning suggests that he thought this to be the case. In any event, if Mill's view is to satisfy the restrictions imposed by the priority of liberty, this is how the argument must go.

I do not wish to criticize Mill's proposal. My account of it is solely for purposes of illustration. His view enables one to see why political equality is sometimes regarded as less essential than equal liberty of conscience or liberty of the person. Government is assumed to aim at the common good, that is, at maintaining conditions and achieving objectives that are similarly to everyone's advantage. To the extent that this presumption holds, and some men can be identified as having superior wisdom and judgment, others are willing to trust them and to concede to their opinion a greater weight. The passengers of a ship are willing to let the captain steer the course, since they believe that he is more knowledgeable and wishes to arrive safely as much as they do. There is both an identity of interests and a noticeably greater skill and judgment in realizing it. Now the ship of state is in some ways analogous to a ship at sea; and to the extent that this is so, the political liberties are indeed subordinate to the other freedoms that, so to say, define the intrinsic good of the passengers. Admitting these assumptions, plural voting may be perfectly just.

Of course, the grounds for self-government are not solely instrumental. Equal political liberty when assured its fair value is bound to have a profound effect on the moral quality of civic life. Citizens' relations to one another are given a secure basis in the manifest constitution of society. The medieval maxim that what touches all concerns all is seen to be taken seriously and declared as the public intention. Political liberty so understood is not designed to satisfy the individual's desire for self-mastery, much less his quest for power. Taking part in political life does not make the individual master of himself, but rather gives him an equal voice along with others in settling how basic social conditions are to be arranged. Nor does it answer to the ambition to dictate to others, since each is now required to moderate his claims by what everyone is able to recognize as just. The public will to consult and to take everyone's beliefs and interests into account lays the foundations for civic friendship and shapes the ethos of political culture.

Moreover, the effect of self-government where equal political rights have their fair value is to enhance the self-esteem and the sense of political competence of the average citizen. His awareness of his own worth developed in the smaller associations of his community is confirmed in the constitution of the whole society. Since he is expected to vote, he is expected to have political opinions. The time and thought that he devotes to forming his views is not governed by the likely material return of his political influence. Rather it is an activity enjoyable in itself that leads to a larger conception of society and to the development of his intellectual and moral faculties. As Mill observed, he is called upon to weigh interests other than his own, and to be guided by some conception of justice and the public good rather than by his own inclinations.[19] Having to explain and justify his views to others, he must appeal to principles that others can accept. Moreover, Mill adds, this education to public spirit is necessary if citizens are to acquire an affirmative sense of political duty and obligation, that is, one that goes beyond the mere willingness to submit to law and government. Without these more inclusive sentiments men become estranged and isolated in their smaller associations, and affective ties may not extend outside the family or a narrow circle of friends. Citizens no longer regard one another as associates with whom one can cooperate to advance some interpretation of the public good; instead, they view themselves as rivals, or else as obstacles to one another's ends. All of these considerations Mill and others have made familiar. They show that equal political liberty is not solely a means. These freedoms strengthen men's sense of their own worth, enlarge their intellectual and moral sensibilities, and lay the basis for a sense of duty and obligation upon which the stability of just institutions depends. The connection of these matters to human good and the sense of justice I shall leave until Part Three. There I shall try to tie these things together under the conception of the good of justice.

19. *Representative Government*, pp. 149–151, 209–211. (These are the end of ch. III, and at the beginning of ch. VIII.)

38. THE RULE OF LAW

I now wish to consider rights of the person as these are protected by the principle of the rule of law.[20] As before my intention is not only to relate these notions to the principles of justice but to elucidate the sense of the priority of liberty. I have already noted (§ 10) that the conception of formal justice, the regular and impartial administration of public rules, becomes the rule of law when applied to the legal system. One kind of unjust action is the failure of judges and others in authority to apply the appropriate rule or to interpret it correctly. It is more illuminating in this connection to think not of gross violations exemplified by bribery and corruption, or the abuse of the legal system to punish political enemies, but rather of the subtle distortions of prejudice and bias as these effectively discriminate against certain groups in the judicial process. The regular and impartial, and in this sense fair, administration of law we may call "justice as regularity." This is a more suggestive phrase than "formal justice."

Now the rule of law is obviously closely related to liberty. We can see this by considering the notion of a legal system and its intimate connection with the precepts definitive of justice as regularity. A legal system is a coercive order of public rules addressed to rational persons for the purpose of regulating their conduct and providing the framework for social cooperation. When these rules are just they establish a basis for legitimate expectations. They constitute grounds upon which persons can rely on one another and rightly object when their expectations are not fulfilled. If the bases of these claims are unsure, so are the boundaries of men's liberties. Of course, other rules share many of these features. Rules of games and of private associations are likewise addressed to rational persons

20. For a general discussion, see Lon Fuller, *The Morality of Law* (New Haven, Yale University Press, 1964), ch. II. The concept of principled decisions in constitutional law is considered by Herbert Wechsler, *Principles, Politics, and Fundamental Law* (Cambridge, Harvard University Press, 1961). See Otto Kirchenheimer, *Political Justice* (Princeton, Princeton University Press, 1961), and J. N. Shklar, *Legalism* (Cambridge, Harvard University Press, 1964), pt. II, for the use and abuse of judicial forms in politics. J. R. Lucas, *The Principles of Politics* (Oxford, The Clarendon Press, 1966), pp. 106–143, contains a philosophical account.

in order to give shape to their activities. Given that these rules are fair or just, then once men have entered into these arrangements and accepted the benefits that result, the obligations which thereby arise constitute a basis for legitimate expectations. What distinguishes a legal system is its comprehensive scope and its regulative powers with respect to other associations. The constitutional agencies that it defines generally have the exclusive legal right to at least the more extreme forms of coercion. The kinds of duress that private associations can employ are strictly limited. Moreover, the legal order exercises a final authority over a certain well-defined territory. It is also marked by the wide range of the activities it regulates and the fundamental nature of the interests it is designed to secure. These features simply reflect the fact that the law defines the basic structure within which the pursuit of all other activities takes place.

Given that the legal order is a system of public rules addressed to rational persons, we can account for the precepts of justice associated with the rule of law. These precepts are those that would be followed by any system of rules which perfectly embodied the idea of a legal system. This is not, of course, to say that existing laws necessarily satisfy these precepts in all cases. Rather, these maxims follow from an ideal notion which laws are expected to approximate, at least for the most part. If deviations from justice as regularity are too pervasive, a serious question may arise whether a system of law exists as opposed to a collection of particular orders designed to advance the interests of a dictator or the ideal of a benevolent despot. Often there is no clear answer to this question. The point of thinking of a legal order as a system of public rules is that it enables us to derive the precepts associated with the principle of legality. Moreover, we can say that, other things equal, one legal order is more justly administered than another if it more perfectly fulfills the precepts of the rule of law. It will provide a more secure basis for liberty and a more effective means for organizing cooperative schemes. Yet because these precepts guarantee only the impartial and regular administration of rules, whatever these are, they are compatible with injustice. They impose rather weak constraints on the basic structure, but ones that are not by any means negligible.

Let us begin with the precept that ought implies can. This precept identifies several obvious features of legal systems. First of all, the actions which the rules of law require and forbid should be of a kind which men can reasonably be expected to do and to avoid. A system of rules addressed to rational persons to organize their conduct concerns itself with what they can and cannot do. It must not impose a duty to do what cannot be done. Secondly, the notion that ought implies can conveys the idea that those who enact laws and give orders do so in good faith. Legislators and judges, and other officials of the system, must believe that the laws can be obeyed; and they are to assume that any orders given can be carried out. Moreover, not only must the authorities act in good faith, but their good faith must be recognized by those subject to their enactments. Laws and commands are accepted as laws and commands only if it is generally believed that they can be obeyed and executed. If this is in question, the actions of authorities presumably have some other purpose than to organize conduct. Finally, this precept expresses the requirement that a legal system should recognize impossibility of performance as a defense, or at least as a mitigating circumstance. In enforcing rules a legal system cannot regard the inability to perform as irrelevant. It would be an intolerable burden on liberty if the liability to penalties was not normally limited to actions within our power to do or not to do.

The rule of law also implies the precept that similar cases be treated similarly. Men could not regulate their actions by means of rules if this precept were not followed. To be sure, this notion does not take us very far. For we must suppose that the criteria of similarity are given by the legal rules themselves and the principles used to interpret them. Nevertheless, the precept that like decisions be given in like cases significantly limits the discretion of judges and others in authority. The precept forces them to justify the distinctions that they make between persons by reference to the relevant legal rules and principles. In any particular case, if the rules are at all complicated and call for interpretation, it may be easy to justify an arbitrary decision. But as the number of cases increases, plausible justifications for biased judgments become more difficult to construct. The requirement of consistency holds of course for the interpretation of all rules and for justifications at all levels. Eventually reasoned arguments for discriminatory judgments become harder to formulate and the attempt to do so less persuasive. This precept holds also in cases of equity, that is, when an exception is to be made when the established rule works an unexpected hardship. But with this proviso: since there is no clear line separating these exceptional cases, there comes a point, as in matters of interpretation, at which nearly any difference will make a difference. In these instances, the principle of authoritative decision applies, and the weight of precedent or of the announced verdict suffices.[21]

The precept that there is no offense without a law (*Nullum crimen sine lege*), and the requirements it implies, also follow from the idea of a legal system. This precept demands that laws be known and expressly promulgated, that their meaning be clearly defined, that statutes be general both in statement and intent and not be used as a way of harming particular individuals who may be expressly named (bills of attainder), that at least the more severe offenses be strictly construed, and that penal laws should not be retroactive to the disadvantage of those to whom they apply. These requirements are implicit in the notion of regulating behavior by public rules. For if, say, statutes are not clear in what they enjoin and forbid, the citizen does not know how he is to behave. Moreover, while there may be occasional bills of attainder and retroactive enactments, these cannot be pervasive or characteristic features of the system, else it must have another purpose. A tyrant might change laws without notice, and punish (if that is the right word) his subjects accordingly, because he takes pleasure in seeing how long it takes them to figure out what the new rules are from observing the penalties he inflicts. But these rules would not be a legal system, since they would not serve to organize social behavior by providing a basis for legitimate expectations.

Finally, there are those precepts defining the notion of natural justice. These are guidelines intended to preserve the integrity of the judicial process.[22] If laws are directives addressed to rational persons for their guidance, courts must be concerned to apply and to enforce these rules in an appropriate way. A conscientious effort must be made to determine whether an infraction has taken place

21. See Lon Fuller, *Anatomy of the Law* (New York, The New American Library, 1969), p. 182.

22. This sense of natural justice is traditional. See H. L. A. Hart, *The Concept of Law* (Oxford, The Clarendon Press, 1961), pp. 156, 202.

and to impose the correct penalty. Thus a legal system must make provisions for conducting orderly trials and hearings; it must contain rules of evidence that guarantee rational procedures of inquiry. While there are variations in these procedures, the rule of law requires some form of due process: that is, a process reasonably designed to ascertain the truth, in ways consistent with the other ends of the legal system, as to whether a violation has taken place and under what circumstances. For example, judges must be independent and impartial, and no man may judge his own case. Trials must be fair and open, but not prejudiced by public clamor. The precepts of natural justice are to insure that the legal order will be impartially and regularly maintained.

Now the connection of the rule of law with liberty is clear enough. Liberty, as I have said, is a complex of rights and duties defined by institutions. The various liberties specify things that we may choose to do, if we wish, and in regard to which, when the nature of the liberty makes it appropriate, others have a duty not to interfere.[23] But if the precept of no crime without a law is violated, say by statutes, being vague and imprecise, what we are at liberty to do is likewise vague and imprecise. The boundaries of our liberty are uncertain. And to the extent that this is so, liberty is restricted by a reasonable fear of its exercise. The same sort of consequences follow if similar cases are not treated similarly, if the judicial process lacks its essential integrity, if the law does not recognize impossibility of performance as a defense, and so on. The principle of legality has a firm foundation, then, in the agreement of

23. It may be disputed whether this view holds for all rights, for example, the right to pick up an unclaimed article. See Hart in *Philosophical Review,* vol. 64, p. 179. But perhaps it is true enough for our purposes here. While some of the basic rights are similarly competition rights, as we may call them—for example, the right to participate in public affairs and to influence the political decisions taken—at the same time everyone has a duty to conduct himself in a certain way. This duty is one of fair political conduct, so to speak, and to violate it is a kind of interference. As we have seen, the constitution aims to establish a framework within which equal political rights fairly pursued and having their fair value are likely to lead to just and effective legislation. When appropriate we can interpret the statement in the text along these lines. On this point see Richard Wollheim, "Equality," *Proceedings of the Aristotelian Society,* vol. 56 (1955–1956), pp. 291ff. Put another way, the right can be redescribed as the right to try to do something under specified circumstances, these circumstances allowing for the fair rivalry of others. Unfairness becomes a characteristic form of interference.

rational persons to establish for themselves the greatest equal liberty. To be confident in the possesssion and exercise of these freedoms, the citizens of a well-ordered society will normally want the rule of law maintained.

We can arrive at the same conclusion in a slightly different way. It is reasonable to assume that even in a well-ordered society the coercive powers of government are to some degree necessary for the stability of social cooperation. For although men know that they share a common sense of justice and that each wants to adhere to the existing arrangements, they may nevertheless lack full confidence in one another. They may suspect that some are not doing their part, and so they may be tempted not to do theirs. The general awareness of these temptations may eventually cause the scheme to break down. The suspicion that others are not honoring their duties and obligations is increased by the fact that, in the absence of the authoritative interpretation and enforcement of the rules, it is particularly easy to find excuses for breaking them. Thus even under reasonably ideal conditions, it is hard to imagine, for example, a successful income tax scheme on a voluntary basis. Such an arrangement is unstable. The role of an authorized public interpretation of rules supported by collective sanctions is precisely to overcome this instability. By enforcing a public system of penalties government removes the grounds for thinking that others are not complying with the rules. For this reason alone, a coercive sovereign is presumably always necessary, even though in a well-ordered society sanctions are not severe and may never need to be imposed. Rather, the existence of effective penal machinery serves as men's security to one another. This proposition and the reasoning behind it we may think of as Hobbes's thesis[24] (§42).

Now in setting up such a system of sanctions the parties in a constitutional convention must weigh its disadvantages. These are of at least two kinds: one kind is the cost of maintaining the agency covered say by taxation; the other is the danger to the liberty of the representative citizen measured by the likelihood that these sanc-

24. See *Leviathan,* chs. 13–18. And also Howard Warrender, *The Political Philosophy of Hobbes* (Oxford, The Clarendon Press, 1957), ch. III; and D. P. Gauthier, *The Logic of Leviathan* (Oxford, The Clarendon Press, 1969), pp. 76–89.

tions will wrongly interfere with his freedom. The establishment of a coercive agency is rational only if these disadvantages are less than the loss of liberty from instability. Assuming this to be so, the best arrangement is one that minimizes these hazards. It is clear that, other things equal, the dangers to liberty are less when the law is impartially and regularly administered in accordance with the principle of legality. While a coercive mechanism is necessary, it is obviously essential to define precisely the tendency of its operations. Knowing what things it penalizes and knowing that these are within their power to do or not to do, citizens can draw up their plans accordingly. One who complies with the announced rules need never fear an infringement of his liberty.

It is clear from the preceding remarks that we need an account of penal sanctions however limited even for ideal theory. Given the normal conditions of human life, some such arrangements are necessary. I have maintained that the principles justifying these sanctions can be derived from the principle of liberty. The ideal conception shows in this case anyway how the nonideal scheme is to be set up; and this confirms the conjecture that it is ideal theory which is fundamental. We also see that the principle of responsibility is not founded on the idea that punishment is primarily retributive or denunciatory. Instead it is acknowledged for the sake of liberty itself. Unless citizens are able to know what the law is and are given a fair opportunity to take its directives into account, penal sanctions should not apply to them. This principle is simply the consequence of regarding a legal system as an order of public rules addressed to rational persons in order to regulate their cooperation, and of giving the appropriate weight to liberty. I believe that this view of responsibility enables us to explain most of the excuses and defenses recognized by the criminal law under the heading of *mens rea* and that it can serve as a guide to legal reform. However, these points cannot be pursued here.[25] It suffices to note that ideal theory requires an account of penal sanctions as a stabilizing device and indicates the manner in which this part of partial compliance theory should be worked out. In particular, the principle of liberty leads to the principle of responsibility.

25. For these matters, consult H. L. A. Hart, *Punishment and Responsibility* (Oxford, The Clarendon Press, 1968), pp. 173–183, whom I follow here.

The moral dilemmas that arise in partial compliance theory are also to be viewed with the priority of liberty in mind. Thus we can imagine situations of an unhappy sort in which it may be permissible to insist less strongly on the precepts of the rule of law being followed. For example, in some extreme eventualities persons might be held liable for certain offenses contrary to the precept ought implies can. Suppose that, aroused by sharp religious antagonisms, members of rival sects are collecting weapons and forming armed bands in preparation for civil strife. Confronted with this situation the government may enact a statute forbidding the possession of firearms (assuming that possession is not already an offense). And the law may hold that sufficient evidence for conviction is that the weapons are found in the defendant's house or property, unless he can establish that they were put there by another. Except for this proviso, the absence of intent and knowledge of possession, and conformity to reasonable standards of care, are declared irrelevant. It is contended that these normal defenses would make the law ineffective and impossible to enforce.

Now although this statute trespasses upon the precept ought implies can it might be accepted by the representative citizen as a lesser loss of liberty, at least if the penalties imposed are not too severe. (Here I assume that imprisonment, say, is a drastic curtailment of liberty, and so the severity of the contemplated punishments must be taken into account.) Viewing the situation from the legislative stage, one may decide that the formation of paramilitary groups, which the passing of the statute may forestall, is a much greater danger to the freedom of the average citizen than being held strictly liable for the possession of weapons. Citizens may affirm the law as the lesser of two evils, resigning themselves to the fact that while they may be held guilty for things they have not done, the risks to their liberty on any other course would be worse. Since bitter dissensions exist, there is no way to prevent some injustices, as we ordinarily think of them, from occurring. All that can be done is to limit these injustices in the least unjust way.

The conclusion once again is that arguments for restricting liberty proceed from the principle of liberty itself. To some degree anyway, the priority of liberty carries over to partial compliance theory. Thus in the situation discussed the greater good of some has not been balanced against the lesser good of others. Nor has a lesser liberty been accepted for the sake of greater economic and social benefits. Rather the appeal has been to the common good in the form of the basic equal liberties of the representative citizen. Unfortunate circumstances and the unjust designs of some necessitate a much lesser liberty than that enjoyed in a well-ordered society. Any injustice in the social order is bound to take its toll; it is impossible that its consequences should be entirely canceled out. In applying the principle of legality we must keep in mind the totality of rights and duties that defines the liberties and adjust its claims accordingly. Sometimes we may be forced to allow certain breaches of its precepts if we are to mitigate the loss of freedom from social evils that cannot be removed, and to aim for the least injustice that conditions allow.

39. THE PRIORITY OF LIBERTY DEFINED

Aristotle remarks that it is a peculiarity of men that they possess a sense of the just and the unjust and that their sharing a common understanding of justice makes a polis.[26] Analogously one might say, in view of our discussion, that a common understanding of justice as fairness makes a constitutional democracy. For I have tried to show, after presenting further arguments for the first principle, that the basic liberties of a democratic regime are most firmly secured by this conception of justice. In each case the conclusions reached are familiar. My aim has been to indicate not only that the principles of justice fit our considered judgments but also that they provide the strongest arguments for freedom. By contrast teleological principles permit at best uncertain grounds for liberty, or at least for equal liberty. And liberty of conscience and freedom of thought should not be founded on philosophical or ethical skepticism, nor on indifference to religious and moral interests. The principles of justice define an appropriate path between dogmatism and intolerance on the one side, and a reductionism which regards religion and morality as mere preferences on the other. And since the theory of justice relies upon weak and widely held presump-

26. *Politics,* bk. I, ch. II, 1253a15.

tions, it may win quite general acceptance. Surely our liberties are most firmly based when they are derived from principles that persons fairly situated with respect to one another can agree to if they can agree to anything at all.

I now wish to examine more carefully the meaning of the priority of liberty. I shall not argue here for this priority (leaving this aside until § 82); instead I wish to clarify its sense in view of the preceding examples, among others. There are several priorities to be distinguished. By the priority of liberty I mean the precedence of the principle of equal liberty over the second principle of justice. The two principles are in lexical order, and therefore the claims of liberty are to be satisfied first. Until this is achieved no other principle comes into play. The priority of the right over the good, or of fair opportunity over the difference principle, is not presently our concern.

As all the previous examples illustrate, the precedence of liberty means that liberty can be restricted only for the sake of liberty itself. There are two sorts of cases. The basic liberties may either be less extensive though still equal, or they may be unequal. If liberty is less extensive, the representative citizen must find this a gain for his freedom on balance; and if liberty is unequal, the freedom of those with the lesser liberty must be better secured. In both instances the justification proceeds by reference to the whole system of the equal liberties. These priority rules have already been noted on a number of occasions.

There is, however, a further distinction that must be made between two kinds of circumstances that justify or excuse a restriction of liberty. First a restriction can derive from the natural limitations and accidents of human life, or from historical and social contingencies. The question of the justice of these constraints does not arise. For example, even in a well-ordered society under favorable circumstances, liberty of thought and conscience is subject to reasonable regulations and the principle of participation is restricted in extent. These constraints issue from the more or less permanent conditions of political life; others are adjustments to the natural features of the human situation, as with the lesser liberty of children. In these cases the problem is to discover the just way to meet certain given limitations.

In the second kind of case, injustice already exists, either in social arrangements or in the conduct of individuals. The question here is what is the just way to answer injustice. This injustice may, of course, have many explanations, and those who act unjustly often do so with the conviction that they pursue a higher cause. The examples of intolerant and of rival sects illustrate this possibility. But men's propensity to injustice is not a permanent aspect of community life; it is greater or less depending in large part on social institutions, and in particular on whether these are just or unjust. A well-ordered society tends to eliminate or at least to control men's inclinations to injustice (see Chapters VIII–IX), and therefore warring and intolerant sects, say, are much less likely to exist, or to be a danger, once such a society is established. How justice requires us to meet injustice is a very different problem from how best to cope with the inevitable limitations and contingencies of human life.

These two kinds of cases raise several questions. It will be recalled that strict compliance is one of the stipulations of the original position; the principles of justice are chosen on the supposition that they will be generally complied with. Any failures are discounted as exceptions (§ 25). By putting these principles in lexical order, the parties are choosing a conception of justice suitable for favorable conditions and assuming that a just society can in due course be achieved. Arranged in this order, the principles define then a perfectly just scheme; they belong to ideal theory and set up an aim to guide the course of social reform. But even granting the soundness of these principles for this purpose, we must still ask how well they apply to institutions under less than favorable conditions, and whether they provide any guidance for instances of injustice. The principles and their lexical order were not acknowledged with these situations in mind and so it is possible that they no longer hold.

I shall not attempt to give a systematic answer to these questions. A few special cases are taken up later (see Chapter VI). The intuitive idea is to split the theory of justice into two parts. The first or ideal part assumes strict compliance and works out the principles that characterize a well-ordered society under favorable circumstances. It develops the conception of a perfectly just basic structure and the corresponding duties and obligations of persons under the fixed constraints of human life. My main concern is with this part of the theory. Nonideal theory, the second part, is worked out after an ideal conception of justice has been chosen; only then do the parties ask which principles to adopt under less happy conditions. This division of the theory has, as I have indicated, two rather different subparts. One consists of the principles for governing adjustments to natural limitations and historical contingencies, and the other of principles for meeting injustice.

Viewing the theory of justice as a whole, the ideal part presents a conception of a just society that we are to achieve if we can. Existing institutions are to be judged in the light of this conception and held to be unjust to the extent that they depart from it without sufficient reason. The lexical ranking of the principles specifies which elements of the ideal are relatively more urgent, and the priority rules this ordering suggests are to be applied to nonideal cases as well. Thus as far as circumstances permit, we have a natural duty to remove any injustices, beginning with the most grievous as identified by the extent of the deviation from perfect justice. Of course, this idea is extremely rough. The measure of departures from the ideal is left importantly to intuition. Still our judgment is guided by the priority indicated by the lexical ordering. If we have a reasonably clear picture of what is just, our considered convictions of justice may fall more closely into line even though we cannot formulate precisely how this greater convergence comes about. Thus while the principles of justice belong to the theory of an ideal state of affairs, they are generally relevant.

The several parts of nonideal theory may be illustrated by various examples, some of which we have discussed. One type of situation is that involving a less extensive liberty. Since there are no inequalities, but all are to have a narrower rather than a wider freedom, the question can be assessed from the perspective of the representative equal citizen. To appeal to the interests of this representative man in applying the principles of justice is to invoke the principle of the common interest. (The common good I think of as certain general conditions that are in an appropriate sense equally to everyone's advantage.) Several of the preceding examples involve a less extensive liberty: the regulation of liberty of conscience and freedom of thought in ways consistent with public order, and the limitation on the scope of majority rule belong to this category (§ § 34, 37). These constraints arise from the permanent conditions of human life and therefore these cases belong to that part of nonideal theory which deals with natural limitations. The two examples of curbing the liberties of the intolerant and of restraining the violence of contending sects, since they involve injustice, belong to the partial compliance part of nonideal theory. In each of these four cases, however, the argument proceeds from the viewpoint of the representative citizen. Following the idea of the lexical ordering, the limitations upon the extent of liberty are for the sake of liberty itself and result in a lesser but still equal freedom.

The second kind of case is that of an unequal liberty. If some have more votes than others, political liberty is unequal; and the same is true if the votes of some are weighted much more heavily, or if a segment of society is without the franchise altogether. In many historical situations a lesser political liberty may have been justified. Perhaps Burke's unrealistic account of representation had an element of validity in the context of eighteenth century society.[27] If so, it reflects the fact that the various liberties are not all on a par, for while at that time unequal political liberty might conceivably have been a permissible adjustment to historical limitations, serfdom and slavery, and religious intolerance, certainly were not. These constraints do not justify the loss of liberty of conscience and the rights defining the integrity of the person. The case for certain political liberties and the rights of fair equality of opportunity is less compelling. As I noted before (§ 11), it may be reasonable to forgo part of these freedoms when the long-run benefits are great enough to transform a less fortunate society into one where the equal liberties can be fully enjoyed. This is especially true when circumstances are not conducive to the exercise of these rights in any case. Under certain conditions that cannot be at present removed, the value of some liberties may not be so high as to rule out the possibility of compensation to those less fortunate. To accept the lexical ordering of the two principles we are not required to deny that the value of liberty depends upon circumstances. But it does have to be shown that as the general conception of justice is followed social conditions are eventually brought about under which a lesser than equal liberty would no longer be accepted. Unequal liberty is then no longer

27. See H. F. Pitkin, *The Concept of Representation*, ch. VIII, for an account of Burke's view.

justified. The lexical order is, so to speak, the inherent long-run equilibrium of a just system. Once the tendency to equality has worked itself out, if not long before, the two principles are to be serially ranked.

In these remarks I have assumed that it is always those with the lesser liberty who must be compensated. We are always to appraise the situation from their point of view (as seen from the constitutional convention or the legislature). Now it is this restriction that makes it practically certain that slavery and serfdom, in their familiar forms anyway, are tolerable only when they relieve even worse injustices. There may be transition cases where enslavement is better than current practice. For example, suppose that city-states that previously have not taken prisoners of war but have always put captives to death agree by treaty to hold prisoners as slaves instead. Although we cannot allow the institution of slavery on the grounds that the greater gains of some outweigh the losses to others, it may be that under these conditions, since all run the risk of capture in war, this form of slavery is less unjust than present custom. At least the servitude envisaged is not hereditary (let us suppose) and it is accepted by the free citizens of more or less equal city-states. The arrangement seems defensible as an advance on established institutions, if slaves are not treated too severely. In time it will presumably be abandoned altogether, since the exchange of prisoners of war is a still more desirable arrangement, the return of the captured members of the community being preferable to the services of slaves. But none of these considerations, however fanciful, tend in any way to justify hereditary slavery or serfdom by citing natural or historical limitations. Moreover, one cannot at this point appeal to the necessity or at least to the great advantage of these servile arrangements for the higher forms of culture. As I shall argue later, the principle of perfection would be rejected in the original position (§ 50).

The problem of paternalism deserves some discussion here, since it has been mentioned in the argument for equal liberty, and concerns a lesser freedom. In the original position the parties assume that in society they are rational and able to manage their own affairs. Therefore they do not acknowledge any duties to self, since this is unnecessary to further their good. But once the ideal conception is chosen, they will want to insure themselves against the possibility that their powers are undeveloped and they cannot rationally advance their interests, as in the case of children; or that through some misfortune or accident they are unable to make decisions for their good, as in the case of those seriously injured or mentally disturbed. It is also rational for them to protect themselves against their own irrational inclinations by consenting to a scheme of penalties that may give them a sufficient motive to avoid foolish actions and by accepting certain impositions designed to undo the unfortunate consequences of their imprudent behavior. For these cases the parties adopt principles stipulating when others are authorized to act in their behalf and to override their present wishes if necessary; and this they do recognizing that sometimes their capacity to act rationally for their good may fail, or be lacking altogether.[28]

Thus the principles of paternalism are those that the parties would acknowledge in the original position to protect themselves against the weakness and infirmities of their reason and will in society. Others are authorized and sometimes required to act on our behalf and to do what we would do for ourselves if we were rational, this authorization coming into effect only when we cannot look after our own good. Paternalistic decisions are to be guided by the individual's own settled preferences and interests insofar as they are not irrational, or failing a knowledge of these, by the theory of primary goods. As we know less and less about a person, we act for him as we would act for ourselves from the standpoint of the original position. We try to get for him the things he presumably wants whatever else he wants. We must be able to argue that with the development or the recovery of his rational powers the individual in question will accept our decision on his behalf and agree with us that we did the best thing for him.

The requirement that the other person in due course accepts his condition is not, however, by any means sufficient, even if this condition is not open to rational criticism. Thus imagine two persons in full possession of their reason and will who affirm different religious or philosophical beliefs; and suppose that there is some psychological process that will convert each to the other's view, despite

---

28. For a discussion of this problem see Gerald Dworkin, "Paternalism," an essay in *Morality and the Law,* ed. R. A. Wasserstrom (Belmont, Calif., Wadsworth Publishing Co., 1971), pp. 107–126.

the fact that the process is imposed on them against their wishes. In due course, let us suppose, both will come to accept conscientiously their new beliefs. We are still not permitted to submit them to this treatment. Two further stipulations are necessary: paternalistic intervention must be justified by the evident failure or absence of reason and will; and it must be guided by the principles of justice and what is known about the subject's more permanent aims and preferences, or by the account of primary goods. These restrictions on the initiation and direction of paternalistic measures follow from the assumptions of the original position. The parties want to guarantee the integrity of their person and their final ends and beliefs whatever these are. Paternalistic principles are a protection against our own irrationality, and must not be interpreted to license assaults on one's convictions and character by any means so long as these offer the prospect of securing consent later on. More generally, methods of education must likewise honor these constraints (§ 78).

The force of justice as fairness would appear to arise from two things: the requirement that all inequalities be justified to the least advantaged, and the priority of liberty. This pair of constraints distinguishes it from intuitionism and teleological theories. Taking the preceding discussion into account, we can reformulate the first principle of justice and conjoin to it the appropriate priority rule. The changes and additions are, I believe, self-explanatory. The principle now reads as follows.

First Principle

Each person is to have an equal right to the most extensive total system of equal basic liberties compatible with a similar system of liberty for all.

Priority Rule

The principles of justice are to be ranked in lexical order and therefore liberty can be restricted only for the sake of liberty. There are two cases: (a) a less extensive liberty must strengthen the total system of liberty shared by all, and (b) a less than equal liberty must be acceptable to those citizens with the lesser liberty.

It perhaps bears repeating that I have yet to give a systematic argument for the priority rule, although I have checked it out in a number of important cases. It appears to fit our considered convictions fairly well. But an argument from the standpoint of the original position I postpone until Part Three when the full force of the contract doctrine can be brought into play (§ 82).

40. THE KANTIAN INTERPRETATION OF JUSTICE AS FAIRNESS

For the most part I have considered the content of the principle of equal liberty and the meaning of the priority of the rights that it defines. It seems appropriate at this point to note that there is a Kantian interpretation of the conception of justice from which this principle derives. This interpretation is based upon Kant's notion of autonomy. It is a mistake, I believe, to emphasize the place of generality and universality in Kant's ethics. That moral principles are general and universal is hardly new with him; and as we have seen these conditions do not in any case take us very far. It is impossible to construct a moral theory on so slender a basis, and therefore to limit the discussion of Kant's doctrine to these notions is to reduce it to triviality. The real force of his view lies elsewhere.[29]

For one thing, he begins with the idea that moral principles are the object of rational choice. They define the moral law that men can rationally will to govern their conduct in an ethical commonwealth. Moral philosophy becomes the study of the conception and outcome of a suitably defined rational decision. This idea has im-

29. To be avoided at all costs is the idea that Kant's doctrine simply provides the general, or formal, elements for a utilitarian (or indeed for any other) theory. See, for example, R. M. Hare, *Freedom and Reason* (Oxford, The Clarendon Press, 1963), pp. 123f. One must not lose sight of the full scope of his view, one must take the later works into consideration. Unfortunately, there is no commentary on Kant's moral theory as a whole; perhaps it would prove impossible to write. But the standard works of H. J. Paton, *The Categorical Imperative* (Chicago, University of Chicago Press, 1948), and L. W. Beck, *A Commentary on Kant's Critique of Practical Reason* (Chicago, University of Chicago Press, 1960), and others need to be further complemented by studies of the other writings. See here M. J. Gregor's *Laws of Freedom* (Oxford, Basil Blackwell, 1963), an account of *The Metaphysics of Morals,* and J. G. Murphy's brief *Kant: The Philosophy of Right* (London, Macmillan, 1970). Beyond this, *The Critique of Judgment, Religion within the Limits of Reason,* and the political writings cannot be neglected without distorting his doctrine. For the last, see *Kant's Political Writings,* ed. Hans Reiss and trans. H. B. Nisbet (Cambridge, The University Press, 1970).

mediate consequences. For once we think of moral principles as legislation for a kingdom of ends, it is clear that these principles must not only be acceptable to all but public as well. Finally Kant supposes that this moral legislation is to be agreed to under conditions that characterize men as free and equal rational beings. The description of the original position is an attempt to interpret this conception. I do not wish to argue here for this interpretation on the basis of Kant's text. Certainly some will want to read him differently. Perhaps the remarks to follow are best taken as suggestions for relating justice as fairness to the high point of the contractarian tradition in Kant and Rousseau.

Kant held, I believe, that a person is acting autonomously when the principles of his action are chosen by him as the most adequate possible expression of his nature as a free and equal rational being. The principles he acts upon are not adopted because of his social position or natural endowments, or in view of the particular kind of society in which he lives or the specific things that he happens to want. To act on such principles is to act heteronomously. Now the veil of ignorance deprives the persons in the original position of the knowledge that would enable them to choose heteronomous principles. The parties arrive at their choice together as free and equal rational persons knowing only that those circumstances obtain which give rise to the need for principles of justice.

To be sure, the argument for these principles does add in various ways to Kant's conception. For example, it adds the feature that the principles chosen are to apply to the basic structure of society; and premises characterizing this structure are used in deriving the principles of justice. But I believe that this and other additions are natural enough and remain fairly close to Kant's doctrine, at least when all of his ethical writings are viewed together. Assuming, then, that the reasoning in favor of the principles of justice is correct, we can say that when persons act on these principles they are acting in accordance with principles that they would choose as rational and independent persons in an original position of equality. The principles of their actions do not depend upon social or natural contingencies, nor do they reflect the bias of the particulars of their plan of life or the aspirations that motivate them. By acting from these principles persons express their nature as free and equal rational beings subject to the general conditions of human life. For to express one's nature as a being of a particular kind is to act on the principles that would be chosen if this nature were the decisive determining element. Of course, the choice of the parties in the original position is subject to the restrictions of that situation. But when we knowingly act on the principles of justice in the ordinary course of events, we deliberately assume the limitations of the original position. One reason for doing this, for persons who can do so and want to, is to give expression to one's nature.

The principles of justice are also categorical imperatives in Kant's sense. For by a categorical imperative Kant understands a principle of conduct that applies to a person in virtue of his nature as a free and equal rational being. The validity of the principle does not presuppose that one has a particular desire or aim. Whereas a hypothetical imperative by contrast does assume this: it directs us to take certain steps as effective means to achieve a specific end. Whether the desire is for a particular thing, or whether it is for something more general, such as certain kinds of agreeable feelings or pleasures, the corresponding imperative is hypothetical. Its applicability depends upon one's having an aim which one need not have as a condition of being a rational human individual. The argument for the two principles of justice does not assume that the parties have particular ends, but only that they desire certain primary goods. These are things that it is rational to want whatever else one wants. Thus given human nature, wanting them is part of being rational; and while each is presumed to have some conception of the good, nothing is known about his final ends. The preference for primary goods is derived, then, from only the most general assumptions about rationality and the conditions of human life. To act from the principles of justice is to act from categorical imperatives in the sense that they apply to us whatever in particular our aims are. This simply reflects the fact that no such contingencies appear as premises in their derivation.

We may note also that the motivational assumption of mutual disinterest accords with Kant's notion of autonomy, and gives another reason for this condition. So far this assumption has been used to characterize the circumstances of justice and to provide a clear conception to guide the reasoning of the parties. We have also seen that the concept of benevolence, being a second-order notion, would not work out well. Now we can add that the assumption of mutual disinterest is to allow for freedom in the choice of a system of final ends.[30] Liberty in adopting a conception of the good is limited only by principles that are deduced from a doctrine which imposes no prior constraints on these conceptions. Presuming mutual disinterest in the original position carries out this idea. We postulate that the parties have opposing claims in a suitably general sense. If their ends were restricted in some specific way, this would appear at the outset as an arbitrary restriction on freedom. Moreover, if the parties were conceived as altruists, or as pursuing certain kinds of pleasures, then the principles chosen would apply, as far as the argument would have shown, only to persons whose freedom was restricted to choices compatible with altruism or hedonism. As the argument now runs, the principles of justice cover all persons with rational plans of life, whatever their content, and these principles represent the appropriate restrictions on freedom. Thus it is possible to say that the constraints on conceptions of the good are the result of an interpretation of the contractual situation that puts no prior limitations on what men may desire. There are a variety of reasons, then, for the motivational premise of mutual disinterest. This premise is not only a matter of realism about the circumstances of justice or a way to make the theory manageable. It also connects up with the Kantian idea of autonomy.

There is, however, a difficulty that should be clarified. It is well expressed by Sidgwick.[31] He remarks that nothing in Kant's ethics is more striking than the idea that a man realizes his true self when he acts from the moral law, whereas if he permits his actions to be determined by sensuous desires or contingent aims, he becomes subject to the law of nature. Yet in Sidgwick's opinion this idea comes to naught. It seems to him that on Kant's view the lives of the saint and the scoundrel are equally the outcome of a free choice (on the part of the noumenal self) and equally the subject of causal laws (as a phenomenal self). Kant never explains why the scoundrel does

30. For this point I am indebted to Charles Fried.
31. See *The Methods of Ethics,* 7th ed. (London, Macmillan, 1907), Appendix, "The Kantian Conception of Free Will" (reprinted from *Mind,* vol. 13, 1888), pp. 511–516, esp. p. 516.

not express in a bad life his characteristic and freely chosen self-hood in the same way that a saint expresses his characteristic and freely chosen selfhood in a good one. Sidgwick's objection is decisive, I think, as long as one assumes, as Kant's exposition may seem to allow, both that the noumenal self can choose any consistent set of principles and that acting from such principles, whatever they are, is sufficient to express one's choice as that of a free and equal rational being. Kant's reply must be that though acting on any consistent set of principles could be the outcome of a decision on the part of the noumenal self, not all such action by the phenomenal self expresses this decision as that of a free and equal rational being. Thus if a person realizes his true self by expressing it in his actions, and if he desires above all else to realize this self, then he will choose to act from principles that manifest his nature as a free and equal rational being. The missing part of the argument concerns the concept of expression. Kant did not show that acting from the moral law expresses our nature in identifiable ways that acting from contrary principles does not.

This defect is made good, I believe, by the conception of the original position. The essential point is that we need an argument showing which principles, if any, free and equal rational persons would choose and these principles must be applicable in practice. A definite answer to this question is required to meet Sidgwick's objection. My suggestion is that we think of the original position as the point of view from which noumenal selves see the world. The parties qua noumenal selves have complete freedom to choose whatever principles they wish; but they also have a desire to express their nature as rational and equal members of the intelligible realm with precisely this liberty to choose, that is, as beings who can look at the world in this way and express this perspective in their life as members of society. They must decide, then, which principles when consciously followed and acted upon in everyday life will best manifest this freedom in their community, most fully reveal their independence from natural contingencies and social accident. Now if the argument of the contract doctrine is correct, these principles are indeed those defining the moral law, or more exactly, the principles of justice for institutions and individuals. The description of the original position interprets the point of view of noumenal selves, of what it means to be a free and equal rational being. Our nature as such beings is displayed when we act from the principles we would choose when this nature is reflected in the conditions determining the choice. Thus men exhibit their freedom, their independence from the contingencies of nature and society, by acting in ways they would acknowledge in the original position.

Properly understood, then, the desire to act justly derives in part from the desire to express most fully what we are or can be, namely free and equal rational beings with a liberty to choose. It is for this reason, I believe, that Kant speaks of the failure to act on the moral law as giving rise to shame and not to feelings of guilt. And this is appropriate, since for him acting unjustly is acting in a manner that fails to express our nature as a free and equal rational being. Such actions therefore strike at our self-respect, our sense of our own worth, and the experience of this loss is shame (§ 67). We have acted as though we belonged to a lower order, as though we were a creature whose first principles are decided by natural contingencies. Those who think of Kant's moral doctrine as one of law and guilt badly misunderstand him. Kant's main aim is to deepen and to justify Rousseau's idea that liberty is acting in accordance with a law that we give to ourselves. And this leads not to a morality of austere command but to an ethic of mutual respect and self-esteem.[32]

The original position may be viewed, then, as a procedural interpretation of Kant's conception of autonomy and the categorical imperative. The principles regulative of the kingdom of ends are those that would be chosen in this position, and the description of this situation enables us to explain the sense in which acting from these principles expresses our nature as free and equal rational persons. No longer are these notions purely transcendent and lacking explicable connections with human conduct, for the procedural conception of the original position allows us to make these ties. It is true that I have departed from Kant's views in several respects. I

32. See B. A. O. Williams, "The Idea of Equality," in *Philosophy, Politics and Society*, Second Series, ed. Peter Laslett and W. G. Runciman (Oxford, Basil Blackwell, 1962), pp. 115f. For confirmation of this interpretation, see Kant's remarks on moral education in *The Critique of Practical Reason*, pt. II. See also Beck, *A Commentary on Kant's Critique of Practical Reason*, pp. 233–236.

shall not discuss these matters here; but two points should be noted. The person's choice as a noumenal self I have assumed to be a collective one. The force of the self's being equal is that the principles chosen must be acceptable to other selves. Since all are similarly free and rational, each must have an equal say in adopting the public principles of the ethical commonwealth. This means that as noumenal selves, everyone is to consent to these principles. Unless the scoundrel's principles would be chosen, they cannot express this free choice, however much a single self might be of a mind to opt for them. Later I shall try to define a clear sense in which this unanimous agreement is best expressive of the nature of even a single self (§ 85). It in no way overrides a person's interests as the collective nature of the choice might seem to imply. But I leave this aside for the present.

Secondly, I have assumed all along that the parties know that they are subject to the conditions of human life. Being in the circumstances of justice, they are situated in the world with other men who likewise face limitations of moderate scarcity and competing claims. Human freedom is to be regulated by principles chosen in the light of these natural restrictions. Thus justice as fairness is a theory of human justice and among its premises are the elementary facts about persons and their place in nature. The freedom of pure intelligences not subject to these constraints, and the freedom of God, are outside the scope of the theory. It might appear that Kant meant his doctrine to apply to all rational beings as such and therefore to God and the angels as well. Men's social situation in the world may seem to have no role in his theory in determining the first principles of justice. I do not believe that Kant held this view, but I cannot discuss this question here. It suffices to say that if I am mistaken, the Kantian interpretation of justice as fairness is less faithful to Kant's intentions than I am presently inclined to suppose.

CHAPTER V. DISTRIBUTIVE SHARES

In this chapter I take up the second principle of justice and describe an arrangement of institutions that fulfills its requirements within the setting of a modern state. I begin by noting that the principles of justice may serve as part of a doctrine of political economy. The utilitarian tradition has stressed this application and we must see how they fare in this regard. I also emphasize that these principles have embedded in them a certain ideal of social institutions, and this fact will be of importance when we consider the values of community in Part Three. As a preparation for subsequent discussions, there are some brief comments on economic systems, the role of markets, and the like. Then I turn to the difficult problem of saving and justice between generations. The essentials are put together in an intuitive way, followed by some remarks devoted to the question of time preference and to some further cases of priority. After this I try to show that the account of distributive shares can explain the place of the common sense precepts of justice. I also examine perfectionism and intuitionism as theories of distributive justice, thus rounding out to some degree the contrast with other traditional views. Throughout the choice between a private-property economy and socialism is left open; from the standpoint of the theory of justice alone, various basic structures would appear to satisfy its principles.

41. THE CONCEPT OF JUSTICE IN
POLITICAL ECONOMY

My aim in this chapter is to see how the two principles work out as a conception of political economy, that is, as standards by which to assess economic arrangements and policies, and their background institutions. (Welfare economics is often defined in the same way.[1] I do not use this name because the term "welfare" suggests that the implicit moral conception is utilitarian; the phrase "social choice" is far better although I believe its connotations are still too narrow.) A doctrine of political economy must include an interpretation of the public good which is based on a conception of justice. It is to guide the reflections of the citizen when he considers questions of economic and social policy. He is to take up the perspective of the constitutional convention or the legislative stage and ascertain how the principles of justice apply. A political opinion concerns what advances the good of the body politic as a whole and invokes some criterion for the just division of social advantages.

From the beginning I have stressed that justice as fairness applies to the basic structure of society. It is a conception for ranking social forms viewed as closed systems. Some decision concerning these background arrangements is fundamental and cannot be avoided. In fact, the cumulative effect of social and economic legislation is to specify the basic structure. Moreover, the social system shapes the wants and aspirations that its citizens come to have. It determines in part the sort of persons they want to be as well as the sort of persons they are. Thus an economic system is not only an institutional device for satisfying existing wants and needs but a way of creating and fashioning wants in the future. How men work together now to satisfy their present desires affects the desires they will have later on, the kind of persons they will be. These matters are, of course, perfectly obvious and have always been recognized. They were stressed by economists as different as Marshall and Marx.[2] Since economic arrangements have these effects, and indeed must do so, the choice of these institutions involves some view of human good

1. Welfare economics is so defined by K. J. Arrow and Tibor Scitovsky in their introduction to *Readings in Welfare Economics* (Homewood, Ill., Richard D. Irwin, 1969), p. 1. For further discussion, see Abram Bergson, *Essays in Normative Economics* (Cambridge, Harvard University Press, 1966), pp. 35–39, 60–63, 68f; and A. K. Sen, *Collective Choice and Social Welfare* (San Francisco, Holden-Day, 1970), pp. 56–59.

2. For a discussion of this point and its consequences for political principles, see Brian Barry, *Political Argument* (London, Routledge and Kegan Paul, 1965), pp. 75–79.

and of the design of institutions to realize it. This choice must, therefore, be made on moral and political as well as on economic
grounds. Considerations of efficiency are but one basis of decision
and often relatively minor at that. Of course, this decision may not
be openly faced; it may be made by default. We often acquiesce
without thinking in the moral and political conception implicit in
the status quo, or leave things to be settled by how contending social
and economic forces happen to work themselves out. But political
economy must investigate this problem even if the conclusion
reached is that it is best left to the course of events to decide.

Now it may seem at first sight that the influence of the social
system upon human wants and men's view of themselves poses a
decisive objection to the contract view. One might think that this
conception of justice relies upon the aims of existing individuals and
regulates the social order by principles that persons guided by these
aims would choose. How, then, can this doctrine determine an
Archimedean point from which the basic structure itself can be
appraised? It might seem as if there is no alternative but to judge
institutions in the light of an ideal conception of the person arrived
at on perfectionist or on a priori grounds. But, as the account of the
original position and its Kantian interpretation makes clear, we
must not overlook the very special nature of that situation and the
scope of the principles adopted there. Only the most general assumptions are made about the aims of the parties, namely, that they take
an interest in primary social goods, in things that men are presumed to want whatever else they want. To be sure, the theory of
these goods depends on psychological premises and these may prove
incorrect. But the idea at any rate is to define a class of goods that are
normally wanted as parts of rational plans of life which may include
the most varied sorts of ends. To suppose, then, that the parties
want these goods, and to found a conception of justice on this
presumption, is not to tie it to a particular pattern of human interests as these might be generated by a particular arrangement of
institutions. The theory of justice does, indeed, presuppose a theory
of the good, but within wide limits this does not prejudge the choice
of the sort of persons that men want to be.

Once the principles of justice are derived, however, the contract doctrine does establish certain limits on the conception of the good. These limits follow from the priority of justice over efficiency and the priority of liberty over social and economic advantages (assuming that serial order obtains). For as I remarked earlier (§6), these priorities mean that desires for things that are inherently unjust, or that cannot be satisfied except by the violation of just arrangements, have no weight. There is no value in fulfilling these wants and the social system should discourage them. Further, one must take into account the problem of stability. A just system must generate its own support. This means that it must be arranged so as to bring about in its members the corresponding sense of justice, an effective desire to act in accordance with its rules for reasons of justice. Thus the requirement of stability and the criterion of discouraging desires that conflict with the principles of justice put further constraints on institutions. They must be not only just but framed so as to encourage the virtue of justice in those who take part in them. In this sense, the principles of justice define a partial ideal of the person which social and economic arrangements must respect. Finally, as the argument for embedding ideals into our working principles has brought out, certain institutions are required by the two principles. They define an ideal basic structure, or the outlines of one, toward which the course of reform should evolve.

The upshot of these considerations is that justice as fairness is not at the mercy, so to speak, of existing wants and interests. It sets up an Archimedean point for assessing the social system without invoking a priori considerations. The long range aim of society is settled in its main lines irrespective of the particular desires and needs of its present members. And an ideal conception of justice is defined since institutions are to foster the virtue of justice and to discourage desires and aspirations incompatible with it. Of course, the pace of change and the particular reforms called for at any given time depend upon current conditions. But the conception of justice, the general form of a just society and the ideal of the person consistent with it are not similarly dependent. There is no place for the question whether men's desires to play the role of superior or inferior might not be so great that autocratic institutions should be accepted, or whether men's perception of the religious practices of

261

others might not be so upsetting that liberty of conscience should not be allowed. We have no occasion to ask whether under reasonably favorable conditions the economic gains of technocratic but authoritarian institutions might be so great as to justify the sacrifice of basic freedoms. Of course, these remarks assume that the general assumptions on which the principles of justice were chosen are correct. But if they are, this sort of question is already decided by these principles. Certain institutional forms are embedded within the conception of justice. This view shares with perfectionism the feature of setting up an ideal of the person that constrains the pursuit of existing desires. In this respect justice as fairness and perfectionism are both opposed to utilitarianism.

Now it may appear that since utilitarianism makes no distinctions between the quality of desires and all satisfactions have some value, it has no criteria for choosing between systems of desires, or ideals of the person. From a theoretical point of view anyway, this is incorrect. The utilitarian can always say that given social conditions and men's interests as they are, and taking into account how they will develop under this or that alternative institutional arrangement, encouraging one pattern of wants rather than another is likely to lead to a greater net balance (or to a higher average) of satisfaction. On this basis the utilitarian selects between ideals of the person. Some attitudes and desires, being less compatible with fruitful social cooperation, tend to reduce the total (or the average) happiness. Roughly speaking, the moral virtues are those dispositions and effective desires that can generally be relied upon to promote the greatest sum of well-being. Thus, it would be a mistake to claim that the principle of utility provides no grounds for choosing among ideals of the person, however difficult it may be to apply the principle in practice. Nevertheless, the choice does depend upon existing desires and present social circumstances and their natural continuations into the future. These initial conditions may heavily influence the conception of human good that should be encouraged. The contrast is that both justice as fairness and perfectionism establish independently an ideal conception of the person and of the basic structure so that not only are some desires and inclinations necessarily discouraged but the effect of the initial circumstances will eventually disappear. With utilitarianism we cannot be sure what will happen. Since there is no ideal embedded in its first principle, the place we start from may always influence the path we are to follow.

By way of summing up, the essential point is that despite the individualistic features of justice as fairness, the two principles of justice are not contingent upon existing desires or present social conditions. Thus we are able to derive a conception of a just basic structure, and an ideal of the person compatible with it, that can serve as a standard for appraising institutions and for guiding the overall direction of social change. In order to find an Archimedean point it is not necessary to appeal to a priori or perfectionist principles. By assuming certain general desires, such as the desire for primary social goods, and by taking as a basis the agreements that would be made in a suitably defined initial situation, we can achieve the requisite independence from existing circumstances. The original position is so characterized that unanimity is possible; the deliberations of any one person are typical of all. Moreover, the same will hold for the considered judgments of the citizens of a well-ordered society effectively regulated by the principles of justice. Everyone has a similar sense of justice and in this respect a well-ordered society is homogeneous. Political argument appeals to this moral consensus.

It may be thought that the assumption of unanimity is peculiar to the political philosophy of idealism.[3] As it is used in the contract view, however, there is nothing characteristically idealist about the supposition of unanimity. This condition is part of the procedural conception of the original position and it represents a constraint on arguments. In this way it shapes the content of the theory of justice, the principles that are to match our considered judgments. Hume and Adam Smith likewise assume that if men were to take up a certain point of view, that of the impartial spectator, they would be led to similar convictions. A utilitarian society may also be well-ordered. For the most part the philosophical tradition, including intuitionism, has assumed that there exists some appropriate perspective from which unanimity on moral questions may be hoped for, at least among rational persons with relevantly similar and sufficient infor-

3. This suggestion is found in K. J. Arrow, *Social Choice and Individual Values*, 2nd ed. (New York, John Wiley and Sons, 1963), pp. 74f, 81–86.

mation. Or if unanimity is impossible, disparities between judgments are greatly reduced once this standpoint is adopted. Different moral theories arise from different interpretations of this point of view, of what I have called the initial situation. In this sense the idea of unanimity among rational persons is implicit throughout the tradition of moral philosophy.

What distinguishes justice as fairness is how it characterizes the initial situation, the setting in which the condition of unanimity appears. Since the original position can be given a Kantian interpretation, this conception of justice does indeed have affinities with idealism. Kant sought to give a philosophical foundation to Rousseau's idea of the general will.[4] The theory of justice in turn tries to present a natural procedural rendering of Kant's conception of the kingdom of ends, and of the notions of autonomy and the categorical imperative (§ 40). In this way the underlying structure of Kant's doctrine is detached from its metaphysical surroundings so that it can be seen more clearly and presented relatively free from objection.

There is another resemblance to idealism: justice as fairness has a central place for the value of community, and how this comes about depends upon the Kantian interpretation. I discuss this topic in Part Three. The essential idea is that we want to account for the social values, for the intrinsic good of institutional, community, and associative activities, by a conception of justice that in its theoretical basis is individualistic. For reasons of clarity among others, we do not want to rely on an undefined concept of community, or to suppose that society is an organic whole with a life of its own distinct from and superior to that of all its members in their relations with one another. Thus the contractual conception of the original position is worked out first. It is reasonably simple and the problem of rational choice that it poses is relatively precise. From this conception, however individualistic it might seem, we must eventually

4. See L. W. Beck, *A Commentary on Kant's Critique of Practical Reason* (Chicago, University of Chicago Press, 1960), pp. 200, 235f; and Ernst Cassirer, *Rousseau, Kant and Goethe* (Princeton, Princeton University Press, 1945), pp. 18–25, 30–35, 58f. Thus among other things, Kant is giving a deeper reading to Rousseau's remark: "to be governed by appetite alone is slavery, while obedience to a law one prescribes to oneself is freedom." *The Social Contract,* bk. I, ch. viii.

explain the value of community. Otherwise the theory of justice cannot succeed. To accomplish this we shall need an account of the primary good of self-respect which relates it to the parts of the theory already developed. But for the time being, I shall leave these problems aside and proceed to consider some further implications of the two principles of justice for the economic aspects of the basic structure.

42. SOME REMARKS ABOUT ECONOMIC SYSTEMS

It is essential to keep in mind that our topic is the theory of justice and not economics, however elementary. We are only concerned with some moral problems of political economy. For example, I shall ask: what is the proper rate of saving over time, how should the background institutions of taxation and property be arranged, or at what level is the social minimum to be set? In asking these questions my intention is not to explain, much less to add anything to, what economic theory says about the working of these institutions. Attempting to do this here would obviously be out of place. Certain elementary parts of economic theory are brought in solely to illustrate the content of the principles of justice. If economic theory is used incorrectly or if the received doctrine is itself mistaken, I hope that for the purposes of the theory of justice no harm is done. But as we have seen, ethical principles depend upon general facts and therefore a theory of justice for the basic structure presupposes an account of these arrangements. It is necessary to make some assumptions and to spell out their consequences if we are to test moral conceptions. These assumptions are bound to be inaccurate and oversimplified, but this may not matter too much if they enable us to uncover the content of the principles of justice and we are satisfied that under a wide range of circumstances the difference principle will lead to acceptable conclusions. In short, questions of political economy are discussed simply to find out the practicable bearing of justice as fairness. I discuss these matters from the point of view of the citizen who is trying to organize his judgments concerning the justice of economic institutions.

In order to avoid misunderstandings and to indicate some of the main problems, I shall begin with a few remarks about economic systems. Political economy is importantly concerned with the public sector and the proper form of the background institutions that regulate economic activity, with taxation and the rights of property, the structure of markets, and so on. An economic system regulates what things are produced and by what means, who receives them and in return for which contributions, and how large a fraction of social resources is devoted to saving and to the provision of public goods. Ideally all of these matters should be arranged in ways that satisfy the two principles of justice. But we have to ask whether this is possible and what in particular these principles require.

To begin with, it is helpful to distinguish between two aspects of the public sector; otherwise the difference between a private-property economy and socialism is left unclear. The first aspect has to do with the ownership of the means of production. The classical distinction is that the size of the public sector under socialism (as measured by the fraction of total output produced by state-owned firms and managed either by state officials or by workers' councils) is much larger. In a private-property economy the number of publicly owned firms is presumably small and in any event limited to special cases such as public utilities and transportation.

A second quite different feature of the public sector is the proportion of total social resources devoted to public goods. The distinction between public and private goods raises a number of intricate points, but the main idea is that a public good has two characteristic features, indivisibility and publicness.[5] That is, there are many individuals, a public so to speak, who want more or less of this good, but if they are to enjoy it at all must each enjoy the same amount. The quantity produced cannot be divided up as private goods can and purchased by individuals according to their preferences for more and less. There are various kinds of public goods depending upon their degree of indivisibility and the size of the relevant public. The polar case of a public good is full indivisibility over the whole society. A standard example is the defense of the nation against (unjustified) foreign attack. All citizens must be provided with this good in the

5. For a discussion of public goods, see J. M. Buchanan, *The Demand and Supply of Public Goods* (Chicago, Rand McNally, 1968), esp. ch. IX. This work contains useful bibliographical appendixes to the literature.

same amount; they cannot be given varying protection depending on their wishes. The consequence of indivisibility and publicness in these cases is that the provision of public goods must be arranged for through the political process and not through the market. Both the amount to be produced and its financing need to be worked out by legislation. Since there is no problem of distribution in the sense that all citizens receive the same quantity, distribution costs are zero.

Various features of public goods derive from these two characteristics. First of all, there is the free-rider problem.[6] Where the public is large and includes many individuals, there is a temptation for each person to try to avoid doing his share.. This is because whatever one man does his action will not significantly affect the amount produced. He regards the collective action of others as already given one way or the other. If the public good is produced his enjoyment of it is not decreased by his not making a contribution. If it is not produced his action would not have changed the situation anyway. A citizen receives the same protection from foreign invasion regardless of whether he has paid his taxes. Therefore in the polar case trade and voluntary agreements cannot be expected to develop.

It follows that arranging for and financing public goods must be taken over by the state and some binding rule requiring payment must be enforced. Even if all citizens were willing to pay their share, they would presumably do so only when they are assured that others will pay theirs as well. Thus once citizens have agreed to act collectively and not as isolated individuals taking the actions of the others as given, there is still the task of tying down the agreement. The sense of justice leads us to promote just schemes and to do our share in them when we believe that others, or sufficiently many of them, will do theirs. But in normal circumstances a reasonable assurance in this regard can only be given if there is a binding rule effectively enforced. Assuming that the public good is to everyone's advantage, and one that all would agree to arrange for, the use of coercion is perfectly rational from each man's point of view. Many of the traditional activities of government, insofar as they can be

6. See Buchanan, ch. V; and also Mancur Olson, *The Logic of Collective Action* (Cambridge, Harvard University Press, 1965), chs. I and II, where the problem is discussed in connection with the theory of organizations.

justified, can be accounted for in this way.[7] The need for the enforcement of rules by the state will still exist even when everyone is moved by the same sense of justice. The characteristic features of essential public goods necessitate collective agreements, and firm assurance must be given to all that they will be honored.

Another aspect of the public goods situation is that of externality. When goods are public and indivisible, their production will cause benefits and losses to others which may not be taken into account by those who arrange for these goods or who decide to produce them. Thus in the polar case, if but a part of the citizenry pays taxes to cover the expenditure on public goods, the whole society is still affected by the items provided. Yet those who agree to these levies may not consider these effects, and so the amount of public expenditure is presumably different from what it would be if all benefits and losses had been considered. The everyday cases are those where the indivisibility is partial and the public is smaller. Someone who has himself inoculated against a contagious disease helps others as well as himself; and while it may not pay him to obtain this protection, it may be worth it to the local community when all advantages are tallied up. And, of course, there are the striking cases of public harms, as when industries sully and erode the natural environment. These costs are not normally reckoned with by the market, so that the commodities produced are sold at much less than their marginal social costs. There is a divergence between private and social accounting that the market fails to register. One essential task of law and government is to institute the necessary corrections.

It is evident, then, that the indivisibility and publicness of certain essential goods, and the externalities and temptations to which they give rise, necessitate collective agreements organized and enforced by the state. That political rule is founded solely on men's propensity to self-interest and injustice is a superficial view. For even among just men, once goods are indivisible over large numbers of individuals, their actions decided upon in isolation from one another will not lead to the general good. Some collective arrangement is necessary and everyone wants assurance that it will be adhered to if he is willingly to do his part. In a large community the

7. See W. J. Baumol, *Welfare Economics and the Theory of the State* (London, Longmans, Green, 1952), chs. I, VII–IX, XII.

degree of mutual confidence in one another's integrity that renders enforcement superfluous is not to be expected. In a well-ordered society the required sanctions are no doubt mild and they may never be applied. Still, the existence of such devices is a normal condition of human life even in this case.

In these remarks I have distinguished between the problems of isolation and assurance.[8] The first sort of problem arises whenever the outcome of the many individuals' decisions made in isolation is worse for everyone than some other course of action, even though, taking the conduct of the others as given, each person's decision is perfectly rational. This is simply the general case of the prisoner's dilemma of which Hobbes's state of nature is the classical example.[9]

8. This distinction is from A. K. Sen, "Isolation, Assurance and the Social Rate of Discount," *Quarterly Journal of Economics,* vol. 81 (1967).

9. The prisoner's dilemma (attributed to A. W. Tucker) is an illustration of a two-person noncooperative, nonzero-sum game; noncooperative because agreements are not binding (or enforceable), and nonzero-sum because it is not the case that what one person gains the other loses. Thus imagine two prisoners who are brought before the attorney general and interrogated separately. They both know that if neither confesses, they will receive a short sentence for a lesser offense and spend a year in prison; but that if one confesses and turns state's evidence, he will be released, the other receiving a particularly heavy term of ten years; if both confess each gets five years. In this situation, assuming mutually disinterested motivation, the most reasonable course of action for them—that neither should confess—is unstable. This can be seen from the following gain-and-loss table (with entries representing years in prison):

| | Second Prisoner | |
First Prisoner	not confess	confess
not confess	1, 1	10, 0
confess	0, 10	5, 5

To protect himself, if not to try to further his own interests, each has a sufficient motive to confess, whatever the other does. Rational decisions from the point of view of each lead to a situation where both prisoners are worse off.

The problem clearly is to find some means of stabilizing the best plan. We may note that if it were shared knowledge between the prisoners that they were either utilitarians, or affirmed the principles of justice (with restricted applications to prisoners), their problem would be solved. Both views in this case support the most sensible arrangement. For a discussion of these matters in connection with the theory of the state, see W. J. Baumol as cited in note 7 above. For an account of the prisoner's dilemma game, see R. D. Luce and Howard Raiffa, *Games and Decisions* (New York, John Wiley and Sons, 1957), ch. V, esp. pp. 94–102. D. P. Gauthier, "Morality and Advantage," *Philosophical Review,* vol. 76 (1967), treats the problem from the standpoint of moral philosophy.

The isolation problem is to identify these situations and to ascertain the binding collective undertaking that would be best from the standpoint of all. The assurance problem is different. Here the aim is to assure the cooperating parties that the common agreement is being carried out. Each person's willingness to contribute is contingent upon the contribution of the others. Therefore to maintain public confidence in the scheme that is superior from everyone's point of view, or better anyway than the situation that would obtain in its absence, some device for administering fines and penalties must be established. It is here that the mere existence of an effective sovereign, or even the general belief in his efficacy, has a crucial role.

A final point about public goods. Since the proportion of social resources devoted to their production is distinct from the question of public ownership of the means of production, there is no necessary connection between the two. A private-property economy may allocate a large fraction of national income to these purposes, a socialist society a small one, and vice versa. There are public goods of many kinds, ranging from military equipment to health services. Having agreed politically to allocate and to finance these items, the government may purchase them from the private sector or from publicly owned firms. The particular list of public goods produced and the procedures taken to limit public harms depend upon the society in question. It is a question not of institutional logic but of political sociology, including under this heading the way in which institutions affect the balance of political advantages.

Having considered briefly two aspects of the public sector, I should like to conclude with a few comments about the extent to which economic arrangements may rely upon a system of markets in which prices are freely determined by supply and demand. Several cases need to be distinguished. All regimes will normally use the market to ration out the consumption goods actually produced. Any other procedure is administratively cumbersome, and rationing and other devices will be resorted to only in special cases. But in a free market system the output of commodities is also guided as to kind and quantity by the preferences of households as shown by their purchases on the market. Goods fetching a greater than normal profit will be produced in larger amounts until the excess is reduced. In a socialist regime planners' preferences or collective decisions often

270

have a larger part in determining the direction of production. Both private-property and socialist systems normally allow for the free choice of occupation and of one's place of work. It is only under command systems of either kind that this freedom is overtly interfered with.

Finally, a basic feature is the extent to which the market is used to decide the rate of saving and the direction of investment, as well as the fraction of national wealth devoted to conservation and to the elimination of irremediable injuries to the welfare of future generations. Here there are a number of possibilities. A collective decision may determine the rate of saving while the direction of investment is left largely to individual firms competing for funds. In both a private-property as well as in a socialist society great concern may be expressed for preventing irreversible damages and for husbanding natural resources and preserving the environment. But again either one may do rather badly.

It is evident, then, that there is no essential tie between the use of free markets and private ownership of the instruments of production. The idea that competitive prices under normal conditions are just or fair goes back at least to medieval times.[10] While the notion that a market economy is in some sense the best scheme has been most carefully investigated by so-called bourgeois economists, this connection is a historical contingency in that, theoretically at least, a socialist regime can avail itself of the advantages of this system.[11] One of these advantages is efficiency. Under certain conditions competitive prices select the goods to be produced and allocate resources to their production in such a manner that there is no way to improve upon either the choice of productive methods by firms, or the distribution of goods that arises from the purchases of households. There exists no rearrangement of the resulting economic configuration that makes one household better off (in view of its preferences) without making another worse off. No further mutually advan-

10. See Mark Blaug, *Economic Theory in Retrospect,* revised edition (Homewood, Ill., Richard D. Irwin, 1968), pp. 31f. See the bibliography, pp. 36f, esp. the articles by R. A. deRoover.

11. For a discussion of this matter, with references to the literature, see Abram Bergson, "Market Socialism Revisited," *Journal of Political Economy,* vol. 75 (1967). See also Jaroslav Vanek, *The General Theory of a Labor Managed Economy* (Ithaca, Cornell University Press, 1970).

tageous trades are possible; nor are there any feasible productive processes that will yield more of some desired commodity without requiring a cutback in another. For if this were not so, the situation of some individuals could be made more advantageous without a loss for anyone else. The theory of general equilibrium explains how, given the appropriate conditions, the information supplied by prices leads economic agents to act in ways that sum up to achieve this outcome. Perfect competition is a perfect procedure with respect to efficiency.[12] Of course, the requisite conditions are highly special ones and they are seldom if ever fully satisfied in the real world. Moreover, market failures and imperfections are often serious, and compensating adjustments must be made by the allocation branch (see § 43). Monopolistic restrictions, lack of information, external economies and diseconomies, and the like must be recognized and corrected. And the market fails altogether in the case of public goods. But these matters need not concern us here. These idealized arrangements are mentioned in order to clarify the related notion of pure procedural justice. The ideal conception may then be used to appraise existing arrangements and as a framework for identifying the changes that should be undertaken.

A further and more significant advantage of a market system is that, given the requisite background institutions, it is consistent with equal liberties and fair equality of opportunity. Citizens have a free choice of careers and occupations. There is no reason at all for the forced and central direction of labor. Indeed, in the absence of some differences in earnings as these arise in a competitive scheme, it is hard to see how, under ordinary circumstances anyway, certain aspects of a command society inconsistent with liberty can be avoided. Moreover, a system of markets decentralizes the exercise of economic power. Whatever the internal nature of firms, whether they are privately or state owned, or whether they are run by entrepreneurs or by managers elected by workers, they take the prices of outputs and inputs as given and draw up their plans accordingly. When markets are truly competitive, firms do not engage in price

12. On the efficiency of competition, see W. J. Baumol, *Economic Theory and Operations Analysis,* 2nd ed. (Englewood Cliffs, N.J., Prentice-Hall, 1965), pp. 355–371; and T. C. Koopmans, *Three Essays on the State of Economic Science* (New York, McGraw-Hill, 1957), the first essay.

wars or other contests for market power. In conformity with political decisions reached democratically, the government regulates the economic climate by adjusting certain elements under its control, such as the overall amount of investment, the rate of interest, and the quantity of money, and so on. There is no necessity for comprehensive direct planning. Individual households and firms are free to make their decisions independently, subject to the general conditions of the economy.

In noting the consistency of market arrangements with socialist institutions, it is essential to distinguish between the allocative and the distributive functions of prices. The former is connected with their use to achieve economic efficiency, the latter with their determining the income to be received by individuals in return for what they contribute. It is perfectly consistent for a socialist regime to establish an interest rate to allocate resources among investment projects and to compute rental charges for the use of capital and scarce natural assets such as land and forests. Indeed, this must be done if these means of production are to be employed in the best way. For even if these assets should fall out of the sky without human effort, they are nevertheless productive in the sense that when combined with other factors a greater output results. It does not follow, however, that there need be private persons who as owners of these assets receive the monetary equivalents of these evaluations. Rather these accounting prices are indicators for drawing up an efficient schedule of economic activities. Except in the case of work of all kinds, prices under socialism do not correspond to income paid over to private individuals. Instead, the income imputed to natural and collective assets accrues to the state, and therefore their prices have no distributive function.[13]

It is necessary, then, to recognize that market institutions are common to both private-property and socialist regimes, and to distinguish between the allocative and the distributive function of prices. Since under socialism the means of production and natural resources are publicly owned, the distributive function is greatly restricted, whereas a private-property system uses prices in varying degrees for

13. For the distinction between the allocative and the distributive functions of prices, see J. E. Meade, *Efficiency, Equality and the Ownership of Property* (London, George Allen and Unwin, 1964), pp. 11–26.

both purposes. Which of these systems and the many intermediate forms most fully answers to the requirements of justice cannot, I think, be determined in advance. There is presumably no general answer to this question, since it depends in large part upon the traditions, institutions, and social forces of each country, and its particular historical circumstances. The theory of justice does not include these matters. But what it can do is to set out in a schematic way the outlines of a just economic system that admits of several variations. The political judgment in any given case will then turn on which variation is most likely to work out best in practice. A conception of justice is a necessary part of any such political assessment, but it is not sufficient.

The ideal scheme sketched in the next several sections makes considerable use of market arrangements. It is only in this way, I believe, that the problem of distribution can be handled as a case of pure procedural justice. Further, we also gain the advantages of efficiency and protect the important liberty of free choice of occupation. At the start I assume that the regime is a property-owning democracy since this case is likely to be better known.[14] But, as I have noted, this is not intended to prejudge the choice of regime in particular cases. Nor, of course, does it imply that actual societies which have private ownership of the means of production are not afflicted with grave injustices. Because there exists an ideal property-owning system that would be just does not imply that historical forms are just, or even tolerable. And, of course, the same is true of socialism.

43. BACKGROUND INSTITUTIONS FOR DISTRIBUTIVE JUSTICE

The main problem of distributive justice is the choice of a social system. The principles of justice apply to the basic structure and regulate how its major institutions are combined into one scheme. Now, as we have seen, the idea of justice as fairness is to use the notion of pure procedural justice to handle the contingencies of par-

14. The term "property-owning democracy" is from Meade, *ibid.*, the title of ch. V.

ticular situations. The social system is to be designed so that the resulting distribution is just however things turn out. To achieve this end it is necessary to set the social and economic process within the surroundings of suitable political and legal institutions. Without an appropriate scheme of these background institutions the outcome of the distributive process will not be just. Background fairness is lacking. I shall give a brief description of these supporting institutions as they might exist in a properly organized democratic state that allows private ownership of capital and natural resources. These arrangements are familiar, but it may be useful to see how they fit the two principles of justice. Modifications for the case of a socialist regime will be considered briefly later.

First of all, I assume that the basic structure is regulated by a just constitution that secures the liberties of equal citizenship (as described in the preceding chapter). Liberty of conscience and freedom of thought are taken for granted, and the fair value of political liberty is maintained. The political process is conducted, as far as circumstances permit, as a just procedure for choosing between governments and for enacting just legislation. I assume also that there is fair (as opposed to formal) equality of opportunity. This means that in addition to maintaining the usual kinds of social overhead capital, the government tries to insure equal chances of education and culture for persons similarly endowed and motivated either by subsidizing private schools or by establishing a public school system. It also enforces and underwrites equality of opportunity in economic activities and in the free choice of occupation. This is achieved by policing the conduct of firms and private associations and by preventing the establishment of monopolistic restrictions and barriers to the more desirable positions. Finally, the government guarantees a social minimum either by family allowances and special payments for sickness and employment, or more systematically by such devices as a graded income supplement (a so-called negative income tax).

In establishing these background institutions the government may be thought of as divided into four branches.[15] Each branch consists of various agencies, or activities thereof, charged with preserving certain social and economic conditions. These divisions do not over-

15. For the idea of branches of government, see R. A. Musgrave, *The Theory of Public Finance* (New York, McGraw-Hill, 1959), ch. I.

lap with the usual organization of government but are to be understood as different functions. The allocation branch, for example, is to keep the price system workably competitive and to prevent the formation of unreasonable market power. Such power does not exist as long as markets cannot be made more competitive consistent with the requirements of efficiency and the facts of geography and the preferences of households. The allocation branch is also charged with identifying and correcting, say by suitable taxes and subsidies and by changes in the definition of property rights, the more obvious departures from efficiency caused by the failure of prices to measure accurately social benefits and costs. To this end suitable taxes and subsidies may be used, or the scope and definition of property rights may be revised. The stabilization branch, on the other hand, strives to bring about reasonably full employment in the sense that those who want work can find it and the free choice of occupation and the deployment of finance are supported by strong effective demand. These two branches together are to maintain the efficiency of the market economy generally.

The social minimum is the responsibility of the transfer branch. Later on I shall consider at what level the minimum should be set; but for the moment a few general remarks will suffice. The essential idea is that the workings of this branch take needs into account and assign them an appropriate weight with respect to other claims. A competitive price system gives no consideration to needs and therefore it cannot be the sole device of distribution. There must be a division of labor between the parts of the social system in answering to the common sense precepts of justice. Different institutions meet different claims. Competitive markets properly regulated secure free choice of occupation and lead to an efficient use of resources and allocation of commodities to households. They set a weight on the conventional precepts associated with wages and earnings, whereas the transfer branch guarantees a certain level of well-being and honors the claims of need. Eventually I will discuss these common sense precepts and how they arise within the context of various institutions. The relevant point here is that certain precepts tend to be associated with specific institutions. It is left to the background system as a whole to determine how these precepts are balanced. Since the principles of justice regulate the whole structure, they also regulate the balance of precepts. In general, then, this balance will vary in accordance with the underlying political conception.

It is clear that the justice of distributive shares depends on the background institutions and how they allocate total income, wages and other income plus transfers. There is with reason strong objection to the competitive determination of total income, since this ignores the claims of need and an appropriate standard of life. From the standpoint of the legislative stage it is rational to insure oneself and one's descendants against these contingencies of the market. Indeed, the difference principle presumably requires this. But once a suitable minimum is provided by transfers, it may be perfectly fair that the rest of total income be settled by the price system, assuming that it is moderately efficient and free from monopolistic restrictions, and unreasonable externalities have been eliminated. Moreover, this way of dealing with the claims of need would appear to be more effective than trying to regulate income by minimum wage standards, and the like. It is better to assign to each branch only such tasks as are compatible with one another. Since the market is not suited to answer the claims of need, these should be met by a separate arrangement. Whether the principles of justice are satisfied, then, turns on whether the total income of the least advantaged (wages plus transfers) is such as to maximize their long-run expectations (consistent with the constraints of equal liberty and fair equality of opportunity).

Finally, there is a distribution branch. Its task is to preserve an approximate justice in distributive shares by means of taxation and the necessary adjustments in the rights of property. Two aspects of this branch may be distinguished. First of all, it imposes a number of inheritance and gift taxes, and sets restrictions on the rights of bequest. The purpose of these levies and regulations is not to raise revenue (release resources to government) but gradually and continually to correct the distribution of wealth and to prevent concentrations of power detrimental to the fair value of political liberty and fair equality of opportunity. For example, the progressive principle might be applied at the beneficiary's end.[16] Doing this would encourage the wide dispersal of property which is a necessary condition, it seems, if the fair value of the equal liberties is to be maintained.

16. See Meade, *Efficiency, Equality and the Ownership of Property*, pp. 56f.

The unequal inheritance of wealth is no more inherently unjust than the unequal inheritance of intelligence. It is true that the former is presumably more easily subject to social control; but the essential thing is that as far as possible inequalities founded on either should satisfy the difference principle. Thus inheritance is permissible provided that the resulting inequalities are to the advantage of the least fortunate and compatible with liberty and fair equality of opportunity. As earlier defined, fair equality of opportunity means a certain set of institutions that assures similar chances of education and culture for persons similarly motivated and keeps positions and offices open to all on the basis of qualities and efforts reasonably related to the relevant duties and tasks. It is these institutions that are put in jeopardy when inequalities of wealth exceed a certain limit; and political liberty likewise tends to lose its value, and representative government to become such in appearance only. The taxes and enactments of the distribution branch are to prevent this limit from being exceeded. Naturally, where this limit lies is a matter of political judgment guided by theory, good sense, and plain hunch, at least within a wide range. On this sort of question the theory of justice has nothing specific to say. Its aim is to formulate the principles that are to regulate the background institutions.

The second part of the distribution branch is a scheme of taxation to raise the revenues that justice requires. Social resources must be released to the government so that it can provide for the public goods and make the transfer payments necessary to satisfy the difference principle. This problem belongs to the distribution branch since the burden of taxation is to be justly shared and it aims at establishing just arrangements. Leaving aside many complications, it is worth noting that a proportional expenditure tax may be part of the best tax scheme.[17] For one thing, it is preferable to an income tax (of any kind) at the level of common sense precepts of justice, since it imposes a levy according to how much a person takes out of the common store of goods and not according to how much he contributes (assuming here that income is fairly earned). Again, a proportional tax on total consumption (for each year say) can contain the usual exemptions for dependents, and so on; and it treats everyone in a

17. See Nicholas Kaldor, *An Expenditure Tax* (London, George Allen and Unwin, 1955).

uniform way (still assuming that income is fairly earned). It may be better, therefore, to use progressive rates only when they are necessary to preserve the justice of the basic structure with respect to the first principle of justice and fair equality of opportunity, and so to forestall accumulations of property and power likely to undermine the corresponding institutions. Following this rule might help to signal an important distinction in questions of policy. And if proportional taxes should also prove more efficient, say because they interfere less with incentives, this might make the case for them decisive if a feasible scheme could be worked out. As before, these are questions of political judgment and not part of a theory of justice. And in any case we are here considering such a proportional tax as part of an ideal scheme for a well-ordered society in order to illustrate the content of the two principles. It does not follow that, given the injustice of existing institutions, even steeply progressive income taxes are not justified when all things are considered. In practice we must usually choose between several unjust, or second best, arrangements; and then we look to nonideal theory to find the least unjust scheme. Sometimes this scheme will include measures and policies that a perfectly just system would reject. Two wrongs can make a right in the sense that the best available arrangement may contain a balance of imperfections, an adjustment of compensating injustices.

The two parts of the distribution branch derive from the two principles of justice. The taxation of inheritance and income at progressive rates (when necessary), and the legal definition of property rights, are to secure the institutions of equal liberty in a property-owning democracy and the fair value of the rights they establish. Proportional expenditure (or income) taxes are to provide revenue for public goods, the transfer branch and the establishment of fair equality of opportunity in education, and the like, so as to carry out the second principle. No mention has been made at any point of the traditional criteria of taxation such as that taxes are to be levied according to benefits received or the ability to pay.[18] The reference to common sense precepts in connection with expenditure taxes is a subordinate consideration. The scope of these criteria is regulated by the principles of justice. Once the problem of distributive shares is

18. For a discussion of these tax criteria, see Musgrave, *The Theory of Public Finance,* chs. IV and V.

recognized as that of designing background institutions, the conventional maxims are seen to have no independent force, however appropriate they may be in certain delimited cases. To suppose otherwise is not to take a sufficiently comprehensive point of view (see § 47 below). It is evident also that the design of the distribution branch does not presuppose the utilitarian's standard assumptions about individual utilities. Inheritance and progressive income taxes, for example, are not predicated on the idea that individuals have similar utility functions satisfying the diminishing marginal principle. The aim of the distribution branch is not, of course, to maximize the net balance of satisfaction but to establish just background institutions. Doubts about the shape of utility functions are irrelevant. This problem is one for the utilitarian, not for contract theory.

So far I have assumed that the aim of the branches of government is to establish a democratic regime in which land and capital are widely though not presumably equally held. Society is not so divided that one fairly small sector controls the preponderance of productive resources. When this is achieved and distributive shares satisfy the principles of justice, many socialist criticisms of the market economy are met. But it is clear that, in theory anyway, a liberal socialist regime can also answer to the two principles of justice. We have only to suppose that the means of production are publicly owned and that firms are managed by workers' councils say, or by agents appointed by them. Collective decisions made democratically under the constitution determine the general features of the economy, such as the rate of saving and the proportion of society's production devoted to essential public goods. Given the resulting economic environment, firms regulated by market forces conduct themselves much as before. Although the background institutions will take a different form, especially in the case of the distribution branch, there is no reason in principle why just distributive shares cannot be achieved. The theory of justice does not by itself favor either form of regime. As we have seen, the decision as to which system is best for a given people depends upon their circumstances, institutions, and historical traditions.

Some socialists have objected to all market institutions as inherently degrading, and they have hoped to set up an economy in which men are moved largely by social and altruistic concerns. In regard to the first, the market is not indeed an ideal arrangement, but certainly given the requisite background institutions, the worst aspects of so-called wage slavery are removed. The question then becomes one of the comparison of possible alternatives. It seems improbable that the control of economic activity by the bureaucracy that would be bound to develop in a socially regulated system (whether centrally directed or guided by the agreements reached by industrial associations) would be more just on balance than control exercised by means of prices (assuming as always the necessary framework). To be sure a competitive scheme is impersonal and automatic in the details of its operation; its particular results do not express the conscious decision of individuals. But in many respects this is a virtue of the arrangement; and the use of the market system does not imply a lack of reasonable human autonomy. A democratic society may choose to rely on prices in view of the advantages of doing so, and then to maintain the background institutions which justice requires. This political decision, as well as the regulation of these surrounding arrangements, can be perfectly reasoned and free.

Moreover the theory of justice assumes a definite limit on the strength of social and altruistic motivation. It supposes that individuals and groups put forward competing claims, and while they are willing to act justly, they are not prepared to abandon their interests. There is no need to elaborate further that this presumption does not imply that men are selfish in the ordinary sense. Rather a society in which all can achieve their complete good, or in which there are no conflicting demands and the wants of all fit together without coercion into a harmonious plan of activity, is a society in a certain sense beyond justice. It has eliminated the occasions when the appeal to the principles of right and justice is necessary.[19] I am not concerned with this ideal case, however desirable it may be. We should note though that even here the theory of justice has an important theoretical role: it defines the conditions under which the spontaneous coherence of the aims and wants of individuals is neither coerced nor contrived but expresses a proper harmony con-

19. Some have interpreted Marx's conception of a full communist society as a society beyond justice in this sense. See R. C. Tucker, *The Marxian Revolutionary Idea* (New York, W. W. Norton, 1969), chs. I and II.

sistent with the ideal good. I cannot pursue these questions further. The main point is that the principles of justice are compatible with quite different types of regime.

A final matter needs to be considered. Let us suppose that the above account of the background institutions is sufficient for our purposes, and that the two principles of justice lead to a definite system of government activities and legal definitions of property together with a schedule of taxes. In this case the total of public expenditures and the necessary sources of revenue is well defined, and the distribution of income and wealth that results is just whatever it is. (See further below §§ 44, 47.) It does not follow, however, that citizens should not decide to make further public expenditures. If a sufficiently large number of them find the marginal benefits of public goods greater than that of goods available through the market, it is appropriate that ways should be found for government to provide them. Since the distribution of income and wealth is assumed to be just, the guiding principle changes. Let us suppose, then, that there is a fifth branch of government, the exchange branch, which consists of a special representative body taking note of the various social interests and their preferences for public goods. It is authorized by the constitution to consider only such bills as provide for government activities independent from what justice requires, and these are to be enacted only when they satisfy Wicksell's unanimity criterion.[20] This means that no public expenditures are voted upon unless at the same time the means of covering their costs are agreed upon, if not unanimously, then approximately so. A motion proposing a new public activity is required to contain one or more alternative arrangements for sharing the costs. Wicksell's idea is that if the public good is an efficient use of social resources, there must be some scheme for distributing the extra taxes among different kinds of taxpayers that will gain unanimous approval. If no

20. This criterion was stated by Knut Wicksell in his *Finanztheoretische Untersuchungen* (Jena, 1896). The major part is translated as "A New Principle of Just Taxation" and included in *Classics in the Theory of Public Finance,* ed. R. A. Musgrave and A. T. Peacock (London, Macmillan, 1958), pp. 72–118, esp. pp. 91–93, where the principle is stated. For some difficulties with it, see Hirafumi Shibata, "A Bargaining Model of the Pure Theory of Public Expenditure," *Journal of Political Economy,* vol. 79 (1971), esp. pp. 27f.

such proposal exists, the suggested expenditure is wasteful and should not be undertaken. Thus the exchange branch works by the principle of efficiency and institutes, in effect, a special trading body that arranges for public goods and services where the market mechanism breaks down. It must be added, however, that very real difficulties stand in the way of carrying this idea through. Even leaving aside voting strategies and the concealment of preferences, discrepancies in bargaining power, income effects, and the like may prevent an efficient outcome from being reached. Perhaps only a rough and approximate solution is possible. I shall, however, leave aside these problems.

Several comments are called for to prevent misunderstandings. First of all, as Wicksell emphasized, the unanimity criterion assumes the justice of the existing distribution of income and wealth, and of the current definition of the rights of property. Without this important proviso, it would have all the faults of the efficiency principle, since it simply expresses this principle for the case of public expenditures. But when this condition is satisfied, then the unanimity principle is sound. There is no more justification for using the state apparatus to compel some citizens to pay for unwanted benefits that others desire than there is to force them to reimburse others for their private expenses. Thus the benefit criterion now applies whereas it did not before; and those who want further public expenditures of various kinds are to use the exchange branch to see whether the requisite taxes can be agreed to. The size of the exchange budget, as distinct from the national budget, is then determined by the expenditures that are eventually accepted. In theory members of the community can get together to purchase public goods up to the point where their marginal value equals that of private goods.

It should be noted that the exchange branch includes a separate representative body. The reason for this is to emphasize that the basis of this scheme is the benefit principle and not the principles of justice. Since the conception of background institutions is to help us organize our considered judgments of justice, the veil of ignorance applies to the legislative stage. The exchange branch is only a trading arrangement. There are no restrictions upon information (except those required to make the scheme more efficient), since it depends upon citizens' knowing their relative valuations of public and private goods. We should also observe that in the exchange branch representatives (and citizens through their representatives) are quite properly guided by their interests. Whereas in describing the other branches, we assume the principles of justice to be applied to institutions solely on the basis of general information. We try to work out what rational legislators suitably constrained by the veil of ignorance, and in this sense impartial, would enact to realize the conception of justice. Ideal legislators do not vote their interests. Strictly speaking, then, the idea of the exchange branch is not part of the four-stage sequence. Nevertheless, there is likely to be confusion between government activities and public expenditures required to uphold just background institutions and those that follow from the benefit principle. With the distinction of branches in mind, the conception of justice as fairness becomes, I believe, more plausible. To be sure, it is often hard to distinguish between the two kinds of government activities, and some public goods may appear to fall into both categories. I leave these problems aside here, hoping that the theoretical distinction is clear enough for present purposes.

44. THE PROBLEM OF JUSTICE BETWEEN GENERATIONS

We must now consider the question of justice between generations. There is no need to stress the difficulties that this problem raises. It subjects any ethical theory to severe if not impossible tests. Nevertheless, the account of justice as fairness would be incomplete without some discussion of this important matter. The problem arises in the present context because the question is still open whether the social system as a whole, the competitive economy surrounded by the appropriate family of background institutions, can be made to satisfy the two principles of justice. The answer is bound to depend, to some degree anyway, on the level at which the social minimum is to be set. But this in turn connects up with how far the present generation is bound to respect the claims of its successors.

So far I have said nothing about how generous the social minimum should be. Common sense might be content to say that the right level depends upon the average wealth of the country and that, other things equal, the minimum should be higher when the average increases. Or one might say that the proper level is determined by customary expectations. But these suggestions are unsatisfactory. The first is not precise enough since it does not say how the minimum depends on average wealth and it overlooks other relevant aspects such as distribution; while the second provides no criterion for telling when customary expectations are themselves reasonable. Once the difference principle is accepted, however, it follows that the minimum is to be set at that point which, taking wages into account, maximizes the expectations of the least advantaged group. By adjusting the amount of transfers (for example, the size of supplementary income payments), it is possible to increase or decrease the prospects of the more disadvantaged, their index of primary goods (as measured by wages plus transfers), so as to achieve the desired result.

Now offhand it might seem that the difference principle requires a very high minimum. One naturally imagines that the greater wealth of those better off is to be scaled down until eventually everyone has nearly the same income. But this is a misconception, although it might hold in special circumstances. The appropriate expectation in applying the difference principle is that of the long-term prospects of the least favored extending over future generations. Each generation must not only preserve the gains of culture and civilization, and maintain intact those just institutions that have been established, but it must also put aside in each period of time a suitable amount of real capital accumulation. This saving may take various forms from net investment in machinery and other means of production to investment in learning and education. Assuming for the moment that a just savings principle is available which tells us how great investment should be, the level of the social minimum is determined. Suppose for simplicity that the minimum is adjusted by transfers paid for by proportional expenditure (or income) taxes. In this case raising the minimum entails increasing the proportion by which consumption (or income) is taxed. Presumably as this fraction becomes larger there comes a point beyond which one of two things happens. Either the appropriate savings cannot be made or the greater taxes interfere so much with economic efficiency that the prospects of the least advantaged in the present generation are no longer improved but begin to decline. In either event the correct minimum has been reached. The difference principle is satisfied and no further increase is called for.

These comments about how to specify the social minimum have led us to the problem of justice between generations. Finding a just savings principle is one aspect of this question.[21] Now I believe that it is not possible, at present anyway, to define precise limits on what the rate of savings should be. How the burden of capital accumulation and of raising the standard of civilization and culture is to be shared between generations seems to admit of no definite answer. It does not follow, however, that certain bounds which impose significant ethical constraints cannot be formulated. As I have said, a moral theory characterizes a point of view from which policies are to be assessed; and it may often be clear that a suggested answer is mistaken even if an alternative doctrine is not ready to hand. Thus it seems evident, for example, that the classical principle of utility leads in the wrong direction for questions of justice between generations. For if one takes the size of the population as variable, and postulates a high

---

21. This problem is often discussed by economists in the context of the theory of economic growth. For an exposition see A. K. Sen, "On Optimizing the Rate of Saving," *Economic Journal,* vol. 71 (1961); James Tobin, *National Economic Policy* (New Haven, Yale University Press, 1966), ch. IX; and R. M. Solow, *Growth Theory* (New York, Oxford University Press, 1970), ch. V. In an extensive literature, see F. P. Ramsey, "A Mathematical Theory of Saving," *Economic Journal,* vol. 38 (1928), reprinted in Arrow and Scitovsky, *Readings in Welfare Economics;* T. C. Koopmans, "On the Concept of Optimal Economic Growth" (1965) in *Scientific Papers of T. C. Koopmans* (Berlin, Springer Verlag, 1970). Sukamoy Chakravarty, *Capital and Development Planning* (Cambridge, M.I.T. Press, 1969), is a theoretical survey which touches upon the normative questions. If for theoretical purposes one thinks of the ideal society as one whose economy is in a steady state of growth (possibly zero), and which is at the same time just, then the savings problem is to choose a principle for sharing the burdens of getting to that growth path (or to such a path if there is more than one), and of maintaining the justice of the necessary arrangements once this is achieved. In the text, however, I do not pursue this suggestion; my discussion is at a more primitive level.

marginal productivity of capital and a very distant time horizon, maximizing total utility may lead to an excessive rate of accumulation (at least in the near future). Since from a moral point of view there are no grounds for discounting future well-being on the basis of pure time preference, the conclusion is all the more likely that the greater advantages of future generations will be sufficiently large to compensate for present sacrifices. This may prove true if only because with more capital and better technology it will be possible to support a sufficiently large population. Thus the utilitarian doctrine may direct us to demand heavy sacrifices of the poorer generations for the sake of greater advantages for later ones that are far better off. But this calculus of advantages, which balances the losses of some against benefits to others, appears even less justified in the case of generations than among contemporaries. Even if we cannot define a precise just savings principle, we should be able to avoid this sort of extreme.

Now the contract doctrine looks at the problem from the standpoint of the original position. The parties do not know to which generation they belong or, what comes to the same thing, the stage of civilization of their society. They have no way of telling whether it is poor or relatively wealthy, largely agricultural or already industrialized, and so on. The veil of ignorance is complete in these respects. Thus the persons in the original position are to ask themselves how much they would be willing to save at each stage of advance on the assumption that all other generations are to save at the same rates. That is, they are to consider their willingness to save at any given phase of civilization with the understanding that the rates they propose are to regulate the whole span of accumulation. In effect, then, they must choose a just savings principle that assigns an appropriate rate of accumulation to each level of advance. Presumably this rate changes depending upon the state of society. When people are poor and saving is difficult, a lower rate of saving should be required; whereas in a wealthier society greater savings may reasonably be expected since the real burden is less. Eventually once just institutions are firmly established, the net accumulation required falls to zero. At this point a society meets its duty of justice by maintaining just institutions and preserving their material base.

Of course, the just savings principle applies to what a society is to save as a matter of justice. If its citizens wish to save for various grand projects, that is another matter.

The question of time preference and matters of priority I shall leave aside until the next sections. For the present I wish to point out the main features of the contractarian approach. First of all, while it is evident that a just savings principle cannot literally be adopted democratically, the conception of the original position achieves the same result. Since no one knows to which generation he belongs, the question is viewed from the standpoint of each and a fair accommodation is expressed by the principle adopted. All generations are virtually represented in the original position, since the same principle would always be chosen. An ideally democratic decision will result, one that is fairly adjusted to the claims of each generation and therefore satisfying the precept that what touches all concerns all. Moreover, it is immediately obvious that every generation, except possibly the first, gains when a reasonable rate of saving is maintained. The process of accumulation, once it is begun and carried through, is to the good of all subsequent generations. Each passes on to the next a fair equivalent in real capital as defined by a just savings principle. (It should be kept in mind here that capital is not only factories and machines, and so on, but also the knowledge and culture, as well as the techniques and skills, that make possible just institutions and the fair value of liberty.) This equivalent is in return for what is received from previous generations that enables the later ones to enjoy a better life in a more just society. Only those in the first generation do not benefit, let us say, for while they begin the whole process, they do not share in the fruits of their provision. Nevertheless, since it is assumed that a generation cares for its immediate descendants, as fathers say care for their sons, a just savings principle, or more accurately, certain limits on such principles, would be acknowledged.

It is also characteristic of the contract doctrine to define a just state of society at which the entire course of accumulation aims. This feature derives from the fact that an ideal conception of a just basic structure is embedded in the principles chosen in the original position. In this respect, justice as fairness contrasts with utilitarian views (§41). The just savings principle can be regarded as an understanding between generations to carry their fair share of the burden of realizing and preserving a just society. The end of the savings process is set up in advance, although only the general outlines can be discerned. Particular circumstances as they arise will in time determine the more detailed aspects. But in any event we are not bound to go on maximizing indefinitely. Indeed, it is for this reason that the savings principle is agreed to after the principles of justice for institutions, even though this principle constrains the difference principle. These principles tell us what to strive for. The savings principle represents an interpretation, arrived at in the original position, of the previously accepted natural duty to uphold and to further just institutions. In this case the ethical problem is that of agreeing on a path over time which treats all generations justly during the whole course of a society's history. What seems fair to persons in the original position defines justice in this instance as in others.

The significance of the last stage of society should not, however, be misinterpreted. While all generations are to do their part in reaching the just state of things beyond which no further net saving is required, this state is not to be thought of as that alone which gives meaning and purpose to the whole process. To the contrary, all generations have their appropriate aims. They are not subordinate to one another any more than individuals are. The life of a people is conceived as a scheme of cooperation spread out in historical time. It is to be governed by the same conception of justice that regulates the cooperation of contemporaries. No generation has stronger claims than any other. In attempting to estimate the fair rate of saving the persons in the original position ask what is reasonable for members of adjacent generations to expect of one another at each level of advance. They try to piece together a just savings schedule by balancing how much at each stage they would be willing to save for their immediate descendants against what they would feel entitled to claim of their immediate predecessors. Thus imagining themselves to be fathers, say, they are to ascertain how much they should set aside for their sons by noting what they would believe themselves entitled to claim of their fathers. When they arrive at an estimate that seems fair from both sides, with due allowance made for the improvement in their circumstances, then the fair rate (or range of rates) for that stage is specified. Now once this is done for all stages, we have defined the just saving principle. When this principle is followed, adjacent generations cannot complain of one another; and in fact no generation can find fault with any other no matter how far removed in time.

The last stage at which saving is called for is not one of great abundance. This consideration deserves perhaps some emphasis. Further wealth might not be superfluous for some purposes; and indeed average income may not, in absolute terms, be very high. Justice does not require that early generations save so that later ones are simply more wealthy. Saving is demanded as a condition of bringing about the full realization of just institutions and the fair value of liberty. If additional accumulation is to be undertaken, it is for other reasons. It is a mistake to believe that a just and good society must wait upon a high material standard of life. What men want is meaningful work in free association with others, these associations regulating their relations to one another within a framework of just basic institutions. To achieve this state of things great wealth is not necessary. In fact, beyond some point it is more likely to be a positive hindrance, a meaningless distraction at best if not a temptation to indulgence and emptiness. (Of course, the definition of meaningful work is a problem in itself. Though it is not a problem of justice, a few remarks in § 79 are addressed to it.)

We should now observe that there is a peculiar feature of the reciprocity principle in the case of just savings. Normally this principle applies when there is an exchange of advantages and each party gives something as a fair return to the other. But in the course of history no generation gives to the preceding generations, the benefits of whose saving it has received. In following the savings principle, each generation makes a contribution to later generations and receives from its predecessors. The first generations may benefit hardly at all, whereas the last generations, those living when no further saving is enjoined, gain the most and give the least. Now this may appear unjust. Herzen remarks that human development is a kind of chronological unfairness, since those who live later profit from the labor of their predecessors without paying the same price. And Kant thought it disconcerting that earlier generations should carry their burdens only for the sake of the later ones and that only the last should have the good fortune to dwell in the completed building.[22] These feelings while entirely natural are misplaced. For although the relation between generations is a special one, it gives rise to no insuperable difficulty.

It is a natural fact that generations are spread out in time and actual exchanges between them take place only in one direction. We can do something for posterity but it can do nothing for us. This situation is unalterable, and so the question of justice does not arise. What is just or unjust is how institutions deal with natural limitations and the way they are set up to take advantage of historical possibilities. Obviously if all generations are to gain (except perhaps the first), they must choose a just savings principle which if followed brings it about that each receives from its predecessors and does its fair share for those which come later. The only reciprocal exchanges between generations are virtual ones, that is, compensating adjustments that can be made in the original position in drawing up the just savings principle. But these adjustments I imagine each generation to make for itself, leaving it to the veil of ignorance and the other constraints to lead any one generation to look out for all.

It is now clear why the difference principle does not apply to the savings problem. There is no way for later generations to improve the situation of the least fortunate first generation. The principle is inapplicable and it would seem to imply, if anything, that there be no saving at all. Thus, the problem of saving must be treated in another fashion. If we imagine that the original position contains representatives from all actual generations, the veil of ignorance would make it unnecessary to change the motivation

22. The remark of Alexander Herzen is from Isaiah Berlin's introduction to Franco Venturi, *Roots of Revolution* (New York, Alfred Knopf, 1960), p. xx. For Kant, see "Idea for a Universal History with a Cosmopolitan Purpose," in *Political Writings*, ed. Hans Reiss and trans. H. B. Nisbet (Cambridge, The University Press, 1970), p. 44.

assumption. But as we noted earlier (§ 24), it is best to take the present time of entry interpretation. Those in the original position know, then, that they are contemporaries, so unless they care at least for their immediate successors, there is no reason for them to agree to undertake any saving whatever. To be sure, they do not know to which generation they belong, but this does not matter. Either earlier generations have saved or they have not; there is nothing the parties can do to affect it. It seems best to preserve the present time of entry interpretation and therefore to adjust the motivation condition. The parties are regarded as representing family lines, say, with ties of sentiment between successive generations. This modification seems natural enough, and has been used already in the argument for equal liberty (§ 33). Although the savings problem presents a special situation, the characterization of justice remains the same. The criteria for justice between generations are those that would be chosen in the original position.

We now have to combine the just savings principle with the two principles of justice. This is done by supposing that this principle is defined from the standpoint of the least advantaged in each generation. It is the representative men from this group as it extends over time who by virtual adjustments are to specify the rate of accumulation. They undertake in effect to constrain the application of the difference principle. In any generation their expectations are to be maximized subject to the condition of putting aside the savings that would be acknowledged. Thus the complete statement of the difference principle includes the savings principle as a constraint. Whereas the first principle of justice and the principle of fair opportunity limit the application of the difference principle within generations, the savings principle limits its scope between them.

Of course, the saving of the less favored need not be done by their taking an active part in the investment process. Rather it normally consists of their approving of the economic and other arrangements necessary for the appropriate accumulation. Saving is achieved by accepting as a political judgment those policies designed to improve the standard of life of later generations of the least advantaged, thereby abstaining from the immediate gains which are available. By supporting these arrangements the required saving can be made, and no representative man in any generation of the most disadvantaged can complain of another for not doing his part. It should also be observed that for much of the time, especially during the earlier stages, the general conception of justice is likely to apply rather than the two principles in serial order. But the same idea holds and I shall not trouble to state it.

So much, then, for a brief sketch of some of the main features of the just savings principle. We can now see that persons in different generations have duties and obligations to one another just as contemporaries do. The present generation cannot do as it pleases but is bound by the principles that would be chosen in the original position to define justice between persons at different moments of time. In addition, men have a natural duty to uphold and to further just institutions and for this the improvement of civilization up to a certain level is required. The derivation of these duties and obligations may seem at first a somewhat farfetched application of the contract doctrine. Nevertheless these requirements would be acknowledged in the original position, and so the conception of justice as fairness covers these matters without any change in its basic idea.

45. TIME PREFERENCE

I have assumed that in choosing a principle of savings the persons in the original position have no pure time preference. We need to consider the reasons for this presumption. In the case of an individual the avoidance of pure time preference is a feature of being rational. As Sidgwick maintains, rationality implies an impartial concern for all parts of our life. The mere difference of location in time, of something's being earlier or later, is not in itself a rational ground for having more or less regard for it. Of course, a present or near future advantage may be counted more heavily on account of its greater certainty or probability, and we should take into consideration how our situation and capacity for particular enjoyments will change. But none of these things justifies our preferring a lesser present to a greater future good simply because of its nearer temporal position[23] (§ 64).

Now Sidgwick thought that the notions of universal good and individual good are in essential respects similar. He held that just as the good of one person is constructed by comparison and integration of the different goods of each moment as they follow one another in time, so the universal good is constructed by the comparison and integration of the good of many different individuals. The relations of the parts to the whole and to each other are analogous in each case, being founded on the aggregative principle of utility.[24] The just savings principle for society must not, then, be affected by pure time preference, since as before the different temporal position of persons and generations does not in itself justify treating them differently.

Since in justice as fairness the principles of justice are not extensions of the principles of rational choice for one person, the argument against time preference must be of another kind. The question is settled by reference to the original position; but once it is seen from this perspective, we reach the same conclusion. There is no reason for the parties to give any weight to mere position in time. They have to choose a rate of saving for each level of civilization. If they make a distinction between earlier and more remote periods because, say, future states of affairs seem less important now, the present state of affairs will seem less important in the future. Although any decision has to be made now, there is no ground for their using today's discount of the future rather than the future's discount of today. The situation is symmetrical and one choice is as arbitrary as the other.[25] Since the persons in the original position take up the standpoint of each period, being subject to the veil of ignorance, this symmetry is clear to them and they will not consent to a principle that weighs nearer periods more or less heavily. Only in this way can they arrive at a consistent agreement from all points of view, for to acknowledge a

23. See *The Methods of Ethics,* 7th ed. (London, Macmillan, 1907), p. 381. Time preference is also rejected by Ramsey, "A Mathematical Theory of Saving."
24. *Methods of Ethics,* p. 382. See also § 30, note 37.
25. See Sen, "On Optimizing the Rate of Savings," p. 482.

principle of time preference is to authorize persons differently situated temporally to assess one another's claims by different weights based solely on this contingency.

As with rational prudence, the rejection of pure time preference is not incompatible with taking uncertainties and changing circumstances into account; nor does it rule out using an interest rate (in either a socialist or a private-property economy) to ration limited funds for investment. The restriction is rather that in first principles of justice we are not allowed to treat generations differently solely on the grounds that they are earlier or later in time. The original position is so defined that it leads to the correct principle in this respect. In the case of the individual, pure time preference is irrational: it means that he is not viewing all moments as equally parts of one life. In the case of society, pure time preference is unjust: it means (in the more common instance when the future is discounted) that the living take advantage of their position in time to favor their own interests.

The contract view agrees, then, with Sidgwick in rejecting time preference as a grounds of social choice. The living may, if they allow themselves to be moved by such considerations, wrong their predecessors and descendants. Now this contention may seem contrary to democratic principles, for it is sometimes said that these require that the wishes of the present generation should determine social policy. Of course, it is assumed that these preferences need to be clarified and ascertained under the appropriate conditions. Collective saving for the future has many aspects of a public good, and the isolation and assurance problems arise in this case.[26] But supposing that these difficulties are overcome and that the informed collective judgment of the present generation is known under the requisite conditions, it may be thought that a democratic view of the state does not countenance the government's intervening for the sake of future generations even when the public judgment is manifestly mistaken.

Whether this contention is correct depends upon how it is interpreted. There can be no objection to it as a description of a

26. See Sen, *ibid.*, p. 479; and S. A. Marglin, "The Social Rate of Discount and the Optimal Rate of Investment," *Quarterly Journal of Economics*, vol. 77 (1963), pp. 100–109.

democratic constitution. Once the public will is clearly expressed in legislation and social policies, the government cannot override it without ceasing to be democratic. It is not authorized to nullify the views of the electorate as to how much saving is to be undertaken. If a democratic regime is justified, then the government's having this power would normally lead to a greater injustice on balance. We are to decide between constitutional arrangements according to how likely it is that they will yield just and effective legislation. A democrat is one who believes that a democratic constitution best meets this criterion. But his conception of justice includes a provision for the just claims of future generations. Even if as a practical matter in the choice of regimes the electorate should have the final say; this is only because it is more likely to be correct than a government empowered to override its wishes. Since, however, a just constitution even under favorable conditions is a case of imperfect procedural justice, the people may still decide wrongly. By causing irreversible damages say, they may perpetuate grave offenses against other generations which under another form of government might have been prevented. Moreover, the injustice may be perfectly evident and demonstrable as such by the same conception of justice that underlies the democratic regime itself. Several of the principles of this conception may actually be more or less explicit in the constitution and frequently cited by the judiciary and informed opinion in interpreting it.

In these cases, then, there is no reason why a democrat may not oppose the public will by suitable forms of noncompliance, or even as a government official try to circumvent it. Although one believes in the soundness of a democratic constitution and accepts the duty to support it, the duty to comply with particular laws may be overridden in situations where the collective judgment is sufficiently unjust. There is nothing sacrosanct about the public decision concerning the level of savings; and its bias with respect to time preference deserves no special respect. In fact the absence of the injured parties, the future generations, makes it all the more open to question. One does not cease to be a democrat unless one thinks that some other form of government would be better and one's efforts are directed to this end. As long as one does not believe this, but thinks instead that appropriate forms of non-compliance, for example, acts of civil disobedience or conscientious refusal, are both necessary and reasonable ways to correct democratically enacted policies, then one's conduct is consistent with accepting a democratic constitution. In the next chapter I shall discuss this matter in more detail. For the moment the essential point is that the collective will concerning the provision for the future is subject, as all other social decisions are, to the principles of justice. The peculiar features of this case do not make it an exception.

We should observe that to reject pure time preference as a first principle is compatible with recognizing that a certain discounting of the future may improve otherwise defective criteria. For example, I have already remarked that the utilitarian principle may lead to an extremely high rate of saving which imposes excessive hardships on earlier generations. This consequence can be to some degree corrected by discounting the welfare of those living in the future. Since the well-being of later generations is made to count for less, not so much need be saved as before. It is also possible to vary the accumulation required by adjusting the parameters in the postulated utility function. I cannot discuss these questions here.[27] Unhappily I can only express the opinion that these devices simply mitigate the consequences of mistaken principles. The situation is in some respects similar to that found with the intuitionistic conception which combines the standard of utility with a principle of equality (see § 7). There the criterion of equality suitably weighted serves to correct the utility criterion when neither principle taken alone would prove acceptable. Thus in an analogous way, having started with the idea that the appropriate rate of saving is the one which maximizes social utility over time (maximizes some integral), we may obtain a more plausible result if the welfare of future generations is weighted less heavily; and the most suitable discount may depend upon how

27. See Chakravarty, *Capital and Development Planning,* pp. 39f, 47, 63–65, 249f. Solow, *Growth Theory,* pp. 79–87, gives an account of the mathematical problem.

swiftly population is growing, upon the productivity of capital, and so on. What we are doing is adjusting certain parameters so as to reach a conclusion more in line with our intuitive judgments. We may find that to achieve justice between generations, these modifications in the principle of utility are required. Certainly introducing time preference may be an improvement in such cases; but I believe that its being invoked in this way is an indication that we have started from an incorrect conception. There is a difference between the situation here and the previously mentioned intuitionistic view. Unlike the principle of equality, time preference has no intrinsic ethical appeal. It is introduced in a purely ad hoc way to moderate the consequences of the utility criterion.

46. FURTHER CASES OF PRIORITY

The problem of just savings may be used to illustrate further cases of the priority of justice. One feature of the contract doctrine is that it places an upper bound on how much a generation can be asked to save for the welfare of later generations. The just savings principle acts as a constraint on the rate of accumulation. Each age is to do its fair share in achieving the conditions necessary for just institutions and the fair value of liberty; but beyond this more cannot be required. Now it may be objected that particularly when the sum of advantages is very great and represents long-term developments, higher rates of saving may be demanded. Some may go further and maintain that inequalities in wealth and authority violating the second principle of justice may be justified if the subsequent economic and social benefits are large enough. To support their view they may point to instances in which we seem to accept such inequalities and rates of accumulation for the sake of the welfare of later generations. Keynes remarks, for example, that the immense accumulations of capital built up before the First World War could never have come about in a society in which wealth was equally divided.[28] Society in the nineteenth century, he

28. See J. M. Keynes, *The Economic Consequences of the Peace* (London, Macmillan, 1919), pp. 18–22.

says, was arranged so as to place the increased income in the hands of those least likely to consume it. The new rich were not brought up to large expenditures and preferred to the enjoyments of immediate consumption the power which investment gave. It was precisely the inequality of the distribution of wealth which made possible the rapid build-up of capital and the more or less steady improvement in the general standard of living of everyone. It is this fact, in Keynes's opinion, that provided the main justification of the capitalist system. If the rich had spent their new wealth on themselves, such a regime would have been rejected as intolerable. Certainly there are more efficient and just ways of raising the level of well-being and culture than that Keynes describes. It is only in special circumstances, including the frugality of the capitalist class as opposed to the self-indulgence of the aristocracy, that a society should obtain investment funds by endowing the rich with more than they feel they can decently spend on themselves. But the essential point here is that Keynes's justification, whether or not its premises are sound, can be made to turn solely on improving the situation of the working class. Although their circumstances appear harsh, Keynes presumably maintains that while there were many ostensible injustices in the system, there was no real possibility that these could have been removed and the conditions of the less advantaged made better. Under other arrangements the position of the laboring man would have been even worse. We need not consider whether these contentions are true. It suffices to note that, contrary to what one might have thought, Keynes does not say that the hardships of the poor are justified by the greater welfare of later generations. And this accords with the priority of justice over efficiency and a greater sum of advantages. Whenever the constraints of justice in the matter of savings are infringed, it must be shown that circumstances are such that not to trespass upon them would lead to an even greater injury to those on whom the injustice falls. This case is analogous to those already discussed under the heading of the priority of liberty (see § 39).

It is clear that the inequalities that Keynes had in mind also violate the principle of fair equality of opportunity. Thus we are led to consider what must be argued to excuse the infringement of this criterion and how to formulate the appropriate priority rule.[29] Many writers hold that fair equality of opportunity would have grave consequences. They believe that some sort of hierarchical social structure and a governing class with pervasive hereditary features are essential for the public good. Political power should be exercised by men experienced in, and educated from childhood to assume, the constitutional traditions of their society, men whose ambitions are moderated by the privileges and amenities of their assured position. Otherwise the stakes become too high and those lacking in culture and conviction contend with one another to control the power of the state for their narrow ends. Thus Burke believed that the great families of the ruling stratum contribute by the wisdom of their political rule to the general welfare from generation to generation.[30] And Hegel thought that restrictions on equality of opportunity such as primogeniture are essential to insure a landed class especially suited to political rule in virtue of its independence from the state, the quest for profit, and the manifold contingencies of civil society.[31] Privileged family and property arrangements prepare those favored by them to take a clearer view of the universal interest for the benefit of the whole society. Of course, one need not favor anything like a rigidly stratified system; one may maintain to the contrary that it is essential for the vigor of the governing class that persons of unusual talents should be able to make their way into it and be fully accepted. But this proviso is compatible with denying the principle of fair opportunity.

Now to be consistent with the priority of fair opportunity over the difference principle, it is not enough to argue, as Burke and Hegel appear to, that the whole of society including the least

29. In this and the next several paragraphs, I am indebted to Michael Lessnoff. See his essay in *Political Studies*, vol. 19 (1971), pp. 75f. The statement and discussion of the priority rules here and in § 39 have benefited from his criticisms.

30. See *Reflections on the Revolution in France* (London, J. M. Dent and Sons, 1910), p. 49; and John Plamenatz, *Man and Society* (London, Longmans, Green, 1963), vol. 1, pp. 346–351.

31. *Philosophy of Right,* §306, trans. T. M. Knox (Oxford, The Clarendon Press, 1942), p. 199.

favored benefit from certain restrictions on equality of opportunity. We must also claim that the attempt to eliminate these inequalities would so interfere with the social system and the operations of the economy that in the long run anyway the opportunities of the disadvantaged would be even more limited. The priority of fair opportunity, as in the parallel case of the priority of liberty, means that we must appeal to the chances given to those with the lesser opportunity. We must hold that a wider range of more desirable alternatives is open to them than otherwise would be the case. The less definite claim that all of society benefits suffices only when circumstances justify giving up the lexical ordering and moving to an intuitive balancing of fair opportunity against social and economic benefits. These circumstances may or may not require us to abandon the lexical ordering of the principles of justice as well. The two orderings may come into play at different times.

I shall not pursue these complications further. We should however note that although the internal life and culture of the family influence, perhaps as much as anything else, a child's motivation and his capacity to gain from education, and so in turn his life prospects, these effects are not necessarily inconsistent with fair equality of opportunity. Even in a well-ordered society that satisfies the two principles of justice, the family may be a barrier to equal chances between individuals. For as I have defined it, the second principle only requires equal life prospects in all sectors of society for those similarly endowed and motivated. If there are variations among families in the same sector in how they shape the child's aspirations, then while fair equality of opportunity may obtain between sectors, equal chances between individuals will not. This possibility raises the question as to how far the notion of equality of opportunity can be carried; but I defer comment on this until later (§ 77). I shall only remark here that following the difference principle and the priority rules it suggests reduces the urgency to achieve perfect equality of opportunity.

I shall not examine whether there are sound arguments overriding the principle of fair equality of opportunity in favor of a hierarchical class structure. These matters are not part of the theory of justice. The relevant point is that while such contentions may sometimes appear self-serving and hypocritical, they have the right form when they exemplify the general conception of justice as it is to be interpreted in the light of the difference principle and the lexical ordering to which it tends. Infringements of fair equality of opportunity are not justified by a greater sum of advantages enjoyed by others or by society as a whole. The claim (whether correct or not) must be that the opportunities of the least favored sectors of the community would be still more limited if these inequalities were removed. One is to hold that they are not unjust, since the conditions for achieving the full realization of the principles of justice do not exist.

Having noted these cases of priority, I now wish to give the final statement of the two principles of justice for institutions. For the sake of completeness, I shall give a full statement including earlier formulations.

First Principle

Each person is to have an equal right to the most extensive total system of equal basic liberties compatible with a similar system of liberty for all.

Second Principle

Social and economic inequalities are to be arranged so that they are both:

(a) to the greatest benefit of the least advantaged, consistent with the just savings principle, and

(b) attached to offices and positions open to all under conditions of fair equality of opportunity.

First Priority Rule (The Priority of Liberty)

The principles of justice are to be ranked in lexical order and therefore liberty can be restricted only for the sake of liberty. There are two cases:

(a) a less extensive liberty must strengthen the total system of liberty shared by all;

(b) a less than equal liberty must be acceptable to those with the lesser liberty.

Second Priority Rule (The Priority of Justice over Efficiency and Welfare)

The second principle of justice is lexically prior to the principle of efficiency and to that of maximizing the sum of advantages; and fair opportunity is prior to the difference principle. There are two cases:

(a) an inequality of opportunity must enhance the opportunities of those with the lesser opportunity;

(b) an excessive rate of saving must on balance mitigate the burden of those bearing this hardship.

General Conception

All social primary goods—liberty and opportunity, income and wealth, and the bases of self-respect—are to be distributed equally unless an unequal distribution of any or all of these goods is to the advantage of the least favored.

By way of comment, these principles and priority rules are no doubt incomplete. Other modifications will surely have to be made, but I shall not further complicate the statement of the principles. It suffices to observe that when we come to nonideal theory, we do not fall back straightway upon the general conception of justice. The lexical ordering of the two principles, and the valuations that this ordering implies, suggest priority rules which seem to be reasonable enough in many cases. By various examples I have tried to illustrate how these rules can be used and to indicate their plausibility. Thus the ranking of the principles of justice in ideal theory reflects back and guides the application of these principles to nonideal situations. It identifies which limitations need to be dealt with first. The drawback of the general conception of justice is that it lacks the definite structure of the two principles in serial order. In more extreme and tangled instances of nonideal theory there may be no alternative to it. At some point the priority of rules for nonideal cases will fail; and indeed, we may be able to find no satisfactory answer at all. But we must try to postpone the day of reckoning as long as possible, and try to arrange society so that it never comes.

47. THE PRECEPTS OF JUSTICE

The sketch of the system of institutions that satisfies the two principles of justice is now complete. Once the just rate of savings is ascertained or the appropriate range of rates specified, we have a criterion for adjusting the level of the social minimum. The sum of transfers and benefits from essential public goods should be arranged so as to enhance the expectations of the least favored consistent with the required savings and the maintenance of equal liberties. When the basic structure takes this form the distribution that results will be just (or at least not unjust) whatever it is. Each receives that total income (earnings plus transfers) to which he is entitled under the public system of rules upon which his legitimate expectations are founded.

Now, as we saw earlier (§ 14), a central feature of this conception of distributive justice is that it contains a large element of pure procedural justice. No attempt is made to define the just distribution of goods and services on the basis of information about the preferences and claims of particular individuals. This sort of knowledge is regarded as irrelevant from a suitably general point of view; and in any case, it introduces complexities that cannot be handled by principles of tolerable simplicity to which men might reasonably be expected to agree. But if the notion of pure procedural justice is to succeed, it is necessary, as I have said, to set up and to administer impartially a just system of surrounding institutions. The reliance on pure procedural justice presupposes that the basic structure satisfies the two principles.

This account of distributive shares is simply an elaboration of the familiar idea that income and wages will be just once a (workably) competitive price system is properly organized and embedded in a just basic structure. These conditions are sufficient. The distribution that results is a case of background justice on the analogy with the outcome of a fair game. But we need to consider whether this conception fits our intuitive ideas of what is just and unjust. In particular we must ask how well it accords with common sense precepts of justice. It seems as if we have ignored these notions altogether. I now wish to show that they can be accounted for and their subordinate place explained.

The problem may be stated in the following way. Mill argued correctly that so long as one remains at the level of common sense precepts, no reconciliation of these maxims of justice is possible. For example, in the case of wages, the precepts to each according to his effort and to each according to his contribution are contrary injunctions taken by themselves. Moreover, if we wish to assign them certain weights, they provide no way to determine how their relative merits are to be ascertained. Thus common sense precepts do not express a determinate theory of just or fair wages.[32] It does not follow, though, as Mill seems to suppose, that one can find a satisfactory conception only by adopting the utilitarian principle. Some higher principle is indeed necessary; but there are other alternatives than that of utility. It is even possible to elevate one of these precepts, or some combination of them, to the level of a first principle, as when it is said: from each according to his ability, to each according to his needs.[33] From the standpoint of the theory of justice, the two principles of justice define the correct higher criterion. Therefore the problem is to consider whether the common sense precepts of justice would arise in a well-ordered society and how they would receive their appropriate weights.

Consider the case of wages in a perfectly competitive economy surrounded by a just basic structure. Assume that each firm (whether publicly or privately owned) must adjust its rates of pay to the long-run forces of supply and demand. The rates firms pay cannot be so high that they cannot afford paying those rates or so low that a sufficient number will not offer their skills in view of the other opportunities available. In equilibrium the relative attractiveness of different jobs will be equal, all things considered. It is easy, then, to see how the various precepts of justice arise. They simply identify features of jobs that are significant on either the demand or the supply side of the market, or both. A firm's demand for workers is determined by the marginal productivity of labor, that is, by the net value of the contribution of a unit of labor measured by the sale price of the commodities that it produces. The worth of this contribution to the firm rests eventually on market conditions, on what households are willing to pay for various goods. Experience and training, natural ability and special

32. *Utilitarianism*, ch. V, par. 30.

33. This precept is cited by Marx in his *Critique of the Gotha Program*, in *Karl Marx and Frederick Engels, Selected Works* (Moscow, Foreign Languages Publishing House, 1955), vol. II, p. 24.

know-how, tend to earn a premium. Firms are willing to pay more to those with these characteristics because their productivity is greater. This fact explains and gives weight to the precept to each according to his contribution, and as special cases, we have the norms to each according to his training, or his experience, and the like. But also, viewed from the supply side, a premium must be paid if those who may later offer their services are to be persuaded to undertake the costs of training and postponement. Similarly jobs which involve uncertain or unstable employment, or which are performed under hazardous and unpleasantly strenuous conditions, tend to receive more pay. Otherwise men cannot be found to fill them. From this circumstance arise such precepts as to each according to his effort, or the risks he bears, and so on. Even when individuals are assumed to be of the same natural ability, these norms will still arise from the requirements of economic activity. Given the aims of productive units and of those seeking work, certain characteristics are singled out as relevant. At any time the wage practices of firms tend to recognize these precepts and, allowing time for adjustment, assign them the weights called for by market conditions.

All of this seems reasonably clear. More important are several further points. For one thing, different conceptions of justice are likely to generate much the same common sense precepts. Thus in a society regulated by the principle of utility all of the above norms would most likely be recognized. So long as the aims of economic agents are sufficiently similar, these precepts are bound to be appealed to, and wage practices will explicitly take them into account. On the other hand, the weights that are assigned to these precepts will not in general be the same. It is here that conceptions of justice diverge. Not only will there be a tendency to operate wage practices in other ways, but the long-term trend of economic events will almost certainly take another course. When the family of background institutions is governed by distinct conceptions, the market forces to which firms and workers have to adjust will not be the same. A different balance of supply and demand will see to it that the various precepts are balanced differently. Thus the contrast between conceptions of justice does not show up at the level of common sense norms but rather in the relative and changing emphasis that these norms receive over time. In no case can the customary or conventional notion of a fair or just balancing be taken as fundamental, since it will depend upon the principles regulating the background system and the adjustments which they require to current conditions.

An example may clarify this point. Suppose that the basic structure of one society provides for fair equality of opportunity while that of a second society does not. Then in the first society the precept to each according to his contribution in the particular form of each according to his training and education will probably receive much less weight. This is likely to be true even if we suppose, as the facts suggest, that persons have different natural abilities. The reason for this is that with many more persons receiving the benefits of training and education, the supply of qualified individuals in the first society is much greater. When there are no restrictions on entry or imperfections in the capital market for loans (or subsidies) for education, the premium earned by those better endowed is far less. The relative difference in earnings between the more favored and the lowest income class tends to close; and this tendency is even stronger when the difference principle is followed. Thus the precept to each according to his training and education is weighted less in the first than in the second society and the precept to each according to his effort is weighted more. Of course, a conception of justice requires that when social conditions change the appropriate balance of precepts normally changes as well. Over time the consistent application of its principles gradually reshapes the social structure so that market forces also shift, thereby resetting the weight of precepts. There is nothing sacrosanct about the existing balance even if it is correct.

Moreover, it is essential to keep in mind the subordinate place of common sense norms. Doing this is sometimes difficult because they are familiar from everyday life and therefore they are likely to have a prominence in our thinking that their derivative status does not justify. None of these precepts can be plausibly raised to a first principle. Each has presumably arisen in answer to a relevant feature connected with certain particular institutions, this feature being but one among many and these institutions of a special kind. Adopting one of them as a first principle is sure to lead to the neglect of other things that should be taken into account. And if all or many precepts are treated as first principles, there is no gain in systematic clarity. Common sense precepts are at the wrong level of generality. In order to find suitable first principles one must step behind them. Admittedly some precepts appear quite general at first. For example, the precept to each according to his contribution covers many cases of distribution in a perfectly competitive economy. Accepting the marginal productivity theory of distribution, each factor of production receives an income according to how much it adds to output (assuming private property in the means of production). In this sense, a worker is paid the full value of the results of his labor, no more and no less. Offhand this strikes us as fair. It appeals to a traditional idea of the natural right of property in the fruits of our labor. Therefore to some writers the precept of contribution has seemed satisfactory as a principle of justice.[34]

It is easy to see, however, that this is not the case. The marginal product of labor depends upon supply and demand. What an individual contributes by his work varies with the demand of firms for his skills, and this in turn varies with the demand for the products of firms. An individual's contribution is also affected by how many offer similar talents. There is no presumption, then, that following the precept of contribution leads to a just outcome unless the underlying market forces, and the availability of opportunities which they reflect, are appropriately regulated. And this implies, as we have seen, that the basic structure as a whole is just. There is no way, then, to give a proper weight to the precepts of justice except by instituting the surrounding arrangements required by the principles of justice. Some institutions may indeed give a special prominence to certain precepts, in the way for example that a competitive economy emphasizes the precept of contribution. But no inference about the justice of the final distribution can be drawn from viewing the use of any precept in isolation. The overall weighting of the many precepts is done by the whole

34. J. B. Clark is often cited as an example. But see the discussion by J. M. Clark in *The Development of Economic Thought*, ed. H. W. Spiegel (New York, John Wiley and Sons, 1952), pp. 598–612.

system. Thus the precept of need is left to the transfer branch; it does not serve as a precept of wages at all. To assess the justice of distributive shares, we must note the total working of the background arrangements, the proportion of income and wealth deriving from each branch.[35]

It may be objected to the preceding account of the common sense precepts and to the idea of pure procedural justice that a perfectly competitive economy can never be realized. Factors of production never in fact receive their marginal products, and under modern conditions anyway industries soon come to be dominated by a few large firms. Competition is at best imperfect and persons receive less than the value of their contribution, and in this sense they are exploited.[36] The reply to this is first that in any case the conception of a suitably regulated competitive economy with the appropriate background institutions is an ideal scheme which shows how the two principles of justice might be realized. It serves to illustrate the content of these principles, and brings out one way in which either a private-property economy or a socialist regime can satisfy this conception of justice. Granting that existing conditions always fall short of the ideal assumptions, we have some notion of what is just. Moreover we are in a better position to assess how serious the existing imperfections are and to decide upon the best way to approximate the ideal.

A second point is this. The sense in which persons are exploited by market imperfections is a highly special one: namely, the precept of contribution is violated, and this happens because the price system is no longer efficient. But as we have just seen, this precept is but one among many secondary norms, and what really counts is the workings of the whole system and whether these defects are compensated for elsewhere. Furthermore, since it is essentially the principle of efficiency that is not fulfilled, one might as well say that the whole community is exploited. But in

35. Thus J. B. Clark's mistake in his reply to Marx is his failure to consider sufficiently the question of background justice. See J. M. Clark, *ibid.*, pp. 610f. Marxian exploitation is compatible with perfect competition, since it is the outcome of a certain structure of property relations.

36. For this definition of exploitation, see A. C. Pigou, *The Economics of Welfare,* 4th ed. (London, Macmillan, 1932), pp. 549–551.

fact the notion of exploitation is out of place here. It implies a deep injustice in the background system and has little to do with the inefficiences of markets.[37]

Finally, in view of the subordinate place of the principle of efficiency in justice as fairness, the inevitable deviations from market perfection are not especially worrisome. It is more important that a competitive scheme gives scope for the principle of free association and individual choice of occupation against a background of fair equality of opportunity, and that it allows the decisions of households to regulate the items to be produced for private purposes. A basic prerequisite is the compatibility of economic arrangements with the institutions of liberty and free association. Thus if markets are reasonably competitive and open, the notion of pure procedural justice is a feasible one to follow. It seems more practicable than other traditional ideals, being explicitly framed to coordinate the multitude of possible criteria into one coherent and workable conception.

48. LEGITIMATE EXPECTATIONS AND MORAL DESERT

There is a tendency for common sense to suppose that income and wealth, and the good things in life generally, should be distributed according to moral desert. Justice is happiness according to virtue. While it is recognized that this ideal can never be fully carried out, it is the appropriate conception of distributive justice, at least as a prime facie principle, and society should try to realize it as circumstances permit.[38] Now justice as fairness rejects this conception. Such a principle would not be chosen in the original position. There seems to be no way of defining the requisite criter-

37. See Mark Blaug, *Economic Theory in Retrospect,* pp. 434f.

38. See, for example, W. D. Ross, *The Right and the Good* (Oxford, The Clarendon Press, 1930), pp. 21, 26–28, 35, 57f. Similarly, Leibniz in "On the Ultimate Origin of Things" (1697) speaks of the law of justice which "declares that each one [each individual] participate in the perfection of the universe and in a happiness of his own in proportion to his own virtue and to the good will he entertains toward the common good." *Leibniz,* ed. P. P. Wiener (New York, Charles Scribner's Sons, 1951), p. 353.

ion in that situation. Moreover, the notion of distribution according to virtue fails to distinguish between moral desert and legitimate expectations. Thus it is true that as persons and groups take part in just arrangements, they acquire claims on one another defined by the publicly recognized rules. Having done various things encouraged by the existing arrangements, they now have certain rights, and just distributive shares honor these claims. A just scheme, then, answers to what men are entitled to; it satisfies their legitimate expectations as founded upon social institutions. But what they are entitled to is not proportional to nor dependent upon their intrinsic worth. The principles of justice that regulate the basic structure and specify the duties and obligations of individuals do not mention moral desert, and there is no tendency for distributive shares to correspond to it.

This contention is borne out by the preceding account of common sense precepts and their role in pure procedural justice (§47). For example, in determining wages a competitive economy gives weight to the precept of contribution. But as we have seen, the extent of one's contribution (estimated by one's marginal productivity) depends upon supply and demand. Surely a person's moral worth does not vary according to how many offer similar skills, or happen to want what he can produce. No one supposes that when someone's abilities are less in demand or have deteriorated (as in the case of singers) his moral deservingness undergoes a similar shift. All of this is perfectly obvious and has long been agreed to.[39] It simply reflects the fact noted before (§17) that it is one of the fixed points of our moral judgments that no one deserves his place in the distribution of natural assets any more than he deserves his initial starting place in society.

Moreover, none of the precepts of justice aims at rewarding virtue. The premiums earned by scarce natural talents, for example, are to cover the costs of training and to encourage the efforts of learning, as well as to direct ability to where it best furthers the common interest. The distributive shares that result do not correlate with moral worth, since the initial endowment of natural assets and the contingencies of their growth and nurture

39. See F. H. Knight, *The Ethics of Competition* (New York, Harper and Brothers, 1935), pp. 54–57.

in early life are arbitrary from a moral point of view. The precept which seems intuitively to come closest to rewarding moral desert is that of distribution according to effort, or perhaps better, conscientious effort.[40] Once again, however, it seems clear that the effort a person is willing to make is influenced by his natural abilities and skills and the alternatives open to him. The better endowed are more likely, other things equal, to strive conscientiously, and there seems to be no way to discount for their greater good fortune. The idea of rewarding desert is impracticable. And certainly to the extent that the precept of need is emphasized, moral worth is ignored. Nor does the basic structure tend to balance the precepts of justice so as to achieve the requisite correspondence behind the scenes. It is regulated by the two principles of justice which define other aims entirely.

The same conclusion may be reached in another way. In the preceding remarks the notion of moral worth as distinct from a person's claims based upon his legitimate expectations has not been explained. Suppose, then, that we define this notion and show that it has no correlation with distributive shares. We have only to consider a well-ordered society, that is, a society in which institutions are just and this fact is publicly recognized. Its members also have a strong sense of justice, an effective desire to comply with the existing rules and to give one another that to which they are entitled. In this case we may assume that everyone is of equal moral worth. We have now defined this notion in terms of the sense of justice, the desire to act in accordance with the principles that would be chosen in the original position (§ 72). But it is evident that understood in this way, the equal moral worth of persons does not entail that distributive shares are equal. Each is to receive what the principles of justice say he is entitled to, and these do not require equality.

The essential point is that the concept of moral worth does not provide a first principle of distributive justice. This is because it cannot be introduced until after the principles of justice and of natural duty and obligation have been acknowledged. Once these principles are on hand, moral worth can be defined as having a

40. See Knight, *ibid.*, p. 56n.

sense of justice; and as I shall discuss later (§66), the virtues can be characterized as desires or tendencies to act upon the corresponding principles. Thus the concept of moral worth is secondary to those of right and justice, and it plays no role in the substantive definition of distributive shares. The case is analogous to the relation between the substantive rules of property and the law of robbery and theft. These offenses and the demerits they entail presuppose the institution of property which is established for prior and independent social ends. For a society to organize itself with the aim of rewarding moral desert as a first principle would be like having the institution of property in order to punish thieves. The criterion to each according to his virtue would not, then, be chosen in the original position. Since the parties desire to advance their conceptions of the good, they have no reason for arranging their institutions so that distributive shares are determined by moral desert, even if they could find an antecedent standard for its definition.

In a well-ordered society individuals acquire claims to a share of the social product by doing certain things encouraged by the existing arrangements. The legitimate expectations that arise are the other side, so to speak, of the principle of fairness and the natural duty of justice. For in the way that one has a duty to uphold just arrangements, and an obligation to do one's part when one has accepted a position in them, so a person who has complied with the scheme and done his share has a right to be treated accordingly by others. They are bound to meet his legitimate expectations. Thus when just economic arrangements exist, the claims of individuals are properly settled by reference to the rules and precepts (with their respective weights) which these practices take as relevant. As we have seen, it is incorrect to say that just distributive shares reward individuals according to their moral worth. But what we can say is that, in the traditional phrase, a just scheme gives each person his due: that is, it allots to each what he is entitled to as defined by the scheme itself. The principles of justice for institutions and individuals establish that doing this is fair.

Now it should be noted that even though a person's claims are regulated by the existing rules, we can still make a distinction between being entitled to something and deserving it in a familiar although nonmoral sense.[41] To illustrate, after a game one often says that the losing side deserved to win. Here one does not mean that the victors are not entitled to claim the championship, or whatever spoils go to the winner. One means instead that the losing team displayed to a higher degree the skills and qualities that the game calls forth, and the exercise of which gives the sport its appeal. Therefore the losers truly deserved to win but lost out as a result of bad luck, or from other contingencies that caused the contest to miscarry. Similarly even the best economic arrangements will not always lead to the more preferred outcomes. The claims that individuals actually acquire inevitably deviate more or less widely from those that the scheme is designed to allow for. Some persons in favored positions, for example, may not have to a higher degree than others the desired qualities and abilities. All this is evident enough. Its bearing here is that although we can indeed distinguish between the claims that existing arrangements require us to honor, given what individuals have done and how things have turned out, and the claims that would have resulted under more ideal circumstances, none of this implies that distributive shares should be in accordance with moral worth. Even when things happen in the best way, there is still no tendency for distribution and virtue to coincide.

No doubt some may still contend that distributive shares should match moral worth at least to the extent that this is feasible. They may believe that unless those who are better off have superior moral character, their having greater advantages is an affront to our sense of justice. Now this opinion may arise from thinking of distributive justice as somehow the opposite of retributive justice. It is true that in a reasonably well-ordered society those who are punished for violating just laws have normally done something wrong. This is because the purpose of the criminal law is to uphold basic natural duties, those which forbid us to injure other persons in their life and limb, or to deprive them of their liberty and property, and punishments are to serve this end. They are not simply a scheme of taxes and burdens designed to put a price on

41. Here I borrow from Joel Feinberg, *Doing and Deserving* (Princeton, Princeton University Press, 1970), pp. 64f.

certain forms of conduct and in this way to guide men's conduct for mutual advantage. It would be far better if the acts proscribed by penal statutes were never done.[42] Thus a propensity to commit such acts is a mark of bad character, and in a just society legal punishments will only fall upon those who display these faults.

It is clear that the distribution of economic and social advantages is entirely different. These arrangements are not the converse, so to speak, of the criminal law, so that just as the one punishes certain offenses, the other rewards moral worth.[43] The function of unequal distributive shares is to cover the costs of training and education, to attract individuals to places and associations where they are most needed from a social point of view, and so on. Assuming that everyone accepts the propriety of self- or group-interested motivation duly regulated by a sense of justice, each decides to do those things that best accord with his aims. Variations in wages and income and the perquisites of position are simply to influence these choices so that the end result accords with efficiency and justice. In a well-ordered society there would be no need for the penal law except insofar as the assurance problem made it necessary. The question of criminal justice belongs for the most part to partial compliance theory, whereas the account of distributive shares belongs to strict compliance theory and so to the consideration of the ideal scheme. To think of distributive and retributive justice as converses of one another is completely misleading and suggests a different justification for distributive shares than the one they in fact have.

49. COMPARISON WITH MIXED CONCEPTIONS

While I have often compared the principles of justice with utilitarianism, I have not yet said anything about the mixed conceptions. It will be recalled that these are defined by substituting the standard of utility and other criteria for the second principle of

42. See H. L. A. Hart, *The Concept of Law* (Oxford, The Clarendon Press, 1961), p. 39; and Feinberg, *Doing and Deserving*, ch. V.
43. On this point, see Feinberg, *ibid.*, pp. 62, 69n.

justice (§21). I must now consider these alternatives, especially since many persons may find them more reasonable than the principles of justice which seem at first anyway to impose rather stringent requirements. But it needs to be emphasized straightway that all the mixed conceptions accept the first principle, and therefore recognize the primary place of the equal liberties. None of these views is utilitarian, for even if the principle of utility is substituted for the second principle, or for some part of it, say the difference principle, the conception of utility still has a subordinate place. Thus insofar as one of the chief aims of justice as fairness is to construct an alternative to the classical utilitarian doctrine, this aim is achieved even if we finally accept a mixed conception rather than the two principles of justice. Moreover, given the importance of the first principle, it seems that the essential feature of the contract theory is preserved in these alternatives.

Now it is evident from these remarks that mixed conceptions are much more difficult to argue against than the principle of utility. Many writers who seem to profess a variant of the utilitarian view, even if it is expressed vaguely as the balancing and harmonizing of social interests, clearly presuppose a fixed constitutional system that guarantees the basic freedoms to a certain minimum degree. Thus they actually hold some mixed doctrine, and therefore the strong arguments from liberty cannot be used as before. The main problem, then, is what can still be said in favor of the second principle over that of utility when both are constrained by the principle of equal liberty. We need to examine the reasons for rejecting the standard of utility even in this instance, although it is clear that these reasons will not be as decisive as those for rejecting the classical and average doctrines.

Consider first a mixed conception that is rather close to the principles of justice: namely, the view arising when the principle of average utility constrained by a certain social minimum is substituted for the difference principle, everything else remaining unchanged. Now the difficulty here is the same as that with intuitionist doctrines generally: how is the social minimum to be selected and adjusted to changing circumstances? Anyone using the two principles of justice might also appear to be striking a balance between maximizing average utility and maintaining an appropriate social minimum. If we attended only to his considered judgments and not to his reason for these judgments, his appraisals might be indistinguishable from those of someone following this mixed conception. There is, I assume, sufficient latitude in the determination of the level of the social minimum under varying conditions to bring about this result. How do we know, then, that a person who adopts this mixed view does not in fact rely on the difference principle? To be sure, he is not conscious of invoking it, and indeed he may even repudiate the suggestion that he does so. But it turns out that the level assigned to the required minimum that constrains the principle of average utility leads to precisely the same consequences that would arise if he were in fact following this criterion. Moreover, he is unable to explain why he chooses the minimum as he does; the best he can say is that he makes the decision that seems most reasonable to him. Now it is going too far to claim that such a person is really using the difference principle, since his judgments may match some other standard. Yet it is true that his conception of justice is still to be identified. The leeway behind the scenes for the determination of the proper minimum leaves the matter unsettled.

Similar things can be said concerning other mixed theories. Thus one might decide to constrain the average principle by setting up some distributional requirement either by itself or in conjunction with some suitably chosen minimum. For example, one might substitute for the difference principle the criterion to maximize the average utility less some fraction (or multiple) of the standard deviation of the resulting distribution.[44] Since this deviation is smallest when everyone achieves the same utility, this criterion indicates a greater concern for the less favored than the average principle. Now the intuitionistic features of this view are also clear, for we need to ask how the fraction (or multiple) of the standard deviation is to be selected and how this parameter is to vary with the average itself. Once again the difference principle may stand in the background. This sort of mixed view is on a par with other intuitionistic conceptions that direct us to follow a plurality of ends. For it holds that provided a certain floor is main-

44. For a view of this kind, see Nicholas Rescher, *Distributive Justice* (New York, Bobbs-Merrill, 1966), pp. 35–38.

tained, greater average well-being and a more equal distribution are both desirable ends. One institution is unambiguously preferable to another if it is better on each count.

Different political views, however, balance these ends differently, and we need criteria for determining their relative weights. The fact is that we do not in general agree to very much when we acknowledge ends of this kind. It must be recognized that a fairly detailed weighting of aims is implicit in a reasonably complete conception of justice. In everyday life we often content ourselves with enumerating common sense precepts and objectives of policy, adding that on particular questions we have to balance them in the light of the general facts of the situation. While this is sound practical advice, it does not express an articulated conception of justice. One is being told in effect to exercise one's judgment as best one can within the framework of these ends as guidelines. Only policies preferable on each score are clearly more desirable. By contrast, the difference principle is a relatively precise conception, since it ranks all combinations of objectives according to how well they promote the prospects of the least favored.

Thus despite the fact that the difference principle seems offhand to be a somewhat special conception, it may still be the criterion which when adjoined to the other principles of justice stands in the background and controls the weights expressed in our everyday judgments as these would be matched by various mixed principles. Our customary way of relying on intuition guided by lower-order standards may obscure the existence of more basic principles that account for the force of these criteria. Of course, whether the two principles of justice, and especially the difference principle, explicate our judgments of distributive justice can only be decided by developing the consequences of these principles in some detail and noting how far we are prepared to accept the weights to which they lead. Possibly there will be no conflict between these consequences and our considered convictions. Certainly there should be none with those judgments that are fixed points, ones that we seem unwilling to revise under any foreseeable circumstances. Otherwise the two principles are not fully acceptable and some revision has to be made.

But perhaps our everyday views do not entail anything very definite about the problem of balancing competing ends. If so, the main question is whether we can assent to the far more exact specification of our conception of justice which the two principles represent. Provided that certain fixed points are preserved, we have to decide the best way to fill in our conception of justice and to extend it to further cases. The two principles of justice may not so much oppose our intuitive convictions as provide a relatively concrete principle for questions that common sense finds unfamiliar and leaves undecided. Thus while the difference principle strikes us as strange at first, reflection upon its implications when it is suitably circumscribed may convince us that it either accords with our considered judgments, or else projects these convictions to new situations in an acceptable way.

In line with these remarks, we may note that it is a political convention of a democratic society to appeal to the common interest. No political party publicly admits to pressing for legislation to the disadvantage of any recognized social group. But how is this convention to be understood? Surely it is something more than the principle of efficiency, and we cannot assume that government affects everyone's interest equally. Since it is impossible to maximize with respect to more than one point of view, it is natural, given the ethos of a democratic society, to single out that of the least advantaged and to further their long-term prospects in the best manner consistent with the equal liberties and fair opportunity. It seems that the policies in the justice of which we have the greatest confidence do at least tend in this direction in the sense that this sector of society would be worse off should they be curtailed. These policies are just throughout even if they are not perfectly just. The difference principle can therefore be interpreted as a reasonable extension of the political convention of a democracy once we face up to the necessity of adopting a reasonably complete conception of justice.

In noting that the mixed conceptions have intuitionistic features, I do not mean that this fact is a decisive objection to them. As I have already observed (§7), such combinations of principles are certainly of great practical value. There is no question but that these conceptions identify plausible standards by reference to which

319

policies may be appraised, and given the appropriate background institutions, they may guide us to sound conclusions. For example, a person who accepts the mixed conception to maximize average well-being less some fraction (or multiple) of the standard deviation will presumably favor fair equality of opportunity, for it seems that having more equal chances for all both raises the average (via increases in efficiency) and decreases inequality. In this instance the substitute for the difference principle supports the other part of the second principle. Furthermore it is evident that at some point we cannot avoid relying upon our intuitive judgments. The difficulty with the mixed conceptions is that they may resort to these judgments too soon and fail to define a clear alternative to the difference principle. In the absence of a procedure for assigning the appropriate weights (or parameters), it is possible that the balance is actually determined by the principles of justice, unless of course these principles yield conclusions that we cannot accept. Should this happen, then some mixed conception despite its appeal to intuition may be preferable, especially if its use helps to introduce order and agreement into our considered convictions.

Another consideration favoring the difference principle is the comparative ease with which it can be interpreted and applied. Indeed to some, part of the attractiveness of mixed criteria is that they are a way to avoid the relatively sharp demands of the difference principle. It is fairly straightforward to ascertain what things will advance the interests of the least favored. This group can be identified by its index of primary goods, and policy questions can be settled by asking how the relevant representative man suitably situated would choose. But to the extent that the principle of utility is given a role, the vagueness in the idea of average (or total) well-being is troublesome. It is necessary to arrive at some estimate of utility functions for different representative persons and to set up an interpersonal correspondence between them, and so on. The problems in doing this are so great and the approximations are so rough that deeply conflicting opinions may seem equally plausible to different persons. Some may claim that the gains of one group outweigh the losses of another, while others may deny it. No one can say what underlying principles account for these differences or how they can be resolved. It is easier for those with the stronger social positions to advance their interests unjustly without being shown to be clearly out of bounds. Of course all this is obvious, and it has always been recognized that ethical principles are vague. Nevertheless they are not all equally imprecise, and the two principles of justice have an advantage in the greater clarity of their demands and in what needs to be done to satisfy them.

It might be thought that the vagueness of the principle of utility can be overcome by a better account of how to measure and to aggregate well-being. I do not wish to stress these much discussed technical problems, since the more important objections to utilitarianism are at another level. But a brief mention of these matters will clarify the contract doctrine. Now there are several ways of establishing an interpersonal measure of utility. One of these (going back at least to Edgeworth) is to suppose that an individual is able to distinguish only a finite number of utility levels.[45] A person is said to be indifferent between alternatives that belong to the same discrimination level, and the cardinal measure of the utility difference between any two alternatives is defined by the number of distinguishable levels that separate them. The cardinal scale that results is unique, as it must be, up to a positive linear transformation. To set up a measure between persons one might assume that the difference between adjacent levels is the same for all individuals and the same between all levels. With this interpersonal correspondence rule the calculations are extremely simple. In comparing alternatives we ascertain the number of levels between them for each individual and then sum, taking account of the pluses and minuses.

This conception of cardinal utility suffers from well-known difficulties. Leaving aside the obvious practical problems and the fact that the detection of a person's discrimination levels depends upon the alternatives actually available, it seems impossible to justify the assumption that the social utility of a shift from one level to another is the same for all individuals. On the one hand, this procedure would weigh identically those changes involving the same number of discriminations that individuals felt differently about, some hav-

45. See A. K. Sen, *Collective Choice and Social Welfare* (San Francisco, Holden-Day, 1970), pp. 93f; for Edgeworth, see *Mathematical Psychics* (London, 1888), pp. 7–9, 60f.

ing stronger feelings than others; while on the other hand, it would count more heavily the changes experienced by those individuals who appear to make more discriminations. Surely it is unsatisfactory to discount the strength of attitudes, and especially to reward so highly the capacity for noting distinctions which may vary systematically with temperament and training.[46] Indeed, the whole procedure seems arbitrary. It has the merit, however, of illustrating the way in which the principle of utility is likely to contain implicit ethical assumptions in the method chosen for establishing the required measure of utility. The concept of happiness and well-being is not sufficiently determinate, and even to define a suitable cardinal measure we may have to look at the moral theory in which it will be used.

Analogous difficulties arise with the Neumann-Morgenstern definition.[47] It can be shown that if an individual's choices between risky prospects satisfy certain postulates, then there exist utility numbers corresponding to the alternatives in such a way that his decisions can be interpreted as maximizing expected utility. He chooses as if he were guided by the mathematical expectation of these utility numbers; and these assignments of utility are unique up to a positive linear transformation. Of course, it is not maintained that the individual himself uses an assignment of utilities in making his decisions. These numbers do not guide his choices, nor do they provide a first-person procedure of deliberation. Rather, given that a person's preferences among prospects fulfill certain conditions, the observing mathematician can, theoretically at least, compute numbers that describe these preferences as maximizing expected utility in the sense defined. So far nothing follows about the actual course of reflection, or the criteria, if any, that the individual relies upon; nor is anything implied about what features of the alternatives the utility numbers correspond to or represent.

Now assuming that we can set up a cardinal utility for each person, how is the interpersonal measure to be established? A familiar

46. For these difficulties, see Sen, *ibid.*, pp. 94f; and W. S. Vickrey, "Utility, Strategy, and Social Decision Rules," *Quarterly Journal of Economics,* vol. 74 (1960), pp. 519–522.

47. For an account of this, see Baumol, *Economic Theory and Operations Analysis,* pp. 512–528; and Luce and Raiffa, *Games and Decisions,* pp. 12–38.

proposal is the zero-one rule: assign the value zero to the individual's worst possible situation and value one to his best situation. Offhand this seems fair, perhaps expressing in another way the idea that each is to count for one and no more than one. Yet there are other proposals with comparable symmetry, for example, that which assigns the value zero to the worst alternative and the value one to the sum of the utilities from all alternatives.[48] Both of these rules seem equally just, since the first postulates equal maximum utility for everyone, the latter equal average utility; but they may lead to different social decisions. Furthermore, these proposals postulate in effect that all individuals have similar capacities for satisfaction, and this seems like an unusual price to pay merely to define an interpersonal measure. These rules clearly determine the concept of well-being in a special way, for the ordinary notion would appear to allow for variations in the sense that a different interpretation of the concept would be equally if not more compatible with common sense. Thus for example the zero-one rule implies that, other things equal, greater social utility results from educating people to have simple desires and to be easily satisfied; and that such persons will generally have the stronger claims. They are pleased with less and so presumably can be brought closer to their highest utility. If one cannot accept these consequences but still wishes to hold the utilitarian view, some other interpersonal measure must be found.

Further, we should observe that while the Neumann-Morgenstern postulates assume that individuals do not enjoy the experience of risk, the actual process of gambling, the resulting measure is nevertheless influenced by attitudes toward uncertainty as defined by the overall probability distribution.[49] Thus if this definition of utility is used in social decisions, men's feelings about taking chances will affect the criterion of well-being that is to be maximized. Once again we see that the conventions defining interpersonal comparisons have unexpected moral consequences. As before the measure of utility is influenced by contingencies that are arbitrary from a moral point of view. The situation is very different from that of

48. See Sen, *Collective Choice and Social Welfare,* p. 98.
49. See Arrow, *Social Choice and Individual Values,* p. 10; and Sen, *ibid.,* pp. 96f.

justice as fairness as shown by its Kantian interpretation, the embedding of ideals in its principles, and its reliance upon primary goods for the necessary interpersonal comparisons.

It would appear, then, that the vagueness of the utilitarian principle is not likely to be satisfactorily removed simply by a more precise measure of utility. To the contrary, once the conventions required for interpersonal comparisons are examined, we see that there are various methods for defining these comparisons. Yet these methods involve strikingly different assumptions and presumably have very different consequences. It is a moral question which of these definitions and correspondence rules, if any, are appropriate for a conception of justice. This is what is meant, I believe, when it is said that interpersonal comparisons depend upon value judgments. While it is obvious that the acceptance of the principle of utility is a matter for moral theory, it is less evident that the very procedures for measuring well-being raise similar problems. Since there is more than one such procedure, the choice depends upon the use to which the measure is to be put; and this means that ethical considerations will eventually be decisive.

Maine's comments on the standard utilitarian assumptions are apropos here. He suggests that the grounds for these assumptions are clear once we see that they are simply a working rule of legislation, and that this is how Bentham regarded them.[50] Given a populous and reasonably homogeneous society and an energetic modern legislature, the only principle that can guide legislation on a large scale is the principle of utility. The necessity to neglect differences between persons, even very real ones, leads to the maxim to count all equally, and to the similarity and marginal postulates. Surely the conventions for interpersonal comparisons are to be judged in the same light. The contract doctrine holds that once we see this, we shall also see that the idea of measuring and summing well-being is best abandoned entirely. Viewed from the perspective of the original position, it is not part of a feasible conception of social justice. Instead the two principles of justice are preferable and far simpler to apply. All things considered, there are still reasons for choosing the difference principle, or the second principle as a

50. These remarks are found in H. S. Maine, *The Early History of Institutions* (London, 1897), pp. 399f.

whole, over that of utility even in the restricted context of a mixed conception.

50. THE PRINCIPLE OF PERFECTION

So far I have said very little about the principle of perfection. But having just considered mixed views, I should now like to examine this conception. There are two variants: in the first it is the sole principle of a teleological theory directing society to arrange institutions and to define the duties and obligations of individuals so as to maximize the achievement of human excellence in art, science, and culture. The principle obviously is more demanding the higher the relevant ideal is pitched. The absolute weight that Nietzsche sometimes gives the lives of great men such as Socrates and Goethe is unusual. At places he says that mankind must continually strive to produce great individuals. We give value to our lives by working for the good of the highest specimens.[51] The second variant found in Aristotle among others has far stronger claims.

This more moderate doctrine is one in which a principle of perfection is accepted as but one standard among several in an intuitionist theory. The principle is to be balanced against others by intuition. The extent to which such a view is perfectionist depends, then, upon the weight given to the claims of excellence and culture. If for example it is maintained that in themselves the achievements of the Greeks in philosophy, science, and art justified the ancient practice of slavery (assuming that this practice was necessary for these achievements), surely the conception is highly perfectionist. The requirements of perfection override the strong claims of liberty. On the other hand, one may use the criterion simply to limit the redistribution of wealth and income under a constitutional re-

51. See the passages cited in G. A. Morgan, *What Nietzsche Means* (Cambridge, Harvard University Press, 1941), pp. 40–42, 369–376. Particularly striking is Nietzsche's statement: "Mankind must work continually to produce individual great human beings—this and nothing else is the task . . . for the question is this: how can your life, the individual life, retain the highest value, the deepest significance? . . . Only by your living for the good of the rarest and most valuable specimens." *Untimely Mediations: Third Essay: Schopenhauer as Educator,* sec. 6, cited from J. R. Hollingsdale, *Nietzsche: The Man and His Philosophy* (Baton Rouge, Louisiana State University Press, 1965), p. 127.

gime. In this case it serves as a counterpoise to egalitarian ideas. Thus it may be said that distribution should indeed be more equal if this is essential for meeting the basic needs of those less favored and only diminishes the enjoyments and pleasures of those better off. But the greater happiness of the less fortunate does not in general justify curtailing the expenditures required to preserve cultural values. These forms of life have greater intrinsic worth than the lesser pleasures, however widely the latter are enjoyed. Under normal conditions a certain minimum of social resources must be kept aside to advance the ends of perfection. The only exception is when these claims clash with the demands of the basic needs. Thus given improving circumstances, the principle of perfection acquires an increasing weight relative to a greater satisfaction of desire. No doubt many have accepted perfectionism in this intuitionist form. It allows for a range of interpretations and seems to express a far more reasonable view than the strict perfectionist theory.[52]

Before considering why the principle of perfection would be rejected, I should like to comment on the relation between the principles of justice and the two kinds of teleological theories, perfectionism and utilitarianism. We may define ideal-regarding principles as those which are not want-regarding principles.[53] That is, they do not take as the only relevant features the overall amount of want-satisfaction and the way in which it is distributed among persons. Now in terms of this distinction, the principles of justice as well as the principle of perfection (either variant) are ideal-regarding principles. They do not abstract from the aims of desires and hold that satisfactions are of equal value when they are equally intense and pleasurable (the meaning of Bentham's remark that, other things equal, pushpin is as good as poetry). As we have seen (§41), a certain ideal is embedded in the principles of justice, and

52. For this kind of view, see Bertrand de Jouvenal, *The Ethics of Redistribution* (Cambridge, The University Press, 1951), pp. 53–56, 62–65. See also Hastings Rashdall, *The Theory of Good and Evil* (London, Oxford University Press, 1907), vol. I, pp. 235–243, who argues for the principle that everyone's good is to count for as much as the like good of anyone else, the criteria of perfection being relevant in determining when persons' goods are equal. The capacity for a higher life is a ground for treating men unequally. See pp. 240–242. A similar view is implicit in G. E. Moore, *Principia Ethica*, ch. VI.

53. The definition is from Barry, *Political Argument*, pp. 39f.

the fulfillment of desires incompatible with these principles has no value at all. Moreover we are to encourage certain traits of character, especially a sense of justice. Thus the contract doctrine is similar to perfectionism in that it takes into account other things than the net balance of satisfaction and how it is shared. In fact, the principles of justice do not even mention the amount or the distribution of welfare but refer only to the distribution of liberties and the other primary goods. At the same time, they manage to define an ideal of the person without invoking a prior standard of human excellence. The contract view occupies, therefore, an intermediate position between perfectionism and utilitarianism.

Turning to the question whether a perfectionist standard would be adopted, we may consider first the strict perfectionist conception, since here the problems are more obvious. Now in order to have a clear sense, this criterion must provide some way of ranking different kinds of achievements and summing their values. Of course this assessment may not be very exact, but it should be accurate enough to guide the main decisions concerning the basic structure. It is at this point that the principle of perfection gets into difficulty. For while the persons in the original position take no interest in one another's interests, they know that they have (or may have) certain moral and religious interests and other cultural ends which they cannot put in jeopardy. Moreover, they are assumed to be committed to different conceptions of the good and they think that they are entitled to press their claims on one another to further their separate aims. The parties do not share a conception of the good by reference to which the fruition of their powers or even the satisfaction of their desires can be evaluated. They do not have an agreed criterion of perfection that can be used as a principle for choosing between institutions. To acknowledge any such standard would be, in effect, to accept a principle that might lead to a lesser religious or other liberty, if not to a loss of freedom altogether to advance many of one's spiritual ends. If the standard of excellence is reasonably clear, the parties have no way of knowing that their claims may not fall before the higher social goal of maximizing perfection. Thus it seems that the only understanding that the persons in the original position can reach is that everyone should have the greatest equal liberty consistent with a similar liberty for others. They cannot risk their freedom by author-izing a standard of value to define what is to be maximized by a teleological principle of justice. This case is entirely different from that of agreeing to an index of primary goods as a basis of inter-personal comparisons. The index plays a subordinate role in any event, and primary goods are things that men generally want in order to achieve their ends whatever they are. Wanting these goods does not distinguish between one person and another. But of course accepting them for the purpose of an index does not establish a standard of excellence.

It is evident, then, that much the same argument that led to the principle of equal liberty requires the rejection of the principle of perfection. But in making this argument I have not contended that the criteria of excellence lack a rational basis from the standpoint of everyday life. Clearly there are standards in the arts and sciences for appraising creative efforts, at least within particular styles and traditions of thought. Very often it is beyond question that the work of one person is superior to that of another. Indeed, the freedom and well-being of individuals, when measured by the excellence of their activities and works, is vastly different in value. This is true not only of actual performance but of potential performance as well. Comparisons of intrinsic value can obviously be made; and although the standard of perfection is not a principle of justice, judgments of value have an important place in human affairs. They are not necessarily so vague that they must fail as a workable basis for assigning rights. The argument is rather that in view of their disparate aims the parties have no reason to adopt the principle of perfection given the conditions of the original position.

In order to arrive at the ethic of perfectionism, we should have to attribute to the parties a prior acceptance of some natural duty, say the duty to develop human persons of a certain style and aesthetic grace, and to advance the pursuit of knowledge and the cultivation of the arts. But this assumption would drastically alter the interpretation of the original position. While justice as fairness allows that in a well-ordered society the values of excellence are recognized, the human perfections are to be pursued within the limits of the principle of free association. Persons join together to further their cultural and artistic interests in the same way that they form religious communities. They do not use the coercive apparatus of the state to win for themselves a greater liberty or larger distributive shares on the grounds that their activities are of more intrinsic value. Perfectionism is denied as a political principle. Thus the social resources necessary to support associations dedicated to advancing the arts and sciences and culture generally are to be won as a fair return for services rendered, or from such voluntary contributions as citizens wish to make, all within a regime regulated by the two principles of justice.

On the contract doctrine, then, the equal liberty of citizens does not presuppose that the ends of different persons have the same intrinsic value, nor that their freedom and well-being is of the same worth. It is postulated though that the parties are moral persons, rational individuals with a coherent system of ends and a capacity for a sense of justice. Since they have the requisite defining properties, it would be superfluous to add that the parties are equally moral persons. We can say if we wish that men have equal dignity, meaning by this simply that they all satisfy the conditions of moral personality expressed by the interpretation of the initial contractual situation. And being alike in this respect, they are to be treated as the principles of justice require (§ 77). But none of this implies that their activities and accomplishments are of equal excellence. To think this is to conflate the notion of moral personality with the various perfections that fall under the concept of value.

I have just noted that persons' being of equal value is not necessary for equal liberty. It should also be observed that their being of equal value is not sufficient either. Sometimes it is said that equality of basic rights follows from the equal capacity of individuals for the higher forms of life; but it is not clear why this should be so. Intrinsic worth is a notion falling under the concept of value, and whether equal liberty or some other principle is appropriate depends upon the conception of right. Now the criterion of perfection insists that rights in the basic structure be assigned so as to maximize the total of intrinsic value. Presumably the configuration of rights and opportunities enjoyed by individuals affects the degree to which they bring to fruition their latent powers and excellences. But it does not follow that an equal distribution of basic freedoms is the best solution.

The situation resembles that of classical utilitarianism: we require postulates parallel to the standard assumptions. Thus even if the latent abilities of individuals were similar, unless the assignment of rights is governed by a principle of diminishing marginal value (estimated in this case by the criteria for excellence), equal rights would not be insured. Indeed, unless there are bountiful resources, the sum of value might be best increased by very unequal rights and opportunities favoring a few. Doing this is not unjust on the perfectionist view provided that it is necessary to produce a greater sum of human excellence. Now a principle of diminishing marginal value is certainly questionable, although perhaps not as much so as that of equal value. There is little reason to suppose that, in general, rights and resources allocated to encourage and to cultivate highly talented persons contribute less and less to the total beyond some point in the relevant range. To the contrary, this contribution may grow (or stay constant) indefinitely. The principle of perfection provides, then, an insecure foundation for the equal liberties and it would presumably depart widely from the difference principle. The assumptions required for equality seem extremely implausible. To find a firm basis for equal liberty, it seems that we must reject the traditional teleological principles, both perfectionist and utilitarian.

So far I have been discussing perfectionism as a single-principle teleological theory. With this variant the difficulties are most evident. The intuitionistic forms are much more plausible, and when the claims of perfection are weighted with moderation, these views are not easy to argue against. The discrepancy from the two principles of justice is much less. Nevertheless similar problems do arise, for each principle of an intuitionistic view must be chosen, and while the consequences are not likely to be so great in this case, there is as before no basis for acknowledging a principle of perfection as a standard of social justice. In addition, criteria of excellence are imprecise as political principles, and their application to public questions is bound to be unsettled and idiosyncratic, however reasonably they may be invoked and accepted within narrower traditions and communities of thought. It is for this reason, among others, that justice as fairness requires us to show that modes of conduct interfere with the basic liberties of others or else violate some obligation or natural duty before they can be restricted. For it is when arguments to this conclusion fail that individuals are tempted to appeal to perfectionist criteria in an ad hoc manner. When it is said, for example, that certain kinds of sexual relationships are degrading and shameful, and should be prohibited on this basis, if only for the sake of the individuals in question irrespective of their wishes, it is often because a reasonable case cannot be made in terms of the principles of justice. Instead we fall back on notions of excellence. But in these matters we are likely to be influenced by subtle aesthetic preferences and personal feelings of propriety; and individual, class, and group differences are often sharp and irreconcilable. Since these uncertainties plague perfectionist criteria and jeopardize individual liberty, it seems best to rely entirely on the principles of justice which have a more definite structure.[54] Thus even in its intuitionistic form, perfectionism would be rejected as not defining a feasible basis of social justice.

Eventually of course we would have to check whether the consequences of doing without a standard of perfection are acceptable, since offhand it may seem as if justice as fairness does not allow enough scope for ideal-regarding considerations. At this point I can only note that public funds for the arts and sciences may be provided through the exchange branch (§ 43). In this instance there are no restrictions on the reasons citizens may have for imposing upon themselves the requisite taxes. They may assess the merits of these public goods on perfectionist principles, since the coercive machinery of government is used in this case only to overcome the problems of isolation and assurance, and no one is taxed without his consent. The criterion of excellence does not serve here as a

---

54. Illustrative of this point is the controversy concerning the so-called enforcement of morals, morality often having the narrow sense of sexual morality. See Patrick Devlin, *The Enforcement of Morals* (London, Oxford University Press, 1965), and H. L. A. Hart, *Law, Liberty and Morality* (Stanford, Calif., Stanford University Press, 1963), who take different positions on this issue. For further discussion see Brian Barry, *Political Argument*, pp. 66–69; Ronald Dworkin, "Lord Devlin and the Enforcement of Morals," *Yale Law Journal*, vol. 75 (1966); and A. R. Louch, "Sins and Crimes," *Philosophy*, vol. 43 (1968).

political principle; and so, if it wishes, a well-ordered society can devote a sizable fraction of its resources to expenditures of this kind. But while the claims of culture can be met in this way, the principles of justice do not permit subsidizing universities and institutes, or opera and the theater, on the grounds that these institutions are intrinsically valuable, and that those who engage in them are to be supported even at some significant expense to others who do not receive compensating benefits. Taxation for these purposes can be justified only as promoting directly or indirectly the social conditions that secure the equal liberties and as advancing in an appropriate way the long-term interests of the least advantaged. This seems to authorize those subsidies the justice of which is least in dispute, and so in these cases anyway there is no evident need for a principle of perfection.

With these remarks I conclude the discussion of how the principles of justice apply to institutions. Clearly there are many further questions that should be considered. Other forms of perfectionism are possible and each problem has been examined only briefly. I should emphasize that my intention is solely to indicate that the contract doctrine may serve well enough as an alternative moral conception. When we check its consequences for institutions, it appears to match our common sense convictions more accurately than its traditional rivals, and to extrapolate to previously unsettled cases in a reasonable way.

CHAPTER VI. DUTY AND OBLIGATION

In the two preceding chapters I have discussed the principles of justice for institutions. I now wish to take up the principles of natural duty and obligation that apply to individuals. The first two sections examine the reasons why these principles would be chosen in the original position and their role in making social cooperation stable. A brief discussion of promising and the principle of fidelity is included. For the most part, however, I shall study the implications of these principles for the theory of political duty and obligation within a constitutional framework. This seems the best way to explain their sense and content for the purposes of a theory of justice. In particular, an account of the special case of civil disobedience is sketched which connects it with the problem of majority rule and the grounds for complying with unjust laws. Civil disobedience is contrasted with other forms of noncompliance such as conscientious refusal in order to bring out its special role in stabilizing a nearly just democratic regime.

51. THE ARGUMENTS FOR THE PRINCIPLES OF NATURAL DUTY

In an earlier chapter (§§ 18–19) I described briefly the principles of natural duty and obligation that apply to individuals. We must now consider why these principles would be chosen in the original position. They are an essential part of a conception of right: they define our institutional ties and how we become bound to one another. The conception of justice as fairness is incomplete until these principles have been accounted for.

From the standpoint of the theory of justice, the most important natural duty is that to support and to further just institutions. This duty has two parts: first, we are to comply with and to do our share in just institutions when they exist and apply to us; and second, we are to assist in the establishment of just arrangements when they do not exist, at least when this can be done with little cost to ourselves. It follows that if the basic structure of society is just, or as just as it is reasonable to expect in the circumstances, everyone has a natural duty to do what is required of him. Each is bound irrespective of his voluntary acts, performative or otherwise. Now our question is why this principle rather than some other would be adopted. As in the case of institutions, there is no way, let us assume, for the parties to examine all the possible principles that might be proposed. The many possibilities are not clearly defined and among them there may be no best choice. To avoid these difficulties I suppose, as before, that the choice is to be made from a short list of traditional and familiar principles. To expedite matters, I shall mention here only the utilitarian alternative for purposes of clarification and contrast, and very much abbreviate the argument.

Now the choice of principles for individuals is greatly simplified by the fact that the principles for institutions have already been adopted. The feasible alternatives are straightway narrowed down to those that constitute a coherent conception of duty and obligation when taken together with the two principles of justice.[1] This restriction is bound to be particularly important in connection with those principles definitive of our institutional ties. Thus let us suppose that the persons in the original position, having agreed to the two principles of justice, entertain the choice of the principle of utility (either variant) as the standard for the acts of individuals. Even if there is no contradiction in this supposition, the adoption of the utilitarian principle would lead to an incoherent conception of right. The criteria for institutions and individuals do not fit together properly. This is particularly clear in situations in which a person holds a social position regulated by the principles of justice. For example, consider the case of a citizen deciding how to vote between political parties, or the case of a legislator wondering whether to favor a certain statute. The assumption is that these in-

1. For clarification on this point I am indebted to Allan Gibbard.

dividuals are members of a well-ordered society that has adopted the two principles of justice for institutions and the principle of utility for individuals. How are they to act? As a rational citizen or legislator, a person should, it seems, support that party or favor that statute which best conforms to the two principles of justice. This means that he should vote accordingly, urge others to do likewise, and so on. The existence of institutions involves certain patterns of individual conduct in accordance with publicly recognized rules. The principles for institutions have, then, consequences for the acts of persons holding positions in these arrangements. But these persons must also regard their actions as governed by the principle of utility. In this case the rational citizen or legislator should support the party or statute whose victory or enactment is most likely to maximize the net balance (or average) of satisfaction. The choice of the utility principle as the standard for individuals leads to contrary directives. To avoid this conflict it is necessary, at least when the individual holds an institutional position, to choose a principle that matches in some suitable way the two principles of justice. Only in noninstitutional situations is the utilitarian view compatible with the agreements already made. Although the principle of utility may have a place in certain duly circumscribed contexts, it is already excluded as a general account of duty and obligation.

The simplest thing to do, then, is to use the two principles of justice as a part of the conception of right for individuals. We can define the natural duty of justice as that to support and to further the arrangements that satisfy these principles; in this way we arrive at a principle that coheres with the criteria for institutions. There is still the question whether the parties in the original position would not do better if they made the requirement to comply with just institutions conditional upon certain voluntary acts on their part, for example, upon their having accepted the benefits of these arrangements, or upon their having promised or otherwise undertaken to abide by them. Offhand a principle with this kind of condition seems more in accordance with the contract idea with its emphasis upon free consent and the protection of liberty. But, in fact, nothing would be gained by this proviso. In view of the lexical ordering of the two principles, the full complement of the equal

335

liberties is already guaranteed. No further assurances on this score are necessary. Moreover, there is every reason for the parties to secure the stability of just institutions, and the easiest and most direct way to do this is to accept the requirement to support and to comply with them irrespective of one's voluntary acts.

These remarks can be strengthened by recalling our previous discussion of public goods (§ 42). We noted that in a well-ordered society the public knowledge that citizens generally have an effective sense of justice is a very great social asset. It tends to stabilize just social arrangements. Even when the isolation problem is overcome and fair large-scale schemes already exist for producing public goods, there are two sorts of tendencies leading to instability. From a self-interested point of view each person is tempted to shirk doing his share. He benefits from the public good in any case; and even though the marginal social value of his tax dollar is much greater than that of the marginal dollar spent on himself, only a small fraction thereof redounds to his advantage. These tendencies arising from self-interest lead to instability of the first kind. But since even with a sense of justice men's compliance with a cooperative venture is predicated on the belief that others will do their part, citizens may be tempted to avoid making a contribution when they believe, or with reason suspect, that others are not making theirs. These tendencies arising from apprehensions about the faithfulness of others lead to instability of the second kind. This instability is particularly likely to be strong when it is dangerous to stick to the rules when others are not. It is this difficulty that plagues disarmament agreements; given circumstances of mutual fear, even just men may be condemned to a condition of permanent hostility. The assurance problem, as we have seen, is to maintain stability by removing temptations of the first kind, and since this is done by public institutions, those of the second kind also disappear, at least in a well-ordered society.

The bearing of these remarks is that basing our political ties upon a principle of obligation would complicate the assurance problem. Citizens would not be bound to even a just constitution unless they have accepted and intend to continue to accept its benefits. Moreover this acceptance must be in some appropriate sense voluntary. But what is this sense? It is difficult to find a plausible account in the case of the political system into which we are born and begin our lives.[2] And even if such an account could be given, citizens might still wonder about one another whether they were bound, or so regarded themselves. The public conviction that all are tied to just arrangements would be less firm, and a greater reliance on the coercive powers of the sovereign might be necessary to achieve stability. But there is no reason to run these risks. Therefore the parties in the original position do best when they acknowledge the natural duty of justice. Given the value of a public and effective sense of justice, it is important that the principle defining the duties of individuals be simple and clear, and that it insure the stability of just arrangements. I assume, then, that the natural duty of justice would be agreed to rather than a principle of utility, and that from the standpoint of the theory of justice, it is the fundamental requirement for individuals. Principles of obligation, while compatible with it, are not alternatives but rather have a complementary role.

There are, of course, other natural duties. A number of these were mentioned earlier (§ 19). Instead of taking up all of these, it may be more instructive to examine a few cases, beginning with the duty of mutual respect, not previously referred to. This is the duty to show a person the respect which is due to him as a moral being, that is, as a being with a sense of justice and a conception of the good. (In some instances these features may be potentialities only, but I leave this complication aside here; see § 77.) Mutual respect is shown in several ways: in our willingness to see the situation of others from their point of view, from the perspective of their conception of their good; and in our being prepared to give reasons for our actions whenever the interests of others are materially affected.[3]

These two ways correspond to the two aspects of moral personality. When called for, reasons are to be addressed to those con-

2. I do not accept the whole of Hume's argument in "Of the Original Contract," but I believe it is correct on this count as applied to political duty for citizens generally. See *Essays: Moral, Political, and Literary*, ed. T. H. Green and T. H. Grose (London, 1875), vol. I, pp. 450–452.

3. On the notion of respect, see B. A. O. Williams, "The Idea of Equality," *Philosophy, Politics, and Society*, Second Series, ed. Peter Laslett and W. G. Runciman (Oxford, Basil Blackwell, 1962), pp. 118f.

cerned; they are to be offered in good faith, in the belief that they are sound reasons as defined by a mutually acceptable conception of justice which takes the good of everyone into account. Thus to respect another as a moral person is to try to understand his aims and interests from his standpoint and to present him with considerations that enable him to accept the constraints on his conduct. Since another wishes, let us suppose, to regulate his actions on the basis of principles to which all could agree, he should be acquainted with the relevant facts which explain the restrictions in this way. Also respect is shown in a willingness to do small favors and courtesies, not because they are of any material value, but because they are an appropriate expression of our awareness of another person's feelings and aspirations. Now the reason why this duty would be acknowledged is that although the parties in the original position take no interest in each other's interests, they know that in society they need to be assured by the esteem of their associates. Their self-respect and their confidence in the value of their own system of ends cannot withstand the indifference much less the contempt of others. Everyone benefits then from living in a society where the duty of mutual respect is honored. The cost to self-interest is minor in comparison with the support for the sense of one's own worth.

Similar reasoning supports the other natural duties. Consider, for example, the duty of mutual aid. Kant suggests, and others have followed him here, that the ground for proposing this duty is that situations may arise in which we will need the help of others, and not to acknowledge this principle is to deprive ourselves of their assistance.[4] While on particular occasions we are required to do things not in our own interests, we are likely to gain on balance at least over the longer run under normal circumstances. In each single instance the gain to the person who needs help far outweighs the loss of those required to assist him, and assuming that the chances of being the beneficiary are not much smaller than those of being the one who must give aid, the principle is clearly in our

4. See *The Foundations of the Metaphysics of Morals*, Academy edition, vol. 4, p. 423. There is a fuller discussion in *The Metaphysics of Morals*, pt. II (*Tugendlehre*), §30, vol. 6, pp. 451f. Kant notes here that the duty of beneficence (as he calls it) is to be public, that is, a universal law. See §23, note 8.

interest. But this is not the only argument for the duty of mutual aid, or even the most important one. A sufficient ground for adopting this duty is its pervasive effect on the quality of everyday life. The public knowledge that we are living in a society in which we can depend upon others to come to our assistance in difficult circumstances is itself of great value. It makes little difference that we never, as things turn out, need this assistance and that occasionally we are called on to give it. The balance of gain, narrowly interpreted, may not matter. The primary value of the principle is not measured by the help we actually receive but rather by the sense of confidence and trust in other men's good intentions and the knowledge that they are there if we need them. Indeed, it is only necessary to imagine what a society would be like if it were publicly known that this duty was rejected. Thus while the natural duties are not special cases of a single principle (or so I have assumed), similar reasons no doubt support many of them when one considers the underlying attitudes they represent. Once we try to picture the life of a society in which no one had the slightest desire to act on these duties, we see that it would express an indifference if not disdain for human beings that would make a sense of our own worth impossible. Once again we should note the great importance of publicity effects.

Taking any natural duty by itself, the reasons favoring its adoption are fairly obvious. At least it is evident why these duties are preferable to no similar requirements at all. Although their definition and systematic arrangement are untidy, there is little question that they would be acknowledged. The real difficulty lies in their more detailed specification and with questions of priority: how are these duties to be balanced when they come into conflict, either with each other or with obligations, and with the good that can be achieved by supererogatory actions? There are no obvious rules for settling these questions. We cannot say, for example, that duties are lexically prior with respect to supererogatory actions, or to obligations. Nor can we simply invoke the utilitarian principle to set things straight. Requirements for individuals so often oppose each other that this would come to much the same thing as adopting the standard of utility for individuals; and, as we have seen, this is ruled out as leading to an incoherent conception of right. I do not know how this problem is to be settled, or even whether a systematic solution formulating useful and practicable rules is possible. It would seem that the theory for the basic structure is actually simpler. Since we are dealing with a comprehensive scheme of general rules, we can rely on certain procedures of aggregation to cancel out the significance of the complicating elements of particular situations once we take the larger long-term view. Therefore in this book I shall not attempt to discuss these questions of priority in full generality. What I shall do is to examine a few special cases in connection with civil disobedience and conscientious refusal under circumstances of what I shall call a nearly just regime. A satisfactory account of these matters is at best only a start; but it may give us some idea of the kinds of obstacles we face and help to focus our intuitive judgments on the right questions.

It seems appropriate at this juncture to note the familiar distinction between a duty other things equal (a so-called prima facie duty), and a duty all things considered. (A parallel distinction holds for obligations.) The formulation of this notion is due to Ross and we may follow him in the main lines.[5] Thus suppose that the full system of principles that would be chosen in the original position is known. It will contain principles for institutions and individuals, and also, of course, priority rules to weigh these principles when they favor contrary sides in given cases. I further suppose that this full conception of right is finite: it consists of a finite number of principles and priority rules. Although there is a sense in which the number of moral principles (virtues of institutions and individuals) is infinite, or indefinitely large, the full conception is approximately complete: that is, the moral considerations that it fails to cover are for the most part of minor importance. Normally they can be neglected without serious risk of error. The significance of the moral reasons that are not accounted for becomes negligible as the conception of right is more fully worked out. Now adjoined to this full conception (finite yet complete in the sense defined) there is a principle asserting its completeness, and, if we like, also a principle enjoining the agent to perform that action which of all those available to him is reasonably judged the

5. See *The Right and the Good* (Oxford, The Clarendon Press, 1930), pp. 18–33, 41f.

right one (or a best one) in the light of the full system (including the priority rules). Here I imagine that the priority rules are sufficient to resolve conflicts of principles, or at least to guide the way to a correct assignment of weights. Obviously, we are not yet in a position to state these rules for more than a few cases; but since we manage to make these judgments, useful rules exist (unless the intuitionist is correct and there are only descriptions). In any case, the full system directs us to act in the light of all the available relevant reasons (as defined by the principles of the system) as far as we can or should ascertain them.

Now with these stipulations in mind, the phrases "other things equal" and "all things considered" (and other related expressions) indicate the extent to which a judgment is based upon the whole system of principles. A principle taken alone does not express a universal statement which always suffices to establish how we should act when the conditions of the antecedent are fulfilled. Rather, first principles single out relevant features of moral situations such that the exemplification of these features lends support to, provides a reason for making, a certain ethical judgment. The correct judgment depends upon all the relevant features as these are identified and tallied up by the complete conception of right. We claim to have surveyed each of these aspects of the case when we say that something is our duty all things considered; or else we imply that we know (or have reason for believing) how this broader inquiry would turn out. By contrast, in speaking of some requirement as a duty other things equal (a so-called prima facie duty), we are indicating that we have so far only taken certain principles into account, that we are making a judgment based on only a subpart of the larger scheme of reasons. I shall not usually signal the distinction between something's being a person's duty (or obligation) other things equal, and its being his duty all things considered. Ordinarily the context can be relied upon to gather what is meant.

I believe that these remarks express the essentials of Ross's concept of prima facie duty. The important thing is that such riders as "other things equal" and "all things considered" (and of course "prima facie") are not operators on single sentences, much less on predicates of actions. Rather they express a relation between sentences, a relation between a judgment and its grounds; or as I have put it above, they express a relation between a judgment and a part or the whole of the system of principles that defines its grounds.[6] This interpretation allows for the point of Ross's notion. For he introduced it as a way of stating first principles so as to allow the reasons they define to support contrary lines of action in particular cases, as indeed they so often do, without involving us in a contradiction. A traditional doctrine found in Kant, or so Ross believed, is to divide the principles that apply to individuals into two groups, those of perfect and imperfect obligation, and then to rank those of the first kind as lexically prior (to use my term) to those of the second kind. Yet not only is it in general false that imperfect obligations (for example, that of beneficence) should always give way to perfect ones (for example, that of fidelity), but we have no answer if perfect obligations conflict.[7] Maybe Kant's theory permits a way out; but in any case, he left this problem aside. It is convenient to use Ross's notion for this purpose. These remarks do not, of course, accept his contention that first principles are self-evident. This thesis concerns how these principles are known, and what sort of derivation they admit of. This question is independent of how principles hang together in one system of reasons and lend support to particular judgments of duty and obligation.

52. THE ARGUMENTS FOR THE PRINCIPLE OF FAIRNESS

Whereas there are various principles of natural duty, all obligations arise from the principle of fairness (as defined in § 18). It will be recalled that this principle holds that a person is under an obligation to do his part as specified by the rules of an institution whenever he has voluntarily accepted the benefits of the scheme or has taken advantage of the opportunities it offers to advance his in-

6. Here I follow Donald Davidson, "How Is Weakness of the Will Possible?" in *Moral Concepts,* ed. Joel Feinberg (London, Oxford University Press, 1969), see p. 109. The whole discussion on pp. 105–110 is relevant here.

7. See *The Right and the Good,* pp. 18f, and *The Foundations of Ethics* (Oxford, The Clarendon Press, 1939), pp. 173, 187.

terests, provided that this institution is just or fair, that is, satisfies the two principles of justice. As noted before, the intuitive idea here is that when a number of persons engage in a mutually advantageous cooperative venture according to certain rules and thus voluntarily restrict their liberty, those who have submitted to these restrictions have a right to a similar acquiescence on the part of those who have benefited from their submission.[8] We are not to gain from the cooperative efforts of others without doing our fair share.

It must not be forgotten that the principle of fairness has two parts: one which states how we acquire obligations, namely, by doing various things voluntarily; and another which lays down the condition that the institution in question be just, if not perfectly just, at least as just as it is reasonable to expect under the circumstances. The purpose of this second clause is to insure that obligations arise only if certain background conditions are satisfied. Acquiescence in, or even consent to, clearly unjust institutions does not give rise to obligations. It is generally agreed that extorted promises are void *ab initio*. But similarly, unjust social arrangements are themselves a kind of extortion, even violence, and consent to them does not bind. The reason for this condition is that the parties in the original position would insist upon it.

Before discussing the derivation of the principle, there is a preliminary matter to straighten out. It may be objected that since the principles of natural duty are on hand, there is no necessity for the principle of fairness. Obligations can be accounted for by the natural duty of justice, for when a person avails himself of an institutional set up, its rules then apply to him and the duty of justice holds. Now this contention is, indeed, sound enough. We can, if we like, explain obligations by invoking the duty of justice. It suffices to construe the requisite voluntary acts as acts by which our natural duties are freely extended. Although previously the scheme in question did not apply to us, and we had no duties in regard to it other than that of not seeking to undermine it, we have now by our deeds enlarged the bonds of natural duty. But it seems appropriate to distinguish between those institutions or aspects thereof which

8. I am indebted here to H. L. A. Hart, "Are There Any Natural Rights?" *Philosophical Review,* vol. 64 (1955), pp. 185f.

must inevitably apply to us since we are born into them and they regulate the full scope of our activity, and those that apply to us because we have freely done certain things as a rational way of advancing our ends. Thus we have a natural duty to comply with the constitution, say, or with the basic laws regulating property (assuming them to be just), whereas we have an obligation to carry out the duties of an office that we have succeeded in winning, or to follow the rules of associations or activities that we have joined. Sometimes it is reasonable to weigh obligations and duties differently when they conflict precisely because they do not arise in the same way. In some cases at least, the fact that obligations are freely assumed is bound to affect their assessment when they conflict with other moral requirements. It is also true that the better-placed members of society are more likely than others to have political obligations as distinct from political duties. For by and large it is these persons who are best able to gain political office and to take advantage of the opportunities offered by the constitutional system. They are, therefore, bound even more tightly to the scheme of just institutions. To mark this fact, and to emphasize the manner in which many ties are freely assumed, it is useful to have the principle of fairness. This principle should enable us to give a more discriminating account of duty and obligation. The term "obligation" will be reserved, then, for moral requirements that derive from the principle of fairness, while other requirements are called "natural duties."

Since in later sections the principle of fairness is mentioned in connection with political affairs, I shall discuss here its relation to promises. Now the principle of fidelity is but a special case of the principle of fairness applied to the social practice of promising. The argument for this begins with the observation that promising is an action defined by a public system of rules. These rules are, as in the case of institutions generally, a set of constitutive conventions. Just as the rules of games do, they specify certain activities and define certain actions.[9] In the case of promising, the basic rule is that governing the use of the words "I promise to do X."

9. On constitutive rules, see J. R. Searle, *Speech Acts* (Cambridge, The University Press, 1969), pp. 33–42. Promising is discussed in ch. III, esp. pp. 57–62.

It reads roughly as follows: if one says the words "I promise to do X" in the appropriate circumstances, one is to do X, unless certain excusing conditions obtain. This rule we may think of as the rule of promising; it may be taken as representing the practice as a whole. It is not itself a moral principle but a constitutive convention. In this respect it is on a par with legal rules and statutes, and rules of games; as these do, it exists in a society when it is more or less regularly acted upon.

The way in which the rule of promising specifies the appropriate circumstances and excusing conditions determines whether the practice it represents is just. For example, in order to make a binding promise, one must be fully conscious, in a rational frame of mind, and know the meaning of the operative words, their use in making promises, and so on. Furthermore, these words must be spoken freely or voluntarily, when one is not subject to threats or coercion, and in situations where one has a reasonably fair bargaining position, so to speak. A person is not required to perform if the operative words are uttered while he is asleep, or suffering delusions, or if he was forced to promise, or if pertinent information was deceitfully withheld from him. In general, the circumstances giving rise to a promise and the excusing conditions must be defined so as to preserve the equal liberty of the parties and to make the practice a rational means whereby men can enter into and stabilize cooperative agreements for mutual advantage. Unavoidably the many complications here cannot be considered. It must suffice to remark that the principles of justice apply to the practice of promising in the same way that they apply to other institutions. Therefore the restrictions on the appropriate conditions are necessary in order to secure equal liberty. It would be wildly irrational in the original position to agree to be bound by words uttered while asleep, or extorted by force. No doubt it is so irrational that we are inclined to exclude this and other possibilities as inconsistent with the concept (meaning) of promising. However, I shall not regard promising as a practice which is just by definition, since this obscures the distinction between the rule of promising and the obligation derived from the principle of fairness. There are many variations of promising just as there are of the law of contract. Whether the particular practice as it is understood by a person, or group of persons, is just remains to be determined by the principles of justice.

With these remarks as a background, we may introduce two definitions. First, a bona fide promise is one which arises in accordance with the rule of promising when the practice it represents is just. Once a person says the words "I promise to do X" in the appropriate circumstances as defined by a just practice, he has made a bona fide promise. Next, the principle of fidelity is the principle that bona fide promises are to be kept. It is essential, as noted above, to distinguish between the rule of promising and the principle of fidelity. The rule is simply a constitutive convention, whereas the principle of fidelity is a moral principle, a consequence of the principle of fairness. For suppose that a just practice of promising exists. Then in making a promise, that is, in saying the words "I promise to do X" in the appropriate circumstances, one knowingly invokes the rule and accepts the benefits of a just arrangement. There is no obligation to make a promise, let us assume; one is at liberty to do so or not. But since by hypothesis the practice is just, the principle of fairness applies and one is to do as the rule specifies, that is, one is to do X. The obligation to keep a promise is a consequence of the principle of fairness.

I have said that by making a promise one invokes a social practice and accepts the benefits that it makes possible. What are these benefits and how does the practice work? To answer this question, let us assume that the standard reason for making promises is to set up and to stabilize small-scale schemes of cooperation, or a particular pattern of transactions. The role of promises is analogous to that which Hobbes attributed to the sovereign. Just as the sovereign maintains and stabilizes the system of social cooperation by publicly maintaining an effective schedule of penalties, so men in the absence of coercive arrangements establish and stabilize their private ventures by giving one another their word. Such ventures are often hard to initiate and to maintain. This is especially evident in the case of covenants, that is, in those instances where one person is to perform before the other. For this person may believe that the second party will not do his part, and therefore the scheme never gets going. It is subject to instability of the second kind even though the person to perform later would in fact carry through. Now in these situations there may be no way of assuring the party who is to perform first except by giving him a promise, that is, by putting oneself under an obligation to carry through later. Only in this way can the scheme be made secure so that both can gain from the benefits of their cooperation. The practice of promising exists for precisely this purpose; and so while we normally think of moral requirements as bonds laid upon us, they are sometimes deliberately self-imposed for our advantage. Thus promising is an act done with the public intention of deliberately incurring an obligation the existence of which in the circumstances will further one's ends. We want this obligation to exist and to be known to exist, and we want others to know that we recognize this tie and intend to abide by it. Having, then, availed ourselves of the practice for this reason, we are under an obligation to do as we promised by the principle of fairness.

In this account of how promising (or entering into covenants) is used to initiate and to stabilize forms of cooperation I have largely followed Prichard.[10] His discussion contains all the essential points. I have also assumed, as he does, that each person knows, or at least reasonably believes, that the other has a sense of justice and so a normally effective desire to carry out his bona fide obligations. Without this mutual confidence nothing is accomplished by uttering words. In a well-ordered society, however, this knowledge is present: when its members give promises there is a reciprocal recognition of their intention to put themselves under an obligation and a shared rational belief that this obligation is honored. It is this reciprocal recognition and common knowledge that enables an arrangement to get started and preserves it in being.

There is no need to comment further on the extent to which a common conception of justice (including the principles of fairness and natural duty), and the public awareness of men's willingness to act in accordance with it, are a great collective asset. I have already noted the many advantages from the standpoint of the assurance problem. It is now equally evident that, having trust

10. See H. A. Prichard, "The Obligation To Keep a Promise," (c. 1940) in *Moral Obligation* (Oxford, The Clarendon Press, 1949), pp. 169–179.

and confidence in one another, men can use their public acceptance of these principles enormously to extend the scope and value of mutually advantageous schemes of cooperation. From the standpoint of the original position, then, it is clearly rational for the parties to agree to the principle of fairness. This principle can be used to secure these ventures in ways consistent with freedom of choice and without unnecessarily multiplying moral requirements. At the same time, given the principle of fairness, we see why there should exist the practice of promising as a way of freely establishing an obligation when this is to the mutual advantage of both parties. Such an arrangement is obviously in the common interest. I shall suppose that these considerations are sufficient to argue for the principle of fairness.

Before taking up the question of political duty and obligation, I should note several further points. First of all, as the discussion of promises illustrates, the contract doctrine holds that no moral requirements follow from the existence of institutions alone. Even the rule of promising does not give rise to a moral obligation by itself. To account for fiduciary obligations we must take the principle of fairness as a premise. Thus along with most other ethical theories, justice as fairness holds that natural duties and obligations arise only in virtue of ethical principles. These principles are those that would be chosen in the original position. Together with the relevant facts of the circumstances at hand, it is these criteria that determine our obligations and duties, and single out what count as moral reasons. A (sound) moral reason is a fact which one or more of these principles identifies as supporting a judgment. The correct moral decision is the one most in line with the dictates of this system of principles when it is applied to all the facts it deems to be relevant. Thus the reason identified by one principle may be supported, overridden, or even canceled (brought to naught) by reasons identified by one or more other principles. I assume, though, that out of the totality of facts, presumably in some sense infinite, a finite or surveyable number are selected as those that bear upon any particular case so that the full system enables us to reach a judgment, all things considered.

By contrast, institutional requirements, and those deriving from social practices generally, can be ascertained from the existing rules and how they are to be interpreted. For example, as citizens our legal duties and obligations are settled by what the law is, insofar as it can be ascertained. The norms applying to persons who are players in a game depend upon the rules of the game. Whether these requirements are connected with moral duties and obligations is a separate question. This is so even if the standards used by judges and others to interpret and to apply the law resemble the principles of right and justice, or are identical with them. It may be, for example, that in a well-ordered society the two principles of justice are used by courts to interpret those parts of the constitution regulating freedom of thought and conscience, and guaranteeing equal protection of the laws.[11] Although in this case it is clear that, should the law satisfy its own standards, we are morally bound, other things equal, to comply with it, the questions what the law demands and what justice requires are still distinct. The tendency to conflate the rule of promising and the principle of fidelity (as a special case arising from the principle of fairness) is particularly strong. At first sight they may seem to be the same thing; but one is defined by the existing constitutive conventions, while the other is explained by the principles that would be chosen in the original position. In this way, then, we can distinguish two kinds of norms. The terms "duty" and "obligation" are used in the context of both kinds; but the ambiguities stemming from this usage should be easy enough to resolve.

Finally, I should like to remark that the preceding account of the principle of fidelity answers a question posed by Prichard. He wondered how it is possible, without appealing to a prior general promise, or agreement to keep agreements, to explain the fact that by uttering certain words (by availing oneself of a convention) one becomes bound to do something, particularly when the action whereby one becomes bound is publicly performed with the very intention, which one wants others to recognize, of bringing about this obligation. Or as Prichard expressed it: what is the something implied in there being bona fide agreements which looks much like an agreement to keep agreements and yet which, strictly speaking, cannot be one (since no such agreement has

11. On this point, see Ronald Dworkin, "The Model of Rules," *University of Chicago Law Review,* vol. 35 (1967), esp. pp. 21–29.

been entered into)?[12] Now the existence of a just practice of promising as a system of public constitutive rules and the principle of fairness suffice for a theory of fiduciary obligations. And neither implies the existence of an actual prior agreement to keep agreements. The adoption of the principle of fairness is purely hypothetical; we only need the fact that this principle would be acknowledged. For the rest, once we assume that a just practice of promising obtains, however it may have come to be established, the principle of fairness is enough to bind those who take advantage of it, given the appropriate conditions already described. Thus what corresponds to the something, which to Prichard looked like a prior agreement but is not, is the just practice of giving one's word in conjunction with the hypothetical agreement on the principle of fairness. Of course, another ethical theory might derive this principle without using the conception of the original position. For the moment I need not maintain that fiduciary ties cannot be explained in some other way. Rather, what I am concerned to show is that even though justice as fairness uses the notion of an original agreement, it is still able to give a satisfactory answer to Prichard's question.

53. THE DUTY TO COMPLY WITH AN UNJUST LAW

There is quite clearly no difficulty in explaining why we are to comply with just laws enacted under a just constitution. In this case the principles of natural duty and the principle of fairness establish the requisite duties and obligations. Citizens generally are bound by the duty of justice, and those who have assumed favored offices and positions, or who have taken advantage of certain opportunities to further their interests, are in addition obligated to do their part by the principle of fairness. The real question is under which circumstances and to what extent we are bound to comply with unjust arrangements. Now it is sometimes said that we are never required to comply in these cases. But this is a mistake. The injustice of a law is not, in general, a sufficient reason for not adhering to it any more than the legal validity of

12. See "The Obligation To Keep a Promise," pp. 172, 178f.

legislation (as defined by the existing constitution) is a sufficient reason for going along with it. When the basic structure of society is reasonably just, as estimated by what the current state of things allows, we are to recognize unjust laws as binding provided that they do not exceed certain limits of injustice. In trying to discern these limits we approach the deeper problem of political duty and obligation. The difficulty here lies in part in the fact that there is a conflict of principles in these cases. Some principles counsel compliance while others direct us the other way. Thus the claims of political duty and obligation must be balanced by a conception of the appropriate priorities.

There is, however, a further problem. As we have seen, the principles of justice (in lexical order) belong to ideal theory (§ 39). The persons in the original position assume that the principles they acknowledge, whatever they are, will be strictly complied with and followed by everyone. Thus the principles of justice that result are those defining a perfectly just society, given favorable conditions. With the presumption of strict compliance, we arrive at a certain ideal conception. When we ask whether and under what circumstances unjust arrangements are to be tolerated, we are faced with a different sort of question. We must ascertain how the ideal conception of justice applies, if indeed it applies at all, to cases where rather than having to make adjustments to natural limitations, we are confronted with injustice. The discussion of these problems belongs to the partial compliance part of nonideal theory. It includes, among other things, the theory of punishment and compensatory justice, just war and conscientious objection, civil disobedience and militant resistance. These are among the central issues of political life, yet so far the conception of justice as fairness does not directly apply to them. Now I shall not attempt to discuss these matters in full generality. In fact, I shall take up but one fragment of partial compliance theory: namely, the problem of civil disobedience and conscientious refusal. And even here I shall assume that the context is one of a state of near justice, that is, one in which the basic structure of society is nearly just, making due allowance for what it is reasonable to expect in the circumstances. An understanding of this admittedly special case may help to clarify the more difficult problems. However, in order to consider civil disobedience and conscientious refusal, we must first discuss several points concerning political duty and obligation.

For one thing, it is evident that our duty or obligation to accept existing arrangements may sometimes be overridden. These requirements depend upon the principles of right, which may justify noncompliance in certain situations, all things considered. Whether noncompliance is justified depends on the extent to which laws and institutions are unjust. Unjust laws do not all stand on a par, and the same is true of policies and institutions. Now there are two ways in which injustice can arise: current arrangements may depart in varying degrees from publicly accepted standards that are more or less just; or these arrangements may conform to a society's conception of justice, or to the view of the dominant class, but this conception itself may be unreasonable, and in many cases clearly unjust. As we have seen, some conceptions of justice are more reasonable than others (see § 49). While the two principles of justice and the related principles of natural duty and obligation define the most reasonable view among those on the list, other principles are not unreasonable. Indeed, some mixed conceptions are certainly adequate enough for many purposes. As a rough rule a conception of justice is reasonable in proportion to the strength of the arguments that can be given for adopting it in the original position. This criterion is, of course, perfectly natural if the original position incorporates the various conditions which are to be imposed on the choice of principles and which lead to a match with our considered judgments.

Although it is easy enough to distinguish these two ways in which existing institutions can be unjust, a workable theory of how they affect our political duty and obligation is another matter. When laws and policies deviate from publicly recognized standards, an appeal to the society's sense of justice is presumably possible to some extent. I argue below that this condition is presupposed in undertaking civil disobedience. If, however, the prevailing conception of justice is not violated, then the situation is very different. The course of action to be followed depends largely on how reasonable the accepted doctrine is and what means are available to change it. Doubtless one can manage to live with a variety of mixed and intuitionistic conceptions, and with utilitarian views when they are not too rigorously interpreted. In other cases, though, as when a society is regulated by principles favoring narrow class interests, one may have no recourse but to oppose the prevailing conception and the institutions it justifies in such ways as promise some success.

Secondly, we must consider the question why, in a situation of near justice anyway, we normally have a duty to comply with unjust, and not simply with just, laws. While some writers have questioned this contention, I believe that most would accept it; only a few think that any deviation from justice, however small, nullifies the duty to comply with existing rules. How, then, is this fact to be accounted for? Since the duty of justice and the principle of fairness presuppose that institutions are just, some further explanation is required.[13] Now one can answer this question if we postulate a nearly just society in which there exists a viable constitutional regime more or less satisfying the principles of justice. Thus I suppose that for the most part the social system is well-ordered, although not of course perfectly ordered, for in this event the question of whether to comply with unjust laws and policies would not arise. Under these assumptions, the earlier account of a just constitution as an instance of imperfect procedural justice (§ 31) provides an answer.

It will be recalled that in the constitutional convention the aim of the parties is to find among the just constitutions (those satisfying the principle of equal liberty) the one most likely to lead to just and effective legislation in view of the general facts about the society in question. The constitution is regarded as a just but imperfect procedure framed as far as the circumstances permit to insure a just outcome. It is imperfect because there is no feasible political process which guarantees that the laws enacted in accordance with it will be just. In political affairs perfect procedural justice cannot be achieved. Moreover, the constitutional

13. I did not note this fact in my essay "Legal Obligation and the Duty of Fair Play" in *Law and Philosophy*, ed. Sidney Hook (New York, New York University Press, 1964). In this section I have tried to make good this defect. The view argued for here is different, however, in that the natural duty of justice is the main principle of political duty for citizens generally, the principle of fairness having a secondary role.

proc/ss must rely, to a large degree, on some form of voting. I assume for simplicity that a variant of majority rule suitably circumscribed is a practical necessity. Yet majorities (or coalitions of minorities) are bound to make mistakes, if not from a lack of knowledge and judgment, then as a result of partial and self-interested views. Nevertheless, our natural duty to uphold just institutions binds us to comply with unjust laws and policies, or at least not to oppose them by illegal means as long as they do not exceed certain limits of injustice. Being required to support a just constitution, we must go along with one of its essential principles, that of majority rule. In a state of near justice, then, we normally have a duty to comply with unjust laws in virtue of our duty to support a just constitution. Given men as they are, there are many occasions when this duty will come into play.

The contract doctrine naturally leads us to wonder how we could ever consent to a constitutional rule that would require us to comply with laws that we think are unjust. One might ask: how is it possible that when we are free and still without chains, we can rationally accept a procedure that may decide against our own opinion and give effect to that of others?[14] Once we take up the point of view of the constitutional convention, the answer is clear enough. First, among the very limited number of feasible procedures that have any chance of being accepted at all, there are none that would always decide in our favor. And second, consenting to one of these procedures is surely preferable to no agreement at all. The situation is analogous to that of the original position where the parties give up any hope of free-rider egoism: this alternative is each person's best (or second best) candidate (leaving aside the constraint of generality), but it is obviously not acceptable to anyone else. Similarly, although at the stage of the constitutional convention the parties are now committed to the principles of justice, they must make some concession to one another to operate a constitutional regime. Even with the best of

14. The metaphor of being free and still without chains is from I. M. D. Little's review of K. J. Arrow, *Social Choice and Individual Values*, in *The Journal of Political Economy*, vol. 60 (1952), p. 431. My remarks here follow Little.

intentions, their opinions of justice are bound to clash. In choosing a constitution, then, and in adopting some form of majority rule, the parties accept the risks of suffering the defects of one another's knowledge and sense of justice in order to gain the advantages of an effective legislative procedure. There is no other way to manage a democratic regime.

Nevertheless, when they adopt the majority principle the parties agree to put up with unjust laws only on certain conditions. Roughly speaking, in the long run the burden of injustice should be more or less evenly distributed over different groups in society, and the hardship of unjust policies should not weigh too heavily in any particular case. Therefore the duty to comply is problematic for permanent minorities that have suffered from injustice for many years. And certainly we are not required to acquiesce in the denial of our own and others' basic liberties, since this requirement could not have been within the meaning of the duty of justice in the original position, nor consistent with the understanding of the rights of the majority in the constitutional convention. Instead, we submit our conduct to democratic authority only to the extent necessary to share equitably in the inevitable imperfections of a constitutional system. Accepting these hardships is simply recognizing and being willing to work within the limits imposed by the circumstances of human life. In view of this, we have a natural duty of civility not to invoke the faults of social arrangements as a too ready excuse for not complying with them, nor to exploit inevitable loopholes in the rules to advance our interests. The duty of civility imposes a due acceptance of the defects of institutions and a certain restraint in taking advantage of them. Without some recognition of this duty mutual trust and confidence are liable to break down. Thus in a state of near justice at least, there is normally a duty (and for some also the obligation) to comply with unjust laws provided that they do not exceed certain bounds of injustice. This conclusion is not much stronger than that asserting our duty to comply with just laws. It does, however, take us a step further, since it covers a wider range of situations; but more important, it gives some idea of the questions that are to be asked in ascertaining our political duty.

355

54. THE STATUS OF MAJORITY RULE

It is evident from the preceding remarks that the procedure of majority rule, however it is defined and circumscribed, has a subordinate place as a procedural device. The justification for it rests squarely on the political ends that the constitution is designed to achieve, and therefore on the two principles of justice. I have assumed that some form of majority rule is justified as the best available way of insuring just and effective legislation. It is compatible with equal liberty (§36) and possesses a certain naturalness; for if minority rule is allowed, there is no obvious criterion to select which one is to decide and equality is violated. A fundamental part of the majority principle is that the procedure should satisfy the conditions of background justice. In this case these conditions are those of political liberty—freedom of speech and assembly, freedom to take part in public affairs and to influence by constitutional means the course of legislation—and the guarantee of the fair value of these freedoms. When this background is absent, the first principle of justice is not satisfied; yet even when it is present, there is no assurance that just legislation will be enacted.[15]

There is nothing to the view, then, that what the majority wills is right. In fact, none of the traditional conceptions of justice have held this doctrine, maintaining always that the outcome of the voting is subject to political principles. Although in given circumstances it is justified that the majority (suitably defined and circumscribed) has the constitutional right to make law, this does not imply that the laws enacted are just. The dispute of substance about majority rule concerns how it is best defined and whether constitutional constraints are effective and reasonable devices for strengthening the overall balance of justice. These limitations may often be used by entrenched

15. For further discussion of majority rule see Herbert McCloskey, "The Fallacy of Majority Rule," *Journal of Politics,* vol. II (1949), and J. R. Pennock, *Liberal Democracy* (New York, Rinehart, 1950), pp. 112–114, 117f. For some of the attractive features of the majority principle from the standpoint of social choice, see A. K. Sen, *Collective Choice and Social Welfare* (San Francisco, Holden-Day, 1970), pp. 68–70, 71–73, 161–186. One problem with this procedure is that it may allow cyclical majorities. But the primary defect from the point of view of justice is that it permits the violation of liberty. Also see Sen, pp. 79–83, 87–89, where his paradox of liberalism is discussed.

minorities to preserve their illicit advantages. This question is one of political judgment and does not belong to the theory of justice. It suffices to note that while citizens normally submit their conduct to democratic authority, that is, recognize the outcome of a vote as establishing a binding rule, other things equal, they do not submit their judgment to it.

I now wish to take up the place of the principle of majority rule in the ideal procedure that forms a part of the theory of justice. A just constitution is defined as a constitution that would be agreed upon by rational delegates in a constitutional convention who are guided by the two principles of justice. When we justify a constitution, we present considerations to show that it would be adopted under these conditions. Similarly, just laws and policies are those that would be enacted by rational legislators at the legislative stage who are constrained by a just constitution and who are conscientiously trying to follow the principles of justice as their standard. When we criticize laws and policies we try to show that they would not be chosen under this ideal procedure. Now since even rational legislators would often reach different conclusions, there is a necessity for a vote under ideal conditions. The restrictions on information will not guarantee agreement, since the tendencies of the general social facts will often be ambiguous and difficult to assess.

A law or policy is sufficiently just, or at least not unjust, if when we try to imagine how the ideal procedure would work out, we conclude that most persons taking part in this procedure and carrying out its stipulations would favor that law or policy. In the ideal procedure, the decision reached is not a compromise, a bargain struck between opposing parties trying to advance their ends. The legislative discussion must be conceived not as a contest between interests, but as an attempt to find the best policy as defined by the principles of justice. I suppose, then, as part of the theory of justice, that an impartial legislator's only desire is to make the correct decision in this regard, given the general facts known to him. He is to vote solely according to his judgment. The outcome of the vote gives an estimate of what is most in line with the conception of justice.

If we ask how likely it is that the majority opinion will be

357

correct, it is evident that the ideal procedure bears a certain analogy to the statistical problem of pooling the views of a group of experts to arrive at a best judgment.[16] Here the experts are rational legislators able to take an objective perspective because they are impartial. The suggestion goes back to Condorcet that if the likelihood of a correct judgment on the part of the representative legislator is greater than that of an incorrect one, the probability that the majority vote is correct increases as the likelihood of a correct decision by the representative legislator increases.[17] Thus we might be tempted to suppose that if many rational persons were to try to simulate the conditions of the ideal procedure and conducted their reasoning and discussion accordingly, a large majority anyway would be almost certainly right. This would be a mistake. We must not only be sure that there is a greater chance of a correct than of an incorrect judgment on the part of the representative legislator, but it is also clear that the votes of different persons are not independent. Since their views will be influenced by the course of the discussion, the simpler sorts of probabilistic reasoning do not apply.

Nevertheless, we normally assume that an ideally conducted discussion among many persons is more likely to arrive at the correct conclusion (by a vote if necessary) than the deliberations of any one of them by himself. Why should this be so? In everyday life the exchange of opinion with others checks our partiality and widens our perspective; we are made to see things from their standpoint and the limits of our vision are brought home to us. But in the ideal process the veil of ignorance means that the legislators are already impartial. The benefits from discussion lie in the fact that even representative legislators are limited in knowledge and the ability to reason. No one of them knows everything the others know, or can make all the same inferences that they can draw in

16. On this point, see K. J. Arrow, *Social Choice and Individual Values*, 2nd ed. (New York, John Wiley and Sons, 1963), pp. 85f. For the notion of legislative discussion as an objective inquiry and not a contest between interests, see F. H. Knight, *The Ethics of Competition* (New York, Harper and Brothers, 1935), pp. 296, 345–347. In both cases see the footnotes.

17. See Duncan Black, *Theory of Committee and Elections*, 2nd ed. (Cambridge, The University Press, 1963), pp. 159–165.

concert. Discussion is a way of combining information and enlarging the range of arguments. At least in the course of time, the effects of common deliberation seem bound to improve matters.

Thus we arrive at the problem of trying to formulate an ideal constitution of public deliberation in matters of justice, a set of rules well-designed to bring to bear the greater knowledge and reasoning powers of the group so as best to approximate if not to reach the correct judgment. I shall not, however, pursue this question. The important point here is that the idealized procedure is part of the theory of justice. I have mentioned some of its features in order to elucidate to some degree what is meant by it. The more definite our conception of this procedure as it might be realized under favorable conditions, the more firm the guidance that the four-stage sequence gives to our reflections. For we then have a more precise idea of how laws and policies would be assessed in the light of general facts about society. Often we can make good intuitive sense of the question how deliberations at the legislative stage, when properly conducted, would turn out.

The ideal procedure is further clarified by noting that it stands in contrast to the ideal market process. Thus, granting that the classical assumptions for perfect competition hold, and that there are no external economies or diseconomies, and the like, an efficient economic configuration results. The ideal market is a perfect procedure with respect to efficiency. A peculiarity of the ideal market process, as distinct from the ideal political process conducted by rational and impartial legislators, is that the market achieves an efficient outcome even if everyone pursues his own advantage. Indeed, the presumption is that this is how economic agents normally behave. In buying and selling to maximize satisfaction or profits, households and firms are not giving a judgment as to what is from a social point of view the most efficient economic configuration, given the initial distribution of assets. Rather they are advancing their ends as the rules allow, and any judgment they make is from their own point of view. It is the system as a whole, so to speak, that makes the judgment of efficiency, this judgment being derived from the many separate sources of information provided by the activities of firms and households. The system provides an answer, even though individuals have no opinion of this question, and often do not know what it means.

Thus despite certain resemblances between markets and elections, the ideal market process and the ideal legislative procedure are different in crucial respects. They are designed to achieve distinct ends, the first leading to efficiency, the latter if possible to justice. And while the ideal market is a perfect process with regard to its objective, even the ideal legislature is an imperfect procedure. There seems to be no way to characterize a feasible procedure guaranteed to lead to just legislation. One consequence of this fact is that whereas a citizen may be bound to comply with the policies enacted, other things equal, he is not required to think that these policies are just, and it would be mistaken of him to submit his judgment to the vote. But in a perfect market system, an economic agent, so far as he has any opinion at all, must suppose that the resulting outcome is indeed efficient. Although the household or firm has gotten everything that it wanted, it must concede that, given the initial distribution, an efficient situation has been attained. But the parallel recognition of the outcome of the legislative process concerning questions of justice cannot be demanded, for although, of course, actual constitutions should be designed as far as possible to make the same determinations as the ideal legislative procedure, they are bound in practice to fall short of what is just. This is not only because, as existing markets do, they fail to conform to their ideal counterpart, but also because this counterpart is that of an imperfect procedure. A just constitution must rely to some extent on citizens and legislators adopting a wider view and exercising good judgment in applying the principles of justice. There seems to be no way of allowing them to take a narrow or group-interested standpoint and then regulating the process so that it leads to a just outcome. So far at least there does not exist a theory of just constitutions as procedures leading to just legislation which corresponds to the theory of competitive markets as procedures resulting in efficiency. And this would seem to imply that the application of economic theory to the actual constitutional process has grave limitations insofar as political conduct is affected by men's sense of justice, as it must be in any viable society, and just legislation is the primary social end (§76). Certainly economic theory does not fit the ideal procedure.[18]

These remarks are confirmed by a further contrast. In the ideal market process some weight is given to the relative intensity of desire. A person can spend a greater part of his income on things he wants more of and in this way, together with other buyers, he encourages the use of resources in ways he most prefers. The market allows for finely graded adjustments in answer to the over-all balance of preferences and the relative dominance of certain wants. There is nothing corresponding to this in the ideal legislative procedure. Each rational legislator is to vote his opinion as to which laws and policies best conform to principles of justice. No special weight is or should be given to opinions that are held with greater confidence, or to the votes of those who let it be known that their being in the minority will cause them great displeasure (§37). Of course, such a voting rule is conceivable, but there are no grounds for adopting it in the ideal procedure. Even among rational and impartial persons, those with greater confidence in their opinion are not, it seems, more likely to be right. Some may be more sensitive to the complexities of the case than others. In defining the criterion for just legislation one should stress the weight of considered collective judgment arrived at when each person does his best under ideal conditions to apply the correct principles. The intensity of desire or the strength of conviction is irrelevant when questions of justice arise.

So much for several differences between the ideal legislative and the ideal market process. I now wish to note the use of the procedure of majority rule as a way of achieving a political settlement. As we have seen, majority rule is adopted as the most feasible way to realize certain ends antecedently defined by the

18. For the economic theory of democracy, see J. A. Schumpeter, *Capitalism, Socialism and Democracy*, 3rd ed. (New York, Harper and Brothers, 1950), chs. 21–23, and Anthony Downs, *An Economic Theory of Democracy* (New York, Harper and Brothers, 1957). The pluralist account of democracy, insofar as the rivalry between interests is believed to regulate the political process, is open to similar objection. See R. A. Dahl, *A Preface to Democratic Theory* (Chicago, University of Chicago Press, 1956), and more recently, *Pluralist Democracy in the United States* (Chicago, Rand McNally, 1967).

principles of justice. Sometimes however these principles are not clear or definite as to what they require. This is not always because the evidence is complicated and ambiguous, or difficult to survey and assess. The nature of the principles themselves may leave open a range of options rather than singling out any particular alternative. The rate of savings, for example, is specified only within certain limits; the main idea of the just savings principle is to exclude certain extremes. Eventually in applying the difference principle we wish to include in the prospects of the least advantaged the primary good of self-respect; and there are a variety of ways of taking account of this value consistent with the difference principle. How heavily this good and others related to it should count in the index is to be decided in view of the general features of the particular society and by what it is rational for its least favored members to want as seen from the legislative stage. In such cases as these, then, the principles of justice set up a certain range within which the rate of savings or the emphasis given to self-respect should lie. But they do not say where in this range the choice should fall.

Now for these situations the principle of political settlement applies: if the law actually voted is, so far as one can ascertain, within the range of those that could reasonably be favored by rational legislators conscientiously trying to follow the principles of justice, then the decision of the majority is practically authoritative, though not definitive. The situation is one of quasi-pure procedural justice. We must rely on the actual course of discussion at the legislative stage to select a policy within the allowed bounds. These cases are not instances of pure procedural justice because the outcome does not literally define the right result. It is simply that those who disagree with the decision made cannot convincingly establish their point within the framework of the public conception of justice. The question is one that cannot be sharply defined. In practice political parties will no doubt take different stands on these kinds of issues. The aim of constitutional design is to make sure, if possible, that the self-interest of social classes does not so distort the political settlement that it is made outside the permitted limits.

55. THE DEFINITION OF CIVIL DISOBEDIENCE

I now wish to illustrate the content of the principles of natural duty and obligation by sketching a theory of civil disobedience. As I have already indicated, this theory is designed only for the special case of a nearly just society, one that is well-ordered for the most part but in which some serious violations of justice nevertheless do occur. Since I assume that a state of near justice requires a democratic regime, the theory concerns the role and the appropriateness of civil disobedience to legitimately established democratic authority. It does not apply to the other forms of government nor, except incidentally, to other kinds of dissent or resistance. I shall not discuss this mode of protest, along with militant action and resistance, as a tactic for transforming or even overturning an unjust and corrupt system. There is no difficulty about such action in this case. If any means to this end are justified, then surely nonviolent opposition is justified. The problem of civil disobedience, as I shall interpret it, arises only within a more or less just democratic state for those citizens who recognize and accept the legitimacy of the constitution. The difficulty is one of a conflict of duties. At what point does the duty to comply with laws enacted by a legislative majority (or with executive acts supported by such a majority) cease to be binding in view of the right to defend one's liberties and the duty to oppose injustice? This question involves the nature and limits of majority rule. For this reason the problem of civil disobedience is a crucial test case for any theory of the moral basis of democracy.

A constitutional theory of civil disobedience has three parts. First, it defines this kind of dissent and separates it from other forms of opposition to democratic authority. These range from legal demonstrations and infractions of law designed to raise test cases before the courts to militant action and organized resistance. A theory specifies the place of civil disobedience in this spectrum of possibilities. Next, it sets out the grounds of civil disobedience and the conditions under which such action is justified in a (more or less) just democratic regime. And finally, a theory should explain the role of civil disobedience within a constitutional system and

363

account for the appropriateness of this mode of protest within a free society.

Before I take up these matters, a word of caution. We should not expect too much of a theory of civil disobedience, even one framed for special circumstances. Precise principles that straightway decide actual cases are clearly out of the question. Instead, a useful theory defines a perspective within which the problem of civil disobedience can be approached; it identifies the relevant considerations and helps us to assign them their correct weights in the more important instances. If a theory about these matters appears to us, on reflection, to have cleared our vision and to have made our considered judgments more coherent, then it has been worthwhile. The theory has done what, for the present, one may reasonably expect it to do: namely, to narrow the disparity between the conscientious convictions of those who accept the basic principles of a democratic society.

I shall begin by defining civil disobedience as a public, nonviolent, conscientious yet political act contrary to law usually done with the aim of bringing about a change in the law or policies of the government.[19] By acting in this way one addresses the sense of justice of the majority of the community and declares that in one's considered opinion the principles of social cooperation among free and equal men are not being respected. A preliminary gloss on this definition is that it does not require that the civilly disobedient act breach the same law that is being protested.[20] It allows for what

19. Here I follow H. A. Bedau's definition of civil disobedience. See his "On Civil Disobedience," *Journal of Philosophy,* vol. 58 (1961), pp. 653–661. It should be noted that this definition is narrower than the meaning suggested by Thoreau's essay, as I note in the next section. A statement of a similar view is found in Martin Luther King's "Letter from Birmingham City Jail" (1963), reprinted in H. A. Bedau, ed., *Civil Disobedience* (New York, Pegasus, 1969), pp. 72–89. The theory of civil disobedience in the text tries to set this sort of conception into a wider framework. Some recent writers have also defined civil disobedience more broadly. For example, Howard Zinn, *Disobedience and Democracy* (New York, Random House, 1968), pp. 119f, defines it as "the deliberate, discriminate violation of law for a vital social purpose." I am concerned with a more restricted notion. I do not at all mean to say that only this form of dissent is ever justified in a democratic state.

20. This and the following gloss are from Marshall Cohen, "Civil Disobedience in a Constitutional Democracy," *The Massachusetts Review,* vol. 10 (1969), pp. 224–226, 218–221, respectively.

some have called indirect as well as direct civil disobedience. And this a definition should do, as there are sometimes strong reasons for not infringing on the law or policy held to be unjust. Instead, one may disobey traffic ordinances or laws of trespass as a way of presenting one's case. Thus, if the government enacts a vague and harsh statute against treason, it would not be appropriate to commit treason as a way of objecting to it, and in any event, the penalty might be far more than one should reasonably be ready to accept. In other cases there is no way to violate the government's policy directly, as when it concerns foreign affairs, or affects another part of the country. A second gloss is that the civilly disobedient act is indeed thought to be contrary to law, at least in the sense that those engaged in it are not simply presenting a test case for a constitutional decision; they are prepared to oppose the statute even if it should be upheld. To be sure, in a constitutional regime, the courts may finally side with the dissenters and declare the law or policy objected to unconstitutional. It often happens, then, that there is some uncertainty as to whether the dissenters' action will be held illegal or not. But this is merely a complicating element. Those who use civil disobedience to protest unjust laws are not prepared to desist should the courts eventually disagree with them, however pleased they might have been with the opposite decision.

It should also be noted that civil disobedience is a political act not only in the sense that it is addressed to the majority that holds political power, but also because it is an act guided and justified by political principles, that is, by the principles of justice which regulate the constitution and social institutions generally. In justifying civil disobedience one does not appeal to principles of personal morality or to religious doctrines, though these may coincide with and support one's claims; and it goes without saying that civil disobedience cannot be grounded solely on group or self-interest. Instead one invokes the commonly shared conception of justice that underlies the political order. It is assumed that in a reasonably just democratic regime there is a public conception of justice by reference to which citizens regulate their political affairs and interpret the constitution. The persistent and deliberate violation of the basic principles of this conception over any extended period of time, especially the infringement of the fundamental equal liberties, invites either submission or resistance. By engaging in civil disobedience a minority forces the majority to consider whether it wishes to have its actions construed in this way, or whether, in view of the common sense of justice, it wishes to acknowledge the legitimate claims of the minority.

A further point is that civil disobedience is a public act. Not only is it addressed to public principles, it is done in public. It is engaged in openly with fair notice; it is not covert or secretive. One may compare it to public speech, and being a form of address, an expression of profound and conscientious political conviction, it takes place in the public forum. For this reason, among others, civil disobedience is nonviolent. It tries to avoid the use of violence, especially against persons, not from the abhorrence of the use of force in principle, but because it is a final expression of one's case. To engage in violent acts likely to injure and to hurt is incompatible with civil disobedience as a mode of address. Indeed, any interference with the civil liberties of others tends to obscure the civilly disobedient quality of one's act. Sometimes if the appeal fails in its purpose, forceful resistance may later be entertained. Yet civil disobedience is giving voice to conscientious and deeply held convictions; while it may warn and admonish, it is not itself a threat.

Civil disobedience is nonviolent for another reason. It expresses disobedience to law within the limits of fidelity to law, although it is at the outer edge thereof.[21] The law is broken, but fidelity to law is expressed by the public and nonviolent nature of the act, by the willingness to accept the legal consequences of one's conduct.[22] This fidelity to law helps to establish to the majority that the act is

21. For a fuller discussion of this point, see Charles Fried, "Moral Causation," *Harvard Law Review*, vol. 77 (1964), pp. 1268f. For clarification below of the notion of militant action, I am indebted to Gerald Loev.

22. Those who define civil disobedience more broadly might not accept this description. See, for example, Zinn, *Disobedience and Democracy*, pp. 27–31, 39, 119f. Moreover he denies that civil disobedience need be nonviolent. Certainly one does not accept the punishment as right, that is, as deserved for an unjustified act. Rather one is willing to undergo the legal consequences for the sake of fidelity to law, which is a different matter. There is room for latitude here in that the definition allows that the charge may be contested in court, should this prove appropriate. But there comes a point beyond which dissent ceases to be civil disobedience as defined here.

indeed politically conscientious and sincere, and that it is intended to address the public's sense of justice. To be completely open and nonviolent is to give bond of one's sincerity, for it is not easy to convince another that one's acts are conscientious, or even to be sure of this before oneself. No doubt it is possible to imagine a legal system in which conscientious belief that the law is unjust is accepted as a defense for noncompliance. Men of great honesty with full confidence in one another might make such a system work. But as things are, such a scheme would presumably be unstable even in a state of near justice. We must pay a certain price to convince others that our actions have, in our carefully considered view, a sufficient moral basis in the political convictions of the community.

Civil disobedience has been defined so that it falls between legal protest and the raising of test cases on the one side, and conscientious refusal and the various forms of resistance on the other. In this range of possibilities it stands for that form of dissent at the boundary of fidelity to law. Civil disobedience, so understood, is clearly distinct from militant action and obstruction; it is far removed from organized forcible resistance. The militant, for example, is much more deeply opposed to the existing political system. He does not accept it as one which is nearly just or reasonably so; he believes either that it departs widely from its professed principles or that it pursues a mistaken conception of justice altogether. While his action is conscientious in its own terms, he does not appeal to the sense of justice of the majority (or those having effective political power), since he thinks that their sense of justice is erroneous, or else without effect. Instead, he seeks by well-framed militant acts of disruption and resistance, and the like, to attack the prevalent view of justice or to force a movement in the desired direction. Thus the militant may try to evade the penalty, since he is not prepared to accept the legal consequences of his violation of the law; this would not only be to play into the hands of forces that he believes cannot be trusted, but also to express a recognition of the legitimacy of the constitution to which he is opposed. In this sense militant action is not within the bounds of fidelity to law, but represents a more profound opposition to the legal order. The basic structure is thought to be so unjust or else to depart so widely from its own professed ideals that one must try to prepare the way for radical or even revolutionary change. And this is to be done by trying to arouse the public to an awareness of the fundamental reforms that need to be made. Now in certain circumstances militant action and other kinds of resistance are surely justified. I shall not, however, consider these cases. As I have said, my aim here is the limited one of defining a concept of civil disobedience and understanding its role in a nearly just constitutional regime.

56. THE DEFINITION OF CONSCIENTIOUS REFUSAL

Although I have distinguished civil disobedience from conscientious refusal, I have yet to explain the latter notion. This will now be done. It must be recognized, however, that to separate these two ideas is to give a narrower definition to civil disobedience than is traditional; for it is customary to think of civil disobedience in a broader sense as any noncompliance with law for conscientious reasons, at least when it is not covert and does not involve the use of force. Thoreau's essay is characteristic, if not definitive, of the traditional meaning.[23] The usefulness of the narrower sense will, I believe, be clear once the definition of conscientious refusal is examined.

Conscientious refusal is noncompliance with a more or less direct legal injunction or administrative order. It is refusal since an order is addressed to us and, given the nature of the situation, whether we accede to it is known to the authorities. Typical examples are the refusal of the early Christians to perform certain acts of piety prescribed by the pagan state, and the refusal of the Jehovah's Witnesses to salute the flag. Other examples are the unwillingness of a pacifist to serve in the armed forces, or of a soldier to obey an order that he thinks is manifestly contrary to the moral law as it applies to war. Or again, in Thoreau's case, the refusal to pay a tax on the grounds that to do so would make him an agent of grave injustice to another. One's action is assumed to be

23. See Henry David Thoreau, "Civil Disobedience" (1848), reprinted in H. A. Bedau, ed., *Civil Disobedience*, pp. 27–48. For a critical discussion, see Bedau's remarks, pp. 15–26.

known to the authorities, however much one might wish, in some cases, to conceal it. Where it can be covert, one might speak of conscientious evasion rather than conscientious refusal. Covert infractions of a fugitive slave law are instances of conscientious evasion.[24]

There are several contrasts between conscientious refusal (or evasion) and civil disobedience. First of all, conscientious refusal is not a form of address appealing to the sense of justice of the majority. To be sure, such acts are not generally secretive or covert, as concealment is often impossible anyway. One simply refuses on conscientious grounds to obey a command or to comply with a legal injunction. One does not invoke the convictions of the community, and in this sense conscientious refusal is not an act in the public forum. Those ready to withhold obedience recognize that there may be no basis for mutual understanding; they do not seek out occasions for disobedience as a way to state their cause. Rather, they bide their time hoping that the necessity to disobey will not arise. They are less optimistic than those undertaking civil disobedience and they may entertain no expectation of changing laws or policies. The situation may allow no time for them to make their case, or again there may not be any chance that the majority will be receptive to their claims.

Conscientious refusal is not necessarily based on political principles; it may be founded on religious or other principles at variance with the constitutional order. Civil disobedience is an appeal to a commonly shared conception of justice, whereas conscientious refusal may have other grounds. For example, assuming that the early Christians would not justify their refusal to comply with the religious customs of the Empire by reasons of justice but simply as being contrary to their religious convictions, their argument would not be political; nor, with similar qualifications, are the views of a pacifist, assuming that wars of self-defense at least are recognized by the conception of justice that underlies a constitutional regime. Conscientious refusal may, however, be grounded on political principles. One many decline to go along with a law thinking that it is so unjust that complying with it is simply out of the question. This would be the case if, say, the law were to enjoin

24. For these distinctions I am indebted to Burton Dreben.

our being the agent of enslaving another, or to require us to submit to a similar fate. These are patent violations of recognized political principles.

It is a difficult matter to find the right course when some men appeal to religious principles in refusing to do actions which, it seems, are required by principles of political justice. Does the pacifist possess an immunity from military service in a just war, assuming that there are such wars? Or is the state permitted to impose certain hardships for noncompliance? There is a temptation to say that the law must always respect the dictates of conscience, but this cannot be right. As we have seen in the case of the intolerant, the legal order must regulate men's pursuit of their religious interests so as to realize the principle of equal liberty; and it may certainly forbid religious practices such as human sacrifice, to take an extreme case. Neither religiosity nor conscientiousness suffices to protect this practice. A theory of justice must work out from its own point of view how to treat those who dissent from it. The aim of a well-ordered society, or one in a state of near justice, is to preserve and strengthen the institutions of justice. If a religion is denied its full expression, it is presumably because it is in violation of the equal liberties of others. In general, the degree of tolerance accorded opposing moral conceptions depends upon the extent to which they can be allowed an equal place within a just system of liberty.

If pacifism is to be treated with respect and not merely tolerated, the explanation must be that it accords reasonably well with the principles of justice, the main exception arising from its attitude toward engaging in a just war (assuming here that in some situations wars of self-defense are justified). The political principles recognized by the community have a certain affinity with the doctrine the pacifist professes. There is a common abhorrence of war and the use of force, and a belief in the equal status of men as moral persons. And given the tendency of nations, particularly great powers, to engage in war unjustifiably and to set in motion the apparatus of the state to suppress dissent, the respect accorded to pacifism serves the purpose of alerting citizens to the wrongs that governments are prone to commit in their name. Even though his views are not altogether sound, the warnings and protests that a pacifist is disposed to express may have the result that on balance the principles of justice are more rather than less secure. Pacifism as a natural departure from the correct doctrine conceivably compensates for the weakness of men in living up to their professions.

It should be noted that there is, of course, in actual situations no sharp distinction between civil disobedience and conscientious refusal. Moreover the same action (or sequence of actions) may have strong elements of both. While there are clear cases of each, the contrast between them is intended as a way of elucidating the interpretation of civil disobedience and its role in a democratic society. Given the nature of this way of acting as a special kind of political appeal, it is not usually justified until other steps have been taken within the legal framework. By contrast this requirement often fails in the obvious cases of legitimate conscientious refusal. In a free society no one may be compelled, as the early Christians were, to perform religious acts in violation of equal liberty, nor must a soldier comply with inherently evil commands while awaiting an appeal to higher authority. These remarks lead up to the question of justification.

57. THE JUSTIFICATION OF CIVIL DISOBEDIENCE

With these various distinctions in mind, I shall consider the circumstances under which civil disobedience is justified. For simplicity I shall limit the discussion to domestic institutions and so to injustices internal to a given society. The somewhat narrow nature of this restriction will be mitigated a bit by taking up the contrasting problem of conscientious refusal in connection with the moral law as it applies to war. I shall begin by setting out what seem to be reasonable conditions for engaging in civil disobedience, and then later connect these conditions more systematically with the place of civil disobedience in a state of near justice. Of course, the conditions enumerated should be taken as presumptions; no doubt there will be situations when they do not hold, and other arguments could be given for civil disobedience.

The first point concerns the kinds of wrongs that are appropri-

ate objects of civil disobedience. Now if one views such disobedience as a political act addressed to the sense of justice of the
community, then it seems reasonable, other things equal, to limit
it to instances of substantial and clear injustice, and preferably to
those which obstruct the path to removing other injustices. For
this reason there is a presumption in favor of restricting civil
disobedience to serious infringements of the first principle of justice, the principle of equal liberty, and to blatant violations of the
second part of the second principle, the principle of fair equality
of opportunity. Of course, it is not always easy to tell whether
these principles are satisfied. Still, if we think of them as guaranteeing the basic liberties, it is often clear that these freedoms
are not being honored. After all, they impose certain strict requirements that must be visibly expressed in institutions. Thus
when certain minorities are denied the right to vote or to hold
office, or to own property and to move from place to place, or
when certain religious groups are repressed and others denied
various opportunities, these injustices may be obvious to all. They
are publicly incorporated into the recognized practice, if not the
letter, of social arrangements. The establishment of these wrongs
does not presuppose an informed examination of institutional
effects.

By contrast infractions of the difference principle are more
difficult to ascertain. There is usually a wide range of conflicting
yet rational opinion as to whether this principle is satisfied. The
reason for this is that it applies primarily to economic and social
institutions and policies. A choice among these depends upon
theoretical and speculative beliefs as well as upon a wealth of statistical and other information, all of this seasoned with shrewd judgment and plain hunch. In view of the complexities of these questions, it is difficult to check the influence of self-interest and
prejudice; and even if we can do this in our own case, it is another
matter to convince others of our good faith. Thus unless tax laws,
for example, are clearly designed to attack or to abridge a basic
equal liberty, they should not normally be protested by civil
disobedience. The appeal to the public's conception of justice is
not sufficiently clear. The resolution of these issues is best left to
the political process provided that the requisite equal liberties are

secure. In this case a reasonable compromise can presumably be reached. The violation of the principle of equal liberty is, then, the more appropriate object of civil disobedience. This principle defines the common status of equal citizenship in a constitutional regime and lies at the basis of the political order. When it is fully honored the presumption is that other injustices, while possibly persistent and significant, will not get out of hand.

A further condition for civil disobedience is the following. We may suppose that the normal appeals to the political majority have already been made in good faith and that they have failed. The legal means of redress have proved of no avail. Thus, for example, the existing political parties have shown themselves indifferent to the claims of the minority or have proved unwilling to accommodate them. Attempts to have the laws repealed have been ignored and legal protests and demonstrations have had no success. Since civil disobedience is a last resort, we should be sure that it is necessary. Note that it has not been said, however, that legal means have been exhausted. At any rate, further normal appeals can be repeated; free speech is always possible. But if past actions have shown the majority immovable or apathetic, further attempts may reasonably be thought fruitless, and a second condition for justified civil disobedience is met. This condition is, however, a presumption. Some cases may be so extreme that there may be no duty to use first only legal means of political opposition. If, for example, the legislature were to enact some outrageous violation of equal liberty, say by forbidding the religion of a weak and defenseless minority, we surely could not expect that sect to oppose the law by normal political procedures. Indeed, even civil disobedience might be much too mild, the majority having already convicted itself of wantonly unjust and overtly hostile aims.

The third and last condition I shall discuss can be rather complicated. It arises from the fact that while the two preceding conditions are often sufficient to justify civil disobedience, this is not always the case. In certain circumstances the natural duty of justice may require a certain restraint. We can see this as follows. If a certain minority is justified in engaging in civil disobedience, then any other minority in relevantly similar circumstances is likewise justified. Using the two previous conditions as the criteria of relevantly similar circumstances, we can say that, other things equal, two minorities are similarly justified in resorting to civil disobedience if they have suffered for the same length of time from the same degree of injustice and if their equally sincere and normal political appeals have likewise been to no avail. It is conceivable, however, even if it is unlikely, that there should be many groups with an equally sound case (in the sense just defined) for being civilly disobedient; but that, if they were all to act in this way, serious disorder would follow which might well undermine the efficacy of the just constitution. I assume here that there is a limit on the extent to which civil disobedience can be engaged in without leading to a breakdown in the respect for law and the constitution, thereby setting in motion consequences unfortunate for all. There is also an upper bound on the ability of the public forum to handle such forms of dissent; the appeal that civilly disobedient groups wish to make can be distorted and their intention to appeal to the sense of justice of the majority lost sight of. For one or both of these reasons, the effectiveness of civil disobedience as a form of protest declines beyond a certain point; and those contemplating it must consider these constraints.

The ideal solution from a theoretical point of view calls for a cooperative political alliance of the minorities to regulate the overall level of dissent. For consider the nature of the situation: there are many groups each equally entitled to engage in civil disobedience. Moreover they all wish to exercise this right, equally strong in each case; but if they all do so, lasting injury may result to the just constitution to which they each recognize a natural duty of justice. Now when there are many equally strong claims which if taken together exceed what can be granted, some fair plan should be adopted so that all are equitably considered. In simple cases of claims to goods that are indivisible and fixed in number, some rotation or lottery scheme may be the fair solution when the number of equally valid claims is too great.[25] But this

25. For a discussion of the conditions when some fair arrangement is called for, see Kurt Baier, *The Moral Point of View* (Ithaca, N.Y., Cornell University Press, 1958), pp. 207–213; and David Lyons, *Forms and Limits of Utilitarianism* (Oxford, The Clarendon Press, 1965), pp. 160–176. Lyons gives an example of a fair rotation scheme and he also observes that (waiving costs of setting them

sort of device is completely unrealistic here. What seems called for is a political understanding among the minorities suffering from injustice. They can meet their duty to democratic institutions by coordinating their actions so that while each has an opportunity to exercise its right, the limits on the degree of civil disobedience are not exceeded. To be sure, an alliance of this sort is difficult to arrange; but with perceptive leadership, it does not appear impossible.

Certainly the situation envisaged is a special one, and it is quite possible that these sorts of considerations will not be a bar to justified civil disobedience. There are not likely to be many groups similarly entitled to engage in this form of dissent while at the same time recognizing a duty to a just constitution. One should note, however, that an injured minority is tempted to believe its claims as strong as those of any other; and therefore even if the reasons that different groups have for engaging in civil disobedience are not equally compelling, it is often wise to presume that their claims are indistinguishable. Adopting this maxim, the circumstance imagined seems more likely to happen. This kind of case is also instructive in showing that the exercise of the right to dissent, like the exercise of rights generally, is sometimes limited by others having the very same right. Everyone's exercising this right would have deleterious consequences for all, and some equitable plan is called for.

Suppose that in the light of the three conditions, one has a right to appeal one's case by civil disobedience. The injustice one protests is a clear violation of the liberties of equal citizenship, or of equality of opportunity, this violation having been more or less deliberate over an extended period of time in the face of normal political opposition, and any complications raised by the question of fairness are met. These conditions are not exhaustive; some allowance still has to be made for the possibility of injury to third parties, to the innocent, so to speak. But I assume that they cover

---

up) such fair procedures may be reasonably efficient. See pp. 169–171. I accept the conclusions of his account, including his contention that the notion of fairness cannot be explained by assimilating it to utility, pp. 176f. The earlier discussion by C. D. Broad, "On the Function of False Hypotheses in Ethics," *International Journal of Ethics*, vol. 26 (1916), esp. pp. 385–390, should also be noted here.

the main points. There is still, of course, the question whether it is wise or prudent to exercise this right. Having established the right, one is now free, as one is not before, to let these matters decide the issue. We may be acting within our rights but nevertheless unwisely if our conduct only serves to provoke the harsh retaliation of the majority. To be sure, in a state of near justice, vindictive repression of legitimate dissent is unlikely, but it is important that the action be properly designed to make an effective appeal to the wider community. Since civil disobedience is a mode of address taking place in the public forum, care must be taken to see that it is understood. Thus the exercise of the right to civil disobedience should, like any other right, be rationally framed to advance one's ends or the ends of those one wishes to assist. The theory of justice has nothing specific to say about these practical considerations. In any event questions of strategy and tactics depend upon the circumstances of each case. But the theory of justice should say at what point these matters are properly raised.

Now in this account of the justification of civil disobedience I have not mentioned the principle of fairness. The natural duty of justice is the primary basis of our political ties to a constitutional regime. As we noted before (§ 52), only the more favored members of society are likely to have a clear political obligation as opposed to a political duty. They are better situated to win public office and find it easier to take advantage of the political system. And having done so, they have acquired an obligation owed to citizens generally to uphold the just constitution. But members of subjected minorities, say, who have a strong case for civil disobedience will not generally have a political obligation of this sort. This does not mean, however, that the principle of fairness will not give rise to important obligations in their case.[26] For not only do many of the requirements of private life derive from this principle, but it comes into force when persons or groups come together for common political purposes. Just as we acquire obligations to others with whom we have joined in various private

26. For a discussion of these obligations, see Michael Walzer, *Obligations: Essays on Disobedience, War, and Citizenship* (Cambridge, Harvard University Press, 1970), ch. III.

associations, those who engage in political action assume obligatory ties to one another. Thus while the political obligation of dissenters to citizens generally is problematical, bonds of loyalty and fidelity still develop between them as they seek to advance their cause. In general, free association under a just constitution gives rise to obligations provided that the ends of the group are legitimate and its arrangements fair. This is as true of political as it is of other associations. These obligations are of immense significance and they constrain in many ways what individuals can do. But they are distinct from an obligation to comply with a just constitution. My discussion of civil disobedience is in terms of the duty of justice alone; a fuller view would note the place of these other requirements.

58. THE JUSTIFICATION OF CONSCIENTIOUS REFUSAL

In examining the justification of civil disobedience I assumed for simplicity that the laws and policies protested concerned domestic affairs. It is natural to ask how the theory of political duty applies to foreign policy. Now in order to do this it is necessary to extend the theory of justice to the law of nations. I shall try to indicate how this can be done. To fix ideas I shall consider briefly the justification of conscientious refusal to engage in certain acts of war, or to serve in the armed forces. I assume that this refusal is based upon political and not upon religious or other principles; that is, the principles cited by way of justification are those of the conception of justice underlying the constitution. Our problem, then, is to relate the just political principles regulating the conduct of states to the contract doctrine and to explain the moral basis of the law of nations from this point of view.

Let us assume that we have already derived the principles of justice as these apply to societies as units and to the basic structure. Imagine also that the various principles of natural duty and of obligation that apply to individuals have been adopted. Thus the persons in the original position have agreed to the principles of right as these apply to their own society and to themselves as members of it. Now at this point one may extend the interpretation of the original position and think of the parties as representatives of different nations who must choose together the fundamental principles to adjudicate conflicting claims among states. Following out the conception of the initial situation, I assume that these representatives are deprived of various kinds of information. While they know that they represent different nations each living under the normal circumstances of human life, they know nothing about the particular circumstances of their own society, its power and strength in comparison with other nations, nor do they know their place in their own society. Once again the contracting parties, in this case representatives of states, are allowed only enough knowledge to make a rational choice to protect their interests but not so much that the more fortunate among them can take advantage of their special situation. This original position is fair between nations; it nullifies the contingencies and biases of historical fate. Justice between states is determined by the principles that would be chosen in the original position so interpreted. These principles are political principles, for they govern public policies toward other nations.

I can give only an indication of the principles that would be acknowledged. But, in any case, there would be no surprises, since the principles chosen would, I think, be familiar ones.[27] The basic principle of the law of nations is a principle of equality. Independent peoples organized as states have certain fundamental equal rights. This principle is analogous to the equal rights of citizens in a constitutional regime. One consequence of this equality of nations is the principle of self-determination, the right of a people to settle its own affairs without the intervention of foreign powers. Another consequence is the right of self-defense against attack, including the right to form defensive alliances to protect this right. A further principle is that treaties are to be kept, provided they are consistent with the other principles governing the relations of states. Thus treaties for self-defense, suitably

27. See. J. L. Brierly, *The Law of Nations,* 6th ed. (Oxford, The Clarendon Press, 1963), esp. chs. IV–V. This work contains all that we need here.

interpreted, would be binding, but agreements to cooperate in an unjustified attack are void *ab initio*.

These principles define when a nation has a just cause in war or, in the traditional phrase, its *jus ad bellum*. But there are also principles regulating the means that a nation may use to wage war, its *jus in bello*.[28] Even in a just war certain forms of violence are strictly inadmissible; and where a country's right to war is questionable and uncertain, the constraints on the means it can use are all the more severe. Acts permissible in a war of legitimate self-defense, when these are necessary, may be flatly excluded in a more doubtful situation. The aim of war is a just peace, and therefore the means employed must not destroy the possibility of peace or encourage a contempt for human life that puts the safety of ourselves and of mankind in jeopardy. The conduct of war is to be constrained and adjusted to this end. The representatives of states would recognize that their national interest, as seen from the original position, is best served by acknowledging these limits on the means of war. This is because the national interest of a just state is defined by the principles of justice that have already been acknowledged. Therefore such a nation will aim above all to maintain and to preserve its just institutions and the conditions that make them possible. It is not moved by the desire for world power or national glory; nor does it wage war for purposes of economic gain or the acquisition of territory. These ends are contrary to the conception of justice that defines a society's legitimate interest, however prevalent they have been in the actual conduct of states. Granting these presumptions, then, it seems reasonable to suppose that the traditional prohibitions incorporating the natural duties that protect human life would be chosen.

Now if conscientious refusal in time of war appeals to these principles, it is founded upon a political conception, and not necessarily upon religious or other notions. While this form of denial may not be a political act, since it does not take place in the public forum, it is based upon the same theory of justice that

28. For a recent discussion, see Paul Ramsey, *War and the Christian Conscience* (Durham, N.C., The Duke University Press, 1961); and also R. B. Potter, *War and Moral Discourse* (Richmond, Va., John Knox Press, 1969). The latter contains a useful bibliographical essay, pp. 87–123.

underlies the constitution and guides its interpretation. Moreover, the legal order itself presumably recognizes in the form of treaties the validity of at least some of these principles of the law of nations. Therefore if a soldier is ordered to engage in certain illicit acts of war, he may refuse if he reasonably and conscientiously believes that the principles applying to the conduct of war are plainly violated. He can maintain that, all things considered, his natural duty not to be made the agent of grave injustice and evil to another outweighs his duty to obey. I cannot discuss here what constitutes a manifest violation of these principles. It must suffice to note that certain clear cases are perfectly familiar. The essential point is that the justification cites political principles that can be accounted for by the contract doctrine. The theory of justice can be developed, I believe, to cover this case.

A somewhat different question is whether one should join the armed forces at all during some particular war. The answer is likely to depend upon the aim of the war as well as upon its conduct. In order to make the situation definite, let us suppose that conscription is in force and that the individual has to consider whether to comply with his legal duty to enter military service. Now I shall assume that since conscription is a drastic interference with the basic liberties of equal citizenship, it cannot be justified by any needs less compelling than those of national security.[29] In a well-ordered society (or in one nearly just) these needs are determined by the end of preserving just institutions. Conscription is permissible only if it is demanded for the defense of liberty itself, including here not only the liberties of the citizens of the society in question, but also those of persons in other societies as well. Therefore if a conscript army is less likely to be an instrument of unjustified foreign adventures, it may be justified on this basis alone despite the fact that conscription infringes upon the equal liberties of citizens. But in any case, the priority of liberty (assuming serial order to obtain) requires that conscription be used only as the security of liberty necessitates. Viewed from the standpoint of the legislature (the appropriate stage for this question), the mechanism of the draft can be defended only

29. I am indebted to R. G. Albritton for clarification on this and other matters in this paragraph.

on this ground. Citizens agree to this arrangement as a fair way of sharing in the burdens of national defense. To be sure, the hazards that any particular individual must face are in part the result of accident and historical happenstance. But in a well-ordered society anyway, these evils arise externally, that is, from unjustified attacks from the outside. It is impossible for just institutions to eliminate these hardships entirely. The most that they can do is to try to make sure that the risks of suffering from these imposed misfortunes are more or less evenly shared by all members of society over the course of their life, and that there is no avoidable class bias in selecting those who are called for duty.

Imagine, then, a democratic society in which conscription exists. A person may conscientiously refuse to comply with his duty to enter the armed forces during a particular war on the ground that the aims of the conflict are unjust. It may be that the objective sought by war is economic advantage or national power. The basic liberty of citizens cannot be interfered with to achieve these ends. And, of course, it is unjust and contrary to the law of nations to attack the liberty of other societies for these reasons. Therefore a just cause for war does not exist, and this may be sufficiently evident that a citizen is justified in refusing to discharge his legal duty. Both the law of nations and the principles of justice for his own society uphold him in this claim. There is sometimes a further ground for refusal based not on the aim of the war but upon its conduct. A citizen may maintain that once it is clear that the moral law of war is being regularly violated, he has a right to decline military service on the ground that he is entitled to insure that he honors his natural duty. Once he is in the armed forces, and in a situation where he finds himself ordered to do acts contrary to the moral law of war, he may not be able to resist the demand to obey. Actually, if the aims of the conflict are sufficiently dubious and the likelihood of receiving flagrantly unjust commands is sufficiently great, one may have a duty and not only a right to refuse. Indeed, the conduct and aims of states in waging war, especially large and powerful ones, are in some circumstances so likely to be unjust that one is forced to conclude that in the foreseeable future one must abjure military service altogether. So understood a form of contingent pacifism may be a perfectly reasonable position: the possibility of a just war is conceded but not under present circumstances.[30]

What is needed, then, is not a general pacifism but a discriminating conscientious refusal to engage in war in certain circumstances. States have not been loath to recognize pacifism and to grant it a special status. The refusal to take part in all war under any conditions is an unworldly view bound to remain a sectarian doctrine. It no more challenges the state's authority than the celibacy of priests challenges the sanctity of marriage.[31] By exempting pacifists from its prescriptions the state may even seem to display a certain magnanimity. But conscientious refusal based upon the principles of justice between peoples as they apply to particular conflicts is another matter. For such refusal is an affront to the government's pretensions, and when it becomes widespread, the continuation of an unjust war may prove impossible. Given the often predatory aims of state power, and the tendency of men to defer to their government's decision to wage war, a general willingness to resist the state's claims is all the more necessary.

59. THE ROLE OF CIVIL DISOBEDIENCE

The third aim of a theory of civil disobedience is to explain its role within a constitutional system and to account for its connection with a democratic polity. As always, I assume that the society in question is one that is nearly just; and this implies that it has some form of democratic government, although serious injustices may nevertheless exist. In such a society I assume that the principles of justice are for the most part publicly recognized as the fundamental terms of willing cooperation among free and equal persons. By engaging in civil disobedience one intends, then, to address the sense of justice of the majority and to serve fair notice that in one's sincere and considered opinion the conditions of

30. See *Nuclear Weapons and Christian Conscience*, ed. Walter Stein (London, The Merlin Press, 1965), for a presentation of this sort of doctrine in connection with nuclear war.
31. I borrow this point from Walzer, *Obligations*, p. 127.

free cooperation are being violated. We are appealing to others to reconsider, to put themselves in our position, and to recognize that they cannot expect us to acquiesce indefinitely in the terms they impose upon us.

Now the force of this appeal depends upon the democratic conception of society as a system of cooperation among equal persons. If one thinks of society in another way, this form of protest may be out of place. For example, if the basic law is thought to reflect the order of nature and if the sovereign is held to govern by divine right as God's chosen lieutenant, then his subjects have only the right of suppliants. They can plead their cause but they cannot disobey should their appeal be denied. To do this would be to rebel against the final legitimate moral (and not simply legal) authority. This is not to say that the sovereign cannot be in error but only that the situation is not one for his subjects to correct. But once society is interpreted as a scheme of cooperation among equals, those injured by serious injustice need not submit. Indeed, civil disobedience (and conscientious refusal as well) is one of the stabilizing devices of a constitutional system, although by definition an illegal one. Along with such things as free and regular elections and an independent judiciary empowered to interpret the constitution (not necessarily written), civil disobedience used with due restraint and sound judgment helps to maintain and strengthen just institutions. By resisting injustice within the limits of fidelity to law, it serves to inhibit departures from justice and to correct them when they occur. A general disposition to engage in justified civil disobedience introduces stability into a well-ordered society, or one that is nearly just.

It is necessary to look at this doctrine from the standpoint of the persons in the original position. There are two related problems which they must consider. The first is that, having chosen principles for individuals, they must work out guidelines for assessing the strength of the natural duties and obligations, and, in particular, the strength of the duty to comply with a just constitution and one of its basic procedures, that of majority rule. The second problem is that of finding reasonable principles for dealing with unjust situations, or with circumstances in which the compliance with just principles is only partial. Now it seems that, given the assumptions characterizing a nearly just society, the parties would agree to the presumptions (previously discussed) that specify when civil disobedience is justified. They would acknowledge these criteria as spelling out when this form of dissent is appropriate. Doing this would indicate the weight of the natural duty of justice in one important special case. It would also tend to enhance the realization of justice throughout the society by strengthening men's self-esteem as well as their respect for one another. As the contract doctrine emphasizes, the principles of justice are the principles of willing cooperation among equals. To deny justice to another is either to refuse to recognize him as an equal (one in regard to whom we are prepared to constrain our actions by principles that we would choose in a situation of equality that is fair), or to manifest a willingness to exploit the contingencies of natural fortune and happenstance for our own advantage. In either case deliberate injustice invites submission or resistance. Submission arouses the contempt of those who perpetuate injustice and confirms their intention, whereas resistance cuts the ties of community. If after a decent period of time to allow for reasonable political appeals in the normal way, citizens were to dissent by civil disobedience when infractions of the basic liberties occurred, these liberties would, it seems, be more rather than less secure. For these reasons, then, the parties would adopt the conditions defining justified civil disobedience as a way of setting up, within the limits of fidelity to law, a final device to maintain the stability of a just constitution. Although this mode of action is strictly speaking contrary to law, it is nevertheless a morally correct way of maintaining a constitutional regime.

In a fuller account the same kind of explanation could presumably be given for the justifying conditions of conscientious refusal (again assuming the context of a nearly just state). I shall not, however, discuss these conditions here. I should like to emphasize instead that the constitutional theory of civil disobedience rests solely upon a conception of justice. Even the features of publicity and nonviolence are explained on this basis. And the same is true of the account of conscientious refusal, although it requires a further elaboration of the contract doctrine. At no point has a reference been made to other than political principles; religious or pacifist conceptions are not essential. While those engaging in civil disobedience have often been moved by convictions of this kind, there is no necessary connection between them and civil disobedience. For this form of political action can be understood as a way of addressing the sense of justice of the community, an invocation of the recognized principles of cooperation among equals. Being an appeal to the moral basis of civic life, it is a political and not a religious act. It relies upon common sense principles of justice that men can require one another to follow and not upon the affirmations of religious faith and love which they cannot demand that everyone accept. I do not mean, of course, that nonpolitical conceptions have no validity. They may, in fact, confirm our judgment and support our acting in ways known on other grounds to be just. Nevertheless, it is not these principles but the principles of justice, the fundamental terms of social cooperation between free and equal persons, that underlie the constitution. Civil disobedience as defined does not require a sectarian foundation but is derived from the public conception of justice that characterizes a democratic society. So understood a conception of civil disobedience is part of the theory of free government.

One distinction between medieval and modern constitutionalism is that in the former the supremacy of law was not secured by established institutional controls. The check to the ruler who in his judgments and edicts opposed the sense of justice of the community was limited for the most part to the right of resistance by the whole society, or any part. Even this right seems not to have been interpreted as a corporate act; an unjust king was simply put aside.[32] Thus the Middle Ages lacked the basic ideas of modern constitutional government, the idea of the sovereign people who have final authority and the institutionalizing of this authority by means of elections and parliaments, and other constitutional forms. Now in much the same way that the modern conception of constitutional government builds upon the medieval, the theory of civil disobedience supplements the purely legal conception of constitutional democracy. It attempts to formulate the grounds upon which legitimate democratic authority may be dis-

32. See J. H. Franklin, ed., *Constitutionalism and Resistance in the Sixteenth Century* (New York, Pegasus, 1969), in the introduction, pp. 11–15.

sented from in ways that while admittedly contrary to law nevertheless express a fidelity to law and appeal to the fundamental political principles of a democratic regime. Thus to the legal forms of constitutionalism one may adjoin certain modes of illegal protest that do not violate the aims of a democratic constitution in view of the principles by which such dissent is guided. I have tried to show how these principles can be accounted for by the contract doctrine.

Some may object to this theory of civil disobedience that it is unrealistic. It presupposes that the majority has a sense of justice, and one might reply that moral sentiments are not a significant political force. What moves men are various interests, the desires for power, prestige, wealth, and the like. Although they are clever at producing moral arguments to support their claims, between one situation and another their opinions do not fit into a coherent conception of justice. Rather their views at any given time are occasional pieces calculated to advance certain interests. Unquestionably there is much truth in this contention, and in some societies it is more true than in others. But the essential question is the relative strength of the tendencies that oppose the sense of justice and whether the latter is ever strong enough so that it can be invoked to some significant effect.

A few comments may make the account presented more plausible. First of all, I have assumed throughout that we have to do with a nearly just society. This implies that there exists a constitutional regime and a publicly recognized conception of justice. Of course, in any particular situation certain individuals and groups may be tempted to violate its principles but the collective sentiment in their behalf has considerable strength when properly addressed. These principles are affirmed as the necessary terms of cooperation between free and equal persons. If those who perpetrate injustice can be clearly identified and isolated from the larger community, the convictions of the greater part of society may be of sufficient weight. Or if the contending parties are roughly equal, the sentiment of justice of those not engaged can be the deciding factor. In any case, should circumstances of this kind not obtain, the wisdom of civil disobedience is highly problematic. For unless one can appeal to the sense of justice of the larger society, the majority may simply be aroused to more repressive measures if the calculation of advantages points in this direction. Courts should take into account the civilly disobedient nature of the protester's act, and the fact that it is justifiable (or may seem so) by the political principles underlying the constitution, and on these grounds reduce and in some cases suspend the legal sanction.[33] Yet quite the opposite may happen when the necessary background is lacking. We have to recognize then that justifiable civil disobedience is normally a reasonable and effective form of dissent only in a society regulated to some considerable degree by a sense of justice.

There may be some misapprehension about the manner in which the sense of justice is said to work. One may think that this sentiment expresses itself in sincere professions of principle and in actions requiring a considerable degree of self-sacrifice. But this supposition asks too much. A community's sense of justice is more likely to be revealed in the fact that the majority cannot bring itself to take the steps necessary to suppress the minority and to punish acts of civil disobedience as the law allows. Ruthless tactics that might be contemplated in other societies are not entertained as real alternatives. Thus the sense of justice affects, in ways we are often unaware of, our interpretation of political life, our perception of the possible courses of action, our will to resist the justified protests of others, and so on. In spite of its superior power, the majority may abandon its position and acquiesce in the proposals of the dissenters; its desire to give justice weakens its capacity to defend its unjust advantages. The sentiment of justice will be seen as a more vital political force once the subtle forms in which it exerts its influence are recognized, and in particular its role in rendering certain social positions indefensible.

In these remarks I have assumed that in a nearly just society there is a public acceptance of the same principles of justice. Fortunately this assumption is stronger than necessary. There can, in fact, be considerable differences in citizens' conceptions of justice provided that these conceptions lead to similar political judgments. And this is possible, since different premises can yield the

33. For a general discussion, see Ronald Dworkin, "On Not Prosecuting Civil Disobedience," *The New York Review of Books,* June 6, 1968.

same conclusion. In this case there exists what we may refer to as overlapping rather than strict consensus. In general, the overlapping of professed conceptions of justice suffices for civil disobedience to be a reasonable and prudent form of political dissent. Of course, this overlapping need not be perfect; it is enough that a condition of reciprocity is satisfied. Both sides must believe that however much their conceptions of justice differ, their views support the same judgment in the situation at hand, and would do so even should their respective positions be interchanged. Eventually, though, there comes a point beyond which the requisite agreement in judgment breaks down and society splits into more or less distinct parts that hold diverse opinions on fundamental political questions. In this case of strictly partitioned consensus, the basis for civil disobedience no longer obtains. For example, suppose those who do not believe in toleration, and who would not tolerate others had they the power, wish to protest their lesser liberty by appealing to the sense of justice of the majority which holds the principle of equal liberty. While those who accept this principle should, as we have seen, tolerate the intolerant as far as the safety of free institutions permits, they are likely to resent being reminded of this duty by the intolerant who would, if positions were switched, establish their own dominion. The majority is bound to feel that their allegiance to equal liberty is being exploited by others for unjust ends. This situation illustrates once again the fact that a common sense of justice is a great collective asset which requires the cooperation of many to maintain. The intolerant can be viewed as free-riders, as persons who seek the advantages of just institutions while not doing their share to uphold them. Although those who acknowledge the principles of justice should always be guided by them, in a fragmented society as well as in one moved by group egoisms, the conditions for civil disobedience do not exist. Still, it is not necessary to have strict consensus, for often a degree of overlapping consensus allows the reciprocity condition to be fulfilled.

There are, to be sure, definite risks in the resort to civil disobedience. One reason for constitutional forms and their judicial interpretation is to establish a public reading of the political conception of justice and an explanation of the application of its principles to social questions. Up to a certain point it is better that the law and its interpretation be settled than that it be settled rightly. Therefore it may be protested that the preceding account does not determine who is to say when circumstances are such as to justify civil disobedience. It invites anarchy by encouraging everyone to decide for himself, and to abandon the public rendering of political principles. The reply to this is that each person must indeed make his own decision. Even though men normally seek advice and counsel, and accept the injunctions of those in authority when these seem reasonable to them, they are always accountable for their deeds. We cannot divest ourselves of our responsibility and transfer the burden of blame to others. This is true on any theory of political duty and obligation that is compatible with the principles of a democratic constitution. The citizen is autonomous yet he is held responsible for what he does (§78). If we ordinarily think that we should comply with the law, this is because our political principles normally lead to this conclusion. Certainly in a state of near justice there is a presumption in favor of compliance in the absence of strong reasons to the contrary. The many free and reasoned decisions of individuals fit together into an orderly political regime.

But while each person must decide for himself whether the circumstances justify civil disobedience, it does not follow that one is to decide as one pleases. It is not by looking to our personal interests, or to our political allegiances narrowly construed, that we should make up our minds. To act autonomously and responsibly a citizen must look to the political principles that underlie and guide the interpretation of the constitution. He must try to assess how these principles should be applied in the existing circumstances. If he comes to the conclusion after due consideration that civil disobedience is justified and conducts himself accordingly, he acts conscientiously. And though he may be mistaken, he has not done as he pleased. The theory of political duty and obligation enables us to draw these distinctions.

There are parallels with the common understandings and conclusions reached in the sciences. Here, too, everyone is autonomous yet responsible. We are to assess theories and hypotheses in the light of the evidence by publicly recognized principles. It is true that there are authoritative works, but these sum up the consensus of many persons each deciding for himself. The absence of a final authority to decide, and so of an official interpretation that all must accept, does not lead to confusion, but is rather a condition of theoretical advance. Equals accepting and applying reasonable principles need have no established superior. To the question, who is to decide? The answer is: all are to decide, everyone taking counsel with himself, and with reasonableness, comity, and good fortune, it often works out well enough.

In a democratic society, then, it is recognized that each citizen is responsible for his interpretation of the principles of justice and for his conduct in the light of them. There can be no legal or socially approved rendering of these principles that we are always morally bound to accept, not even when it is given by a supreme court or legislature. Indeed each constitutional agency, the legislature, the executive, and the court, puts forward its interpretation of the constitution and the political ideals that inform it.[34] Although the court may have the last say in settling any particular case, it is not immune from powerful political influences that may force a revision of its reading of the constitution. The court presents its doctrine by reason and argument; its conception of the constitution must, if it is to endure, persuade the major part of the citizens of its soundness. The final court of appeal is not the court, nor the executive or the legislature, but the electorate as a whole. The civilly disobedient appeal in a special way to this body. There is no danger of anarchy so long as there is a sufficient working agreement in citizens' conceptions of justice and the conditions for resorting to civil disobedience are respected. That men can achieve such an understanding and honor these limits when the basic political liberties are maintained is an assumption implicit in a democratic polity. There is no way to avoid entirely the danger of divisive strife, any more than one can rule out the possibility of profound scientific controversy. Yet if justified civil disobedience seems to threaten civic concord, the responsibility falls not upon those who protest but upon those whose abuse of

34. For a presentation of this view to which I am indebted, see A. M. Bickel, *The Least Dangerous Branch* (New York, Bobbs-Merrill, 1962), esp. chs. V and VI.

authority and power justifies such opposition. For to employ the coercive apparatus of the state in order to maintain manifestly unjust institutions is itself a form of illegitimate force that men in due course have a right to resist.

With these remarks we have reached the end of our discussion of the content of the principles of justice. Throughout this part my aim has been to describe a scheme of institutions that satisfies these principles and to indicate how duties and obligations arise. These things must be done to see if the theory of justice put forward matches our considered judgments and extends them in an acceptable way. We need to check whether it defines a workable political conception and helps to focus our reflections on the most relevant and basic moral concerns. The account in this part is still highly abstract, but I hope to have provided some guidance as to how the principles of justice apply in practice. However, we should not forget the limited scope of the theory presented. For the most part I have tried to develop an ideal conception, only occasionally commenting on the various cases of nonideal theory. To be sure the priority rules suggest directives in many instances, and they may be useful if not pressed too far. Even so, the only question of nonideal theory examined in any detail is that of civil disobedience in the special case of near justice. If ideal theory is worthy of study, it must be because, as I have conjectured, it is the fundamental part of the theory of justice and essential for the nonideal part as well. I shall not pursue these matters further. We have still to complete the theory of justice by seeing how it is rooted in human thought and feeling, and tied in with our ends and aspirations.

PART THREE. ENDS

CHAPTER VII. GOODNESS AS RATIONALITY

In this final part I proceed as follows. First, I present in more detail the theory of the good which has already been used to characterize primary goods and the interests of the persons in the original position. Since a more comprehensive view is required for the subsequent argument, this theory must be given a firmer foundation. The next chapter is largely concerned with moral psychology and the acquisition of the sentiment of justice. Once these matters have been dealt with, we are in a position to discuss the relative stability of justice as fairness and to argue in the last chapter that, in a sense to be defined, justice and goodness are congruent, at least in the circumstances of a well-ordered society. Last of all I explain how the theory of justice connects up with the social values and the good of community. Sometimes in this part the overall direction of the exposition may seem less clear, and the transition from one topic to another more abrupt. It might help to keep in mind that the central aim is to prepare the way to settle the questions of stability and congruence, and to account for the values of society and the good of justice.

60. THE NEED FOR A THEORY OF THE GOOD

So far I have said very little about the concept of goodness. It was briefly mentioned earlier when I suggested that a person's good is determined by what is for him the most rational plan of life given reasonably favorable circumstances (§15). All along I have assumed that in a well-ordered society citizens' conceptions of their good conform to the principles of right publicly recognized and include an appropriate place for the various primary goods. But the concept of goodness has been used only in a rather thin sense. And in fact I shall distinguish between two theories of the good. The reason for doing this is that in justice as fairness the concept of right is prior to that of the good. In contrast with teleological theories, something is good only if it fits into ways of life consistent with the principles of right already on hand. But to establish these principles it is necessary to rely on some notion of goodness, for we need assumptions about the parties' motives in the original position. Since these assumptions must not jeopardize the prior place of the concept of right, the theory of the good used in arguing for the principles of justice is restricted to the bare essentials. This account of the good I call the thin theory: its purpose is to secure the premises about primary goods required to arrive at the principles of justice. Once this theory is worked out and the primary goods accounted for, we are free to use the principles of justice in the further development of what I shall call the full theory of the good.

In order to clarify these matters, let us recall where a theory of the good has already played a role. First of all, it is used to define the least favored members of society. The difference principle assumes that this can be done. It is true that the theory need not define a cardinal measure of welfare. We do not have to know how disadvantaged the least fortunate are, since once this group is singled out, we can take their ordinal preferences (from the appropriate point of view) as determining the proper arrangement of the basic structure (§ 15). Nevertheless, we must be able to identify this group. Further, the index of well-being and the expectations of representative men are specified in terms of primary goods. Rational individuals, whatever else they want, desire certain things as prerequisites for carrying out their plans of life. Other things equal, they prefer a wider to a narrower liberty and opportunity, and a greater rather than a smaller share of wealth and income. That these things are good seems clear enough. But I have also said that self-respect and a sure confidence in the sense of one's own worth is perhaps the most important primary good. And this suggestion has been used in the argument for the two principles of justice (§ 29). Thus the initial definition of expectations solely by reference to such things as liberty and wealth is provisional; it is necessary to include other kinds of primary goods and these raise deeper questions. Obviously an account of the good is required for this; and it must be the thin theory.

Again, some view of goodness is used in defending justice as fairness against various objections. For example, it may be said that the persons in the original position know so little about their situation that a rational agreement upon principles of justice is impossible. Since they do not know what their aims are, they may find their plans utterly ruined by the principles to which they consent. Therefore how can they reach a sensible decision? One might reply that the rationality of a person's choice does not depend upon how much he knows, but only upon how well he reasons from whatever information he has, however incomplete. Our decision is perfectly rational provided that we face up to our circumstances and do the best we can. Thus the parties can in fact make a rational decision, and surely some of the alternative conceptions of justice are better than others. Nevertheless, the thin theory of the good which the parties are assumed to accept shows that they should try to secure their liberty and self-respect, and that, in order to advance their aims, whatever these are, they normally require more rather than less of the other primary goods. In entering into the original agreement, then, the parties suppose that their conceptions of the good have a certain structure, and this is sufficient to enable them to choose principles on a rational basis.

Summing up these points, we need what I have called the thin theory of the good to explain the rational preference for primary goods and to explicate the notion of rationality underlying the choice of principles in the original position. This theory is necessary to support the requisite premises from which the principles of justice are derived. But looking ahead to other questions yet to be discussed, a more comprehensive account of the good is essential. Thus the definition of beneficent and supererogatory acts depends upon such a theory. So likewise does the definition of the moral worth of persons. This is the third main concept of ethics and we must find a place for it within the contract view. Eventually we shall have to consider whether being a good person is a good thing for that person, if not in general, then under what conditions. In some circumstances at least, for example those of a society well-ordered or in a state of near justice, it turns out, I believe, that being a good person is indeed a good. This fact is intimately connected with the good of justice and the problem of the congruence of a moral theory. We need an account of the good to spell all this out. The characteristic feature of this full theory, as I have said, is that it takes the principles of justice as already secured, and then uses these principles in defining the other moral concepts in which the notion of goodness is involved. Once the principles of right are on hand, we may appeal to them in explaining the concept of moral worth and the good of the moral virtues. Indeed, even rational plans of life which determine what things are good for human beings, the values of human life so to speak, are themselves constrained by the principles of justice. But clearly, to avoid moving in a circle, we must distinguish between the thin and the full theory, and always keep in mind which one we are relying upon.

Finally, when we come to the explanation of the social values and the stability of a conception of justice, a wider interpretation of the good is required. For example, one basic psychological principle is that we have a tendency to love those who manifestly love us, those who with evident intention advance our good. In this instance our good comprises final ends and not only primary goods. Moreover, in order to account for the social values, we need a theory that explains the good of activities, and in particular the good of everyone's willingly acting from the public conception of justice in affirming their social institutions. When we consider these questions we can work within the full theory. Sometimes we are examining the processes by which the sense of justice and moral sentiments are acquired; or else we are noting that the collective activities of a just society are also good. There is no reason for not using the full theory, since the conception of justice is available.

However, when we ask whether the sense of justice is a good, the important question clearly is that defined by the thin theory. We want to know whether having and maintaining a sense of justice is a good (in the thin sense) for persons who are members of a well-ordered society. Surely if the sentiment of justice is ever a good, it is a good in this special case. And if within the thin theory it turns out that having a sense of justice is indeed a good, then a well-

398

ordered society is as stable as one can hope for. Not only does it generate its own supportive moral attitudes, but these attitudes are desirable from the standpoint of rational persons who have them when they assess their situation independently from the constraints of justice. This match between justice and goodness I refer to as congruence; and I shall examine this relation when we take up the good of justice (§ 86).

61. THE DEFINITION OF GOOD FOR SIMPLER CASES

Rather than proceeding immediately to the application of the concept of rationality to the assessment of plans, it seems best to illustrate the definition I shall use by first considering simpler cases. Doing this will bring out several distinctions that are necessary for a clear understanding of its sense. Thus I suppose the definition to have three stages as follows (for simplicity these stages are formulated using the concept of goodness rather than that of better than): (1) A is a good X if and only if A has the properties (to a higher degree than the average[1] or standard X) which it is rational to want in an X, given what X's are used for, or expected to do, and the like (whichever rider is appropriate); (2) A is a good X for K (where K is some person) if and only if A has the properties which it is rational for K to want in an X, given K's circumstances, abilities, and plan of life (his system of aims), and therefore in view of what he intends to do with an X, or whatever; (3) the same as 2 but adding a clause to the effect that K's plan of life, or that part of it relevant in the present instance, is itself rational. What rationality means in the case of plans has yet to be determined and will be discussed later on. But according to the definition, once we establish that an object has the properties that it is rational for someone with a rational plan of life to want, then we have shown that it is good for him. And if certain sorts of things satisfy this condition for persons generally, then these things are human goods. Eventually we want to be assured that liberty and

1. See W. D. Ross, *The Right and the Good* (Oxford, The Clarendon Press, 1930), p. 67.

opportunity, and a sense of our own worth, fall into this category.[2]

Now for a few comments on the first two stages of the definition. We tend to move from the first stage to the second whenever it is necessary to take into account the special features of a person's situation which the definition defines to be relevant. Typically these features are his interests, abilities, and circumstances. Although the principles of rational choice have not yet been set out, the everyday notion seems clear enough for the time being. In general, there is a reasonably precise sense in speaking simply of a good object of a certain kind, a sense explained by the first stage, provided that there is enough similarity of interests and circumstances among persons concerned with objects of this kind so that recognized standards can be established. When these conditions are met, saying that something is good conveys useful information. There is sufficient common experience with or knowledge of these things for us to have an understanding of the desired features exemplified by an average or standard object. Often there are conventional cri-

2. As I have remarked, there is wide agreement, with many variations, on an account of the good along these lines. See Aristotle, *Nicomachean Ethics*, bks. I and X; and Aquinas, *Summa Theologica*, I-I, q. 5–6, *Summa Contra Gentiles*, bk. III, chs. 1–63, and *Treatise on Happiness*, trans. J. A. Oesterle (Englewood Cliffs, N.J., Prentice-Hall, Inc., 1964). For Kant, *The Fundamental Principles of the Metaphysics of Morals*, Academy Edition, vol. IV, pp. 415–419; and *The Critique of Practical Reason*, first part of ch. II, bk. I of pt. I. See H. J. Paton's discussion of Kant, *In Defense of Reason* (London, George Allen and Unwin, Ltd., 1951), pp. 157–177. For Sidgwick, *Methods of Ethics*, 7th ed. (London, Macmillan, 1907), bk. I, ch. IX, and bk. III, ch. XIV. This kind of view is held by idealists and those influenced by them. See, for example, F. H. Bradley, *Ethical Studies*, 2nd ed. (Oxford, The Clarendon Press, 1926), ch. II; and Josiah Royce, *The Philosophy of Loyalty* (New York, Macmillan, 1908), lect. II. And more recently, H. J. Paton, *The Good Will* (London, George Allen and Unwin, 1927), bks. II and III, esp. chs. VIII and IX; W. D. Lamont, *The Value Judgment* (Edinburgh, The University Press, 1955); and J. N. Findlay, *Values and Intentions* (London, George Allen and Unwin, 1961), ch. V, secs. I and III, and ch. VI. For the so-called naturalists in value theory, see John Dewey, *Human Nature and Conduct* (New York, Henry Holt, 1922), pt. III; R. B. Perry, *General Theory of Value* (New York, Longmans, Green, 1926), chs. XX-XXII; and C. I. Lewis, *An Analysis of Knowledge and Valuation* (LaSalle, Ill., Open Court Publishing Co., 1946), bk. III. My account is indebted to J. O. Urmson, "On Grading," *Mind*, vol. 59 (1950); Paul Ziff, *Semantic Analysis* (Ithaca, N.Y., Cornell University Press, 1960), ch. VI; and Philippa Foot, "Goodness and Choice," *Proceedings of the Aristotelian Society*, supp. vol. 35 (1961), though they may not approve of what I say.

teria founded upon commercial or other practice which define these properties.[3] By taking up various examples we could no doubt see how these criteria evolve and the relevant standards determined. The essential point, however, is that these criteria depend upon the nature of the objects in question and upon our experience with them; and therefore we say that certain things are good without further elaboration only when a certain background is presupposed or some particular context is taken for granted. The basic value judgments are those made from the standpoint of persons, given their interests, abilities, and circumstances. Only insofar as a similarity of conditions permits can we safely abstract from anyone's special situation. In cases of any complexity, when the thing to be chosen should be adjusted to specific wants and situations, we move to the second stage of the definition. Our judgments of value are tailored to the agent in question as this stage requires.

These remarks may be illustrated by looking at several examples from certain typical categories: artifacts, functional parts of systems, and occupations and roles. Among artifacts, a good watch, say, is one that has the features which it is rational to want in a watch. There are clearly a number of desired features here, in addition to that of keeping accurate time. It must not be excessively heavy, for example. These features must be measured somehow and assigned appropriate weights in the overall assessment. I shall not consider here how these things are done. It is worth noting, however, that if we take the definition of good in the traditional sense as an analysis, that is, as a statement of concept identity, and if we suppose that by definition a watch is an article used to tell time, and that by definition rationality is taking effective means to achieve one's ends, then it is analytic that a good watch is one that keeps accurate time. This fact is established solely by virtue of truths of logic and definitions of concepts. But since I do not wish to take the definition of good in this sense but rather as a rough guideline for constructing substitute expressions that can be used to say what on reflection we want to say, I do not count this statement as analytic. In fact, for our present purposes I shall sidestep this question entirely and simply take certain facts about watches (or whatever) as common knowledge. There is no occa-

3. See Urmson, "On Grading," pp. 148–154.

sion to ask whether the statements that express them are analytic. On this account, then, it is certainly true that a good watch keeps accurate time and this correspondence with everyday facts suffices to confirm the propriety of the definition.

Again, it is plain that the letter "X" in the phrase "a good X" often has to be replaced by various noun phrases depending on the context. Thus it is usually not enough to speak of good watches, since we frequently need a more fine-grained classification. We are called upon to assess wrist watches, stop watches, and so on; or even wrist watches to go with a particular kind of evening dress. In all these cases special interests give rise to certain appropriate classifications and standards. These complications are ordinarily gathered from the circumstances and are explicitly mentioned when it seems necessary. With things that are not artifacts some elaboration is usually called for to explain one's meaning since it is not provided by the reference to the object. Thus, for example, the statement that Wildcat is a good mountain may require the kind of amplification provided by adding that it is a good mountain for skiing. Or the observation that it is a good night may call for the explanation that it is a good night for seeing the stars, since it is a clear and dark night. Some terms suggest the appropriate expansion. Consider an example: if we compare the statement that a body is a good corpse with the statement that it is a good cadaver, the sense of the first is not clear, whereas referring to something as a cadaver conveys its use in the study of anatomy. A good cadaver is presumably a corpse having the properties (whatever they are) which it is rational to want for this purpose.[4] It may be noted in passing that we can understand at least part of what is meant by calling something good even though we do not know what are the desired features of the object being evaluated.

There always stands in the background a point of view from which an artifact, functional part, or role is being appraised, although of course this point of view need not be made explicit. This perspective is characterized by identifying the persons whose concerns are relevant for making the judgment, and then by describing the interests which they take in the object. For example, in the case of parts of the body (functional parts of systems), we normally

4. The example is from Ziff, *Semantic Analysis,* p. 211.

take up the point of view of the person in question and presume that his interest is the normal one. Thus good eyes and ears are those having the properties that it is rational to want in one's own eyes and ears when one wishes to see and hear well. Similarly with animals and plants: when we say that they have a good coat, or good roots, we appear to adopt the point of view of the animal or plant. No doubt there is some artificiality in doing this, especially in the case of plants. On the other hand, perhaps there are other perspectives that would explain these judgments more naturally. But the definition is likely to be more suitable for some cases than others, and this fact need not worry us too much so long as it is satisfactory for the purposes of the theory of justice. Turning to the category of occupations, in some instances anyway while the desired properties are those of persons belonging to the occupation, the persons whose point of view we take up do not belong to it. Thus a good doctor is one who has the skills and abilities that it is rational for his patients to want in a doctor. The skills and abilities are the doctor's, the interest in the restoration of health by which they are assessed are the patients'. These illustrations show that the point of view varies from case to case and the definition of goodness contains no general formula for determining it. These matters are explained as the occasion arises or gathered from the context.

A further comment is that there is nothing necessarily right, or morally correct, about the point of view from which things are judged to be good or bad.[5] One may say of a man that he is a good spy, or a good assassin, without approving of his skills. Applying the definition to this case, we would be interpreted as saying that the individual referred to has the attributes that it is rational to want in a spy, or assassin, given what spies and assassins are expected to do. There is no implication that it is proper to want spies and assassins to do what they do. Normally it is governments and conspirators and the like who employ spies and assassins. We are simply evaluating certain proficiencies and talents from the point of view of governments and conspirators. Whether a spy or assassin is a good person is a separate question altogether; to answer it we

5. On this point, see Ross, *The Right and the Good,* p. 67. A somewhat different view is expressed by A. E. Duncan-Jones, "Good Things and Good Thieves," *Analysis,* vol. 27 (1966), pp. 113–118.

should have to judge the cause for which he works and his motives for doing so.

Now this moral neutrality of the definition of good is exactly what we should expect. The concept of rationality by itself is not an adequate basis for the concept of right; and in contract theory the latter is derived in another way. Moreover, to construct the conception of moral goodness, the principles of right and justice must be introduced. It is easy to see that with many occupations and roles moral principles have an important place in characterizing the desired properties. For example, a good judge has a strong desire to give justice, to decide cases fairly in accordance with what the law requires. He possesses the judicial virtues which his position demands: he is impartial, able to assess the evidence fairly, not prejudiced or moved by personal considerations. These attributes may not suffice but they are generally necessary. The characterizations of a good father or wife, friend or associate, and so on indefinitely, rely upon a theory of the virtues and therefore presuppose the principles of right. These matters belong to the full theory. In order for goodness as rationality to hold for the concept of moral worth, it must turn out that the virtues are properties that it is rational for persons to want in one another when they adopt the requisite point of view. I shall try to show in due course that this is in fact the case (§ 66).

62. A NOTE ON MEANING

I shall supplement this account of the thin theory with a few words about the meaning of judgments of value. These matters are not central to our inquiry but several comments may prevent misunderstanding. Perhaps the chief issue is whether these judgments represent a descriptive or a prescriptive use of language. Unfortunately the notions of a descriptive and a prescriptive use are obscure, but I shall try to come to the main point straightway.[6]

6. For the most part my account follows J. R. Searle, "Meaning and Speech Acts," *Philosophical Review*, vol. 71 (1962). See also his *Meaning and Speech Acts* (Cambridge, The University Press, 1969), ch. VI; and Ziff, *Semantic Analysis*, ch. VI.

All sides seem to agree upon two general facts. First, the terms "good" and "bad" and the like are typically used in giving advice and counsel, and to praise and extol, and so on. To be sure, these terms are not always used in this manner, since they may appear in conditional statements, in commands and questions, as well as in other remarks that have no practical bearings. Still, their role in giving advice and counsel and in praising and extolling is characteristic. Second, the criteria for evaluation vary from one kind of thing to another. What is wanted in dwellings is not what is wanted in clothes. A satisfactory definition of the goodness must fit these two facts.

Now I shall simply define a descriptive theory as maintaining the following pair of theses. First, despite the variation in criteria from object to object, the term "good" has a constant sense (or meaning) that, for philosophical purposes, is of the same kind as that of other predicates normally counted as descriptive. Indeed, this constant sense enables us to understand why and how the criteria for evaluation vary from one kind of thing to another. The other thesis is that the propriety of using the term "good" (and its relatives) in giving advice and counsel, and in expressions of commendation, is explained by this constant sense together with a general theory of meaning. I assume that this theory includes an account of speech acts and illocutionary forces along the lines suggested by Austin.[7] A descriptive theory holds that the constant descriptive meaning of good accounts for its being used, when in fact it is properly used, to praise and to advise, and the like. There is no necessity to assign "good" a special kind of meaning which is not already explained by its constant descriptive sense and the general theory of speech acts.

Goodness as rationality is a descriptive theory in this sense. In the required way, it explains the two general facts which everyone recognizes. The constant sense of "good" is characterized by the definition in its several stages. Thus something's being good is its having the properties that it is rational to want in things of its kind, plus further elaborations depending on the case. In the light of this definition it is easy to account for the fact that the criteria

7. See J. L. Austin, *How To Do Things with Words* (Oxford, The Clarendon Press, 1962), esp. pp. 99–109, 113–116, 145f.

of evaluation differ from one kind of thing to another. Since we want things for different purposes, it is obviously rational to assess them by different features. It is helpful to think of the sense of "good" as being analogous to that of a function sign.[8] We can then view the definition as assigning to each kind of thing a set of properties by which instances of that kind are to be assessed, namely, the properties which it is rational to want in things of that kind.

Furthermore, the account of goodness as rationality explains why the term "good" appears in statements of advice and counsel, and in remarks of praise and approval. Thus, for example, when we are asked for advice someone wishes to have our opinion as to which course of action, say, is best for him. He wants to know what we think is rational for him to do. A climber who advises another about the equipment and route to use on a difficult pitch takes up the other's standpoint and recommends what he thinks is a sensible plan of attack. The meaning of "good" and of related expressions does not change in those statements that are counted as advisory. It is the context that converts what we say into advice even though the sense of our words is the same. Climbers, for example, have a duty of mutual aid to help one another, and hence they have a duty to offer their considered opinion in urgent circumstances. In these situations their words become advisory. And so as the situation warrants, what we say may be, and in some cases must be, reckoned as advice and counsel. Accepting the theory of right already sketched, the constant descriptive sense together with the general reasons why persons seek out the views of others explain these characteristic uses of "good." At no point must we appeal to a special kind of prescriptive or emotive meaning.

It may be objected to these remarks that the theory of illocutionary forces allows all that has been claimed by those who have proposed a prescriptive or an emotive theory of meaning. If so, there may be no disagreement. I have not denied that the understanding of the illocutionary forces of the various uses of "good," its being employed in statements of praise and advice, and the like, is relevant to grasping the meaning of the term. Nor do I oppose

8. Here I borrow from P. T. Geach, "Good and Evil," *Analysis,* vol. 17 (1956), pp. 37f.

the view that a certain illocutionary force is central to "good," in the sense that one cannot accept as true the statement that something is good and at the same time dissent from its illocutionary force (assuming this force to obtain in the context).[9] The question is how these facts are to be explained.

Thus the descriptive theory maintains that "good" is characteristically used with the force of a recommendation or advice, and the like, precisely because of its descriptive sense as given by the definition. The descriptive meaning of "good" is not simply a family of lists of properties, a list for each kind of thing according to convention or preference. Rather in the way that the definition explains, these lists are formed in the light of what it is rational to want in objects of various kinds. Therefore understanding why the word "good" (and its relatives) is employed in these speech acts is part of understanding this constant sense. Similarly, certain illocutionary forces are central to "good" as a result of its descriptive meaning, just as the force of factual narration belongs to some utterances in virtue of their descriptive meaning. For if we assent to the statement that something is best for us when it is offered as advice, say, we will indeed accept this advice and act upon it if we are rational. The dispute, if there is one, is not about these recognized facts but concerns the place of the descriptive meaning of "good" in explaining them. The descriptive theory holds that conjoined to a general theory of speech acts the definition of "good" yields an adequate account of these facts. There is no occasion to introduce a distinct kind of meaning.

63. THE DEFINITION OF GOOD FOR PLANS OF LIFE

To this point I have discussed only the first stages of the definition of good in which no questions are raised about the rationality of the ends taken as given. A thing's being a good X for K is treated as equivalent to its having the properties which it is rational for K to want in an X in view of his interests and aims. Yet we often assess the rationality of a person's desires, and the definition must be ex-

9. For these and other points, see J. O. Urmson, *The Emotive Theory of Ethics* (London, Hutchinson University Library, 1968), pp. 136–145.

tended to cover this fundamental case if it is to serve the purposes of the theory of justice. Now the basic idea at the third stage is to apply the definition of good to plans of life. The rational plan for a person determines his good. Here I adapt Royce's thought that a person may be regarded as a human life lived according to a plan. For Royce an individual says who he is by describing his purposes and causes, what he intends to do in his life.[10] If this plan is a rational one, then I shall say that the person's conception of his good is likewise rational. In his case the real and the apparent good coincide. Similarly his interests and aims are rational, and it is appropriate to take them as stopping points in making judgments that correspond to the first two stages of the definition. These suggestions are quite straightforward but unfortunately setting out the details is somewhat tedious. In order to expedite matters I shall start off with a pair of definitions and then explain and comment on them over the next several sections.

These definitions read as follows: first, a person's plan of life is rational if, and only if, (1) it is one of the plans that is consistent with the principles of rational choice when these are applied to all the relevant features of his situation, and (2) it is that plan among those meeting this condition which would be chosen by him with full deliberative rationality, that is, with full awareness of the relevant facts and after a careful consideration of the consequences.[11] (The notion of deliberative rationality is discussed in the next sec-

10. See *The Philosophy of Loyalty,* lect. IV, sec. IV. Royce uses the notion of a plan to characterize the coherent, systematic purposes of the individual, what makes him a conscious, unified moral person. In this Royce is typical of the philosophical usage found in many of the writers cited in §61, note 2, Dewey and Perry, for example. And I shall do the same. The term is given no technical sense, nor are the structures of plans invoked to get other than obvious common sense results. These are matters I do not investigate. For a discussion of plans, see G. A. Miller, Eugene Galanter, and K. H. Pribram, *Plans and the Structure of Behavior* (New York, Henry Holt, 1960); and also Galanter's *Textbook of Elementary Psychology* (San Francisco, Holden-Day, 1966), ch. IX. The notion of a plan may prove useful in characterizing intentional action. See, for example, Alvin Goldman, *A Theory of Action* (Englewood Cliffs, N.J., Prentice-Hall, 1970), pp. 56–73, 76–80; but I do not consider this question.

11. For simplicity I assume that there is one and only one plan that would be chosen, and not several (or many) between which the agent would be indifferent, or whatever. Thus I speak throughout of the plan that would be adopted with deliberative rationality.

tion.) Secondly, a person's interests and aims are rational if, and only if, they are to be encouraged and provided for by the plan that is rational for him. Note that in the first of these definitions I have implied that a rational plan is presumably but one of many possible plans that are consistent with the principles of rational choice. The reason for this complication is that these principles do not single out one plan as the best. We have instead a maximal class of plans: each member of this class is superior to all plans not included in it, but given any two plans in the class, neither is superior or inferior to the other. Thus to identify a person's rational plan, I suppose that it is that plan belonging to the maximal class which he would choose with full deliberative rationality. We criticize someone's plan, then, by showing either that it violates the principles of rational choice, or that it is not the plan that he would pursue were he to assess his prospects with care in the light of a full knowledge of his situation.

Before illustrating the principles of rational choice, I should say a few things about the rather complex notion of a rational plan. It is fundamental for the definition of good, since a rational plan of life establishes the basic point of view from which all judgments of value relating to a particular person are to be made and finally rendered consistent. Indeed, with certain qualifications (§ 83) we can think of a person as being happy when he is in the way of a successful execution (more or less) of a rational plan of life drawn up under (more or less) favorable conditions, and he is reasonably confident that his plan can be carried through. Someone is happy when his plans are going well, his more important aspirations being fulfilled, and he feels sure that his good fortune will endure. Since plans which it is rational to adopt vary from person to person depending upon their endowments and circumstances, and the like, different individuals find their happiness in doing different things. The gloss concerning favorable circumstances is necessary because even a rational arrangement of one's activities can be a matter of accepting the lesser evil if natural conditions are harsh and the demands of other men oppressive. The achievement of happiness in the larger sense of a happy life, or of a happy period of one's life, always presumes a degree of good fortune.

Several further points about long-term plans should be mentioned.

The first relates to their time structure. A plan will, to be sure, make some provision for even the most distant future and for our death, but it becomes relatively less specific for later periods. Certain broad contingencies are insured against and general means provided for, but the details are filled in gradually as more information becomes available and our wants and needs are known with greater accuracy. Indeed, one principle of rational choice is that of postponement: if in the future we may want to do one of several things but are unsure which, then, other things equal, we are to plan now so that these alternatives are both kept open. We must not imagine that a rational plan is a detailed blueprint for action stretching over the whole course of life. It consists of a hierarchy of plans, the more specific subplans being filled in at the appropriate time.

The second point is connected with the first. The structure of a plan not only reflects the lack of specific information but it also mirrors a hierarchy of desires proceeding in similar fashion from the more to the less general. The main features of a plan encourage and secure the fulfillment of the more permanent and general aims. A rational plan must, for example, allow for the primary goods, since otherwise no plan can succeed; but the particular form that the corresponding desires will take is usually unknown in advance and can wait for the occasion. Thus while we know that over any extended period of time we shall always have desires for food and drink, it is not until the moment comes that we decide to have a meal consisting of this or that course. These decisions depend on the choices available, on the menu that the situation allows.

Thus planning is in part scheduling.[12] We try to organize our activities into a temporal sequence in which each is carried on for a certain length of time. In this way a family of interrelated desires can be satisfied in an effective and harmonious manner. The basic resources of time and energy are allotted to activities in accordance with the intensity of the wants that they answer to and the contribution that they are likely to make to the fulfillment of other ends. The aim of deliberation is to find that plan which best organizes our activities and influences the formation of our subsequent wants

12. See J. D. Mabbott, "Reason and Desire," *Philosophy*, vol. 28 (1953), for a discussion of this and other points to which I am indebted.

so that our aims and interests can be fruitfully combined into one scheme of conduct. Desires that tend to interfere with other ends, or which undermine the capacity for other activities, are weeded out; whereas those that are enjoyable in themselves and support other aims as well are encouraged. A plan, then, is made up of subplans suitably arranged in a hierarchy, the broad features of the plan allowing for the more permanent aims and interests that complement one another. Since only the outlines of these aims and interests can be foreseen, the operative parts of the subplans that provide for them are finally decided upon independently as we go along. Revisions and changes at the lower levels do not usually reverberate through the entire structure. If this conception of plans is sound, we should expect that the good things in life are, roughly speaking, those activities and relationships which have a major place in rational plans. And primary goods should turn out to be those things which are generally necessary for carrying out such plans successfully whatever the particular nature of the plan and of its final ends.

These remarks are unhappily too brief. But they are intended only to prevent the more obvious misunderstandings of the notion of a rational plan, and to indicate the place of this notion in a theory of the good. I must now try to convey what is meant by the principles of rational choice. These principles are to be given by enumeration so that eventually they replace the concept of rationality. The relevant features of a person's situation are identified by these principles and the general conditions of human life to which plans must be adjusted. At this point I shall mention those aspects of rationality that are most familiar and seem least in dispute. And for the moment I shall assume that the choice situation relates to the short term. The question is how to fill in the more or less final details of a subplan to be executed over a relatively brief period of time, as when we make plans for a holiday. The larger system of desires may not be significantly affected, although of course some desires will be satisfied in this interval and others will not.

Now for short-term questions anyway, certain principles seem perfectly straightforward and not in dispute. The first of these is that of effective means. Suppose that there is a particular objective that is wanted, and that all the alternatives are means to achieve it, while they are in other respects neutral. The principle holds that we are to adopt that alternative which realizes the end in the best way. More fully: given the objective, one is to achieve it with the least expenditure of means (whatever they are); or given the means, one is to fulfill the objective to the fullest possible extent. This principle is perhaps the most natural criterion of rational choice. Indeed, as we shall note later, there is some tendency to suppose that deliberation must always take this form, being regulated ultimately by a single final end (§83). Otherwise it is thought that there is no rational way to balance a plurality of aims against one another. But this question I leave aside for the present.

The second principle of rational choice is that one (short-term) plan is to be preferred to another if its execution would achieve all of the desired aims of the other plan and one or more further aims in addition. Perry refers to this criterion as the principle of inclusiveness and I shall do the same.[13] Thus we are to follow the more inclusive plan if such a plan exists. To illustrate, suppose that we are planning a trip and we have to decide whether to go to Rome or Paris. It seems impossible to visit both. If on reflection it is clear that we can do everything in Paris that we want to do in Rome, and some other things as well, then we should go to Paris. Adopting this plan will realize a larger set of ends and nothing is left undone that might have been realized by the other plan. Often, however, neither plan is more inclusive than the other; each may achieve an aim which the other does not. We must invoke some other principle to make up our minds, or else subject our aims to further analysis (§83).

A third principle we may call that of the greater likelihood. Suppose that the aims which may be achieved by two plans are roughly the same. Then it may happen that some objectives have a greater chance of being realized by one plan than the other, yet at the same time none of the remaining aims are less likely to be attained. For example, although one can perhaps do everything one wants to do in both Rome and Paris, some of the things one wishes to do seem more likely to meet with success in Paris, and for the rest it is roughly the same. If so, the principle holds that

13. See *General Theory of Value* (New York, Longmans, Green, 1926), pp. 645–649.

412

one should go to Paris. A greater likelihood of success favors a plan just as the more inclusive end does. When these principles work together the choice is as obvious as can be. Suppose that we prefer a Titian to a Tintoretto, and that the first of two lottery tickets gives the larger chance to Titian while the second assigns it to the Tintoretto. Then one **must** prefer the first ticket.

So far we have been considering the application of the principles of rational choice to the short-term case. I now wish to examine the other extreme in which one has to adopt a long-term plan, even a plan of life, as when we have to choose a profession or occupation. It may be thought that having to make such a decision is a task imposed only by a particular form of culture. In another society this choice might not arise. But in fact the question of what to do with our life is always there, although some societies force it upon us more obviously than others and at a different time of life. The limit decision to have no plan at all, to let things come as they may, is still theoretically a plan that may or may not be rational. Accepting the idea of a long-term plan, then, it seems clear that such a scheme is to be assessed by what it will probably lead to in each future period of time. The principle of inclusiveness in this case, therefore, runs as follows: one long-term plan is better than another for any given period (or number of periods) if it allows for the encouragement and satisfaction of all the aims and interests of the other plan and for the encouragement and satisfaction of some further aim or interest in addition. The more inclusive plan, if there is one, is to be preferred: it comprehends all the ends of the first plan and at least one other end as well. If this principle is combined with that of effective means, then together they define rationality as preferring, other things equal, the greater means for realizing our aims, and the development of wider and more varied interests assuming that these aspirations can be carried through. The principle of greater likelihood supports this preference even in situations when we cannot be sure that the larger aims can be executed, provided that the chances of execution are as great as with the less comprehensive plan.

The application of the principles of effective means and the greater likelihood to the long-term case seems sound enough. But the use of the principle of inclusiveness may seem problematical.

With a fixed system of ends in the short run, we assume that we already have our desires and given this fact we consider how best to satisfy them. But in long-term choice, although we do not yet have the desires which various plans will encourage, we are nevertheless directed to adopt that plan which will develop the more comprehensive interests on the assumption that these further aims can be realized. Now a person may say that since he does not have the more inclusive interests, he is not missing anything in not deciding to encourage and to satisfy them. He may hold that the possible satisfaction of desires that he can arrange never to have is an irrelevant consideration. Of course, he might also contend that the more inclusive system of interests subjects him to a greater risk of dissatisfaction; but this objection is excluded since the principle assumes that the larger pattern of ends is equally likely to be attained.

There are two considerations that seem to favor the principle of inclusiveness in the long-term case. First of all, assuming that how happy a person is depends in part upon the proportion of his aims that are achieved, the extent to which his plans are carried through, it follows that pursuing the principle of inclusiveness tends to raise this proportion and thereby enhance a person's happiness. This effect is absent only in the case where all of the aims of the less inclusive plan are already safely provided for. The other consideration is that, in accordance with the Aristotelian Principle (explained below in § 65), I assume that human beings have a higher-order desire to follow the principle of inclusiveness. They prefer the more comprehensive long-term plan because its execution presumably involves a more complex combination of abilities. The Aristotelian Principle states that, other things equal, human beings enjoy the exercise of their realized capacities (their innate or trained abilities), and that this enjoyment increases the more the capacity is realized, or the greater its complexity. A person takes pleasure in doing something as he becomes more proficient at it, and of two activities which he performs equally well, he prefers the one that calls upon the greater number of more subtle and intricate discriminations. Thus the desire to carry out the larger pattern of ends which brings into play the more finely developed talents is an aspect of the Aristotelian Principle. And this desire, along with the higher-order desires to act upon other principles of rational choice, is one of the regulative ends that moves us to engage in rational deliberation and to follow its outcome.

Many things in these remarks call for further explanation. It is clear, for example, that these three principles are not in general sufficient to rank the plans open to us. Means may not be neutral, inclusive plans may not exist, the aims achieved may not be sufficiently similar, and so on. To apply these principles we view our aims as we are inclined to describe them, and more or less count the number realized by this or that plan, or estimate the likelihood of success. For this reason I shall refer to these criteria as counting principles. They do not require a further analysis or alteration of our desires, nor a judgment concerning the relative intensity of our wants. These matters I put aside for the discussion of deliberative rationality. It seems best to conclude this preliminary account by noting what seems to be reasonably clear: namely that we can choose between rational plans of life. And this means that we can choose now which desires we shall have at a later time.

One might suppose at first that this is not possible. We sometimes think that our major desires at least are fixed and that we deliberate solely about the means to satisfy them. Of course, it is obvious that deliberation leads us to have some desires that we did not have before, for example, the desire to avail ourselves of certain means that we have on reflection come to see as useful for our purposes. Furthermore, it is clear that taking thought may lead us to make a general desire more specific, as when a desire for music becomes a desire to hear a particular work. But let us suppose that, except for these sorts of exceptions, we do not choose now what to desire now. Nevertheless, we can certainly decide now to do something that we know will affect the desires that we shall have in the future. At any given time rational persons decide between plans of action in view of their situation and beliefs, all in conjunction with their present major desires and the principles of rational choice. Thus we choose between future desires in the light of our existing desires, including among these the desire to act on rational principles. When an individual decides what to be, what occupation or profession to enter, say, he adopts a particular plan of life. In time his choice will lead him to acquire a definite pattern of wants and

415

aspirations (or the lack thereof), some aspects of which are peculiar to him while others are typical of his chosen occupation or way of life. These considerations appear evident enough, and simply parallel in the case of the individual the deep effects that a choice of a conception of justice is bound to have upon the kinds of aims and interests encouraged by the basic structure of society. Convictions about what sort of person to be are similarly involved in the acceptance of principles of justice.

64. DELIBERATIVE RATIONALITY

I have already noted that the simpler principles of rational choice (the counting principles) do not suffice to order plans. Sometimes they do not apply, since there may be no inclusive plan, say, or else the means are not neutral. Or it often happens that we are left with a maximal class. In these cases further rational criteria may of course be invoked, and some of these I shall discuss below. But I shall suppose that while rational principles can focus our judgments and set up guidelines for reflection, we must finally choose for ourselves in the sense that the choice often rests on our direct self-knowledge not only of what things we want but also of how much we want them. Sometimes there is no way to avoid having to assess the relative intensity of our desires. Rational principles can help us to do this, but they cannot always determine these estimates in a routine fashion. To be sure, there is one formal principle that seems to provide a general answer. This is the principle to adopt that plan which maximizes the expected net balance of satisfaction. Or to express the criterion less hedonistically, if more loosely, one is directed to take that course most likely to realize one's most important aims. But this principle also fails to provide us with an explicit procedure for making up our minds. It is clearly left to the agent himself to decide what it is that he most wants and to judge the comparative importance of his several ends.

At this point I introduce the notion of deliberative rationality following an idea of Sidgwick's. He characterizes a person's future good on the whole as what he would now desire and seek if the consequences of all the various courses of conduct open to him were, at the present point of time, accurately foreseen by him and adequately realized in imagination. An individual's good is the hypothetical composition of impulsive forces that results from deliberative reflection meeting certain conditions.[14] Adjusting Sidgwick's notion to the choice of plans, we can say that the rational plan for a person is the one (among those consistent with the counting principles and other principles of rational choice once these are established) which he would choose with deliberative rationality. It is the plan that would be decided upon as the outcome of careful reflection in which the agent reviewed, in the light of all the relevant facts, what it would be like to carry out these plans and thereby ascertained the course of action that would best realize his more fundamental desires.

In this definition of deliberative rationality it is assumed that there are no errors of calculation or reasoning, and that the facts are correctly assessed. I suppose also that the agent is under no misconceptions as to what he really wants. In most cases anyway, when he achieves his aim, he does not find that he no longer wants it and wishes that he had done something else instead. Moreover, the agent's knowledge of his situation and the consequences of carrying out each plan is presumed to be accurate and complete. No relevant circumstances are left out of account. Thus the best plan for an individual is the one that he would adopt if he possessed full information. It is the objectively rational plan for him and determines his real good. As things are, of course, our knowledge of what will happen if we follow this or that plan is usually incomplete. Often we do not know what is the rational plan for us; the most that we can have is a reasonable belief as to where our good lies, and sometimes we can only conjecture. But if the agent does the best that a rational person can do with the information available to him, then the plan he follows is a subjectively rational plan. His choice may be an unhappy one, but if so it is because his beliefs are understandably mistaken or his knowledge insufficient, and not because he drew hasty and fallacious inferences or was confused as to what he really wanted. In this case a person is not to be faulted for any discrepancy between his apparent and his real good.

14. See *The Methods of Ethics*, 7th ed. (London, Macmillan, 1907), pp. 111f.

The notion of deliberative rationality is obviously highly complex, combining many elements. I shall not attempt to enumerate here all the ways in which the process of reflection may go wrong. One could if necessary classify the kinds of mistakes that can be made, the sorts of tests that the agent might apply to see if he has adequate knowledge, and so on. It should be noted, however, that a rational person will not usually continue to deliberate until he has found the best plan open to him. Often he will be content if he forms a satisfactory plan (or subplan), that is, one that meets various minimum conditions.[15] Rational deliberation is itself an activity like any other, and the extent to which one should engage in it is subject to rational decision. The formal rule is that we should deliberate up to the point where the likely benefits from improving our plan are just worth the time and effort of reflection. Once we take the costs of deliberation into account, it is unreasonable to worry about finding the best plan, the one that we would choose had we complete information. It is perfectly rational to follow a satisfactory plan when the prospective returns from further calculation and additional knowledge do not outweigh the trouble. There is even nothing irrational in an aversion to deliberation itself provided that one is prepared to accept the consequences. Goodness as rationality does not attribute any special value to the process of deciding. The importance to the agent of careful reflection will presumably vary from one individual to another. Nevertheless, a person is being irrational if his unwillingness to think about what is the best (or a satisfactory) thing to do leads him into misadventures that on consideration he would concede that he should have taken thought to avoid.

In this account of deliberative rationality I have assumed a certain competence on the part of the person deciding: he knows the general features of his wants and ends both present and future, and he is able to estimate the relative intensity of his desires, and to decide if necessary what he really wants. Moreover, he can envisage the alternatives open to him and establish a coherent ordering of them: given any two plans he can work out which one he prefers or whether he is indifferent between them, and these

---

15. On this point, see H. A. Simon, "A Behavioral Model of Rational Choice," *Quarterly Journal of Economics,* vol. 69 (1955).

preferences are transitive. Once a plan is settled upon, he is able to adhere to it and he can resist present temptations and distractions that interfere with its execution. These assumptions accord with the familiar notion of rationality that I have used all along (§25). I shall not examine here these aspects of being rational. It seems more useful to mention briefly some ways of criticizing our ends which may often help us to estimate the relative intensity of our desires. Keeping in mind that our overall aim is to carry out a rational plan (or subplan), it is clear that some features of desires make doing this impossible. For example, we cannot realize ends the descriptions of which are meaningless, or contradict well-established truths. Since π is a transcendental number, it would be pointless to try to prove that it is an algebraic number. To be sure, a mathematician in attempting to prove this proposition might discover by the way many important facts, and this achievement might redeem his efforts. But insofar as his end was to prove a falsehood, his plan would be open to criticism; and once he became aware of this, he would no longer have this aim. The same thing holds for desires that depend upon our having incorrect beliefs. It is not excluded that mistaken opinions may have a beneficial effect by enabling us to proceed with our plans, being so to speak useful illusions. Nevertheless, the desires that these beliefs support are irrational to the degree that the falsehood of these beliefs makes it impossible to execute the plan, or prevents superior plans from being adopted. (I should observe here that in the thin theory the value of knowing the facts is derived from their relation to the successful execution of rational plans. So far at least there are no grounds for attributing intrinsic value to having true beliefs.)

We may also investigate the circumstances under which we have acquired our desires and conclude that some of our aims are in various respects out of line.[16] Thus a desire may spring from excessive generalization, or arise from more or less accidental associations. This is especially likely to be so in the case of aversions developed when we are younger and do not possess enough experience and maturity to make the necessary corrections. Other wants may be inordinate, having acquired their peculiar urgency as an

16. For the remarks in this paragraph, I am indebted to R. B. Brandt.

overreaction to a prior period of severe deprivation or anxiety. The study of these processes and their disturbing influence on the normal development of our system of desires is not our concern here. They do however suggest certain critical reflections that are important devices of deliberation. Awareness of the genesis of our wants can often make it perfectly clear to us that we really do desire certain things more than others. As some aims seem less important in the face of critical scrutiny, or even lose their appeal entirely, others may assume an assured prominence that provides sufficient grounds for choice. Of course, it is conceivable that despite the unfortunate conditions under which some of our desires and aversions have developed, they may still fit into and even greatly enhance the fulfillment of rational plans. If so, they turn out to be perfectly rational after all.

Finally, there are certain time-related principles that also can be used to select among plans. The principle of postponement I have already mentioned. It holds that, other things equal, rational plans try to keep our hands free until we have a clear view of the relevant facts. And the grounds for rejecting pure time preference we have also considered (§45). We are to see our life as one whole, the activities of one rational subject spread out in time. Mere temporal position, or distance from the present, is not a reason for favoring one moment over another. Future aims may not be discounted solely in virtue of being future, although we may, of course, ascribe less weight to them if there are reasons for thinking that, given their relation to other things, their fulfillment is less probable. The intrinsic importance that we assign to different parts of our life should be the same at every moment of time. These values should depend upon the whole plan itself as far as we can determine it and should not be affected by the contingencies of our present perspective.

Two other principles apply to the overall shape of plans through time. One of these is that of continuity.[17] It reminds us that since a plan is a scheduled sequence of activities, earlier and later activities are bound to affect one another. The whole plan has a certain unity, a dominant theme. There is not, so to speak, a

17. This name is taken from Jan Tinbergen, "Optimum Savings and Utility Maximization over Time," *Econometrica,* vol. 28 (1960).

separate utility function for each period. Not only must effects between periods be taken into account, but substantial swings up and down are presumably to be avoided. A second closely related principle holds that we are to consider the advantages of rising, or at least of not significantly declining, expectations. There are various stages of life, each ideally with its own characteristic tasks and enjoyments. Other things equal, we should arrange things at the earlier stages so as to permit a happy life at the later ones. It would seem that for the most part rising expectations over time are to be preferred. If the value of an activity is assessed relative to its own period, assuming that this is possible, we might try to explain this preference by the relatively greater intensity of the pleasures of anticipation over those of memory. Even though the total sum of enjoyment is the same when enjoyments are estimated locally, increasing expectations provide a measure of contentment that makes the difference. But even leaving this element aside, the rising or at least the nondeclining plan appears preferable since later activities can often incorporate and bind together the results and enjoyments of an entire life into one coherent structure as those of a declining plan cannot.

In these remarks about the devices of deliberation and time-related principles I have tried to fill in Sidgwick's notion of a person's good. In brief, our good is determined by the plan of life that we would adopt with full deliberative rationality if the future were accurately foreseen and adequately realized in the imagination. The matters we have just discussed are connected with being rational in this sense. Here it is worth stressing that a rational plan is one that would be selected if certain conditions were fulfilled. The criterion of the good is hypothetical in a way similar to the criterion of justice. When the question arises as to whether doing something accords with our good, the answer depends upon how well it fits the plan that would be chosen with deliberative rationality.

Now one feature of a rational plan is that in carrying it out the individual does not change his mind and wish that he had done something else instead. A rational person does not come to feel an aversion for the foreseen consequences so great that he regrets following the plan he has adopted. The absence of this sort of regret is not however sufficient to insure that a plan is rational. There may be another plan open to us such that were we to consider it we would find it much better. Nevertheless, if our information is accurate and our understanding of the consequences complete in relevant respects, we do not regret following a rational plan, even if it is not a good one judged absolutely. In this instance the plan is objectively rational. We may, of course, regret something else, for example, that we have to live under such unfortunate circumstances that a happy life is impossible. Conceivably we may wish that we had never been born. But we do not regret that, having been born, we followed the best plan as bad as it may be when judged by some ideal standard. A rational person may regret his pursuing a subjectively rational plan, but not because he thinks his choice is in any way open to criticism. For he does what seems best at the time, and if his beliefs later prove to be mistaken with untoward results, it is through no fault of his own. There is no cause for self-reproach. There was no way of knowing which was the best or even a better plan.

Putting these reflections together, we have the guiding principle that a rational individual is always to act so that he need never blame himself no matter how his plans finally work out. Viewing himself as one continuing being over time, he can say that at each moment of his life he has done what the balance of reasons required, or at least permitted.[18] Therefore any risks he assumes must be worthwhile, so that should the worst happen that he had any reason to foresee, he can still affirm that what he did was above criticism. He does not regret his choice, at least not in the sense that he later believes that at the time it would have been more rational to have done otherwise. This principle will not certainly prevent us from taking steps that lead to misadventure. Nothing can protect us from the ambiguities and limitations of our knowledge, or guarantee that we find the best alternative open to us. Acting with deliberative rationality can only insure that our conduct is above reproach, and that we are responsible to ourselves as

18. For this and other points in this paragraph see Charles Fried, *An Anatomy of Values* (Cambridge, Harvard University Press, 1970), pp. 158–169, and Thomas Nagel, *The Possibility of Altruism* (Oxford, The Clarendon Press, 1970), esp. ch. VIII.

one person over time. We should indeed be surprised if someone said that he did not care about how he will view his present actions later any more than he cares about the affairs of other people (which is not much, let us suppose). One who rejects equally the claims of his future self and the interests of others is not only irresponsible with respect to them but in regard to his own person as well. He does not see himself as one enduring individual.

Now looked at in this way, the principle of responsibility to self resembles a principle of right: the claims of the self at different times are to be so adjusted that the self at each time can affirm the plan that has been and is being followed. The person at one time, so to speak, must not be able to complain about actions of the person at another time. This principle does not, of course, exclude the willing endurance of hardship and suffering; but it must be presently acceptable in view of the expected or achieved good. From the standpoint of the original position the relevance of responsibility to self seems clear enough. Since the notion of deliberative rationality applies there, it means that the parties cannot agree to a conception of justice if the consequences of applying it may lead to self-reproach should the least happy possibilities be realized. They should strive to be free from such regrets. And the principles of justice as fairness seem to meet this requirement better than other conceptions, as we can see from the earlier discussion of the strains of commitment (§29).

A final observation about goodness as rationality. It may be objected that this conception implies that one should be continually planning and calculating. But this interpretation rests upon a misunderstanding. The first aim of the theory is to provide a criterion for the good of the person. This criterion is defined chiefly by reference to the rational plan that would be chosen with full deliberative rationality. The hypothetical nature of the definition must be kept in mind. A happy life is not one taken up with deciding whether to do this or that. From the definition alone very little can be said about the content of a rational plan, or the particular activities that comprise it. It is not inconceivable that an individual, or even a whole society, should achieve happiness moved entirely by spontaneous inclination. With great luck and good fortune some men might by nature just happen to hit upon the way of living that they would adopt with deliberative rationality. For the most part, though, we are not so blessed, and without taking thought and seeing ourselves as one person with a life over time, we shall almost certainly regret our course of action. Even when a person does succeed in relying on his natural impulses without misadventure, we still require a conception of his good in order to assess whether he has really been fortunate or not. He may think so, but he may be deluded; and to settle this matter, we have to examine the hypothetical choices that it would have been rational for him to make, granting due allowance for whatever benefits he may have obtained from not worrying about these things. As I noted before, the value of the activity of deciding is itself subject to rational appraisal. The efforts we should expend making decisions will depend like so much else on circumstances. Goodness as rationality leaves this question to the person and the contingencies of his situation.

65. THE ARISTOTELIAN PRINCIPLE

The definition of the good is purely formal. It simply states that a person's good is determined by the rational plan of life that he would choose with deliberative rationality from the maximal class of plans. Although the notion of deliberative rationality and the principles of rational choice rely upon concepts of considerable complexity, we still cannot derive from the definition of rational plans alone what sorts of ends these plans are likely to encourage. In order to draw conclusions about these ends, it is necessary to take note of certain general facts.

First of all, there are the broad features of human desires and needs, their relative urgency and cycles of recurrence, and their phases of development as affected by physiological and other circumstances. Second, plans must fit the requirements of human capacities and abilities, their trends of maturation and growth, and how they are best trained and educated for this or that purpose. Moreover, I shall postulate a basic principle of motivation which I shall refer to as the Aristotelian Principle. Finally, the general facts of social interdependency must be reckoned with. The basic structure of society is bound to encourage and support certain kinds of plans more than others by rewarding its members for contributing to the common good in ways consistent with justice. Taking account of these contingencies narrows down the alternative plans so that the problem of decision becomes, in some cases anyway, reasonably definite. To be sure, as we shall see, a certain arbitrariness still remains, but the priority of right limits it in such a way that it is no longer a problem from the standpoint of justice (§68).

The general facts about human needs and abilities are perhaps clear enough and I shall assume that common sense knowledge suffices for our purposes here. Before taking up the Aristotelian Principle, however, I should comment briefly on the human goods (as I shall call them) and the constraints of justice. Given the definition of a rational plan, we may think of these goods as those activities and ends that have the features whatever they are that suit them for an important if not a central place in our life.[19] Since in the full theory rational plans must be consistent with the principles of justice, the human goods are similarly constrained. Thus the familiar values of personal affection and friendship, meaningful work and social cooperation, the pursuit of knowledge and the fashioning and contemplation of beautiful objects, are not only prominent in our rational plans but they can for the most part be advanced in a manner which justice permits. Admittedly to attain and to preserve these values, we are often tempted to act unjustly; but achieving these ends involves no inherent injustice. In contrast with the desire to cheat and to degrade others, doing something unjust is not included in the description of the human goods (§66).

The social interdependency of these values is shown in the fact that not only are they good for those who enjoy them but they are likely to enhance the good of others. In achieving these ends we generally contribute to the rational plans of our associates. In this sense, they are complementary goods, and this accounts for their being singled out for special commendation. For to commend something is to praise it, to recount the properties that make it

19. For the explanation of these goods I have drawn from C. A. Campbell, "Moral and Non-Moral Values," *Mind,* vol. 44 (1935); see pp. 279–291.

good (rational to want) with emphasis and expressions of approval. These facts of interdependency are further reasons for including the recognized values in long-term plans. For assuming that we desire the respect and good will of other persons, or at least to avoid their hostility and contempt, those plans of life will tend to be preferable which further their aims as well as our own.

Turning now to our present topic, it will be recalled that the Aristotelian Principle runs as follows: other things equal, human beings enjoy the exercise of their realized capacities (their innate or trained abilities), and this enjoyment increases the more the capacity is realized, or the greater its complexity.[20] The intuitive idea here is that human beings take more pleasure in doing something as they become more proficient at it, and of two activities they do equally well, they prefer the one calling on a larger repertoire of more intricate and subtle discriminations. For example, chess is a more complicated and subtle game than checkers, and algebra is more intricate than elementary arithmetic. Thus the principle says that someone who can do both generally prefers playing chess to playing checkers, and that he would rather study algebra than arithmetic. We need not explain here why the Aris-

20. The name "Aristotelian Principle" seems to me appropriate in view of what Aristotle says about the relations between happiness, activity, and enjoyment in the *Nicomachean Ethics,* bk. VII, chs. 11–14, and bk. X, chs. 1–5. Yet since he does not state such a principle explicitly, and some of it is at best only implied, I have not called it "Aristotle's Principle." Nevertheless, Aristotle certainly affirms two points that the principle conveys: (1) that enjoyment and pleasure are not always by any means the result of returning to a healthy or normal state, or of making up deficiencies; rather many kinds of pleasure and enjoyment arise when we exercise our faculties; and (2) that the exercise of our natural powers is a leading human good. Further, (3) the idea that the more enjoyable activities and the more desirable and enduring pleasures spring from the exercise of greater abilities involving more complex discriminations is not only compatible with Aristotle's conception of the natural order, but something like it usually fits the judgments of value he makes, even when it does not express his reasons. For a discussion of Aristotle's account of enjoyment and pleasure, see W. F. R. Hardie, *Aristotle's Ethical Theory* (Oxford, The Clarendon Press, 1968), ch. XIV. The interpretation of Aristotle's doctrine given by G. C. Field, *Moral Theory* (London, Methuen, 1932), pp. 76–78, strongly suggests what I have called the Aristotelian Principle. Mill comes very close to stating it in *Utilitarianism.* ch. II, pars. 4–8. Important here is the concept of effectance motivation introduced by R. W. White, "Ego and Reality in Psychoanalytic Theory," *Psychological Issues,* vol. III (1963), ch. III, upon which I have relied. See also pp. 173–175, 180f. I am indebted to J. M. Cooper for discussion on the interpretation of this principle and the propriety of its name.

totelian Principle is true. Presumably complex activities are more enjoyable because they satisfy the desire for variety and novelty of experience, and leave room for feats of ingenuity and invention. They also evoke the pleasures of anticipation and surprise, and often the overall form of the activity, its structural development, is fascinating and beautiful. Moreover, simpler activities exclude the possibility of individual style and personal expression which complex activities permit or even require, for how could everyone do them in the same way? That we should follow our natural bent and the lessons of our past experience seems inevitable if we are to find our way at all. Each of these features is well illustrated by chess, even to the point where grand masters have their characteristic style of play. Whether these considerations are explanations of the Aristotelian Principle or elaboration of its meaning, I shall leave aside. I believe that nothing essential for the theory of the good depends upon this question.

It is evident that the Aristotelian Principle contains a variant of the principle of inclusiveness. Or at least the clearest cases of greater complexity are those in which one of the activities to be compared includes all the skills and discriminations of the other activity and some further ones in addition. Once again, we can establish but a partial order, since each of several activities may require abilities not used in the others. Such an ordering is the best that we can have until we possess some relatively precise theory and measure of complexity that enables us to analyze and compare seemingly disparate activities. I shall not, however, discuss this problem here, but assume instead that our intuitive notion of complexity will suffice for our purposes.

The Aristotelian Principle is a principle of motivation. It accounts for many of our major desires, and explains why we prefer to do some things and not others by constantly exerting an influence over the flow of our activity. Moreover, it expresses a psychological law governing changes in the pattern of our desires. Thus the principle implies that as a person's capacities increase over time (brought about by physiological and biological maturation, for example, the development of the nervous system in a young child), and as he trains these capacities and learns how to exercise them, he will in due course come to prefer the more complex activities that he can now engage in which call upon his newly realized abilities. The simpler things he enjoyed before are no longer sufficiently interesting or attractive. If we ask why we are willing to undergo the stresses of practice and learning, the reason may be (if we leave out of account external rewards and penalties) that having had some success at learning things in the past, and experiencing the present enjoyments of the activity, we are led to expect even greater satisfaction once we acquire a greater repertoire of skills. There is also a companion effect to the Aristotelian Principle. As we witness the exercise of well-trained abilities by others, these displays are enjoyed by us and arouse a desire that we should be able to do the same things ourselves. We want to be like those persons who can exercise the abilities that we find latent in our nature.

Thus it would appear that how much we learn and how far we educate our innate capacities depends upon how great these capacities are and how difficult is the effort of realizing them. There is a race, so to speak, between the increasing satisfaction of exercising greater realized ability and the increasing strains of learning as the activity becomes more strenuous and difficult. Assuming that natural talents have an upper bound, whereas the hardships of training can be made more severe without limit, there must be some level of achieved ability beyond which the gains from a further increase in this level are just offset by the burdens of the further practice and study necessary to bring it about and to maintain it. Equilibrium is reached when these two forces balance one another, and at this point the effort to achieve greater realized capacity ceases. It follows that if the pleasures of the activity increase too slowly with rising ability (an index let us suppose of a lower level of innate ability), then the correspondingly greater efforts of learning will lead us to give up sooner. In this case we will never engage in certain more complex activities nor acquire the desires evoked by taking part in them.

Now accepting the Aristotelian Principle as a natural fact, it will generally be rational, in view of the other assumptions, to realize and train mature capacities. Maximal or satisfactory plans are almost certainly plans that provide for doing this in significant measure. Not only is there a tendency in this direction postulated by the Aristotelian Principle, but the plain facts of social inter-dependency and the nature of our interests more narrowly construed incline us in the same way. A rational plan—constrained as always by the principles of right—allows a person to flourish, so far as circumstances permit, and to exercise his realized abilities as much as he can. Moreover, his fellow associates are likely to support these activities as promoting the common interest and also to take pleasure in them as displays of human excellence. To the degree, then, that the esteem and admiration of others is desired, the activities favored by the Aristotelian Principle are good for other persons as well.

There are several points to keep in mind in order to prevent misunderstandings of this principle. For one thing, it formulates a tendency and not an invariable pattern of choice, and like all tendencies it may be overridden. Countervailing inclinations can inhibit the development of realized capacity and the preference for more complex activities. Various hazards and risks, both psychological and social, are involved in training and prospective accomplishment, and apprehensions about these may outweigh the original propensity. We must interpret the principle so as to allow for these facts. Yet if it is a useful theoretical notion, the tendency postulated should be relatively strong and not easily counterbalanced. I believe that this is indeed the case, and that in the design of social institutions a large place has to be made for it, otherwise human beings will find their culture and form of life dull and empty. Their vitality and zest will fail as their life becomes a tiresome routine. And this seems borne out by the fact that the forms of life which absorb men's energies, whether they be religious devotions or purely practical matters or even games and pastimes, tend to develop their intricacies and subtleties almost without end. As social practices and cooperative activities are built up through the imagination of many individuals, they increasingly call forth a more complex array of abilities and new ways of doing things. That this process is carried along by the enjoyment of natural and free activity seems to be verified by the spontaneous play of children and animals which shows all the same features.

A further consideration is that the principle does not assert that any particular kind of activity will be preferred. It says only that we

429

prefer, other things equal, activities that depend upon a larger repertoire of realized capacities and that are more complex. More precisely, suppose that we can order a certain number of activities in a chain by the inclusion relation. This means that the nth activity exercises all the skills of the n–1th activity and some further ones in addition. Now there are indefinitely many such chains with no elements in common, let us say; and moreover, numerous chains may start from the same activity representing different ways in which this activity can be built upon and enriched. What the Aristotelian Principle says is that whenever a person engages in an activity belonging to some chain (and perhaps to several chains) he tends to move up the chain. In general, he will prefer doing the nth to doing the n–1th activity; and this tendency will be stronger the more his capacity is yet to be realized and the less onerous he finds the strains of learning and training. Presumably there is a preference for ascending the chain or chains which offer the greatest prospects of exercising the higher abilities with the least stress. The actual course that a person follows, the combination of activities that he finds most appealing, is decided by his inclinations and talents and by his social circumstances, by what his associates appreciate and are likely to encourage. Thus natural assets and social opportunities obviously influence the chains that individuals eventually prefer. By itself the principle simply asserts a propensity to ascend whatever chains are chosen. It does not entail that a rational plan includes any particular aims, nor does it imply any special form of society.

Again, we may suppose, although it is probably not essential, that every activity belongs to some chain. The reason for this is that human ingenuity can and normally will discover for each activity a continuing chain that elicits a growing inventory of skills and discriminations. We stop moving up a chain, however, when going higher will use up resources required for raising or for maintaining the level of a preferred chain. And resources here is to be taken broadly, so that among the most important ones are time and energy. This is the reason why, for example, we are content to lace our shoes or to tie our tie in a straightforward way, and do not ordinarily make complex rituals of these daily actions. There are only so many hours in a day, and this prevents our ascending to the upper limits of our capacity all the chains that are open to us. But then a prisoner in a cell might take time with daily routines and invent ways of doing them that he would not otherwise bother with. The formal criterion is that a rational individual selects a preferred pattern of activities (compatible with the principle of justice) and proceeds along each of its chains up to the point where no further improvement results from any feasible change in the schedule. This overall standard does not, of course, tell us how to decide; rather it emphasizes the limited resources of time and energy, and explains why some activities are slighted in favor of others even though, in the form in which we engage in them, they allow for further elaboration.

Now it may be objected that there is no reason to suppose that the Aristotelian Principle is true. Like the idealist notion of self-realization, to which it bears a certain resemblance, it may have the ring of a philosopher's principle with little to support it. But it seems to be borne out by many facts of everyday life, and by the behavior of children and some of the higher animals. Moreover, it appears to be susceptible to an evolutionary explanation. Natural selection must have favored creatures of whom this principle is true. Aristotle says that men desire to know. Presumably we have acquired this desire by a natural development, and indeed, if the principle is sound, a desire to engage in more complex and demanding activities of any kind as long as they are within our reach.[21] Human beings enjoy the greater variety of experience, they take pleasure in the novelty and surprises and the occasions for ingenuity and invention that such activities provide. The multiplicity of spontaneous activities is an expression of the delight that we take in imagination and creative fantasy. Thus the Aristotelian Principle characterizes human beings as importantly moved not only by the pressure of bodily needs, but also by the desire to do things enjoyed simply for their own sakes, at least when the urgent and pressing wants are satisfied. The marks of such enjoyed activities are many, varying from the manner and way in which they are done to the persistence with which they are returned to at a later

21. See B. G. Campbell, *Human Evolution* (Chicago, Aldine Publishing Co., 1966), pp. 49–53; and W. H. Thorpe, *Science, Man, and Morals* (London, Methuen, 1965), pp. 87–92. For animals see Irenäus Eibl-Eibesfeldt, *Ethology*, trans. Erich Klinghammer (New York, Holt, Rinehart, and Winston, 1970), pp. 217–248.

time. Indeed, we do them without the incentive of evident reward, and allowing us to engage in them can itself act often as a reward for doing other things.[22] Since the Aristotelian Principle is a feature of human desires as they now exist, rational plans must take it into account. The evolutionary explanation, even if it is correct, is not of course a justification for this aspect of our nature. In fact, the question of justification does not arise. The question is rather: granted that this principle characterizes human nature as we know it, to what extent is it to be encouraged and supported, and how is it to be reckoned with in framing rational plans of life?

The role of the Aristotelian Principle in the theory of the good is that it states a deep psychological fact which, in conjunction with other general facts and the conception of a rational plan, accounts for our considered judgments of value. The things that are commonly thought of as human goods should turn out to be the ends and activities that have a major place in rational plans. The principle is part of the background that regulates these judgments. Provided that it is true, and leads to conclusions matching our convictions about what is good and bad (in reflective equilibrium), it has a proper place in moral theory. Even if this conception should not be true of some persons, the idea of a rational long-term plan still applies. We can work out what is good for them in much the same way as before. Thus imagine someone whose only pleasure is to count blades of grass in various geometrically shaped areas such as park squares and well-trimmed lawns. He is otherwise intelligent and actually possesses unusual skills, since he manages to survive by solving difficult mathematical problems for a fee. The definition of the good forces us to admit that the good for this man is indeed counting blades of grass, or more accurately, his good is determined by a plan that gives an especially prominent place to this activity. Naturally we would be surprised that such a person should exist. Faced with his case, we would try out other hypotheses. Perhaps he is peculiarly neurotic and in early life acquired an aversion to human fellowship, and so he counts blades of grass to avoid having to deal with other people. But if we allow that his nature is to enjoy this activity and not to enjoy any other, and that there is no feasible way to alter his condition, then surely a rational

22. This seems also to be true of monkeys. See, Eibl-Eibesfeldt, *ibid.,* p. 239.

plan for him will center around this activity. It will be for him the end that regulates the schedule of his actions, and this establishes that it is good for him. I mention this fanciful case only to show that the correctness of the definition of a person's good in terms of the rational plan for him does not require the truth of the Aristotelian Principle. The definition is satisfactory, I believe, even if this principle should prove inaccurate, or fail altogether. But by assuming the principle we seem able to account for what things are recognized as good for human beings taking them as they are. Moreover, since this principle ties in with the primary good of self-respect, it turns out to have a central position in the moral psychology underlying justice as fairness (§ 67).

66. THE DEFINITION OF GOOD APPLIED TO PERSONS

Having defined a person's good as the successful execution of a rational plan of life, and his lesser goods as parts thereof, we are in a position to introduce further definitions. In this way the concept of goodness is applied to other subjects that have an important place in moral philosophy. But before doing this we should note the assumption that the primary goods can be accounted for by the thin theory of the good. That is, I suppose that it is rational to want these goods whatever else is wanted, since they are in general necessary for the framing and the execution of a rational plan of life. The persons in the original position are assumed to accept this conception of the good, and therefore they take for granted that they desire greater liberty and opportunity, and more extensive means for achieving their ends. With these objectives in mind, as well as that of securing the primary good of self-respect (§ 67), they evaluate the conceptions of justice available to them in the original position.

That liberty and opportunity, income and wealth, and above all self-respect are primary goods must indeed be explained by the thin theory. The constraints of the principles of justice cannot be used to draw up the list of primary goods that serves as part of the description of the initial situation. The reason is, of course, that this list is one of the premises from which the choice of the principles of right is derived. To cite these principles in explaining the list would be a circular argument. We must assume, then, that the list of primary goods can be accounted for by the conception of goodness as rationality in conjunction with the general facts about human wants and abilities, their characteristic phases and requirements of nurture, the Aristotelian Principle, and the necessities of social interdependence. At no point can we appeal to the constraints of justice. But once we are satisfied that the list of primary goods can be arrived at in this way, then in all further applications of the definition of good the constraints of right may be freely invoked. I shall not argue the case for the list of primary goods here, since their claims seem evident enough. I shall, however, come back to this point from time to time, especially in connection with the primary good of self-respect. In what follows I take the list as established and apply the full theory of the good. The test of this theory is that it should fit our considered judgments of value in reflective equilibrium.

Two fundamental cases for the theory of the good remain to be considered. We must see whether the definition holds for both persons and societies. In this section I discuss the case of persons, leaving the question of a good society for the last chapter when all parts of justice as fairness can be brought to bear. Now many philosophers have been willing to accept some variant of goodness as rationality for artifacts and roles, and for such nonmoral values as friendship and affection, the pursuit of knowledge and the enjoyment of beauty, and the like. Indeed, I have emphasized that the main elements of goodness as rationality are extremely common, being shared by philosophers of markedly different persuasions. Nevertheless, it is often thought that this conception of the good expresses an instrumental or economic theory of value that does not hold for the case of moral worth. When we speak of the just or the benevolent person as morally good, a different concept of goodness is said to be involved.[23] I wish to argue, however, that once the principles of right and justice are on hand, the full theory of goodness as rationality can in fact cover these judgments. The

23. See C. A. Campbell, "Moral and Non-Moral Values," *Mind,* vol. 44 (1935); and R. M. Hare, "Geach on Good and Evil," *Analysis,* vol. 18 (1957).

reason why the so-called instrumental or economic theory fails is that what is in effect the thin theory is applied directly to the problem of moral worth. What we must do instead is to use this theory only as a part of the description of the original position from which the principles of right and justice are derived. We can then apply the full theory of the good without restrictions and are free to use it for the two basic cases of a good person and a good society. Developing the thin into the full theory via the original position is the essential step.

Several ways suggest themselves for extending the definition to the problem of moral worth, and I believe that at least one of these will serve well enough. First of all, we might identify some basic role or position, say that of citizen, and then say that a good person is one who has to a higher degree than the average the properties which it is rational for citizens to want in one another. Here the relevant point of view is that of a citizen judging other citizens in the same role. Second, the notion of a good person could be interpreted as requiring some general or average assessment so that a good person is one who performs well in his various roles, especially those that are considered more important. Finally, there may exist properties which it is rational to want in persons when they are viewed with respect to almost any of their social roles. Let us say that such properties, if they exist, are broadly based.[24] To illustrate this idea in the case of tools, the broadly based properties are efficiency, durability, ease of maintenance, and so on. These features are desirable in tools of almost any kind. Much less broadly based properties are properties such as keeps its cutting edge, does not rust, and so on. The question whether some tools have these would not even arise. By analogy, a good person, in contrast to a good doctor or a good farmer, and the like, is one who has to a higher degree than the average person the broadly based properties (yet to be specified) that it is rational for persons to want in one another.

Offhand it seems that the last suggestion is the most plausible one. It can be made to include the first as a special case and to capture the intuitive idea of the second. There are, however, certain

24. For the notion of broadly based properties and its use here, I am indebted to T. M. Scanlon.

complications in working it out. The first thing is to identify the point of view from which the broadly based properties are rationally preferred and the assumptions upon which this preference is founded. I note straightway that the fundamental moral virtues, that is, the strong and normally effective desires to act on the basic principles of right, are undoubtedly among the broadly based properties. At any rate, this seems bound to be true so long as we suppose that we are considering a well-ordered society, or one in a state of near justice, as I shall indeed take to be the case. Now since the basic structure of such a society is just, and these arrangements are stable with respect to the society's public conception of justice, its members will in general have the appropriate sense of justice and a desire to see their institutions affirmed. But it is also true that it is rational for each person to act on the principles of justice only on the assumption that for the most part these principles are recognized and similarly acted upon by others. Therefore the representative member of a well-ordered society will find that he wants others to have the basic virtues, and in particular a sense of justice. His rational plan of life is consistent with the constraints of right, and he will surely want others to acknowledge the same restrictions. In order to make this conclusion absolutely firm, we should also like to be sure that it is rational for those belonging to a well-ordered society who have already acquired a sense of justice to maintain and even to strengthen this moral sentiment. I shall discuss this question later (§86); for the present I suppose that it is the case. Thus with all these presumptions on hand, it seems clear that the fundamental virtues are among the broadly based properties that it is rational for members of a well-ordered society to want in one another.

A further complication must be considered. There are other properties that are presumably as broadly based as the virtues, for example, intelligence and imagination, strength and endurance. Indeed, a certain minimum of these attributes is necessary for right conduct, since without judgment and imagination, say, benevolent intentions may easily lead to harm. On the other hand, unless intellect and vigor are regulated by a sense of justice and obligation, they may only enhance one's capacity to override the legitimate claims of others. Certainly it would not be rational to want some

436

to be so superior in these respects that just institutions would be jeopardized. Yet the possession of these natural assets in the appropriate degree is clearly desirable from a social point of view; and therefore within limits these attributes are also broadly based. Thus while the moral virtues are included in the broadly based properties, they are not the only ones in this class.

It is necessary, then, to distinguish the moral virtues from the natural assets. The latter we may think of as natural powers developed by education and training, and often exercised in accordance with certain characteristic intellectual or other standards by reference to which they can be roughly measured. The virtues on the other hand are sentiments and habitual attitudes leading us to act on certain principles of right. We can distinguish the virtues from each other by means of their corresponding principles. I assume, then, that the virtues can be singled out by using the conception of justice already established; once this conception is understood, we can rely on it to define the moral sentiments and to mark them off from the natural assets.

A good person, then, or a person of moral worth, is someone who has to a higher degree than the average the broadly based features of moral character that it is rational for the persons in the original position to want in one another. Since the principles of justice have been chosen, and we are assuming strict compliance, each knows that in society he will want the others to have the moral sentiments that support adherence to these standards. Thus we could say alternatively that a good person has the features of moral character that it is rational for members of a well-ordered society to want in their associates. Neither of these interpretations introduces any new ethical notions, and so the definition of goodness as rationality has been extended to persons. In conjunction with the theory of justice which has the thin account of the good as a subpart, the full theory seems to give a satisfactory rendering of moral worth, the third main concept of ethics.

Some philosophers have thought that since a person qua person has no definite role or function, and is not to be treated as an instrument or object, a definition along the lines of goodness as rationality must fail.[25] But as we have seen, it is possible to de-

25. See, for example, Hare, "Geach on Good and Evil," pp. 109ff.

velop a definition of this sort without supposing that persons hold some particular role, much less that they are things to be used for some ulterior purpose. It is true, of course, that the extension of the definition to the case of moral worth makes many assumptions. In particular, I assume that being a member of some community and engaging in many forms of cooperation is a condition of human life. But this presumption is sufficiently general so as not to compromise a theory of justice and moral worth. Indeed, it is entirely proper, as I have noted previously, that an account of our considered moral judgments should draw upon the natural circumstances of society. In this sense there is nothing a priori about moral philosophy. It suffices to recall by way of summation that what permits this definition of the good to cover the notion of moral worth is the use of the principles of justice already derived. Moreover, the specific content and mode of derivation of these principles is also relevant. The main idea of justice as fairness, that the principles of justice are those that would be agreed to by rational persons in an original position of equality, prepares the way for extending the definition of good to the larger questions of moral goodness.

It seems desirable to indicate the way in which the definition of good might be extended to other cases. Doing this will give us more confidence in its application to persons. Thus let us suppose that for each person there is a rational plan of life that determines his good. We can now define a good act (in the sense of a beneficent act) as one which we are at liberty to do or not to do, that is, no requirements of natural duty or obligation constrain us either to do it or not to do it, and which advances and is intended to advance another's good (his rational plan). Taking a further step, we can define a good action (in the sense of a benevolent action) as a good act performed for the sake of the other person's good. A beneficent act promotes another's good; and a benevolent action is done from the desire that the other should have this good. When the benevolent action is one that brings much good for the other person and when it is undertaken at considerable loss or risk to the agent as estimated by his interests more narrowly construed, then the action is supererogatory. An act which would be very good for another, especially one which protects him from great harm or injury, is a natural duty required by the principle of mutual aid, provided that the sacrifice and hazards to the agent are not very great. Thus a supererogatory act may be thought of as one which a person does for the sake of another's good even though the proviso that nullifies the natural duty is satisfied. In general, supererogatory actions are ones that would be duties were not certain exempting conditions fulfilled which make allowance for reasonable self-interest. Eventually, of course, for a complete contractarian account of right, we would have to work out from the standpoint of the original position what is to count as reasonable self-interest. But I shall not pursue this question here.

Finally, the full theory of the good enables us to distinguish different sorts of moral worth, or the lack of it. Thus we can distinguish between the unjust, the bad, and the evil man. To illustrate, consider the fact that some men strive for excessive power, that is, authority over others which goes beyond what is allowed by the principles of justice and which can be exercised arbitrarily. In each of these cases there is a willingness to do what is wrong and unjust in order to achieve one's ends. But the unjust man seeks dominion for the sake of aims such as wealth and security which when appropriately limited are legitimate. The bad man desires arbitrary power because he enjoys the sense of mastery which its exercise gives to him and he seeks social acclaim. He too has an inordinate desire for things which when duly circumscribed are good, namely, the esteem of others and the sense of self-command. It is his way of satisfying these ambitions that makes him dangerous. By contrast, the evil man aspires to unjust rule precisely because it violates what independent persons would consent to in an original position of equality, and therefore its possession and display manifest his superiority and affront the self-respect of others. It is this display and affront which is sought after. What moves the evil man is the love of injustice: he delights in the impotence and humiliation of those subject to him and he relishes being recognized by them as the willful author of their degradation. Once the theory of justice is joined to the theory of the good in what I have called the full theory, we can make these and other distinctions. There seems to be no reason to fear that the numerous variations of moral worth cannot be accounted for.

67. SELF-RESPECT, EXCELLENCES, AND SHAME

On several occasions I have mentioned that perhaps the most important primary good is that of self-respect. We must make sure that the conception of goodness as rationality explains why this should be so. We may define self-respect (or self-esteem) as having two aspects. First of all, as we noted earlier (§29), it includes a person's sense of his own value, his secure conviction that his conception of his good, his plan of life, is worth carrying out. And second, self-respect implies a confidence in one's ability, so far as it is within one's power, to fulfill one's intentions. When we feel that our plans are of little value, we cannot pursue them with pleasure or take delight in their execution. Nor plagued by failure and self-doubt can we continue in our endeavors. It is clear then why self-respect is a primary good. Without it nothing may seem worth doing, or if some things have value for us, we lack the will to strive for them. All desire and activity becomes empty and vain, and we sink into apathy and cynicism. Therefore the parties in the original position would wish to avoid at almost any cost the social conditions that undermine self-respect. The fact that justice as fairness gives more support to self-esteem than other principles is a strong reason for them to adopt it.

The conception of goodness as rationality allows us to characterize more fully the circumstances that support the first aspect of self-esteem, the sense of our own worth. These are essentially two: (1) having a rational plan of life, and in particular one that satisfies the Aristotelian Principle; and (2) finding our person and deeds appreciated and confirmed by others who are likewise esteemed and their association enjoyed. I assume then that someone's plan of life will lack a certain attraction for him if it fails to call upon his natural capacities in an interesting fashion. When activities fail to satisfy the Aristotelian Principle, they are likely to seem dull and flat, and to give us no feeling of competence or a sense that they are worth doing. A person tends to be more confident of his value when his abilities are both fully realized and organized in ways of suitable complexity and refinement.

But the companion effect of the Aristotelian Principle influences the extent to which others confirm and take pleasure in what we do.

For while it is true that unless our endeavors are appreciated by our associates it is impossible for us to maintain the conviction that they are worthwhile, it is also true that others tend to value them only if what we do elicits their admiration or gives them pleasure. Thus activities that display intricate and subtle talents, and manifest discrimination and refinement, are valued by both the person himself and those around him. Moreover the more someone experiences his own way of life as worth fulfilling, the more likely he is to welcome our attainments. One who is confident in himself is not grudging in the appreciation of others. Putting these remarks together, the conditions for persons respecting themselves and one another would seem to require that their common plans be both rational and complementary: they call upon their educated endowments and arouse in each a sense of mastery, and they fit together into one scheme of activity that all can appreciate and enjoy.

Now it may be thought that these stipulations cannot be generally satisfied. One might suppose that only in a limited association of highly gifted individuals united in the pursuit of common artistic, scientific, or social ends is anything of this sort possible. There would seem to be no way to establish an enduring basis of self-respect throughout society. Yet this surmise is mistaken. The application of the Aristotelian Principle is always relative to the individual and therefore to his natural assets and particular situation. It normally suffices that for each person there is some association (one or more) to which he belongs and within which the activities that are rational for him are publicly affirmed by others. In this way we acquire a sense that what we do in everyday life is worthwhile. Moreover, associative ties strengthen the second aspect of self-esteem, since they tend to reduce the likelihood of failure and to provide support against the sense of self-doubt when mishaps occur. To be sure, men have varying capacities and abilities, and what seems interesting and challenging to some will not seem so to others. Yet in a well-ordered society anyway, there are a variety of communities and associations, and the members of each have their own ideals appropriately matched to their aspirations and talents. Judged by the doctrine of perfectionism, the activities of many groups may not display a high degree of excellence. But no matter. What counts is that the internal life of these associations is suitably adjusted to the abilities and wants of those belonging to them, and provides a secure basis for the sense of worth of their members. The absolute level of achievement, even if it could be defined, is irrelevant. But in any case, as citizens we are to reject the standard of perfection as a political principle, and for the purposes of justice avoid any assessment of the relative value of one another's way of life (§ 50). Thus what is necessary is that there should be for each person at least one community of shared interests to which he belongs and where he finds his endeavors confirmed by his associates. And for the most part this assurance is sufficient whenever in public life citizens respect one another's ends and adjudicate their political claims in ways that also support their self-esteem. It is precisely this background condition that is maintained by the principles of justice. The parties in the original position do not adopt the principle of perfection, for rejecting this criterion prepares the way to recognize the good of all activities that fulfill the Aristotelian Principle (and are compatible with the principles of justice). This democracy in judging each other's aims is the foundation of self-respect in a well-ordered society.

Later on I shall relate these matters to the idea of social union and the place of the principles of justice in human good (§§ 79–82). Here I wish to discuss the connections between the primary good of self-respect, the excellences, and shame, and consider when shame is a moral as opposed to a natural emotion. Now we may characterize shame as the feeling that someone has when he experiences an injury to his self-respect or suffers a blow to his self-esteem. Shame is painful since it is the loss of a prized good. There is a distinction however between shame and regret that should be noted. The latter is a feeling occasioned by the loss of most any sort of good, as when we regret having done something either imprudently or inadvertently that resulted in harm to ourselves. In explaining regret we focus say on the opportunities missed or the means squandered. Yet we may also regret having done something that put us to shame, or even having failed to carry out a plan of life that established a basis for our self-esteem. Thus we may regret the lack of a sense of our own worth. Regret is the general feeling aroused by the loss or absence of what we think good for us, whereas shame is the emotion evoked by shocks to our self-respect, a special kind of good.

Now both regret and shame are self-regarding, but shame implies an especially intimate connection with our person and with those upon whom we depend to confirm the sense of our own worth.[26] Also, shame is sometimes a moral feeling, a principle of right being cited to account for it. We must find an explanation of these facts. Let us distinguish between things that are good primarily for us (for the one who possesses them) and attributes of our person that are good both for us and for others as well. These two classes are not exhaustive but they indicate the relevant contrast. Thus commodities and items of property (exclusive goods) are goods mainly for those who own them and have use of them, and for others only indirectly. On the other hand, imagination and wit, beauty and grace, and other natural assets and abilities of the person are goods for others too: they are enjoyed by our associates as well as ourselves when properly displayed and rightly exercised. They form the human means for complementary activities in which persons join together and take pleasure in their own and one another's realization of their nature. This class of goods constitutes the excellences: they are the characteristics and abilities of the person that it is rational for everyone (including ourselves) to want us to have. From our standpoint, the excellences are goods since they enable us to carry out a more satisfying plan of life enhancing our sense of mastery. At the same time these attributes are appreciated by those with whom we associate, and the pleasure they take in our person and in what we do supports our self-esteem. Thus the excellences are a condition of human flourishing; they are goods from everyone's point of view. These facts relate them to the con-

26. My definition of shame is close to William McDougall, *An Introduction to Social Psychology* (London, Methuen, 1908), pp. 124–128. On the connection between self-esteem and what I have called the Aristotelian Principle, I have followed White, "Ego and Reality in Psychoanalytic Theory," ch.7. On the relation of shame to guilt, I am indebted to Gerhart Piers and Milton Singer, *Shame and Guilt* (Springfield, Ill. Charles C. Thomas, 1953), though the setting of my discussion is quite different. See also Erik Erikson, "Identity and the Life Cycle," *Psychological Issues*, vol. 1 (1959), pp. 39–41, 65–70. For the intimacy of shame, see Stanley Cavell, "The Avoidance of Love," in *Must We Mean What We Say?* (New York, Charles Scribner's Sons, 1969), pp. 278, 286f.

ditions of self-respect, and account for their connection with our confidence in our own value.

Considering first natural shame, it arises not from a loss or absence of exclusive goods, or at least not directly, but from the injury to our self-esteem owing to our not having or failing to exercise certain excellences. The lack of things primarily good for us would be an occasion for regret but not for shame. Thus one may be ashamed of his appearance or slow-wittedness. Normally these attributes are not voluntary and so they do not render us blameworthy; yet given the tie between shame and self-respect, the reason for being downcast by them is straightforward. With these defects our way of life is often less fulfilling and we receive less appreciative support from others. Thus natural shame is aroused by blemishes in our person, or by acts and attributes indicative thereof, that manifest the loss or lack of properties that others as well as ourselves would find it rational for us to have. However, a qualification is necessary. It is our plan of life that determines what we feel ashamed of, and so feelings of shame are relative to our aspirations, to what we try to do and with whom we wish to associate.[27] Those with no musical ability do not strive to be musicians and feel no shame for this lack. Indeed it is no lack at all, not at least if satisfying associations can be formed by doing other things. Thus we should say that given our plan of life, we tend to be ashamed of those defects in our person and failures in our actions that indicate a loss or absence of the excellences essential to our carrying out our more important associative aims.

Turning now to moral shame, we have only to put together the account of the notion of a good person (in the previous section) and the remarks above concerning the nature of shame. Thus someone is liable to moral shame when he prizes as excellences of his person those virtues that his plan of life requires and is framed to encourage. He regards the virtues, or some of them anyway, as properties that his associates want in him and that he wants in himself. To possess these excellences and to express them in his actions are among his regulative aims and are felt to be a condition of his being valued and esteemed by those with whom he cares to asso-

27. See William James, *The Principles of Psychology,* vol. I (New York, 1890), pp. 309f.

ciate. Actions and traits that manifest or betray the absence of these attributes in his person are likely then to occasion shame, and so is the awareness or recollection of these defects. Since shame springs from a feeling of the diminishment of self, we must explain how moral shame can be so regarded. First of all, the Kantian interpretation of the original position means that the desire to do what is right and just is the main way for persons to express their nature as free and equal rational beings. And from the Aristotelian Principle it follows that this expression of their nature is a fundamental element of their good. Combined with the account of moral worth, we have, then, that the virtues are excellences. They are good from the standpoint of ourselves as well as from that of others. The lack of them will tend to undermine both our self-esteem and the esteem that our associates have for us. Therefore indications of these faults will wound one's self-respect with accompanying feelings of shame.

It is instructive to observe the differences between the feelings of moral shame and guilt. Although both may be occasioned by the same action, they do not have the same explanation (§73). Imagine for example someone who cheats or gives in to cowardice and then feels both guilty and ashamed. He feels guilty because he has acted contrary to his sense of right and justice. By wrongly advancing his interests he has transgressed the rights of others, and his feelings of guilt will be more intense if he has ties of friendship and association to the injured parties. He expects others to be resentful and indignant at his conduct, and he fears their righteous anger and the possibility of reprisal. Yet he also feels ashamed because his conduct shows that he has failed to achieve the good of self-command, and he has been found unworthy of his associates upon whom he depends to confirm his sense of his own worth. He is apprehensive lest they reject him and find him contemptible, an object of ridicule. In his behavior he has betrayed a lack of the moral excellences he prizes and to which he aspires.

We see, then, that being excellences of our person which we bring to the affairs of social life, all of the virtues may be sought and their absence may render us liable to shame. But some virtues are joined to shame in a special way, since they are peculiarly indicative of the failure to achieve self-command and its attendant

445

excellences of strength, courage, and self-control. Wrongs manifesting the absence of these qualities are especially likely to subject us to painful feelings of shame. Thus while the principles of right and justice are used to describe the actions disposing us to feel both moral shame and guilt, the perspective is different in each case. In the one we focus on the infringement of the just claims of others and the injury we have done to them, and on their probable resentment or indignation should they discover our deed. Whereas in the other we are struck by the loss to our self-esteem and our inability to carry out our aims: we sense the diminishment of self from our anxiety about the lesser respect that others may have for us and from our disappointment with ourself for failing to live up to our ideals. Moral shame and guilt, it is clear, both involve our relations to others, and each is an expression of our acceptance of the first principles of right and justice. Nevertheless, these emotions occur within different points of view, our circumstances being seen in contrasting ways.

68. SEVERAL CONTRASTS BETWEEN THE RIGHT AND THE GOOD

In order to bring out the structural features of the contract view, I shall now mention several contrasts between the concepts of the right and the good. Since these concepts enable us to explain moral worth, they are the two fundamental concepts of the theory. The structure of an ethical doctrine depends upon how it relates these two notions and defines their differences. The distinctive features of justice as fairness can be shown by noting these points.

One difference is that whereas the principles of justice (and the principles of right generally) are those that would be chosen in the original position, the principles of rational choice and the criteria of deliberative rationality are not chosen at all. The first task in the theory of justice is to define the initial situation so that the principles that result express the correct conception of justice from a philosophical point of view. This means that the typical features of this situation should represent reasonable constraints on arguments for accepting principles and that the principles agreed to should match our considered convictions of justice in reflective equilibrium. Now, the analogous problem for the theory of the good does not arise. There is, to begin with, no necessity for an agreement upon the principles of rational choice. Since each person is free to plan his life as he pleases (so long as his intentions are consistent with the principles of justice), unanimity concerning the standards of rationality is not required. All the theory of justice assumes is that, in the thin account of the good, the evident criteria of rational choice are sufficient to explain the preference for the primary goods, and that such variations as exist in conceptions of rationality do not affect the principles of justice adopted in the original position.

Nevertheless, I have assumed that human beings do recognize certain principles and that these standards may be taken by enumeration to replace the notion of rationality. We can, if we wish, allow certain variations in the list. Thus there is disagreement as to the best way to deal with uncertainty.[28] There is no reason, though, why individuals in making their plans should not be thought of as following their inclinations in this case. Therefore any principle of choice under uncertainty which seems plausible can be added to the list, so long as decisive arguments against it are not forthcoming. It is only in the thin theory of the good that we have to worry about these matters. Here the notion of rationality must be interpreted so that the general desire for the primary goods can be established and the choice of the principles of justice demonstrated. But even in this case, I have suggested that the conception of justice adopted is insensitive with respect to conflicting interpretations of rationality. But in any event, once the principles of justice are chosen, and we are working within the full theory, there is no need to set up the account of the good so as to force unanimity on all the standards of the rational choice. In fact, it would contradict the freedom of choice that justice as fairness assures to individuals and groups within the framework of just institutions.

A second contrast between the right and the good is that it is, in general, a good thing that individuals' conceptions of their good should differ in significant ways, whereas this is not so for conceptions of right. In a well-ordered society citizens hold the same prin-

28. See the discussion in R. D. Luce and Howard Raiffa, *Games and Decisions* (New York, John Wiley and Sons, 1957), pp. 278–306.

ciples of right and they try to reach the same judgment in particular cases. These principles are to establish a final ordering among the conflicting claims that persons make upon one another and it is essential that this ordering be identifiable from everyone's point of view, however difficult it may be in practice for everyone to accept it. On the other hand, individuals find their good in different ways, and many things may be good for one person that would not be good for another. Moreover, there is no urgency to reach a publicly accepted judgment as to what is the good of particular individuals. The reasons that make such an agreement necessary in questions of justice do not obtain for judgments of value. Even when we take up another's point of view and attempt to estimate what would be to his advantage, we do so as an adviser, so to speak. We try to put ourselves in the other's place, and imagining that we have his aims and wants, we attempt to see things from his standpoint. Cases of paternalism aside, our judgment is offered when it is asked for, but there is no conflict of right if our advice is disputed and our opinion is not acted upon.

In a well-ordered society, then, the plans of life of individuals are different in the sense that these plans give prominence to different aims, and persons are left free to determine their good, the views of others being counted as merely advisory. Now this variety in conceptions of the good is itself a good thing, that is, it is rational for members of a well-ordered society to want their plans to be different. The reasons for this are obvious. Human beings have various talents and abilities the totality of which is unrealizable by any one person or group of persons. Thus we not only benefit from the complementary nature of our developed inclinations but we take pleasure in one another's activities. It is as if others were bringing forth a part of ourselves that we have not been able to cultivate. We have had to devote ourselves to other things, to only a small part of what we might have done (§ 79). But the situation is quite otherwise with justice: here we require not only common principles but sufficiently similar ways of applying them in particular cases so that a final ordering of conflicting claims can be defined. Judgments of justice are advisory only in special circumstances.

The third difference is that many applications of the principles of justice are restricted by the veil of ignorance, whereas evaluations

448

of a person's good may rely upon a full knowledge of the facts. Thus, as we have seen, not only must the principles of justice be chosen in the absence of certain kinds of particular information, but when these principles are used in designing constitutions and basic social arrangements, and in deciding between laws and policies, we are subject to similar although not as strict limitations. The delegates to a constitutional convention, and ideal legislators and voters, are also required to take up a point of view in which they know only the appropriate general facts. An individual's conception of his good, on the other hand, is to be adjusted from the start to his particular situation. A rational plan of life takes into account our special abilities, interests, and circumstances, and therefore it quite properly depends upon our social position and natural assets. There is no objection to fitting rational plans to these contingencies, since the principles of justice have already been chosen and constrain the content of these plans, the ends that they encourage and the means that they use. But in judgments of justice, it is only at the judicial and administrative stage that all restrictions on information are dropped, and particular cases are to be decided in view of all the relevant facts.

In the light of these contrasts we may further clarify an important difference between the contract doctrine and utilitarianism. Since the principle of utility is to maximize the good understood as the satisfaction of rational desire, we are to take as given existing preferences and the possibilities of their continuation into the future, and then to strive for the greatest net balance of satisfaction. But as we have seen, the determination of rational plans is indeterminate in important ways (§ 64). The more evident and easily applied principles of rational choice do not specify the best plan; a great deal remains to be decided. This indeterminacy is no difficulty for justice as fairness, since the details of plans do not affect in any way what is right or just. Our way of life, whatever our particular circumstances, must always conform to the principles of justice that are arrived at independently. Thus the arbitrary features of plans of life do not affect these principles, or how the basic structure is to be arranged. The indeterminacy in the notion of rationality does not translate itself into legitimate claims that men can impose on one another. The priority of the right prevents this.

The utilitarian, on the other hand, must concede the theoretical possibility that configurations of preferences allowed by this indeterminacy may lead to injustice as ordinarily understood. For example, assume that the larger part of society has an abhorrence for certain religious or sexual practices, and regards them as an abomination. This feeling is so intense that it is not enough that these practices be kept from the public view; the very thought that these things are going on is enough to arouse the majority to anger and hatred. Even when these attitudes are unsupportable on moral grounds, there appears to be no sure way to exclude them as irrational. Seeking the greatest satisfaction of desire may, then, justify harsh repressive measures against actions that cause no social injury. To defend individual liberty in this case the utilitarian has to show that given the circumstances the real balance of advantages in the long run still lies on the side of freedom; and this argument may or may not be successful.

In justice as fairness, however, this problem never arises. The intense convictions of the majority, if they are indeed mere preferences without any foundation in the principles of justice antecedently established, have no weight to begin with. The satisfaction of these feelings has no value that can be put in the scales against the claims of equal liberty. To have a complaint against the conduct and belief of others we must show that their actions injure us, or that the institutions that authorize what they do treat us unjustly. And this means that we must appeal to the principles that we would acknowledge in the original position. Against these principles neither the intensity of feeling nor its being shared by the majority counts for anything. On the contract view, then, the grounds of liberty are completely separate from existing preferences. Indeed, we may think of the principles of justice as an agreement not to take into account certain feelings when assessing the conduct of others. As I noted before (§ 50), these points are familiar elements of the classical liberal doctrine. I have mentioned them again in order to show that the indeterminacy in the full theory of the good is no cause for objection. It may leave a person unsettled as to what to do, since it cannot provide him with instructions as to how to decide. But since the aim of justice is not to maximize the fulfillment of rational plans, the content of justice is not in any way affected. Of course, it cannot be denied that prevailing social attitudes tie the statesman's hands. The convictions and passions of the majority may make liberty impossible to maintain. But bowing to these practical necessities is a different thing from accepting the justification that if these feelings are strong enough and outweigh in intensity any feelings that might replace them, they should carry the decision. By contrast, the contract view requires that we move toward just institutions as speedily as the circumstances permit irrespective of existing sentiments. A definite scheme of ideal institutions is embedded in its principles of justice (§ 41).

It is evident from these contrasts that in justice as fairness the concepts of the right and the good have markedly distinct features. These differences arise from the structure of contract theory and the priority of right and justice that results. I do not suggest, however, that the terms "right" and "good" (and their relatives) are normally used in ways that reflect these distinctions. Although our ordinary speech may tend to support the account of these concepts, this correspondence is not needed for the correctness of the contract doctrine. Rather, two things suffice. First, there is a way of mapping our considered judgments into the theory of justice such that in reflective equilibrium the counterparts of these convictions turn out to be true, to express judgments that we can accept. And second, once we understand the theory, we can acknowledge these interpretations as suitable renderings of what on reflection we now wish to maintain. Even though we would not normally use these replacements, perhaps because they are too cumbersome, or would be misunderstood, or whatever, we are prepared to grant that they cover in substance all that wants to be said. Certainly these substitutes may not mean the same as the ordinary judgments with which they are paired. How far this is the case is a question that I shall not examine. Moreover, the replacements may indicate a shift more or less drastic from our initial moral judgments as they existed prior to philosophical reflection. Some changes anyway are bound to have taken place as philosophical criticism and construction lead us to revise and extend our views.

But what counts is whether the conception of justice as fairness, better than any other theory presently known to us, turns out to lead to true interpretations of our considered judgments, and provides a mode of expression for what we want to affirm.

CHAPTER VIII. THE SENSE OF JUSTICE

Having presented an account of the good, I now turn to the problem of stability. I shall treat it in two stages. In this chapter I discuss the acquisition of the sense of justice by the members of a well-ordered society, and I consider briefly the relative strength of this sentiment when defined by different moral conceptions. The final chapter examines the question of congruence, that is, whether the sense of justice coheres with the conception of our good so that both work together to uphold a just scheme. It is well to keep in mind that much of this chapter is preparation and that various topics are touched upon only to indicate the more basic points that are relevant for the philosophical theory. I begin with a definition of a well-ordered society and with some brief remarks about the meaning of stability. Then I sketch the development of the sense of justice as it presumably would take place once just institutions are firmly established and recognized to be just. The principles of moral psychology also receive some discussion; I emphasize the fact that they are reciprocity principles and connect this with the question of relative stability. The chapter concludes with an examination of the natural attributes in virtue of which human beings are owed the guarantees of equal justice, and which define the natural basis of equality.

69. THE CONCEPT OF A WELL-ORDERED SOCIETY

At the beginning (§1) I characterized a well-ordered society as one designed to advance the good of its members and effectively regulated by a public conception of justice. Thus it is a society in which everyone accepts and knows that the others accept the same principles of justice, and the basic social institutions satisfy and are known to satisfy these principles. Now justice as fairness is framed to accord with this idea of society. The persons in the original position are to assume that the principles chosen are public, and so they must assess conceptions of justice in view of their probable effects as the generally recognized standards (§ 23). Conceptions that might work out well enough if understood and followed by a few or even by all, so long as this fact were not widely known, are excluded by the publicity condition. We should also note that since principles are consented to in the light of true general beliefs about men and their place in society, the conception of justice adopted is acceptable on the basis of these facts. There is no necessity to invoke theological or metaphysical doctrines to support its principles, nor to imagine another world that compensates for and corrects the inequalities which the two principles permit in this one. Conceptions of justice must be justified by the conditions of our life as we know it or not at all.[1]

Now a well-ordered society is also regulated by its public conception of justice. This fact implies that its members have a strong and normally effective desire to act as the principles of justice require. Since a well-ordered society endures over time, its conception of justice is presumably stable: that is, when institutions are just (as defined by this conception), those taking part in these arrangements acquire the corresponding sense of justice and desire to do their part in maintaining them. One conception of justice is more stable than another if the sense of justice that it tends to generate is stronger and more likely to override disruptive inclinations and if the institutions it allows foster weaker impulses and temptations to act unjustly. The stability of a conception depends upon a balance of motives: the sense of justice that it cultivates and the aims that it encourages must normally win out against propensities toward injustice. To estimate the stability of a conception of jus-

---

1. It follows that such devices as Plato's Noble Lie in the *Republic*, bk. III, 414–415, are ruled out, as well as the advocacy of religion (when not believed) to buttress a social system that could not otherwise survive, as by the Grand Inquisitor in Dostoevsky's *The Brothers Karamazov*.

tice (and the well-ordered society that it defines), one must examine the relative strength of these opposing tendencies.

It is evident that stability is a desirable feature of moral conceptions. Other things equal, the persons in the original position will adopt the more stable scheme of principles. However attractive a conception of justice might be on other grounds, it is seriously defective if the principles of moral psychology are such that it fails to engender in human beings the requisite desire to act upon it. Thus in arguing further for the principles of justice as fairness, I should like to show that this conception is more stable than other alternatives. This argument from stability is for the most part in addition to the reasons so far adduced (except for considerations presented in § 29). I wish to consider this notion in more detail both for its own sake and to prepare the way for the discussion of other matters such as the basis of equality and the priority of liberty.

To be sure, the criterion of stability is not decisive. In fact, some ethical theories have flouted it entirely, at least on some interpretations. Thus Bentham is occasionally said to have held both the classical principle of utility and the doctrine of psychological egoism. But if it is a psychological law that individuals pursue only interests in themselves, it is impossible for them to have an effective sense of justice (as defined by the principle of utility). The best that the ideal legislator can do is to design social arrangements so that from self- or group-interested motives citizens are persuaded to act in ways that maximize the sum of well-being. In this conception the identification of interests that results is truly artificial: it rests upon the artifice of reason, and individuals comply with the institutional scheme solely as a means to their separate concerns.[2]

This sort of divergence between principles of right and justice and human motives is unusual, although instructive as a limiting

2. While Bentham is sometimes interpreted as a psychological egoist, he is not by Jacob Viner, "Bentham and J.S. Mill: The Utilitarian Background" (1949), reprinted in *The Long View and the Short* (Glencoe, Ill., Free Press, 1958); see pp. 312–314. Viner also gives what must be the correct rendering of Bentham's conception of the role of the legislator, pp. 316–319.

case. Most traditional doctrines hold that to some degree at least human nature is such that we acquire a desire to act justly when we have lived under and benefited from just institutions. To the extent that this is true, a conception of justice is psychologically suited to human inclinations. Moreover, should it turn out that the desire to act justly is also regulative of a rational plan of life, then acting justly is part of our good. In this event the conceptions of justice and goodness are compatible and the theory as a whole is congruent. The task of this chapter is to explain how justice as fairness generates its own support and to show that it is likely to have greater stability than the traditional alternatives, since it is more in line with the principles of moral psychology. To this end, I shall describe briefly how human beings in a well-ordered society might acquire a sense of justice and the other moral sentiments. Inevitably we shall have to take up some rather speculative psychological questions; but all along I have assumed that general facts about the world, including basic psychological principles, are known to the persons in the original position and relied upon by them in making their decisions. By reflecting on these problems here we survey these facts as they affect the initial agreement.

It may prevent misunderstanding if I make a few remarks about the concepts of equilibrium and stability. Both of these ideas admit of considerable theoretical and mathematical refinement but I shall use them in an intuitive way.[3] The first thing to note perhaps is that they are applied to systems of some kind. Thus it is a system that is in equilibrium, and it is so when it has reached a state that persists indefinitely over time so long as no external forces impinge upon it. In order to define an equilibrium state

3. For the notions of equilibrium and stability applied to systems, see, for example, W. R. Ashby, *Design for a Brain,* 2nd ed. revised (London, Chapman and Hall, 1960), chs. 2–4, 19–20. The concept of stability I use is actually that of quasi-stability: if an equilibrium is stable, then all the variables return to their equilibrium values after a disturbance has moved the system away from equilibrium; a quasi-stable equilibrium is one in which only some of the variables return to their equilibrium configuration. For this definition, see Harvey Leibenstein, *Economic Backwardness and Economic Growth* (New York, John Wiley and Sons, 1957), p. 18. A well-ordered society is quasi-stable with respect to the justice of its institutions and the sense of justice needed to maintain this condition. While a shift in social circumstances may render its institutions no longer just, in due course they are reformed as the situation requires, and justice is restored.

precisely, the boundaries of the system have to be carefully drawn and its determining characteristics clearly set out. Three things are essential: first, to identify the system and to distinguish between internal and external forces; second, to define the states of the system, a state being a certain configuration of its determining characteristics; and third, to specify the laws connecting the states.

Some systems have no equilibrium states, while others have many. These matters depend upon the nature of the system. Now an equilibrium is stable whenever departures from it, caused say by external disturbances, call into play forces within the system that tend to bring it back to this equilibrium state, unless of course the outside shocks are too great. By contrast, an equilibrium is unstable when a movement away from it arouses forces within the system that lead to even greater changes. Systems are more or less stable depending upon the strength of the internal forces that are available to return them to equilibrium. Since in practice all social systems are subject to disturbances of some kind, they are practically stable, let us say, if the departures from their preferred equilibrium positions caused by normal disturbances elicit forces sufficiently strong to restore these equilibria after a decent length of time, or else to stay sufficiently close to them. These definitions are unhappily vague but they should serve our purposes.

The relevant systems here, of course, are the basic structures of the well-ordered societies corresponding to the different conceptions of justice. We are concerned with this complex of political, economic, and social institutions when it satisfies, and is publicly known by those engaged in it to satisfy, the appropriate principles of justice. We must try to assess the relative stability of these systems. Now I assume that the boundaries of these schemes are given by the notion of a self-contained national community. This supposition is not relaxed until the derivation of the principles of justice for the law of nations (§ 58), but the wider problems of international law I shall not further discuss. It is also essential to note that in the present case equilibrium and stability are to be defined with respect to the justice of the basic structure and the moral conduct of individuals. The stability of a conception of justice does not imply that the institutions and practices of the well-ordered society do not alter. In fact, such a society will presumably contain great diversity and adopt different arrangements from time to time. In this context stability means that however institutions are changed, they still remain just or approximately so, as adjustments are made in view of new social circumstances. The inevitable deviations from justice are effectively corrected or held within tolerable bounds by forces within the system. Among these forces I assume that the sense of justice shared by the members of the community has a fundamental role. To some degree, then, moral sentiments are necessary to insure that the basic structure is stable with respect to justice.

I now turn to how these sentiments are formed, and on this question there are, broadly speaking, two main traditions. The first stems historically from the doctrine of empiricism and is found in the utilitarians from Hume to Sidgwick. In its most recent and developed form it is represented by social learning theory. One main contention is that the aim of moral training is to supply missing motives: the desire to do what is right for its own sake, and the desire not to do what is wrong. Right conduct is conduct generally beneficial to others and to society (as defined by the principle of utility) for the doing of which we commonly lack an effective motive, whereas wrong conduct is behavior generally injurious to others and to society for the doing of which we often have a sufficient motive. Society must somehow make good these defects. This is achieved by the approbation and disapprobation of parents and of others in authority, who when necessary use rewards and punishments ranging from bestowal and withdrawal of affection to the administration of pleasures and pains. Eventually by various psychological processes we acquire a desire to do what is right and an aversion to doing what is wrong. A second thesis is that the desire to conform to moral standards is normally aroused early in life before we achieve an adequate understanding of the reasons for these norms. Indeed some persons may never grasp the grounds for them in the utilitarian principle.[4] The conse-

4. This sketch of moral learning draws from James Mill, the section of the *Fragment on Mackintosh* which J. S. Mill included in a footnote to ch. XXIII of his father's *Analysis of the Phenomena of the Human Mind* (1869). The passage is in [J. S.] *Mill's Ethical Writings*, ed. J. B. Schneewind (New York, Collier Books, 1965), pp. 259–270. For an account of social learning theory, see Albert Bandura, *Principles of Behavior Modification* (New York, Holt, Rinehart, and Winston, 1969).

quence is that our subsequent moral sentiments are likely to bear the scars of this early training which shapes more or less roughly our original nature.

Freud's theory is similar in important respects to this view. He holds that the processes by which the child comes to have moral attitudes center around the oedipal situation and the deep conflicts to which it gives rise. The moral precepts insisted upon by those in authority (in this case the parents) are accepted by the child as the best way to resolve his anxieties, and the resulting attitudes represented by the superego are likely to be harsh and punitive reflecting the stresses of the oedipal phase.[5] Thus Freud's account supports the two points that an essential part of moral learning occurs early in life before a reasoned basis for morality can be understood, and that it involves the acquisition of new motives by psychological processes marked by conflict and stress. Indeed, his doctrine is a dramatic illustration of these features. It follows that since parents and others in authority are bound to be in various ways misguided and self-seeking in their use of praise and blame, and rewards and punishments generally, our earlier and unexamined moral attitudes are likely to be in important respects irrational and without justification. Moral advance in later life consists partly in correcting these attitudes in the light of whatever principles we finally acknowledge to be sound.

The other tradition of moral learning derives from rationalist thought and is illustrated by Rousseau and Kant, and sometimes by J. S. Mill, and more recently by the theory of Piaget. Moral learning is not so much a matter of supplying missing motives as one of the free development of our innate intellectual and emotional capacities according to their natural bent. Once the powers of understanding mature and persons come to recognize their place in society and are able to take up the standpoint of others, they

---

For a recent survey of moral learning, see Roger Brown, *Social Psychology* (New York, The Free Press, 1965), ch. VIII; and Martin L. Hoffman, "Moral Development," in *Carmichael's Manual of Psychology,* ed. Paul H. Mussen, 3rd ed. (New York, John Wiley and Sons, 1970), vol. 2, ch. 23; pp. 282–332 is on social learning theory.

5. For accounts of Freud's theory of moral learning, see Roger Brown, *Social Psychology,* pp. 350–381; and Ronald Fletcher, *Instinct in Man* (New York, International Universities Press, 1957), ch. VI, esp. pp. 226–234.

appreciate the mutual benefits of establishing fair terms of social cooperation. We have a natural sympathy with other persons and an innate susceptibility to the pleasures of fellow feeling and self-mastery, and these provide the affective basis for the moral sentiments once we have a clear grasp of our relations to our associates from an appropriately general perspective. Thus this tradition regards the moral feelings as a natural outgrowth of a full appreciation of our social nature.[6]

Mill expresses the view as follows: the arrangements of a just society are so suited to us that anything which is obviously necessary for it is accepted much like a physical necessity. An indispensable condition of such a society is that all shall have consideration for the others on the basis of mutually acceptable principles of reciprocity. It is painful for us when our feelings are not in union with those of our fellows; and this tendency to sociality provides in due course a firm basis for the moral sentiments. Moreover, Mill adds, to be held accountable to the principles of justice in one's dealings with others does not stunt our nature. Instead it realizes our social sensibilities and by exposing us to a larger good enables us to control our narrower impulses. It is only when we are restrained not because we injure the good of others but by their mere displeasure, or what seems to us their arbitrary authority, that our nature is blunted. If the reasons for moral injunctions are made plain in terms of the just claims of others, these constraints do us no injury but are seen to be compatible with our good.[7] Moral learning is not so much a matter of acquir-

6. For Rousseau, see *Emile*, trans. Barbara Foxley (London, J. M. Dent and Sons, 1908), esp. pp. 46–66 (in bk. II), 172–196, 244–258 (in bk. IV); for Kant, *The Critique of Practical Reason*, pt. II, with the misleading name: The Methodology of Pure Practical Reason; and J. S. Mill as cited below, note 7. For Jean Piaget, see *The Moral Judgment of the Child*, trans. Majorie Gabain (London, Kegan Paul, Trench, Trubner, 1932). Further development of this approach is found in Lawrence Kohlberg; see "The Development of Children's Orientation toward a Moral Order: 1. Sequence in the Development of Moral Thought," *Vita Humana*, vol. 6 (1963); and "Stage and Sequence: The Cognitive Developmental Approach to Socialization," in *Handbook of Socialization Theory and Research*, ed. D. A. Goslin (Chicago, Rand McNally, 1969), ch. VI. For a critique, see Hoffman, "Moral Development," pp. 264–275 (on Piaget), pp. 276–281 (on Kohlberg).

7. For Mill's view, see *Utilitarianism*, chs. III and V, pars. 16–25; *On Liberty*, ch. III, par. 10; and *Mill's Ethical Writings*, ed. J. B. Schneewind, pp. 257–259.

ing new motives, for these will come about of themselves once the requisite developments in our intellectual and emotional capacities has taken place. It follows that a full grasp of moral conceptions must await maturity; the child's understanding is always primitive and the characteristic features of his morality fall away in later stages. The rationalist tradition presents a happier picture, since it holds that the principles of right and justice spring from our nature and are not at odds with our good, whereas the other account would seem to include no such guarantee.

I shall not try to assess the relative merits of these two conceptions of moral learning. Surely there is much that is sound in both and it seems preferable to try to combine them in a natural way. It must be emphasized that a moral view is an extremely complex structure of principles, ideals, and precepts, and involves all the elements of thought, conduct, and feeling. Certainly many kinds of learning ranging from reinforcement and classical conditioning to highly abstract reasoning and the refined perception of exemplars enter into its development. Presumably at some time or other each has a necessary role. In the next several sections (§§ 70–72) I sketch the course of moral development as it might occur in a well-ordered society realizing the principles of justice as fairness. I am concerned solely with this special case. Thus my aim is to indicate the major steps whereby a person would acquire an understanding of and an attachment to the principles of justice as he grows up in this particular form of well-ordered society. These steps I take to be identified by the main structural features of the complete scheme of principles, ideals, and precepts, as these are applied to social arrangements. As I shall explain, we are led to distinguish between the moralities of authority, of association, and of principles. The account of moral development is tied throughout to the conception of justice which is to be learned, and therefore presupposes the plausibility if not the correctness of this theory.[8]

8. While the view of moral development to follow in §§70–72 is designed to fit the theory of justice, I have borrowed from several sources. The idea of three stages the content of which is given by precepts, role ideals, and principles is similar to William McDougall, *An Introduction to Social Psychology* (London, Methuen, 1908), chs. VII–VIII. Piaget's *The Moral Judgment of the Child* suggested to me the contrast between the morality of authority and the moralities of association and principles, and much of the description of these stages. See also Kohlberg's further elaboration

A caveat is apropos here similar to that I made before in regard to the remarks on economic theory (§42). We want the psychological account of moral learning to be true and in accordance with existing knowledge. But of course it is impossible to take the details into account; I sketch at best only the main outlines. One must keep in mind that the purpose of the following discussion is to examine the question of stability and to contrast the psychological roots of the various conceptions of justice. The crucial point is how the general facts of moral psychology affect the choice of principles in the original position. Unless the psychological account is defective in a way that would call into question the acknowledgment of the principles of justice rather than the standard of utility, say, no irreparable difficulty should ensue. I also hope that none of the further uses of psychological theory will prove too wide of the mark. Particularly important among these is the account of the basis of equality.

70. THE MORALITY OF AUTHORITY

The first stage in the sequence of moral development I shall refer to as the morality of authority. While certain aspects of this morality are preserved at later stages for special occasions, we can regard the morality of authority in its primitive form as that of the child. I assume that the sense of justice is acquired gradually by the younger members of society as they grow up. The succession of generations and the necessity to teach moral attitudes (however simple) to children is one of the conditions of human life.

Now I shall assume that the basic structure of a well-ordered

---

of this type of theory in the references cited in note 6 above, esp. pp. 369–389, on his six stages. In the last several paragraphs of §75 I note some differences between the view I present and these writers. Concerning Kohlberg's theory, I should add here that I believe the morality of association is parallel to his stages three to five. Development within this stage is being able to assume more complex, demanding, and comprehensive roles. But more important, I assume that the final stage, the morality of principles, may have different contents given by any of the traditional philosophical doctrines we have discussed. It is true that I argue for the theory of justice as superior, and work out the psychological theory on this presumption; but this superiority is a philosophical question and cannot, I believe, be established by the psychological theory of development alone.

society includes the family in some form, and therefore that children are at first subject to the legitimate authority of their parents. Of course, in a broader inquiry the institution of the family might be questioned, and other arrangements might indeed prove to be preferable. But presumably the account of the morality of authority could, if necessary, be adjusted to fit these different schemes. In any event, it is characteristic of the child's situation that he is not in a position to assess the validity of the precepts and injunctions addressed to him by those in authority, in this case his parents. He lacks both the knowledge and the understanding on the basis of which their guidance can be challenged. Indeed, the child lacks the concept of justification altogether, this being acquired much later. Therefore he cannot with reason doubt the propriety of parental injunctions. But since we are assuming that the society is well-ordered we may suppose, so as to avoid needless complications, that these precepts are on the whole justified. They accord with a reasonable interpretation of familial duties as defined by the principles of justice.

The parents, we may suppose, love the child and in time the child comes to love and to trust his parents. How does this change in the child come about? To answer this question I assume the following psychological principle: the child comes to love the parents only if they manifestly first love him.[9] Thus the child's actions are motivated initially by certain instincts and desires, and his aims are regulated (if at all) by rational self-interest (in a suitably restricted sense). Although the child has the potentiality for love, his love of the parents is a new desire brought about by his recognizing their evident love of him and his benefiting from the actions in which their love is expressed.

The parents' love of the child is expressed in their evident intention to care for him, to do for him as his rational self-love would incline, and in the fulfillment of these intentions. Their love is displayed by their taking pleasure in his presence and supporting his sense of competence and self-esteem. They encourage his ef-

9. The formulation of this psychological law is drawn from Rousseau's *Emile*, p. 174. Rousseau says that while we like from the start what contributes to our preservation, this attachment is quite unconscious and instinctive. "Ce que transforme cet instinct en sentiment, l'attachement en amour, l'aversion en haine, c'est l'intention manifestée de nous nuire ou de nous être utile."

forts to master the tasks of growing up and they welcome his assuming his own place. In general, to love another means not only to be concerned for his wants and needs, but to affirm his sense of the worth of his own person. Eventually, then, the love of the parents for the child gives rise to his love in return. The child's love does not have a rational instrumental explanation: he does not love them as a means to achieve his initial self-interested ends. With this aim in view he could conceivably act as if he loved them, but his doing so would not constitute a transformation of his original desires. By the stated psychological principle, a new affection is in time called into being by the evident love of the parents.

There are several ways in which this psychological law may be analyzed into further elements. Thus it is unlikely that the child's recognition of parental affection causes directly a returning sentiment. We may conjecture several other steps as follows: when the parents' love of the child is recognized by him on the basis of their evident intentions, the child is assured of his worth as a person. He is made aware that he is appreciated for his own sake by what are to him the imposing and powerful persons in his world. He experiences parental affection as unconditional; they care for his presence and spontaneous acts, and the pleasure they take in him is not dependent upon disciplined performances that contribute to the well-being of others. In due course, the child comes to trust his parents and to have confidence in his surroundings; and this leads him to launch out and to test his maturing abilities, all the while supported by their affection and encouragement. Gradually he acquires various skills and develops a sense of competence that affirms his self-esteem. It is in the course of this whole process that the child's affection for his parents develops. He connects them with the success and enjoyment that he has had in sustaining his world, and with his sense of his own worth. And this brings about his love for them.

We must now consider how the child's love and trust will show itself. At this point it is necessary to keep in mind the peculiar features of the authority situation. The child does not have his own standards of criticism, since he is not in a position to reject precepts on rational grounds. If he loves and trusts his parents, he will tend to accept their injunctions. He will also strive to be like them, assuming that they are indeed worthy of esteem and adhere to the precepts which they enjoin. They exemplify, let us suppose, superior knowledge and power, and set forth appealing examples of what is demanded. The child, therefore, accepts their judgment of him and he will be inclined to judge himself as they do when he violates their injunctions. At the same time, of course, his desires exceed the bonds of what is permitted, for otherwise there would be no need for these precepts. Thus parental norms are experienced as constraints and the child may rebel against them. After all, he may see no reason why he should comply with them; they are in themselves arbitrary prohibitions and he has no original tendency to do the things he is told to do. Yet if he does love and trust his parents, then, once he has given in to temptation, he is disposed to share their attitude toward his misdemeanors. He will be inclined to confess his transgression and to seek reconciliation. In these various inclinations are manifested the feelings of (authority) guilt. Without these and related inclinations, feelings of guilt would not exist. But it is also true that the absence of these feelings would indicate a lack of love and trust. For given the nature of the authority situation and the principles of moral psychology connecting the ethical and the natural attitudes, love and trust will give rise to feelings of guilt once the parental injunctions are disobeyed. Admittedly in the case of the child it is sometimes difficult to distinguish feelings of guilt from the fear of punishment, and especially from the dread of the loss of parental love and affection. The child lacks the concepts for understanding moral distinctions and this will reflect itself in his behavior. I have supposed, however, that even in the child's case we can separate (authority) guilt feelings from fear and anxiety.

In the light of this sketch of the development of the morality of authority, it seems that the conditions favoring its being learned by the child are these.[10] First, the parents must love the child and be worthy objects of his admiration. In this way they arouse in him a sense of his own value and the desire to become the sort of person that they are. Secondly, they must enunciate clear and intelligible

10. Here I borrow and adapt from E. E. Maccoby, "Moral Values and Behavior in Childhood," in *Socialization and Society,* ed. J. A. Clausen (Boston, Little, Brown, 1968), and Hoffman, "Moral Development," pp. 282–319.

(and of course justifiable) rules adapted to the child's level of comprehension. In addition they should set out the reasons for these injunctions so far as these can be understood, and they must also follow these precepts insofar as they apply to them as well. The parents should exemplify the morality which they enjoin, and make explicit its underlying principles as time goes on. Doing this is required not only to arouse the child's inclination to accept these principles at a later time, but also to convey how they are to be interpreted in particular cases. Presumably moral development fails to take place to the extent that these conditions are absent, and especially if parental injunctions are not only harsh and unjustified, but enforced by punitive and even physical sanctions. The child's having a morality of authority consists in his being disposed without the prospect of reward or punishment to follow certain precepts that not only may appear to him largely arbitrary but which in no way appeal to his original inclinations. If he acquires the desire to abide by these prohibitions, it is because he sees them as addressed to him by powerful persons who have his love and trust, and who also act in conformity with them. He then concludes that they express forms of action that characterize the sort of person he should want to be. In the absence of affection, example, and guidance, none of these processes can take place, and certainly not in loveless relationships maintained by coercive threats and reprisals.

The child's morality of authority is primitive because for the most part it consists of a collection of precepts, and he cannot comprehend the larger scheme of right and justice within which the rules addressed to him are justified. But even a developed morality of authority in which the basis of the rules can be understood shows many of the same features, and contains similar virtues and vices. There is typically an authoritative person who is loved and trusted, or at least who is accepted as worthy of his position, and whose precepts it is one's duty to follow implicitly. It is not for us to consider the consequences, this being left for those in authority. The prized virtues are obedience, humility, and fidelity to authoritative persons; the leading vices are disobedience, self-will, and temerity. We are to do what is expected without questioning, for not so to act expresses doubt and distrust, and a certain arrogance and tendency to suspicion. Clearly the morality of authority must be subordinate to the principles of right and justice which alone can determine when these extreme requirements, or analogous constraints, are justified. The child's morality of authority is temporary, a necessity arising from his peculiar situation and limited understanding. Moreover, the theological parallel is a special case which, in view of the principle of equal liberty, does not apply to the basic structure of society (§ 33). Thus the morality of authority has but a restricted role in fundamental social arrangements and can be justified only when the unusual demands of the practice in question make it essential to give certain individuals the prerogatives of leadership and command. In all cases, the scope of this morality is governed by the principles of justice.

71. THE MORALITY OF ASSOCIATION

The second stage of moral development is that of the morality of association. This stage covers a wide range of cases depending on the association in question and it may even include the national community as a whole. Whereas the child's morality of authority consists largely of a collection of precepts, the content of the morality of association is given by the moral standards appropriate to the individual's role in the various associations to which he belongs. These standards include the common sense rules of morality along with the adjustments required to fit them to a person's particular position; and they are impressed upon him by the approval and disapproval of those in authority, or by the other members of the group. Thus at this stage the family itself is viewed as a small association, normally characterized by a definite hierarchy, in which each member has certain rights and duties. As the child becomes older he is taught the standards of conduct suitable for one in his station. The virtues of a good son or a good daughter are explained, or at least conveyed by parental expectations as shown in their approvals and disapprovals. Similarly there is the association of the school and the neighborhood, and also such short-term forms of cooperation, though not less important for this, as games and play with peers. Corresponding to these arrangements one learns the virtues of a good student and classmate, and the ideals of a good sport and companion. This type of moral view extends to the ideals adopted in later life, and so to one's various adult statuses and occupations, one's family position, and even to one's place as a member of society. The content of these ideals is given by the various conceptions of a good wife and husband, a good friend and citizen, and so on. Thus the morality of association includes a large number of ideals each defined in ways suitable for the respective status or role. Our moral understanding increases as we move in the course of life through a sequence of positions. The corresponding sequence of ideals requires increasingly greater intellectual judgment and finer moral discriminations. Clearly some of these ideals are also more comprehensive than others and make quite different demands upon the individual. As we shall see, having to follow certain ideals quite naturally leads up to a morality of principles.

Now each particular ideal is presumably explained in the context of the aims and purposes of the association to which the role or position in question belongs. In due course a person works out a conception of the whole system of cooperation that defines the association and the ends which it serves. He knows that others have different things to do depending upon their place in the cooperative scheme. Thus he eventually learns to take up their point of view and to see things from their perspective. It seems plausible, then, that acquiring a morality of association (represented by some structure of ideals) rests upon the development of the intellectual skills required to regard things from a variety of points of view and to think of these together as aspects of one system of cooperation. In fact, when we consider it, the requisite array of abilities is quite complex.[11] First of all, we must recognize that these different points of view exist, that the perspectives of others are not the same as ours. But we must not only learn that things look different to them, but that they have different wants

11. For the following remarks, I am indebted to John Flavell, *The Development of Role-Taking and Communication Skills in Children* (New York, John Wiley and Sons, 1968), pp. 208–211. See also G. H. Mead, *Mind, Self and Society* (Chicago, University of Chicago Press, 1934), pp. 135–164.

and ends, and different plans and motives; and we must learn how to gather these facts from their speech, conduct, and countenance. Next, we need to identify the definitive features of these perspectives, what it is that others largely want and desire, what are their controlling beliefs and opinions. Only in this way can we understand and assess their actions, intentions, and motives. Unless we can identify these leading elements, we cannot put ourselves into another's place and find out what we would do in his position. To work out these things, we must, of course, know what the other person's perspective really is. But finally, having understood another's situation, it still remains for us to regulate our own conduct in the appropriate way by reference to it.

Doing these things to a certain minimum degree at least comes easily to adults, but it is difficult for children. No doubt this explains in part why the precepts of the child's primitive morality of authority are usually expressed in terms referring to external behavior, and why motives and intentions are largely neglected by children in their appraisal of actions. The child has not yet mastered the art of perceiving the person of others, that is, the art of discerning their beliefs, intentions, and feelings, so that an awareness of these things cannot inform his interpretation of their behavior. Moreover, his ability to put himself in their place is still untutored and likely to lead him astray. It is no surprise, then, that these elements, so important from the final moral point of view, are left out of account at the earliest stage.[12] But this lack is gradually overcome as we assume a succession of more demanding roles with their more complex schemes of rights and duties. The corresponding ideals require us to view things from a greater multiplicity of perspectives as the conception of the basic structure implies.

I have touched upon these aspects of intellectual development for the sake of completeness. I cannot consider them in any detail, but we should note that they obviously have a central place in the acquisition of moral views. How well the art of perceiving the person is learned is bound to affect one's moral sensibility; and it is equally important to understand the intricacies of social coopera-

12. For a discussion of these points, see Roger Brown, *Social Psychology*, pp. 239–244.

tion. But these abilities are not sufficient. Someone whose designs are purely manipulative, and who wishes to exploit others for his own advantage, must likewise, if he lacks overwhelming force, possess these skills. The tricks of persuasion and gamesmanship call upon the same intellectual accomplishments. We must, then, examine how we become attached to our fellow associates and later to social arrangements generally. Consider the case of an association the public rules of which are known by all to be just. Now how does it come about that those taking part in the arrangement are bound by ties of friendship and mutual trust and that they rely on one another to do their part? We may suppose that these feelings and attitudes have been generated by participation in the association. Thus once a person's capacity for fellow feeling has been realized by his acquiring attachments in accordance with the first psychological law, then as his associates with evident intention live up to their duties and obligations, he develops friendly feelings toward them, together with feelings of trust and confidence. And this principle is a second psychological law. As individuals enter the association one by one over a period of time, or group by group (suitably limited in size), they acquire these attachments when others of longer standing membership do their part and live up to the ideals of their station. Thus if those engaged in a system of social cooperation regularly act with evident intention to uphold its just (or fair) rules, bonds of friendship and mutual trust tend to develop among them, thereby holding them ever more securely to the scheme.

Once these ties are established, a person tends to experience feelings of (association) guilt when he fails to do his part. These feelings show themselves in various ways, for example, in the inclination to make good the harms caused to others (reparation), if such harms have occurred, as well as in a willingness to admit that what one has done is unfair (wrong) and to apologize for it. Feelings of guilt are also manifest in conceding the propriety of punishment and censure, and in finding it more difficult to be angry and indignant with others when they likewise fail to do their share. The absence of these inclinations would betray an absence of ties of friendship and mutual trust. It would indicate a readiness to associate with others in disregard of the standards and criteria of legitimate expectations that are publicly recognized and used by all to adjudicate their disagreements. A person without these feelings of guilt has no qualms about the burdens that fall on others, nor is he troubled by the breaches of confidence by which they are deceived. But when relations of friendship and trust exist, such inhibitions and reactions tend to be aroused by the failure to fulfill one's duties and obligations. If these emotional constraints are missing, there is at best only a show of fellow feeling and mutual trust. Thus just as in the first stage certain natural attitudes develop toward the parents, so here ties of friendship and confidence grow up among associates. In each case certain natural attitudes underlie the corresponding moral feelings: a lack of these feelings would manifest the absence of these attitudes.

The second psychological law presumably takes hold in ways similar to the first. Since the arrangements of an association are recognized to be just (and in the more complex roles the principles of justice are understood and serve to define the ideal appropriate), thereby insuring that all of its members benefit and know that they benefit from its activities, the conduct of others in doing their part is taken to be to the advantage of each. Here the evident intention to honor one's obligations and duties is seen as a form of good will, and this recognition arouses feelings of friendship and trust in return. In due course the reciprocal effects of everyone's doing his share strengthen one another until a kind of equilibrium is reached. But we may also suppose that the newer members of the association recognize moral exemplars, that is, persons who are in various ways admired and who exhibit to a high degree the ideal corresponding to their position. These individuals display skills and abilities, and virtues of character and temperament, that attract our fancy and arouse in us the desire that we should be like them, and able to do the same things. Partly this desire to emulate springs from viewing their attributes as prerequisites for their more privileged positions, but it is also a companion effect to the Aristotelian Principle, since we enjoy the display of more complex and subtle activities and these displays tend to elicit a desire in us to do these things ourselves. Thus when the moral ideals belonging to the various roles of a just association are lived up to with evident intention by attractive and admirable persons, these ideals are likely to be adopted by those who witness their realization. These conceptions are perceived as a form of good will and the activity in which they are exemplified is shown to be a human excellence that others likewise can appreciate. The same two psychological processes are present as before: other persons act with evident intention to affirm our well-being and at the same time they exhibit qualities and ways of doing things that appeal to us and arouse the desire to model ourselves after them.

The morality of association takes many forms depending upon the association and role in question, and these forms represent many levels of complexity. But if we consider the more demanding offices that are defined by the major institutions of society, the principles of justice will be recognized as regulating the basic structure and as belonging to the content of a number of important ideals. Indeed, these principles apply to the role of citizen held by all, since everyone, and not only those in public life, is meant to have political views concerning the common good. Thus we may suppose that there is a morality of association in which the members of society view one another as equals, as friends and associates, joined together in a system of cooperation known to be for the advantage of all and governed by a common conception of justice. The content of this morality is characterized by the cooperative virtues: those of justice and fairness, fidelity and trust, integrity and impartiality. The typical vices are graspingness and unfairness, dishonesty and deceit, prejudice and bias. Among associates, giving in to these faults tends to arouse feelings of (association) guilt on the one side and resentment and indignation on the other. These moral attitudes are bound to exist once we become attached to those cooperating with us in a just (or fair) scheme.

72. THE MORALITY OF PRINCIPLES

Someone attaining to the more complex forms of the morality of association, as expressed say by the ideal of equal citizen, has an understanding certainly of the principles of justice. He has also developed an attachment to many particular individuals and communities, and he is disposed to follow the moral standards that apply to him in his various positions and which are upheld by social approval and disapproval. Having become affiliated with others and aspiring to live up to these ethical conceptions, he is concerned to win acceptance for his conduct and aims. It would seem that while the individual understands the principles of justice, his motive for complying with them, for some time at least, springs largely from his ties of friendship and fellow feeling for others, and his concern for the approbation of the wider society. I should now like to consider the process whereby a person becomes attached to these highest-order principles themselves, so that just as during the earlier phase of the morality of association he may want to be a good sport, say, he now wishes to be a just person. The conception of acting justly, and of advancing just institutions, comes to have for him an attraction analogous to that possessed before by subordinate ideals.

In conjecturing how this morality of principles might come about (principles here meaning first principles such as those considered in the original position), we should note that the morality of association quite naturally leads up to a knowledge of the standards of justice. In a well-ordered society anyway not only do those standards define the public conception of justice, but citizens who take an interest in political affairs, and those holding legislative and judicial and other similar offices, are constantly required to apply and to interpret them. They often have to take up the point of view of others, not simply with the aim of working out what they will want and probably do, but for the purpose of striking a reasonable balance between competing claims and for adjusting the various subordinate ideals of the morality of association. To put the principles of justice into practice requires that we adopt the standpoints defined by the four-stage sequence (§31). As the situation dictates, we take up the perspective of a constitutional convention, or of a legislature, or whatever. Eventually one achieves a mastery of these principles and understands the values they secure and the way in which they are to everyone's advantage. Now this leads to an acceptance of these principles by a third psychological law. This law states that once the attitudes of love and trust, and of friendly feelings and mutual confidence, have been generated in accordance with the two preceding psychological laws, then the recognition that we and those for whom we care are the beneficiaries of an established and enduring just institution tends to engender in us the corresponding sense of justice. We develop a desire to apply and to act upon the principles of justice once we realize how social arrangements answering to them have promoted our good and that of those with whom we are affiliated. In due course we come to appreciate the ideal of just human cooperation.

Now a sense of justice shows itself in at least two ways. First, it leads us to accept the just institutions that apply to us and from which we and our associates have benefited. We want to do our part in maintaining these arrangements. We tend to feel guilty when we do not honor our duties and obligations, even though we are not bound to those of whom we take advantage by any ties of particular fellow feeling. It may be that they have not yet had sufficient opportunity to display an evident intention to do their share, and are not therefore the objects of such feelings by the second law. Or, again, the institutional scheme in question may be so large that particular bonds never get widely built up. In any case, the citizen body as a whole is not generally bound together by ties of fellow feeling between individuals, but by the acceptance of public principles of justice. While every citizen is a friend to some citizens, no citizen is a friend to all. But their common allegiance to justice provides a unified perspective from which they can adjudicate their differences. Secondly, a sense of justice gives rise to a willingness to work for (or at least not to oppose) the setting up of just institutions, and for the reform of existing ones when justice requires it. We desire to act on the natural duty to advance just arrangements. And this inclination goes beyond the support of those particular schemes that have affirmed our good. It seeks to extend the conception they embody to further situations for the good of the larger community.

When we go against our sense of justice we explain our feelings of guilt by reference to the principles of justice. These feelings, then, are accounted for quite differently than the emotions of authority and association guilt. The complete moral development has now taken place and for the first time we experience feelings of guilt in the strict sense; and the same is true of the other moral emotions. In the child's case, the notion of a moral ideal, and the relevance of intentions and motives, are not understood, and so the appropriate setting for feelings of (principle) guilt does not exist. And in the morality of association, moral feelings depend essentially on ties of friendship and trust to particular individuals or communities, and moral conduct is based in large part on wanting the approval of one's associates. This may still be true even in the more demanding phases of this morality. Individuals in their role as citizens with a full understanding of the content of the principles of justice may be moved to act upon them largely because of their bonds to particular persons and an attachment to their own society. Once a morality of principles is accepted, however, moral attitudes are no longer connected solely with the well-being and approval of particular individuals and groups, but are shaped by a conception of right chosen irrespective of these contingencies. Our moral sentiments display an independence from the accidental circumstances of our world, the meaning of this independence being given by the description of the original position and its Kantian interpretation.

But even though moral sentiments are in this sense independent from contingencies, our natural attachments to particular persons and groups still have an appropriate place. For within the morality of principles the infractions which earlier gave rise to (association) guilt and resentment, and to the other moral feelings, now occasion these feelings in the strict sense. A reference to the relevant principle is made in explaining one's emotions. When the natural ties of friendship and mutual trust are present, however, these moral feelings are more intense than if they are absent. Existing attachments heighten the feeling of guilt and indignation, or whatever feeling is called for, even at the stage of the morality of principles. Now granting that this heightening is appropriate, it follows that violations of these natural ties are wrongs. For if we suppose that, say, a rational feeling of guilt (that is, a feeling of guilt arising from applying the correct moral principles in the light of true or reasonable beliefs) implies a fault on our part, and that a greater feeling of guilt implies a greater fault, then indeed breach of trust and the betrayal of friendships, and the like, are especially forbidden. The violation of these ties to particular individuals and groups arouses more intense moral feelings, and this entails that these offenses are worse. To be sure, deceit and infidelity are always wrong, being contrary to natural duties and obligations. But they

475

are not always equally wrong. They are worse whenever bonds of affection and good faith have been formed, and this consideration is relevant in working out the appropriate priority rules.

It may seem strange at first that we should come to have the desire to act from a conception of right and justice. How is it possible that moral principles can engage our affections? In justice as fairness there are several answers to this question. First of all, as we have seen (§ 25), moral principles are bound to have a certain content. Since they are chosen by rational persons to adjudicate competing claims, they define agreed ways of advancing human interests. Institutions and actions are appraised from the standpoint of securing these ends; and therefore pointless principles, for example, that one is not to look up at the sky on Tuesdays, are rejected as burdensome and irrational constraints. In the original position rational persons have no reason for acknowledging standards of this kind. But secondly, it is also the case that the sense of justice is continuous with the love of mankind. I noted earlier (§ 30) that benevolence is at a loss when the many objects of its love oppose one another. The principles of justice are needed to guide it. The difference between the sense of justice and the love of mankind is that the latter is supererogatory, going beyond the moral requirements and not invoking the exemptions which the principles of natural duty and obligation allow. Yet clearly the objects of these two sentiments are closely related, being defined in large part by the same conception of justice. If one of them seems natural and intelligible, so is the other. Moreover, feelings of guilt and indignation are aroused by the injuries and deprivations of others unjustifiably brought about either by ourselves or third parties, and our sense of justice is offended in the same way. The content of the principles of justice accounts for this. Finally, the Kantian interpretation of these principles shows that by acting upon them men express their nature as free and equal rational beings (§ 40). Since doing this belongs to their good, the sense of justice aims at their well-being even more directly. It supports those arrangements that enable everyone to express his common nature. Indeed, without a common or overlapping sense of justice civic friendship cannot exist. The desire to act justly is not, then, a form of blind obedience to arbitrary principles unrelated to rational aims.

I should not, of course, contend that justice as fairness is the only doctrine that can interpret the sense of justice in a natural way. As Sidgwick notes, a utilitarian never regards himself as acting merely for the sake of an impersonal law, but always for the welfare of some being or beings for whom he has some degree of fellow feeling.[13] The utilitarian view, and no doubt perfectionism as well, meets the condition that the sentiment of justice can be characterized so that it is psychologically understandable. Best of all, a theory should present a description of an ideally just state of affairs, a conception of a well-ordered society such that the aspiration to realize this state of affairs, and to maintain it in being, answers to our good and is continuous with our natural sentiments. A perfectly just society should be part of an ideal that rational human beings could desire more than anything else once they had full knowledge and experience of what it was.[14] The content of the principles of justice, the way in which they are derived, and the stages of moral development, show how in justice as fairness such an interpretation is possible.

It would seem, then, that the doctrine of the purely conscientious act is irrational. This doctrine holds, first, that the highest moral motive is the desire to do what is right and just simply because it is right and just, no other description being appropriate; and second, that while other motives certainly have moral value, for example the desire to do what is right because doing this increases human happiness, or because it tends to promote equality, these desires are less morally worthy than that to do what is right solely in virtue of its being right. Ross holds that the sense of right is a desire for a distinct (and unanalyzable) object, since a specific (and unanalyzable) property characterizes actions that are our duty. The other morally worthy desires, while indeed desires for things necessarily connected with what is right, are not desires for the right as such.[15]

13. *Methods of Ethics*, 7th ed. (London, Macmillan, 1907), p. 501.

14. On this point, see G. C. Field, *Moral Theory*, 2nd ed. (London, Methuen, 1932), pp. 135f, 141f.

15. For the notion of the purely conscientious act, see W. D. Ross, *The Right and the Good* (Oxford, The Clarendon Press, 1930), pp. 157–160, and *The Foundations of Ethics* (Oxford, The Clarendon Press, 1939), pp. 205f. That this notion makes the right an arbitrary preference, I borrow from J. N. Findlay, *Values and Intentions* (London, George Allen and Unwin, 1961), pp. 213f.

But on this interpretation the sense of right lacks any apparent reason; it resembles a preference for tea rather than coffee. Although such a preference might exist, to make it regulative of the basic structure of society is utterly capricious; and no less so because it is masked by a fortunate necessary connection with reasonable grounds for judgments of right.

But for one who understands and accepts the contract doctrine, the sentiment of justice is not a different desire from that to act on principles that rational individuals would consent to in an initial situation which gives everyone equal representation as a moral person. Nor is it different from wanting to act in accordance with principles that express men's nature as free and equal rational beings. The principles of justice answer to these descriptions and this fact allows us to give an acceptable interpretation to the sense of justice. In the light of the theory of justice we understand how the moral sentiments can be regulative in our life and have the role attributed to them by the formal conditions on moral principles. Being governed by these principles means that we want to live with others on terms that everyone would recognize as fair from a perspective that all would accept as reasonable. The ideal of persons cooperating on this basis exercises a natural attraction upon our affections.

Finally, we may observe that the morality of principles takes two forms, one corresponding to the sense of right and justice, the other to the love of mankind and to self-command. As we have noted, the latter is supererogatory, while the former is not. In its normal form of right and justice the morality of principles includes the virtues of the moralities of authority and association. It defines the last stage at which all the subordinate ideals are finally understood and organized into a coherent system by suitably general principles. The virtues of the other moralities receive their explanation and justification within the larger scheme; and their respective claims are adjusted by the priorities assigned by the more comprehensive conception. The morality of supererogation has two aspects depending upon the direction in which the requirements of the morality of principles are willingly surpassed. On the one hand, the love of mankind shows itself in advancing the common good in ways that go well beyond our natural duties and obligations. This morality is not one for ordinary persons, and its peculiar virtues are those of benevolence, a heightened sensitivity to the feelings and wants of others, and a proper humility and unconcern with self. The morality of self-command, on the other hand, in its simplest form is manifest in fulfilling with complete ease and grace the requirements of right and justice. It becomes truly supererogatory when the individual displays its characteristic virtues of courage, magnanimity, and self-control in actions presupposing great discipline and training. And this he may do either by freely assuming offices and positions which call upon these virtues if their duties are to be well performed; or else by seeking superior ends in a manner consistent with justice but surpassing the demands of duty and obligation. Thus the moralities of supererogation, those of the saint and the hero, do not contradict the norms of right and justice; they are marked by the willing adoption by the self of aims continuous with these principles but extending beyond what they enjoin.[16]

73. FEATURES OF THE MORAL SENTIMENTS

In the next sections I discuss several aspects of the three stages of morality in more detail. The concept of a moral sentiment, the nature of the three psychological laws, and the process whereby they take hold call for further comment. Turning to the first of these matters, I should explain that I shall use the older term "sentiment" for permanent ordered families of governing dispositions, such as the sense of justice and the love of mankind (§30), and for lasting attachments to particular individuals or associations that have a central place in a person's life. Thus there are both moral and natural sentiments. The term "attitude" I use more broadly. Like sentiments, attitudes are ordered families of dispositions either moral or natural, but in their case the tendencies need not be so regulative or enduring. Finally, I shall use the phrases

16. In this account of the aspects of the morality of supererogation I have drawn upon J. O. Urmson, "Saints and Heros," in *Essays in Moral Philosophy*, ed. A. I. Melden (Seattle, University of Washington Press, 1958). The notion of self-command is taken from Adam Smith, *The Theory of the Moral Sentiments*, pt. VI, sec. III, which may be found in *Adam Smith's Moral and Political Philosophy*, ed. H. W. Schneider (New York, Hafner, 1948), pp. 251–277.

"moral feeling" and "moral emotion" for the feelings and emotions that we experience on particular occasions. I wish to clarify the connection between moral sentiments, attitudes, and feelings, and the relevant moral principles.

The main features of moral sentiments can perhaps be best elucidated by considering the various questions that arise in trying to characterize them and the various feelings in which they are manifested.[17] It is worthwhile to observe the ways in which they are distinguished both from each other and from those natural attitudes and feelings with which they are likely to be confused. Thus, first of all, there are such questions as the following. (a) What are the linguistic expressions that are used to give voice to having a particular moral feeling, and the significant variations, if any, in these expressions? (b) What are the characteristic behavioral indications of a given feeling, and what are the ways in which a person typically betrays how he feels? (c) What are the characteristic sensations and kinesthetic feelings, if any, that are connected with moral emotions? When a person is angry, for example, he may feel hot; he may tremble and experience a tightening of the stomach. He may be unable to speak without his voice shaking; and perhaps he cannot suppress certain gestures. If there are such characteristic sensations and behavioral manifestations for a moral feeling, these do not constitute the feeling of guilt, shame, indignation, or whatever. Such characteristic sensations and manifestations are neither necessary nor sufficient in particular instances for someone to feel guilty, ashamed, or indignant. This is not to deny that some characteristic sensations and behavioral manifestations of disturbance may be

17. These questions are suggested by applying to the concept of the moral feelings the kind of inquiry carried out by Wittgenstein in the *Philosophical Investigations* (Oxford, Basil Blackwell, 1953). See also, for example, G. E. M. Anscombe, "Pretending," *Proceedings of the Aristotelian Society,* supp. vol. 32 (1958), pp. 285–289; Phillipa Foot, "Moral Beliefs," *Proceedings of the Aristotelian Society,* vol. 59 (1958–1959), pp. 86–89; and George Pitcher, "On Approval," *Philosophical Review,* vol. 67 (1958). See also B. A. O. Williams, "Morality and the Emotions," *Inaugural Lecture,* Bedford College, University of London, 1965. It may be a difficulty with the emotive theory of ethics as presented by C. L. Stevenson in *Ethics and Language* (New Haven, Yale University Press, 1944) that it cannot identify and distinguish the moral from the nonmoral feelings. For a discussion of this question, see W. P. Alston, "Moral Attitudes and Moral Judgments," *Nous,* vol. 2 (1968).

necessary if one is to be overwhelmed by feelings of guilt, shame, or indignation. But to have these feelings it is often sufficient that a person sincerely say that he feels guilty, ashamed or indignant, and that he is prepared to give an appropriate explanation of why he feels as he does (assuming of course that he accepts this explanation as correct).

This last consideration introduces the main question in distinguishing the moral feelings from other emotions and from each other, namely: (d) What is the definitive type of explanation required for having a moral feeling, and how do these explanations differ from one feeling to another? Thus when we ask someone why he feels guilty, what sort of answer do we want? Certainly not any reply is acceptable. A reference merely to expected punishment is not enough; this might account for fear or anxiety, but not for guilt feelings. Similarly, mention of harms or misadventures that have fallen upon oneself as a consequence of one's past actions explains feelings of regret but not those of guilt, and much less those of remorse. To be sure, fear and anxiety often accompany feelings of guilt for obvious reasons, but these emotions must not be confused with the moral feelings. We should not suppose, then, that the experience of guilt is somehow a mixture of fear, anxiety, and regret. Anxiety and fear are not moral feelings at all, and regret is connected with some view of our own good, being occasioned, say, by failures to further our interests in sensible ways. Even such phenomena as neurotic guilt feelings, and other deviations from the standard case, are accepted as feelings of guilt and not simply as irrational fears and anxieties because of the special type of explanation for the departure from the norm. It is always supposed in such cases that a deeper psychological investigation will uncover (or has uncovered) the relevant similarity to other guilt feelings.

In general, it is a necessary feature of moral feelings, and part of what distinguishes them from the natural attitudes, that the person's explanation of his experience invokes a moral concept and its associated principles. His account of his feeling makes reference to an acknowledged right or wrong. When we question this, we are likely to offer various forms of guilt feelings as counterexamples. This is easy to understand since the earliest forms of guilt feelings are those of authority guilt, and we are unlikely to grow up without having what one may call residue guilt feelings. For example, a person raised in a strict religious sect may have been taught that going to the theater is wrong. While he no longer believes this, he tells us that he still feels guilty when attending the theater. But these are not proper guilt feelings, since he is not about to apologize to anyone, or to resolve not to see another play, and so on. Indeed, he should say rather that he has certain sensations and feelings of uneasiness, and the like, which resemble those which he has when he feels guilty. Assuming, then, the soundness of the contract view, the explanation of some moral feelings relies on principles of right that would be chosen in the original position, while the other moral feelings are related to the concept of goodness. For example, a person feels guilty because he knows that he has taken more than his share (as defined by some just scheme), or has treated others unfairly. Or a person feels ashamed because he has been cowardly and not spoken out. He has failed to live up to a conception of moral worth which he has set himself to achieve (§ 68). What distinguishes the moral feelings from one another are the principles and faults which their explanations typically invoke. For the most part, the characteristic sensations and behavioral manifestations are the same, being psychological disturbances and having the common features of these.

It is worthwhile to note that the same action may give rise to several moral feelings at once provided that, as is often the case, the appropriate explanation for each one can be given (§ 67). For example, a person who cheats may feel both guilty and ashamed: guilty because he has violated a trust and unfairly advanced himself, his guilt being in answer to the injuries done to others; ashamed because by resorting to such means he has convicted himself in his own eyes (and in those of others) as weak and untrustworthy, as someone who resorts to unfair and covert means to further his ends. These explanations appeal to different principles and values, thus distinguishing the corresponding feelings; but both explanations frequently apply. We may add here that for a person to have a moral feeling, it is not necessary that everything asserted in his explanation be true; it is sufficient that he accepts the explanation. Someone may be in error, then, in thinking that he has taken more than his share. He may not be guilty. Nevertheless, he feels guilty since his explanation is of the right sort, and although mistaken, the beliefs he expresses are sincere.

Next, there is a group of questions concerning the relation of moral attitudes to action: (e) What are the characteristic intentions, endeavors, and inclinations of a person experiencing a given feeling? What sorts of things does he want to do, or find himself unable to do? An angry man characteristically tries to strike back, or to block the purposes of the person at whom he is angry. When plagued by feelings of guilt, say, a person wishes to act properly in the future and strives to modify his conduct accordingly. He is inclined to admit what he has done and to ask for reinstatement, and to acknowledge and accept reproofs and penalties; and he finds himself less able to condemn others when they behave wrongly. The particular situation will determine which of these dispositions are realized; and we may also suppose that the family of dispositions which may be elicited varies according to the morality of the individual. It is clear, for example, that the typical expressions of guilt and the appropriate explanations will be quite different as the ideals and roles of the morality of association become more complex and demanding; and these feelings in turn will be distinct from the emotions connected with the morality of principles. In justice as fairness, these variations are accounted for in the first instance by the content of the corresponding moral view. The structure of precepts, ideals, and principles shows what sorts of explanations are required.

Further, we can ask: (f) What emotions and responses does a person having a particular feeling expect on the part of other persons? How does he anticipate that they will react toward him, as this is shown, say, in various characteristic distortions in his interpretation of others' conduct toward him? Thus, one who feels guilty, recognizing his action as a transgression of the legitimate claims of others, expects them to resent his conduct and to penalize him in various ways. He also assumes that third parties will be indignant with him. Someone who feels guilty, then, is apprehensive about the resentment and indignation of others, and the uncertainties which thereby arise. By contrast, someone who feels ashamed anticipates derision and contempt. He has fallen short of a standard of excellence, given in to weakness, and shown himself unworthy of association with others who share his ideals. He is apprehensive lest he be cut off and rejected, made an object of scorn and ridicule. Just as the feelings of guilt and shame have different principles in their explanations, they lead us to anticipate different attitudes in other persons. In general, guilt, resentment, and indignation invoke the concept of right, whereas shame, contempt, and derision appeal to the concept of goodness. And these remarks extend in the obvious way to feelings of duty and obligation (if there are such), and to proper pride and a sense of one's own worth.

Finally, we can ask: (g) What are the characteristic temptations to actions that give rise to the moral feeling and how is the feeling typically resolved? Here again there are marked differences between the moral emotions. Feelings of guilt and shame have different settings and are overcome in distinct ways, and these variations reflect the defining principles with which they are connected and their peculiar psychological bases. Thus, for example, guilt is relieved by reparation and the forgiveness that permits reconciliation; whereas shame is undone by proofs of defects made good, by a renewed confidence in the excellence of one's person. It is also clear, for example, that resentment and indignation have their characteristic resolutions, since the first is aroused by what we regard as wrongs done to ourselves, the second is concerned with wrongs done to others.

Yet the contrasts between the feelings of guilt and shame are so striking that it is helpful to note how they fit in with the distinctions made between different aspects of morality. As we have seen, a breach of any virtue may give rise to shame; it suffices that one prizes the form of action among one's excellences (§67). Analogously, a wrong can always occasion guilt whenever others are in some way harmed, or their rights violated. Thus guilt and shame reflect the concern with others and with one's person that must be present in all moral conduct. Nevertheless, some virtues, and so those moralities that emphasize them, are more typical of the standpoint of one feeling than the other, and therefore are more closely connected with it. Thus in particular, the moralities of supererogation provide the stage for shame; for they represent the higher forms of moral excellence, the love of humankind and self-command, and in choosing them one risks failure from their very nature. It would be a mistake, however, to emphasize the perspective of one feeling more than the other in the complete moral conception. For the theory of right and justice is founded on the notion of reciprocity which reconciles the points of view of the self and of others as equal moral persons. This reciprocity has the consequence that both perspectives characterize moral thought and feeling, usually in roughly even measure. Neither concern for others nor for self has priority, for all are equal; and the balance between persons is given by the principles of justice. And where this balance moves to one side, as with the moralities of supererogation, it does so from the election of self, which freely takes on the larger part. Thus while we may think of the points of view of the self and of others as characteristic of some moralities historically, or of certain perspectives within a full conception, a complete moral doctrine includes both. All by themselves, a morality of shame or of guilt is but a part of a moral view.

In these remarks I have stressed two main points. First of all, the moral attitudes are not to be identified with characteristic sensations and behavioral manifestations, even if these exist. Moral feelings require certain types of explanations. Thus, second, the moral attitudes involve the acceptance of specific moral virtues; and the principles which define these virtues are used to account for the corresponding feelings. The judgments that elucidate different emotions are distinguished from one another by the standards cited in their explanation. Guilt and shame, remorse and regret, indignation and resentment, either appeal to principles belonging to different parts of morality or invoke them from contrasting points of view. An ethical theory must explain and find a place for these distinctions, although presumably each theory will try to do so in its own way.

74. THE CONNECTION BETWEEN MORAL AND NATURAL ATTITUDES

There is a further aspect of moral attitudes that I have noted in the sketch of the development of the sense of justice, namely, their connection with certain natural attitudes.[18] Thus in examining a

18. Throughout this section, and indeed on the subject of the moral emotions generally, I am very much indebted to David Sachs.

moral feeling we should ask: what if any are the natural attitudes to which it is related? Now there are two questions here, one the converse of the other. The first asks about the natural attitudes that are shown to be absent when a person fails to have certain moral feelings. Whereas the second asks which natural attitudes are evidenced to be present when someone experiences a moral emotion. In sketching the three stages of morality I have been concerned only with the first question, since its converse raises other and more difficult problems. I have held that, in the context of the authority situation, the child's natural attitudes of love and trust for those in authority lead to feelings of (authority) guilt when he violates the injunctions addressed to him. The absence of these moral feelings would evidence a lack of these natural ties. Similarly, within the framework of the morality of association, the natural attitudes of friendship and mutual trust give rise to feelings of guilt for not fulfilling the duties and obligations recognized by the group. The absence of these feelings would imply the absence of these attachments. These propositions must not be mistaken for their converses, for while feelings of indignation and guilt, say, can often be taken as evidence for such affections, there may be other explanations. In general, moral principles are affirmed for various reasons and their acceptance is normally sufficient for the moral feelings. To be sure, on the contract theory principles of right and justice have a certain content, and as we have just seen, there is a sense in which acting in accordance with them can be interpreted as acting from a concern for mankind, or for the good of other persons. Whether this fact shows that one acts in part from certain natural attitudes, especially as these involve attachments to particular individuals, and not simply from the general forms of sympathy and benevolence, is a question that I shall leave aside here. Certainly the preceding account of the development of morality supposes that affection for particular persons plays an essential part in the acquisition of morality. But how far these attitudes are required for later moral motivation can be left open, although it would, I think, be surprising if these attachments were not to some degree necessary.

Now the connection between the natural attitudes and the moral sentiments may be expressed as follows: these sentiments and attitudes are both ordered families of characteristic dispositions, and these families overlap in such a manner that the absence of certain moral feelings evidences the absence of certain natural ties. Or alternatively, the presence of certain natural attachments gives rise to a liability to certain moral emotions once the requisite moral development has taken place. We can see how this is so by an example. If A cares for B, then failing a special explanation A is afraid for B when B is in danger and tries to come to B's assistance. Again, if C plans to treat B unjustly, A is indignant with C and attempts to prevent his plans from succeeding. In both cases, A is disposed to protect B's interests. Further, unless there are special circumstances, A is joyful when together with B, and when B suffers injury or dies, A is stricken with grief. If the injury to B is A's responsibility, A will feel remorse. Love is a sentiment, a hierarchy of dispositions to experience and to manifest these primary emotions as the occasion elicits and to act in the appropriate way.[19] To confirm the connection between the natural attitudes and the moral sentiments one simply notes that the disposition on A's part to feel remorse when he injures B, or guilt when he violates B's legitimate claims, or A's disposition to feel indignation when C seeks to deny B's right, are as closely related psychologically with the natural attitudes of love as the disposition to be joyful in the other's presence, or to feel sorrow when he suffers. The moral sentiments are in some ways more complex. In their complete form they presuppose an understanding and an acceptance of certain principles and an ability to judge in accordance with them. But assuming these things, the liability to moral feelings seems to be as much a part of the natural sentiments as the tendency to be joyful, or the liability to grief. Love sometimes expresses itself in sorrow, at other times in indignation. Either one without the other would be equally unusual. The content of rational moral principles is such as to render these connections intelligible.

Now one main consequence of this doctrine is that the moral feelings are a normal feature of human life. We could not do away with them without at the same time eliminating certain natural

19. On this point, see A. F. Shand, *The Foundations of Character*, 2nd ed. (London, Macmillan, 1920), pp. 55f.

attitudes. Among persons who never acted in accordance with their duty of justice except as reasons of self-interest and expediency dictated there would be no bonds of friendship and mutual trust. For when these attachments exist, other reasons are acknowledged for acting fairly. This much seems reasonably obvious. But it also follows from what has been said that, barring self-deception, egoists are incapable of feeling resentment and indignation. If either of two egoists deceives the other and this is found out, neither of them has a ground for complaint. They do not accept the principles of justice, or any other conception that is reasonable from the standpoint of the original position; nor do they experience any inhibition from guilt feelings for breaches of their duties. As we have seen, resentment and indignation are moral feelings and therefore they presuppose an explanation by reference to an acceptance of the principles of right and justice. But by hypothesis the appropriate explanations cannot be given. To deny that self-interested persons are incapable of resentment and indignation is not of course to say that they cannot be angry and annoyed with one another. A person without a sense of justice may be enraged at someone who fails to act fairly. But anger and annoyance are distinct from indignation and resentment; they are not, as the latter are, moral emotions. Nor should it be denied that egoists may want others to recognize the bonds of friendship and to treat them in a friendly way. But these desires are not to be mistaken for ties of affection that lead one to make sacrifices for one's friends. No doubt there are difficulties in distinguishing between resentment and anger, and between apparent and real friendship. Certainly the overt manifestations and actions may seem the same when viewing a limited span of conduct. Yet in the longer run the difference can usually be made out.

One may say, then, that a person who lacks a sense of justice, and who would never act as justice requires except as self-interest and expediency prompt, not only is without ties of friendship, affection, and mutual trust, but is incapable of experiencing resentment and indignation. He lacks certain natural attitudes and moral feelings of a particularly elementary kind. Put another way, one who lacks a sense of justice lacks certain fundamental attitudes and capacities included under the notion of humanity. Now the moral

feelings are admittedly unpleasant, in some extended sense of unpleasant; but there is no way for us to avoid a liability to them
without disfiguring ourselves. This liability is the price of love and
trust, of friendship and affection, and of a devotion to institutions
and traditions from which we have benefited and which serve the
general interests of mankind. Further, assuming that persons are
possessed of interests and aspirations of their own, and that they
are prepared in the pursuit of their own ends and ideals to press
their claims on one another—that is, so long as the conditions
giving rise to questions of justice obtain among them—it is inevitable that, given temptation and passion, this liability will be
realized. And since being moved by ends and ideals of excellence
implies a liability to humiliation and shame, and an absence of a
liability to humiliation and shame implies a lack of such ends and
ideals, one can say of shame and humiliation also that they are a
part of the notion of humanity. Now the fact that one who lacks
a sense of justice, and thereby a liability to guilt, lacks certain
fundamental attitudes and capacities is not to be taken as a reason
for acting as justice dictates. But it has this significance: by understanding what it would be like not to have a sense of justice—that
it would be to lack part of our humanity too—we are led to accept
our having this sentiment.

It follows that the moral sentiments are a normal part of human
life. One cannot do away with them without at the same time dis-
mantling the natural attitudes as well. And we have also seen
(§§30, 72) that the moral sentiments are continuous with these
attitudes in the sense that the love of mankind and the desire to
uphold the common good include the principles of right and
justice as necessary to define their object. None of this is to deny
that our existing moral feelings may be in many respects irrational
and injurious to our good. Freud is right in his view that these
attitudes are often punitive and blind, incorporating many of the
harsher aspects of the authority situation in which they were first
acquired. Resentment and indignation, feelings of guilt and remorse, a sense of duty and the censure of others, often take per-
verse and destructive forms, and blunt without reason human
spontaneity and enjoyment. When I say that moral attitudes are
part of our humanity, I mean those attitudes that appeal to sound

principles of right and justice in their explanation. The reasonableness of the underlying ethical conception is a necessary condition; and so the appropriateness of moral sentiments to our nature is determined by the principles that would be consented to in the original position.[20] These principles regulate moral education and the expression of moral approval and disapproval, just as they govern the design of institutions. Yet even if the sense of justice is the normal outgrowth of natural human attitudes within a well-ordered society, it is still true that our present moral feelings are liable to be unreasonable and capricious. However, one of the virtues of a well-ordered society is that, since arbitrary authority has disappeared, its members suffer much less from the burdens of oppressive conscience.

75. THE PRINCIPLES OF MORAL PSYCHOLOGY

We must soon examine the relative stability of justice as fairness in the light of the sketch of moral development. But before doing this I should like to make a few remarks about the three psychological laws. It will help to have a statement of them before us. Taking for granted that they represent tendencies and are effective other things being equal, they can be rendered as follows.

First law: given that family institutions are just, and that the parents love the child and manifestly express their love by caring for his good, then the child, recognizing their evident love of him, comes to love them.

Second law: given that a person's capacity for fellow feeling has been realized by acquiring attachments in accordance with the first law, and given that a social arrangement is just and publicly known by all to be just, then this person develops ties of friendly feeling and trust toward others in the association as they with evident intention comply with their duties and obligations, and live up to the ideals of their station.

20. Mill observes in *On Liberty,* ch. III, par. 10, that while being held to rigid rules of justice for the sake of others develops the social part of our nature, and therefore is compatible with our well-being, being restrained in ways not for their good but because of their mere displeasure blunts our nature if acquiesced in.

Third law: given that a person's capacity for fellow feeling has been realized by his forming attachments in accordance with the first two laws, and given that a society's institutions are just and are publicly known by all to be just, then this person acquires the corresponding sense of justice as he recognizes that he and those for whom he cares are the beneficiaries of these arrangements.

Perhaps the most striking feature of these laws (or tendencies) is that their formulation refers to an institutional setting as being just, and in the last two, as being publicly known to be such. The principles of moral psychology have a place for a conception of justice; and different formulations of these principles result when different conceptions are used. Thus some view of justice enters into the explanation of the development of the corresponding sentiment; hypotheses about this psychological process incorporate moral notions even if these are understood only as part of the psychological theory. This much seems straightforward, and assuming that ethical ideas can be stated clearly, there is no difficulty in seeing how there can be laws of this kind. The preceding outline of moral development indicates how these matters can be worked out. After all, the sense of justice is a settled disposition to adopt and to want to act from the moral point of view insofar at least as the principles of justice define it. It is hardly surprising that these principles should be involved in the formation of this regulative sentiment. Indeed, it seems likely that our understanding of moral learning cannot far exceed our grasp of the moral conceptions that are to be learned. Analogously, our understanding of how we learn our language is limited by what we know about its grammatical and semantic structure. Just as psycholinguistics depends upon linguistics, so the theory of moral learning depends upon an account of the nature of morality and its various forms. Our common sense ideas about these matters do not suffice for the aims of theory.

No doubt some prefer that social theories avoid the use of moral notions. For instance, they may wish to explain the formation of affective ties by laws referring to the frequency of interaction among those engaged in some common task, or to the regularity with which some persons take the initiative or exercise

491

authoritative guidance. Thus one law may state that among equals cooperating together, where equality is defined by the accepted rules, the more often individuals interact with one another, the more likely it is that friendly feelings develop between them. Another law may assert that the more someone in a position of authority uses his powers and leads those subject to him, the more they come to respect him.[21] But since these laws (or tendencies) do not mention the justice (or fairness) of the arrangement in question, they are bound to be very limited in scope. Those subject to another exercising authority will surely regard him differently depending upon whether the whole arrangement is just and well designed to advance what they take to be their legitimate interests. And the same is true of cooperation among equals. Institutions are patterns of human conduct defined by public systems of rules, and the very holding of the offices and positions which they define normally indicates certain intentions and aims. The justice or injustice of society's arrangements and men's beliefs about these questions profoundly influence the social feelings; to a large extent they determine how we regard another's accepting or rejecting an institution, or his attempt to reform or defend it.

It may be objected that much social theory does well enough without using any moral ideas. The obvious example is economics. However, the situation in economic theory is peculiar in that one can often assume a fixed structure of rules and constraints that define the actions open to individuals and firms, and certain simplifying motivational assumptions are highly plausible. The theory of price (its more elementary parts anyway) is an illustration. One does not consider why buyers and sellers behave in accordance with the rules of law governing economic activity; or how preferences get formed or legal norms established. For the most part, these matters are taken as given, and at a certain level there is no objection to this. On the other hand, the so-called economic theory of democracy, the view that extends the basic ideas and methods of price theory to the political process, must for

21. For examples of suggested laws (or tendencies) of this type, see G. C. Homans, *The Human Group* (New York, Harcourt, Brace, 1950), pp. 243, 247, 249, 251. In a later book, however, the notion of justice is explicitly brought in. See *Social Behavior: Its Elementary Forms* (New York, Harcourt, Brace and World, 1961), pp. 295f, which applies the theory developed at pp. 232–264.

all its merits be regarded with caution.[22] For a theory of a constitutional regime cannot take the rules as given, nor simply assume that they will be followed. Clearly the political process is importantly one of enacting and revising rules and of trying to control the legislative and executive branches of government. Even if everything is done in accordance with constitutional procedures, we need to explain why these are accepted. Nothing analogous to the constraints of a competitive market holds for this case; and there are no legal sanctions in the ordinary sense for many sorts of unconstitutional actions by parliaments and chief executives, and the political forces they represent. The leading political actors are guided therefore in part by what they regard as morally permissible; and since no system of constitutional checks and balances succeeds in setting up an invisible hand that can be relied upon to guide the process to a just outcome, a public sense of justice is to some degree necessary. It would appear, then, that a correct theory of politics in a just constitutional regime presupposes a theory of justice which explains how moral sentiments influence the conduct of public affairs. I touched upon this question in connection with the role of civil disobedience; it suffices to add here that one test of the contract doctrine is how well it serves this purpose.

A second point about the psychological laws is that they govern changes in the affective ties which belong to our final ends. To clarify this, we may observe that to explain an intentional action is to show how, given our beliefs and the available alternatives, it accords with our plan of life, or with that subpart of it relevant in the circumstances. Often this is done by a series of explanations saying that a first thing is done in order to achieve a second; that the second thing is done in order to achieve a third, and so on, the series being finite and ending at an aim for the sake of which the previous things are done. In accounting for our various actions, we may cite many different chains of reasons, and these normally stop at different points given the complexity of a plan of life and its plurality of ends. Moreover, a chain of reasons may have several

22. For references to this theory of democracy, see §31, note 2, and §54, note 18. Of course, those who have developed the theory are aware of this limitation. See, for example, Anthony Downs, "The Public Interest: Its Meaning in a Democracy," *Social Research,* vol. 29 (1962).

branches, since an action may be done to advance more than one end. How activities furthering the many ends are scheduled and balanced against each other is settled by the plan itself and the principles upon which it is based.

Now among our final ends are the attachments we have for persons, the interests we take in the realization of their interests, and the sense of justice. The three laws describe how our system of desires comes to have new final ends as we acquire affective ties. These changes are to be distinguished from our forming derivative desires as a consequence of additional knowledge or further opportunities, or from our determining our existing wants in a more specific way. For example, someone wishing to travel to a certain place is informed that a certain route is the best. Upon accepting this advice, he has a desire to proceed in a particular direction. Derivative desires of this sort have a rational explanation. They are desires to do what in view of the evidence on hand will most effectively realize our present aims, and they shift along with knowledge and belief, and the available opportunities. The three psychological laws do not provide rational explanations of desires in this sense; rather they characterize transformations of our pattern of final ends that arise from our recognizing the manner in which institutions and the actions of others affect our good. Of course, whether an aim is final or derivative is not always easy to ascertain. The distinction is made on the basis of a person's rational plan of life and the structure of this plan is not generally obvious, even to him. Yet for our purposes here, the distinction is clear enough.

A third observation is that the three laws are not merely principles of association or of reinforcement. While they have a certain resemblance to these learning principles, they assert that the active sentiments of love and friendship, and even the sense of justice, arise from the manifest intention of other persons to act for our good. Because we recognize that they wish us well, we care for their well-being in return. Thus we acquire attachments to persons and institutions according to how we perceive our good to be affected by them. The basic idea is one of reciprocity, a tendency to answer in kind. Now this tendency is a deep psychological fact. Without it our nature would be very different and fruitful social cooperation fragile if not impossible. For surely a rational person is not indifferent to things that significantly affect his good; and supposing that he develops some attitude toward them, he acquires either a new attachment or a new aversion. If we answered love with hate, or came to dislike those who acted fairly toward us, or were averse to activities that furthered our good, a community would soon dissolve. Beings with a different psychology either have never existed or must soon have disappeared in the course of evolution. A capacity for a sense of justice built up by responses in kind would appear to be a condition of human sociability. The most stable conceptions of justice are presumably those for which the corresponding sense of justice is most firmly based on these tendencies (§ 76).

Finally, several comments about the account of moral development as a whole. The reliance upon the three principles of moral psychology is of course a simplification. A fuller account would distinguish between different kinds of learning and therefore between instrumental conditioning (reinforcement) and classical conditioning, so likely to shape our emotions and feelings. A consideration of modeling and imitation, and the learning of concepts and principles, would also be necessary.[23] There is no reason to deny the significance of these forms of learning. For our purposes, though, the three-stage schema may suffice. Insofar as it stresses the forming of attachments as final ends, the sketch of moral learning resembles the empiricist tradition with its emphasis on the importance of acquiring new motives.

There are also ties with what I have called the rationalistic view. For one thing, the acquisition of the sense of justice takes place in stages connected with the growth of knowledge and understanding. One must develop a conception of the social world and of what is just and unjust if the sentiment of justice is to be acquired. The manifest intentions of others are recognized against a background of public institutions as interpreted by one's view of the self and its situation. I have not maintained, however, that the stages of development are innate or determined by psychological mechanisms. Whether various native propensities influence these stages is a matter I have left aside. Rather a theory of right and justice is used to de-

23. See Brown, *Social Psychology*, pp. 411f.

scribe what the expected course of development might be. The manner in which a well-ordered society is arranged, and the full system of principles, ideals, and precepts that govern the complete scheme, provide a way of distinguishing the three levels of morality. It seems plausible that, in a society regulated by the contract doctrine, moral learning would follow the order presented. The stages are determined by the structure of what is to be learned, proceeding from the simpler to the more complex as the requisite capacities are realized.

Last of all, by founding the account of moral learning explicitly upon a particular ethical theory, it is evident in what sense the sequence of stages represents a progressive development and not simply a regular sequence. Just as persons gradually formulate rational plans of life that answer to their deeper interests, so they come to know the derivation of moral precepts and ideals from the principles that they would accept in an initial situation of equality. Ethical norms are no longer experienced merely as constraints, but are tied together into one coherent conception. The connection between these standards and human aspirations is now comprehended, and persons understand their sense of justice as an extension of their natural attachments, and as a way of caring about the collective good. The many chains of reasons with their various stopping points are no longer simply distinct but are seen as elements of a systematic view. These remarks assume, however, a particular theory of justice. Those who espouse a different one will favor another account of these matters. But in any case, some conception of justice surely has a place in explaining moral learning, even if this conception belongs solely to the psychological theory and is not itself accepted as philosophically correct.

76. THE PROBLEM OF RELATIVE STABILITY

I now turn to the comparison between justice as fairness and other conceptions with respect to stability. It may be useful to recall that the problem of stability arises because a just scheme of cooperation may not be in equilibrium, much less stable. To be sure, from the standpoint of the original position, the principles of justice are collectively rational; everyone may expect to improve his situation if all comply with these principles, at least in comparison with what his prospects would be in the absence of any agreement. General egoism represents this no-agreement point. Nevertheless, from the perspective of any one man, both first-person and free-rider egoism would be still better. Of course given the conditions of the original position neither of these options is a serious candidate (§23). Yet in everyday life an individual, if he is so inclined, can sometimes win even greater benefits for himself by taking advantage of the cooperative efforts of others. Sufficiently many persons may be doing their share so that when special circumstances allow him not to contribute (perhaps his omission will not be found out), he gets the best of both worlds: on these occasions anyway things proceed much as if free-rider egoism had been acknowledged.

Just arrangements may not be in equilibrium then because acting fairly is not in general each man's best reply to the just conduct of his associates. To insure stability men must have a sense of justice or a concern for those who would be disadvantaged by their defection, preferably both. When these sentiments are sufficiently strong to overrule the temptations to violate the rules, just schemes are stable. Meeting one's duties and obligations is now regarded by each person as the correct answer to the actions of others. His rational plan of life regulated by his sense of justice leads to this conclusion.

As I remarked earlier, Hobbes connected the question of stability with that of political obligation. One may think of the Hobbesian sovereign as a mechanism added to a system of cooperation which would be unstable without it. The general belief in the sovereign's efficacy removes the two kinds of instability (§42). Now it is evident how relations of friendship and mutual trust, and the public knowledge of a common and normally effective sense of justice, bring about the same result. For given these natural attitudes and the desire to do what is just, no one wishes to advance his interests unfairly to the disadvantage of others; this removes instability of the first kind. And since each recognizes that these inclinations and sentiments are prevalent and effective, there is no reason for anyone to think that he must violate the rules to protect his legitimate interests; so instability of the second kind is likewise absent. Of course, some infractions will presumably occur, but when they do feelings of guilt arising from friendship and mutual trust and the sense of justice tend to restore the arrangement.

Moreover, a society regulated by a public sense of justice is inherently stable: other things equal, the forces making for stability increase (up to some limit) as time passes. This inherent stability is a consequence of the reciprocal relation between the three psychological laws. The more effective operation of one law strengthens that of the other two. For example, when the second law leads to stronger attachments, the sense of justice acquired by the third law is reinforced because of the greater concern for the beneficiaries of just institutions. And going the other way, a more effective sense of justice leads to a more secure intention to do one's share, and the recognition of this fact arouses more intense feelings of friendship and trust. Again, it seems that with a firmer assurance of one's own worth and a livelier capacity for fellow feeling brought about by more favorable conditions for the first law, the effects governed by the other two laws should be similarly enhanced. Conversely, persons who have developed a regulative sense of justice and are confident in their self-esteem are more likely to care for their children with manifest intention. Thus all three psychological principles conspire together to support the institutions of a well-ordered society.

There seems to be no doubt then that justice as fairness is a reasonably stable moral conception. But a decision in the original position depends on a comparison: other things equal, the preferred conception of justice is the most stable one. Ideally we should compare the contract view with all its rivals in this respect, but as so often I shall only consider the principle of utility. In order to do this, it is useful to recall three elements that enter into the operation of the psychological laws: namely, an unconditional caring for our good, a clear awareness of the reasons for moral precepts and ideals (aided by explanation and instruction, and the possibility of giving precise and convincing justifications), and the recognition that those complying with these precepts and ideals, and doing their part in social arrangements, both accept these norms and express in their life and character forms of human good which evoke our admiration and esteem (§70). The resulting sense of justice is stronger the more these three elements are realized. The first enlivens the sense of our own worth strengthening the tendency to answer in kind, the second presents the moral conception so that it can be readily understood, and the third displays the adherence to it as attractive. The most stable conception of justice, therefore, is presumably one that is perspicuous to our reason, congruent with our good, and rooted not in abnegation but in affirmation of the self.

Now several things suggest that the sense of justice corresponding to justice as fairness is stronger than the parallel sentiment inculcated by the other conceptions. First of all, the unconditional concern of other persons and institutions for our good is far stronger on the contract view. The restrictions contained in the principle of justice guarantee everyone an equal liberty and assure us that our claims will not be neglected or overridden for the sake of a larger sum of benefits, even for the whole society. We have only to keep in mind the various priority rules, and the meaning of the difference principle as rendered by its Kantian interpretation (persons are not to be treated as means at all) and its relation to the idea of fraternity (§§29, 17). The effect of these aspects of justice as fairness is to heighten the operation of the reciprocity principle. As we have noted, a more unconditional caring for our good and a clearer refusal by others to take advantage of accident and happenstance, must strengthen our self-esteem; and this greater good must in turn lead to a closer affiliation with persons and institutions by way of an answer in kind. These effects are more intense than in the case of the utility principle, and so the resulting attachments should be stronger.

We can confirm this suggestion by considering the well-ordered society paired with the principle of utility. In this case, the three psychological laws have to be altered. For example, the second law now holds that persons tend to develop friendly feelings toward those who with evident intention do their part in cooperative schemes publicly known to maximize the sum of advantages, or the average well-being (whichever variant is used). In either case the resulting psychological law is not as plausible as before. For suppose that certain institutions are adopted on the public understanding that the greater advantages of some counterbalance the lesser losses of others. Why should the acceptance of the principle of utility (in either form) by the more fortunate inspire the less advantaged to have friendly feelings toward them? This response would seem in fact to be rather surprising, especially if those in a better situation have pressed their claims by maintaining that a greater sum (or average) of well-being would result from their satisfaction. No reciprocity principle is at work in this case and the appeal to utility may simply arouse suspicion. The concern which is expressed for all persons by counting each as one (by weighing everyone's utility equally) is weak compared to that conveyed by the principles of justice. Thus the attachments generated within a well-ordered society regulated by the utility criterion are likely to vary widely between one sector of society and another. Some groups may acquire little if any desire to act justly (now defined by the utilitarian principle) with a corresponding loss in stability.

To be sure, in any kind of well-ordered society the strength of the sense of justice will not be the same in all social groups. Yet to insure that mutual ties bind the entire society, each and every member of it, one must adopt something like the two principles of justice. It is evident why the utilitarian stresses the capacity for sympathy. Those who do not benefit from the better situation of others must identify with the greater sum (or average) of satisfaction else they will not desire to follow the utility criterion. Now such altruistic inclinations no doubt exist. Yet they are likely to be less strong than those brought about by the three psychological laws formulated as reciprocity principles; and a marked capacity for sympathetic identification seems relatively rare. Therefore these feelings provide less support for the basic structure of society. In addition, as we have seen, following the utilitarian conception tends to be destructive of the self-esteem of those who lose out, particularly when they are already less fortunate (§29). Now it is characteristic of the morality of authority when conceived as a morality for the social order as a whole to demand self-sacrifice for the sake of a higher good and to deprecate the worth of the individual and lesser associations. The emptiness of the self is to be overcome in the service of larger ends. This doctrine is likely to encourage self-hatred with its destructive consequences. Certainly utilitarianism does not go to this extreme, but there is bound to be a similar effect which further weakens the capacity for sympathy and distorts the development of affective ties.

By contrast, in a social system regulated by justice as fairness, identification with the good of others, and an appreciation of what they do as an element in our own good (§ 79), might be quite strong. But this is possible only because of the mutuality already implicit in the principles of justice. With the constant assurance expressed by these principles, persons will develop a secure sense of their own worth that forms the basis for the love of humankind. By appealing straightway to the capacity for sympathy as a foundation of just conduct in the absence of reciprocity, the principle of utility not only requires more than justice as fairness but depends upon weaker and less common inclinations. Two other elements affect the strength of the sense of justice: the clarity of the moral conception and the attractiveness of its ideals. I shall consider the latter in the next chapter. There I try to show that the contract view is more congruent with our good than its rivals; and assuming this conclusion here, it lends further support to the preceding considerations. The greater clarity of the principles of justice was considered earlier (§ 49). I noted that in comparison with teleological doctrines, the principles of justice define a perspicuous conception. By contrast, the idea of maximizing the aggregate of well-being, or of attaining the greatest perfection, is vague and amorphous. It is easier to ascertain when the equal liberties are infringed and to establish discrepancies from the difference principle than it is to decide whether unequal treatment increases social welfare. The more definite structure of the two principles (and the various priority rules) offers them with greater sharpness to the intellect and thereby secures their hold on the mind. The explanations and reasons given for them are more easily understood and accepted; the conduct expected of us is more clearly defined by publicly acknowledged criteria. On all three counts, then, the contract view seems to possess greater stability.

It is remarkable that Mill appears to agree with this conclusion. He notes that with the advance of civilization persons come more and more to recognize that society between human beings is manifestly impossible on any other basis than that the interests of all are to be consulted. The improvement in political institutions removes the opposition of interests and the barriers and inequalities that encourage individuals and classes to disregard one another's claims. The natural end of this development is a state of the human mind in which each person has a feeling of unity with others. Mill maintains that when this state of mind is perfected, it leads the individual to desire for himself only those things in the benefits of which others are included. One of a person's natural wants is that there should be harmony between his feelings and those of his fellow citizens. He desires to know that his aims and theirs are not in opposition, that he is not setting himself against their good but is furthering what they really wish for. [24]

Now the desire Mill characterizes here is the desire to act upon the difference principle (or some similar criterion), and not a desire to act on the principle of utility. Mill does not notice the discrepancy; but he seems intuitively to recognize that a perfectly just society in which men's aims are reconciled in ways acceptable to them all would be one that follows the notion of reciprocity expressed by the principles of justice. His remarks accord with the idea that a stable conception of justice which elicits men's natural sentiments of unity and fellow feeling is more likely to incorporate these principles than the utilitarian standard. And this conclusion is borne out by Mill's account of the roots of the sense of justice, for he believes that this sentiment arises not only from sympathy but also from the natural instinct of self-protection and the desire for security.[25] This double origin suggests that, in his view, justice strikes a balance between altruism and the claims of self and therefore involves a notion of reciprocity. The contract doctrine achieves the same result, but it does so not by an ad hoc weighing of two competing tendencies, but by a theoretical construction which leads to the appropriate reciprocity principles as a conclusion.

In arguing for the greater stability of the principles of justice I have assumed that certain psychological laws are true, or approximately so. I shall not pursue the question of stability beyond this point. We may note however that one might ask how it is that human beings have acquired a nature described by these psycho-

24. *Utilitarianism,* ch. III, pars. 10–11.
25. *Ibid.,* ch. V, pars. 16–25.

logical principles. The theory of evolution would suggest that it is the outcome of natural selection; the capacity for a sense of justice and the moral feelings is an adaption of mankind to its place in nature. As ethologists maintain, the behavior patterns of a species, and the psychological mechanisms of their acquisition, are just as much its characteristics as are the distinctive features of its bodily structures; and these patterns of behavior have an evolution exactly as organs and bones do.[26] It seems clear that for members of a species which lives in stable social groups, the ability to comply with fair cooperative arrangements and to develop the sentiments necessary to support them is highly advantageous, especially when individuals have a long life and are dependent on one another. These conditions guarantee innumerable occasions when mutual justice consistently adhered to is beneficial to all parties.[27]

The crucial question here, however, is whether the principles of justice are closer to the tendency of evolution than the principle of utility. Offhand it would seem that if selection is always of individuals and of their genetic lines, and if the capacity for the various forms of moral behavior has some genetic basis, then altruism in the strict sense would generally be limited to kin and the smaller face-to-face groups. In these cases the willingness to make considerable self-sacrifice would favor one's descendants and tend to be selected. Turning to the other extreme, a society which had a strong propensity to supererogatory conduct in its relations with other societies would jeopardize the existence of its own distinctive culture and its members would risk domination. Therefore one

26. See Konrad Lorenz, his introduction to Darwin's *The Expression of the Emotions in Man and Animals* (Chicago, University of Chicago Press, 1965), pp. xii-xiii.

27. Biologists do not always distinguish between altruism and other kinds of moral conduct. Frequently behavior is classified as either altruistic or egoistic. Not so, however, R. B. Trivers in "Evolution of Reciprocal Altruism," *Quarterly Review of Biology*, vol. 46 (1971). He draws a distinction between altruism and reciprocal altruism (or what I should prefer to call simply reciprocity). The latter is the biological analogue of the cooperative virtues of fairness and good faith. Trivers discusses the natural conditions and selective advantages of reciprocity and the capacities that sustain it. See also G. C. Williams, *Adaptation and Natural Selection* (Princeton, Princeton University Press, 1966), pp. 93–96, 113, 195–197, 247. For a discussion of mutualism between species, see Irenäus Eibl-Eibesfeldt, *Ethology*, trans. Erich Klinghammer (New York, Holt, Rinehart and Winston, 1970), pp. 146f, 292–302.

might conjecture that the capacity to act from the more universal forms of rational benevolence is likely to be eliminated, whereas the capacity to follow the principles of justice and natural duty in relations between groups and individuals other than kin would be favored. We can also see how the system of the moral feelings might evolve as inclinations supporting the natural duties and as stabilizing mechanisms for just schemes.[28] If this is correct, then once again the principles of justice are more securely based.

These remarks are not intended as justifying reasons for the contract view. The main grounds for the principles of justice have already been presented. At this point we are simply checking whether the conception already adopted is a feasible one and not so unstable that some other choice might be better. We are in the second part of the argument in which we ask if the acknowledgment previously made should be reconsidered (§25). I do not contend then that justice as fairness is the most stable conception of justice. The understanding required to answer this question is far beyond the primitive theory I have sketched. The conception agreed to need only be stable enough.

77. THE BASIS OF EQUALITY

I now turn to the basis of equality, the features of human beings in virtue of which they are to be treated in accordance with the principles of justice. Our conduct toward animals is not regulated by these principles, or so it is generally believed. On what grounds then do we distinguish between mankind and other living things and regard the constraints of justice as holding only in our relations to human persons? We must examine what determines the range of application of conceptions of justice.

To clarify our question, we may distinguish three levels where the concept of equality applies. The first is to the administration of institutions as public systems of rules. In this case equality is essentially justice as regularity. It implies the impartial application and consistent interpretation of rules according to such precepts as to treat similar cases similarly (as defined by statutes and precedents)

28. On this last point, see Trivers, *ibid.*, pp. 47–54.

and the like (§ 38). Equality at this level is the least controversial element in the common sense idea of justice.[29] The second and much more difficult application of equality is to the substantive structure of institutions. Here the meaning of equality is specified by the principles of justice which require that equal basic rights be assigned to all persons. Presumably this excludes animals; they have some protection certainly but their status is not that of human beings. But this outcome is still unexplained. We have yet to consider what sorts of beings are owed the guarantees of justice. This brings us to the third level at which the question of equality arises.

The natural answer seems to be that it is precisely the moral persons who are entitled to equal justice. Moral persons are distinguished by two features: first they are capable of having (and are assumed to have) a conception of their good (as expressed by a rational plan of life); and second they are capable of having (and are assumed to acquire) a sense of justice, a normally effective desire to apply and to act upon the principles of justice, at least to a certain minimum degree. We use the characterization of the persons in the original position to single out the kind of beings to whom the principles chosen apply. After all, the parties are thought of as adopting these criteria to regulate their common institutions and their conduct toward one another; and the description of their nature enters into the reasoning by which these principles are selected. Thus equal justice is owed to those who have the capacity to take part in and to act in accordance with the public understanding of the initial situation. One should observe that moral personality is here defined as a potentiality that is ordinarily realized in due course. It is this potentiality which brings the claims of justice into play. I shall return to this point below.

We see, then, that the capacity for moral personality is a sufficient condition for being entitled to equal justice.[30] Nothing beyond

29. See Sidgwick, *Methods of Ethics*, p. 496.

30. This fact can be used to interpret the concept of natural rights. For one thing, it explains why it is appropriate to call by this name the rights that justice protects. These claims depend solely on certain natural attributes the presence of which can be ascertained by natural reason pursuing common sense methods of inquiry. The existence of these attributes and the claims based upon them is established independently from social conventions and legal norms. The

the essential minimum is required. Whether moral personality is also a necessary condition I shall leave aside. I assume that the capacity for a sense of justice is possessed by the overwhelming majority of mankind, and therefore this question does not raise a serious practical problem. That moral personality suffices to make one a subject of claims is the essential thing. We cannot go far wrong in supposing that the sufficient condition is always satisfied. Even if the capacity were necessary, it would be unwise in practice to withhold justice on this ground. The risk to just institutions would be too great.

It should be stressed that the sufficient condition for equal justice, the capacity for moral personality, is not at all stringent. When someone lacks the requisite potentiality either from birth or accident, this is regarded as a defect or deprivation. There is no race or recognized group of human beings that lacks this attribute. Only scattered individuals are without this capacity, or its realization to the minimum degree, and the failure to realize it is the consequence of unjust and impoverished social circumstances, or fortuitous contingencies. Furthermore, while individuals presumably have varying capacities for a sense of justice, this fact is not a reason for depriving those with a lesser capacity of the full protection of justice. Once a certain minimum is met, a person is entitled to equal liberty on a par with everyone else. A greater capacity for a sense of justice, as shown say in a greater skill and facility in applying the principles of justice and in marshaling arguments in particular cases, is a natural asset like any other ability. The special advantages a person receives for its exercise are to be governed by

propriety of the term "natural" is that it suggests the contrast between the rights identified by the theory of justice and the rights defined by law and custom. But more than this, the concept of natural rights includes the idea that these rights are assigned in the first instance to persons, and that they are given a special weight. Claims easily overridden for other values are not natural rights. Now the rights protected by the first principle have both of these features in view of the priority rules. Thus justice as fairness has the characteristic marks of a natural rights theory. Not only does it ground fundamental rights on natural attributes and distinguish their bases from social norms, but it assigns rights to persons by principles of equal justice, these principles having a special force against which other values cannot normally prevail. Although specific rights are not absolute, the system of equal liberties is absolute practically speaking under favorable conditions.

the difference principle. Thus if some have to a preeminent degree the judicial virtues of impartiality and integrity which are needed in certain positions, they may properly have whatever benefits should be attached to these offices. Yet the application of the principle of equal liberty is not affected by these differences. It is sometimes thought that basic rights and liberties should vary with capacity, but justice as fairness denies this: provided the minimum for moral personality is satisfied, a person is owed all the guarantees of justice.

This account of the basis of equality calls for a few comments. First of all, it may be objected that equality cannot rest on natural attributes. There is no natural feature with respect to which all human beings are equal, that is, which everyone has (or which sufficiently many have) to the same degree. It might appear that if we wish to hold a doctrine of equality, we must interpret it in another way, namely as a purely procedural principle. Thus to say that human beings are equal is to say that none has a claim to preferential treatment in the absence of compelling reasons. The burden of proof favors equality: it defines a procedural presumption that persons are to be treated alike. Departures from equal treatment are in each case to be defended and judged impartially by the same system of principles that hold for all; the essential equality is thought to be equality of consideration.

There are several difficulties with this procedural interpretation.[31] For one thing, it is nothing more than the precept of treating similar cases similarly applied at the highest level, together with an assignment of the burden of proof. Equality of consideration puts no restrictions upon what grounds may be offered to justify inequalities. There is no guarantee of substantive equal treatment, since slave and caste systems (to mention extreme cases) may satisfy this conception. The real assurance of equality lies in the content of the principles of justice and not in these procedural presumptions. The placing of the burden of proof is not sufficient. But further, even if the procedural interpretation imposed some genuine

31. For a discussion of these, see S. I. Benn, "Egalitarianism and the Equal Consideration of Interests," *Nomos IX: Equality*, ed. J. R. Pennock and J. W. Chapman (New York, Atherton Press, 1967), pp. 62–64, 66–68; and W. K. Frankena, "Some Beliefs about Justice" (The Lindley Lecture, The University of Kansas, 1966), pp. 16f.

restrictions on institutions, there is still the question why we are to follow the procedure in some instances and not others. Surely it applies to creatures who belong to some class, but which one? We still need a natural basis for equality so that this class can be identified.

Moreover, it is not the case that founding equality on natural capacities is incompatible with an egalitarian view. All we have to do is to select a range property (as I shall say) and to give equal justice to those meeting its conditions. For example, the property of being in the interior of the unit circle is a range property of points in the plane. All points inside this circle have this property although their coordinates vary within a certain range. And they equally have this property, since no point interior to a circle is more or less interior to it than any other interior point. Now whether there is a suitable range property for singling out the respect in which human beings are to be counted equal is settled by the conception of justice. But the description of the parties in the original position identifies such a property, and the principles of justice assure us that any variations in ability within the range are to be regarded as any other natural asset. There is no obstacle to thinking that a natural capacity constitutes the basis of equality.

How then can it seem plausible that founding equality on natural attributes undermines equal justice? The notion of a range property is too obvious to be overlooked. There must be a deeper explanation. The answer, I think, is that a teleological theory is often taken for granted. Thus, if the right is to maximize the net balance of satisfaction, say, then rights and duties are to be assigned so as to achieve this end. Among the relevant aspects of the problem are men's different productive skills and capacities for satisfaction. It may happen that maximizing aggregate welfare requires adjusting basic rights to variations in these features. Of course, given the standard utilitarian assumptions, there is a tendency to equality. The relevant thing, however, is that in either case the correct natural basis and the appropriate assignment of rights depends upon the principle of utility. It is the content of the ethical doctrine, and the fact that it is a maximizing notion, that allows variations in capacity to justify unequal fundamental rights, and not the idea that equality is founded on natural attributes. An examination of perfectionism would, I believe, lead to the same conclusion. But justice as fairness is not a maximizing theory. We are not directed to look for differences in natural features that affect some maximand and therefore serve as possible grounds for different grades of citizenship. Although agreeing with many teleological theories in the relevance of natural attributes, the contract view needs much weaker assumptions about their distribution to establish equal rights. It is enough that a certain minimum is generally fulfilled.

Several further points should be noted briefly. First, the conception of moral personality and the required minimum may often prove troublesome. While many concepts are vague to some degree, that of moral personality is likely to be especially so. But these matters are, I think, best discussed in the context of definite moral problems. The nature of the specific issue and the structure of the available general facts may suggest a fruitful way to settle them. In any case, one must not confuse the vagueness of a conception of justice with the thesis that basic rights should vary with natural capacity.

I have said that the minimal requirements defining moral personality refer to a capacity and not to the realization of it. A being that has this capacity, whether or not it is yet developed, is to receive the full protection of the principles of justice. Since infants and children are thought to have basic rights (normally exercised on their behalf by parents and guardians), this interpretation of the requisite conditions seems necessary to match our considered judgments. Moreover, regarding the potentiality as sufficient accords with the hypothetical nature of the original position, and with the idea that as far as possible the choice of principles should not be influenced by arbitrary contingencies. Therefore it is reasonable to say that those who could take part in the initial agreement, were it not for fortuitous circumstances, are assured equal justice.

Now of course none of this is literally argument. I have not set out the premises from which this conclusion follows, as I have tried to do, albeit not very rigorously, with the choice of conceptions of justice in the original position. Nor have I tried to prove that the characterization of the parties must be used as the basis of equality. Rather this interpretation seems to be the natural completion of justice as fairness. A full discussion would take up the various special cases of lack of capacity. That of children I have already com mented upon briefly in connection with paternalism (§39). The problem of those who have lost their realized capacity temporarily through misfortune, accident, or mental stress can be regarded in a similar way. But those more or less permanently deprived of moral personality may present a difficulty. I cannot examine this problem here, but I assume that the account of equality would not be materially affected.

I should like to conclude this section with a few general comments. First of all, the simplicity of the contract view of the basis of equality is worth emphasizing. The minimum capacity for the sense of justice insures that everyone has equal rights. The claims of all are to be adjudicated by the principles of justice. Equality is supported by the general facts of nature and not merely by a procedural rule without substantive force. Nor does equality presuppose an assessment of the intrinsic worth of persons, or a comparative evaluation of their conceptions of the good. Those who can give justice are owed justice.

The advantages of these straightforward propositions become more evident when other accounts of equality are examined. For example, one might think that equal justice means that society is to make the same proportionate contribution to each person's realizing the best life which he is capable of.[32] Offhand this may seem an attractive suggestion. It suffers however from serious difficulties. For one thing it not only requires a method of estimating the relative goodness of plans of life, but it also presupposes some way of measuring what counts as an equal proportionate contribution to persons with different conceptions of their good. The problems in applying this standard are obvious. A more important difficulty is that the greater abilities of some may give them a stronger claim on social resources irrespective of compensating advantages to others. One must assume that variations in natural assets will affect what is necessary to provide equal proportionate assistance to those with different plans of life. But in addition to violating the principle of mutual advantage, this conception of equality means that the strength of men's claims is directly influenced by the distribution of

32. For this idea, see W. K. Frankena, "Some Beliefs about Justice," pp. 14ff; and J. N. Findlay, *Values and Intentions,* pp. 301f.

natural abilities, and therefore by contingencies that are arbitrary from a moral point of view. The basis of equality in justice as fairness avoids these objections. The only contingency which is decisive is that of having or not having the capacity for a sense of justice. By giving justice to those who can give justice in return, the principle of reciprocity is fulfilled at the highest level.

A further observation is that we can now more fully reconcile two conceptions of equality. Some writers have distinguished between equality as it is invoked in connection with the distribution of certain goods, some of which will almost certainly give higher status or prestige to those who are more favored, and equality as it applies to the respect which is owed to persons irrespective of their social position.[33] Equality of the first kind is defined by the second principle of justice which regulates the structure of organizations and distributive shares so that social cooperation is both efficient and fair. But equality of the second kind is fundamental. It is defined by the first principle of justice and by such natural duties as that of mutual respect; it is owed to human beings as moral persons. The natural basis of equality explains its deeper significance. The priority of the first principle over the second enables us to avoid balancing these conceptions of equality in an ad hoc manner, while the argument from the standpoint of the original position shows how this precedence comes about (§ 82).

The consistent application of the principle of fair opportunity requires us to view persons independently from the influences of their social position.[34] But how far should this tendency be carried? It seems that even when fair opportunity (as it has been defined) is satisfied, the family will lead to unequal chances between individuals (§ 46). Is the family to be abolished then? Taken by itself and given a certain primacy, the idea of equal opportunity inclines in this direction. But within the context of the theory of justice as a whole, there is much less urgency to take this course. The acknowledgment of the difference principle redefines the grounds for social inequalities as conceived in the system of liberal equality;

33. See B. A. O. Williams, "The Idea of Equality," *Philosophy, Politics, and Society,* second series, ed. Peter Laslett and W. G. Runciman (Oxford, Basil Blackwell, 1962), pp. 129–131; and W. G. Runciman, *Relative Deprivation and Social Justice* (London, Routledge and Kegan Paul, 1966), pp. 274–284.

34. See Williams, *ibid.,* pp. 125–129.

and when the principles of fraternity and redress are allowed their appropriate weight, the natural distribution of assets and the contingencies of social circumstances can more easily be accepted. We are more ready to dwell upon our good fortune now that these differences are made to work to our advantage, rather than to be downcast by how much better off we might have been had we had an equal chance along with others if only all social barriers had been removed. The conception of justice, should it be truly effective and publicly recognized as such, seems more likely than its rivals to transform our perspective on the social world and to reconcile us to the dispositions of the natural order and the conditions of human life.

Last of all, we should recall here the limits of a theory of justice. Not only are many aspects of morality left aside, but no account is given of right conduct in regard to animals and the rest of nature. A conception of justice is but one part of a moral view. While I have not maintained that the capacity for a sense of justice is necessary in order to be owed the duties of justice, it does seem that we are not required to give strict justice anyway to creatures lacking this capacity. But it does not follow that there are no requirements at all in regard to them, nor in our relations with the natural order. Certainly it is wrong to be cruel to animals and the destruction of a whole species can be a great evil. The capacity for feelings of pleasure and pain and for the forms of life of which animals are capable clearly imposes duties of compassion and humanity in their case. I shall not attempt to explain these considered beliefs. They are outside the scope of the theory of justice, and it does not seem possible to extend the contract doctrine so as to include them in a natural way. A correct conception of our relations to animals and to nature would seem to depend upon a theory of the natural order and our place in it. One of the tasks of metaphysics is to work out a view of the world which is suited for this purpose; it should identify and systematize the truths decisive for these questions. How far justice as fairness will have to be revised to fit into this larger theory it is impossible to say. But it seems reasonable to hope that if it is sound as an account of justice among persons, it cannot be too far wrong when these broader relationships are taken into consideration.

CHAPTER IX. THE GOOD OF JUSTICE

In this chapter I take up the second and last part of the problem of stability. This concerns the question whether justice as fairness and goodness as rationality are congruent. It remains to be shown that given the circumstances of a well-ordered society, a person's rational plan of life supports and affirms his sense of justice. I approach this problem by discussing in turn the various desiderata of a well-ordered society and the ways in which its just arrangements contribute to the good of its members. Thus I note first that such a society allows for persons' autonomy and the objectivity of their judgments of right and justice. I indicate next how justice combines with the ideal of social union, mitigates the propensity to envy and spite, and defines an equilibrium in which the priority of liberty obtains. Finally, by an examination of the contrast between justice as fairness and hedonistic utilitarianism, I attempt to show how just institutions provide for the unity of the self and enable human beings to express their nature as free and equal moral persons. Taking these features together, I then argue that in a well-ordered society an effective sense of justice belongs to a person's good, and so tendencies to instability are kept in check if not eliminated.

78. AUTONOMY AND OBJECTIVITY

Before taking up the various features of a well-ordered society, I should emphasize that I am concerned with the problem of congruence only for this social form. We are therefore still limiting ourselves to strict compliance theory. Yet this case is the first one to examine, for if congruence fails for a well-ordered society it seems bound to fail everywhere. On the other hand, it is by no means a foregone conclusion even in this instance that the right and the good are congruent. For this relation implies that the members of a well-ordered society, when they appraise their plan of life by the principles of rational choice, will decide to maintain their sense of justice as regulative of their conduct toward one another. The requisite match exists between the principles of justice that would be agreed to in the absence of information and the principles of rational choice that are not chosen at all and applied with full knowledge. Principles accounted for in strikingly different ways nevertheless fit together when those of justice are perfectly realized. Of course, this congruence has its explanation in how the contract doctrine is set up. But the relation is not a matter of course and its basis needs to be worked out.

I shall proceed by examining a number of features of a well-ordered society which all told lead rational persons to confirm their sense of justice. The argument is cumulative and depends upon a convergence of observations the force of which is not summed up until later (§86).

I begin by noting that we sometimes doubt the soundness of our moral attitudes when we reflect on their psychological origins. Thinking that these sentiments have arisen in situations marked say by submission to authority, we may wonder whether they should not be rejected altogether. Since the argument for the good of justice depends upon the members of a well-ordered society having an effective desire to act justly, we must allay these uncertainties. Imagine then that someone experiences the promptings of his moral sense as inexplicable inhibitions which for the moment he is unable to justify. Why should he not regard them as simply neurotic compulsions? If it should turn out that these scruples are indeed largely shaped and accounted for by the contingencies of early childhood, perhaps by the course of our family history and class situation, and that there is nothing to add on their behalf, then there is surely no reason why they should govern our lives. But of course to someone in a well-ordered society there are many things to say. One can point out to him the essential features of the development of the sentiment of justice and how eventually the morality of principles is to be understood. Moreover his moral education itself has been regulated by the principles of right and justice to which he would consent in an initial situation in which all have equal representation as moral persons. As we have seen, the moral conception adopted is independent of natural contingencies and accidental social circumstances; and therefore the psychological processes by which his moral sense has been acquired conform to principles that he himself would choose under conditions that he would concede are fair and undistorted by fortune and happenstance.

Nor can someone in a well-ordered society object to the practices of moral instruction that inculcate a sense of justice. For in agreeing to principles of right the parties in the original position at the same time consent to the arrangements necessary to make these principles effective in their conduct. Indeed, the adaptability of these arrangements to the limitations of human nature is an important consideration in choosing a conception of justice. Thus no one's moral convictions are the result of coercive indoctrination. Instruction is throughout as reasoned as the development of understanding permits, just as the natural duty of mutual respect requires. None of the ideals, principles, and precepts upheld in the society takes unfair advantage of human weakness. A person's sense of justice is not a compulsive psychological mechanism cleverly installed by those in authority in order to insure his unswerving compliance with rules designed to advance their interests. Nor is the process of education simply a causal sequence intended to bring about as an end result the appropriate moral sentiments. As far as possible each stage foreshadows in its teaching and explanations the conception of right and justice at which it aims and by reference to which we will later recognize that the moral standards presented to us are justified.

These observations are evident consequences of the contract doctrine and the fact that its principles regulate the practices of moral instruction in a well-ordered society. Following the Kantian interpretation of justice as fairness, we can say that by acting from these principles persons are acting autonomously: they are acting from principles that they would acknowledge under conditions that best express their nature as free and equal rational beings. To be sure, these conditions also reflect the situation of individuals in the world and their being subject to the circumstances of justice. But this simply means that the conception of autonomy is that fitting for human beings; the notion suited to superior or inferior natures is most likely different (§ 40). Thus moral education is education for autonomy. In due course everyone will know why he would adopt the principles of justice and how they are derived from the conditions that characterize his being an equal in a society of moral persons. It follows that in accepting these principles on this basis we are not influenced primarily by tradition and authority, or the opinions of others. However necessary these agencies may be in order for us to reach complete understanding, we eventually come to hold a conception of right on reasonable grounds that we can set out independently for ourselves.

Now on the contract view the notions of autonomy and objectivity are compatible: there is no antinomy between freedom and reason.[1] Both autonomy and objectivity are characterized in a consistent way by reference to the original position. The idea of the initial situation is central to the whole theory and other basic notions are defined in terms of it. Thus acting autonomously is acting from principles that we would consent to as free and equal rational beings, and that we are to understand in this way. Also, these principles are objective. They are the principles that we would want everyone (including ourselves) to follow were we to take up together the appropriate general point of view. The original position defines this perspective, and its conditions also embody those of objectivity: its stipulations express the restrictions on arguments that force us to consider the choice of principles unencumbered by the singularities of the circumstances in which we find ourselves. The veil of ignorance prevents us from shaping our moral view to accord with our own particular attachments and interests. We do not look at the social order from our situation but take up a point of view that everyone can adopt on an equal footing. In this sense we look at our society and our place in it objectively: we share a common standpoint along with others and do not make our judg-

1. The question of the compatibility of autonomy and objectivity is discussed by H. D. Aiken in his essay "The Concept of Moral Objectivity," in *Reason and Conduct* (New York, Alfred Knopf, 1962), pp. 134–170. See also Huntington Terrell, "Moral Objectivity and Freedom," *Ethics,* vol. 76 (1965), pp. 117–127, for a discussion to which I am indebted.

ments from a personal slant. Thus our moral principles and convictions are objective to the extent that they have been arrived at and tested by assuming this general standpoint and by assessing the arguments for them by the restrictions expressed by the conception of the original position. The judicial virtues such as impartiality and considerateness are the excellences of intellect and sensibility that enable us to do these things well.

One consequence of trying to be objective, of attempting to frame our moral conceptions and judgments from a shared point of view, is that we are more likely to reach agreement. Indeed, other things equal, the preferred description of the initial situation is that which introduces the greatest convergence of opinion. It is partly for this reason that we accept the constraints of a common standpoint, since we cannot reasonably expect our views to fall into line when they are affected by the contingencies of our different circumstances. But of course our judgments will not coincide on all questions, and in fact many if not most social issues may still be insoluble, especially if viewed in their full complexity. This is why the numerous simplifications of justice as fairness are acknowledged. We have only to recall the reasons for such notions as the veil of ignorance, pure procedural justice (as opposed to allocative justice), lexical ordering, the division of the basic structure into two parts, and so on. Taken all together the parties hope that these and other devices will simplify political and social questions so that the resulting balance of justice, made possible by the greater consensus, outweighs what may have been lost by ignoring certain potentially relevant aspects of moral situations. The complexity of problems of justice is up to the persons in the original position to decide. Although ethical differences are bound to remain, seeing the social world from the original position does permit essential understandings to be reached. The acceptance of the principles of right and justice forges the bonds of civic friendship and establishes the basis of comity amidst the disparities that persist. Citizens are able to recognize one another's good faith and desire for justice even though agreement may occasionally break down on constitutional questions and most certainly on many issues of policy. But unless there existed a common perspective, the assumption of which narrowed differences of opinion, reasoning and argument would be pointless and we would have no rational grounds for believing in the soundness of our convictions.

It is clear that this interpretation of autonomy and objectivity depends upon the theory of justice. The idea of the original position is used to give a consistent rendering of both notions. Of course, if it is believed that the principles of justice would not be chosen, the content of these conceptions would have to be suitably altered. One who holds that the principle of utility would be consented to thinks that our autonomy is expressed by following this criterion. Nevertheless, the general idea will be the same, and both autonomy and objectivity are still explicated by reference to the initial situation. But some have characterized autonomy and objectivity in an entirely different way. They have suggested that autonomy is the complete freedom to form our moral opinions and that the conscientious judgment of every moral agent ought absolutely to be respected. Objectivity is then attributed to those judgments which satisfy all the standards that the agent himself has in his liberty decided are relevant.[2] These standards may or may not have anything to do with taking up a common point of view that others might reasonably be expected to share; nor of course is the corresponding idea of autonomy connected with such a perspective. I mention these other interpretations only to indicate by contrast the nature of the contract doctrine.

From the standpoint of justice as fairness it is not true that the conscientious judgments of each person ought absolutely to be respected; nor is it true that individuals are completely free to form their moral convictions. These contentions are mistaken if they mean that, having arrived at our moral opinions conscientiously (as we believe), we always have a claim to be allowed to act on them. In discussing conscientious objection, we noted that the problem here is that of deciding how one is to answer those who strive to act as their erring conscience directs them (§ 56). How do we ascertain that their conscience and not ours is mistaken, and under what circumstances can they be compelled to desist? Now the answer to these questions is found by ascending to the original position: a person's conscience is misguided when he seeks to impose on us conditions that violate the principles to which we

2. See Aiken, *ibid.,* pp. 162–169.

would each consent in that situation. And we can resist his plans in those ways that would be authorized when the conflict is viewed from that perspective. We are not literally to respect the conscience of an individual. Rather we are to respect him as a person and we do this by limiting his actions, when this proves necessary, only as the principles we would both acknowledge permit. In the original position the parties agree to be held responsible for the conception of justice that is chosen. There is no violation of our autonomy so long as its principles are properly followed. Moreover, these principles stipulate that on many occasions we cannot shift the responsibility for what we do onto others. Those in authority are accountable for the policies they pursue and the instructions they lay down. And those who acquiesce in carrying out unjust commands or in abetting evil designs cannot in general plead that they did not know better or that the fault rests solely with those in higher positions. The details concerning these matters belong to partial compliance theory. The essential point here is that the principles that best conform to our nature as free and equal rational beings themselves establish our accountability. Otherwise autonomy is likely to lead to a mere collision of self-righteous wills, and objectivity to the adherence to a consistent yet idiosyncratic system.

Here we should note that in times of social doubt and loss of faith in long established values, there is a tendency to fall back on the virtues of integrity: truthfulness and sincerity, lucidity and commitment, or, as some say, authenticity. If no one knows what is true, at least we can make our beliefs our own in our own way and not adopt them as handed to us by others. If the traditional moral rules are no longer relevant and we cannot agree which ones should take their place, we can in any event decide with a clear head how we mean to act and stop pretending that somehow or other it is already decided for us and we must accept this or that authority. Now of course the virtues of integrity are virtues, and among the excellences of free persons. Yet while necessary, they are not sufficient; for their definition allows for most any content: a tyrant might display these attributes to a high degree, and by doing so exhibit a certain charm, not deceiving himself by political pretenses and excuses of fortune. It is impossible to construct a moral view from these virtues alone; being virtues of form they are in a sense secondary. But joined to the appropriate conception of justice, one that allows for autonomy and objectivity correctly understood, they come into their own. The idea of the original position, and the principles chosen there, show how this is achieved.

In conclusion then a well-ordered society affirms the autonomy of persons and encourages the objectivity of their considered judgments of justice. Any doubts that its members may entertain about the soundness of their moral sentiments when they reflect upon how these dispositions were acquired may be dispelled by seeing that their convictions match the principles which would be chosen in the original position or, if they do not, by revising their judgments so that they do.

79. THE IDEA OF SOCIAL UNION

We have already seen that despite the individualistic features of justice as fairness, the two principles of justice provide an Archimedean point for appraising existing institutions as well as the desires and aspirations which they generate. These criteria provide an independent standard for guiding the course of social change without invoking a perfectionist or an organic conception of society (§ 41). But the question remains whether the contract doctrine is a satisfactory framework for understanding the values of community and for choosing among social arrangements to realize them. It is natural to conjecture that the congruence of the right and the good depends in large part upon whether a well-ordered society achieves the good of community. I shall take up several aspects of this question in this and the three following sections.

We may begin by recalling that one of the conditions of the original position is that the parties know that they are subject to the circumstances of justice. They assume that each has a conception of his good in the light of which he presses claims against the rest. So although they view society as a cooperative venture for mutual advantage, it is typically marked by a conflict as well as by an identity of interests. Now there are two ways of viewing these suppositions. The first is that taken by the theory of justice: the idea is to derive satisfactory principles from the weakest possible assumptions. The premises of the theory should be simple and reasonable conditions that everyone or most everyone would grant, and for which convincing philosophical arguments can be given. At the same time, the greater the initial collision of claims into which the principles can introduce an acceptable order, the more comprehensive the theory is likely to be. Therefore a deep opposition of interests is presumed to obtain.

The other way to think of these suppositions is to regard them as describing a certain kind of social order, or a certain aspect of the basic structure that is actually realized. Thus we are led to the notion of private society.[3] Its chief features are first that the persons comprising it, whether they are human individuals or associations, have their own private ends which are either competing or independent, but not in any case complementary. And second, institutions are not thought to have any value in themselves, the activity of engaging in them not being counted as a good but if anything as a burden. Thus each person assesses social arrangements solely as a means to his private aims. No one takes account of the good of others, or of what they possess; rather everyone prefers the most efficient scheme that gives him the largest share of assets. (Expressed more formally, the only variables in an individual's utility function are commodities and assets held by him, and not items possessed by others nor their level of utility.)

We may suppose also that the actual division of advantages is determined largely by the balance of power and strategic position resulting from existing circumstances. Yet this division may of course be perfectly fair and satisfy the claims of mutuality. By good fortune the situation may happen to lead to this outcome. Public goods consist largely of those instrumentalities and conditions maintained by the state for everyone to use for his own purposes as his means permit, in the same manner that each has his own destination when traveling along the highways. The theory of com-

3. The notion of private society, or something like it, is found in many places. Well-known examples are in Plato, *The Republic*, 369–372, and Hegel, *Philosophy of Right*, trans. T. M. Knox (Oxford, The Clarendon Press, 1942), §§ 182–187, under the heading of civil society. The natural habitat of this notion is in economic theory (general equilibrium), and Hegel's discussion reflects his reading of Adam Smith, *The Wealth of Nations*.

petitive markets is a paradigm description of this type of society. Since the members of this society are not moved by the desire to act justly, the stability of just and efficient arrangements when they exist normally requires the use of sanctions. Therefore the alignment of private and collective interests is the result of stabilizing institutional devices applied to persons who oppose one another as indifferent if not hostile powers. Private society is not held together by a public conviction that its basic arrangements are just and good in themselves, but by the calculations of everyone, or of sufficiently many to maintain the scheme, that any practicable changes would reduce the stock of means whereby they pursue their personal ends.

It is sometimes contended that the contract doctrine entails that private society is the ideal, at least when the division of advantages satisfies a suitable standard of reciprocity. But this is not so, as the notion of a well-ordered society shows. And as I have just said, the idea of the original position has another explanation. The account of goodness as rationality and the social nature of mankind also requires a different view. Now the sociability of human beings must not be understood in a trivial fashion. It does not imply merely that society is necessary for human life, or that by living in a community men acquire needs and interests that prompt them to work together for mutual advantage in certain specific ways allowed for and encouraged by their institutions. Nor is it expressed by the truism that social life is a condition for our developing the ability to speak and think, and to take part in the common activities of society and culture. No doubt even the concepts that we use to describe our plans and situation, and even to give voice to our personal wants and purposes, often presuppose a social setting as well as a system of belief and thought that are the outcome of the collective efforts of a long tradition. These facts are certainly not trivial; but to use them to characterize our ties to one another is to give a trivial interpretation of human sociability. For all of these things are equally true of persons who view their relations purely instrumentally.

The social nature of mankind is best seen by contrast with the conception of private society. Thus human beings have in fact shared final ends and they value their common institutions and activities as good in themselves. We need one another as partners in ways of life that are engaged in for their own sake, and the successes and enjoyments of others are necessary for and complimentary to our own good. These matters are evident enough, but they call for some elaboration. In the account of goodness as rationality we came to the familiar conclusion that rational plans of life normally provide for the development of at least some of a person's powers. The Aristotelian Principle points in this direction. Yet one basic characteristic of human beings is that no one person can do everything that he might do; nor a fortiori can he do everything that any other person can do. The potentialities of each individual are greater than those he can hope to realize; and they fall far short of the powers among men generally. Thus everyone must select which of his abilities and possible interests he wishes to encourage; he must plan their training and exercise, and schedule their pursuit in an orderly way. Different persons with similar or complementary capacities may cooperate so to speak in realizing their common or matching nature. When men are secure in the enjoyment of the exercise of their own powers, they are disposed to appreciate the perfections of others, especially when their several excellences have an agreed place in a form of life the aims of which all accept.

Thus we may say following Humboldt that it is through social union founded upon the needs and potentialities of its members that each person can participate in the total sum of the realized natural assets of the others. We are led to the notion of the community of humankind the members of which enjoy one another's excellences and individuality elicited by free institutions, and they recognize the good of each as an element in the complete activity the whole scheme of which is consented to and gives pleasure to all. This community may also be imagined to extend over time, and therefore in the history of a society the joint contributions of successive generations can be similarly conceived.[4] Our predeces-

4. This idea must have occurred to many and is surely implicit in numerous writings. Yet I have been able to find but a few definite formulations of it as expressed in this section. See Wilhelm von Humboldt, *The Limits of State Action*, ed. J. W. Burrow (Cambridge, The University Press, 1969), pp. 16f, for a clear statement. He says: "Every human being, then, can act with only one dominant faculty at a time; or rather, our whole nature disposes us at any given time to some single form of spontaneous activity. It would therefore seem to follow from

sors in achieving certain things leave it up to us to pursue them further; their accomplishments affect our choice of endeavors and define a wider background against which our aims can be under-

this, that man is inevitably destined to a partial cultivation, since he only enfeebles his energies by directing them to a multiplicity of objects. But man has it in his power to avoid this one-sidedness, by attempting to unite the distinct and generally separately exercised faculties of his nature, by bringing into spontaneous cooperation, at each period of his life, the dying sparks of one activity, and those which the future will kindle, and endeavoring to increase and diversify the powers with which he works, by harmoniously combining them, instead of looking for mere variety of objects for their separate exercise. What is achieved, in the case of the individual, by the union of past and future with the present, is produced in society by the mutual cooperation of its different members; for, in all stages of his life, each individual can achieve only one of those perfections, which represent the possible features of human character. It is through a social union, therefore, based on the internal wants and capacities of its members, that each is enabled to participate in the rich collective resources of all the others"(pp. 16f). As a pure case to illustrate this notion of social union, we may consider a group of musicians every one of whom could have trained himself to play equally as well as the others any instrument in the orchestra, but who each have by a kind of tacit agreement set out to perfect their skills on the one they have chosen so as to realize the powers of all in their joint performances. This idea also has a central place in Kant's "Idea for a Universal History," in *Kant's Political Writings,* ed. Hans Reiss and trans. H. B. Nisbet (Cambridge, The University Press, 1970). See pp. 42f where he says that every individual man would have to live for a vast length of time if he were to learn how to make complete use of all his natural capacities, and therefore it will require perhaps an incalculable series of generations of men. I have not been able to find this idea expressly stated where I would expect to, for example, in Schiller's *Letters on the Aesthetic Education of Man,* ed. and trans. E. M. Wilkinson and L. A. Willoughby (Oxford, The Clarendon Press, 1967), esp. the sixth and twenty-seventh letters. Nor, I think, in Marx's early writings, particularly the *Economic and Philosophical Manuscripts.* See *Karl Marx: Early Writings,* trans. and ed. T. B. Bottomore (London, C. A. Watts, 1963), pp. 126–129, 154, 156–157, 189, 202f. However, Marx is interpreted to hold a notion like this by Shlomo Avineri, *The Social and Political Thought of Karl Marx* (Cambridge, The University Press, 1969), pp. 231f. Yet Marx tends, I think, to view full communist society as one in which each person completely realizes his nature, in which he himself expresses all of his powers. In any event, it is important not to confuse the idea of social union with the high value put upon human diversity and individuality, as found in Mill's *On Liberty,* ch. III, and in German Romanticism—see A. O. Lovejoy, *The Great Chain of Being* (Cambridge, Harvard University Press, 1936), ch. X; or with the conception of the good as the harmonious fulfillment of natural powers by (complete) individuals; nor, finally, with gifted individuals, artists, and statesmen, and so on, achieving this for the rest of mankind. Rather, in the limiting case where the powers of each are similar, the group achieves, by a coordination of activities among peers, the same totality of capacities latent in each. Or when these powers differ and are in suitable ways complementary, stood. To say that man is a historical being is to say that the realizations of the powers of human individuals living at any one time takes the cooperation of many generations (or even societies) over a long period of time. It also implies that this cooperation is guided at any moment by an understanding of what has been done in the past as it is interpreted by social tradition. By contrast with humankind, every individual animal can and does do what for the most part it might do, or what any other of its kind might or can do that lives at the same time. The range of realized abilities of a single individual of the species is not in general materially less than the potentialities of others similar to it. The striking exception is the difference of sex. This is perhaps why sexual affinity is the most obvious example of the need of individuals both human and animal for each other. Yet this attraction may take but a purely instrumental form, each individual treating the other as a means to his own pleasure or the continuation of his line. Unless this attachment is fused with elements of affection and friendship, it will not exhibit the characteristic features of social union.

Now many forms of life possess the characteristics of social union, shared final ends and common activities valued for themselves. Science and art provide ready-to-hand illustrations. Likewise families, friendships, and other groups are social unions. There is some advantage though in thinking about the simpler instances of games. Here we can easily distinguish four sorts of ends: the aim of the game as defined by its rules, say to score the most runs; the various motives of the players in playing the game, the excitement they get from it, the desire for exercise, and so on, which may be different for each person; the social purposes served by the game which may be unintended and unknown to the players, or even to anyone in the society, these being matters for the reflective observer to ascertain; and then finally, the shared end, the common desire of all the players that there should be a good play of the game. This shared end can be realized only if the game is played

---

they express the sum of potentialities of the membership as a whole in activities that are intrinsically good and not merely cooperation for social or economic gain. (On this last, see Smith, *Wealth of Nations*, bk. I, chs. I–II.) In either case, persons need one another since it is only in active cooperation with others that one's powers reach fruition. Only in a social union is the individual complete.

fairly according to the rules, if the sides are more or less evenly matched, and if the players all sense that they are playing well. But when this aim is attained, everyone takes pleasure and satisfaction in the very same thing. A good play of the game is, so to speak, a collective achievement requiring the cooperation of all.

Now the shared end of a social union is clearly not merely a common desire for the same particular thing. Grant and Lee were one in their desire to hold Richmond but this desire did not establish community between them. Persons generally want similar sorts of things, liberty and opportunity, shelter and nourishment, yet these wants may put them at odds. Whether individuals have a shared end depends upon the more detailed features of the activity to which their interests incline them as these are regulated by principles of justice. There must be an agreed scheme of conduct in which the excellences and enjoyments of each are complementary to the good of all. Each can then take pleasure in the actions of the others as they jointly execute a plan acceptable to everyone. Despite their competitive side, many games illustrate this type of end in a clear way: the public desire to execute a good and fair play of the game must be regulative and effective if everyone's zest and pleasure are not to languish.

The development of art and science, of religion and culture of all kinds, high and low, can of course be thought of in much the same way. Learning from one another's efforts and appreciating their several contributions, human beings gradually build up systems of knowledge and belief; they work out recognized techniques for doing things and elaborate styles of feeling and expression. In these cases the common aim is often profound and complex, being defined by the respective artistic, scientific, or religious tradition; and to understand this aim often takes years of discipline and study. The essential thing is that there be a shared final end and accepted ways of advancing it which allow for the public recognition of the attainments of everyone. When this end is achieved, all find satisfaction in the very same thing; and this fact together with the complementary nature of the good of individuals affirms the tie of community.

I do not wish to stress, however, the cases of art and science, and high forms of religion and culture. In line with the rejection of the principle of perfection and the acceptance of democracy in the assessment of one another's excellences, they have no special merit from the standpoint of justice. Indeed the reference to games not only has the virtue of simplicity but in some ways is more appropriate. It helps to show that the primary concern is that there are many types of social union and from the perspective of political justice we are not to try to rank them in value. Moreover these unions have no definite size; they range from families and friendships to much larger associations. Nor are there limits of time and space, for those widely separated by history and circumstance can nevertheless cooperate in realizing their common nature. A well-ordered society, and indeed most societies, will presumably contain countless social unions of many different kinds.

With these remarks as a preface, we can now see how the principles of justice are related to human sociability. The main idea is simply that a well-ordered society (corresponding to justice as fairness) is itself a form of social union. Indeed, it is a social union of social unions. Both characteristic features are present: the successful carrying out of just institutions is the shared final end of all the members of society, and these institutional forms are prized as good in themselves. Let us consider these features in turn. The first is quite straightforward. In much the same way that players have the shared end to execute a good and fair play of the game, so the members of a well-ordered society have the common aim of cooperating together to realize their own and another's nature in ways allowed by the principles of justice. This collective intention is the consequence of everyone's having an effective sense of justice. Each citizen wants everyone (including himself) to act from principles to which all would agree in an initial situation of equality. This desire is regulative, as the condition of finality on moral principles requires; and when everyone acts justly, all find satisfaction in the very same thing.

The explanation of the second feature is more involved, yet clear enough from what has been said. We have only to note the various ways in which the fundamental institutions of society, the just constitution and the main parts of the legal order, can be found good in themselves once the idea of social union is applied to the basic structure as a whole. Thus first of all, the Kantian interpretation enables us to say that everyone's acting to uphold just institutions is for the good of each. Human beings have a desire to express their nature as free and equal moral persons, and this they do most adequately by acting from the principles that they would acknowledge in the original position. When all strive to comply with these principles and each succeeds, then individually and collectively their nature as moral persons is most fully realized, and with it their individual and collective good.

But further, the Aristotelian Principle holds for institutional forms as well as for any other human activity. Seen in this light, a just constitutional order, when adjoined to the smaller social unions of everyday life, provides a framework for these many associations and sets up the most complex and diverse activity of all. In a well-ordered society each person understands the first principles that govern the whole scheme as it is to be carried out over many generations; and all have a settled intention to adhere to these principles in their plan of life. Thus the plan of each person is given a more ample and rich structure than it would otherwise have; it is adjusted to the plans of others by mutually acceptable principles. Everyone's more private life is so to speak a plan within a plan, this superordinate plan being realized in the public institutions of society. But this larger plan does not establish a dominant end, such as that of religious unity or the greatest excellence of culture, much less national power and prestige, to which the aims of all individuals and associations are subordinate. The regulative public intention is rather that the constitutional order should realize the principles of justice. And this collective activity, if the Aristotelian Principle is sound, must be experienced as a good.

We have seen that the moral virtues are excellences, attributes of the person that it is rational for persons to want in themselves and in one another as things appreciated for their own sake, or else as exhibited in activities so enjoyed (§§ 66–67). Now it is clear that these excellences are displayed in the public life of a well-ordered society. Therefore the companion principle to the

Aristotelian Principle implies that men appreciate and enjoy these attributes in one another as they are manifested in cooperating to affirm just institutions. It follows that the collective activity of justice is the preeminent form of human flourishing. For given favorable conditions, it is by maintaining these public arrangements that persons best express their nature and achieve the widest regulative excellences of which each is capable. At the same time just institutions allow for and encourage the diverse internal life of associations in which individuals realize their more particular aims. Thus the public realization of justice is a value of community.

As a final comment, I should note that a well-ordered society does not do away with the division of labor in the most general sense. To be sure, the worst aspects of this division can be surmounted: no one need be servilely dependent on others and made to choose between monotonous and routine occupations which are deadening to human thought and sensibility. Each can be offered a variety of tasks so that the different elements of his nature find a suitable expression. But even when work is meaningful for all, we cannot overcome, nor should we wish to, our dependence on others. In a fully just society persons seek their good in ways peculiar to themselves, and they rely upon their associates to do things they could not have done, as well as things they might have done but did not. It is tempting to suppose that everyone might fully realize his powers and that some at least can become complete exemplars of humanity. But this is impossible. It is a feature of human sociability that we are by ourselves but parts of what we might be. We must look to others to attain the excellences that we must leave aside, or lack altogether. The collective activity of society, the many associations and the public life of the largest community that regulates them, sustains our efforts and elicits our contribution. Yet the good attained from the common culture far exceeds our work in the sense that we cease to be mere fragments: that part of ourselves that we directly realize is joined to a wider and just arrangement the aims of which we affirm. The division of labor is overcome not by each becoming complete in himself, but by willing and meaningful work within a just social union of social unions in which all can freely participate as they so incline.

80. THE PROBLEM OF ENVY

Throughout I have assumed that the persons in the original position are not moved by certain psychological propensities (§ 25). A rational individual is not subject to envy, at least when the differences between himself and others are not thought to be the result of injustice and do not exceed certain limits. Nor are the parties influenced by different attitudes toward risk and uncertainty, or by various tendencies to dominate or to submit, and the like. These special psychologies I have also imagined to be behind the veil of ignorance along with the parties' knowledge of their conception of the good. One explanation for these stipulations is that as far as possible the choice of a conception of justice should not be affected by accidental contingencies. The principles adopted should be invariant with respect to differences in these inclinations for the same reason that we want them to hold irrespective of individual preferences and social circumstances.

These assumptions tie in with the Kantian interpretation of justice as fairness and greatly simplify the argument from the standpoint of the original position. The parties are not swayed by individual differences in these propensities, thereby avoiding the complications in the bargaining process that would result. Without rather definite information about which configuration of attitudes existed, one might not be able to say what agreement if any would be reached. In each case it would be contingent upon the particular hypothesis laid down. Unless we could show some distinctive merit from a moral point of view in the postulated array of special psychologies, the principles adopted would be arbitrary, no longer the outcome of reasonable conditions. And since envy is generally regarded as something to be avoided and feared, at least when it becomes intense, it seems desirable that, if possible, the choice of principles should not be influenced by this trait. Therefore, for reasons both of simplicity and moral theory, I have assumed an absence of envy and a lack of knowledge of the special psychologies.

Nevertheless these inclinations do exist and in some way they must be reckoned with. Thus I have split the argument for the principles of justice into two parts: the first part proceeds on the presumptions just mentioned, and is illustrated by most of the argument so far; the second part asks whether the well-ordered society corresponding to the conception adopted will actually generate feelings of envy and patterns of psychological attitudes that will undermine the arrangements it counts to be just. At first we reason as if there is no problem of envy and the special psychologies; and then having ascertained which principles would be settled upon, we check to see whether just institutions so defined are likely to arouse and encourage these propensities to such an extent that the social system becomes unworkable and incompatible with human good. If so, the adoption of the conception of justice must be reconsidered. But should the inclinations engendered support just arrangements, or be easily accommodated by them, the first part of the argument is confirmed. The essential advantage of the two-step procedure is that no particular constellation of attitudes is taken as given. We are simply checking the reasonableness of our initial assumptions and the consequences we have drawn from them in the light of the constraints imposed by the general facts of our world.

I shall discuss the problem of envy as an illustration of the way in which the special psychologies enter into the theory of justice. While each special psychology raises no doubt different questions, the general procedure may be much the same. I begin by noting the reason why envy poses a problem, namely, the fact that the inequalities sanctioned by the difference principle may be so great as to arouse envy to a socially dangerous extent. To clarify this possibility it is useful to distinguish between general and particular envy. The envy experienced by the least advantaged towards those better situated is normally general envy in the sense that they envy the more favored for the kinds of goods and not for the particular objects they possess. The upper classes say are envied for their greater wealth and opportunity; those envying them want similar advantages for themselves. By contrast, particular envy is typical of rivalry and competition. Those who lose out in the quest for office and honor, or for the affections of another, are liable to envy the success of their rivals and to covet the very same thing that they have won. Our problem then is whether the principles of justice, and especially the difference principle with fair equality

531

of opportunity, is likely to engender in practice too much destructive general envy.

I now turn to the definition of envy that seems appropriate for this question. To fix ideas, suppose that the necessary interpersonal comparisons are made in terms of the objective primary goods, liberty and opportunity, income and wealth, which for simplicity I have normally used to define expectations in applying the difference principle. Then we may think of envy as the propensity to view with hostility the greater good of others even though their being more fortunate than we are does not detract from our advantages. We envy persons whose situation is superior to ours (estimated by some agreed index of goods as noted above) and we are willing to deprive them of their greater benefits even if it is necessary to give up something ourselves. When others are aware of our envy, they may become jealous of their better circumstances and anxious to take precautions against the hostile acts to which our envy makes us prone. So understood envy is collectively disadvantageous: the individual who envies another is prepared to do things that make them both worse off, if only the discrepancy between them is sufficiently reduced. Thus Kant, whose definition I have pretty much followed, quite properly discusses envy as one of the vices of hating mankind.[5]

This definition calls for comment. First of all, as Kant observes, there are many occasions when we openly speak of the greater good of others as enviable. Thus we may remark upon the enviable harmony and happiness of a marriage or a family. Similarly, one might say to another that one envies his greater opportunities or attainments. In these cases, those of benign envy as I shall refer to them, there is no ill will intended or expressed. We do not wish, for example, that the marriage or family should be less happy or harmonious. By these conventional expressions we are affirming the value of certain things that others have. We are indicating that, although we possess no similar good of equal value, they are

5. *The Metaphysics of Morals*, pt. II, § 36. In the edition trans. M. G. Gregor (New York, Harper and Row, 1964), p. 127. Aristotle notes that envy and spite as passions do not admit of a mean; their names already imply badness. *Nicomachean Ethics*, 1107a11.

indeed worth striving for. Those to whom we address these remarks are expected to receive them as a kind of praise and not as a foretaste of our hostility. A somewhat different case is that of emulative envy which leads us to try to achieve what others have. The sight of their greater good moves us to strive in socially beneficial ways for similar things for ourselves.[6] Thus envy proper, in contrast with benign envy which we freely express, is a form of rancor that tends to harm both its object and its subject. It is what emulative envy may become under certain conditions of defeat and sense of failure.

A further point is that envy is not a moral feeling. No moral principle need be cited in its explanation. It is sufficient to say that the better situation of others catches our attention. We are downcast by their good fortune and no longer value as highly what we have; and this sense of hurt and loss arouses our rancor and hostility. Thus one must be careful not to conflate envy and resentment. For resentment is a moral feeling. If we resent our having less than others, it must be because we think that their being better off is the result of unjust institutions, or wrongful conduct on their part. Those who express resentment must be prepared to show why certain institutions are unjust or how others have injured them. What marks off envy from the moral feelings is the different way in which it is accounted for, the sort of perspective from which the situation is viewed (§ 73).

We should note also the nonmoral feelings connected with envy but not to be mistaken for it. In particular, jealousy and grudgingness are reverse, so to speak, to envy. A person who is better off may wish those less fortunate than he to stay in their place. He is jealous of his superior position and begrudges them the greater advantages that would put them on a level with himself. And should this propensity extend to denying them benefits that he does not need and cannot use himself, then he is moved by spite.[7] These

---

6. For the distinction between emulation and envy, see Bishop Butler, *Sermons,* I, in *British Moralists,* ed. L. A. Selby-Bigge (Oxford, 1897), vol. I, p. 205.

7. Aristotle, *Nicomachean Ethics,* 1108b1–6, characterizes spite as being pleased at the bad fortune of others, whether deserved or not. For the idea that jealousy, grudgingness, and spite are the reverse of envy, the feelings of those envied and who possess what is wanted, I am indebted to G. M. Foster.

inclinations are collectively harmful in the way that envy is, since the grudging and spiteful man is willing to give up something to maintain the distance between himself and others.

So far I have considered envy and grudgingness as vices. As we have seen, the moral virtues are among the broadly based traits of character which it is rational for persons to want in one another as associates (§66). Thus vices are broadly based traits that are not wanted, spitefulness and envy being clear cases, since they are to everyone's detriment. The parties will surely prefer conceptions of justice the realization of which does not arouse these propensities. We are normally expected to forbear from the actions to which they prompt us and to take the steps necessary to rid ourselves of them. Yet sometimes the circumstances evoking envy are so compelling that given human beings as they are no one can reasonably be asked to overcome his rancorous feelings. A person's lesser position as measured by the index of objective primary goods may be so great as to wound his self-respect; and given his situation, we may sympathize with his sense of loss. Indeed, we can resent being made envious, for society may permit such large disparities in these goods that under existing social conditions these differences cannot help but cause a loss of self-esteem. For those suffering this hurt, envious feelings are not irrational; the satisfaction of their rancor would make them better off. When envy is a reaction to the loss of self-respect in circumstances where it would be unreasonable to expect someone to feel differently, I shall say that it is excusable. Since self-respect is the main primary good, the parties would not agree, I shall assume, to count this sort of subjective loss as irrelevant. Therefore the question is whether a basic structure which satisfies the principles of justice is likely to arouse so much excusable envy that the choice of these principles should be reconsidered.

81. ENVY AND EQUALITY

We are now ready to examine the likelihood of excusable general envy in a well-ordered society. I shall only discuss this case, since our problem is whether the principles of justice are a reasonable

534

undertaking in view of the propensities of human beings, in particular their aversion to disparities in objective goods. Now I assume that the main psychological root of the liability to envy is a lack of self-confidence in our own worth combined with a sense of impotence. Our way of life is without zest and we feel powerless to alter it or to acquire the means of doing what we still want to do.[8] By contrast, someone sure of the worth of his plan of life and his ability to carry it out is not given to rancor nor is he jealous of his good fortune. Even if he could, he has no desire to level down the advantages of others at some expense to himself. This hypothesis implies that the least favored tend to be more envious of the better situation of the more favored the less secure their self-respect and the greater their feeling that they cannot improve their prospects. Similarly the particular envy aroused by competition and rivalry is likely to be stronger the worse one's defeat, for the blow to one's self-confidence is more severe and the loss may seem irretrievable. It is general envy, however, that mainly concerns us here.

There are three conditions, I assume, that encourage hostile outbreaks of envy. The first of these is the psychological condition we have just noted: persons lack a sure confidence in their own value and in their ability to do anything worthwhile. Second (and one of two social conditions), many occasions arise when this psychological condition is experienced as painful and humiliating. The discrepancy between oneself and others is made visible by the social structure and style of life of one's society. The less fortunate are therefore often forcibly reminded of their situation, sometimes leading them to an even lower estimation of themselves and their mode of living. And third, they see their social position as allowing no constructive alternative to opposing the favored circumstances of the more advantaged. To alleviate their feelings of anguish and inferiority, they believe they have no choice but to impose a loss

8. This sort of hypothesis has been proposed by various writers. See, for example, Nietzsche, *On the Genealogy of Morals,* trans. Walter Kaufmann and R. J. Hollingdale (New York, Random House, 1967), I, secs. 10, 11, 13, 14, 16; II, sec. 11; III, secs. 14–16; and Max Scheler, *Ressentiment,* trans. W. W. Holdheim (Glencoe, Ill., The Free Press, 1961), pp. 45–50. For a discussion of Nietzsche's notion of ressentiment, see Walter Kaufmann, *Nietzsche* (Princeton, Princeton University Press, 1950), pp. 325–331.

on those better placed even at some cost to themselves, unless of course they are to relapse into resignation and apathy.

Now many aspects of a well-ordered society work to mitigate if not to prevent these conditions. In regard to the first condition, it is clear that, although it is a psychological state, social institutions are a basic instigating cause. But I have maintained that the contract conception of justice supports the self-esteem of citizens generally more firmly than other political principles. In the public forum each person is treated with the respect due to a sovereign equal; and everyone has the same basic rights that would be acknowledged in an initial situation regarded as fair. The members of the community have a common sense of justice and they are bound by ties of civic friendship. I have already discussed these points in connection with stability (§§ 75–76). We can add that the greater advantages of some are in return for compensating benefits for the less favored; and no one supposes that those who have a larger share are more deserving from a moral point of view. Happiness according to virtue is rejected as a principle of distribution (§ 48). And so likewise is the principle of perfection: regardless of the excellences that persons or associations display, their claims to social resources are always adjudicated by principles of mutual justice (§ 50). For all these reasons the less fortunate have no cause to consider themselves inferior and the public principles generally accepted underwrite their self-assurance. The disparities between themselves and others, whether absolute or relative, should be easier for them to accept than in other forms of polity.

Turning to the second condition, both the absolute and the relative differences allowed in a well-ordered society are probably less than those that have often prevailed. Although in theory the difference principle permits indefinitely large inequalities in return for small gains to the less favored, the spread of income and wealth should not be excessive in practice, given the requisite background institutions (§ 26). Moreover the plurality of associations in a well-ordered society, each with its secure internal life, tends to reduce the visibility, or at least the painful visibility, of variations in men's prospects. For we tend to compare our circumstances with others in the same or in a similar group as ourselves, or in

536

positions that we regard as relevant to our aspirations. The various associations in society tend to divide it into so many noncomparing groups, the discrepancies between these divisions not attracting the kind of attention which unsettles the lives of those less well placed. And this ignoring of differences in wealth and circumstance is made easier by the fact that when citizens do meet one another, as they must in public affairs at least, the principles of equal justice are acknowledged. Moreover in everyday life the natural duties are honored so that the more advantaged do not make an ostentatious display of their higher estate calculated to demean the condition of those who have less. After all, if the disposing conditions for envy are removed, so probably are those for jealousy, grudgingness, and spite, the converses of envy. When the less fortunate segments of society lack the one, the more fortunate will lack the other. Taken together these features of a well-ordered regime diminish the number of occasions when the less favored are likely to experience their situation as impoverished and humiliating. Even if they have some liability to envy, it may never be strongly evoked.

Finally, considering the last condition, it would seem that a well-ordered society as much as any other offers constructive alternatives to hostile outbreaks of envy. The problem of general envy anyway does not force us to reconsider the choice of the principles of justice. As for particular envy, to a certain extent it is endemic to human life; being associated with rivalry, it may exist in any society. The more specific problem for political justice is how pervasive are the rancor and jealousy aroused by the quest for office and position, and whether it is likely to distort the justice of institutions. It is difficult to settle this matter in the absence of the more detailed knowledge of social forms available at the legislative stage. But there seems to be no reason why the hazards of particular envy should be worse in a society regulated by justice as fairness than by any other conception.

I conclude, then, that the principles of justice are not likely to arouse excusable general envy (nor particular envy either) to a troublesome extent. By this test, the conception of justice again seems relatively stable. I should now like to examine briefly the possible connections between envy and equality, taking equality to be defined in various ways as specified by the theory of justice in question. While there are many forms of equality, and egalitarianism admits of degrees, there are conceptions of justice that are recognizably egalitarian, even though certain significant disparities are permitted. The two principles of justice fall, I assume, under this heading.

Many conservative writers have contended that the tendency to equality in modern social movements is the expression of envy.[9] In this way they seek to discredit this trend, attributing it to collectively harmful impulses. Before this thesis can be seriously entertained, however, one must first argue that the form of equality objected to is indeed unjust and bound in the end to make everyone including the less advantaged worse off. Yet to insist upon equality as the two principles of justice define it is not to give voice to envy. This is shown by the content of these principles and the characterization of envy. It is also evident from the nature of the parties in the original position: the conception of justice is chosen under conditions where by hypothesis no one is moved by rancor and spite (§ 25). Thus the claims to equality supported by the two principles do not spring from these feelings. The claims of those affirming the principles may sometimes express resentment, but this as we have seen is another matter.

In order to show that the principles of justice are based in part on envy it would have to be established that one or more of the conditions of the original position arise from this propensity. Since the question of stability does not force a reconsideration of the choice already made, the case for the influence of envy must be made by reference to the first part of the theory. But each of the stipulations of the original position has a justification which makes no mention of envy. For example, one invokes the function of moral principles as being a suitably general and public way of ordering claims (§ 23). To be sure, there may be forms of equality that do spring from envy. Strict egalitarianism, the doctrine which insists upon an equal distribution of all primary goods, conceivably derives from this propensity. What this means is that this concep-

9. See, for example, Helmut Schoeck, *Envy: A Theory of Social Behavior*, trans. Michael Glenny and Betty Ross (London, Secker and Warburg, 1969). Chapters XIV–XV contain many references. At one point even Marx thought of the first stage of communism as the expression of envy. See *Early Writings*, pp. 153f.

tion of equality would be adopted in the original position only if the parties are assumed to be sufficiently envious. This possibility in no way affects the two principles of justice. The different conception of equality which they define is acknowledged on the supposition that envy does not exist.[10]

The importance of separating envy from the moral feelings can be seen from several examples. Suppose first that envy is held to be pervasive in poor peasant societies. The reason for this, it may be suggested, is the general belief that the aggregate of social wealth is more or less fixed, so that one person's gain is another's loss. The social system is interpreted, it might be said, as a naturally established and unchangeable zero-sum game. Now actually, if this belief were widespread and the stock of goods were generally thought to be given, then a strict opposition of interests would be assumed to obtain. In this case, it would be correct to think that justice requires equal shares. Social wealth is not viewed as the outcome of mutually advantageous cooperation and so there is no fair basis for an unequal division of advantages. What is said to be envy may in fact be resentment which might or might not prove to be justified.

Freud's speculations about the origin of the sense of justice suffer from the same defect. He remarks that this sentiment is the outgrowth of envy and jealousy. As some members of the social group jealously strive to protect their advantages, the less favored are moved by envy to take them away. Eventually everyone recognizes that they cannot maintain their hostile attitudes toward one another without injury to themselves. Thus as a compromise they settle upon the demand of equal treatment. The sense of justice is a reaction-formation: what was originally jealousy and envy is transformed into a social feeling, the sense of justice that insists upon equality for all. Freud believes that this process is exemplified in the nursery and in many other social circumstances.[11] Yet the plausibility of his account assumes that the initial attitudes are correctly described. With a few changes, the underlying features of

10. In this and the next several paragraphs I am indebted to R. A. Schultz for helpful suggestions.

11. See *Group Psychology and the Analysis of the Ego*, rev. ed., trans. James Strachey (London, The Hogarth Press, 1959), pp. 51f.

the examples he depicts correspond to those of the original position. That persons have opposing interests and seek to advance their own conception of the good is not at all the same thing as their being moved by envy and jealousy. As we have seen, this sort of opposition gives rise to the circumstances of justice. Thus if children compete for the attention and affection of their parents, to which one might say they justly have an equal claim, one cannot assert that their sense of justice springs from jealousy and envy. Certainly children are often envious and jealous; and no doubt their moral notions are so primitive that the necessary distinctions are not grasped by them. But waiving these difficulties, we could equally well say that their social feeling arises from resentment, from a sense that they are unfairly treated.[12] And similarly one could say to conservative writers that it is mere grudgingness when those better circumstanced reject the claims of the less advantaged to greater equality. But this contention also calls for careful argument. None of these charges and countercharges can be given credence without first examining the conceptions of justice sincerely held by individuals and their understanding of the social situation in order to see how far these claims are indeed founded on these motives.

None of these remarks is intended to deny that the appeal to justice is often a mask for envy. What is said to be resentment may really be rancor. But rationalizations of this sort present a further problem. In addition to showing that a person's conception of justice is not itself founded on envy, we must determine whether the principles of justice cited in his explanation are sincerely held as this is shown in their being applied by him to other cases in which he is not involved, or even better, in which he would suffer a loss from their being followed. Freud means to assert more than the truism that envy often masquerades as resentment. He wants to say that the energy that motivates the sense of justice is borrowed from that of envy and jealousy, and that without this energy, there would be no (or much less) desire to give justice. Conceptions of justice have few attractions for us other than those deriving from

12. See Rousseau, *Emile*, trans. Barbara Foxley (London, J. M. Dent and Sons, 1911), pp. 61–63. And also J. N. Shklar, *Men and Citizens* (Cambridge, The University Press, 1969), p. 49.

these and similar feelings. It is this claim that is supported by erroneously conflating envy and resentment.

Unhappily the problem of the other special psychologies must go untouched. They should in any case be treated in much the same way as envy. One tries to assess the configuration of attitudes toward risk and uncertainty, domination and submission, and the like, that just institutions are likely to generate, and then to estimate whether they are likely to render these institutions unworkable or ineffective. We also need to ask whether, from the point of view of the persons in the original position, the conception chosen is acceptable or at least tolerable whatever our special proclivities may turn out to be. The most favorable alternative is that which allows a place for all these different tendencies insofar as they are likely to be encouraged by a just basic structure. There is a division of labor so to speak between persons with contrary inclinations. Of course some of these attitudes may earn a premium in the way that certain trained abilities do, as for example the willingness to be adventuresome and to take unusual risks. But if so, the problem is on all fours with the return to natural assets and it is covered by the discussion of distributive shares (§ 47). What a social system must not do clearly is to encourage propensities and aspirations that it is bound to repress and disappoint. So long as the pattern of special psychologies elicited by society either supports its arrangements or can be reasonably accommodated by them, there is no need to reconsider the choice of a conception of justice. I believe, though I have not shown, that the principles of justice as fairness pass this test.

82. THE GROUNDS FOR THE PRIORITY OF LIBERTY

In presenting the principles of justice I have usually ranked them in lexical order with the first principle taking priority over the second. The meaning of this precedence I have already explained and incorporated into the priority rules (§§ 39, 46). I have referred to the principles when ranked serially as the special as opposed to the general conception of justice (§§ 11, 26). But I have yet to tie together the grounds for this ordering, although I have mentioned its theoretical convenience and I have tried to show that its consequences match fairly closely our considered judgments. Moreover, the discussion of the first principle brought out reasons why the persons in the original position give pride of place to their interest in the equal freedoms. Now that all the elements of the theory of justice have been set out, it is time to consider the general argument for this priority.

Earlier I noted the intuitive idea behind the precedence of liberty (§26). The supposition is that if the persons in the original position assume that their basic liberties can be effectively exercised, they will not exchange a lesser liberty for an improvement in their economic well-being, at least not once a certain level of wealth has been attained. It is only when social conditions do not allow the effective establishment of these rights that one can acknowledge their restriction. The denial of equal liberty can be accepted only if it is necessary to enhance the quality of civilization so that in due course the equal freedoms can be enjoyed by all. The lexical ordering of the two principles is the long-run tendency of the general conception of justice consistently pursued under reasonably favorable conditions. Eventually there comes a time in the history of a well-ordered society beyond which the special form of the two principles takes over and holds from then on. What must be shown then is the rationality of this ranking from the standpoint of the parties in the original position. Clearly the conception of goodness as rationality and the principles of moral psychology have a part in answering this question.

Now the basis for the priority of liberty is roughly as follows: as the conditions of civilization improve, the marginal significance for our good of further economic and social advantages diminishes relative to the interests of liberty, which become stronger as the conditions for the exercise of the equal freedoms are more fully realized. Beyond some point it becomes and then remains irrational from the standpoint of the original position to acknowledge a lesser liberty for the sake of greater material means and amenities of office. Let us note why this should be so. First of all, as the general level of well-being rises (as indicated by the index of primary goods the less favored can expect) only the less urgent wants remain to be met by further advances, at least insofar as men's wants are not largely created by institutions and social forms. At the same time the obstacles to the exercise of the equal liberties decline and a growing insistence upon the right to pursue our spiritual and cultural interests asserts itself. Increasingly it becomes more important to secure the free internal life of the various communities of interests in which persons and groups seek to achieve, in modes of social union consistent with equal liberty, the ends and excellences to which they are drawn. In addition men come to aspire to some control over the laws and rules that regulate their association, either by directly taking part themselves in its affairs or indirectly through representatives with whom they are affiliated by ties of culture and social situation.

To be sure, it is not the case that when the priority of liberty holds, all material wants are satisfied. Rather these desires are not so compelling as to make it rational for the persons in the original position to agree to satisfy them by accepting a less than equal freedom. The account of the good enables the parties to work out a hierarchy among their several interests and to note which kinds of ends should be regulative in their rational plans of life. Until the basic wants of individuals can be fulfilled, the relative urgency of their interest in liberty cannot be firmly decided in advance. It will depend on the claims of the least favored as seen from the constitutional and legislative stages. But under favorable circumstances the fundamental interest in determining our plan of life eventually assumes a prior place. One reason for this I have discussed in connection with liberty of conscience and freedom of thought. And a second reason is the central place of the primary good of self-respect and the desire of human beings to express their nature in a free social union with others. Thus the desire for liberty is the chief regulative interest that the parties must suppose they all will have in common in due course. The veil of ignorance forces them to abstract from the particulars of their plans of life, thereby leading to this conclusion. The serial ordering of the two principles then follows.

Now it might seem that even though the desire for an absolute increase in economic advantages declines, men's concern for their relative place in the distribution of wealth will persist. In fact, if we suppose that everyone wishes a greater proportionate share, the result could be a growing desire for material abundance all the same. Since each strives for an end that cannot be collectively attained, society might conceivably become more and more preoccupied with raising productivity and improving economic efficiency. And these objectives might become so dominant as to undermine the precedence of liberty. Some have objected to the tendency to equality on precisely this ground, that it is thought to arouse in individuals an obsession with their relative share of social wealth. But while it is true that in a well-ordered society there is most likely a trend to greater equality, its members take little interest in their relative position as such. As we have seen, they are not much affected by envy and jealousy, and for the most part they do what seems best to them as judged by their own plan of life without being dismayed by the greater amenities and enjoyments of others. Thus there are no strong psychological propensities prompting them to curtail their liberty for the sake of greater absolute or relative economic welfare. The desire for a higher relative place in the distribution of material means should be sufficiently weak that the priority of liberty is not affected.

Of course, it does not follow that in a just society everyone is unconcerned with matters of status. The account of self-respect as perhaps the main primary good has stressed the great significance of how we think others value us. But in a well-ordered society the need for status is met by the public recognition of just institutions, together with the full and diverse internal life of the many free communities of interests that equal liberty allows. The basis for self-esteem in a just society is not then one's income share but the publicly affirmed distribution of fundamental rights and liberties. And this distribution being equal, everyone has a similar and secure status when they meet to conduct the common affairs of the wider society. No one is inclined to look beyond the constitutional affirmation of equality for further political ways of securing his status. Nor, on the other hand, are men disposed to acknowledge a less than equal liberty. For one thing, doing this would put them at a disadvantage and weaken their political position from a strategic point of view. It would also have the effect of publicly establishing their inferiority as defined by the basic structure of society. This subordinate ranking in the public forum experienced in the attempt to take part in political and economic life, and felt in dealing with those who have a greater liberty, would indeed be humiliating and destructive of self-esteem. And so by acquiescing in a less than equal liberty one might lose on both counts. This is particularly likely to be true as a society becomes more just, since equal rights and the public attitudes of mutual respect have an essential place in maintaining a political balance and in assuring citizens of their own worth. Thus while the social and economic differences between the various sectors of society, the noncomparing groups as we may think of them, are not likely to generate animosity, the hardships arising from political and civic inequality, and from cultural and ethnic discrimination, cannot be easily accepted. When it is the position of equal citizenship that answers to the need for status, the precedence of the equal liberties becomes all the more necessary. Having chosen a conception of justice that seeks to eliminate the significance of relative economic and social advantages as supports for men's self-confidence, it is essential that the priority of liberty be firmly maintained. So for this reason too the parties are led to adopt a serial ordering of the two principles.

In a well-ordered society then self-respect is secured by the public affirmation of the status of equal citizenship for all; the distribution of material means is left to take care of itself in accordance with the idea of pure procedural justice. Of course doing this assumes the requisite background institutions which narrow the range of inequalities so that excusable envy does not arise. Now this way of dealing with the problem of status has several noteworthy features which may be brought out as follows. Suppose to the contrary that how one is valued by others depends upon one's relative place in the distribution of income and wealth. In this case having a higher status implies having more material means than a larger fraction of society. Thus not everyone can have the highest status, and to improve one person's position is to lower that of someone else. Social cooperation to increase the conditions of self-respect is impossible. The means of status, so to speak, are fixed, and each man's gain is another's loss. Clearly this situation is a great misfortune. Persons are set at odds with one another in the pursuit of their self-esteem. Given the preeminence of this primary good, the parties in the original position surely do not want to find themselves so opposed.

It would tend, for one thing, to make the good of social union difficult if not impossible to achieve. Moreover, as I mentioned in the discussion of envy, if the means of providing a good are indeed fixed and cannot be enlarged by cooperation, then justice seems to require equal shares, other things the same. But an equal division of all primary goods is irrational in view of the possibility of bettering everyone's circumstances by accepting certain inequalities. Thus the best solution is to support the primary good of self-respect as far as possible by the assignment of the basic liberties that can indeed be made equal, defining the same status for all. At the same time, distributive justice as frequently understood, justice in the relative shares of material means, is relegated to a subordinate place. Thus we arrive at another reason for factoring the social order into two parts as indicated by the principles of justice. While these principles permit inequalities in return for contributions that are for the benefit of all, the precedence of liberty entails equality in the social bases of esteem.

Now it is quite possible that this idea cannot be carried through completely. To some extent men's sense of their own worth may hinge upon their institutional position and their income share. If, however, the account of social envy and jealousy is sound, then with the appropriate background arrangements, these inclinations should not be excessive, at least not when the priority of liberty is effectively upheld. But theoretically we can if necessary include self-respect in the primary goods, the index of which defines expectations. Then in applications of the difference principle, this index can allow for the effects of excusable envy (§ 80); the expectations of the less advantaged are lower the more severe these effects. Whether some adjustment for self-respect has to be made is best decided from the standpoint of the legislative stage where the parties have more information about social circumstances and the principle of political determination applies. Admittedly this problem is an unwelcome complication. Since simplicity is itself desirable in a public conception of justice, the conditions that elicit excusable envy should if possible be avoided. I have mentioned this point not to settle it, but only to note that when necessary the expectations of the less advantaged can be understood so as to include the primary good of self-esteem.

Now some may want to object to this account of the priority of liberty that societies have other ways of affirming self-respect and of coping with envy and other disruptive inclinations. Thus in a feudal or in a caste system each person is believed to have his allotted station in the natural order of things. His comparisons are presumably confined to within his own estate or caste, these ranks becoming in effect so many noncomparing groups established independently of human control and sanctioned by religion and theology. Men resign themselves to their position should it ever occur to them to question it; and since all may view themselves as assigned their vocation, everyone is held to be equally fated and equally noble in the eyes of providence.[13] This conception of society solves the problem of social justice by eliminating in thought the circumstances that give rise to it. The basic structure is said to be already determined, and not something for human beings to affect. On this view, it misconceives men's place in the world to suppose that the social order should match principles which they would as equals consent to.

Now contrary to this idea, I have assumed all along that the parties are to be guided in their choice of a conception of justice by a knowledge of the general facts about society. They take for granted then that institutions are not fixed but change over time, altered by natural circumstances and the activities and conflicts of social groups. The constraints of nature are recognized, but men are not powerless to shape their social arrangements. This assumption is likewise part of the background of the theory of justice. It follows that certain ways of dealing with envy and other aberrant propensities are closed to a well-ordered society. For example, it cannot keep them in check by promulgating false or unfounded beliefs. For our problem is how society should be arranged if it is to conform to principles that rational persons with true general beliefs would acknowledge in the original position. The publicity condition requires the parties to assume that as members of society

13. On this point, see Max Weber, *Economy and Society,* ed. Guenther Roth and Claus Wittich (New York, Bedminster Press, 1968), vol. II, pp. 435f, 598f. See pp. 490–499 for general comments on the things looked for in religions by different social strata. Also consult Ernst Troeltsch, *The Social Teaching of the Christian Churches,* trans. Olive Wyon (London, George Allen and Unwin, 1931), vol. I, pp. 120–127, 132f, 134–138; and Scheler, *Ressentiment,* pp. 56f.

they will also know the general facts. The reasoning leading up to the initial agreement is to be accessible to public understanding. Of course, in working out what the requisite principles are, we must rely upon current knowledge as recognized by common sense and the existing scientific consensus. But there is no reasonable alternative to doing this. We have to concede that as established beliefs change, it is possible that the principles of justice which it seems rational to choose may likewise change. Thus when the belief in a fixed natural order sanctioning a hierarchical society is abandoned, assuming here that this belief is not true, a tendency is set up that points in the direction of the two principles of justice in serial order. The effective protection of the equal liberties becomes increasingly of first importance.

83. HAPPINESS AND DOMINANT ENDS

In order to be in a position to take up the question of the good of justice, I shall discuss the manner in which just institutions frame our choice of a rational plan and incorporate the regulative element of our good. I shall approach this topic in a roundabout fashion by returning in this section to the concept of happiness and noting the temptation to think of it as determined by a dominant end. Doing this will lead naturally into the problems of hedonism and of the unity of the self. How these matters are connected should be apparent in due course.

Earlier I said that, with certain qualifications, a person is happy when he is in the way of a successful execution (more or less) of a rational plan of life drawn up under (more or less) favorable conditions, and he is reasonably confident that his intentions can be carried through (§ 63). Thus we are happy when our rational plans are going well, our more important aims being fulfilled, and we are with reason quite sure that our good fortune will continue. The achievement of happiness depends upon circumstances and luck, and hence the gloss about favorable conditions. While I shall not discuss the concept of happiness in any detail, we should consider a few further points to bring out the connection with the problem of hedonism.

First of all, happiness has two aspects: one is the successful execution of a rational plan (the schedule of activities and aims) which a person strives to realize, the other is his state of mind, his sure confidence supported by good reasons that his success will endure. Being happy involves both a certain achievement in action and a rational assurance about the outcome.[14] This definition of happiness is objective: plans are to be adjusted to the conditions of our life and our confidence must rest upon sound beliefs. Alternatively, happiness might be defined subjectively as follows: a person is happy when he believes that he is in the way of a successful execution (more or less) of a rational plan, and so on as before, adding the rider that if he is mistaken or deluded, then by contingency and coincidence nothing happens to disabuse him of his misconceptions. By good luck he is not cast out of his fool's paradise. Now the definition to be preferred is that which best fits the theory of justice and coheres with our considered judgments of value. At this point it suffices to observe, as I indicated a few pages back (§82), that we have assumed that the parties in the original position have correct beliefs. They acknowledge a conception of justice in the light of general truths about persons and their place in society. Thus it seems natural to suppose that in framing their plans of life they are similarly lucid. Of course none of this is strictly argument. Eventually one has to appraise the objective definition as a part of the moral theory to which it belongs.

Adopting this definition, and keeping in mind the account of rational plans presented earlier (§§63–65), we can interpret the special characteristics sometimes attributed to happiness.[15] For example, happiness is self-contained: that is, it is chosen solely for its own sake. To be sure, a rational plan will include many (or at least several) final aims, and any of these may be pursued partly because it complements and furthers one or more other aims as well. Mutual support among ends pursued for their own sake is an important feature of rational plans, and therefore these ends are not

14. For this point see Anthony Kenny, "Happiness," *Proceedings of the Aristotelian Society*, vol. 66 (1965–1966), pp. 101f.

15. Notably by Aristotle, *Nicomachean Ethics*, 1097a15–b21. For a discussion of Aristotle's account of happiness, see W. F. R. Hardie, *Aristotle's Ethical Theory* (Oxford, The Clarendon Press, 1968), ch. II.

usually sought solely for themselves. Nevertheless executing the entire plan, and the enduring confidence with which this is done, is something that we want to do and to have only for itself. All considerations including those of right and justice (using here the full theory of good) have already been surveyed in drawing up the plan. And therefore the whole activity is self-contained.

Happiness is also self-sufficient: a rational plan when realized with assurance makes a life fully worthy of choice and demands nothing further in addition. When circumstances are especially favorable and the execution particularly successful, one's happiness is complete. Within the general conception one sought to follow, there is nothing essential that is lacking, no way in which it could have been distinctly better. So even if the material means that support our mode of life can always be imagined to be greater, and a different pattern of aims might often have been chosen, still the actual fulfillment of the plan itself may have, as compositions, paintings, and poems often do, a certain completeness which though marred by circumstance and human failing is evident from the whole. Thus some become exemplars of human flourishing and models for emulation, their lives being as instructive in how to live as any philosophical doctrine.

A person is happy then during those periods when he is successfully carrying through a rational plan and he is with reason confident that his efforts will come to fruition. He may be said to approach blessedness to the extent that conditions are supremely favorable and his life complete. Yet it does not follow that in advancing a rational plan one is pursuing happiness, not at least as this is normally meant. For one thing, happiness is not one aim among others that we aspire to, but the fulfillment of the whole design itself. But also I have supposed first that rational plans satisfy the constraints of right and justice (as the full theory of the good stipulates). To say of someone that he seeks happiness does not, it seems, imply that he is prepared either to violate or to affirm these restrictions. Therefore the acceptance of these limits should be made explicit. And secondly, the pursuit of happiness often suggests the pursuit of certain sorts of ends, for example, life, liberty, and one's own welfare.[16] Thus persons who devote them-

16. For these two qualifications, see Kenny, "Happiness," pp. 98f.

selves selflessly to a righteous cause, or who dedicate their lives to furthering the well-being of others, are not normally thought to seek happiness. It would be misleading to say this of saints and heroes, or of those whose plan of life is in some marked degree supererogatory. They do not have the kinds of aims that fall under this heading, admittedly not sharply defined. Yet saints and heroes, and persons whose intentions acknowledge the limits of right and justice, are in fact happy when their plans succeed. Although they do not strive for happiness, they may nevertheless be happy in advancing the claims of justice and the well-being of others, or in attaining the excellences to which they are attracted.

But how in general is it possible to choose among plans rationally? What procedure can an individual follow when faced with this sort of decision? I now want to return to this question. Previously I said that a rational plan is one that would be chosen with deliberative rationality from among the class of plans all of which satisfy the principles of rational choice and stand up to certain forms of critical reflection. We eventually reach a point though where we just have to decide which plan we most prefer without further guidance from principle (§ 64). There is however one device of deliberation that I have not yet mentioned, and this is to analyze our aims. That is, we can try to find a more detailed or more illuminating description of the object of our desires hoping that the counting principles will then settle the case. Thus it may happen that a fuller or deeper characterization of what we want discloses that an inclusive plan exists after all.

Let us consider again the example of planning a holiday (§ 63). Often when we ask ourselves why we wish to visit two distinct places, we find that certain more general ends stand in the background and that all of them can be fulfilled by going to one place rather than the other. Thus we may want to study certain styles of art, and further reflection may bring out that one plan is superior or equally good on all these counts. In this sense we may discover that our desire to go to Paris is more intense than our desire to go to Rome. Often however a finer description fails to be decisive. If we want to see both the most famous church in Christendom and the most famous museum, we may be stuck. Of course these desires too may be examined further. Nothing in the way that most desires are expressed shows whether there exists a more revealing characterization of what we really want. But we have to allow for the possibility, indeed for the probability, that sooner or later we will reach incomparable aims between which we must choose with deliberative rationality. We may trim, reshape, and transform our aims in a variety of ways as we try to fit them together. Using the principles of rational choice as guidelines, and formulating our desires in the most lucid form we can, we may narrow the scope of purely preferential choice, but we cannot eliminate it altogether.

The indeterminacy of decision seems to arise, then, from the fact that a person has many aims for which there is no ready standard of comparison to decide between them when they conflict. There are many stopping points in practical deliberation and many ways in which we characterize the things we want for their own sake. Thus it is easy to see why the idea of there being a single dominant end (as opposed to an inclusive end) at which it is rational to aim is highly appealing.[17] For if there exists such an end to which all other ends are subordinate, then presumably all desires, insofar as they are rational, admit of an analysis which shows the counting principles to apply. The procedure for making a rational choice, and the conception of such a choice, would then be perfectly clear: deliberation would always concern means to ends, all lesser ends in turn being ordered as means to one single dominant end. The many finite chains of reasons eventually converge and meet at the same point. Hence a rational decision is always in principle possible, since only difficulties of computation and lack of information remain.

Now it is essential to understand what the dominant-end theorist wants: namely, a method of choice which the agent himself can always follow in order to make a rational decision. Thus there are three requirements: the conception of deliberation must specify (1) a first-person procedure which is (2) generally applicable and (3) guaranteed to lead to the best result (at least under favorable conditions of information and given the ability to calculate). We have no procedures meeting these conditions. A random device

17. The terminology of "dominant" and "inclusive" ends is from W. F. R. Hardie, "The Final Good in Aristotle's Ethics," *Philosophy*, vol. 40 (1965). This usage is not adhered to in his *Aristotle's Ethical Theory*.

provides a general method but it would be rational only in special circumstances. In everyday life we employ schemes of deliberation acquired from our culture and modified during the course of our personal history. But there is no assurance that these forms of reflection are rational. Perhaps they only meet various minimum standards which enable us to get by, all the while falling far short of the best that we might do. Thus if we seek a general procedure by which to balance our conflicting aims so as to single out, or at least to identify in thought, the best course of action, the idea of a dominant end seems to give a simple and natural answer.

Let us consider then what this dominant end might be. It cannot be happiness itself, since this state is attained by executing a rational plan of life already set out independently. The most we can say is that happiness is an inclusive end, meaning that the plan itself, the realization of which makes one happy, includes and orders a plurality of aims, whatever these are. On the other hand, it is most implausible to think of the dominant end as a personal or social objective such as the exercise of political power, or the achievement of social acclaim, or maximizing one's material possessions. Surely it is contrary to our considered judgments of value, and indeed inhuman, to be so taken with but one of these ends that we do not moderate the pursuit of it for the sake of anything else. For a dominant end is at least lexically prior to all other aims and seeking to advance it always takes absolute precedence. Thus Loyola holds that the dominant end is serving God, and by this means saving our soul. He is consistent in recognizing that furthering the divine intentions is the sole criterion for balancing subordinate aims. It is for this reason alone that we should prefer health to sickness, riches to poverty, honor to dishonor, a long life to a short one, and, one might add, friendship and affection to hatred and animosity. We must be indifferent, he says, to all attachments whatsoever, for these become inordinate once they prevent us from being like equalized scales in a balance, ready to take the course that we believe is most for the glory of God.[18]

It should be observed that this principle of indifference is com-

18. See *The Spiritual Exercises,* The First Week, the remarks under the heading "Principle and Foundation"; and The Second Week, the remarks under the heading "Three Occasions When a Wise Choice Can Be Made."

patible with our enjoying lesser pleasures and allowing ourselves to engage in play and amusements. For these activities relax the mind and rest the spirit so that we are better fitted to advance more important aims. Thus although Aquinas believes that the vision of God is the last end of all human knowledge and endeavor, he concedes play and amusements a place in our life. Nevertheless these pleasures are permitted only to the extent that the superordinate aim is thereby advanced, or at least not hindered. We should arrange things so that our indulgences in frivolity and jest, in affection and friendship, do not interfere with the fullest attainment of our final end.[19]

The extreme nature of dominant-end views is often concealed by the vagueness and ambiguity of the end proposed. Thus if God is conceived (as surely he must be) as a moral being, then the end of serving him above all else is left unspecified to the extent that the divine intentions are not clear from revelation, or evident from natural reason. Within these limits a theological doctrine of morals is subject to the same problems of balancing principles and determining precedence which trouble other conceptions. Since disputed questions commonly lie here, the solution propounded by the religious ethic is only apparent. And certainly when the dominant end is clearly specified as attaining some objective goal such as political power or material wealth, the underlying fanaticism and inhumanity are manifest. Human good is heterogeneous because the aims of the self are heterogeneous. Although to subordinate all our aims to one end does not strictly speaking violate the principles of rational choice (not the counting principles anyway), it still strikes us as irrational, or more likely as mad. The self is disfigured and put in the service of one of its ends for the sake of system.

84. HEDONISM AS A METHOD OF CHOICE

Traditionally hedonism is interpreted in one of two ways: either as the contention that the sole intrinsic good is pleasurable feeling, or as the psychological thesis that the only thing individuals strive for is pleasure. However I shall understand hedonism in a third

19. *Summa Contra Gentiles,* bk. III, ch. XXV.

way, namely, as trying to carry through the dominant-end conception of deliberation. It attempts to show how a rational choice is always possible, at least in principle. Although this effort fails, I shall examine it briefly for the light it throws upon the contrast between utilitarianism and the contract doctrine.

I imagine the hedonist to reason as follows. First he thinks that, if human life is to be guided by reason, there must exist a dominant end. There is no rational way to balance our competing aims against one another except as means to some higher end. Second, he interprets pleasure narrowly as agreeable feeling. Pleasantness as an attribute of feeling and sensation is thought to be the only plausible candidate for the role of the dominant end, and therefore it is the only thing good in itself. That, so conceived, pleasure alone is good is not postulated straightway as a first principle and then held to accord with our considered judgments of value. Rather pleasure is arrived at as the dominant end by a process of elimination. Granting that rational choices are possible, such an end must exist. At the same time this end cannot be happiness or any objective goal. To avoid the circularity of the one and the inhumanity and fanaticism of the other, the hedonist turns inwards. He finds the ultimate end in some definite quality of sensation or feeling identifiable by introspection. We can suppose, if we like, that pleasantness can be ostensively defined as that attribute which is common to the feelings and experiences toward which we have a favorable attitude and wish to prolong, other things equal. Thus, for purposes of illustration, one might say that pleasantness is that feature which is common to the experience of smelling roses, of tasting chocolate, of requited affection, and so on, and analogously for the opposite attribute of painfulness.[20]

The hedonist maintains, then, that a rational agent knows exactly how to proceed in determining his good: he is to ascertain which of the plans open to him promises the greatest net balance of pleasure over pain. This plan defines his rational choice, the best way to order his competing aims. The counting principles now apply trivially, since all good things are homogeneous and therefore comparable as means to the one end of pleasure. Of course these

20. The illustration is from C. D. Broad, *Five Types of Ethical Theory* (London, Routledge and Kegan Paul, 1930), pp. 186f.

assessments are plagued by uncertainties and lack of information, and normally only the crudest estimates can be made. Yet for hedonism this is not a real difficulty: what counts is that the maximum of pleasure provides a clear idea of the good. We are now said to know the one thing the pursuit of which gives rational form to our life. Largely for these reasons Sidgwick thinks that pleasure must be the single rational end that is to guide deliberation.[21]

It is important to note two points. First, when pleasure is regarded as a special attribute of feeling and sensation, it is conceived as a definite measure on which calculations can be based. By reckoning in terms of the intensity and duration of pleasant experiences, the necessary computations can theoretically be made. The method of hedonism provides a first-person procedure of choice as the standard of happiness does not. Second, taking pleasure as the dominant end does not imply that we have any particular objective goals. We find pleasure in the most varied activities and in the quest for any number of things. Therefore aiming to maximize pleasurable feeling seems at least to avoid the appearance of fanaticism and inhumanity while still defining a rational method for first-person choice. Furthermore, the two traditional interpretations of hedonism are now easily accounted for. If pleasure is indeed the only end the pursuit of which enables us to identify rational plans, then surely pleasure would appear to be the sole intrinsic good, and so we would have arrived at the principle of hedonism by an argument from the conditions of rational deliberation. A variant of psychological hedonism also follows: for although it is going too far to say that rational conduct would always consciously aim at pleasure, it would in any case be regulated by a schedule of activities designed to maximize the net balance of pleasurable feeling. Since it leads to the more familiar interpretations, the thesis that the pursuit of pleasure provides the only rational method of deliberation seems to be the fundamental idea of hedonism.

It seems obvious that hedonism fails to define a reasonable dominant end. We need only note that once pleasure is conceived, as it must be, in a sufficiently definite way so that its intensity and

21. *The Methods of Ethics*, 7th ed. (London, Macmillan, 1907), pp. 405–407, 479.

duration can enter into the agent's calculations, then it is no longer plausible that it should be taken as the sole rational aim.[22] Surely the preference for a certain attribute of feeling or sensation above all else is as unbalanced and inhuman as an overriding desire to maximize one's power over others or one's material wealth. No doubt it is for this reason that Sidgwick is reluctant to grant that pleasantness is a particular quality of feeling; yet he must concede this if pleasure is to serve, as he wants it to, as the ultimate criterion to weigh ideal values such as knowledge, beauty, and friendship against one another.[23]

And then too there is the fact that there are different sorts of agreeable feelings themselves incomparable, as well as the quantitative dimensions of pleasure, intensity and duration. How are we to balance these when they conflict? Are we to choose a brief but intense pleasant experience of one kind of feeling over a less intense but longer pleasant experience of another? Aristotle says that the good man if necessary lays down his life for his friends, since he prefers a short period of intense pleasure to a long one of mild enjoyment, a twelvemonth of noble life to many years of humdrum existence.[24] But how does he decide this? Further, as Santayana observes, we must settle the relative worth of pleasure and pain. When Petrarch says that a thousand pleasures are not worth one pain, he adopts a standard for comparing them that is more basic than either. The person himself must make this decision, taking into account the full range of his inclinations and desires, present and future. Clearly we have made no advance beyond deliberative rationality. The problem of a plurality of ends arises all over again within the class of subjective feelings.[25]

22. As Broad observes in *Five Types of Ethical Theory*, p. 187.

23. In *Methods of Ethics*, p. 127, Sidgwick denies that pleasure is a measurable quality of feeling independent of its relation from volition. This is the view of some writers, he says, but one he cannot accept. He defines pleasure "as a feeling which, when experienced by intelligent beings, is at least apprehended as desirable or—in cases of comparison—preferable." It would seem that the view he here rejects is the one he relies upon later as the final criterion to introduce coherence among ends. See pp. 405–407, 479. Otherwise the hedonist method of choice no longer provides instructions that can be followed.

24. *Nicomachean Ethics*, 1169a17–26.

25. *The Life of Reason in Common Sense* (New York, Charles Scribners, 1905), pp. 237f.

It may be objected that in economics and decision theory these problems are overcome. But this contention is based on a misunderstanding. In the theory of demand, for example, it is assumed that the consumer's preferences satisfy various postulates: they define a complete ordering over the set of alternatives and exhibit the properties of convexity and continuity, and the like. Given these assumptions, it can be shown that a utility function exists which matches these preferences in the sense that one alternative is chosen over another if and only if the value of the function for the selected alternative is greater. This function characterizes the individual's choices, what he in fact prefers, granted that his preferences meet certain stipulations. It asserts nothing at all about how a person arranges his decisions in such a coherent order to begin with, nor clearly can it claim to be a first-person procedure of choice that someone might reasonably follow, since it only records the outcome of his deliberations. At best the principles that economists have supposed the choices of rational individuals to satisfy can be presented as guidelines for us to consider when we make our decisions. But so understood, these criteria are just the principles of rational choice (or their analogues) and we are back once again with deliberative rationality.[26]

It seems indisputable, then, that there is no dominant end the pursuit of which accords with our considered judgments of value. The inclusive end of realizing a rational plan of life is an entirely different thing. But the failure of hedonism to provide a rational procedure of choice should occasion no surprise. Wittgenstein showed that it is a mistake to postulate certain special experiences to explain how we distinguish memories from imaginings, beliefs from suppositions, and so on for other mental acts. Similarly, it is antecedently unlikely that certain kinds of agreeable feeling can

26. Thus to the objection that price theory must fail because it seeks to predict the unpredictable, the decisions of persons with free will, Walras says: "Actually, we have never attempted to predict decisions made under conditions of perfect freedom; we have only tried to express the effects of such decisions in terms of mathematics. In our theory each trader may be assumed to determine his utility or want curves as he pleases." *Elements of Pure Economics,* trans. William Jaffé (Homewood, Ill., Richard D. Irwin, 1954), p. 256. See also P. A. Samuelson, *Foundations of Economic Analysis* (Cambridge, Harvard University Press, 1947), the remarks pp. 90–92, 97f; and R. D. Luce and Howard Raiffa, *Games and Decisions* (New York, John Wiley and Sons, 1957), pp. 16, 21–24, 38.

define a unit of account the use of which explains the possibility of rational deliberation. Neither pleasure nor any other determinate end can play the role that the hedonist would assign it.[27]

Now philosophers have supposed that characteristic experiences exist and guide our mental life for many different reasons. So while it seems a simple matter to show that hedonism gets us nowhere, the important thing is to see why one might be driven to resort to such a desperate expedient. I have already noted one possible reason: the desire to narrow down the scope of purely preferential choice in determining our good. In a teleological theory any vagueness or ambiguity in the conception of the good is transferred to that of the right. Hence if the good of individuals is something that, so to speak, is just up to them to decide as individuals, so likewise within certain limits is that which is right. But it is natural to think that what is right is not a matter of mere preference, and therefore one tries to find a definite conception of the good.

There is, however, another reason: a teleological theory needs a way to compare the diverse goods of different individuals so that the total good can be maximized. How can these assessments be made? Even if certain ends serve to organize the plans of individuals taken singly, they do not suffice to define a conception of right. It would appear, then, that the turn inwards to the standard of agreeable feeling is an attempt to find a common denominator among the plurality of persons, an interpersonal currency as it

27. See *The Philosophical Investigations* (Oxford, Basil Blackwell, 1953). The argument against postulating special experiences is made throughout for many different cases. For the application to pleasure, see the remarks of G. E. M. Anscombe, *Intention* (Oxford, Basil Blackwell, 1957). Anscombe says: "We might adapt a remark of Wittgenstein's about meaning and say 'Pleasure cannot be an impression; for no impression could have the consequences of pleasure.' They [the British Empiricists] were saying that something which they thought of as like a particular tickle or itch was quite obviously the point of doing anything whatsoever" (p. 77). See also Gilbert Ryle, "Pleasure," *Proceedings of the Aristotelian Society*, supp. vol. 28 (1954), and *Dilemmas* (Cambridge, The University Press, 1954), ch. IV; Anthony Kenny, *Action, Emotion and Will* (London, Routledge and Kegan Paul, 1963), ch. VI; and C. C. W. Taylor, "Pleasure," *Analysis*, supp. vol. (1963). These studies present what seems to be the more correct view. In the text I try to explain the motivation from the standpoint of moral philosophy of the so-called British Empiricist conception of pleasure. That it is fallacious I pretty much take for granted, as the writers mentioned have, I believe, shown.

were, by means of which the social ordering can be specified. And this suggestion is all the more compelling if it is already maintained that this standard is the aim of each person to the extent that he is rational.

By way of conclusion, I should not say that a teleological doctrine is necessarily driven to some form of hedonism in order to define a coherent theory. Yet it does seem that the tendency in this direction has a certain naturalness. Hedonism is, one might say, the symptomatic drift of teleological theories insofar as they try to formulate a clear and applicable method of moral reasoning. The weakness of hedonism reflects the impossibility of defining an appropriate definite end to be maximized. And this suggests that the structure of teleological doctrines is radically misconceived: from the start they relate the right and the good in the wrong way. We should not attempt to give form to our life by first looking to the good independently defined. It is not our aims that primarily reveal our nature but rather the principles that we would acknowledge to govern the background conditions under which these aims are to be formed and the manner in which they are to be pursued. For the self is prior to the ends which are affirmed by it; even a dominant end must be chosen from among numerous possibilities. There is no way to get beyond deliberative rationality. We should therefore reverse the relation between the right and the good proposed by teleological doctrines and view the right as prior. The moral theory is then developed by working in the opposite direction. I shall now try to explain these last remarks in the light of the contract doctrine.

85. THE UNITY OF THE SELF

The outcome of the preceding discussion is that there is no one aim by reference to which all of our choices can reasonably be made. Significant intuitionist elements enter into determining the good, and in a teleological theory these are bound to affect the right. The classical utilitarian tries to avoid this consequence by the doctrine of hedonism, but to no avail. We cannot, however, stop here; we must find a constructive solution to the problem of choice which hedonism seeks to answer. Thus we are faced once again with the question: if there is no single end that determines the appropriate pattern of aims, how is a rational plan of life actually to be identified? Now the answer to this question has already been given: a rational plan is one that would be chosen with deliberative rationality as defined by the full theory of the good. It remains to make sure that, within the context of a contract doctrine, this answer is perfectly satisfactory and that the problems which beset hedonism do not arise.

As I have said, moral personality is characterized by two capacities: one for a conception of the good, the other for a sense of justice. When realized, the first is expressed by a rational plan of life, the second by a regulative desire to act upon certain principles of right. Thus a moral person is a subject with ends he has chosen, and his fundamental preference is for conditions that enable him to frame a mode of life that expresses his nature as a free and equal rational being as fully as circumstances permit. Now the unity of the person is manifest in the coherence of his plan, this unity being founded on the higher-order desire to follow, in ways consistent with his sense of right and justice, the principles of rational choice. Of course, a person shapes his aims not all at once but only gradually; but in ways that justice allows, he is able to formulate and to follow a plan of life and thereby to fashion his own unity.

The distinctive feature of a dominant-end conception is how it supposes the self's unity is achieved. Thus in hedonism the self becomes one by trying to maximize the sum of pleasurable experiences within its psychic boundaries. A rational self must establish its unity in this manner. Since pleasure is the dominant end, the individual is indifferent to all aspects of himself, viewing his natural assets of mind and body, and even his natural inclinations and attachments, as so many materials for obtaining pleasant experiences. Moreover, it is not by aiming at pleasure as his pleasure but simply as pleasure that gives unity to the self. Whether it is his pleasure or that of others as well which is to be advanced raises a further matter that can be put aside so long as we are dealing with one person's good. But once we consider the problem of social choice, the utilitarian principle in its hedonistic form is perfectly

561

natural. For if any one individual must order his deliberations by seeking the dominant end of pleasure and can secure his rational personhood in no other way, then it seems that a number of persons in their joint efforts should strive to order their collective actions by maximizing the pleasurable experiences of the group. Thus just as one saint when alone is to work for the glory of God, so the members of an association of saints are to cooperate together to do whatever is necessary for the same end. The difference between the individual and the social case is that the resources of the self, its mental and physical capacities and its emotional sensibilities and desires, are placed in a different context. In both instances these materials are in the service of the dominant end. But depending on the other agencies available to cooperate with them, it is the pleasure of the self or of the social group that is to be maximized.

Further, if the same sorts of considerations that lead to hedonism as a theory of first-person choice are applied to the theory of right, the principle of utility seems quite plausible. For let us suppose first that happiness (defined in terms of agreeable feeling) is the sole good. Then, as even intuitionists concede, it is at least a prima facie principle of right to maximize happiness. If this principle is not alone regulative, there must be some other criterion such as distribution which is to be assigned some weight. But by reference to what dominant end of social conduct are these standards to be balanced? Since this end must exist if judgments of right are to be reasoned and not arbitrary, the principle of utility appears to specify the required goal. No other principle has the features necessary to define the ultimate end of right conduct. I believe that it is essentially this reasoning that underlies Mill's so-called proof of utility.[28]

28. See *Utilitarianism*, ch. IV. This much-discussed chapter, and especially par. 3, is noteworthy for the fact that Mill seems to believe that if he can establish that happiness is the sole good, he has shown that the principle of utility is the criterion of right. The chapter title refers to the proof of the principle of utility; but what we are given is an argument to the effect that happiness alone is good. Now nothing so far follows about the conception of right. It is only by looking back at the first chapter of the essay, and attending to Mill's notion of the structure of a moral theory, as I discussed it in § 8 and outlined it in the text above, that we can set out all the premises in the light of which Mill thought his argument a proof.

Now in justice as fairness a complete reversal of perspective is brought about by the priority of right and the Kantian interpretation. To see this we have only to recall the features of the original position and the nature of the principles that are chosen. The parties regard moral personality and not the capacity for pleasure and pain as the fundamental aspect of the self. They do not know what final aims persons have, and all dominant-end conceptions are rejected. Thus it would not occur to them to acknowledge the principle of utility in its hedonistic form. There is no more reason for the parties to agree to this criterion than to maximize any other particular objective. They think of themselves as beings who can and do choose their final ends (always plural in number). Just as one person is to decide upon his plan of life in the light of full information (no restrictions being imposed in this case), so a plurality of persons are to settle the terms of their cooperation in a situation that gives all fair representation as moral beings. The parties' aim in the original position is to establish just and favorable conditions for each to fashion his own unity. Their fundamental interest in liberty and in the means to make fair use of it is the expression of their seeing themselves as primarily moral persons with an equal right to choose their mode of life. Thus they acknowledge the two principles of justice to be ranked in serial order as circumstances permit.

We must now connect these remarks with the problem of the indeterminacy of choice with which we began. The main idea is that given the priority of right, the choice of our conception of the good is framed within definite limits. The principles of justice and their realization in social forms define the bounds within which our deliberations take place. The essential unity of the self is already provided by the conception of right. Moreover, in a well-ordered society this unity is the same for all; everyone's conception of the good as given by his rational plan is a subplan of the larger comprehensive plan that regulates the community as a social union of social unions. The many associations of varying sizes and aims, being adjusted to one another by the public conception of justice, simplify decision by offering definite ideals and forms of life that have been developed and tested by innumerable individuals, sometimes for generations. Thus in drawing up our plan of life we do not start de novo; we are not required to choose from countless possibilities without given structure or fixed contours. So while there is no algorithm for settling upon our good, no first-person procedure of choice, the priority of right and justice securely constrains these deliberations so that they become more manageable. Since the basic rights and liberties are already firmly established, our choices cannot distort our claims upon one another.

Now given the precedence of right and justice, the indeterminacy of the conception of the good is much less troublesome. In fact, the considerations that lead a teleological theory to embrace the notion of a dominant end lose their force. First of all, the purely preferential elements in choice, while not eliminated, are nevertheless confined within the constraints of right already on hand. Since men's claims on one another are not affected, the indeterminacy is relatively innocuous. Moreover, within the limits allowed by the principles of right, there need be no standard of correctness beyond that of deliberative rationality. If a person's plan of life meets this criterion and if he succeeds in carrying it out, and in doing so finds it worthwhile, there are no grounds for saying that it would have been better if he had done something else. We should not simply assume that our rational good is uniquely determined. From the standpoint of the theory of justice, this assumption is unnecessary. Secondly, we are not required to go beyond deliberative rationality in order to define a clear and workable conception of right. The principles of justice have a definite content and the argument supporting them uses only the thin account of the good and its list of primary goods. Once the conception of justice is established, the priority of right guarantees the precedence of its principles. Thus the two considerations that make dominant-end conceptions attractive for teleological theories are both absent in the contract doctrine. Such is the effect of the reversal of structure.

Earlier when introducing the Kantian interpretation of justice as fairness, I mentioned that there is a sense in which the unanimity condition on the principles of justice is suited to express even the nature of a single self (§ 40). Offhand this suggestion seems paradoxical. How can the requirement of unanimity fail to be a constraint? One reason is that the veil of ignorance insures that everyone should reason in the same way and so the condition is

564

satisfied as a matter of course. But a deeper explanation lies in the fact that the contract doctrine has a structure opposite to that of a utilitarian theory. In the latter each person draws up his rational plan without hindrance under full information, and society then proceeds to maximize the aggregate fulfillment of the plans that result. In justice as fairness, on the other hand, all agree ahead of time upon the principles by which their claims on one another are to be settled. These principles are then given absolute precedence so that they regulate social institutions without question and each frames his plans in conformity with them. Plans that happen to be out of line must be revised. Thus the prior collective agreement sets up from the first certain fundamental structural features common to everyone's plan. The nature of the self as a free and equal moral person is the same for all, and the similarity in the basic form of rational plans expresses this fact. Moreover, as shown by the notion of society as a social union of social unions, the members of a community participate in one another's nature: we appreciate what others do as things we might have done but which they do for us, and what we do is similarly done for them. Since the self is realized in the activities of many selves, relations of justice that conform to principles which would be assented to by all are best fitted to express the nature of each. Eventually then the requirement of a unanimous agreement connects up with the idea of human beings who as members of a social union seek the values of community.

It may be thought that once the principles of justice are given precedence, then there is a dominant end that organizes our life after all. Yet this idea is based on a misunderstanding. To be sure the principles of justice are lexically prior to that of efficiency, and the first principle has precedence over the second. It follows that an ideal conception of the social order is set up which is to regulate the direction of change and the efforts of reform (§41). But it is the principles of individual duty and obligation that define the claim of this ideal upon persons and these do not make it all controlling. Furthermore, I have all along assumed that the proposed dominant end belongs to a teleological theory in which by definition the good is specified independently from the right. The role of this end is in part to make the conception of right reasonably precise. In justice as fairness there can be no dominant end in this sense, nor as we have seen is one needed for this purpose. Finally, the dominant end of a teleological theory is so defined that we can never finally achieve it and therefore the injunction to advance it always applies. Recall here the earlier remarks as to why the principle of utility is not really suitable for a lexical ordering: the later criteria will never come into play, except in special cases to break ties. The principles of justice, on the other hand, represent more or less definite social aims and restrictions (§8). Once we realize a certain structure of institutions, we are at liberty to determine and to pursue our good within the limits which its arrangements allow.

In view of these reflections, the contrast between a teleological theory and the contract doctrine may be expressed in the following intuitive way: the former defines the good locally, for example, as a more or less homogeneous quality or attribute of experience, and regards it as an extensive magnitude which is to be maximized over some totality; whereas the latter moves in the opposite fashion by identifying a sequence of increasingly specific structural forms of right conduct each set within the preceding one, and in this manner working from a general framework for the whole to a sharper and sharper determination of its parts. Hedonistic utilitarianism is the classical instance of the first procedure and illustrates it with compelling simplicity. Justice as fairness exemplifies the second possibility. Thus the four-stage sequence (§31) formulates an order of agreements and enactments designed to build up in several steps a hierarchical structure of principles, standards, and rules, which when consistently applied and adhered to, lead to a definite constitution for social action.

Now this sequence does not aim at the complete specification of conduct. Rather the idea is to approximate the boundaries, however vague, within which individuals and associations are at liberty to advance their aims and deliberative rationality has free play. Ideally the approximation should converge in the sense that with further steps the cases left unaccounted for become of less and less importance. The notion guiding the entire construction is that of the original position and its Kantian interpretation: this notion contains within itself the elements that select which information is relevant at each stage, and generate a sequence of adjustments appropriate to the contingent conditions of the existing society.

86. THE GOOD OF THE SENSE OF JUSTICE

Now that all the parts of the theory of justice are before us, the argument for congruence can be completed. It suffices to tie together the various aspects of a well-ordered society and to see them in the appropriate context. The concepts of justice and goodness are linked with distinct principles and the question of congruence is whether these two families of criteria fit together. More precisely, each concept with its associated principles defines a point of view from which institutions, actions, and plans of life can be assessed. A sense of justice is an effective desire to apply and to act from the principles of justice and so from the point of view of justice. Thus what is to be established is that it is rational (as defined by the thin theory of the good) for those in a well-ordered society to affirm their sense of justice as regulative of their plan of life. It remains to be shown that this disposition to take up and to be guided by the standpoint of justice accords with the individual's good.

Whether these two points of view are congruent is likely to be a crucial factor in determining stability. But congruence is not a foregone conclusion even in a well-ordered society. We must verify it. Of course, the rationality of choosing the principles of justice in the original position is not in question. The argument for this decision has already been made; and if it is sound, just institutions are collectively rational and to everyone's advantage from a suitably general perspective. It is also rational for each to urge others to support these arrangements and to fulfill their duties and obligations. The problem is whether the regulative desire to adopt the standpoint of justice belongs to a person's own good when viewed in the light of the thin theory with no restrictions on information. We should like to know that this desire is indeed rational; being rational for one, it is rational for all, and therefore no tendencies to instability exist. More precisely, consider any given person in a well-ordered society. He knows, I assume, that institutions are just and that others have (and will continue to have) a sense of justice similar to his, and therefore that they comply (and will continue to comply) with these arrangements. We want to show that on these suppositions it is rational for someone, as defined by the thin theory, to affirm his sense of justice. The plan of life which does this is his best reply to the similar plans of his associates; and being rational for anyone, it is rational for all.

It is important not to confuse this problem with that of justifying being a just man to an egoist. An egoist is someone committed to the point of view of his own interests. His final ends are related to himself: his wealth and position, his pleasures and social prestige, and so on. Such a man may act justly, that is, do things that a just man would do; but so long as he remains an egoist, he cannot do them for the just man's reasons. Having these reasons is inconsistent with being an egoist. It merely happens that on some occasions the point of view of justice and that of his own interests lead to the same course of action. Therefore I am not trying to show that in a well-ordered society an egoist would act from a sense of justice, nor even that he would act justly because so acting would best advance his ends. Nor, again, are we to argue that an egoist, finding himself in a just society, would be well advised, given his aims, to transform himself into a just man. Rather, we are concerned with the goodness of the settled desire to take up the standpoint of justice. I assume that the members of a well-ordered society already have this desire. The question is whether this regulative sentiment is consistent with their good. We are not examining the justice or the moral worth of actions from certain points of view; we are assessing the goodness of the desire to adopt a particular point of view, that of justice itself. And we must evaluate this desire not from the egoist's standpoint, whatever this might be, but in the light of the thin theory of the good.

I shall assume that human actions spring from existing desires and that these can be changed only gradually. We cannot just decide at a given moment to alter our system of ends (§63). We act now as the sort of person we are and from the wants we have now, and not as the sort of person we might have been or from desires we would have had if earlier we had only chosen differently. Regulative aims are especially subject to this constraint. Thus we must decide well in advance whether to affirm our sense of justice by trying to assess our situation over a fairly extensive future. We cannot have things both ways. We cannot preserve a sense of justice and all that this implies while at the same time holding ourselves ready to act unjustly should doing so promise some personal advantage. A just person is not prepared to do certain things, and if he is tempted too easily, he was prepared after all.[29] Our question concerns then only those with a certain psychology and system of desires. It would obviously be demanding too much to require that stability should not depend upon definite restrictions in this respect.

Now on one interpretation the question has an obvious answer. Supposing that someone has an effective sense of justice, he will then have a regulative desire to comply with the corresponding principles. The criteria of rational choice must take this desire into account. If a person wants with deliberative rationality to act from the standpoint of justice above all else, it is rational for him so to act. Therefore in this form the question is trivial: being the sorts of persons they are, the members of a well-ordered society desire more than anything to act justly and fulfilling this desire is part of their good. Once we acquire a sense of justice that is truly final and effective, as the precedence of justice requires, we are confirmed in a plan of life that, insofar as we are rational, leads us to preserve and to encourage this sentiment. Since this fact is public knowledge, instability of the first kind does not exist, and hence neither does that of the second. The real problem of congruence is what happens if we imagine someone to give weight to his sense of justice only to the extent that it satisfies other descriptions which connect it with reasons specified by the thin theory of the good. We should not rely on the doctrine of the pure conscientious act (§72). Suppose, then, that the desire to act justly is not a final desire like that to avoid pain, misery, or apathy, or the desire to fulfill the inclusive interest. The theory of justice supplies other descriptions of what the sense of justice is a desire for; and we must use these to show that a person following the thin theory of

29. See Philippa Foot, "Moral Beliefs," *Proceedings of the Aristotelian Society,* vol. 59 (1958–1959), p. 104. I am much indebted to this essay, although I have not followed it on all counts.

the good would indeed confirm this sentiment as regulative of his plan of life.

So much then for defining the question. I now wish to note the grounds of congruence by reviewing various points already made. First of all, as the contract doctrine requires, the principles of justice are public: they characterize the commonly recognized moral convictions shared by the members of a well-ordered society (§23). We are not concerned with someone who is questioning these principles. By hypothesis, he concedes as everyone else does that they are the best choice from the standpoint of the original position. (Of course, this can always be doubted but it raises an entirely different matter.) Now since others are assumed to have (and to continue to have) an effective sense of justice, our hypothetical individual is considering in effect a policy of pretending to have certain moral sentiments, all the while being ready to act as a free-rider whenever the opportunity arises to further his personal interests. Since the conception of justice is public, he is debating whether to set out on a systematic course of deception and hypocrisy, professing without belief, as it suits his purpose, the accepted moral views. That deception and hypocrisy are wrongs does not, I assume, bother him; but he will have to reckon with the psychological cost of taking precautions and maintaining his pose, and with the loss of spontaneity and naturalness that results.[30] In most societies as things are, such pretensions may not have a high price, since the injustice of institutions and the often squalid behavior of others renders one's own deceits easier to endure; but in a well-ordered society there is not this comfort.

These remarks are supported by the fact that there is a connection between acting justly and natural attitudes (§74). Given the content of the principles of justice and the laws of moral psychology, wanting to be fair with our friends and wanting to give justice to those we care for is as much a part of these affections as the desire to be with them and to feel sad at their loss. Assuming therefore that one needs these attachments, the policy contemplated is presumably that of acting justly only toward those to whom we are bound by ties of affection and fellow feeling, and of respecting ways of life to which we are devoted. But in a well-

30. See Foot, *ibid.,* p. 104.

ordered society these bonds extend rather widely, and include ties to institutional forms, assuming here that all three psychological laws are fully effective. In addition, we cannot in general select who is to be injured by our unfairness. For example, if we cheat on paying our taxes, or if we find some way to avoid doing our fair share for the community, everyone is hurt, our friends and associates along with the rest. To be sure, we might consider covertly passing on part of our gains to those we especially like, but this becomes a dubious and involved affair. Thus in a well-ordered society where effective bonds are extensive both to persons and to social forms, and we cannot select who is to lose by our defections, there are strong grounds for preserving one's sense of justice. Doing this protects in a natural and simple way the institutions and persons we care for and leads us to welcome new and broader social ties.

Another basic consideration is this: it follows from the Aristotelian Principle (and its companion effect) that participating in the life of a well-ordered society is a great good (§ 79). This conclusion depends upon the meaning of the principles of justice and their precedence in everyone's plans as well as upon the psychological features of our nature. It is the details of the contract view which establish this connection. Because such a society is a social union of social unions, it realizes to a preeminent degree the various forms of human activity; and given the social nature of humankind, the fact that our potentialities and inclinations far surpass what can be expressed in any one life, we depend upon the cooperative endeavors of others not only for the means of well-being but to bring to fruition our latent powers. And with a certain success all around, each enjoys the greater richness and diversity of the collective activity. Yet to share fully in this life we must acknowledge the principles of its regulative conception, and this means that we must affirm our sentiment of justice. To appreciate something as ours, we must have a certain allegiance to it. What binds a society's efforts into one social union is the mutual recognition and acceptance of the principles of justice; it is this general affirmation which extends the ties of identification over the whole community and permits the Aristotelian Principle to have its wider effect. Individual and group accomplishments are no longer seen as just so many separate personal goods. Whereas not to confirm our sense of justice is to limit ourselves to a narrow view.

Finally, there is the reason connected with the Kantian interpretation: acting justly is something we want to do as free and equal rational beings (§40). The desire to act justly and the desire to express our nature as free moral persons turn out to specify what is practically speaking the same desire. When someone has true beliefs and a correct understanding of the theory of justice, these two desires move him in the same way. They are both dispositions to act from precisely the same principles: namely, those that would be chosen in the original position. Of course, this contention is based on a theory of justice. If this theory is unsound, the practical identity fails. But since we are concerned only with the special case of a well-ordered society as characterized by the theory, we are entitled to assume that its members have a lucid grasp of the public conception of justice upon which their relations are founded.

Let us suppose that these are the chief reasons (or typical thereof) which the thin account of the good allows for maintaining one's sense of justice. The question now arises whether they are decisive. Here we confront the familiar difficulty of a balance of motives which in many ways is similar to a balance of first principles. Sometimes the answer is found by comparing one balance of reasons with another, for surely if the first balance clearly favors one course of action then the second will also, should its reasons supporting this alternative be stronger and its reasons supporting the other alternatives be weaker. But arguing from such comparisons presupposes some configurations of reasons which evidently go one way rather than another to serve as a bench mark. Failing these, we cannot get beyond conditional comparisons: if the first balance favors a certain choice, then the second does also.

Now at this point it is obvious that the content of the principles of justice is a crucial element in the decision. Whether it is for a person's good that he have a regulative sense of justice depends upon what justice requires of him. The congruence of the right and the good is determined by the standards by which each concept is specified. As Sidgwick notes, utilitarianism is more strict than common sense in demanding the sacrifice of the agent's private interests when this is necessary for the greater happiness of all.[31] It is also more exacting than the contract theory, for while beneficent acts going beyond our natural duties are good actions and evoke our esteem, they are not required as a matter of right. Utilitarianism may seem to be a more exalted ideal, but the other side of it is that it may authorize the lesser welfare and liberty of some for the sake of a greater happiness of others who may already be more fortunate. A rational person, in framing his plan, would hesitate to give precedence to so stringent a principle. It is likely both to exceed his capacity for sympathy and to be hazardous to his freedom. Thus however improbable the congruence of the right and the good in justice as fairness, it is surely more probable than on the utilitarian view. The conditional balance of reasons favors the contract doctrine.

A somewhat different point is suggested by the following doubt: namely, that while the decision to preserve our sentiment of justice might be rational, we may in the end suffer a very great loss or even be ruined by it. As we have seen, a just person is not prepared to do certain things, and so in the face of evil circumstances he may decide to chance death rather than to act unjustly. Yet although it is true enough that for the sake of justice a man may lose his life where another would live to a later day, the just man does what all things considered he most wants; in this sense he is not defeated by ill fortune the possibility of which he foresaw. The question is on a par with the hazards of love; indeed, it is simply a special case. Those who love one another, or who acquire strong attachments to persons and to forms of life, at the same time become liable to ruin: their love makes them hostages to misfortune and the injustice of others. Friends and lovers take great chances to help each other; and members of families willingly do the same. Their being so disposed belongs to their attachments as much as any other inclination. Once we love we are vulnerable: there is no such thing as loving while being ready to consider whether to love, just like that. And the loves that may hurt the least are not the best loves. When we love we accept the dangers of injury and loss. In view of our general knowledge of the likely course of life, we do not

31. *Methods of Ethics*, pp. 246–253, 499.

think these risks so great as to cause us to cease loving. Should evils occur, they are the object of our aversion, and we resist those whose machinations bring them about. If we are loving we do not regret our love. Now if these things are true of love as the world is, or very often is, then a fortiori they would appear to be true of loves in a well-ordered society, and so of the sense of justice too. For in a society where others are just our loves expose us mainly to the accidents of nature and the contingency of circumstances. And similarly for the sentiment of justice which is connected to these affections. Taking as a bench mark the balance of reasons that leads us to affirm our loves as things are, it seems that we should be ready once we come of age to maintain our sense of justice in the more favorable conditions of a just society.

One special feature of the desire to express our nature as moral persons strengthens this conclusion. With other inclinations of the self, there is a choice of degree and scope. Our policy of deception and hypocrisy need not be completely systematic; our affective ties to institutions and to other persons can be more or less strong, and our participation in the wider life of society more or less full. There is a continuum of possibilities and not an all or nothing decision, although for simplicity I have spoken pretty much in these terms. But the desire to express our nature as a free and equal rational being can be fulfilled only by acting on the principles of right and justice as having first priority. This is a consequence of the condition of finality: since these principles are regulative, the desire to act upon them is satisfied only to the extent that it is likewise regulative with respect to other desires. It is acting from this precedence that expresses our freedom from contingency and happenstance. Therefore in order to realize our nature we have no alternative but to plan to preserve our sense of justice as governing our other aims. This sentiment cannot be fulfilled if it is compromised and balanced against other ends as but one desire among the rest. It is a desire to conduct oneself in a certain way above all else, a striving that contains within itself its own priority. Other aims can be achieved by a plan that allows a place for each, since their satisfaction is possible independent of their place in the ordering. But this is not the case with the sense of right and justice; and therefore acting wrongly is always liable to arouse feelings of guilt and shame, the emotions aroused by the defeat of our regulative moral sentiments. Of course, this does not mean that the realization of our nature as a free and rational being is itself an all or nothing affair. To the contrary, how far we succeed in expressing our nature depends upon how consistently we act from our sense of justice as finally regulative. What we cannot do is express our nature by following a plan that views the sense of justice as but one desire to be weighed against others. For this sentiment reveals what the person is, and to compromise it is not to achieve for the self free reign but to give way to the contingencies and accidents of the world.

One last question must be mentioned. Suppose that even in a well-ordered society there are some persons for whom the affirmation of their sense of justice is not a good. Given their aims and wants and the peculiarities of their nature, the thin account of the good does not define reasons sufficient for them to maintain this regulative sentiment. It has been argued that to these persons one cannot truthfully recommend justice as a virtue.[32] And this is surely correct, assuming such a recommendation to imply that rational grounds (identified by the thin theory) counsel this course for them as individuals. But then the further question remains whether those who do affirm their sense of justice are treating these persons unjustly in requiring them to comply with just institutions.

Now unhappily we are not yet in a position to answer this query properly, since it presupposes a theory of punishment and I have said very little about this part of the theory of justice (§ 39). I have assumed strict compliance with any conception that would be chosen and then considered which one on the list presented would be adopted. However, we may reason much as we did in the case of civil disobedience, another part of partial compliance theory. Thus granting that adherence to whatever conception is acknowledged will be imperfect if left completely voluntary, under what conditions would the persons in the original position agree that stabilizing penal devices can be employed? Would they insist that a person can be required to do only what is to his advantage as defined by the thin theory?

It seems clear, in the light of the contract doctrine as a whole, that they would not. For this restriction amounts in effect to gen-

32. See Foot, pp. 99–104.

eral egoism which, as we have seen, would be rejected. Moreover, the principles of right and justice are collectively rational; and it is in the interest of each that everyone else should comply with just arrangements. It is also the case that the general affirmation of the sense of justice is a great social asset, establishing the basis for mutual trust and confidence from which all normally benefit. Thus in agreeing to penalties that stabilize a scheme of cooperation the parties accept the same kind of constraint on self-interest that they acknowledge in choosing the principles of justice in the first place. Having agreed to these principles in view of the reasons already surveyed, it is rational to authorize the measures needed to maintain just institutions, assuming that the constraints of equal liberty and the rule of law are duly recognized (§§38–39). Those who find that being disposed to act justly is not a good for them cannot deny these contentions. It is, of course, true that in their case just arrangements do not fully answer to their nature, and therefore, other things equal, they will be less happy than they would be if they could affirm their sense of justice. But here one can only say: their nature is their misfortune.

The main point then is that to justify a conception of justice we do not have to contend that everyone, whatever his capacities and desires, has a sufficient reason (as defined by the thin theory) to preserve his sense of justice. For our good depends upon the sorts of persons we are, the kinds of wants and aspirations we have and are capable of. It can even happen that there are many who do not find a sense of justice for their good; but if so, the forces making for stability are weaker. Under such conditions penal devices will play a much larger role in the social system. The greater the lack of congruence, the greater the likelihood, other things equal, of instability with its attendant evils. Yet none of this nullifies the collective rationality of the principles of justice; it is still to the advantage of each that everyone else should honor them. At least this holds true so long as the conception of justice is not so unstable that some other conception would be preferable. But what I have tried to show is that the contract doctrine is superior to its rivals on this score, and therefore that the choice of principles in the original position need not be reconsidered. In fact, granted a reasonable interpretation of human sociability (provided by the account of how a sense of justice is acquired and by the idea of social union), justice as fairness appears to be a sufficiently stable conception. The hazards of the generalized prisoner's dilemma are removed by the match between the right and the good. Of course, under normal conditions public knowledge and confidence are always imperfect. So even in a just society it is reasonable to admit certain constraining arrangements to insure compliance, but their main purpose is to underwrite citizens' trust in one another. These mechanisms will seldom be invoked and will comprise but a minor part of the social scheme.

We are now at the end of this rather lengthy discussion of the stability of justice as fairness. The only further point to note is that congruence allows us to complete the sequence of applications of the definition of goodness. We can say first that, in a well-ordered society, being a good person (and in particular having an effective sense of justice) is indeed a good for that person; and second that this form of society is a good society. The first assertion follows from congruence; the second holds since a well-ordered society has the properties that it is rational to want in a society from the two relevant points of view. Thus a well-ordered society satisfies the principles of justice which are collectively rational from the perspective of the original position; and from the standpoint of the individual, the desire to affirm the public conception of justice as regulative of one's plan of life accords with the principles of rational choice. These conclusions support the values of community, and in reaching them my account of justice as fairness is completed.

87. CONCLUDING REMARKS ON JUSTIFICATION

I shall not try to summarize the presentation of the theory of justice. Instead I should like to end with a few comments about the kind of argument I have offered for it. Now that the whole conception is before us, we are in a position to note in a general way the sorts of things that can be said on its behalf. Doing this will clarify several points which may still be in doubt.

Philosophers commonly try to justify ethical theories in one of two ways. Sometimes they attempt to find self-evident principles from which a sufficient body of standards and precepts can be derived to account for our considered judgments. A justification of this kind we may think of as Cartesian. It presumes that first principles can be seen to be true, even necessarily so; deductive reasoning then transfers this conviction from premises to conclusion. A second approach (called naturalism by an abuse of language) is to introduce definitions of moral concepts in terms of presumptively non-moral ones, and then to show by accepted procedures of common sense and the sciences that the statements thus paired with the asserted moral judgments are true. Although on this view the first principles of ethics are not self-evident, the justification of moral convictions poses no special difficulties. They can be established, granting the definitions, in the same fashion as other statements about the world.

I have not adopted either of these conceptions of justification. For while some moral principles may seem natural and even obvious, there are great obstacles to maintaining that they are necessarily true, or even to explaining what is meant by this. Indeed, I have held that these principles are contingent in the sense that they are chosen in the original position in the light of general facts (§26). More likely candidates for necessary moral truths are the conditions imposed on the adoption of principles; but actually it seems best to regard these conditions simply as reasonable stipulations to be assessed eventually by the whole theory to which they belong. There is no set of conditions or first principles that can be plausibly claimed to be necessary or definitive of morality and thereby especially suited to carry the burden of justification. On the other hand, the method of naturalism so-called must first distinguish moral from non-moral concepts and then gain acceptance for the definitions laid down. For the justification to succeed, a clear theory of meaning is presupposed and this seems to be lacking. And in any case, definitions become the main part of the ethical doctrine, and thus in turn they need to be justified.

Therefore we do better, I think, to regard a moral theory just as any other theory, making due allowances for its Socratic aspects (§9). There is no reason to suppose that its first principles or assumptions need to be self-evident, or that its concepts and criteria can be replaced by other notions which can be certified as non-moral.[33] Thus while I have maintained, for example, that something's being right, or just, can be understood as its being in accordance with the relevant principles that would be acknowledged in the original position, and that we can in this way replace the former notions by the latter, these definitions are set up within the theory itself (§ 18). I do not hold that the conception of the original position is itself without moral force, or that the family of concepts it draws upon is ethically neutral (§ 23). This question I simply leave aside. I have not proceeded then as if first principles, or conditions thereon, or definitions either, have special features that permit them a peculiar place in justifying a moral doctrine. They are central elements and devices of theory, but justification rests upon the entire conception and how it fits in with and organizes our considered judgments in reflective equilibrium. As we have noted before, justification is a matter of the mutual support of many considerations, of everything fitting together into one coherent view (§ 4). Accepting this idea allows us to leave questions of meaning and definition aside and to get on with the task of developing a substantive theory of justice.

The three parts of the exposition of this theory are intended to make a unified whole by supporting one another in roughly the following way. The first part presents the essentials of the theoretical structure, and the principles of justice are argued for on the basis of reasonable stipulations concerning the choice of such conceptions. I urged the naturalness of these conditions and presented reasons why they are accepted, but it was not claimed that they are self-evident, or required by the analysis of moral concepts or the meaning of ethical terms. In the second part I examined the sorts of institutions that justice enjoins and the kinds of duties and obligations it imposes on individuals. The aim throughout was to show that the theory proposed matches the fixed points of our

33. The view proposed here accords with the account in § 9 which follows "Outline for Ethics" (1951). But it has benefited from the conception of justification found in W. V. Quine, *Word and Object* (Cambridge, M.I.T. Press, 1960), ch. 1 and elsewhere. See also his *Ontological Relativity and Other Essays* (New York, Columbia University Press, 1969), Essay 4. For a development of this conception to include explicitly moral thought and judgment, see Morton White, *Toward Reunion in Philosophy* (Cambridge, Harvard University Press, 1956), pt. III, esp. pp. 254–258, 263, 266f.

considered convictions better than other familiar doctrines, and that it leads us to revise and extrapolate our judgments in what seem on reflection to be more satisfactory ways. First principles and particular judgments appear on balance to hang together reasonably well, at least in comparison with alternative theories. Finally we checked to see in the third part if justice as fairness is a feasible conception. This forced us to raise the question of stability and whether the right and the good as defined are congruent. These considerations do not determine the initial acknowledgment of principles in the first part of the argument, but confirm it (§81). They show that our nature is such as to allow the original choice to be carried through. In this sense we might say that humankind has a moral nature.

Now some may hold that this kind of justification faces two sorts of difficulties. First, it is open to the general complaint that it appeals to the mere fact of agreement. Second, there is the more specific objection to the argument I have presented that it depends upon a particular list of conceptions of justice between which the parties in the original position are to choose, and it assumes not only an agreement among persons in their considered judgments, but also in what they regard as reasonable conditions to impose on the choice of first principles. It may be said that the agreement in considered convictions is constantly changing and varies between one society, or part thereof, and another. Some of the so-called fixed points may not really be fixed, nor will everyone accept the same principles for filling in the gaps in their existing judgments. And any list of conceptions of justice, or consensus about what counts as reasonable conditions on principles, is surely more or less arbitrary. The case presented for justice as fairness, so the contention runs, does not escape these limitations.

In regard to the general objection the reply is that justification is argument addressed to those who disagree with us, or to ourselves when we are of two minds. It presumes a clash of views between persons or within one person, and seeks to convince others, or ourselves, of the reasonableness of the principles upon which our claims and judgments are founded. Being designed to reconcile by reason, justification proceeds from what all parties to the discussion hold in common. Ideally, to justify a conception of justice to someone is to give him a proof of its principles from premises that we both accept, these principles having in turn consequences that match our considered judgments. Thus mere proof is not justification. A proof simply displays logical relations between propositions. But proofs become justification once the starting points are mutually recognized, or the conclusions so comprehensive and compelling as to persuade us of the soundness of the conception expressed by their premises.

It is perfectly proper, then, that the argument for the principles of justice should proceed from some consensus. This is the nature of justification. Yet the more specific objections are correct in implying that the force of the argument depends on the features of the consensus appealed to. Here several points deserve notice. To begin with, while it should be granted that any list of alternatives may be to some extent arbitrary, the objection is mistaken if it is read as holding that all lists are equally so. A list that includes the leading traditional theories is less arbitrary than one which leaves out the more obvious candidates. Certainly the argument for the principles of justice would be strengthened by showing that they are still the best choice from a more comprehensive list more systematically evaluated. I do not know how far this can be done. I doubt, however, that the principles of justice (as I have defined them) will be the preferred conception on anything resembling a complete list. (Here I assume that, given an upper bound on complexity and other constraints, the class of reasonable and practicable alternatives is effectively finite.) Even if the argument I have offered is sound, it only shows that a finally adequate theory (if such exists) will look more like the contract view than any of the other doctrines we discussed. And even this conclusion is not proved in any strict sense.

Nevertheless, in comparing justice as fairness with these conceptions, the list used is not simply ad hoc: it includes representative theories from the tradition of moral philosophy which comprises the historical consensus about what so far seem to be the more reasonable and practicable moral conceptions. With time further possibilities will be worked out, thereby providing a more convincing basis for justification as the leading conception is subjected to a more severe test. But these things we can only anticipate. For the present it is appropriate to try to reformulate the contract doctrine and to compare it with a few familiar alternatives. This procedure is not arbitrary; we can advance in no other way.

Turning to the particular difficulty about the consensus on reasonable conditions, one should point out that one of the aims of moral philosophy is to look for possible bases of agreement where none seem to exist. It must attempt to extend the range of some existing consensus and to frame more discriminating moral conceptions for our consideration. Justifying grounds do not lie ready to hand: they need to be discovered and suitably expressed, sometimes by lucky guesses, sometimes by noting the requirements of theory. It is with this aim in mind that the various conditions on the choice of first principles are brought together in the notion of the original position. The idea is that by putting together enough reasonable constraints into a single conception, it will become obvious that one among the alternatives presented is to be preferred. We should like it to happen that the superiority of a particular view (among those currently known) is the result, perhaps the unexpected result, of this newly observed consensus.

Again, the set of conditions incorporated into the notion of the original position is not without an explanation. It is possible to maintain that these requirements are reasonable and to connect them with the purpose of moral principles and their role in establishing the ties of community. The grounds for ordering and finality, say, seem clear enough. And we can now see that publicity can be explained as insuring that the process of justification can be perfectly carried through (in the limit so to speak) without untoward effects. For publicity allows that all can justify their conduct to everyone else (when their conduct is justifiable) without self-defeating or other disturbing consequences. If we take seriously the idea of a social union and of society as a social union of such unions, then surely publicity is a natural condition. It helps to establish that a well-ordered society is one activity in the sense that its members follow and know of one another, that they follow the same regulative conception; and everyone shares in the benefits of the endeavors of all in ways to which each is known to consent. Society is not partitioned with respect to the mutual recognition of its first principles. And, indeed, this must be so if the binding action of the conception of justice and of the Aristotelian principle (and its companion effect) are to take place.

To be sure, the function of moral principles is not uniquely defined; it admits of various interpretations. We might try to choose between them by seeing which one uses the weakest set of conditions to characterize the initial situation. The difficulty with this suggestion is that while weaker conditions are indeed to be preferred, other things equal, there is no weakest set; a minimum does not exist short of no conditions at all and this is of no interest. Therefore we must look for a constrained minimum, a set of weak conditions that still enables us to construct a workable theory of justice. Certain parts of justice as fairness should be viewed in this way. I have several times noted the minimal nature of the conditions on principles when taken singly. For example, the assumption of mutually disinterested motivation is not a demanding stipulation. Not only does it enable us to base the theory upon a reasonably precise notion of rational choice, but it asks little of the parties: in this way the principles chosen can adjust wider and deeper conflicts, an obvious desideratum (§ 40). It has the further advantage of separating off the more evident moral elements of the original position in the form of general conditions and the veil of ignorance and the like, so that we can see more clearly how justice requires us to go beyond a concern for our own interests.

The discussion of freedom of conscience illustrates most clearly the assumption of mutual disinterest. Here the opposition of the parties is very great, yet one can still show that if any agreement is possible, it is that on the principle of equal liberty. And, as we noted, this idea can be extended to conflicts between moral doctrines as well (§ 33). If the parties assume that in society they affirm some moral conception (the content of which is unknown to them), they can still assent to the first principle. This principle therefore appears to hold a special place among moral views; it defines an agreement in the limit once we postulate sufficiently wide disparities consistent with certain minimal conditions for a practical conception of justice.

I should now like to take note of several objections that are independent from the method of justification and concern instead certain features of the theory of justice itself. One of these is the criticism that the contract view is a narrowly individualistic doctrine. To this difficulty, the preceding remarks supply the answer. For once the point of the assumption of mutual disinterest is understood, the objection seems misplaced. Within the framework of justice as fairness we can reformulate and establish Kantian themes by using a suitably general conception of rational choice. For example, we have found interpretations of autonomy and of the moral law as an expression of our nature as free and equal rational beings; the categorical imperative also has its analogue, as does the idea of never treating persons as means only, or indeed as means at all. Further, in the last part the theory of justice has been shown to account for the values of community as well; and this strengthens the earlier contention that embedded in the principles of justice there is an ideal of the person that provides an Archimedean point for judging the basic structure of society (§ 41). These aspects of the theory of justice are developed slowly beginning from what looks like an unduly rationalistic conception that makes no provision for social values. The original position is first used to determine the content of justice, the principles which define it. Not until later is justice seen as part of our good and connected with our natural sociability. The merits of the idea of the original position cannot be assessed by focusing on some single feature of it, but, as I have often observed, only by the whole theory which is built upon it.

If justice as fairness is more convincing than the older presentations of the contract doctrine, I believe that it is because the original position, as indicated above, unites in one conception a reasonably clear problem of choice with conditions that are widely recognized as fitting to impose on the adoption of moral principles. This initial situation combines the requisite clarity with the relevant ethical constraints. It is partly to preserve this clarity that I have avoided attributing to the parties any ethical motivation. They decide solely on the basis of what seems best calculated to further their interests so far as they can ascertain them. In this way we can exploit the intuitive idea of rational prudential choice. We can, however, define ethical variations of the initial situation by supposing the parties to be influenced by moral considerations. It is a mistake to object that the notion of the original agreement would no longer be ethically neutral. For this notion already includes moral features and must do so, for example, the formal conditions on principles and the veil of ignorance. I have simply divided up the description of the original position so that these elements do not occur in the characterization of the parties, although even here there might be a question as to what counts as a moral element and what does not. There is no need to settle this problem. What is important is that the various features of the original position should be expressed in the simplest and most compelling way.

Occasionally I have touched upon some possible ethical variations of the initial situation (§ 17). For example, one might assume that the parties hold the principle that no one should be advantaged by unmerited assets and contingencies, and therefore they choose a conception of justice that mitigates the effects of natural accident and social fortune. Or else they may be said to accept a principle of reciprocity requiring that distributive arrangements always lie on the upward sloping portion of the contribution curve. Again, some notion of fair and willingly cooperation may limit the conceptions of justice which the parties are prepared to entertain. There is no a priori reason for thinking that these variations must be less convincing, or the moral constraints they express less widely shared. Moreover, we have seen that the possibilities just mentioned appear to confirm the difference principle, lending further support to it. Although I have not proposed a view of this kind, they certainly deserve further examination. The crucial thing is not to use principles that are contested. Thus to reject the principle of average utility by imposing a rule against taking chances in the original position would render the method fruitless, since some philosophers have sought to justify this principle by deriving it as the consequence of the appropriate impersonal attitude in certain risk situations. We must find other arguments against the utility criterion: the propriety of taking chances is among the things in dispute (§ 28). The idea of the initial agreement can only succeed if its conditions are in fact widely recognized, or can become so.

Another fault, some may contend, is that the principles of justice are not derived from the notion of respect for persons, from a recognition of their inherent worth and dignity. Since the original position (as I have defined it) does not include this idea, not explicitly anyway, the argument for justice as fairness may be thought unsound. I believe, however, that while the principles of justice will be effective only if men have a sense of justice and do therefore respect one another, the notion of respect or of the inherent worth of persons is not a suitable basis for arriving at these principles. It is precisely these ideas that call for interpretation. The situation is analogous to that of benevolence: without the principles of right and justice, the aims of benevolence and the requirements of respect are both undefined; they presuppose these principles already independently derived (§ 30). Once the conception of justice is on hand, however, the ideas of respect and of human dignity can be given a more definite meaning. Among other things, respect for persons is shown by treating them in ways that they can see to be justified. But more than this, it is manifest in the content of the principles to which we appeal. Thus to respect persons is to recognize that they possess an inviolability founded on justice that even the welfare of society as a whole cannot override. It is to affirm that the loss of freedom for some is not made right by a greater welfare enjoyed by others. The lexical priorities of justice represent the value of persons that Kant says is beyond all price.[34] The theory of justice provides a rendering of these ideas but we cannot start out from them. There is no way to avoid the complications of the original position, or of some similar construction, if our notions of respect and the natural basis of equality are to be systematically presented.

These remarks bring us back to the common sense conviction, which we noted at the outset, that justice is the first virtue of social institutions (§ 1). I have tried to set forth a theory that enables us to understand and to assess these feelings about the primacy of justice. Justice as fairness is the outcome: it articulates these opinions and supports their general tendency. And while, of course, it is not a fully satisfactory theory, it offers, I believe, an alternative to the utilitarian view which has for so long held the preeminent place in our moral philosophy. I have tried to present the theory of justice as a viable systematic doctrine so that the idea of maximizing the good does not hold sway by default. The criticism of teleo-

34. See *The Foundations of the Metaphysics of Morals*, pp. 434–436, vol. IV of the Academy Edition.

logical theories cannot fruitfully proceed piecemeal. We must attempt to construct another kind of view which has the same virtues of clarity and system but which yields a more discriminating interpretation of our moral sensibilities.

Finally, we may remind ourselves that the hypothetical nature of the original position invites the question: why should we take any interest in it, moral or otherwise? Recall the answer: the conditions embodied in the description of this situation are ones that we do in fact accept. Or if we do not, then we can be persuaded to do so by philosophical considerations of the sort occasionally introduced. Each aspect of the original position can be given a supporting explanation. Thus what we are doing is to combine into one conception the totality of conditions that we are ready upon due reflection to recognize as reasonable in our conduct with regard to one another (§4). Once we grasp this conception, we can at any time look at the social world from the required point of view. It suffices to reason in certain ways and to follow the conclusions reached. This standpoint is also objective and expresses our autonomy (§78). Without conflating all persons into one but recognizing them as distinct and separate, it enables us to be impartial, even between persons who are not contemporaries but who belong to many generations. Thus to see our place in society from the perspective of this position is to see it *sub specie aeternitatis:* it is to regard the human situation not only from all social but also from all temporal points of view. The perspective of eternity is not a perspective from a certain place beyond the world, nor the point of view of a transcendent being; rather it is a certain form of thought and feeling that rational persons can adopt within the world. And having done so, they can, whatever their generation, bring together into one scheme all individual perspectives and arrive together at regulative principles that can be affirmed by everyone as he lives by them, each from his own standpoint. Purity of heart, if one could attain it, would be to see clearly and to act with grace and self-command from this point of view.

INDEX

Civil disobedience, § 55:363–368, § 57:371–377, § 59:382–391; defined, 364ff, 368; to oppose savings policies, 296f; as problem for democratic theory, 363; three parts of theory of, 363f; and sense of justice, 364, 374, 386f; as a political act, 365f; and fidelity to law, 366f; distinguished from militant action, 367f; appropriate objects of, 371ff; three conditions of justification of, 371–375; problem of fairness in, 373ff; wisdom of, 376; and principle of fairness, 376f; role of in maintaining democratic constitution, 382–386; theory of founded on conception of justice, 384f; place of in constitutional theory, 385f; and types of consensus, 387f; citizen's responsibility in, 388–391

Civility, duty of, 355

Clark, J. B., 308n, 309n

Clark, J. M., 308n, 309n

Close-knitness, 80–83

Cohen, Marshall, 364n

Commending, 425f

Common good, defined, 233, 246

Common interest, principle of: defined, 97, 246; and equal citizenship, 97; and toleration, 211–216; as political convention, 319

Completeness, approximative, defined, 340f, 566f

Complexity, limits on, 45, 132, 142, 517

Condorcet, Marquis de, 358

Congruence: concept of defined, 398f, 456; problem of defined, 513f, 567–570; argument for, 570–575. See also Sense of justice, good of

Conscience: see Equal liberty of

Conscientious evasion, 369f

Conscientious refusal: § 56:368–371, § 58:377–382; defined, 368ff; distinguished from conscientious evasion, 369; contrasted with civil disobedience, 369f; toleration of and erring conscience, 370f; general pacifism as natural departure, 370f; law of nations derived, 377ff; justification of in case of particular war, 379–382; and conscription, 380f; and contingent pacifism, 381f; discriminating preferred to general pacificism, 382

Conscription, 380f

Consensus, 18f, 387f, 517, 580ff

Considered judgments: defined, 47f; fixed points of, 19f, 319, 579ff; role of in justification, 19ff, 120, 579ff; and reflective equilibrium, 20f, 48ff; as facts to be explained by moral theory, 51

Constant, Benjamin, 201, 222

Constitution: justice of, 197f, 221–234, 357; case of imperfect procedural justice, 197f, 221, 353f, 360; majority rule in, 228–231, 354–357; of ideal procedure of public deliberation, 359

Constitutional convention, stage of, 196–199

Constitutional democracy: defined, 222f, 227; example of just basic structure, 195; constitutional devices of, 224; historical failure of, 226f; and sense of justice, 243; liberties of, best founded on justice, 243f; and just savings problems, 295ff; place of majority rule in, 354–357; economic theory of, 360f, 492ff; place of civil disobedience in theory of, 363, 385f; role of civil disobedience in, 382–386. See also Equal participation, principle of

Constitutive rules, 56f, 344f

Content of conceptions of right: pointless excluded, 149f; and psychological understandability, 476ff, 487

Contingencies of social circumstance: and intuitive idea of the principles of justice, 15; in system of natural liberty, 72f; in liberal equality, 73f; in democratic equality and difference principle, 75, 79, 102ff, 585

Continuity, principle of, 420f

Contribution, precept of, 305f, 307, 308f, 311

Contribution curve, 76f, 104, 585

Coordination, problem of, 6

Cooper, J. M., 426n

Counter-examples, limited usefulness of, 52

Counting principles of rational choice, 415, 416; in first-person procedure of choice, 551f; and dominant ends, 554f; in hedonism, 555f

Culture: claims of in justice as fairness, 101f, 328f, 331f, 441f; claims of in perfectionism, 248, 325f, 328;

Equality (*cont'd*)
of equality, 511f; and limits of
justice as fairness, 512
Equality, tendency to § 17:100–108;
principle of redress, 100ff; distribution of natural talents as a common
asset, 101f, 179, 511f, 585; and
reciprocity, 102–105; and harmony
of interests, 104f; principle of
fraternity, 105f; difference principle
prevents meritocratic society, 106f;
eugenics, 107f; and envy, 537–541
Equality of consideration, 507f
Equality of fair opportunity, § 14:83–
89, § 46:298–303; defined, 73f; and
the family, 74, 300f, 511f; and pure
procedural justice, 83–89; role of in
background justice, 84f, 87f; contrasted with allocative justice, 88;
lexically prior to difference principle,
89; cases illustrating priority of,
299ff; priority rule for stated, 302f;
and two conceptions of equality,
511f
Equality of opportunity, formal, *see*
Careers open to talents
Equilibrium, 119f, 456ff
Equity, 237f
Erikson, Erik, 443n
Erring conscience, 370f, 518f
Eternity, perspective of, 587
Ethics of creation, 159f
Eugenics, 107f
Evil man, 439
Evolution, 431f, 502ff
Exchange branch, 282ff, 331f
Excellences, 442–446; defined, 443f;
and natural shame, 444; relation to
moral virtues and moral shame, 444f;
and virtues of self-command, 445f.
See also Self-respect; Shame
Expectations, defined, 64f; and
representative persons, 64f; utili-
tarianism and accurate measure of,
90f; how based on index of primary
goods, 92–95; index problem for,
93f; reasons for using primary goods
as basis for, 94f; lack of unity of in
average utility, 173ff. *See also*
Primary goods
Exploitation, 309f

Fair political conduct, duty of, 239n
Fairness, principle of, § 18:111–114,
§ 52:342–350; two parts of defined,

111f, 342f; covers all obligation,
112; Locke on and background
justice, 112; characteristic features
of, 113; political obligation for
citizens generally problematical,
113f, 335f; rejected as sole
basis of political ties, 335ff; permits
more discriminating account of
requirements, 343f; explains obligation to keep promises, 344–348;
argument for, 346ff; requirements
not founded on institutions alone,
348f; and Prichard's question, 349f;
and political obligation for members
of groups, 376f
Falk, W. D., 131n
Family, institution of: and fair equality
of opportunity, 74, 300f, 511f; and
fraternity, 105; persons in original
position as heads of, 128f; in
morality of authority, 463; in moral
ity of association, 467f
Feinberg, Joel, 314n, 315n
Fellner, William, 154n, 169n, 173n
Fidelity, principle of, *see* Promises
Fidelity to law, 366f, 383f
Field, G. H., 426n, 477n
Finality, as formal condition, 135; in
argument for two principles, 175–
178; in argument for congruence,
569, 574f
Findlay, J. N., 400n, 477n, 510n
First principle of justice: first statement of, 60f; final statement of, 250,
302; applies to first part of basic
structure, 61, 199; as criterion for
use in constitutional convention,
199; and equal liberty of conscience,
205–221; and political justice, 221–
234; and rule of law, 235–243;
meaning of priority of, 243–251;
affirmed by mixed conceptions, 316;
and perfectionism, 327–331; violations of, as appropriate object of
civil disobedience, 372. *See also*
Equal liberty of conscience; Political
justice
Firth, Roderick, 184n, 185n
Fixed natural characteristics, 99
Fixed points, of considered judgments,
19f, 319, 579f
Flavell, John, 468n
Fletcher, Ronald, 459n
Foot, Philippa, 149n, 400n, 479n, 569n,
570n, 575n

Publicity (*cont'd*)
    dition, 130n, 133, 454; in argument
    for stability, 177–182; of general
    beliefs, 454, 547f; and envy, 547f; in
    argument for congruence, 570; and
    justifications in social union, 582
Punishment, 241, 314f, 575f
Purely conscientious act, doctrine of,
    477f, 569
Purely preferential choice, *see* Indeter-
    minacy of choice
Purity of heart, 587

Quasi-stability, 456n
Quine, W. V., 111n, 131n, 579n

Raiffa, Howard, 85n, 152n, 173n, 269n,
    322n, 447n, 558n
Ramsey, F. P., 286n, 294n
Ramsey, Paul, 379n
Rancor, *see* Envy
Raphael, D. D., 100n
Rashdall, Hastings, 326n
Rational choice, principles of: apply
    to plans of life, 408f; at best deter-
    mine maximal class, 409, 416; time-
    related principles defined, 410, 420f;
    counting principles defined, 411–415;
    specify higher-order desires, 414f;
    not unanimously chosen, 446f; for
    choice under uncertainty, 447; and
    veil of ignorance, 448f. *See also*
    Uncertainty, choice under
Rationality of the parties, § 25:142–
    150; defined, 142f; and envy, 143f,
    530–541; and mutual disinterested-
    ness, 144f; how related to strict com-
    pliance condition, 145; elements of
    initial situation and variations listed,
    146f; an aspect of theoretically de-
    fined individuals, 147; relation to
    egoism and benevolence, 147ff; and
    content of morality, 149f
Reciprocity: utilitarianism incompatible
    with, 14, 33, 499f; in difference prin-
    ciple, 102ff; in harmony of interests,
    104f; in argument from stability and
    mutual respect, 178f; and just savings
    principle, 290ff; in conditions of
    consensus, 388; as characterizing
    psychological laws, 494f, 499ff; and
    the basis of equality, 511; as ethical
    variation of initial situation, 585
Redress, principle of, 100ff

Reflective equilibrium, 20f, 48–51, 120,
    432, 434, 579
Region of positive contributions, 79,
    82, 104f
Regret, 422, 442f, 444, 481
Relevant social positions, § 16:95–100;
    defined, 95f; and starting places, 96f,
    100; two main cases of, 96f, 99;
    equal citizenship as, 96ff; least ad-
    vantaged as defined, 97f; and fixed
    natural characteristics, 99; need for
    account of, 100
Remorse, 481
Representative persons, defined, 64f
Requirements, 111–117
Rescher, Nicholas, 34n, 317n
Resentment, 475, 484, 533, 534, 539ff
Responsibility, principle of, 241, 389f,
    519
Responsibility to self, principle of, 423
Retributive justice, 314f
Right, complete conception of, 108ff,
    340ff, 348
Right, concept of: contract definition
    of, 111, 184f; formal constraints of,
    130–136; generality, 131f; univer-
    sality, 132f; publicity, 133; ordering,
    133f; finality, 135; ideal observer
    definition of, 184f
    contrasted with the good, § 68:
    446–452; with respect to need for
    agreement, 446f, to diversity of con-
    ceptions of, 447f; and veil of igno-
    rance, 448f; priority of right in
    contrast to utilitarianism, 30–33,
    499ff; and analysis of meaning, 451f
Rightness as fairness, 17, 111
Rodes, Robert, 74n
Ross, W. D., 34n, 40, 43n, 310n, 340ff,
    399n, 403n, 477
Rousseau, J. J., 11, 140n, 215f, 264,
    459f, 463n, 540n
Royce, Josiah, 400n, 408
Ruggiero, Guido, 201n
Rule of law, § 38:235–243; legal system
    defined, 235f; precept of ought im-
    plies can, 236f; precept of similar
    cases, 237f; precept of no offense
    without a law, 238; precepts of natu-
    ral justice, 238f; relation to liberty,
    239ff; and penal sanctions and prin-
    ciple of responsibility, 241; and cases
    illustrating priority of liberty, 242f
Runciman, W. G., 511n
Ryle, Gilbert, 559n